THE ETERNAL SPIRIT

God Living In Us

WILLEM J. OUWENEEL

AN EVANGELICAL INTRODUCTION TO
REFORMATIONAL THEOLOGY
VOLUME II/3

PART II: GOD:
THE PERSONAL SOURCE BEHIND THEOLOGY

AN EVANGELICAL INTRODUCTION TO REFORMATIONAL THEOLOGY

Part I: Scripture: The Revealed Source For Theology
   I/1 *The Eternal Word:* God Speaking To Us
   I/2 *The Eternal Torah:* Living Under God

Part II: God: The Personal Source Behind Theology
   II/1 *The Eternal God:* God Revealing Himself To Us
   II/2 *The Eternal Christ:* God With Us
   II/3 *The Eternal Spirit:* God Living In Us

Part III: Redemption: The Christ-Centered Heart of Theology
   III/1 *The Eternal Purpose:* Living In Christ
   III/2 *Eternal Righteousness:* Living Before God
   III/3 *Eternal Salvation:* Christ Dying For Us
   III/4 *Eternal Life:* Christ Living In Us

Part IV: Consummation: The Lived Shape of Theology
   IV/1a *The Eternal People:* God in Relation To Israel: Israel in the Tanakh and the New Testament
   IV/1b *The Eternal People:* God in Relation To Israel: Post-New Testament Israel
   IV/2 *The Eternal Covenant:* Living With God
   IV/3 *The Eternal Kingdom:* Living Under Christ

Part V: Method: The Comprehensive Foundation of Theology
   V/1 *Eternal Truth:* The Prolegomena of Theology

THE ETERNAL SPIRIT

God Living In Us

WILLEM J. OUWENEEL

The Eternal Spirit: God Living In Us

This English edition is a publication of Paideia Press (P.O. Box 500, Jordan Station, Ontario, Canada L0R 1S0). Copyright © 2023 by Paideia Press. All rights reserved. Except for brief quotations in critical publications or reviews, no part of this book may be reproduced in any manner without prior written permission from Paideia Press at the address above.

Unless otherwise indicated, Scripture quotations are from the ESV® Bible (The Holy Bible, English Standard Version®). Copyright © 2001 by Crossway, a publishing ministry of Good News Publishers. Used by permission. All rights reserved.

Scripture quotations or references marked as NKJV are taken from the New King James Version®. Copyright © 1982 by Thomas Nelson, Inc. Used by permission. All rights reserved.

Scripture quotations or references marked as NIV are taken from the Holy Bible, New International Version®, NIV®. Copyright © 1973, 1978, 1984, 2011 by Biblica, Inc.™ Used by permission of Zondervan. All rights reserved worldwide. www.zondervan.com. The "NIV" and "New International Version" are trademarks registered in the United States Patent and Trademark Office by Biblica, Inc.™

Book Design by: Steven R. Martins

ISBN 978-0-88815-330-2

*. . . Christ, who through the **eternal Spirit** offered himself without blemish to God.*

Hebrews 9:14

*My **Spirit** that is upon you,
 and my words that I have put in your mouth,
shall not depart out of your mouth,
 or out of the mouth of your offspring,
from this time forth
 and **forevermore**.*

Isaiah 59:21

*I will ask the Father, and he will give you another Helper, to be with you **forever**, even the **Spirit** of truth.*

John 14:16–17

*[T]he one who sows to the **Spirit** will from the Spirit reap **eternal** life*

Galatians 6:8

Table of Contents

Table of Contents (Expanded)	
Series Preface	i
Author's Preface	v
Abbreviations	ix
Introduction	1
Chapter 1 — Earlier Pneumatology	9
Chapter 2 — Later Pneumatology	43
Chapter 3 — The Person of the Spirit	85
Chapter 4 — The Power of the Spirit	131
Chapter 5 — The Earlier Work of the Spirit	177
Chapter 6 — Christ and the Holy Spirit	223
Chapter 7 — The Coming of the Spirit	277
Chapter 8 — Believing Through the Holy Spirit	325
Chapter 9 — Walking By the Holy Spirit	381
Chapter 10 — The Dwelling Place of the Holy Spirit	443
Chapter 11 — Being Filled With the Spirit	503
Chapter 12 — The Gifts of the Holy Spirit	551
Bibliography	605
Scripture Index	641
Subject Index	671

Table of Contents

Series Preface	i
Author's Preface	v
Abbreviations	ix
Introduction	1
1 Earlier Pneumatology	9
1.1 Place in Systematic Theology	10
1.1.1 The "Forgotten God"	10
1.1.2 East and West	12
1.2 Neglect of the Spirit	14
1.2.1 First Explanation	14
1.2.2 Second Explanation	15
1.2.3 Third Explanation	16
1.2.4 Fourth Explanation	17
1.3 Pneumatology and Spirituality	18
1.3.1 Spirit-Driven Pneumatology	18
1.3.2 "Hear What the Spirit Says"	19
1.4 Early Charismatics	21
1.4.1 Charismatic versus Institutionalized	21
1.4.2 Montanus	23
1.4.3 Nicaea and Constantinople	24
1.4.4 Augustine	26
1.5 The Schism	28
1.5.1 Introduction	28
1.5.2 Evaluation	29
1.5.3 Other Aspects	32

	1.6	*Filioque*	34
		1.6.1 Introduction	34
		1.6.2 Division	35
		1.6.3 Dualism	37
	1.7	Summary	39
		1.7.1 Two Realms	39
		1.7.2 No Speculations	40
2	Later Pneumatology		43
	2.1	The Reformers	44
		2.1.1 Luther	44
		2.1.2 Calvin: "Theologian of the Spirit"?	46
		2.1.3 The Internal Testimony of the Holy Spirit	48
	2.2	Protestant Scholasticism	50
		2.2.1 Word and Spirit	50
		2.2.2 The Anabaptists	52
	2.3	Dutch Theologians	55
		2.3.1 Abraham Kuyper	55
		2.3.2 Johan Herman Bavinck	58
		2.3.3 Reformed Successors in the Netherlands	61
		2.3.4 Recent Developments	63
	2.4	The Pentecostal and Charismatic Movement	65
		2.4.1 Precursors and Beginnings	65
		2.4.2 Missions and Evangelism	68
		2.4.3 Ecstatic Experience	71
	2.5	More Recent Developments	73
		2.5.1 Causes and Expressions	73

	2.5.2 International Churches	75
	2.5.3 Lutheran and Modern Theologies	76
2.6	Types of Pneumatology	78
	2.6.1 Various Approaches	78
	2.6.2 Paul on the Spirit	80
	2.6.3 Theological and Biblical	82

3 The Person of the Spirit — 85

- 3.1 God is Spirit — 86
  - 3.1.1 God's Spirit, God's Being — 86
  - 3.1.2 In What Sense *Pneuma*? — 88
  - 3.1.3 Anthropological Parallel — 89
- 3.2 The Spirit and the Trinity — 92
  - 3.2.1 Stating the Problem — 92
  - 3.2.2 Terminology — 94
- 3.3 The Personality of the Holy Spirit — 95
  - 3.3.1 Thinking, Feeling, Willing — 95
  - 3.3.2 A Distinct Person — 97
- 3.4 The Perfect Deity of the Holy Spirit — 99
  - 3.4.1 Divine Attributes — 99
  - 3.4.2 Involved in God's Works — 101
  - 3.4.3 The Spirit and YHWH — 103
- 3.5 Prayer and Worship to the Spirit — 104
  - 3.5.1 Six Hints — 104
  - 3.5.2 Historical Examples — 106
- 3.6 Names of the Holy Spirit — 108
  - 3.6.1 References to Persons — 108
  - 3.6.2 References to Attributes — 109
- 3.7 The Maternal Metaphor — 111

		3.7.1 The Feminine Spirit	111
		3.7.2 Other Feminine Characteristics	113
	3.8	Chokmah and Shekhinah	116
		3.8.1 Wisdom Literature and the Kabbalah	116
		3.8.2 Early Christian Traditions	118
		3.8.3 The Shekhinah and the Spirit	119
		3.8.4 The Shekhinah and the Church	122
	3.9	"Lady Spirit"	124
		3.9.1 Women in Revelation	124
		3.9.2 The World Soul	126
4	The Power of the Spirit		131
	4.1	Basic Metaphors of the Spirit	132
		4.1.1 Air, Water, and Fire	132
		4.1.2 Breath, Wind: Old Testament	133
		4.1.3 Breath, Wind: New Testament	135
	4.2	Water	138
		4.2.1 Outpouring of the Spirit	138
		4.2.2 Dew, Rain, Wells, Rivers	140
		4.2.3 Cleansing	141
	4.3	Fire	142
		4.3.1 Old Testament Passages	142
		4.3.2 New Testament Passages	144
		4.3.3 Historical Comparisons	146
	4.4	Evaluation	147
		4.4.1 The Use of Metaphors	147
		4.4.2 Person As Well As Force	150
	4.5	Oil	153
		4.5.1 Medicine or Sacrament?	153

	4.5.2 Old Testament Passages	154
	4.5.3 New Testament Passages	156
	4.5.4 The Elect Messiah	157
	4.5.5 Elect Believers	159
4.6	Wine	161
	4.6.1 "Drunk" with the Spirit	161
	4.6.2 Historical References	163
	4.6.3 Quantification	165
4.7	Dove	167
	4.7.1 The Dove On the Lamb	167
	4.7.2 Ancient Parallels	169
4.8	Other Images	171
	4.8.1 Seal	171
	4.8.2 Hand and Finger	173
	4.8.3 Ear, Pearl, Key, Milk, Honey	175
5	**The Earlier Work of the Spirit**	**177**
5.1	Creation	178
	5.1.1 *Tohu Wabohu*	178
	5.1.2 Creator Spirit	180
	5.1.3 *Tehom*	181
5.2	After Creation	182
	5.2.1 Providential Upholding	182
	5.2.2 History and Culture	184
5.3	Flood and Exodus	186
	5.3.1 The Noahic Flood	186
	5.3.2 The Exodus from Egypt	188
	5.3.3 The Spirit Journeying with Israel	189
	5.3.4 The New Garden	191

	5.4	The Spirit in the Pentateuch and Judges	192
		5.4.1 The Pentateuch	192
		5.4.2 The Book of Judges	193
	5.5	The Prophets	195
		5.5.1 Samuel and David	195
		5.5.2 Messiah-Prophet	197
		5.5.3 Prophetesses	200
	5.6	The Temple of Solomon	201
		5.6.1 David the Man of God	201
		5.6.2 Building the Temple	203
	5.7	The Second Temple	205
		5.7.1 Haggai	205
		5.7.2 Zechariah	207
	5.8	Word and Spirit	209
		5.8.1 Wisdom, Torah, Logos	209
		5.8.2 More Parallels	211
		5.8.3 Spirit: Uppercase or Lowercase S?	212
	5.9	Dwelling in People?	215
		5.9.1 Three Differences	215
		5.9.2 Dwelling and Working	217
		5.9.3 Temporary Anointing	219
6	Christ and the Holy Spirit		223
	6.1	Jesus' Beginnings in This World	224
		6.1.1 The Incarnation of the Word	224
		6.1.2 The Virgin Birth	226
		6.1.3 Jesus' Baptism	228
	6.2	Jesus and the Spirit in Isaiah	230
		6.2.1 Isaiah 11	230

	6.2.2 Isaiah 42	233
	6.2.3 Isaiah 61	234
6.3	The Holy Spirit and Jesus' Death	237
	6.3.1 Exodus and Baptism	237
	6.3.2 "The Eternal Spirit"	238
6.4	The Holy Spirit and Jesus' Resurrection	240
	6.4.1 1 Peter 3:18	240
	6.4.2 1 Peter 3:19–20	242
	6.4.3 Romans 1:3–4	243
6.5	The Holy Spirit in the Synoptic Gospels	244
	6.5.1 Matthew 10:19–20; Mark 13:11; Luke 12:11–12	244
	6.5.2 Matthew 12:28, 31–32; Mark 3:29	247
	6.5.3 Luke 11:13	250
6.6	The Holy Spirit in John 4 and 7	252
	6.6.1 John 4:10, 14	252
	6.6.2 John 7:37–38	254
	6.6.3 John 7:39	256
6.7	The Holy Spirit in John 14	258
	6.7.1 The "Advocate"	258
	6.7.2 The "Other Paraclete"	260
	6.7.3 Other Aspects	261
6.8	The Holy Spirit in John 15	263
	6.8.1 John 15:26–27	263
	6.8.2 Comparison with 1 John 5:6–8	265
6.9	The Holy Spirit in John 16	266
	6.9.1 To the Disciples' Benefit	266
	6.9.2 Threefold Legal Proof	268
	6.9.3 Guiding Into the Truth	270

	6.10	The Holy Spirit in John 19 and 20	271
		6.10.1 John 19:30	271
		6.10.2 John 20:22	273
7	The Coming of the Spirit		277
	7.1	Spirit Baptism Announced	278
		7.1.1 By John the Baptist (Synoptic Gospels)	278
		7.1.2 By John the Baptist (Gospel of John)	281
		7.1.3 By Jesus Himself	282
	7.2	Parallels Between Jesus and the Church	285
		7.2.1 Preparation	285
		7.2.2 The Anointing With the Spirit	286
		7.2.3 The Works of the Spirit	287
	7.3	The First Outpouring	289
		7.3.1 Sinai and Zion	289
		7.3.2 Torah and Spirit	291
		7.3.3 The One Hundred Twenty	293
	7.4	The Three Thousand	295
		7.4.1 Peter's Sermon	295
		7.4.2 The People's Response	297
		7.4.3 Gift and Gifts	299
	7.5	The Samaritans	301
		7.5.1 The Gospel in Samaria	301
		7.5.2 Spirit Baptism for the Samaritans	303
		7.5.3 False Inferences	304
		7.5.4 The Meaning of the Samaritan Events	306
	7.6	Two Individuals	307

	7.6.1 The Ethiopian Eunuch	307
	7.6.2 Saul of Tarsus	309
7.7	A Gentile Pentecost	310
	7.7.1 Cornelius and His Friends	310
	7.7.2 The Sequence of Events	312
	7.7.3 The Disciples at Ephesus	313
7.8	The Holy Spirit and Some Key Terms	316
	7.8.1 The Kingdom of God	316
	7.8.2 Witnessing	320
	7.8.3 Signs and Wonders	322
8	Believing Through the Holy Spirit	325
8.1	Introduction	326
	8.1.1 A Twofold Work of the Spirit	326
	8.1.2 Even Today No Automatism	328
	8.1.3 Aspects of Conversion	329
8.2	The Holy Spirit and Rebirth	332
	8.2.1 John 3	332
	8.2.2 A New Nature	334
	8.2.3 Made Alive by the Spirit	336
	8.2.4 Sanctification and Justification by the Spirit	338
8.3	Related Expressions	340
	8.3.1 Obedience, Circumcision	340
	8.3.2 Released, Set Free	342
	8.3.3 The Spirit of Faith	343
8.4	Receiving the Spirit at Conversion	344
	8.4.1 General Remarks	344
	8.4.2 The Indwelling of the Spirit	347
	8.4.3 The Spirit of Sonship	349

		8.4.4 The Ministry of the Spirit	351
	8.5	Firstfruits and Measures	353
		8.5.1 Firstfruits of the Spirit	353
		8.5.2 Four "Measures" of the Spirit	355
		8.5.3 Partakers of the Spirit	356
	8.6	"Baptism" in 1 Corinthians 12	358
		8.6.1 Which Baptism?	358
		8.6.2 Unity Through Spirit Baptism	360
	8.7	A "Second Blessing"?	362
		8.7.1 Believing and Sealing	362
		8.7.2 Romans 7 and 8	364
	8.8	Time Between Rebirth and Spirit baptism	366
		8.8.1 Five Cases	366
		8.8.2 Again: Rebirth and Spirit Baptism	368
	8.9	The Fullness of the Spirit	370
		8.9.1 Five Groups	370
		8.9.2 Evaluation	372
	8.10	Terminological Confusion	374
		8.10.1 Second Blessing? Baptized? Filled?	374
		8.10.2 John Wimber	376
		8.10.3 Luke Versus Paul?	378
9	Walking By the Holy Spirit		381
	9.1	Guidance By the Spirit	382
		9.1.1 The Pillar of the Cloud	382
		9.1.2 Guidance in the Book of Acts	385
		9.1.3 Paul's Visit to Jerusalem	387
	9.2	Guidance in Church History	389

	9.2.1 Earlier Centuries	389
	9.2.2 Recent Centuries	392
	9.2.3 Same Bible, Different Applications	394
	9.2.4 Different Times, Different Views	397
9.3	Exegesis and the Spirit's Guidance	399
	9.3.1 Hermeneutical Developments	399
	9.3.2 Is There Meaning In the Text?	401
	9.3.3 The New Hermeneutics and the Spirit	402
	9.3.4 Self-Reflection	404
9.4	Spirit Guidance in Romans 8	406
	9.4.1 Flesh and Spirit	406
	9.4.2 Mortifying Evil Actions	409
	9.4.3 Other Pauline Passages	411
9.5	*Theosis*	412
	9.5.1 A Step Beyond Justification	412
	9.5.2 The Fullness of God	414
9.6	The Conflict Between Flesh and Spirit	417
	9.6.1 Receiving and Walking	417
	9.6.2 Two Antagonists	418
	9.6.3 A Fine Balance	420
9.7	The Fruit of the Spirit	422
	9.7.1 Introduction	422
	9.7.2 Inner Excellency	425
	9.7.3 Benevolence Toward Others	427
	9.7.4 Other Moral Features	428
9.8	The Remainder of Galatians 5	430
	9.8.1 The Fruit and the Law	430
	9.8.2 In Step With the Spirit	432

	9.8.3 The Harvest of the Spirit	433
9.9	Some Remaining Aspects	435
	9.9.1 Practical Sanctification	435
	9.9.2 Praying in the Spirit	437
	9.9.3 Glossolalia in Romans 8?	438
10 The Dwelling Place of the Holy Spirit		443
10.1	God's Dwelling Places	444
	10.1.1 Eden, Sinai, Moriah	444
	10.1.2 Jesus the New Temple	446
	10.1.3 From Garden to Garden	448
10.2	A Holy Temple	450
	10.2.1 Dwelling Place of the Holy Spirit	450
	10.2.2 Dwelling and Ministry	451
10.3	Dwelling "In God"	454
	10.3.1 Four Aspects	454
	10.3.2 Eternal Life	455
10.4	Spiritual Leadership in the Church	458
	10.4.1 Overseers	458
	10.4.2 Prophets	461
	10.4.3 The New Testament Church "Office"	463
	10.4.4 The Correlativity of Gifts and Offices	465
10.5	The Unity of the Church	467
	10.5.1 Body, House, Family	467
	10.5.2 Ephesians 4:3–6	469
	10.5.3 Philippians 2:1–5	470
10.6	Worship	471
	10.6.1 John 4	471

10.6.2 The Collective Aspect	473
10.6.3 The Creative Aspect	474
10.7 Jesus and the Church	475
10.7.1 Six Similarities	475
10.7.2 Another Six Similarities	477
10.7.3 Jesus as Prototype	479
10.7.4 Proper Preparation	480
10.8 The Sacraments	481
10.8.1 What Are Sacraments?	481
10.8.2 How the Sacraments Work	483
10.8.3 Sacraments and the Spirit	485
10.9 The Universal Spirit and Christ	487
10.9.1 The Spirit's Omnipresence	487
10.9.2 Barth and Some Opponents	489
10.10 Creation and Re-Creation	491
10.10.1 No Dualism	491
10.10.2 One Word of God	492
10.10.3 *Creatio Continua?*	494
10.10.4 *Creatio Nova?*	495
10.11 The Spirit Blows Where He Wishes	497
10.11.1 Working Outside the Church	497
10.11.2 Aslan and Emeth	499
10.11.3 The Spirit Is Universal	500
11 Being Filled With the Spirit	503
11.1 Filling	504
11.1.1 What Is It?	504
11.1.2 Ecstasy	506
11.1.3 "Prophesying"	507

11.2	Fasting	509
	11.2.1 Asceticism	509
	11.2.2 Preparation	511
11.3	Effects of Being Filled (1)	513
	11.3.1 Introduction	513
	11.3.2 Power	514
	11.3.3 The Service of God	515
	11.3.4 Obedience and Dedication	516
11.4	Effects of Being Filled (2)	517
	11.4.1 Compassion	517
	11.4.2 Worship	518
	11.4.3 Spiritual Warfare	519
11.5	Effects of Being Filled (3)	520
	11.5.1 Prophecy	520
	11.5.2 Witnessing	521
	11.5.3 Miraculous Works	522
	11.5.4 Preaching	523
11.6	The Transfer of the *Dynamis*	525
	11.6.1 Healing Through Hands	525
	11.6.2 God's Hands	527
	11.6.3 Other Ways of Transfer	528
11.7	Parallels With the Occult	530
	11.7.1 The Magicians of Egypt	530
	11.7.2 Simon the Magician	531
	11.7.3 The Spirit and the Physical	532
11.8	Special Manifestations	535
	11.8.1 Being "Slain in the Spirit"	535
	11.8.2 The Human Spirit Versus the Divine Spirit	536

11.9 Psycho-Physical Relationships		538
11.9.1 Natural-Scientific		538
11.9.2 Biblical Application		540
11.9.3 Trembling and Falling		541
11.9.4 Again: Prophetic Ecstasy		543
11.10 Empowering		545
11.10.1 Various Anointings		545
11.10.2 Vulnerability		546
11.10.3 Oppression		548
12 The Gifts of the Holy Spirit		**551**
12.1 Gifts and Ministries		552
12.1.1 *Pneumatika*		552
12.1.2 Trinitarian Involvement		554
12.1.3 Enumeration		555
12.2 *Charismata*		557
12.2.1 Gifts of Grace		557
12.2.2 What Is "Gift"?		559
12.2.3 Old Testament Gifts		561
12.3 Gifts of Illumination		563
12.3.1 Introduction		563
12.3.2 [1] A Word of Wisdom		564
12.3.3 [2] A Word of Knowledge		566
12.3.4 [7] Discerning the Spirits		567
12.4 Gifts of Action		570
12.4.1 [3] Faith		570
12.4.2 [4] Gifts of Healing		572
12.4.3 [5] Performing Miracles		574
12.5 Gifts of Communication		575

12.5.1 [6] Prophecy	575
12.5.2 [8] Various Kinds of Tongues	577
12.5.3 [9] Interpretation of Tongues	580
12.6 Gifts of the Church	581
12.6.1 The Five Ministries	581
12.6.2 The Gifts Are for All	584
12.6.3 Are Miracle Workers More Spiritual?	586
12.7 Were the Gifts Only for the Apostolic Age?	587
12.7.1 Cessationism	587
12.7.2 Historical Notes	589
12.8 The Spirit in 1 Corinthians 13	591
12.8.1 The "More Excellent Way"	591
12.8.2 "The Perfect"	593
12.9 The Spirit in 1 Corinthians 14	595
12.9.1 *Pneuma, Pneumata, Pneumatikos*	595
12.9.2 1 Corinthians 14 on Glossolalia	598
12.9.3 The Spiritual Utterances of Verses 6 and 26	600
12.9.4 Order and Freedom	601
Bibliography	605
Scripture Index	641
Subject Index	671

Series Preface

BY MEANS OF THIS PREFACE, the editor and publisher of this series wish to help the reader both understand and process the content of these volumes.

The capacities and erudition of Dr. Willem J. Ouweneel need no demonstration or defense from us. His voluminous work and prodigious writing stand as a testimony to his love for the Lord Jesus Christ, God's Word, and God's people.

But these volumes present ideas that will surprise some, anger others, and possibly confuse still others. Both the editor and publisher disagree with some of Dr. Ouweneel's assertions and conclusions, but this is not the place for offering our counter-arguments. That requires an altogether different venue. Nevertheless, discerning readers will legitimately wonder why this editor and publisher invested effort and resources in putting these volumes into print.

At least three reasons justify that investment. Each of them is very sensitive.

The first reason is: *self-examination*. Some of our readers may conclude that, in presenting his exegetical, doctrinal, and historical case, Dr. Ouweneel is "coloring outside the lines" of what they have come to believe. He challenges deeply and firmly held convictions and beliefs, like those associated with Israel, with the law of God, with election and reprobation, with infant baptism, with covenant theology, and with justification. At each point, his challenges call us readers to self-examination, regarding our love for Scripture, for the God of Scripture, and for the Truth revealed and incarnated personally in Jesus Christ. One of Ouweneel's challenges is for us believers in Jesus Christ who are Reformed and Presbyterian church members to recognize that there are millions, even billions, of Jesus-believers who disagree with us *and are nevertheless genuine Christians*. And they ought to be acknowledged as such.

The second reason is: *repentance*. Coming, as they do, from one who lives and teaches outside the orbit of many of our readers, Dr. Ouweneel's observations about the state of our (numerous) churches and of our (interminable) doctrinal squabbles ought to embarrass us Reformed and Presbyterian church members. Our incessant polemicizing, our cantankerous stridency, and our offenses against the unity of Christ's church seriously compromise the gospel's witness to the watching world. Brothers and sisters, we must repent of these, for the sake of the gospel, for the sake of the church's witness, and for the sake of our children.

The third reason is: *ecumenicity*. This reason may indeed strike you as strange, but one of the salutary outcomes of reading Dr. Ouweneel's arguments can be this: *not* that you surrender your commitments and convictions that are being challenged, but instead that you come to *respect* and *love* those Jesus-believers who don't share them with you. These Christians are those whose spiritual pilgrimage and gospel-guided history have not brought them to the same place on the road, but who nonetheless are walking the same road as we.

You may well be asking: How, then, is this different from advocating doctrinal relativism? If these distinctive features of Reformed confession and theology are biblical, then why is Dr. Ouweneel being given a microphone for proclaiming his criticisms and rejections of these distinctive emphases of Reformed teaching? The short answer is this: So that from this brother in Christ, this close cousin in the faith, this fellow pilgrim-soldier, we may learn how to lock arms with other Jesus-believers as we face unbelief in our day, even if we can't hold hands. So that we may learn what it means to be Jesus-believers *first*, Reformed or Presbyterian confessors *second*, and only then, *thirdly*, *theological advocates*.

So we leave you with this challenge: Why do you believe what you believe? What is your biblical warrant? Dr. Ouweneel presents fairly the various positions prevalent within Christianity. The reader will learn why others believe what they believe, and why they don't emphasize certain teachings in the same way that we do.

These books, then, are *not* for the faint of faith. But they *are* for those wanting to grow up and mature into the unity of faith in our Lord Jesus Christ (John 17: 20-23; Eph. 4:13).

Nelson D. Kloosterman, editor
John Hultink, publisher

Author's Preface

THIS IS THE SIXTH VOLUME of our series on the "unseen, eternal" things of God (cf. 2 Cor. 4:18). It was Zophar who asked Job: "Can you find out the deep things of God? Can you find out the limit of the Almighty?" (Job 11:7). Insofar as it is given to humanity to grasp these things to some extent, such is possible only through the Holy Spirit: "[A]s it is written, 'What no eye has seen, nor ear heard, nor the heart of man imagined, what God has prepared for those who love him' — these things God has revealed to us through the Spirit. For the Spirit searches everything, even the depths of God. . . . [N]o one comprehends the thoughts of God except the Spirit of God" (1 Cor. 2:9-11). At the same time, the *Spirit himself* is part of these depths of God. If all true theology can be performed through the Spirit alone, pneumatology (the theological study of the Holy Spirit), too, can be performed through this Spirit alone. It is through the Spirit that we know the Spirit.

Those who read an edifying essay concerning the Holy Spirit expect to see the fire of the Spirit burning, to feel the warmth of the Spirit, to hear the wind of the Spirit blowing, and sense the water of the Spirit flowing. Today, such books and articles appear in great numbers in Western countries. I myself have tried to make a contribution to this with my book *Meer Geest in de gemeenten* (*More Spirit in the Churches*).[1] Such books are much needed because the fire, the warmth, and the wind of the Spirit have often been too little felt in our churches. It is a reason for gratitude that this has been changing during recent decades. This development is described in the present book.

On other occasions it is good to take a step back. I mean a step that leads to critical reflection and to thorough theological investigation concerning the biblical doctrine of the person and the work of the Holy Spirit. The resulting publications may help us separate the pneumatological wheat from the chaff. Does all Christian fire and warmth really come from the Holy Spirit? Is everything that blows and flows always from the Spirit? Who and what, actually, *is* the Holy Spirit? What is the Spirit's significance for God's work in this world, for churches and congregations, and for believers' personal lives?

The source of answers to such questions can only be Holy Scripture, as Christian theology has understood it throughout the centuries, and as we, too, try to understand it today. Such understanding is less easy than biblicistic approaches often suggest. From our modern context we try to build a bridge to the context of the apostles and prophets. This is cumbersome labor. The present book is the humble product of such labor. Whether it is a useful contribution to the theological discussion readers must judge for themselves.

There are various differences between devotional books and theological studies. First, in general devotional books are more easily accessible, whereas digesting theological studies requires the reader to expend greater effort. These studies are harder stuff; they demand more reflection. These books are not for bedtime reading.

Second, the difference between them resembles the difference between the eater and the chemist. The person who eats

---

1. Ouweneel (2004).

bread profits from it: that bread nourishes and strengthens the person. The one who chemically analyzes that bread is not edified and does not edify. Yet that person's task is indispensable: such a person continually tests the bread's nutritional quality and the possible presence of damaging substances. The ordinary eater distinguishes between tasteful and less tasteful bread. The chemist distinguishes between healthy and less healthy bread — and concludes that often, "tasteful" and "healthy" are not identical qualities. The chemist's task does not nourish, but may help us find the bread that best nourishes us, no matter how it tastes.

Third, it is incorrect to claim that devotional books touch the heart, whereas theological books touch only the mind. This is a false contrast, since good theology must ultimately touch the heart as well. In the Bible, this heart is as much the seat of our rational deliberations as it is the seat of our feelings, affections, and emotions. Theology touches the heart not through feeling but through reason. Pneumatology X may feel better than Y, but on the basis of rational arguments, X may turn out to be less biblical. To investigate this is the task of theology. Theology moves the heart through reason. In a time when feeling and the will are often valued above reason, such investigation may not be very popular — just as in earlier centuries the opposite was sometimes the case: reason was overestimated so strongly that little room existed for genuinely biblical experience (called so eloquently by many Dutch Calvinists: *bevinding*).

As I said, good theology is led in its investigation by the One who is the very subject of pneumatological study: the Holy Spirit. In this respect, a Spirit-led theologian is usually alert to the danger of self-deception. Therefore, theologians must regularly, humbly, and impartially check their own heart, including their theological starting points and methodology, — insofar as this is at all possible — in the light of God's Word and Spirit. Where this matter is brought up I try to account for this in the present book.

This volume is a re-working and expansion of volume 1 of my *Evangelisch-Dogmatische Reeks* (Evangelical Dogmatic Series, published in Dutch by Medema [Heerenveen], consisting of twelve volumes in total).[2] My intention in writing this series was, and is, to offer an Evangelical analysis of various subjects that traditionally have played a great role in Reformational—especially Calvinist—thinking: the law, the covenant, justification, predestination, the kingdom, and the Holy Spirit. The order of the volumes is rather arbitrary. I may add that especially the latter two subjects, God's kingdom and God's Spirit, seem to rank highly on God's agenda since the second half of the twentieth century. It is my impression that this is realized better in many free church Evangelical circles than in many traditional Protestant circles.

Bible quotations in this book are usually from the English Standard Version.

I thank Dr. Nelson D. Kloosterman again very warmly for his expert editorial work on the manuscript of this book. And I am again deeply thankful to my publisher, John Hultink, for his constant encouragement in this entire project.

Willem J. Ouweneel
Spring 2017

---

2. Ouweneel (2007a).

Abbreviations

Bible Versions

AMP	Amplified Bible
AMPC	Amplified Bible, Classic Edition
ASV	American Standard Version
BRG	BRG Bible
CEB	Common English Bible
CEV	Contemporary English Version
CJB	Complete Jewish Bible
DARBY	Darby Translation
DLNT	Disciples' Literal New Translation
DRA	Douay-Rheims 1899 American Edition
ERV	Easy-to-Read Version
ESV	English Standard Version
EXB	Expanded Bible
GNT	Good News Translation
GNV	1599 Geneva Bible
GW	God's Word Translation
HCSB	Holman Christian Standard Bible
ICB	International Children's Bible
ISV	International Standard Version
JUB	Jubilee Bible 2000
KJ21	21st Century King James Version

KJV	King James Version
LEB	Lexham English Bible
MEV	Modern English Version
MOUNCE	Mounce Reverse-Interlinear New Testament
MSG	The Message
NABRE	New American Bible (Revised Edition)
NASB	New American Standard Bible
NCV	New Century Version
NET	New English Translation
NIV	New International Version
NLV	New Life Version
NKJV	New King James Version
NOG	Names of God Bible
NRSV	New Revised Standard Version
OJB	Orthodox Jewish Bible
RSV	Revised Standard Version
TLB	Living Bible
TLV	Tree of Life Version
VOICE	The Voice
WE	Worldwide English (New Testament)
WEB	World English Bible
WYC	Wycliffe Bible
YLT	Young's Literal Translation

Other Sources

BT	Kelly, W., ed. *The Bible Treasury*. Winschoten: H. L. Heijkoop.
CNT	Commentaar op het Nieuwe Testament
COT	Commentaar op het Oude Testament
CD	Barth, K. 2009. *Church Dogmatics. Study*

	Edition. Translated by G. W. Bromiley et al. Vols. I/1–IV/1. New York, NY: T&T Clark. (Editor'scNote: The original fourteen volumes have been published in the *Study Edition* as thirty-one volumes. For citation purposes, the original volume enumeration is followed by the number of the equivalent new volume: e.g., III/3=18. The sections [§] are identical in both editions. The final number[s] refer[s] to the page[s] in the new *Study Edition*. Sample citation convention: *CD* III/3=18, §51.2:130.)
CR	*Corpus Reformatorum*. 1st series and 2nd series. Vols. 1–87. Brunswick: Schwetschke, 1834–1900.
CW	Darby, J. N. n.d. *The Collected Writings of J. N. Darby*. Edited by W. Kelly. London: G. Morrish.
EBC	The Expositor's Bible Commentary
EDR	Evangelisch-Dogmatische Reeks
EGT	Expositor's Greek Testament
KV	Korte Verklaring der Heilige Schrift
NICNT	*New International Commentary on the New Testament*
NICOT	New International Commentary on the Old Testament
NIDNTT	Brown, C., ed. 1992. *The New International Dictionary of New Testament Theology*. 4 vols. Carlisle: Paternoster.
NIGTC	New International Greek Testament Commentary
RD	Bavinck, H. 2002–2008. *Reformed*

	Dogmatics. Edited by J. Bolt. Translated by J. Vriend. 4 vols. Grand Rapids, MI: Baker Academic.
RGG	Galling, K., ed. *Die Religion in Geschichte und Gegenwart: Handwörterbuch für Theologie und Religionswissenschaft*. Stuttgart: UTB.
RT	Ouweneel, W. J. Forthcoming. *An Evangelical Introduction to Reformational Theology*. Edited by N. D. Kloosterman. 13 vols. Jordan Station, ON: Paideia Press.
TDNT	Kittel, G. et al., eds. 1964–1976. *Theological Dictionary of the New Testament*. Translated by G. W. Bromiley. 10 vols. Grand Rapids, MI: Eerdmans.

Introduction

SOMETIME DURING THE 1990s, while staying in Rome, I entered the Sant'Ignazio Church, that gorgeous church of the Jesuits. It was late Friday afternoon, and I had no other purpose than to admire that wonderful church again. To my utter amazement, the church was filled with people, perhaps fifteen hundred in number. Moreover, they were singing (in Italian) a well-known evangelical song written by American songwriter Carl Tuttle: "Hosanna, Hosanna, Hosanna in the highest." For a moment, I thought I was in an Evangelical church. I asked the people at the information desk near the church's entrance what was going on. The reply was: *Cattolici carismatici*, "Charismatic Catholics." How Charismatic they were was evident from their "happy clappy" singing. How Catholic they were became clear when a bit later they began praying the rosary.

What struck me most were the long lines, about ten of them scattered throughout the church, of people who were waiting in front of the confessionals. These confessionals were simply chairs arranged in pairs, visible to everyone. Thus, everybody could see the priest and his visitor talking together. Such a conversation lasted ten minutes easily, but the people in line did not care; they had all the time of the world. While waiting in line, they participated in singing and praying. The thought struck me that, thanks to this kind of confession, Charismatic Catholics presumably needed fewer psychotherapists than typical Western Protestants.

This event was my first encounter with one of those remarkable phenomena belonging to the Spirit-led renewals of the last half-century. I met them again when I was walking as a "pilgrim" in Spain on my way to Santiago de Compostela (2005). Since then, I have met them in other countries as well, and I began to hear about the Belgian Cardinal Leo Suenens, who played a great role in the Charismatic movement, and influenced even the Belgian royal family in this regard. In the Netherlands, since 1972, Catholic and Reformed Charismatics work together happily in the *Charismatische Werkgemeenschap Nederland* (The Netherlands Charismatic Cooperative).

The Charismatic movement has had an enormous impact. Fifty or sixty years ago, there were about one thousand Pentecostals in my own country, the Netherlands, but at present there are — taking the term in its widest sense — more than one hundred times as many. According to Patrick Johnstone of WEC International and Operation World in England, in 2005 the Netherlands had almost 400,000 Charismatic Christians (again, taking the term in its widest sense) among a population of 16 million; this constituted about 2.5% of the population. Only 25% of them belonged to Pentecostal and related churches; the rest was found in traditional churches.[1] Johnstone described "Charismatics" as Christians who have undergone an experience of renewal by the Holy Spirit and have received special gifts from the Spirit (glossolalia, healing, prophecy, miracles). According to the Pew Research Center, Pentecostals and Charismatic Christians numbered more than 584 million worldwide in 2011, which constituted 25% of the world's two billion Christians; this was, for instance, about seven times the number of Calvinists worldwide.[2] Statisticians expect that by 2020, the number of "Renewalists" (Pentecostals, Charismatics, etc. — in 1970 about 63 million)

---

1. Quoted by Siebesma in Doornenbal and Siebesma (2005, 233–34).
2. Pew Forum (2011, 67).

will approach 700 million; this will be almost half of all regular churchgoers, and approximately 10% of the entire world population.[3] We should be careful in drawing far-reaching conclusions from these numbers, but the trend is certainly remarkable.

In chapter 1 of this book, I will observe that, in systematic theology and church history, the Holy Spirit is the "major unknown factor." British theologian Michael Green began his own book, *I Believe in the Holy Spirit*, by stating that many Christians today would be greatly embarrassed by Paul's question: "Did you receive the Holy Spirit when you believed?" (Acts 19:2); they would have to answer: "Nay, we did not so much as hear whether the Holy Spirit was [given]" (v. 2b ASV[4]).[5] I have heard traditional Protestants complain that in their churches the Holy Spirit is hardly ever mentioned — except, of course, on Pentecost Sunday, when the pastor cannot avoid the subject. But even then, he usually preaches on Acts 2 or on the Spirit's work in regeneration. No wonder this is the case; neither John Calvin's *Institutes of the Christian Religion*[6] and Abraham Kuyper's *The Work of the Holy Spirit*,[7] goes much further than to discuss the Spirit's work of regeneration, justification, and sanctification, aside from the doctrines of the Trinity and of the inspiration of Scripture.

Before Michael Green, Lesslie Newbigin gave his own application of Acts 19:2. In a challenging way, he stated that the apostle's Roman Catholic successors would ask their future members: "Were the hands that were laid upon you indeed

---

3   See http://www.gordonconwell.edu/ockenga/research/documents/2ChristianityinitsGlobalContext.pdf.
4. I prefer this rendering to the traditional translation (e.g., ESV: "No, we have not even heard that there is a Holy Spirit"). Why would disciples of John the Baptist not have known about the Holy Spirit (cf. Matt. 3:11; John 1:32–33)? What they did not know was whether he had already *descended* (cf. John 7:38–39).
5. Green (1975, 11).
6. See http://www.ccel.org/ccel/calvin/institutes/.
7. See http://www.ccel.org/ccel/kuyper/holy_spirit.html.

our hands?," while Paul's Protestant successors would ask instead, "Did you indeed believe precisely what we taught?" If the responses are satisfactory, both types of successors assure their converts that they have received the Holy Spirit, even if the latter have not the slightest awareness of this.[8] Dutch (Pentecostal, later Dutch Reformed) theologian Jean-Jacques Suurmond put it this way: The first question of Catholics for identifying Christians is: "Did you receive the sacraments?" The first question of Protestants is: "Do you have the right doctrine?" The first question of Pentecostals is: "Did you receive the Holy Spirit?"[9]

Nowadays, more than sixty years after Newbigin's statement, the situation has improved significantly; many Catholics and traditional Protestants have come to realize that experiencing the power of the Holy Spirit in the Christian life is at least as important as receiving the sacraments or having correct Christian doctrine. However, the situation is still far from ideal. There are still too many Christians who believe purely theoretically that they have received the Holy Spirit, without knowing the power of the Spirit in their personal lives. But we are on the right road.

Stanley Burgess claimed that, after centuries of indifference, the Western churches of the twentieth century have experienced a dramatic rebirth in their interest concerning the nature and work of the Holy Spirit, and in their experience of his presence and power. Burgess also quoted the British theologian F. D. Maurice, who made a remarkable prediction: he believed that this new awareness of the Spirit would in turn lead to a reformation even more profound and effective than that of the sixteenth century.[10] Suurmond expressed the same expectation.[11] He said that, in the 1960s, nobody would have expected that, by the end of the twentieth century, the Holy

---

8. Newbigin (1954, 104).
9. Suurmond (1995, 99).
10. Burgess (1989, 1).
11. Suurmond (1995, 74).

Spirit would play such a prominent role again in the Christian world. If the present trend were to continue (and today we know that it did), this would imply a revolutionary turn in the direction that the church had taken since the third century. Suurmond, too, suggested that this would be a more radical event than the Reformation because the Reformers had left the church's *structure* basically intact. This structure was oriented more toward "order" (the Word, the right doctrine, the right offices) than toward the work of the Spirit (other than regeneration, justification, and sanctification).

I write this introduction after having just preached at a renewal conference in the Netherlands that is part of the international "New Wine" movement. In my country, the movement was initiated by the Kuyperian Reformed pastor Dick Westerkamp. There were about 6,000 (!) participants, mainly from the Protestant Church in the Netherlands and from Reformed churches of Kuyperian orientation (Liberated Reformed [Dutch *Gereformeerd vrijgemaakt*], Netherlands Reformed [Dutch *Nederlands Gereformeerd*]), in addition to a number of Baptists and free church Evangelicals. The conference included, among many other things, seminars on glossolalia, on healing ministry, and on (charismatic) worship. Those who were concerned in earlier decades with liberal tendencies among Dutch Kuyperians may now have another reason for concern: charismatic tendencies!

During the Pentecost season of the church year, there is a weekend conference in the Netherlands that is attended by 50,000 to 65,000 (!) Christians. I have preached there several times. This *Opwekkingsconferentie* (Revival Conference) began in 1970 with about 250 Pentecostals. Today, 60-70% of the participants come from traditional (Reformed) denominations.

One special reason for gratitude is that this new interest in the Holy Spirit has a strongly ecumenical character. It brings conservative orthodox Christians together from many different denominational backgrounds. In 1977, Patrick Regan wrote that church history had exhibited many "charismatic" renewal movements, but that these usually led to various splinter groups—such as the Pentecostal churches earlier in the twentieth century—instead of being integrated into the Christian establishment.[12] This is now changing very rapidly. There are still books being written *against* Pentecostals and Charismatics, but at the same time there is a growing interest in what is *taught* by these Christians. Stanley Burgess stated that it is no longer acceptable to adopt that snobby attitude that misjudged the charismatic dimension of spirituality as a movement consisting merely of extremists and enthusiasts.[13] In 2007, the secretary of the Protestant Church in the Netherlands (Bas Plaisier) and the chairman of the United Pentecostal and Evangelical Congregations (Peter Sleebos) publicly asked *each other's* forgiveness for the way they had looked down upon each other in the past.

Just as traditional churches have begun to listen to Charismatic preachers, the (free church) Charismatic movement and, more widely, the entire (free church) Evangelical movement have become less anti-theological and anti-establishment. Here, too, more and more Christians are listening to what has been preserved by a theological tradition of almost two thousand years. This self-critical attention and respect for the theological tradition is indeed a great gain. And this is a matter not only of listening to each other but also of praying and worshiping together. Clark Pinnock rightly wrote that the Spirit is known not only through study, but also through prayer, and that we therefore have to become people of prayer, who are prepared to be open not only to their fellow Christians but first and foremost to God.[14]

There is an entirely new movement of listening to each other, of opening up to one another's arguments, of reexamining views that have been thoughtlessly adopted from pre-

---

12. Regan (1977, 333–34).
13. Burgess (1997, 8).
14. Pinnock (1996, 13).

decessors but that turn out to be no longer tenable, and of learning to read various Bible portions in a fresh way. The present book aims to be a modest contribution to this movement. Its subject matter—shedding light on the person and the work of the Holy Spirit for the Church of the twenty-first century—is more than worth it.

Chapter 1
Earlier Pneumatology

In the beginning,
  God created the heavens and the earth.
The earth was without form and void,
  and darkness was over the face of the deep.
And the Spirit of God was hovering
  over the face of the waters.
And God said, "Let there be light,"
  and there was light.
                                    Genesis 1:1–3

Summary: *The Holy Spirit has been referred to as the "forgotten God" and the "unknown God," especially in the Western church; in the Eastern church, his place was always far more important because of different emphases in its theology. Several explanations are offered for the neglect of the Spirit in the history of theology. One is the different place of spirituality; the point is not only what the church has to say about the Spirit, but what the Spirit has to say to the church. In the early church, tension arose between the free utterances of the Spirit and the increasing institutionalization of the church. Attention is given to Montanism, the Council of Constantinople (381), and Augustine's views. Of dramatic significance was* the Schism between East and West (1054), which involved the issue of *filioque* (whether the Spirit proceeded from Father **and** the Son, or from the Father alone). The deeper causes were much wider, and the consequences of the Schism were enormous.

1.1 Place in Systematic Theology
1.1.1 The "Forgotten God"

PNEUMATOLOGY IS THE DOCTRINE of the Holy Spirit, as an "-ology" comparable to other theological "ologies": anthropology (doctrine of humanity), hamartiology (doctrine of sin), Christology, soteriology (doctrine of salvation), ecclesiology (doctrine of the church), eschatology (doctrine of the last things), theology proper (doctrine of God). However, whereas within systematic theology each of these "-ologies" occupies its own assigned space, in general this is not the case with pneumatology. Other than Pentecostal and Charismatic systematic-theological handbooks, current Roman Catholic, Lutheran, and Calvinist handbooks usually do not contain their own separate chapter(s) on pneumatology. What we are told about the Holy Spirit in such works is mentioned under the *doctrine of God*, where he is discussed as a member of the divine Trinity, the *doctrine of revelation*, where he is discussed in relation to the inspiration of Scripture, and the *doctrine of salvation*, where the Spirit's activity in regeneration, conversion, justification, and sanctification is described.

Sometimes, the Holy Spirit is also discussed under the *doctrine of the church*. This has to do with the fact that, in ancient creeds (the Apostles' Creed and the Nicene Creed), the confession of the Holy Spirit is directly followed by the confession about the church, as if these are closely related, if not identical. Thus, for instance, the Apostles' Creed (Latin version) says, "I believe in the Holy Spirit, the [or, a] holy, universal church" (Lat. *credo in Spiritum Sanctum, sanctam ecclesiam catholicam*). Some suggest that this refers to the Spirit not as a divine person only, but also as the power that makes the church a holy, universal, apostolic church[1] — the church as the "embodiment" (or, as some have said, the "incarnation") of the Holy Spirit. The forgiveness of sins, the resurrection of the body, and everlasting life, mentioned after the church, could all be considered to depend on the Holy Spirit.[2]

In my view, the fact that the great handbooks of systematic theology usually do not contain a separate discussion about the Holy Spirit is symptomatic. Perhaps it is a token of a lack of interest, but more likely it is a token of a certain ignorance, or embarrassment. Quite a few pneumatological treatments that do exist therefore begin with stating that the study of the person and work of the Holy Spirit has been strongly neglected in church history.[3] The Cappadocian theologian Gregory of Nazianzus described the Spirit as the "undescribed God" (Gk. *theos agraptos*), the God about whom no one writes. Augustine, too, claimed that, until his own time, far less attention had been paid to the Holy Spirit than to the Father and the Son.[4] The philosopher Nikolai Berdayev, of Russian Orthodox descent, described pneumatology as "the last uninvestigated theological boundary."[5]

Some nineteenth-century Roman Catholic theologians called the Holy Spirit the "forgotten God."[6] Elizabeth Johnson spoke of the faceless, shadow-like, ghost-like, anonymous, unknown or semi-known, homeless God.[7] She also wrote that forgetting the Spirit is not disowning a faceless, shadow-like third hypostasis (i.e., person within the Godhead), but rather to disown the mystery of God, which is nearer to us than we are to ourselves, and comes closer and passes in quickening, liberation compassion.[8] Since the time of the church fathers,

---

1. Congar (1997, 2.5–6).
2. Ibid., 2.123.
3. Kärkkäinen (2002, 16–18).
4. Augustine, *De fide et symbolo* 9.18–19.
5. Berdayev (1964, 22).
6. Gelpi (1992, 185).
7. Johnson (2002, 130, with references).
8. Ibid., 131.

others have spoken of the "Unknown Third One" (cf. the "unknown third variable" in algebra). Still others, in our own day, have described the Holy Spirit as the Cinderella of the Trinity: whereas the other two sisters are allowed to go to the theological ball, Cinderella must stay home.

The Spirit has indeed been treated in a neglectful manner.[9] In the liturgy, there are many lines in which the Father and the Son are praised, followed by the Latin phrase *cum Sancto Spiritu* ("with the Holy Spirit"), as a kind of afterthought (see §3.5.2).[10] (In Latin phrases such as *Gloria Patri et Filio et Spiritui Sancto*, though, the Spirit is praised along with the Father and the Son.) In every church tradition, the practical meaning of Pentecost is much less than that of Christmas and Easter. Yet, the Spirit is significant in every Christian feast: in terms of Christmas, Jesus was begotten by the Spirit (Matt. 1:20), in relation to Good Friday, he offered himself through the eternal Spirit (Heb. 9:14), and on Easter, he was raised in the power of the Spirit (cf. Rom. 1:4; 1 Pet. 3:18).

1.1.2 East and West

The Western church shares more blame than the Eastern church for the neglect of pneumatology. Stanley Burgess emphasized that pneumatology always constituted the heart of Eastern Christian theology.[11] Even before the great Schism (1054), Eastern theologians reproached their Western colleagues for their "forgetfulness" with regard to the Holy Spirit. The latter were more occupied with Trinitarian themes, especially the procession of the Spirit (see §§1.5 and 1.6), than with pneumatological subjects as such. In more recent times, too, Eastern theologians reproached the Western church for a kind of Christomonism, a strong focus upon Christ at the expense of the Holy Spirit.

---

9. Sirks (1957); cf. Moltmann (1992, 1); Johnson (2002, 130–31).
10. Pinnock (1996, 10). Incidentally, the musical tradition does devote significant attention to the Lat. phrase *cum Sancto Spiritu* in the *Gloria* part of the mass, by treating the words in an exuberant, often fugue-like way.
11. Burgess (1989, 1).

Among Western Christians Christology comes first, while among Eastern Christians pneumatology comes first; this has been the case since the time of the Eastern church fathers, Athanasius of Alexandria, Basil the Great, and Cyril of Alexandria. This is especially the consequence of the more radical Western view of the Fall, leading to a stronger emphasis on soteriology, and only then on pneumatology. Without oversimplifying, we might say that Western theology focused on the question: "How do I receive salvation?," whereas Eastern theology focused on the question: "How do I receive the Holy Spirit?" Of course, the two questions are related — there is no reception of the Spirit apart from salvation, and *vice versa* — yet, the emphasis is quite different.

One could also put it this way: in general, Western Christians start from Genesis 3: the Fall and the restoration of it through the work of Christ. Eastern Christians start from Genesis 1: the image of God, and the manifestation of it in believers through the work of the Holy Spirit. Or, as Jean-Jacques Suurmond put it,[12] the West worked from the Augustinian starting point of the sinful individual, who, judged by the Word of God, must be justified and sanctified. Thus, a strong emphasis came to be placed on the guilt and unworthiness of humans, and faith often degenerated into a joyless moral code. By contrast, the East always beat the festival drum more loudly because they retained more firmly the early Christian emphasis on the Spirit. Whereas in the West the gifts of the Spirit were soon considered to be a kind of accessories, no longer needed since the church could stand on its own legs, the East always continued to regard the *charismata* as constitutive for the church.

In light of this tremendous difference, leading to the underestimation of the Spirit among Western Christians, it is no wonder that in Western Christianity the most "charismatic" pneumatological contributions came from the "outer edges"

---

12. Suurmond (1995, 68).

of the church: mystics, Cathars, the prophetic women (e.g., Hildegard of Bingen, Catherine of Siena, and the apocalyptics (Joachim of Fiore, much later Thomas Müntzer).[13] Even more boldly, one might argue that, in certain respects, the free church movements in the West, including the Charismatic movement, link up better with the pneumatological tradition of the Eastern tradition than with Roman Catholicism and traditional Protestantism.[14]

1.2 Neglect of the Spirit
1.2.1 First Explanation

Pneumatological treatises of recent decades often begin with the complaint concerning the modest place traditionally assigned to the Holy Spirit in systematic theology. Even if a systematic-theological work contains many references to Scriptural passages about the Spirit, this is not evidence that in such a work true justice is being done to pneumatology. But sometimes that number of references is in fact very limited.[15] People may write about the "essence of Christianity," or "the essence of (neo-)Calvinism" as a theology and a worldview, with few if any references to the Holy Spirit,[16] and so on.

No *locus* (topic) within systematic theology remains the same if it is thoroughly reflected upon and re-worked in a pneumatological sense.[17] So important and decisive are the place and role of the Spirit. Therefore, the twofold solution for (as the Germans say) our *Geistvergessenheit* (our having forgotten the Spirit) is the inclusion of a distinct pneumatological *locus*, and the pneumatological leavening of all the other *loci*. Just as surely as every systematic-theological *locus* has

---

13. Burgess (1997, 5–6).
14. I will return to the position of Eastern Christianity concerning the Spirit in §§1.3 and 1.4.
15. L. Berkhof (1996); De Graaf (1940); Rahner (1978); Spykman (1992); Dijk (n.d.); Geisler (2011).
16. Wielenga (n.d.); Kuyper (1899).
17. Grudem (1994) writes about the Holy Spirit under the headings of "God," "Christ," and "the Church."

a Christological basis, so too each ought to have an equally strong pneumatological basis.

Several explanations may be mentioned for what has been referred to as the "pneumatological deficit" (see this and the following sections).[18] The first is a *theological* one, and involves what the Eastern Orthodox theologian John Meyendorff has described as the *kenosis* of the Holy Spirit.[19] The term *kenosis*, from the Greek verb *kenoō*, "to empty (oneself)," goes back to Philippians 2:7, where it is said of Christ that he emptied himself in his incarnation. In an analogous way, some people speak of the kenosis of the Spirit, who supposedly took the "form of a servant" when he was poured out. In this position, he only points away from himself to Christ (cf. John 16:14–15), and thus disappears somewhat into the background. As Hendrikus Berkhof put it: "The Spirit constantly leads our attention away from himself to Jesus Christ. So he hides himself, on the one hand, in Christ; and, on the other hand, he hides himself in his operations in the life of the church and the lives of individuals. As a consequence, the Spirit is rarely mentioned in most of the confessions and in most of the dogmatical handbooks."[20] However, the kenosis of the Spirit[21] does not justify such a neglect of pneumatology.

1.2.2 Second Explanation

A second explanation has to do with what is called the history of theologians, or with (what is closely related to it) the history of (church) dogma. It goes back to the way in which Victorinus of Pettau first, and Augustine later, approached the topic of the Holy Spirit. The former described him as the "bond between the Father and the Son" (*patris et filii copula*), a description that does insufficient justice to the Holy Spirit as

---

18. Hilberath (1992, 445–52).
19. On this, see R. L. Dabney (1997).
20. Berkhof (1964, 10).
21. Presuming we could justify this expression in any sense—which is doubtful, since there is no "incarnation" of the Spirit. On this point, the comparison with the Son fails.

a person equal to the Father and the Son.

In the wake of Victorinus, Augustine described the Spirit as the "bond of love" (*vinculum amoris*) between the Father and the Son (see §1.4.4). Again, this description has not helped very much to underscore the significance of the Holy Spirit: he who speaks of the Spirit as the "bond" existing between two divine persons cannot do justice to the personality of the Spirit himself.[22]

In this connection, the Holy Spirit has been called the "great bridge builder" (Lat. *pontifex maximus*), first between Father and Son, then between God and humanity.[23] It is difficult to see how a person who is "only" the bond or bridge between two other persons can be just as important as these two other persons.[24]

1.2.3 Third Explanation

A third explanation has to do with church history. The establishment of an ordered clergy within the church (second century) led gradually to less room for the free working of the Spirit in the church. At first, the hierarchical[25] and the charismatic elements seemed to remain in a rather good balance. However, the strong rejection of the Montanists (see §1.4.2) indicated that the charismatic line was losing ground. Later church historians and dogmaticians also liked to suggest that, with the rise of the ordered, hierarchical clergy—and according to some, with the closing of the New Testament canon (§12.8.2)—the *charismata* were no longer needed.

The churches of the Reformation, too, introduced a strictly ordered clergy, which again curtailed the free work of the Spirit. Apparently, this was done not out of theological conviction but out of fear of disorder and loss of control. The

---

22. Hilberath (1992, 446–47; 1998, 2–4).
23. See Veenhof (1978).
24. Pinnock seems initially to adopt Augustine's idea (1996, 35), but later distances himself from it (40).
25. Ibid., 119–20; later he uses the word "sacramental," but speaks also of a synergism of gift/charisma and office/institute (140).

most abused Scripture is here 1 Corinthians 14:33, "God is not a God of confusion but of peace" (or, as it is sometimes wrongly rendered, "a God of order"; see AMP, CEV, VOICE, WE). People who appeal to this passage fail to realize that this chapter deals with the *regulation*, not the *suppression*, of spiritual gifts.[26]

Some thought one of the causes of the neglect of the Spirit to be fear of (supposed) religious fanaticism (Montanists, Anabaptists, Quakers, [extreme] Pentecostals, [extreme] Charismatics) as well as fear of the nineteenth-century theological liberalism. In the wake of the German philosopher G. F. Hegel, this liberalism preached its own kind of spirituality (especially Friedrich Schleiermacher), in which the "liberal mind" was no longer Christocentric, and seemed to be merely an extension of the human mind.[27] Similarly, it cannot be denied that certain extreme forms of Charismatism (sometimes called Charismania, or Charismagic) seem to be more Spiritocentric than Christocentric.

1.2.4 Fourth Explanation

A fourth explanation is *socio-cultural*, identified by Roman Catholic feminist theologian Elizabeth Johnson: in her view, the neglect of the Holy Spirit was connected with, among other things, the marginalization of women throughout church history. The scant attention paid by the church to the special place, role, and significance of women was directly related to the scant attention paid to the Holy Spirit, who exhibits such strong feminine traits. For instance, the Hebrew word *ruach* ("spirit") is a feminine word; some apocryphal works and medieval mystics used various feminine metaphors for the Spirit. Believers are "born of the Spirit" (John 3:5; cf. the same expression in Gal. 4:4, "born of a woman"; see on this subject extensively §3.4).

---

26. Cf. Suurmond (1995, 63–66).
27. Berkhof (1964, 11); Van de Beek (1987, 180–81).

1.3 Pneumatology and Spirituality
1.3.1 Spirit-Driven Pneumatology

Virtually every recent pneumatological treatise rejects a scholastic, strictly intellectual approach to the study of the Holy Spirit. In opposition to such an approach, emphasis is placed on the personal and collective (ecclesial) experience of the Spirit; that is, upon true biblical spirituality.[28] Of course, it is no coincidence that the word "spirituality" was derived from the Latin word *spiritus*, "spirit" or "Spirit." Biblical spirituality must be the alpha and omega of all theological pneumatology. The value of any theological pneumatology depends not (only) on the way in which it has managed to order the biblical data in a systematic way, but (also) on the extent to which it manages, through the power of the Spirit, to make the living Word accessible to common believers.

True pneumatology not only theorizes—or even speculates—about the Spirit, but is driven by the Spirit. Speculating about the Spirit has a long history; Augustine stands at its cradle (see §1.4.4). Instead of such speculation, we should instead reverently listen to the Spirit, and should remain reverently silent where the Spirit does not reveal about himself as much as we might wish.

In addition to the scholastic intellectual approach, a real danger exists in the over-institutionalization of many denominations (cf. §12.9). It is refreshing, for instance, to hear Roman Catholic theologians acknowledge this danger. Yves Congar contrasted two principles: the "personal principle," that is, the role that individuals with their personal experiences play within the community, and the "institutional principle," which places more emphasis on the church as a community of people led by the Holy Spirit.[29] In addition, I would like to distinguish further between the church as an institutionalized *organization* and the church as a living *organism*. Congar rightly sought a balance between these personal and institutional

---
28. See, e.g., Moltmann (1992).
29. Congar (1997, 2.152–53).

principles, that is, between the Spirit's work in the lives of individual believers as well as in the community of the church as a whole.

Elsewhere I have tried to explain why God, and in this case, the Holy Spirit, *as such* can never be the object of scientific analysis.[30] The object of theological investigation consists in *statements* about the Holy Spirit—first, statements in the Bible inspired by the Spirit himself, and second, statements in theological literature throughout the centuries. In pneumatological studies, it is instead the Holy Spirit himself who searches the "depths of God" (1 Cor. 2:10), and searches even our own hearts (Rom. 8:27). As one theologian expressed it, the Spirit is breath, not a complete treatise, and therefore he only wishes to breathe through us, not to present himself to us as an object; he wishes not to be seen but to be in us as the seeing eye of grace.[31]

Another theologian[32] recalled Ludwig Wittgenstein's famous paradoxical line: "Whereof one cannot speak, thereof one must be silent,"[33] and commented that we must acknowledge that, although there is little that we could say about the Holy Spirit, what cannot be said is even more profound and significant. If ever the limitations of human language and theologizing can be easily acknowledged, it is in pneumatological investigation. But of course, this recognition does not keep us from saying something about what is ineffable. After all, the Bible itself speaks about the Holy Spirit, and we can—and must—endeavor to process what has been spoken.

1.3.2 "Hear What the Spirit Says"

At the end of each of the seven letters of Revelation 2 and 3, the author says seven times: "He who has an ear, let him hear what the Spirit says to the churches" (2:7, 11, 17, 29; 3:6, 13, 22).

---

30. Ouweneel (2013, chapter 7).
31. Von Balthasar (1993, 111).
32. Kärkkäinen (2002, 175–76).
33. *Tractatus logico-philosophicus* 7.

It is more important to hear what the Spirit says to Christians than what theologians have to say about the Spirit. Especially Pentecostals and Charismatics have strongly emphasized that Christians must indeed reconsider their pneumatology, but that it is far more important that they experience the working of the Holy Spirit, personally and ecclesiastically. Spirituality precedes pneumatology. Good spirituality often—not always—leads to theological reflection upon it, that is, to pneumatology, but unfortunately, the reverse occurs much less frequently. It is possible that a pneumatological orthodoxy is maintained for centuries—"I believe in the Holy Spirit"—whereas the Spirit as a living reality is virtually unknown.

Conversely, we cannot avoid pointing out that, within the Pentecostal and Charismatic movement, theological pneumatology often was not their strong suit. But this has changed, too: New Testament scholars such as Gordon Fee[34] and James Dunn[35] had a Pentecostal background, but as theologians they made a name far beyond their own circle, also in the field of pneumatology.

Many have pleaded before for a healthy balance between pneumatology and spirituality. Our spirituality must be checked by a pneumatology that does justice to the Word; and conversely, such a pneumatology must prove its value in the spiritual practice of individual and church life. As Joseph Ratzinger put it: our experience must be tested and checked so that someone's "own spirit" will not take the place of the Holy Spirit.[36]

Of course, he sees this evaluation as a special task assigned to the church (read: the Roman Catholic Church). There is much truth in this. Conversely, we must not underestimate the prophetic testimony of individuals who can call the church to order.[37] To this end, such individuals must be

---

34. See Fee (1987; 1994; 1999).
35. See Dunn (1970; 1975; 1993; 1998).
36. Ratzinger (1998, 325).
37. In my view, Kärkkäinen (2002, 16) emphasizes this point too little.

led by the Spirit in such an evident way that the church is indeed prepared to listen to them. Church history has witnessed enough so-called prophets whose self-chosen calling had little effect, and rightly so. However, the church can err, too. We may be thankful for prophets to whom (part of) the church did listen: Athanasius, Symeon the New Theologian, Martin Luther, John of the Cross, Seraphim of Sarov, as well as Charles F. Parham, William J. Seymour, Dennis Bennett, and other voices who, in the twentieth century, called the church back to the order of the Spirit.

1.4   Early Charismatics[38]
1.4.1   Charismatic versus Institutionalized

Church history has witnessed various movements that have departed from traditional, established Christianity with its rigid church structure, and have propounded a charismatic type of Christianity. It is difficult to get a clear picture of such movements because the available information often comes only from representatives of institutional Christianity, which took a very critical stand against such "fanatic" movements. In spite of this, one gets the impression that, after the first century, charismatic spiritual Christianity played a much larger role than has often been assumed.

Around the middle of the second century, Justin Martyr testified that prophecy and other *charismata* still existed and functioned.[39] In AD 180, Irenaeus reported about miraculous *charismata* in the church, and around 190 about prophecy and glossolalia.[40] Miltiades (end of the second century) believed that prophecy and the other *charismata* would remain among Christians throughout church history.[41] Although the church was already at that time exhibiting an increasingly outspoken hierarchical structure, with an ordered clergy, this did not yet

---
38. Cf. recently Thiselton (2015, chapter 12).
39. See extensively, Congar (1997, 2.65–72).
40. *Adversus Haereses* V.6.1.
41. Quoted by Eusebius, *Historia Ecclesiae* V.XVII.4.

necessarily impede the functioning of the *charismata*. On the contrary, church and clergy themselves were deemed to be charismatic.

Indeed, in 248, Origen reported that Christians still drove out evil spirits, healed the sick, and gave prophecies.[42] In 252, Cyprian said of the Council of Carthage that it had taken decisions "under the inspiration of the Holy Spirit and according to the warnings given by the Lord in many visions."[43] In the same century, Novatian wrote that the Spirit raised up prophets in the church, instructed the teachers of the church, encouraged tongues, granted strength and health, worked miracles in the church, brought discernment of the spirits, helped those who ruled the church, inspired the councils of the church, and granted the other gifts.[44]

This changed when the following happened: "No longer is it the one whom God destines by the gift of the Spirit who is ordained for the ministry; the one who, in the proper way, has been instituted in the office, henceforth guaranteed the Spirit of God."[45] So first it was: if you had the Spirit, you obtained the office (cf. Acts 20:28). Later it became: if you had the office, you were supposed to automatically possess and distribute the Spirit. Henceforth those who emphasized the necessity of the former — that is, the charismatically minded Christians — were considered to be sectarians. Before this it had been: "Where the Spirit of God is, there is the universal church and all grace."[46] Now it became: where the [hierarchical, institutionalized] church is, there is the Spirit.[47] One could

---

42. *Contra Celsus* I.46.
43. *Letters* LXII.5.
44. Novatian, *De Trinitate*, lib. 29.
45. Schweizer (1968, 451).
46. Irenaeus, *Adversus haereses* 3.24.1.
47. Regarding the Eastern churches: Symeon the New Theologian (c. 1000) still strongly emphasized the individual, charismatic experience of the Spirit; see Congar (1997, 1.93–103); but according to Nicolas Cabasilas (fourteenth century), life in the Spirit can be experienced only through the hierarchical-sacramental church system; see Burgess (1989, 77).

speak here of the "domestication" of the Spirit—to which we may add that, later, scholastic, and still later, liberal and charismatic theology developed their own forms of "domestication."[48]

1.4.2 Montanus

Montanus (second century), the founder of a new charismatic movement within the church, was the first to make a distinction between the church of the Spirit and the church of the bishops. Montanism originated around 160–170 in Phrygia. We possess sharp condemnations of it by various opponents, such as Basil the Great, who asserted that Montanus identified himself with the Paraklete of John 14–16. Unfortunately, we cannot evaluate what in this accusation is true. In addition, we have a more positive evaluation by Tertullian, who is esteemed for his theological writings to this day. Some have claimed that he himself joined Montanism, but others believe this is incorrect. He has remained an influential Catholic authority.

In his judgment of Montanism, Tertullian touched a point that has been disputed to this day: did the gift of prophecy cease when the canon was closed, or does it exist today as well? If the latter, do we possess the complete revelation of God in the canon of the Bible, or can genuine prophets of God pass on new revelations today as well (cf. 1 Cor. 14:29–30)? (a) If no, is the task of present-day "prophets" only the exposition and practical application of Scripture (cf. 1 Cor. 14:3)? (b) If yes, are such prophetic revelations on the same level as those of Scripture, or are they of a lower order? It seems that Tertullian did accept that the doctrinal truth of God lies enclosed and completed in the canon, but that new revelations are possible with regard to the practical life of faith (see further §§10.4.2, 11.5.1, and 12.5.1).

Another point of dispute regarded the biblical assessment of "ecstasis." Here again, the discussion is quite timely be-

---
48 Green (1975, 11–13).

cause the two conceivable positions still occur. Can ecstasis be evidence of the presence and activity of the Holy Spirit? Or must we ascribe ecstasis—think, for instance, of the contemporaneous phenomenon of the *Toronto blessing* (being "slain in the Spirit")—to demonic activity? The opinions were and are very diverse, some preferring to appeal to a middle explanation, in which the phenomena are explained psychologically. In such an explanation, spiritual phenomena, including glossolalia, are thought to come neither from the Spirit nor from the devil, but from the minds of persons themselves (see further §11.8).

1.4.3 Nicaea and Constantinople

The early church fought many battles en route to developing a clear understanding of the personality and divinity of the Holy Spirit (see §§3.3 and 3.4).[49] In line with the Old Testament testimony concerning the Holy Spirit (see, e.g., Ps. 51:11; Isa. 11:2; 30:1; 32:15; 34:16; 40:13; 42:1; 44:3; 48:16; 59:21; 63:10–11; Mal. 2:15), many viewed the Spirit more as a divine force than as a divine person. We cannot elaborate on this extensively, because the story of this battle belongs to the doctrine of God (Lat. *theologia propria*). But a few words about this may be helpful.

At the Council of Nicaea (325), the question of the Holy Spirit did not yet appear on the agenda; the fathers were occupied with describing the relationship between the Father and the Son. However, in the course of that fourth century, the church encountered the doctrine of the Pneumatomachians ("fighters against the Spirit"), the followers of bishop Macedonius, who argued against the doctrine of the Spirit's divinity. At the Council of Constantinople (381), this doctrine was condemned. In the original Nicene Creed, the church confesses the Holy Spirit as "Lord and making alive" (Lat. *Dominum et vivificantem*), the One "who proceeds from the Father" (Lat.

---

49. See Meijering (2002) on the development of trinitarian doctrine, and the summary by Congar (1997, 1.73–84; more extensively, 3.19–132).

qui ex Patre procedit) and "who is worshiped and glorified together with the Father and the Son" (Lat. *qui cum Patre et Fílio simul adoratur et conglorificatur*; cf. §§1.5 and 1.6).

Although not explicitly stated, the confession implies that the Holy Spirit is God because only God is worshiped (Lat. *adoratur*). And since the church was already convinced that not only the Father but also the Son is God, the implication was the doctrine of the divine Trinity: one God, three persons (entities, subsistences). As it was expressed in what is called the Athanasian Creed (late fifth or early sixth century):

> We worship one God in Trinity, and Trinity in Unity; neither confounding the persons; nor dividing the essence. For there is one person of the Father; another of the Son; and another of the Holy Ghost. But the Godhead of the Father, of the Son, and of the Holy Ghost, is all one; the glory equal, the majesty co-eternal. Such as the Father is, such is the Son, and such is the Holy Ghost. The Father uncreated, the Son uncreated, and the Holy Ghost uncreated. The Father unlimited, the Son unlimited, and the Holy Ghost unlimited. The Father eternal, the Son eternal, and the Holy Ghost eternal. And yet they are not three eternals; but one eternal. As also there are not three uncreated; nor three infinites, but one uncreated; and one infinite. So likewise the Father is Almighty; the Son Almighty; and the Holy Ghost Almighty. And yet they are not three Almighties; but one Almighty. So the Father is God; the Son is God; and the Holy Ghost is God. And yet they are not three Gods; but one God. So likewise the Father is Lord; the Son Lord; and the Holy Ghost Lord. And yet not three Lords; but one Lord.

Especially Athanasius and the three Cappadocians (Basil the Great, his brother Gregory of Nyssa, and Gregory of Nazianzus, fourth century) had paved the way for this doctrinal development. They confessed one divine being consisting of three distinct divine persons. The full development of the doctrine of the Holy Spirit required first that the personality of the Spirit be properly distinguished, and then that this person be recognized as a divine person, equal in being to the Father and the Son, that is, not subordinate to them (see §§3.3 and 3.4).

1.4.4 Augustine

The doctrine of the Trinity reached its apex in the work of Augustine, who wrote about the Spirit especially in his work *De Trinitate* (*On the Trinity*, 399–419). In fact, he sought not to proclaim any novelties but merely to expound and summarize the work of the earlier fathers. He did, however, develop an entirely new doctrine concerning the Holy Spirit, which cannot be found explicitly in the Bible but nevertheless acquired an important place in theological tradition, and which has always been ascribed to Augustine. It is the doctrine of the Holy Spirit as the "bond of love" (Lat. *vinculum amoris*) between the Father and the Son.[50]

Augustine's reasoning is as follows. On the one hand, he stated that the Father and the Son have a number of characteristics and relationships in common that the Spirit does not possess. Thus, the Father is the Father of the Son but not the Father of the Spirit. And the Son is the Son of the Father but not the Son of the Spirit. On the other hand, the Spirit is both the Spirit of the Father (Matt. 10:20; Eph. 3:14, 16) and the Spirit of the Son (Gal. 4:6; cf. Acts 16:7; Rom. 8:9; Phil. 1:19; 1 Pet. 1:11). Thus, the Spirit is clearly distinct from both the Father and the Son, at the same time being that which the two have in common; he is their shared holiness and love. To put it more strongly: "God is Spirit" (John 4:24), so the Father is Spirit, the Son is Spirit, and the Holy Spirit is Spirit, that is, he is what Father and Son have in common. In other words: he is the *communion* between them ("the consubstantial and co-eternal communion as such," Lat. *ipsa communio consubstantialis et coaeterna*). Next, he is also the *communion* between believers and God, and between believers mutually.

---

50. Congar (1997, 1.77–92). Bernard of Clairvaux called the Holy Spirit the Father's "kiss" of the Son; Burgess (1997, 53, 55, 57).

Augustine considers "love" to be basically a biblical term for the Spirit (cf. Rom. 15:30, "the love of the Spirit," which might be read as "love, namely, the Spirit"[51]). "God is love" (1 John 4:8, 16). This is true for the Triune God, and in particular for the Holy Spirit. Here, too, the "evidence" is ingenious. According to 1 John 4:12 ("[I]f we love one another, God abides in us")" and verse 16 ("God is love, and whoever abides in love abides in God"), the "abiding" is an effect of love, but in verse 13 ("By this we know that we abide in him and he in us, because he has given us of his Spirit") the "abiding" is an effect of the Holy Spirit. In other words, the Holy Spirit coincides with love. Romans 5:5 ("God's love has been poured into our hearts through the Holy Spirit who has been given to us") seems to support this argument: sending the Spirit of God into our hearts (cf. Gal. 4:6) is equal to pouring God's love into our hearts.

This theory has acquired a fixed place in the pneumatological tradition of the Western established churches, but it does not persuade the reader who is less attached to this tradition. From the side of Eastern Orthodoxy, the fear has been expressed — understandably so — that, if the Holy Spirit is not clearly distinguished as a separate person *alongside* Father and Son, but rather as the "We" of Father and Son, the personality of the Spirit disappears.[52] Yet, Augustine drew some conclusions from his deliberations that do appeal to us, such as that the church is the temple of the Holy Spirit (1 Cor. 3:16; Eph. 2:20-22; see §10.2.1). Every fight and dissent within the church conflicts with the unity of the Spirit (Eph. 4:3), which is the same as saying that it conflicts with love (§10.5.2). The church is, as it were, the embodiment of the Spirit — and she is similarly the embodiment of love.

Since the Spirit is the Spirit of both the Father and the

---

51. For an example of this genitive of apposition, see 2 Cor. 1:22, literally, "the earnest [= guarantee] of the Spirit" (KJV), i.e., "the guarantee, namely, the Spirit."
52. See Pannenberg (1991, 1:315–17).

Son, and is the bond of love between these two, he must also "proceed" from both. This conclusion played a great role in the history of the church, especially because the question became one of the main causes of the great Schism between the Western and the Eastern churches (see §1.5). In the Western church, the authority of Augustine was so enormous that the great medieval thinkers, such as Anselm of Canterbury, Peter Abelard, Bonaventura, and Thomas Aquinas did not add anything essentially new to his pneumatological ideas. One could also put it this way: the medieval Christian thinkers have badly neglected pneumatology.

1.5 The Schism
1.5.1 Introduction

In what way is the Holy Spirit related to the other divine persons within the Trinity? This question occupied the early fathers. The answer ultimately formulated in the extended Nicene Creed was that the Holy Spirit "proceeds from the Father and the Son," while the Athanasian Creed says in article 22: "The Holy Spirit is of the Father and the Son: neither made, nor created, nor begotten, but proceeding." This verb "to proceed" (Gk. *ekporeuomai*) is derived from John 15:26, "the Spirit of truth, who proceeds [Gk. *ekporeuetai*; Vulgate: *procedit*] from the Father."

This *procession* (Lat. *processio*, "proceeding," from the verb *procedere*) was also described as *pnoē* (cf. Gk. *pneuma*), which means "wind" (Acts 2:2) or "breath" (17:25), or in this case "breathing (out)": the Spirit is viewed as "proceeding" from the Father and the Son, just like a person's breath "proceeds" (is "breathed out"). Therefore, the Latin church introduced the term *spiratio* ("breathing [out]"), which is related to the word *spiritus* ("spirit," originally "breath, wind"). A person's breath of life is breathed out continually, yet is never completely severed from the person; a person's breath "remains" in that person until physical death (cf. 1 Kings 17:17). Similarly, the Holy Spirit was described as "proceeding" continually from the Father and the Son by a kind of "breathing out," yet remaining one with them. This *procession* seems to be supported by 1 Corinthians 2:12, "the Spirit who is from God" (Gk. *to pneuma to ek tou theou*, where the preposition *ek*, "out of," is the same preposition found in *ekporeuomai* in John 15:26). Neither 1 Corinthians 2:12 nor John 15:26 proves an eternal *procession* of the Spirit (see next section), but they both agree with this idea.

1.5.2 Evaluation

Through the Ecumenical Creeds, the idea of the procession of the Holy Spirit has become a fixed element of belief in the Roman Catholic Church and the churches of the Reformation. Yet, I believe that no contemporaneous theologian would have arrived at this idea unless he had been instructed in the traditional teaching of his church. For it is obvious that the only Bible passage speaking of the Spirit's procession from the Father (John 15:26) clearly is *not* speaking of an eternal procession, but of the event of Acts 2, as various theologians have admitted.[53]

Herman Bavinck uses John 15:26 as an argument for an eternal procession of the Spirit in the following way:

> But this "being sent" [of the Spirit by the Father and the Son] in time is a reflection of the immanent relations of the three persons in the divine being and is grounded in generation [i.e., the eternal generation of the Son by the Father] and spiration [i.e., the procession of the Spirit]. The incarnation of the Word has its eternal archetype in the generation of the Son, and the outpouring of the Holy Spirit is a weak analogy of the procession from the Father and the Son. The church fathers, accordingly, derived the eternal and immanent relations existing between the persons from the relations that were manifest before the human eye in time. And rightly so.[54]

---

53. Bavinck (*RD* 2.277); Althaus (1952, 699); Pannenberg (19991, 1:306).
54. Bavinck (*RD* 2.320–21); see also Chafer (1983, 6.10).

Bavinck may believe so—and he underscores this with quotations from Augustine[55]—but the reader may definitely expect some more direct Scriptural arguments. These are not available, but the following considerations may be useful. First, there is, of course, a parallel with the doctrine of the eternal generation of the Son by the Father.[56] Some form of generation seems necessarily implied in the very notions of Father and Son. These terms do not necessarily imply masculinity, or the need of a mother, or sexual intercourse—but they do seem to imply some form of generation. The Father–Son relationship can hardly imply only an eternal, intimate love relationship because, in that case, it would be totally obscure why the one is called Father and the other Son. Else, why would not the metaphor of a Husband–Wife, or of Two-Friends, or Two-Brothers be more relevant in this case? In an analogous way, the quality of being eternally "breathed" or "blown" seems to be necessarily implied in the term "Spirit" (Heb. *ruach*, Gk. *pneuma*, both "breath, wind"). Why is the Spirit called "breath" if he is not "breathed"?

This meaning of "breath" is often quite prominent in God's *ruach*: notice Job 15:30, "the *ruach* of his mouth," 27:3, "the *ruach* of God is in my nostrils," Psalm 33:6, "the *ruach* of [God's] mouth," and Isaiah 40:7, "the *ruach* of the LORD blows." Also notice the parallelism with *neshamah* in Job 27:3, 32:8, 33:4, and 34:14, which underscores the element of "breath."[57] In certain passages, the meanings of wind, breath and s/Spirit intermingle in a striking manner (cf. Exod. 14:21 and 15:8, 10; Ezek. 37:1, 5–6, 8–10, 14). The association of *ruach* with "breath" might also be present in 2 Samuel 23:2, "The *ruach* of the LORD speaks by me; his word is on my tongue," as if God's breath forms the words on David's tongue. This

---

55. Van Genderen and Velema (2008, 155–58) and Pinnock (1996, 42) believe the matter is equally self-evident.
56. See extensively, Ouweneel (2007b, §§8.3–8.5).
57. In some passages, the "breath" of God is *neshamah* (Job 4:9; 32:8; 34:14; 37:10; Ps. 18:15; Isa. 30:33).

meaning might be present at other places as well: God's *ruach* hovering (several translations: God's wind sweeping) over the waters (Gen. 1:2) is in the next verse the breath through which he speaks (cf. 1 Kings 22:24; Ezek. 2:2; 3:24; Matt. 10:20; Mark 13:11; John 16:13).

Of course, we are dealing here with a metaphor; but a metaphor must express something about reality. And this is exactly what happens in passages that speak of the *ruach* or the *pneuma* of God's nose or mouth (see extensively, §4.1). But here, too, we must ponder the fact that none of these Bible passages refers to an eternal *procession*, but only to historical actions of God. Can we really derive the idea of an eternal procession from them?

Eternal generation is not necessarily the only possible explanation of the Father–Son relationship; in principle, eternal adoption is another possible explanation. I point here to the parallel with an adoption within time in 2 Samuel 7:14 (cf. Heb. 1:5, Ps. 2:7, and 89:26–27), and to the fact that, in the New Testament, the believers' childhood is linked with begetting and birth (e.g., John 1:12–13), whereas their sonship is linked with adoption (Rom. 8:15, 23; Gal. 4:5; Eph. 1:5). If the eternal generation of the Son is less evident than the tradition might think, the eternal procession of the Spirit is not so evident either. From the fact that literal breath must have a source (mouth, nose), can we conclude that this must also be true for the Spirit? *Ruach* and *pneuma* also mean "wind"; does the literal wind have an identifiable source? Actually not.[58] Jesus said of the *pneuma* (i.e., both Spirit and wind): "The *pneuma* blows where it wishes, and you hear its sound, but you do not know where it comes from or where it goes" (John 3:8). In light of this, could we not say that the idea of an eternal spiration or procession is nothing else than a vain, speculative

---

58. Only in metaphorical language is there such a thing as the "storehouses" of the snow and the hail, or "the place . . . where the east wind is scattered upon the earth" (Job 38:22, 24). *If* such places exist at all, the point of Job 38 is that no human knows anything about it.

attempt to say where the *pneuma* "comes from"?

1.5.3 Other Aspects

It has been argued that, if there is no eternal generation of the Son and no eternal procession of the Spirit, it is difficult to avoid tritheism (the belief in three gods). In this case, we could still say that the three divine persons participate in the same Godhead, but how could this Godhead be more than a merely generic unity of the three persons, just like a marriage or a family is a unity? However, if there is an eternal generation and an eternal procession, we understand how, within the one Godhead, the Father from eternity generates the Son, and the Spirit from eternity proceeds from the Father.

The underlying difficulty is broader than the question of generation and procession. Speaking of the *one* God and the *three* persons within the Godhead has always been a matter of striking a balance somewhere between tritheism and Sabellianism (or modalism).[59] That is, either we fall into the snare of factually speaking of three gods; in the light of the modern psychological description of persons as independent individuals it is hardly possible to refer to divine persons without falling into tritheism (see §3.3.2). Or we fall into the snare of viewing the three divine entities only as sides or modes or manifestations of the one Godhead.

From ancient times, people have claimed that the doctrine of eternal generation and procession is needed in order to avoid tritheism. However, could we not claim with equally persuasive power that the doctrine of eternal generation and procession must be rejected in order to avoid Sabellianism (modalism)? I believe it is possible to maintain the doctrine of eternal generation and procession without becoming a Sabellian, as long as one maintains the ontic distinction between the three members of the Trinity. I also believe it is possible to reject the doctrine of eternal generation and procession as

---

59. Sabellius (early third century) taught that God is one Person, who manifests himself in three modes (faces, masks): Father, Son, and Spirit.

speculative without becoming a tritheist, as long as one maintains that God is ontically and numerically one. A person is not necessarily a Sabellian who believes that it is rationally inexplicable how the one Godhead can be three distinct subsistences. Similarly, a person is not necessarily a tritheist who believes that it is rationally inexplicable how the three subsistences can be ontically and numerically one.

People have claimed that the Holy Spirit's relationship to the Son is comparable to that between the Son and the Father. Just as "the Son can do nothing of his own accord, but only what he sees the Father doing" (John 5:19; cf. vv. 26, 30; 8:28; 12:49; 14:10), so it is said of the Spirit: "[H]e will not speak on his own authority, but whatever he hears he will speak, . . . he will take what is mine and declare it to you" (16:13-14). Just as the Son bears witness about the Father (1:18; 17:4, 6, 8), so the Holy Spirit bears witness about the Son (15:26; 16:14). Just as no one can come to the Father except through the Son (14:6; Matt. 11:27), so no one can say that Jesus is Lord except through the Holy Spirit (1 Cor. 12:3). Those who have accepted the doctrine of the eternal procession of the Spirit can view these considerations as evidence that this procession is not only from the Father but also from the Son (see §1.6). Just as the Son is sent by the Father (John 3:17, 34; 4:34; 5:23-24, 30, 36-38), so the Holy Spirit is sent both by the Father and by the Son (John 14:26; 15:26; cf. 20:22; Acts 2:33). The Son never sends the Father, and the Holy Spirit never sends the Father or the Son.

Insofar as one accepts the doctrine of eternal generation and procession, one may view this order in sending as parallel with it: the generation is that of the Son from the Father, not the reverse, and the procession is that of the Father (and the Son? see §1.6), not the reverse. However, all these considerations are at best circumstantial evidence, but not proof, for the doctrine of eternal generation and procession. Therefore let me conclude this section with a hymn by Adam of Saint Victor:

> *Digne loqui de personis*
> *Vim transcendit rationis,*
> *Excedit ingenia.*
> *Quid sit gigni, quid processus*
> *Me nescire sum professus.*

> To speak worthily about the [divine] persons
> transcends the power of reason
> [and] exceeds the intellect.
> I profess that I do not know
> what generation is, and what procession is.[60]

1.6 Filioque
1.6.1 Introduction

All of the foregoing convinces us that the indications—to say nothing about evidence and proof—for the eternal procession of the Spirit are even more meager than those for the eternal generation of the Son. The idea of eternal procession is a significant paradigm that explains various matters in an elegant way. However, it is not based on direct Scriptural evidence but merely on logical deductions. Moreover, in principle, all the evidence that is adduced can also be explained in a different way; one could argue that it does not *need* to be explained in terms of an explication of the origin of the Holy Spirit.

At any rate, the consciences of ordinary believers may not be bound by any single paradigm of this kind—this is true for *every* theological paradigm. Even less may such a paradigm be presented as a condition for eternal salvation, as is unfortunately done in the Athanasian Creed. The latter starts with the famous words: "Whosoever wants to be saved. . ." (Lat. *Quicunque vult salvus esse. . .*), and then identifies believing the eternal generation of the Son and the procession of the Spirit as essential to saving faith. Does this mean, for instance, that all Eastern Orthodox Christians are eternally lost because they reject the *filioque* (see below)?

---
60. Quoted in Congar (1997, 3.8).

Even the greatest heresy is never an excuse for requiring an orthodoxy that goes beyond what can be shown from Scripture. Therefore, it was irresponsible for the Protestant "church father" Johann Gerhard to assert that without the *knowledge* of the doctrine of the Trinity no one can be saved.[61] Otto Weber pointed out that such claims may be the expression of a hubris in dogmatics that is usually followed by secularization—as indeed occurred during the Enlightenment.[62] Theological claims that are far too bold often have a counterproductive effect. *Modesty* is not one of the characteristics for which Christian theology has been known throughout the centuries.

Traditional theology has not only accepted the doctrine of the eternal procession of the Spirit but also speculated about it in an immodest way.[63] G. H. Joyce therefore rightly remarked that this doctrine was entirely due to Augustine (i.e., it is not in the Bible). It is never encountered among the Greek church fathers. The doctrine does harmonize with all the truths of faith, and it is admirably suited to help us understand more fully the foundations of Christianity, but it does not enjoy the sanction of divine revelation.[64] This description is perfectly true. It is all the more regrettable that this very doctrine of the proceeding of the Spirit caused the lamentable schism between the Eastern and the Western churches.

1.6.2 Division

As is generally known, the direct reason for the split between the Western and the Eastern churches in 1054 was the question involving whether the Spirit proceeds from the Father (*ex patro*) alone, or from the Father *and* the Son (Lat. *ex patro filioque*). The former was and is the view of the Eastern church, the latter the view of the Western church. Apart from the his-

---

61. Joh. Gerhard, *Loci theologici* III.209 etc.
62. Weber (1981, 371–72).
63. Cf. Bavinck (*RD* 2.316–17).
64. Joyce (1912, 55–56).

torical, psychological, and sociological aspects of the debate, the central problem was a purely theological debate, which soared high above the heads of many ordinary Christians.[65]

Elsewhere,[66] I have explained how, after the year 1000, an antithesis arose between the realm of temporal, natural things and the realm of eternal, supernatural things. In the practical sense, the former realm is manifested in the state, and the latter in the church.[67] Behind this, there was not only a changed theoretical insight, but also *metahistorical* changes, as became visible first of all in the schism mentioned. The question about the *filioque* was especially remarkable because, as we have seen, there is not the slightest biblical evidence for either view. Nevertheless, the entire Christian world was torn apart in 1054 because of this one word: *filioque*. How could this happen?

The Nicene Creed spoke of the Spirit proceeding only from the Father (Gk. *ek tou patris ekporeuomenon*). The first formal creed in which the word *filioque* was encountered was the Symbol of Toledo (*Symbolum Toletanum*), which had been formulated by the First Synod of the Spanish city of Toledo (400). The Third Synod of Toledo was held in 589, during the reign of the Visigothic King Reccared I, who ruled from 586 to 601 over the larger part of present-day Spain and the south-eastern part of present-day France. At this Synod, Arianism was formally repressed, and the Christianity of Reccared's domain was declared to be Roman Catholic. Moreover, the term *filioque* was officially inserted into the Nicene Creed — an action with dramatic consequences. Such an insertion was not only formally wrong — as was admitted by pope Leo III, who advised Charlemagne to drop it from the Creed — but was in fact an abuse of power.[68] Only in 1014 (!) did pope Benedict VIII, upon the urging of the German emperor Henry II, give the

---

65. See extensively, Congar (1997, 3.49–214).
66. See Ouweneel (2016, §§6.2–6.4).
67. See extensively, Ouweneel (2017a).
68. Pinnock (1996, 196–97).

term *filioque* the status of official dogma of the Western (Roman Catholic) church.⁶⁹ This was only forty years before the schism. The consequences of this action have been disastrous, since the Eastern church could not and would not accept this insertion.

The Eastern church was certainly prepared to accept that the procession of the Spirit, though being from the Father (Gk. *ek patros*), was through the Son (Gk. *dia tou huiou*); thus, for instance, Cyril of Alexandria and John of Damascus.⁷⁰ The Western church did not object to this; however, it wished to emphasize that the Father and the Son are "one principle" as well as "one beginning" (both phrases render the Lat. *unum principium*) with regard to the Spirit's procession. In this, the Father was supposed to be "the principle without principle/beginning" (*principium sine principio*), and the Son "the principle from principle" (Lat. *principium ex principio*); that is, the Son's capacity to make the Spirit proceed also from the Son was granted to the Son by the Father. In opposition to this, the Eastern church accused the Western church of starting from two principles (Lat. *principia* or Gk. *aitia*, "causes").⁷¹

1.6.3 Dualism

It is quite remarkable to see how both Western (Roman Catholic as well as Protestant) and Eastern theologians have tried to reduce the *entire* Eastern and Western sentiment, respectively, to the debate about *filioque*.⁷² How would things have developed if the Western and the Eastern churches had remained united, and had retained the original reading of the Nicene Creed? For instance, imagine the possibility of a sixteenth-century Reformation that could also have permeated Eastern Christianity! How different might the entire world,

---

69. See Bavinck (*RD* 2.316); Kasper (1983, 214–22, 296–98); Schlink (1983, 756–57); Kettler (1986, 1030–31).
70. Cf. Kasper (1983, 222), who is prepared to accept this formula.
71. Cf. Bavinck (*RD* 3.316–17); Schlink (1986, 1038).
72. Cf. Ouweneel (2017).

including the non-Christian world, have looked today.[73]

Both the Western and the Eastern reproaches amounted to accusing the other party of a deeply rooted *dualism*. Thus, various Western theologians have endeavored to show that the rejection of *filioque* had the greatest *practical* consequences for ordinary Orthodox Christians. The argument goes as follows: because Eastern Christians sever the Holy Spirit from the Son, a dualism arises between the (objectivistic) orthodoxy and the (subjectivistic) mysticism of the Eastern church. This view allegedly implies two ways to the Father: one leading through the Son to *knowledge* (of the Father), and one leading through the Spirit to *enjoyment* (i.e., communion with the Father).[74]

I have serious doubts about the correctness of this allegation. Knowledge of the Father is not primarily objectivistic-theological knowledge, but the knowledge intended in John 17:3: knowing God as Father, and Jesus Christ as the Son of the Father. This very knowledge implies communion with the Father and the Son, which is the whole point of 1 John 1:1–4. Accusing the East of such a dualism tells us more about the dangers of Western thinking itself.

Indeed, the Eastern church's accusation with regard to the Western church implies that the Western church assumes two causes (sources, principles, starting points) for the work of the Holy Spirit. Various Eastern theologians, such as Lew Karsawin, have attempted to reduce the inner contrasts within Western culture to this alleged dualism. Such a contrast is especially the antithesis, growing later into a cleavage, between personal faith and rationalist science (including theology), which has led to the dechristianization of the Western world.[75] In essence, this is the reproach of scholastic thinking. While Westerners accuse Easterners of an orthodoxy–mysticism dualism, we may wonder whether it is not far more ap-

---

73. See rather extensively, Van de Beek (1987, 280–94).
74. See Bavinck (*RD* 2.317); Barth (*CD* I/1=2, §12.2:167–68); Van Niftrik (1961, 259); Wentsel (1987, 388); and Van Genderen and Velema (2008, 157–58).
75. See especially Karsawin (1925, 356–65).

propriate to accuse the Western Christians of this very dualism, or of the comparable dualism of theoretical theology and the practical life of faith.

Karl Barth blamed the Russian theologians and philosophers of religion for erasing all boundaries between philosophy and theology, between reason and revelation, between church tradition and immediate enlightenment, between mind and nature, between faith (Gk. *pistis*) and knowledge (Gk. *gnosis*).[76] However, this very reproach makes me suspicious. If Barth presumes that this blotting out is a consequence of the Russian rejection of *filioque*, I wonder if Barth's own (and the usual Catholic and Protestant) *scholastic* separations between philosophy and theology, between reason and revelation, between mind and nature, between faith and knowledge,[77] have not been caused by — or are at least related to — the *acceptance* of *filioque*.

Clark Pinnock saw another danger of the greatest practical importance: *filioque* may threaten our understanding of the Spirit's universality. It might suggest that the Spirit is not universally the Father's gift to creation but a gift limited to the realm of the Son, or the realm of the church. It might give the impression that the Spirit is not present in the entire world but restricted to Christian domains.[78] (On this important question of the Spirit's universality, see more extensively, §10.9.)

1.7 Summary
1.7.1 Two Realms

While the theological debate about *filioque* may make a speculative impression, and may in fact seem basically irrelevant, the *metahistorical* backgrounds of the debate are all the more fascinating. It is much telling that Eastern theologians identify the acceptance of *filioque* with the acceptance of two divine principles or starting points, and with the distinction (and

---

76. Barth (*CD* I/1=2, § 12.2, 190).
77. See extensively, Ouweneel (2013).
78. Pinnock (1996, 196).

separation) of two spiritual worlds, the sacred world and the secular one. It is not so strange—as Barth thought—that Karsawin links Kantianism with *filioque* because Immanuel Kant, too, was still occupied with the distinction between the sacred and the secular, that is, the distinction between the higher and the lower realms of the spirit. The former is the domain of the church, but also of theology, faith, divine revelation, and the Holy Spirit. The latter is the domain of the state, but also of philosophy, reason, nature, and the body.

Indeed, who can deny that these distinctions have everything to do with the late-medieval and more recent spiritual developments in the Western world? Under the Carolingian and Ottonian emperors, the world (Gk. *oikoumenē*) was still the one, undivided, Christian community. True, it was ruled by both the emperor and the pope, but some distinction between church and state was still foreign. However, in the eleventh and twelfth centuries, this distinction did arise: church and state began to be viewed as *two* distinct worlds of the Spirit.

This is why the *filioque* debate in 1054 was of eminent importance. It was a matter of the greatest metahistorical significance. Whereas the Eastern world clung to the one, undivided (Eastern) Christendom under the twofold leadership of emperor and patriarch, the Western world developed into a partition of church and state, of two realms, not of the Spirit but *of the spirits*. The one realm is the supernatural realm of grace, while the other one is the realm of nature. This latter realm is the world that, during the late Middle Ages, came to be divided *politically* into the first nation states of Europe, each with its own angelic prince, and fell into the grip *ideologically* of the humanistic totalitarian ideal of the emerging natural sciences.[79]

1.7.2 No Speculations

The conclusion of systematic theologian Paul Althaus is tenable: "Because we do not speak of an eternal 'procession' of the

---
79. See further on this, Ouweneel (2017a; 2017f, from §6.4.2).

Spirit anyway, the ancient doubtful point [of debate between East and West] *formally* does not exist for us."[80] Edmund Schlink dubbed the conflict a matter of "drawing conclusions from conclusions."[81] Gotthold Hasenhüttl rightly said: "Due to the battle around the Holy Spirit, the unity [between East and West] was abolished, and the Spirit was quenched because of the Spirit [cf. 1 Thess. 5:19]. A very doubtful speculation destroyed the fellowship, which was in fact already being held together only by a thread."[82]

With all due respect for the great creeds of the early church, with which every Christian can largely agree, I would ask: Has not the time come to dethrone *theological paradigms*, and even more so, metaphysical speculation, as rulers over the faith and the eternal destiny of Christians, as currently happens with these creeds? If this insight is correctly applied, it will lead to greater practical unity than, for instance, the proposal of the Eastern and Western theologians during the *Faith and Order* conference of 1978–1979, urging us to accept as normative the original form of the Nicene Creed, that is, without *filioque*.[83]

---

80. Althaus (1952, 700).
81. Schlink (1983, 758).
82. Hasenhüttl (1979, 110).
83. Cf. Pannenberg (1991, 1:318–19); Berkhof (1986, 338–39).

Chapter 2
Later Pneumatology

*He who has an ear, let him hear
what the Spirit says to the churches.*
Revelation 2:7

*I, Jesus, have sent my angel
to testify to you about these things for the churches.
I am the root and the descendant of David,
the bright morning star.
The Spirit and the Bride say, "Come."
And let the one who hears say, "Come."
And let the one who is thirsty come;
let the one who desires take the water of life
without price.*
Revelation 22:16–17

Summary: *The Reformers as well as the Anabaptists have contributed more to pneumatology than their medieval predecessors; Calvin was called a "theologian of the Holy Spirit." His main new contribution concerned the internal testimony of the Holy Spirit, which gave rise to a long debate about the relationship between*

Word and Spirit. For the Netherlands, the work of Abraham Kuyper and many successors must be mentioned. Some of them interacted theologically with the emerging Pentecostal and Charismatic movements (twentieth century). The latter's precursors and beginnings are considered, along with their greatest significance, namely, in missions and evangelism. Recent theological developments in traditional churches and in modern theological movements are discussed, as well as various types of pneumatology that have been developed.

2.1 The Reformers
2.1.1 Luther

IN MEDIEVAL THEOLOGY, relatively little attention was paid to the Holy Spirit; such attention as there was did not surpass what Augustine had already provided in his pneumatological work. To find exciting ideas in medieval pneumatology requires one to consult the great mystics, such as St. Bernard of Clairvaux, St. Hildegard of Bingen, St. Bonaventure, and St. Catherine of Siena.[1]

It is gratifying to see that the Reformers paid far more attention to the Holy Spirit. As a consequence of the doctrine of justification by faith alone, Martin Luther emphasized the renewal of life (i.e., sanctification) by the power of the Holy Spirit. Especially Regin Prenter has shown how attention to the Holy Spirit can be found in every part of Luther's theology.[2] However, although the Reformers elevated the written Word so highly, they seemed to have been quite apprehensive about any supposed speaking and working of the Spirit apart from the written Word. The Spirit works through the preaching of the gospel and through the sacraments. Luther rejected not only the Roman Catholics who cried *Kirche! Kirche!* ("church, church!"), but also the religious "enthusiasts" who cried *Geist! Geist!* ("Spirit, Spirit!"), who claimed some unique work of the Spirit apart from Word and sacraments.[3]

---

1. Burgess (1997, Parts 2 and 3); Kärkkäinen (2002, 49–55).
2. Prenter (1954).
3. Cf. Congar (1997, 2.138–140).

This objection is very ancient. Thomas Aquinas raised it with regard to Joachim of Fiore, who claimed that, after the Age of the Father (the Old Testament period) and the Age of the Son (between Christ and 1260), the Age of the Holy Spirit would dawn. Up to today, the same objection has been leveled by traditional theologians against all "enthusiast" movements, including contemporary Pentecostals and Charismatics (see §§2.2 and 2.4). Tradition has safely encased the Holy Spirit within the established order, and traditional churches are generally quite afraid of that genie being released from its bottle. Conveniently for them, there are enough excesses to which they may point as a warning: Thomas Aquinas found them with Joachim of Fiore, Luther with Thomas Müntzer, present-day traditionalists with certain Pentecostal and Charismatic leaders. No wonder: little movement yields very little activity in the wrong direction, while much movement unfortunately produces very much activity that may be moving in the wrong direction. Excesses are eagerly criticized by traditionalists.

The consequences of the strict Lutheran linking of the Spirit to the Word can be easily identified. Hendrikus Berkhof wrote that the Roman Catholics encased the Spirit in the church, and the Protestants in the Word.[4] And Hans-Emil Weber wrote that the Word seems to have been banned to, and locked up in, Scripture, and what is worse: in dogma and preaching. As a result, people yearn for the Spirit rather than the letter of Scripture (cf. Rom. 2:29; 7:6; 2 Cor. 3:6), and long for the immediate knowledge of the Spirit and for new revelations.[5]

Jean-Jacques Suurmond gave a striking example of how Luther encased the Spirit in the written Word and in the established church order. In 1524, the German Peasants' War broke out under the militant leadership of Thomas Müntzer

---

4. Berkhof (1982, 15). Suurmond (1995, 69) added: the Eastern Orthodox imprisoned the Spirit in the liturgy.
5. Weber (1965, 146).

because the serfs, inspired by Word and Spirit, emancipated themselves from their inhumane situation. However, Luther ruthlessly suppressed them with an appeal to the established order. Since then, the Lutheran Church has largely remained conservative in political respects, and has consistently lived in the shadow of the political authorities. This partly explained the shocking obedience of so many Lutherans to the Nazi regime in the Germany of the 1930s and 1940s. This attitude favoring the status quo was further strengthened by the theological development of the seventeenth century. In both Lutheran and Calvinist theology, the enthusiasm of the Reformers yielded to rationalism and to a neo-scholastic emphasis on order that Luther himself had opposed.[6]

2.1.2 Calvin: "Theologian of the Spirit"?

Even more than Luther, John Calvin, just like Ulrich Zwingli,[7] has been called a "theologian of the Holy Spirit."[8] Hartvelt pointed out that, in the time of the Reformation, especially the Lutherans included the Calvinists among the spiritualists.[9] Yet, just like Luther, Calvin bound the Spirit strongly to the Word in opposition to the enthusiasts. Just as in Luther's case, virtually every part of Calvin's theology mentions the Holy Spirit; I refer especially to his doctrine of God, the doctrines of justification and sanctification, the inspiration of Scripture, and the sacraments. The main emphasis is no doubt on soteriology. Calvin referred to the Spirit particularly as the One who works rebirth and faith in the elect, and strengthens the elect in sanctification, in which they confirm their election (cf. 2 Pet. 1:10).

If Calvin is indeed the "theologian of the Holy Spirit," this should be evident especially from his *Institutes of the Chris-*

---

6. Suurmond (1995, 70–71).
7. Schmidt-Clausing (1965, 82–112).
8. Van der Linde (1943, 1), following B. B. Warfield (1909, 14).
9. Hartvelt (1978, 40); Dutch Protestant theologian Noordmans (1949, 8) even called the Reformed, in this respect, the "twin brother" of the Anabaptist Christian.

tian Religion. Its third volume deals with the way the grace of Christ is received. It begins with two chapters on the Holy Spirit and on faith, respectively, two subjects that Calvin saw as closely linked. In the fourth volume, the Holy Spirit occupies the central place as the One who applies to us what Christ has accomplished. By the Spirit, Christ himself works in believers, shares himself with them, and comes to dwell in them. Calvin says beautiful things on these matters. Yet, the work of the Spirit is virtually limited to soteriology. For this and many other reasons, I cannot agree with the claim of Reformed theologian Jan van Genderen, that "the doctrine of the Holy Spirit has received a central place in the church of the Reformation."[10] If this were so, this would be evident from Van Genderen's own handbook of dogmatics, co-authored with W. H. Velema.[11] This work lacks a separate chapter on the Holy Spirit. It refers to the Holy Spirit only in connection with the inspiration of Scripture and the divine Trinity, with ecclesiology and the sacraments, and with soteriology. There is little evidence of this supposed "central place" of the Holy Spirit in Reformed theology.

As to Calvin's view of the *charismata*, Reformed theologian Cornelis Graafland said, "I even think that we must regret that Calvin's influence on our Reformed tradition, in many respects so blessed, has also worked in this point [viz., 1 Cor. 12], but then in a less blessed way. For this [influence] has not involved any positive contribution to the spiritual well-being of the church."[12] It is therefore no wonder that, in nineteenth-century America, it was precisely Calvinist theologians such as Charles Hodge and Benjamin Warfield[13] — the same who called Calvin a "theologian of the Holy Spirit"! — who opposed the beginnings of Pentecostalism.

If we were to search in the Reformed tradition for more at-

---

10. Van Genderen (1958, 405).
11. Van Genderen and Velema (2008).
12. Graafland (1999, 312).
13. Warfield (1953).

tention paid to the special work of the Spirit, we would think first of Martin Bucer,[14] then of the English Calvinist theologian John Owen,[15] and the great Puritan Revival preachers Jonathan Edwards and George Whitefield, the leaders of the Great Awakening.[16] Edwards' balanced work has lost hardly any of its power.[17] Some late nineteenth-century Calvinist treatises on the Holy Spirit were those by Abraham Kuyper (see §2.3) and George Smeaton.[18]

2.1.3 The Internal Testimony of the Holy Spirit

Perhaps, Calvin's most original contribution to pneumatology was his doctrine of the internal testimony of the Holy Spirit (Lat. *testimonium Spiritus Sancti internum*). This doctrine was inspired by Romans 8:16, "The Spirit himself bears witness with our spirit that we are children of God."[19] Remarkably enough, German Reformed theologian Otto Weber called this doctrine the only new element that Reformational theology contributed to the doctrine of the authority of Scripture.[20] Here, the interesting crucial question arises whether this teaching of Calvin does in fact imply some testimony by the Spirit within the believer's heart *apart from Scripture's own testimony*. No Reformed theologian ever seems to have answered this question affirmatively, but claims instead that such an idea would be equivalent to mysticism or spiritualism.[21]

Nonetheless, according to Weber,[22] Calvin sometimes moved along the edge of this tempting view, but in the end

---

14. See Lang (1900, 120–21); Anrich (1914, 138); Stephens (1970); Van 't Spijker (1970, 333–41).
15. Owen (2012).
16. On Puritan pneumatology in general, see Nuttall (1992).
17. Edwards (2011).
18. Kuyper (1900); Smeaton (2010).
19. Calvin, *Institutes* 1.7, especially sections 4–5; cf. Dee (1918, 114–16); Krusche (1957). Incidentally, the idea may well go back to Luther (cf. Drescher [1883] 30/2.688).
20. Weber (1981, 241–42).
21. Cf. Althaus (1967, 211); Heyns (1976, 127).
22. Weber (1981, 242).

withstood the temptation. From the internal testimony of the Holy Spirit he referred back to Scripture. That is to say, only when one who is a believer hears the testimony of the Spirit does one know that God is speaking directly to the believer in Scripture, but only in Scripture does one learn what God's speaking to the believer entails. In this sense, the testimonies of Scripture and Spirit are in the end identical.[23] There can be no such thing as an independent criterion of an internal testimony of the Spirit *alongside* a Scripture witnessing to itself. The assurance of faith does not rest on two distinct testimonies but on the one, internal testimony of the Spirit *through* Scripture. Thus, the testimony of Scripture is nothing without the Spirit, but at the same time, the testimony of the Spirit is nothing without Scripture. The two are inextricably joined.

Otto Weber linked the internal testimony of the Spirit with the question of the so-called "hermeneutical circle."[24] The belief that Scripture is the Word of God cannot be proven objectively, by means of rational arguments (nor can the belief that Scripture is *not* God's Word, for that matter). Our arguments to account for this belief are *a posteriori* arguments. That is, only *after* we have accepted Scripture as Word of God we can interpret this experience, first pre-theoretically, then theologically, but never other than by our *a priori*, transcendent belief. Indeed, each genuine belief and testimony with regard to Scripture is the work of the Holy Spirit. That is, the Spirit is operative both in the Word that comes to the believer and in the believer's heart response[25] to it (what Calvin called the "internal testimony of the Spirit").

Of course, it would be easy to criticize such an identification between the external and the internal testimonies of the Spirit, as did, for instance, David Friedrich Strauß. Karl Barth responded, "What Strauss failed to see is that there is no Prot-

---

23. Althaus (1967, 212).
24. Weber (1981, 240–41; cf. 250–51); cf. Ouweneel (2012b, §§1.3.2 and 1.4).
25. German *Antwort*, Dutch *antwoord*, derived from *Wort* and *woord*, respectively.

estant 'system,' but that the Protestant Church and Protestant doctrine has necessarily and gladly chosen to leave his question unanswered, because there at its weakest point, where it can only acknowledge and confess, it has all its indestructible strength."[26] More precisely, what seems to be weak here is the absence of rational arguments—but what is strong here is that the testimony concerning Scripture ultimately, at the suprarational, transcendent level of faith, surpasses the entire (immanent-rational) dilemma of the internal testimony versus the external testimony.[27]

2.2 Protestant Scholasticism
2.2.1 Word and Spirit

The Protestant suppression of the freely working Spirit entailed imprisoning the Spirit within a Bible that had been reduced to a legal code, and within dogmas and the sacraments. No wonder that this led to a reaction emphasizing the personal experience of faith and the sanctification of life. In Germany this reaction was called Pietism, in the Netherlands, the "Second Reformation" (*Nadere Reformatie*), in the Anglo-Saxon countries, Puritanism. The Quakers, the Methodists, and the holiness movements followed. Implicitly or explicitly all these movements sought more room for the Spirit. We are dealing here with a universal phenomenon, widespread throughout the Christian world: the monasteries, the seventh-century travelling Irish monks,[28] Pentecostal and Charismatic movements, and the Roman Catholic "basic communities" of recent decades[29] were, and are, similar spiritual reactions.[30] Suurmond concluded: "[N]ot the church possesses the Spirit, but the Spirit possesses the church—and time and again the

---

26. Barth (*CD* I/2, 537).
27. See extensively, Ouweneel (Wisdom / Theology).
28. The Northumbrian Irish monk Willibrord, who became the "Apostle to the Frisians," i.e., in the modern Netherlands.
29. See http://www.encyclopedia.com/humanities/encyclopedias-almanacs-transcripts-and-maps/christian-base-communities.
30. Suurmond (1995, 70–74).

latter turns out to be much wider than the official church orders indicate."³¹

In the meantime, scholastic Protestant theologians indefatigably continued speculating about the relationship between Word and Spirit. In 1621, Hermann Rathmann ventured the thesis that Scripture offers only an external communication of God's Word, but by itself does not work the enlightenment that leads to conversion.³² This enlightenment is the exclusive work of the Holy Spirit, which is *new* (additional) with regard to the testifying work of Scripture. He called Scripture an axe that functions only when guided by an arm. The naive reader may call this self-evident. However, every suggestion of a Spirit working apart from Scripture—even if it is only the Spirit who applies Scripture—led opponents to suspect mysticism and spiritualism. Rathmann's opponents argued that the Word of God is operative not only when it is being used (*in usu,* "in use," that is, when Scripture is read, preached, or heard) but also before and apart from its use (*ante et extra usum,* "preceding, and apart from, the use").

Karl Barth pointed out that, if Rathmann was guilty of one extreme, these opponents were guilty of the other extreme.³³ Thus, Andreas Quenstedt viewed Scripture and preaching as the means (Lat. *media*) that inherently possess the highest strength and efficacy Lat. (*summa vis et efficacia*). David Hollaz spoke of Scripture possessing a supernatural strength (Lat. *vis huperphysica*). Such views come dangerously close to treating Scripture as something that works magically (a problem of which Quenstedt was aware).

We encounter the same danger in a related discussion among early Protestants. The Lutherans believed that the Spirit works through the Word (*per verbum*). However, the Calvinists believed that the Spirit works together with the

---

31. Ibid., 71.
32. See Weber (1981, 284–85), and references there.
33. Barth (*CD* I/1=1, §4.2:107–108), including references to Quenstedt and Hollaz.

Word (*cum verbo*). The former view can easily lead to an automatic working of the Word, and the latter may lead to a de-spiritualization of the Word and the idea of an autonomous working of the Spirit.[34] Nevertheless, both views do contain elements of truth. In other words, it is not the faithful intention behind such views that constitutes them as dangerous, but rather the pretense of theoretical thought seeking to capture suprarational truths in rational-theological formulas. Ultimately, all such rationalistic speculations inadvertently paved the way for Enlightenment theology, which discarded the suprarational element altogether.

Reformed theologian Ben Wentsel summarized the underlying problem very well. He stated that it is wrong, on the one hand, to describe Scripture as a book that in itself is dead and must repeatedly be resuscitated by the Spirit, and on the other hand, to assert that the Spirit is identical with Scripture, or lies confined within its letters, constituting a kind of incarnation of the Spirit. The former leads to a denial of the Bible's inspiration, the latter leads to bibliolatry.[35] In order to avoid both dangers, we cannot possibly improve on the following careful, practical statements: (a) Scripture is God's Word, independent of, and superior to, subjective experience. (b) Scripture always has divine power, also in opposition to unbelief, just as the sun produces heat behind the clouds, and seeds retain their strength in infertile ground (Hollaz). (c) This power is the power of the Holy Spirit, which subjectively strikes the target if there is faith. The dilemma whether Scripture has inherent power, or whether its power belongs to the Holy Spirit, is simply false.

2.2.2 The Anabaptists

One way to know how the Reformers thought about the Holy Spirit is to consider how they thought about the Anabaptists.

---

34. Berkhof (1986, 66; cf. 1964, 36–38; Hoenderdaal (1968, especially chapter 6).
35. Wentsel (1981, 195–96).

As in the case of the Montanists, the judgment of present-day theologians is strongly tainted by the negative judgment of their opponents. The Anabaptists were rejected by both the Roman Catholic Church and the Protestant churches.[36] The reproach that echoes even today is twofold. First, the enthusiasts—in this case, the Anabaptists—are accused of claiming that the Spirit speaks apart from the Word. Second, they are accused of attaching more value to subjective experience than to the objective Word[37] (an accusation that, incidentally, also has been leveled at hyper-Calvinists). From the sixteenth century until today, the question has always been whether these accusations were appropriate. Each has a correct element: Christians must always beware of a so-called speaking of the Spirit that *goes against Scripture*, and of advocating experiences that *go against Scripture*.

The crux lies in the italicized words. All prophecy, throughout church history, is genuine prophecy only if it does not simply repeat and apply Scripture. The Spirit can certainly reveal things that are not written in the Bible. Agabus foretold "by the Spirit that there would be a great famine over all the world" (Acts 11:28), and: "Thus says the Holy Spirit, 'This is how the Jews at Jerusalem will bind the man who owns this belt and deliver him into the hands of the Gentiles'" (21:11). What biblical reason is there to assert that such prophecies could be uttered only as long as the canon of the New Testament was not yet completed? The New Testament does not supply us with such concrete prophecies in view of concrete circumstances, neither in view of the time of the apostles, nor of our own times. Therefore, we need people like Agabus just as much as Paul's time needed them. The idea of post-canonical revelation does not at all diminish the unique divine reve-

---

36. See Badcock (1997); cf. Kärkkäinen (2002, 55–57).
37. These are also some of the arrows shot from the bow of John MacArthur (1992, 31–35, 54–60) in his fierce, one-sided, and unfair attack against Pentecostal and Charismatic Christians.

lation that we have in the inscripturated Word of God.[38]

The apostle Paul emphasizes: "Do not quench the Spirit. Do not despise prophecies, but test everything; hold fast what is good" (1 Thess. 5:19-21). This implies two things. On the one hand, those who suppress the prophetic ministry — a unique channel through which the Spirit flows — risk quenching the Spirit. On the other hand, what is presented as prophecy must be evaluated. As far as I can see, this means first that the uttered words must not conflict with the written Word (cf. Deut. 13:1-5); and second, the uttered words must eventually come true (cf. 1 Kings 22:17-28, especially the concluding verse).

The second accusation of the established churches toward the enthusiasts was that they attached more value to subjective experience than to the objective Word. The reply to this must be that experience itself is not dangerous. On the contrary, the Second Reformation within Calvinism, as well as Pietism and Puritanism, always emphasized that true Christian life must include genuine experience (in Dutch, the term is *bevinding*). But to be sure, this experience may never go beyond or against the written Word, and must therefore be carefully evaluated.

Despite what some critics may have asserted, Anabaptists, like present-day Pentecostals and Charismatics, undoubtedly assigned to the Bible the highest priority. Their reverence for Scripture was so strong, and their obedience to it so strict, that their Protestant siblings sometimes reproached them for biblicism. These very Anabaptists in turn blamed the Lutherans and Calvinists for remaining too close to Rome and for holding on to certain ecclesiastical traditions more strongly than Scripture. One of these Anabaptist complaints was that, also among Lutherans and Calvinists, ecclesiastical institutions

---

38. If certain "revelations" (Matt. 16:17; Luke 2:26; 1 Cor. 14:6, 26, 30; 2 Cor. 12:1, 7; Gal. 1:12; 2:2) were neither derived from the Old Testament, nor later included in the New Testament, then there *is* revelation apart from the Old and New Testament canon.

and offices were considered to be more important than the spontaneous working of the Holy Spirit. They believed that in this respect Lutherans and Calvinists did not differ essentially from Rome.

The Anabaptists, and later the Mennonites (named after the Frisian pastor Menno Simons, d. 1561), laid great emphasis on the work of the Holy Spirit, not only in faith and justification but also in the practical lives of individual believers and of the congregations. Thus, they assigned insight into Scripture that the Spirit produces to be of higher value than insight into Scripture that theological education produces. Incidentally, this opinion was, and still is, shared by both hyper-Calvinists and many Evangelical Christians.

Anabaptists also attached great value to prophecy and spontaneous worship, and concomitantly less value to the sacraments and a strongly formal liturgy. In this respect, too, they viewed Lutherans and Calvinists as remaining (too) close to Rome; they themselves resembled far more the later free church Evangelical world. It is indeed remarkable that initially, Anabaptists were seen as a movement on the margins of the Reformation. However, as precursors of later Methodism, Evangelicalism, and Pentecostalism, in due time they acquired an enormous influence. Ultimately, in terms of membership numbers, their influence vastly exceeded that of Lutheranism and Calvinism. As Clark Pinnock states so poignantly, the Spirit's fire often burns outside the fireplaces of historic institutions.[39]

2.3 Dutch Theologians
2.3.1 Abraham Kuyper

If John Calvin has been called a "theologian of the Holy Spirit," the neo-Calvinist Abraham Kuyper shares this honorary title with him.[40] It is remarkable that Calvinists have been re-

---

39. Pinnock (1996, 119: "The fire [of the Spirit] often burns outside the hearth of historic institutions.").
40. See Velema (1957, 7).

peatedly acclaimed for their devotion to the Holy Spirit. The same honor has been paid to other Dutch Reformed theologians as well, like O. Noordmans, A. A. van Ruler, and J. P. Versteeg.[41] According to J. Veenhof, attention to the Holy Spirit and linking Spirit and Word are characteristics of Reformed thought.[42] Is such an honorific claim justified?

Kuyper did write a three-volume treatise containing — in my Dutch edition — no fewer than nine hundred pages on the work of the Holy Spirit,[43] aside from what he wrote about this subject in many of his other writings. In volume 1 of this work, Kuyper dealt with the role of the Spirit in creation, in inspiration, in the incarnation, and in the work of atonement, and with the outpouring of the Spirit, the apostolate, and the church. In this last part, we find a mere six (!) pages devoted to discussing the spiritual gifts,[44] with the following conclusion: "The charismata now existing in the Church are those pertaining to the ministry of the Word; the ordinary charismata of increased exercise of faith and love; those of wisdom, knowledge, and discernment of spirits; that of self-restraint; and lastly, that of healing the sick suffering from nervous and psychological diseases. The others for the present are inactive." Incredibly, Kuyper thereby simply swept aside the miraculous *charismata*, that is, *words* of wisdom, *words* of knowledge, gifts of healing, the working of miracles, prophecy, glossolalia, and the interpretation of tongues (see chapter 12).

In volume 2, Kuyper dealt with sin, rebirth, calling, conversion, justification, and faith, and in volume 3, with sanctification, love, and prayer. The treatise on the work of the Holy Spirit ends at this point.[45] Here again, entirely accord-

---

41. The same honor was paid to Basil the Great, Martin Bucer, Thomas Müntzer, Philip Jakob Spener, Seraphim of Sarov, Friedrich Schleiermacher, Auguste Sabatier, Karl Barth, and Yves Congar.
42. Veenhof (1992, 82).
43. Kuyper (1900).
44. Ibid., 1.184-89.
45. It went exactly like this in De Groot (1949). In his *Dogmatiek* (1988), Heyns has a chapter on the person and work of the Holy Spirit, in which this "work,"

ing to Calvinist tradition, pneumatology goes no further than soteriology. We hear nothing about the significance of the Spirit for the subsequent Christian life, about the battle between flesh and Spirit (e.g., Rom. 8:1-17; Gal. 5:16-25), about spiritual growth and maturity (e.g., 2 Cor. 3:17-18), about the forming of the new self (e.g., Eph. 5:17-32 KJV)—not to mention the baptism in the Spirit (e.g., Acts 1:5; 11:16), and being filled with the Spirit (e.g., Acts 2:4; 4:8, 31; 9:17; 13:9, 52). These omissions are understandable in view of the fact that the great renewal movement of the Holy Spirit had not yet arrived when Kuyper wrote these volumes—but they are not understandable when we see that these matters are dealt with extensively in the Bible.

Incidentally, perhaps we should not judge Kuyper's attitude toward the person and the work of the Holy Spirit on the basis of this kind of writing, but rather on the basis of his sermons and meditations. Kuyperian Reformed pastor D. G. Molenaar wrote about Kuyper:

> Even though he theoretically rejected the baptism with the Holy Spirit,[46] he no doubt has known this baptism in his experience. This may be concluded from his collections of meditations: 'To Be Near God'....[47] In *E Voto Dordraceno*, he had written about '... a sacred experience of the workings of the consolations of the Holy Spirit in the depth of the mind, operating in the experiences and enjoyments of blissful love, elevating our soul all the way to the spheres of majesty, and setting us aglow with a holy Pentecostal fire.'[48] ... Kuyper was a mystic, and lived out of the fullness of the Spirit.[49]

---

as with De Groot, does not go any further than so-called perseverance. Verkuil (1992) has a chapter on the Holy Spirit and his work, which does not go any further than faith, hope, and love.
46. Kuyper (1900, 1:127).
47. Kuyper (1918).
48. Kuyper (1893, 2:106).
49. Molenaar (1963, 61–62).

2.3.2 Johan Herman Bavinck

What kind of building upon this foundation occurred subsequently in the Netherlands? In 1949 there appeared a work of more than 450 pages, entitled *De Heilige Geest* (*The Holy Spirit*), under the editorship of J. H. Bavinck, P. Prins, and G. Brillenburg Wurth, containing contributions from some twenty Reformed authors.[50] Each of its chapters dealt with a certain aspect—exegetical, systematic theological, dogma historical, and practical—of pneumatology. To me, the most interesting part of this work is the epilogue by Bavinck. In this he said, "[A]t this moment we are in a low-tide period of the work of the Holy Spirit in his church" (referring to his own denomination [the Kuyperian *Gereformeerde Kerken in Nederland*] and related denominations). Bavinck continued: "[T]here remains sufficient ground for humility, and even for concern. . . . [G]enerally speaking we must take note of a certain weariness and powerlessness in the church of our day, also in the church in our fatherland [i.e., the Netherlands]."[51]

This statement is gratifying, although our satisfaction is tempered by the fact that Bavinck ascribed the troubles particularly to a lack of a sense of sin and of the assurance of salvation. Yet, he also mentioned "our lack of confidence in the power of the Spirit. . . . Therefore, as soon as we take account of the strength of the Holy Spirit, the 'power from on high' [Luke 24:49], there is very little ground left for feelings of powerlessness and discouragement."[52] He concludes by saying: "Somewhere within us, fountains must have been stopped up [cf. Gen. 26:15, 18], so that the work of the Spirit cannot manifest itself in its glory. Somewhere, obstacles must have been raised [2 Cor. 10:5 NET]. For the church of our days, it is of the greatest importance to investigate the causes, and then, in humble obedience, set our feet on this track."[53]

---

50. Bavinck et al. (1949).
51. Ibid., 439–40.
52. Ibid., 443.
53. Ibid., 452.

I read these comments with warm pleasure. Unfortunately, however, this epilogue hardly covers the contents of this book. Cessationism, the theological view that claims that the miraculous gifts ceased at the end of the apostolic period (see §12.7), prevails throughout the book. For instance, pastor A. Ringnalda wrote of the prophets, "No doubt, their work was of great importance during the time when there was not yet the written New Testament, but could cease afterwards. Therefore, in God's providence, New Testament prophecy lasted no longer than about AD 200."[54] (This is still rather late, considering the fact that the canon had been closed more than a hundred years earlier!) And pastor Arie B. W. M. Kok wrote: "As to glossolalia, healing prayer, prophecy—according to their nature and aim, they belong to the first period of the Christian church, and do not constitute essential characteristics of the church itself. . . . Together with the other peculiar gifts of the Spirit, [glossolalia] disappeared when it was no longer needed."[55]

We can hardly blame these pastors, for their teachers and leaders, Abraham Kuyper and Herman Bavinck,[56] had presented the same viewpoint. Today the situation is very different. After hundreds of studies, who today could still defend the same position without explaining *why*, with the closing of the canon, the miraculous gifts should have ceased functioning? In what sense does a complete canon make the gifts of prophecy (in the sense of predictions), healing, and glossolalia superfluous? The two—canon and *charismata*—are simply not related. The claim about the gifts ceasing with the closing of the canon has been parroted by generations of theologians who because they did not witness these gifts functioning in their own denominations *therefore* concluded that these gifts had apparently ceased (see chapter 12).

---

54. Ibid., 119.
55. Ibid., 294. Cessationism is defended also by Vellenga and Kret (1957, 34–37, 64–66).
56. Bavinck (*RD* 3.501–503; 4.247, 299, 337).

Thus, this remarkable book by J. H. Bavinck and colleagues evidenced an important deficiency—and at the same time obstructed the route toward correcting it. This was observed fourteen years later by Reformed (!) pastor D. G. Molenaar, who had also been formed by Kuyper and Bavinck.[57] He wrote,

> He who himself was allowed to discover new perspectives is astonished that, on this point, Reformed theologians were sometimes struck with blindness. It would enhance preaching if theology would do full justice to the significance of the baptism and filling with the Holy Spirit, and it would, to an important extent, further a revival that is so much needed in the church.

We are able to see how Johan H. Bavinck continued to wrestle with this matter in his booklet *Ik geloof in de Heilige Geest* (*I believe in the Holy Spirit*). On the one hand, he made a remarkable attempt to portray the gifts of the Spirit as purely natural phenomena (thereby robbing them of their miraculous character).[58] At certain points he showed a clear inclination toward cessationism,[59] claiming that, in the present "world period," the church must not expect certain gifts of the Spirit as something normal.[60] On the other hand, he wrote, "[T]here can be no question of a caesura [at the end of the apostolic period]. The Bible says nothing about the idea that, after Pentecost, there would be some other thoroughgoing change in the redemptive work of Christ, and that everything would then become duller, less vivid. . . . It therefore seems clear enough that there is no caesura. In our day, we can still expect the very same signs of the Spirit as the believers in the day of the apostles. In principle, nothing has changed. It is the same Spirit. Therefore, if we in our day do not receive the same signs, this is only our own fault"[61]—a statement that Bavinck

---

57. See Molenaar (1963, 5–6).
58. Bavinck (n.d., 60, 63).
59. Ibid., 65.
60. Ibid., 92.
61. Ibid., 86–87.

subsequently weakened with a number of qualifications.

Yet, one of his conclusions is this: "In principle, nothing has changed in the position of the church. In our day, the Spirit can display in the church the same miracles that he did in those days" — though with this addition: "However, there is reason to suppose that some of those signs were not intended as an indication of the situation in which the church lives in this [present] world period, but were seeking to sketch very emphatically the ultimate goal that God has appointed for his church."[62]

2.3.3 Reformed Successors in the Netherlands

In addition to the 1949 work by Bavinck and colleagues, other important Reformed pneumatological works appeared after World War II, specifically publications by O. Noordmans, A. A. van Ruler, H. Berkhof, G. J. Hoenderdaal, J. P. Versteeg, and A. van de Beek.[63] Most of these works appeared, however, before the great renewal within pneumatology began. In these publications we encounter many traditionalist, and sometimes modernist, views, but no real spiritual breakthrough.

A true precursor of the renewal for which many Reformed people had longed appeared in the work by Reformed pastor D. G. Molenaar, published in the 1960s.[64] Molenaar had brought his manuscript to the publisher two weeks before his untimely death (1961), a fact that makes its testimony all the more impressive. Here is the testimony of one crying in the wilderness, one that still speaks after his death. He was not alone, but could echo other hopeful voices of his time. Thus he signaled that G. C. Berkouwer fundamentally rejected ces-

---

62. Ibid., 92–93.
63. Noordmans (1955); see also Van der Kooi (2018); Van Ruler (1969 [lecture given in 1961]; 1973); Berkhof (1964; this book contains the Annie Kinkead Warfield lectures that Berkhof gave in 1964 at Princeton Theological Seminary); Hoenderdaal (1968); Versteeg (1973; 1976; 1978; 1979; 1980; 1984); Van de Beek (1987).
64. Molenaar (1968).

sationism as follows:

> Thus, God, even after the establishment of salvation in Christ, wills to go His way and to build the Church through signs and miracles. And we find nothing in the Scriptures to indicate a line that we can draw through a definite period to mark off a boundary between the time of miracles and the time of the absence of miracles.[65]

Reformed theologian J. L. Koole tied in with this as expressed in these remarkable words: "[W]e ourselves believe that we should not fail to strongly exhort the authoritative organs in the church... to carefully give heed to the development of the events, and accurately notice when 'wonders' and 'signs' seem to be revealed."[66] Also notice the sympathetic-critical attitude of Reformed pastor Wim W. Verhoef toward the Pentecostal and Charismatic movement.[67]

In the Reformed world within the Netherlands this was going to be the decisive question: is cessationism right or wrong? No doubt, ground-breaking work was done here by Reformed pastors K. J. Kraan and P. C. van Leeuwen, and afterwards by Reformed theologian M-J. Paul about the "healing ministry," in which the other charismata were dealt with as well.[68] Other Reformed theologians, J. P. Versteeg and L. Floor, clearly rejected cessationism.[69]

Especially refreshing were the words by highly esteemed Reformed theologian C. Graafland, who wrote the following:

> [T]he Spirit has remained the same, whereas the once Re-formed church is anew on the decline. Therefore, would and could the Spirit not bring about a new re-formation? Precisely because we know of God's great deeds in the past [read: the Reformation.

---

65. Berkouwer (1952, 241).
66. Koole (1955, 79).
67. Verhoef (1974; 1977).
68. Kraan (1970; 1974; 1983–1984); Van Leeuwen (1989); Paul (1997; 2002; n.d.).
69. Versteeg (1976, 94); Floor (1982, 179–85).

> WJO] we have expectation for the present. Therefore we intensely long for this new reformation. This expectation is not from ourselves but we have it from God, from Jesus Christ, and from his Spirit.[70]

Later, he wrote,

> Those [Charismatic] churches have little difficulty with 1 Corinthians 12. We have much more. Is it not high time that this changes, in some way or another? The point here is not so much that we no longer understand what these gifts that Paul mentions have been. The point is rather that we no longer recognize them as being present in the church, *and* that we acquiesce in this, whereas Scripture presents them to us.[71]

Another signal of change within the Reformed world was the book entitled *Gaven voor de gemeente* (*Gifts for the Church*),[72] featuring contributions of Reformed theologians like R. Doornenbal, P. Siebesma, J. Hoek, M-J. Paul, and A. Romkes. Moreover, the Evangelisch Werkverband (Evangelical Working Alliance) within the Protestant Church in the Netherlands (a denomination that emerged from the Dutch Reformed Church, the Kuyperian Reformed Churches, and the Dutch Lutherans) has shown clear openness to the miraculous manifestations of the Holy Spirit.[73] According to its website, its aim is to "prayerfully seek and work toward a spiritual revival for the entire church, in order that, being oriented toward God's glory, the church can fulfill its calling in the world in obedience to its Lord Jesus Christ and in the power of the Holy Spirit."

2.3.4 Recent Developments

Beyond the Protestant Church but still within the Reformed world in the Netherlands, we must especially mention New

---

70. Graafland, in Den Boer and Bouw (1986, 58).
71. Graafland (1999, 316).
72. Doornenbal and Siebesma (2005).
73. http://www.ewv.nl.

Wine Netherlands, an organization linked to the charismatic New Wine movement within the Anglican Church of England. The British New Wine conferences are attended annually by tens of thousands of Christians, who are being instructed in the work of the Holy Spirit. The most recent New Wine conference in the Netherlands (2017) was attended by six thousand Christians, mainly Reformed (of various kinds). Its aim, according to its website,[74] is the renewal "of Christians and churches in the Netherlands in the joy of knowing and worshiping Jesus Christ, equipping them to announce his kingdom in the love of God the Father and in the power and the gifts of the Holy Spirit."

Much more could be mentioned, such as the teaching position for the theology of charismatic renewal at the (originally Reformed) Free University at Amsterdam; its first occupant was Reformed theologian C. van der Kooi (until 2008).[75] He delivered the 2014 Warfield Lectures at Princeton Theological Seminary, entitled "This Incredible Benevolent Force: The Holy Spirit in Reformed Theology and Spirituality."[76] In addition, since 2002 the Azusa Theological Seminary of the Pentecostal congregations in the Netherlands has been integrated into the Free University, and its director, C. van der Laan, was professor of Pentecostalism at the same university.[77]

There is also movement in the Gereformeerde Kerken Vrijgemaakt (Reformed Churches in the Netherlands, Liberated, related to the American and Canadian Reformed Churches). Within this denomination, the book by pastor G. Hutten, *Verrast door de Geest* (*Surprised by the Spirit*), caused quite a stir.[78] Hutten is part of a remarkable charismatic renewal movement within this group of churches, which group includes pastors J. Douma, H. Smit, and P. Troost. The latter wrote an interest-

---

74. http://www.new-wine.nl/over-new-wine/
75. See Van der Kooi (2003).
76. Van der Kooi (2018).
77. See Van der Laan (1989).
78. Hutten (2004).

ing book on what the Reformed and the Charismatics could learn from one another.[79]

Given the much stronger relationships today between the many denominations within the Reformed world, as well as between this world and the Evangelical world, those committed to charismatic renewal can interact more easily today than they did a few decades ago. We see clear signs of an evangelical-charismatic renewal movement within many denominations and congregations. The proponents of this movement interact at numerous conferences. After decades of tension between the Pentecostal world and the Reformed world, this tension has recently been melting like snow in springtime. A fruitful dialogue is developing, in which both sides are learning from each other and are becoming more aware of the weaknesses in their own traditions.

2.4 The Pentecostal and Charismatic Movement
2.4.1 Precursors and Beginnings

Remarkably, according to some historians, the Pentecostal movement began on the very first day of the twentieth century. On January 1, 1901, a number of students at Charles F. Parham's Bethel Bible School in Topeka, Kansas, after a thorough study of the book of Acts, began speaking in tongues. In 1906, the movement advanced much more strongly with the preaching of William J. Seymour, the son of two former American slaves. He was raised Roman Catholic and Baptist, successively, was converted among the Methodists, joined a Holiness movement, and was formed at a Bible school led by Charles F. Parham in Houston, Texas. In 1906, Seymour founded a congregation in Los Angeles, which met first in North Bonnie Brae Street, then in a building on Azusa Street. The latter location gave the movement its name of the Azusa Street Revival. This congregation included people who were baptized in the Holy Spirit and began speaking in tongues.

From there, the news of a new outpouring of the Holy

---

79. Troost (2006).

Spirit spread across every continent.[80] In fact, opinions differ about which preacher or which group began speaking in tongues first; perhaps we should say that the work began more or less simultaneously at a number of locations. The theological roots of this new movement are difficult to trace, but we should mention sources like John Wesley, Charles G. Finney, Reuben A. Torrey, and more generally the nineteenth-century Holiness movements, although some Holiness leaders rejected the emerging Pentecostalism.

Some historians or theologians have discerned relationships with the great mystic traditions, which continued especially within the Roman Catholic Church.[81] In addition, we may think here of the Syriacs Ephrem and Philoxenus of Mabbug, the free church Messalians (fourth and fifth centuries), the Egyptian (?) Pseudo-Macarius (late fourth century), who had great influence on John Wesley, the Assyrian Nestorian Isaac of Nineve, and the Russian Seraphim of Sarov. The latter taught that the great aim of Christian life was to receive the baptism of the Spirit, and to enter into the sphere of the Spirit.[82] Especially in the Eastern churches, there have been many precursors of modern Pentecostalism, even if early Pentecostals were completely unaware of them.

Before the 1960s, Christians who practiced speaking in tongues were forced to leave existing churches and congregations, and to join Pentecostal congregations, a great variety of which existed by this time. This changed in 1960, when the so-called "Charismatic renewal" or "Charismatic movement" began. It started with Dennis Bennett, an Episcopalian pastor at St. Mark's Church in Van Nuys, California, who received the Spirit baptism and began speaking in tongues but insisted on remaining in the Episcopalian tradition. From here,

---

80. The early history of the Pentecostal movement has been described many times; I would mention only the studies of Bloch-Hoell (1964), Hollenweger (1969), and Williams (1972).
81. Bruner (1970, 35–55); Kärkkäinen (2002, 87–88).
82. Burgess (1989, 62, 81–82, 103, 107, 148–49, 187, 197, 214–15).

Later Pneumatology

the movement spread throughout other Protestant churches, first the free church Evangelicals, then Lutheran churches, Reformed and Presbyterian churches (think of the Sovereign Grace Churches), the Roman Catholic Church (since about 1967), and finally the Eastern Orthodox Church.[83]

It has been to the credit of the Pentecostal and Charismatic movement that, in spite of its own theological shortcomings, it re-assigned to the Holy Spirit the place that he deserves. Indeed, these Christians had their predecessors, but it was they who spread renewed pneumatology throughout the world, to every corner of the Christian church. As Alister McGrath wrote, in almost all large denominations the rise of the Charismatic movement has caused the subject of the Holy Spirit to be moved near the top of the theological agenda. The new experience of the reality and power of the Spirit has exerted an enormous influence on the theological discussion concerning the person and work of the Holy Spirit.[84] Clark Pinnock, who himself was a Baptist, described his own pneumatological book as "charismatic" because it celebrates Pentecostalism as a mighty twentieth-century outpouring of the Spirit; he even called this outpouring the most important development in modern Christianity.[85]

Unfortunately, the Pentecostal and Charismatic movement has suffered a number of divisions, and at present contains a large variety of denominations, some of which exclude the others. Some of these advocate definitely heretical ideas, such as Unitarianism ("Jesus is Father, Son, and Holy Spirit"). Pinnock thought it was remarkable that Pentecostalism could be such a truly great revival movement, while at the same time overflow with so many errors.[86] I would put it this way (in a somewhat unnuanced fashion): the early church was a work of the Spirit, while the resulting Roman Catholic Church

---

83. See the critical evaluation by Veenhof et al. (1978); Welker (1992, 7–15).
84. McGrath (2017, xxxiii–xxxiv, 290).
85. Pinnock (1996, 18).
86. Pinnock (1996, 267).

and the Eastern Orthodox churches were the work of people. Similarly, the Reformation was a work of the Spirit, while resulting Protestantism, with its many strands, was the work of people. Similarly, the revivals of 1906 and 1960 were a work of the Spirit, while the resulting Pentecostal and Charismatic denominations were the work of people.

2.4.2 Missions and Evangelism

In general, the strongest point of the Pentecostal and Charismatic movements is hardly their theological precision but rather their strong emphasis on spirituality, and on missions and evangelism. These two matters are intertwined: the Pentecostals were, and are, convinced that Spirit baptism supplies power needed not only for believers' personal lives but especially for missions and gospel preaching (cf. especially Acts 1:8).[87] To any theological objections raised against this view, these Christians will respond that at least their doctrine appears to work, given their enormous missionary success.

Indeed, the contribution of the mainline churches to world missions is minimal, whereas Evangelicals worldwide among *all* religious currents are experiencing the fastest growth. Depending on how one defines them, they number between 300 and 800 million Christians. Some estimate the number of American Evangelicals to be 90–100 million, or about 30–35% of the population.[88] These numbers suggest that, after the Roman Catholic Church, the Evangelicals are internationally the second largest Christian community, dispersed among many denominations. The World Evangelical Alliance claims that it embraces 600 million Christians in 129 countries.[89]

Within this growth of Evangelicalism, especially in the Third World, signs and wonders play an essential role. In 1988, Peter Wagner of the Fuller School of World Missions

---

87. Menzies and Menzies (2005, 27).
88. http://www.wheaton.edu/ISAE/Defining-Evangelicalism/How-Many-Are-There.
89. http://www.worldea.org/whoweare/introduction.

described how during the preceding thirty-five years most Christian converts had been converted through "power evangelism," that is, through signs and wonders.[90] In 1997, Wagner claimed that we live in a time of a more extensive outpouring of the Holy Spirit than on the Day of Pentecost: (a) every *day* about 140,000 people come to Christ (more modest estimations say 80–90,000); this is forty-six times as many as in Acts 2; (b) more people had become Christians in the past ten years (i.e., between 1987 and 1997) than in all previous church history; (c) more signs and wonders occur now than ever before.[91]

In 1900, Latin America had only 50,000 Protestants, but today there are more than one thousand (!) times as many, and three-fourths of them are Pentecostals and Charismatics. Since 1950 (when the foreign missionaries were chased out), the fastest growth of Christianity in all of its history is occurring in China through the house churches. In 1950 there were about four million Christians in China, and in 2012 they were at least fifty million, and according to some, closer to one hundred million. About 85% of Chinese Christians seem to be familiar with miracles and wonders. In Africa, where Christianity is also experiencing phenomenal growth, this percentage seems to be even higher.[92] Michael Green is another author who links the rapid growth of Christianity in the Third World with miraculous gifts, and explains this by the fact that this part of the world is still largely untouched by Western skepticism with regard to supernatural powers, both good and bad.[93]

John Wimber said something similar: "power evangelism" is so effective in the Third World partly because people are more open to spiritual activities from *both* sides, both good and evil. This means that they easily accept supernat-

---

90. Wagner (1988a; see also 1988b; 1988c).
91. http://www. evanwiggs.com/revival/history/mission.html.
92. Wimber and Springer (1991, 203–204).
93. In his preface to Wimber and Springer (1991, 8–9).

ural healings, believe dreams and visions, acknowledge the existence of demons, and so on. We, Western people, do not notice supernatural powers, or we argue them away. This is what many have done, for example, with demon possession, whose symptoms they have reduced to psychiatric phenomena. Therefore, many no longer believe that demons are cast out through the power of Christ. Many have overlooked the entire supernatural dimension, and are unaware of the spiritual battle that surrounds us.

In Western culture, there is suspicion concerning almost everything that is spiritual. We have been raised to doubt the supernatural, and to invent a natural explanation for healings, prophecies, evil spirits, and the like. In this way, the *normal* forms in which the kingdom of God is manifested, such as healing, prayer, and prophecy (Matt. 4:23; 9:35; 12:28; Acts 8:5-12), are viewed as *abnormal* by many Western Christians. No wonder that Western Europe and North America are not experiencing revival to the extent that we find it today in other parts of the world (Asia, Africa, South America).[94] In other words, many Western objections seem to be clothed in the robes of theology, but in reality they are instead wrapped in psychological and rationalist garb.

The cautious but open attitude of Reformed Baptist preacher John Piper seems most helpful at this point: "[W]hat I think I can say for our guidance is this. 1. On the one hand, we ought to honor the uniqueness of Jesus and the apostles and of that revelatory moment in history that gave us the foundational doctrines of faith and life in the New Testament. 2. On the other hand we ought to be open to the real possibility that this [present time] too might be a unique moment in history, and in this moment it may well be God's purpose to pour out his Spirit in unprecedented revival—revival of love to Christ and zeal for worship and compassion for lost people and a missionary thrust with signs and wonders."[95]

---

94. Ibid., 204–205.
95. http://www.desiringgod.org/messages/are-signs-and-wonders-for-today.

2.4.3 Ecstatic Experience

Typical Pentecostal spirituality is expressed in ecstatic enthusiasm, especially during congregational worship. With the exception of singing in tongues, though, its typical expressions, such as clapping, raising arms, shouting "Amen" and "Hallelujah," have also become common in many Evangelical congregations that have no Pentecostal or Charismatic background. Incidentally, according to Eddie Ensley,[96] from the ninth to the sixteenth century spontaneous worship, improvised songs of jubilee, clapping, and even dancing, as well as a kind of glossolalia, were common among saints, mystics, and many simple believers.

Apart from the theological characteristics that Pentecostals have in common with other orthodox Christians, these are the most specific Pentecostal doctrines:

(a) *Spirit baptism* is a separate experience *after* conversion, often called the "second blessing."

(b) *Speaking in tongues* is a gift that is the evidence of this Spirit baptism, a gift that is intended for all believers.

(c) The conviction that *healing* is included in the work of atonement, and thus can be promised to all people on the condition of faith.

(d) Emphasis on the other gifts of the Spirit, especially *prophecy*, including dreams, visions, "images."

The matter is not clear-cut; with regard to each separate point we may notice a variety of views, also because after the 1960s various new movements have arisen. Some of these, in the 1980s, have been referred to as the "Third Wave," following the Pentecostal and Charismatic movements.[97] Each of these movements has made its unique contribution to the theological discussion. Some of these contributions will be discussed later. In particular these involve points (a): is Spirit baptism indeed a "second blessing" *after* conversion?; and

---

96. Ensley (1977).
97. Wagner (1988b); Nathan and Wilson (1995).

(b): is glossolalia indeed *the* proof of Spirit baptism, and is it indeed intended for *all* believers (see §8.7)? To this we may add point (c): can we promise converts their physical healing to the same extent that we can promise them the forgiveness of their sins?

It is not difficult to imagine the dangers to which Pentecostal and Charismatic faith and practice are continually exposed—dangers that to some extent can be signaled in the *entire* Evangelical world as well as the subjectivist wings of established churches (e.g., hyper-Calvinism).[98]

(a) The first danger is subjectivistic anti-intellectualism and anti-theologism, accompanied by biblicism, that is, quoting and applying Bible verses apart from their redemptive-historical and grammatical context, apart from the literary genre characteristics, and without comparing Scripture with Scripture.[99] Appealing to this very Holy Spirit, the apostle Peter warns against one's "own interpretation" of Scripture (2 Pet. 1:20–21).

(b) Next, the danger exists of a certain sensational (that is, carnal!) striving for special experiences, which often seem to be the product of the mind rather than of the Spirit.

(c) Concomitantly, there is an exuberant striving for certain *gifts* of the Spirit, more than for the *fruit* of the Spirit. The longing for especially glossolalia is often quite disproportionate to the attention the subject receives in the New Testament.

(d) We also have to shun what Cornelis Aalders has called the passionate hunger for spiritual experiences (Lat. *passio experientiae*)[100] which are sometimes sought at the expense of Scripture and thorough theological analysis.

(e) Finally, Pentecostal and Charismatic teaching and practice are occasionally guilty of a particular compulsion: each believer *must* undergo the "second blessing," and one

---

98. See Bakker (2005, especially 181–94).
99. Cf. Bakker (2005, 211–16).
100. Aalders (1977, 96).

must demonstrate this by speaking in tongues (see §8.7). This is linked to the frequent phenomenon of the authoritarian (because "Spirit-filled") pastor.

Signaling these dangers of the flesh does not at all diminish respect for the tremendous work of the Holy Spirit in the Charismatic renewal movement—the most extensive renewal movement that has ever occurred in all of church history, a work that continues today.

2.5 More Recent Developments
2.5.1 Causes and Expressions

In recent decades, interest in the Holy Spirit has arisen throughout the Christian church in a manner that is almost unparalleled in church history. This has occurred partly under the influence of the Pentecostal and Charismatic movements, partly through theological dynamics of various denominations. Already in his day, Karl Barth called pneumatology "the future of Christian theology."[101] Jean-Jacques Suurmond saw at least three causes of this new interest.[102]

(1) The effects of the Enlightenment ideals of emancipation and democracy, which today touch every facet of society, have also clearly permeated church life. Stated in my own words, the emancipation of the ordinary church members has minimized the distance between them and the clergy, and the values of democracy lead to much greater participation of church members in church government, and especially in the church's liturgy. In other words, worship services are marked less by a rigid order and liturgy (which order and liturgy some allege as nurturing a silent congregation of listeners), and more by the spontaneous working of the Spirit and the contributions of a great variety of *charismata*.

(2) A re-evaluation of the holistic approach to reality.

---

101. Quoted in Kärkkäinen (2002, 13n7). However, H. Berkhof complained that in Barth's theology, pneumatology had been swallowed up by Christology, as it were (quoted by Hartveld [1978, 34]); cf. also Suurmond (1986).
102. Suurmond (1995, 74).

Again, in my own words, this means a balanced attention to Word *and* Spirit, to reason *and* feeling, to mind *and* body, to orthodoxy *and* religious experience (mysticism), to doctrine *and* living, to order *and* spontaneity, to church *and* society, to hierarchical *and* charismatic church life. A fascinating example is the role of religious dancing in ancient Israel (as well as, e.g., among the Chasidim), in pre-Reformational churches, and among Pentecostals and Charismatics, in contrast to the rejection of religious dancing by all those denominations that, like the ancient Greeks, elevate the mind above the body.[103]

(3) As a consequence of secularization, the church loses its influence within the established order of society. This means a loss of *power*. This may mean that Christians learn anew what it is to be spiritually and materially poor, for only in this way will they learn to open themselves to what the Spirit wishes to give them. The less they have, or the less is left to them, the more they will be prepared to receive.

The renewed interest for the Holy Spirit comes to expression in at least three ways.[104]

(a) *Individually:* Millions of Christians have a longing for greater intimacy with God, more spiritual growth, more dedication to Christ in the power of the Holy Spirit, and more awareness of all blessings that the Spirit can offer them.

(b) *Ecclesiastically:* In many denominations, there is a great longing for inner renewal of spiritual life and of the liturgy, for a deeper insight into the gifts of the Spirit and their functioning in the church, for more genuine praise and worship. Many churches are searching for their spiritual roots.

(c) *Theologically:* Closely related to these is vigorous theological (and philosophical) activity, which comes to light in a flood of publications on the Holy Spirit. These no longer come mainly from Pentecostals and Charismatics, but appear across the entire spectrum of academic theology, not least

---

103. Ibid., 99–100.
104. Dreyer (1998, 1).

from Roman Catholic, as well as Lutheran, Calvinist, and free church Evangelical theologians.

2.5.2 International Churches

There are several characteristics of the strongly renewed interest in the Holy Spirit in various segments of the church (besides Pentecostals and Charismatics).

(a) The *Eastern Orthodox Churches* had always emphasized the Holy Spirit. Through their membership in the World Council of Churches as well as their renewed contacts with the Roman Catholic Church, they have become more familiar to those within Western Christianity. In this way, the rich pneumatological inheritance of these churches has come within easy reach of Western Catholics and Protestants.

One of the most remarkable aspects of this is the typically Eastern Orthodox view of *theosis*, or "deification." This notion does not imply that believers become God, but that they become *like* God. Of course, this is intended in the sense not of Genesis 3:5 (Satan's falsehood), but of 1:26-27: the image of God is renewed in them, and they become "partakers of the divine nature" (2 Pet. 1:4; cf. Rom. 8:29; 1 Cor. 11:7; 15:49; 2 Cor. 3:18; Col. 3:10) — a far-reaching expression indeed.[105] The path to *theosis* requires being fashioned also by the Holy Spirit. One modern Orthodox pneumatologist who has drawn attention to these things far beyond their own circle is John D. Zizioulas, the bishop of Pergamon (Greece).[106]

(b) One of the most striking characteristics of the Charismatic movement was its widespread influence within the *Roman Catholic Church*.[107] In the Catholic tradition, there was a strong tendency to identify the Spirit with the church, exemplified strongly in the writings of Joseph Ratzinger, the for-

---

105. See Lossky (1985). Among the ascetic mystics, this *theosis* is the experience of only a moment; so Maxim the Confessor; see Burgess (1989, 44).
106. Zizioulas (1985; 2009).
107. See Laurentin (1977); for a sympathetic-critical Catholic assessment of the movement, see Congar (1997, 2.149–212).

mer pope Benedict XVI.[108] This approach changed when the Charismatic movement entered the Roman Catholic Church, and the Spirit could demonstrate his own character within (and over against) the church. Perhaps this was also caused by the fact that pope John XXIII called the bishops together for a council (Vatican II) "as for a new Pentecost."[109] In Western Europe especially the Belgian cardinal Leo Suenens was energized by this movement.[110] Pope John Paul II asked that the year 1998 be a year of special devotion to the Holy Spirit in preparation for the new millennium.[111] Important Roman Catholic pneumatologists were Karl Rahner, Hans Urs von Balthasar, Yves Congar, and Heribert Mühlen.[112]

(c) In 1991, the World Council of Churches (WCC) paid special attention to pneumatology under the motto: "Come, Holy Spirit, renew creation." In 1993, a meeting of its Faith and Order Commission was held in Santiago de Compostela, and was devoted to the Spirit and the church community. The 1997 WCC General Assembly in Harare (Zimbabwe) dealt with pneumatological subjects, and established a study group consisting of, on the one hand, Pentecostals and Charismatics and, on the other hand, people of the WCC.[113]

2.5.3 Lutheran and Modern Theologies

(d) In the *Lutheran Church* of Germany, several leading thinkers have expressed renewed interest in the Holy Spirit. I would mention *The Spirit of Life* by Jürgen Moltmann (b. 1926),[114] in which he began not with the theological concept of the Holy Spirit but with the collective experience of the Spirit

---

108. Ratzinger (1968, 275); according to him, the third part of the Apostles' Creed refers not to the person of the Holy Spirit as such, but to the Spirit as a gift of God who manifests himself in the church.
109. Congar (1997, 2.149).
110. See his collected work on the charismatic renewal (Suenens [2001]).
111. See Thigpar (1997).
112. Rahner (1966); Von Balthasar (1993; 2005); Congar (1997); Mühlen (1969; 1974).
113. See more extensively, Kärkkäinen (2002, 98–104).
114. Moltmann (1991).

as a foundation for theology.[115] Another important theologian is Wolfhart Pannenberg, who, in his three-volume *Systematic Theology*, described all the important loci of dogmatics from a pneumatological viewpoint.[116] Here, the absence of a separate chapter on pneumatology is not a defect because pneumatology, just like Christology, has become an integrating element of his entire systematic-theological edifice.[117] A third German pneumatologist of importance is Michael Welker (b. 1947), who offered a biblical theology of the Spirit.[118]

(e) Finally, we encounter a flood of publications from more specialized theologians. Contributions to pneumatology have been made in the fields of liberation theology,[119] process theology,[120] political theology,[121] feminist theology,[122] and ecological theology.[123] In all of them, the significance of the Holy Spirit is explained in relation to various theological topics (see §10.10).

Nevertheless, we should observe that, just as occurred in the nineteenth century, the "spirit" of revolution or of the environmental movement, for instance, is all too easily identified with the Holy Spirit.[124] These cases illustrate that it is essential to interpret pneumatology in a Christological way: there is no activity of the Spirit apart from the rule of Christ.[125] Therefore, the Holy Spirit does not engage in his own activ-

---

115. See Kärkkäinen (2002, 125–32).
116. Pannenberg (1991); see Kärkkäinen (2002, 117–25). In the Trinitarian construction of his abridged dogmatics, Van Niftrik (1961, 249–426) gave ecclesiology, the doctrine of the covenant and the sacraments, soteriology, and eschatology a pneumatological form.
117. A similar approach in Evangelical circles is found with Pinnock (1996); see Kärkkäinen (2002, 139–45); cf. also Bloesch (1992) and Erickson (1985).
118. Welker (1992); see Kärkkäinen (2002, 132–39).
119. Comblin (1989); see Kärkkäinen (2002, 154–58).
120. Cobb and Griffin (1976); Reynolds (1990); see Kärkkäinen (2002, 148–54).
121. Volf (1991); Mueller-Fahrenholz (1995).
122. Elizabeth Johnson (2002); see Kärkkäinen (2002, 164–69).
123. Wallace (1996); see Kärkkäinen (2002, 159–64).
124. Floor (1982, 222–23).
125. For this central notion, see Ouweneel (2017a).

ity apart from Christ in Hinduism, Buddhism, or Islam, except that within these religions the Spirit sometimes prepares people spiritually for encountering Christ. Since the Day of Pentecost, all activity of the Spirit is Christocentric,[126] though we must add that this Christocentric working of the Spirit is *universal* in scope (see §§5.2 and 10.9).

2.6 Types of Pneumatology
2.6.1 Various Approaches

Christian pneumatology necessarily involves a multiplicity of insights, such that all one-sidedness must be avoided. Pentecostals and Charismatics emphasize seeking the power of the Holy Spirit, and this is good. However, in this quest, they may easily manifest a rather individualistic and even "Christofugal" tendency.

In opposition to this, the Evangelical (non-Charismatic) movement is often strongly Jesucentric, and this is good. However, this feature can easily obscure the work of the Holy Spirit. This, too, is one-sided.

In traditional Calvinism, the Lord (or the LORD, or YHWH) occupies the center, and this is good; however, if this name is identified with any single person of the Trinity, that would likely be especially the Father. This, too, is one-sided (see §3.5.1).

The Roman Catholic tradition emphasizes the significance of the church as the community of the Holy Spirit, and this is good. However, it risks underestimating the personal experience of the Spirit, or sacrificing it to ecclesiastical control.

Eastern Orthodox Churches emphasize *theosis* (deification) in the power of the Spirit, and this is good. However, in so doing, they must not erase the boundary between God and human beings.

Liberation theology hopes for a Spirit-wrought freedom, and this is good. However, it must not confuse spiritual free-

---

126. Green (1975, 49–50).

dom with political freedom.

Feminist theology emphasizes the equal value of man and woman as grounded in the masculine-feminine primordial image in God, and this is good. However, they must not make God or the Spirit a "she," for God is neither female nor male, even though we refer to God as "he" and "him," just as the Bible does.

At virtually no time in church history have the various movements been so busy learning to listen to each other, and thus to become more aware of the shortcomings and imbalances in one's own tradition. This may come to expression in a variegated pneumatology that does justice to the insights from different emphases.

In 1987, the Reformed Dutch theologian Abraham van de Beek tried to distinguish a number of approaches to pneumatology, comparable to a similar variety of approaches to Christology.[127] First, one could try to design a pneumatology-from-above, one that begins with the active Spirit, who at his own initiative intervenes in the cosmos and in the personal life of an individual. Second, in opposition to this, one could try to design a pneumatology-from-below, one that begins with human religious experience and recognizes in it the work of the Spirit. Van de Beek assigns his own approach, but also that of Paul Tillich,[128] to this second category (to which the view of Moltmann could be added).

Third, one could try to design a pneumatology-from-behind; the most common version of this is a pneumatology-from-above-from-behind. That model views the work of the Spirit by following the sequence of redemptive history. From either Genesis 1 or Acts 2, one looks forward along the line of the Bible's history. Fourth, in opposition to this, one could try to design a pneumatology-from-before, one that begins with church history, and from there looks back to view

---

127. Van de Beek (1987, 24).
128. Tillich (1968, vol. 3).

the work of the Spirit in retrospect (this approach is found particularly in classical Roman Catholic ecclesiology, but also, e.g., with G. Lampe[129]), or one that begins with the consummation of history and looks back (e.g., O. Noordmans[130]).

2.6.2 Paul on the Spirit

More distinctions could be made, such as beginning with the relationship of pneumatology to other loci in systematic theology. Here we think especially of its relationship to *ecclesiology* (see above on Roman Catholic pneumatology), or to *eschatology* (e.g., the eschatological pneumatology of O. Noordmans), or to *anthropology* (e.g., that of A. A. van Ruler), and particularly to *Christology*. It belongs to the essence of pneumatology that it must always be thoroughly Christocentric.[131] "A Reformed pneumatology can be pure only if it views the connection between Kyrios and Pneuma properly," W. H. Velema wrote[132] — and, of course, this holds for any type of Christian pneumatology, not just a Reformed one. However, such a claim does not yet indicate *how* this connection between pneumatology and Christology must be viewed.

Let us take our starting point in the following difficult statements by the apostle Paul: "[T]he Lord is the Spirit" (2 Cor. 3:17, *ho kyrios to pneuma estin*[133]), and ". . . from [the] Lord Spirit" (thus literally in v. 18, *apo kyriou pneumatos*). Two exegetical approaches can be distinguished here: one in which Christology is almost a function of pneumatology (here, the Spirit is the acting subject, and Christ is the object of the acting), and one in which pneumatology is almost a function of Christology (here, Christ is the acting subject, and the Spirit is the object of the acting).[134] In the former approach, which is

---

129. Lampe (1977).
130. Noordmans (1955).
131. See Floor (1982, 35–50); Van de Beek (1987, 30–52).
132. Velema (1957, 246); cf. Versteeg (1980, 205–13).
133. Notice that the Gk. word *pneuma* has the article, so that the phrase is reciprocal; cf. "the life was the light" (Gk. *hē zōē ēn to phōs*, John 1:4).
134. Cf. Kasper (1974, 54).

characteristic of the Synoptic Gospels, the Spirit is the starting point. He is at work before the Man Jesus appears on the scene, and it is he who descends upon Jesus and grants him his power and authority (e.g., Luke 3:21-22; 4:1, 14). In the latter approach, which is characteristic of the Gospel of John, Christ is the starting point. Apart from John 1:32-33, the emphasis is on him who announces the Spirit, and sends him from the Father into this world (John 7:39; 14:26; 15:26; 16:13-15).[135]

These two lines converge with Paul, for in his letters Jesus is both the One who, "according to the Spirit of holiness," was declared to be the Son of God in power (Rom. 1:4; cf. 1 Tim. 3:16), and the One who grants the *gift* (Gk. *dōrea*) of the Spirit (i.e., the Spirit himself is the gift; Acts 2:38; 10:45) and the *gifts* (Gk. *charismata*) of the Spirit (i.e., the gifts worked by the Spirit; 1 Cor. 12:4). Two very different pnuematologies arise if one emphasizes either the former, more traditional line, or the latter, more charismatic line, each at the expense of the other. And a third type of pneumatology arises if, through misunderstanding 2 Corinthians 3:17, one ultimately identifies Christ and the Spirit entirely, as did, for instance, Ingo Hermann.[136] H. Berkhof seemed to express a large measure of agreement with Hermann, though for Berkhof the risen Lord always surpasses his function of being the "life-giving s/Spirit" (1 Cor. 15:45).[137]

In the relationship between pneumatology and Christology, the Christian's *position* is this: the believer is in Christ, and the Spirit is in the believer. One's *practical* realization is that one is more in Christ as the Spirit works more in one; and the Spirit works more in a person as that person is more in Christ.

We should not devote isolated attention, however, to the relationship between the exalted Kyrios and the Pneuma. Very important as well is the relationship between the hu-

---

135. Cf. Ridderbos (1975, 88–89); extensively, Versteeg (1980); Floor (1982, 36).
136. Hermann (1961); see Congar (1997, 1.39).
137. Berkhof (1964, 25–29); on this entire subject, see Floor (1982, chapter 3).

miliated Jesus and the Spirit. The church in Corinth seemed to be carried away by its own theology of the Spirit, whereas it seemed allergic to a theology of the cross.[138] Conversely, many traditional Protestant denominations seem to boast in a theology of the cross or more broadly, of suffering (*theologia crucis*) — which may give the appearance of a real humility — but to be allergic to a theology of the Holy Spirit, which emphasizes spiritual strength and fullness. Suffering rather than power, acquiescence rather than faith, resignation rather than victory, seem to be the slogans.[139]

2.6.3 Theological and Biblical

Finally, we might make another distinction, namely, between a more theological and a more biblical pneumatology. The former is more characteristic of (continental European) traditional theology, the latter more of (Anglo-Saxon) Evangelical theology. In the former case, we are dealing with theologians who design a pneumatology with academic creativity and literary expertise, as well as with deep knowledge of theological literature. Such a design is based on what one considers to be the great themes of God's revelation but, for this very reason, it has a pronounced personal bias.

A good example is supplied by Van de Beek, who extensively contrasts the pneumatologies of two contemporaneous thinkers from the same Reformed tradition in the Netherlands, namely, those of Oepke Noordmans and Arnold A. van Ruler, and calls the one the reverse of the other.[140] Both pneumatologies cannot be true, and perhaps neither is true, since each one evidences its author's strong personal bias.

A biblical pneumatology is much more closely tied to Old and New Testament exegesis. However, this may come at the expense of grasping the great redemptive- and revelation-historical lines in Scripture. In other words, such a pneumatolo-

---

138. Ernst Käsemann, quoted by Green (1975, 56).
139. See extensively, Ouweneel (2005a, §3.3).
140. Van de Beek (1987, 232–34, 266).

gy is strongly based upon the exegesis of Bible passages dealing with the Spirit, but less upon the theology of the Old and New Testaments. Blades of grass are inspected close to the ground, with a magnifying glass; prairies are inspected from the heights, with binoculars.

Pinnock rightly said of pneumatology that exegesis alone cannot furnish the full perspective that is demanded by the Christian community. The investigation must also take into account historical, theological, philosophical, cultural, and mystical dimensions.[141] In the pneumatology of this volume, I am seeking to articulate a middle way between these two approaches.

---

141. Pinnock (1996, 17).

Chapter 3
The Person of the Spirit

And I will ask the Father,
and he will give you another Helper,
to be with you forever,
even the Spirit of truth, ...
You know him,
for he dwells with you
and will be in you. . . .
. . . the Helper, the Holy Spirit,
whom the Father will send in my name,
he will teach you all things
and bring to your remembrance
all that I have said to you.
                               John 14:16–17, 26

Summary: *God's being is Spirit, God has a Spirit, and the Spirit is one of the three persons within the Godhead; how do these statements relate? In what sense is God Spirit? How does this relate to human beings? How did the early church arrive at the doctrine of the Trinity? It demonstrated that the Holy Spirit is a person, a divine person, equal to the Father and the Son. All the features that make a person a person apply to the Holy Spirit. Moreover, he pos-*

sesses the same divine attributes as the Father and the Son do. YHWH is the name of the Triune God, including the Holy Spirit. Because he is God it is possible to pray to, and to worship, the Holy Spirit. In the Bible, the Holy Spirit has many names.

Of special interest is the metaphor of "mother" as applied not only to the Holy Spirit, but also to Chokmah/Sophia (Wisdom) and to the Shekhinah (God's glorious presence). Early Christianity was still very aware of the maternal aspects of the Holy Spirit, and their relation to Chokmah/Sophia and Shekhinah. This was due partly to neo-Platonic and Gnostic influences.

3.1 God is Spirit
3.1.1 God's Spirit, God's Being

WHEN WE SPEAK OF THE TRIUNE GOD, and more specifically of the Holy Spirit, we can say two different things about the relationship between God and the Spirit: God both has a Spirit and God is (a) s/Spirit.[1] When God says, "My spirit" (e.g., Gen. 6:3), this is the same as saying that God has a Spirit, just as his saying "my Son" (e.g., Luke 3:22) implies that he has a Son. But when Jesus says, "God is (a) s/Spirit" (John 4:24), this says something about God's very being, about the being of the Triune God. When we hear about the "Spirit of God" (e.g., Gen. 1:2), this may mean either God has a Spirit or God is Spirit.

In John 4:23–24, Jesus told the Samaritan woman: "[T]he hour is coming, and is now here, when the true worshipers will worship the Father in spirit and truth, for the Father is seeking such people to worship him. God is spirit [or "Spirit," GNT; or "a spirit," ERV; or "a Spirit," KJV], and those who worship him must worship in spirit and truth" (John 4:23–24). In my view, the indefinite article is undesirable here, because it might suggest that God is a spirit among other spirits.[2] Jesus

---
1. Pinnock (1996, 24–28, 35).
2. Morris (1971, 271); Tenney (1981, 56n24); the latter points out that this is one of the four "God is + noun" statements in the New Testament, in addition to "God is light" (1 John 1:5), "God is love" (4:8, 16), and "God is a consuming fire" (Heb. 12:29), to which may be added "God is [my] witness" (Rom.

is pointing out here not how God is related to possible other spirits, or how he belongs to a higher category (*genus proximum*, here: that of "spirits"). Rather, he is explaining how the entire question of worship must be severed from the earthly-material level at which the Samaritan woman was thinking, and must be transferred to the heavenly-spiritual level. The point is not to what higher category God belongs, but what his being is. "Spirit" is his spiritual essence (*essentia spiritualis*).³

With this statement by Jesus we may compare this statement by Paul: "For who knows a person's thoughts except the spirit of that person, which is in him? So also no one comprehends the thoughts of God except the Spirit of God" (1 Cor. 2:11). The CEV puts it this way: "You are the only one who knows what is in your own mind, and God's Spirit is the only one who knows what is in God's mind." The Greek expression *ta tou theou* can also mean "the [things] of God," that which is of God, what is proper to him. Factually, the "spirit of that person" is not much different from that person himself: no one knows the mind (or the being) of a person except he himself. Similarly, no one knows the mind (or the being) of God except God himself. The "Spirit of God" is in this case not primarily a pneumatological or a Trinitarian term, but an ontological term; it is God himself in his being. God is s/Spirit; no one knows him except his s/Spirit, that is, he himself. Only God knows God.

In verse 12 this *becomes* a pneumatological statement when Paul says that "we" have received "the Spirit who is from God" (*to ek tou theou*).⁴ Thus, the Spirit is, first, the being of God himself (the Spirit *of* God), second, the One who comes "*from* God" to us (or, to say the same thing in different words, it is God who in his Spirit comes to us), and third, the Spirit

---

1:9; Phil. 1:8; 1 Thess. 2:5).
3. However, Keener (1997, 154) does not want to view this as an "ontological philosophical statement," but as a claim that God is manifested in his Spirit.
4. Cf. Fee (1987, 112).

is the Third Person within the Godhead. Of course, the three expressions overlap extensively, yet they must be carefully distinguished.

3.1.2 In What Sense *Pneuma*?

What does it mean that God is *pneuma*? Etymology does not take us very far here, for if God is "breath," metaphorically speaking (cf. §4.1), we hasten to add that he is incomparably more. On the one hand, it is true that we can speak of God in an "idea-like" or "analogical" (less accurately: "metaphorical"[5]) way. That is, terms such as Hebrew *ruach* and Greek *pneuma* are taken from material (human, but also animal and inanimate) reality and are applied to God. This is possible not only because humans were created in the image and after the likeness of God, but also because we cannot speak of God other than in terms taken from our earthly reality. On the other hand, God is more dissimilar than similar to whatever we know in this world as spirit.[6] God is always more than what the terms we use for him can express; they merely give us an *idea* (image, impression, representation) of him.

But what kind of idea is this? Can we say anything more about this? Following Platonism and Philo, at an early stage in church history, that is, from Origen, the thought arose that God is primarily "mind" (*nous*, with connotations of intellect and thought), particularly to counteract the thought that God would be "matter" in any sense.[7] This thought could arise all the more easily because in Isaiah 40:13 the Septuagint rendered the Hebrew phrase *ruach* YHWH as the Greek phrase *nous Kyriou*. This discussion played some role in early Protestantism. However, Johannes Crellius established the elementary fact that the terms *ruach* and *pneuma* themselves never mean intellect or consciousness.[8] In the basic meaning of "wind" or

---

5. See Ouweneel (2014; 2015).
6. Johnson (2002, 131).
7. Pannenberg (1991, 1:371–72; 1991, 2:185–87).
8. Pannenberg (1991, 1:373). Jewish sources (Kimchi, Metsudath David) understand the phrase in Isa. 40:13 to refer to the divine will; see Slotki (1983,

"breath," we instead encounter the idea that God, or God's Spirit, is the source of all vital energy. We are dealing much more with a biotic than with a logical idea.

This is beautifully illustrated in the comparison between verses 29 and 30 of Psalm 104: "When you hide your face, they [i.e., God's creatures] are dismayed; when you take away their breath [*ruach*], they die and return to their dust. When you send forth your breath [or Spirit; *ruach*], they are created, and you renew the face of the ground."[9] "Their" *ruach* is the life principle in God's creatures; when it is taken away they die. But "your *ruach*" is the life-giving principle in God. As Elihu said, "The Spirit [*ruach*] of God has made me, and the breath [*neshamah*] of the Almighty gives me life" (Job 33:4).

Jesus, too, used the metaphor with strictly biotic connotations: "It is the Spirit [*pneuma*] who gives life. . . . The words that I have spoken to you are spirit [*pneuma*] and life" (John 6:63). The apostle Paul calls the Holy Spirit the "Spirit of life" (Rom. 8:2; cf. v. 6). He calls the risen Christ a "life-giving spirit [*pneuma*]" (1 Cor. 15:45).

3.1.3 Anthropological Parallel

When it comes to God's *pneuma*, a clear parallel can be observed between anthropology and the doctrine of God (*theologia propria*). As I have argued elsewhere, the Reformed philosopher in the Netherlands, Herman Dooyeweerd, has done groundbreaking work here.[10] The human *pneuma* (here in the sense of human "being") is not to be located, *contra* Aristotelian-Thomistic thought, in human *reason* (Gk. *nous*, Lat. *anima rationalis*) but in the human *heart*, the human religious personality, the focal point of human existence. In Scripture, this concentration point is alternately referred to as the "soul" — at least in the existential meaning of the word (e.g., Matt. 10:28) — or as the "inner person" (Gk. *ho esō anthrōpos*, "inner

---

188).
9. "Yahweh's breath is creative power of life"; Wolff (1973, 61).
10. See Ouweneel (2016).

self," "inner being," "inner human"; Rom. 7:22; 2 Cor. 4:16; Eph. 3:16), and especially the "heart," from which "flow the springs [KJ21: outflowings; Heb. *tōtseōt*] of life" (Prov. 4:23), and in which God has put "[the awareness of] eternity" (*olam*, Eccl.3:11 CJB).

No theory or concept of this "heart" can be constructed simply from Scripture; such a theory can be approximated in a scholarly fashion only to the extent that it is *manifested* in all of human temporal existence. Only in this way is it possible to form a suprarational, religious *idea* — not a "concept" — of the heart that transcends the theoretical. This heart (soul, spirit) does not exist in a dualistic relation to the human body, but the entire human temporal bodily existence finds its inner unity, concentration, and integration in the human heart. Conversely, this transcendent heart is manifested in the many immanent functions of human existence. This heart *is* the person in his transcendent unity, just like the bodily existence *is* the person in his immanent diversity. Here, every form of dualism has been severed *a priori* at the root.[11]

Humans have been created as God's image and after his likeness (Gen. 1:26-27; 5:1; 9:6; 1 Cor. 11:7; Col. 3:10; James 3:9). Concomitantly, just like with humans, the divine "Spirit" (Gk. *pneuma*) is not primarily "mind" (Gk. *nous*) but "heart" (Heb. *leb(ab)*; Gk. *kardia*). Indeed, we do read several times about the "heart" of God: "[T]he LORD regretted that he had made man on the earth, and it grieved him to his heart" (Gen. 6:6). God said of the First Temple: "My eyes and my heart will be there for all time" (1 Kings 9:3). To the prince of Tyre he said, "[Y]ou make your heart like the heart of a god [KJV: of God; NIV: as wise as a god]" (Ezek. 28:2, 6). In these passages, the heart of God is associated with emotion (grief), with loving attention, and with wisdom, respectively.

Whether God's "breath" (Gk. *pneuma*) implies a certain form of (ethereal) corporality, or exists in a dualistic relation to

---

11. See ibid.

a certain form of (common physical) corporality, or excludes any form of corporality whatsoever, involves an evaluation of ancient substantialism and the Aristotelian-Thomistic soul-body dualism.[12] Just as human corporality finds its concentration point in the human heart (or spirit), so too all biblical talk about God's hands, eyes, ears, face, nostrils, arms, and so on, no matter how understood (metaphorically, anthropomorphically), finds its concentration point in God's *pneuma*, that is here, his "heart." "God is Spirit" does not mean "God is immaterial" or "God is non-corporeal," but that God is a mighty wind, the power in and behind creation, a reservoir of inexhaustible life, the power that calls things into existence that did not exist before (Rom. 4:17) and calls the dead to life (8:11).[13]

In some passages, the *ruach* of mortals is explicitly contrasted to that of God, as for instance, in Psalm 104:29–30 (quoted in §3.1.2), where God's *ruach* is the source of the human *ruach*, in the sense of Genesis 2:7 (God "breathed [*vayyippach*] into his nostrils the breath of life [*nishmat chayyim*]"). At death, the human *ruach* "returns to God who gave it" (Eccl. 12:7). This is even more remarkable in Job 27:3, where Job speaks of God's *ruach* that is in *his* (Job's) own nostrils. In Job 32:8; 33:4, and 34:14, *ruach* and *neshamah* ("breath") are used in a parallel way; this underscores the fact that the human *ruach* proceeds from God's *ruach*, to such an extent that the human breath can be called "*ruach* of God."[14]

Returning to what I said at the beginning of this section, this entire discussion about the "pneumatic being" of God must be kept clearly separate from all Trinitarian distinctions pertaining to God. God as *pneuma* is just as much Father and Son as he is Holy Spirit. Each of the three persons within the

---

12. See Congar (1997, 1.3): The Greeks thought in categories of substance, but the Jews thought of power, energy, and the principle of acting. The spirit-breath always refers to an energy of life.
13. Pinnock (1996, 24–25); J. Daniélou, quoted in Congar (1997, 1.4).
14. Hildebrandt (1995, 56).

Godhead, including the *pneuma hagion* (Holy Spirit), participates in the divine being, which is *pneuma*, energy of life. Put it this way: God's "heart" beats in the Father as well as in the Son as well as in the Holy Spirit. It is quite remarkable that, within the one *pneuma*, which is God, both the Father and the Son assume an additional name, but the Holy Spirit does not.

3.2 The Spirit and the Trinity
3.2.1 Stating the Problem

The doctrine of the divine Trinity is one of the most fundamental doctrines of the Christian faith. Within this teaching, an essential role is played by the claim that the Holy Spirit is fully and eternally a person, a divine person. If the Holy Spirit were not this, if he were not *God* the Holy Spirit, then there would not be three divine persons (entities, subsistences), and there would be no divine Trinity. The doctrine of the Trinity came to mature formulation only after the church had become aware of the fact *that* the Holy Person is not simply a person but a divine person, in close relationship with the Father and the Son, and just as personal and divine as they are.

The development of this insight took a long time. In AD 380, Gregory of Nazianzus wrote that many orthodox theologians were not sure whether they were allowed to call the Holy Spirit "God." They were convinced that the Holy Spirit was the Spirit of God, and as such was divine. But they were not sure that the Holy Spirit was a divine person, closely connected with but at the same time distinct from the Father and the Son, a person who could be called "God" just like the Father is called "God" and the Son is called "God." A year later, the well-known Council of Constantinople issued a statement in which the divine properties of the Holy Spirit were clearly established, though the fathers did not (yet) use the *term* "God" for the Holy Spirit (§1.4.3).

The doctrine that the Holy Spirit is a divine person is important because of the intimate relationship that he has to people. He is a person who works regeneration (John 3:5), conviction about sin (16:8–11), inner renewal (Titus 3:5), sanctification (1 Cor. 6:11; 1 Pet. 1:2), adoption as God's children (Rom. 8:15), awareness of possessing the love of God (Rom. 5:5), spiritual fruit (Gal. 5:22), sealing (2 Cor. 1:22; Eph. 1:13; 4:30), anointing (2 Cor. 1:21), resurrection (Rom. 8:11). Are all these works due to some merely impersonal power or influence, or perhaps to some creature of God (no matter how "exalted")? Is some impersonal influence or a creature the source of new life, or of sanctification, or of resurrection? We will have to face these questions, not only because the doctrine of the Trinity is at stake, but so too is human salvation.

As to the Holy Spirit's position within the Trinity, there are in principle two major problems. First, the Spirit is either a real person, or only a description of the mind (spirit, thought) of God, the power of God, some divine influence emanating from God, a gift of God, and so on. Second, if the Holy Spirit is indeed a person, he is either a created person, just like angels and human beings, and therefore non-eternal, or he is an eternal, non-created person. In other words, we have the following alternatives:

(a) The Holy Spirit is a non-eternal, and therefore created, impersonal emanation ("outflowing"), power, or gift of God.

(b) The Holy Spirit is a non-eternal, and therefore created, person.

(c) The Holy Spirit is an eternal, and therefore uncreated, yet impersonal emanation ("outflowing"), power, or gift of God.

(d) The Holy Spirit is an eternal, and therefore uncreated, divine person.

It is helpful to point out that the early church appropriated option (d) that is being defended here only through a long and cumbersome process. Generally speaking, the second- and third-century church fathers were very unclear on the matter. This was not because Scripture was insufficiently clear on the matter, but because the fathers apparently could not reconcile the biblical data with their preconceived ideas, which had been shaped by (neo-)Platonism and Stoicism.

3.2.2 Terminology

Also during the period around the Council of Nicaea (AD 325), there was much uncertainty about the deity of the Holy Spirit. First, this concerned the Spirit's *hypostatic subsistence*, that is, his distinct existence as a divine person. The second uncertainty concerned the Spirit's *homo-ousia*, that is, his being equal to (the same being as) the Father and the Son.[15] It was Athanasius who, not until the year 350, confessed the ontic equality of the Spirit, and rejected all subordinationism within the Trinity, that is, the alleged subordination of the Spirit to the Father and the Son, or of the Spirit and the Son to the Father.

Of course, we must consider here the fact that Greek terms such as *hypostasis, (homo-)ousia,* and *physis,* and Latin terms such as *persona, essentia, natura, substantia,* and *subsistentia,* are merely human attempts to approximate in an *idea-like* way something that surpasses human *conceptualization*. Therefore, such terms always necessarily have their disadvantages. Thus, the term "person" with respect to the Trinity may never be taken in a psychological sense as if we were dealing here with three autonomous "subjects," "personalities," or "consciousnesses," for this would lead to tritheism, the belief in three distinct gods. Paul Tillich had a point when he emphasized[16] that we can better speak of the *personae* within the Godhead than of *persons,* apparently because the early-Christian term *persona* did not involve the risks of the modern psychological term "person."[17]

Robert Jenson preferred to speak of three "identities,"[18] but Wolfhart Pannenberg felt that this approach paid inadequate

---

15. Cf. Schmidt (1986).
16. Tillich (1968, 2.166); cf. Pinnock (1996, 30, 36).
17. Cf. Barth (*CD* I/1=2, §8.2:37–38); Van Niftrik (1961, 422); Buri (1978, 591–95); Kasper (1983, 285–90).
18. Jenson (1982, 108–10).

attention to the mutual self-distinction of the three divine persons.[19] Therefore, Jenson's way of speaking would lead to "modalism" (Sabellianism), according to which Father, Son, and Spirit are only three *modes* (aspects or modes of manifestation) of the Godhead. Clark Pinnock believed he could discern a tendency to modalism with Augustine, and also with Karl Barth, Karl Rahner, and Hans Küng.[20] The difficulty with such accusations is always that those who level them raise the suspicion that they themselves are guilty of a tendency toward tritheism. The proposal of Albrecht Ritschl to use terms like "person" or "mode of being" as little as possible is not very helpful, either. We cannot work without distinguishing terms, which is not a problem as long as we carefully describe and define them.

Hendrikus Berkhof noticed the same problems in the concept of person with regard to the Holy Spirit, and solved them by discarding the entire notion within pneumatology: "The Spirit is Person because he is God acting as a Person. However, we cannot say that the Spirit is a Person distinct from God the Father. He is a Person in relation to us, not in relation to God; for he is of the personal God himself in relation to us."[21] In this way, as far as I can see, Berkhof, too, is clearly in danger of slipping into modalism.[22]

3.3 The Personality of the Holy Spirit
3.3.1 Thinking, Feeling, Willing

There are numerous Bible passages implying that the Holy Spirit is not just some impersonal emanation of God, a vague force or power, but a real person, distinct but not separated from the Father and the Son. As the Advocate (Gk. *paraklētos*) he helps, he assists, he encourages, he comforts—this is all implied in the Greek verb *parakaleō*—and he instructs and

---

19. Pannenberg (1991, 1:319).
20. Pinnock (1996, 33–34).
21. Berkhof (1964, 116).
22. Ibid., 131–32.

witnesses, he hears, speaks and convicts (John 14:16, 26; 15:26; 16:7-8; cf. Rev. 2:7). He leads (Mark 1:12; Luke 4:1, 14; John 16:13), and can raise the question concerning his own *being* led and counseled (Isa. 40:13). He is sent by the Father and the Son (John 14:16, 26; 15:26), and he himself sends prophets (Isa. 48:16) and apostles (Acts 13:2). He lifts a standard against the enemies (Isa. 59:19 NKJV).

The Holy Spirit may be grieved (Isa. 63:10; Eph. 4:30). He dwells in believers individually (John 14:17; 1 Cor. 6:19), and in the church as a whole (1 Cor. 3:16; Eph. 2:21-22). He forms a judgment in a certain matter (Acts 15:28). He searches the depths of God (1 Cor. 2:10-11). He intercedes (Rom. 8:27). He bears witness (Rom. 8:16; 1 John 5:6), and so on.[23] He *thinks, feels*, and *wills*, that is, has wisdom and understanding (Isa. 11:2; 1 Cor. 2:10-11), emotions (Isa. 63:10; Micah 2:7;[24] Zech. 6:8; Rom. 15:30; Eph. 4:30; cf. Col. 1:8), and his own will (John 3:8; 1 Cor. 12:11).

Another consideration is that, although the Greek word *pneuma* is neuter, the Bible refers to the Holy Spirit not as an "it" (which grammatically would be correct), but as a "he" (Gk. *ekeinos*, John 15:26; 16:13-14). Therefore, the "he" in the statement "he who is in you is greater than he who is in the world" (1 John 4:4) definitely refers back to the "Spirit of God" in verse 2.[25] Incidentally, the "he" in John 15 and 16 can also be simply explained from the masculine gender of the Greek masculine noun *Paraklētos*.[26]

It is also interesting that in 1 John 5:8 (lit., "the Spirit and the water and the blood, and the three are unto one"), the participle "are testifying" (*hoi martyrountes*) is *masculine* plural, although "the Spirit" (*to pneuma*), "the water" (*to hudōr*), and "the blood" (*to haima*), as well as "one" (*to hen*) are all

---

23. Cf. Kasper (1983, 210–14).
24. Cf. NASB, RSV: "Is the Spirit of the LORD impatient [NLV: angry]?"
25. *Contra* Marshall (1978, 208n16); Lalleman (2005, 188), but see 1 John 3:24; 4:12, 15–16.
26. Pinnock (1996, 15).

four neuter nouns.[27] The Spirit is put on the same level as the Son when the Lord refers to him as *allon Paraklēton*, "another Helper," the One who, in this quality, takes the place of the Son on earth (John 14:16). In the same way, the Holy Spirit can use first person pronouns, just as the Father and the Son and each angel and every human being can: "[T]he Holy Spirit said, 'Set apart *for me* Barnabas and Saul for the work to which *I* have called them'" (Acts 13:2).

It is one of the clearest indications of being a person to be able to refer to oneself in the first person. At the same time, the essential question is, of course, whether this really involves a person distinct from the Father and the Son, both of whom also speak in the first person. If I say "I," what difference does it make if I say that my spirit says "I"? If God says, "My Spirit shall not abide in [or, with] man forever" (Gen. 6:3),[28] how different is this—if we assume that the Holy Spirit is intended (cf. 1:2)—from saying: "*I* shall not abide in man forever"? Similarly, "of my Spirit" does not mean much more than "of me" (Isa. 30:1b; see the parallel with v. 1a). "My Spirit remains in your midst" (Hag. 2:5) does not mean much more than "*I* remain in your midst (cf. GNV: "*I* am still with you), and "have set my Spirit at rest" (Zech. 6:8) not much more than "have set *myself* to rest" (cf. GNT: "have quieted the LORD's anger").

3.3.2 A Distinct Person

If we possessed only those Bible passages just mentioned, I wonder whether we would have ever arrived at the idea that God's Spirit is a distinct person. We may add that in the New Testament the Spirit is strongly linked with the Father and with the Son, respectively. He is the Spirit of the Father (Matt. 10:20; cf. Eph. 3:14, 16), and he is the Spirit of the Son (Gal. 4:6), or the Spirit of Christ (Rom. 8:9; Phil. 1:19; 1 Pet. 1:11), of Jesus (Acts 16:7; cf. v. 6), and of Jesus Christ (Phil. 1:19).

---

27. Smith (1979, 195).
28. Compare, however, MSG "I'm not going to breathe life into men and women endlessly" (cf. CEB, CEV; and see Gen. 2:7).

Such expressions must be properly understood: the "Spirit of Christ," that is, the Holy Spirit, is very different from the *human* spirit of the *Man* Christ Jesus (cf. Mark 8:12; Luke 1:80; 23:46; John 11:33; 13:21), and from Christ as a "life-giving spirit" (1 Cor. 15:45).

Moreover, the expression that the Lord (Jesus) is the Spirit (2 Cor. 3:17–18) can be easily misunderstood. First, it does not necessarily mean anything more than that the Father, the Son, and the Spirit are closely linked as members of the one Godhead; this expression provides no evidence against the doctrine of the Trinity. To give an example: in John 14:18, Jesus identified himself with the Spirit by saying, "I will come to you," apparently meaning: "I will come to you in the person of the Holy Spirit," or "The Spirit will come to you" (at least this is the way many — not all — expositors read the verse; see §6.7.3). However, in John 15:25 he distinguished himself from the Spirit as the One who would send the Spirit from the Father. In 16:13–14 the Spirit comes to glorify the Son, thus distinguishing himself from the Son.

Second, for the very reason why the Holy Spirit is called both the Spirit of the Father and the Spirit of the Son, whereas Father and Son are clearly distinguished persons, the Holy Spirit cannot be identical to either the Father or the Son. When a person says, "My spirit," this usually amounts to saying, "I." However, when the Holy Spirit says "I," it is not the Father or the Son saying "I," but a person who is distinct from them.

Moreover, the baptismal formula in Matthew 28:19, which places the three persons of the Godhead alongside each other as equal,[29] makes it hardly possible to assert that one of the three is nothing but the "I" of one of the other two, or of both. The same holds for other passages where the other two are mentioned, such as John 16:13–15 (the Spirit of truth, the Son,

---

29. This claim assumes the comprehensive integrity of the Gospels; to view the baptismal formula of Matt. 28:19 as a gloss because of theological doubts is to commit the fallacy of *petitio principii* (begging the question).

the Father), 1 Corinthians 12:4-6 (the Spirit, the Lord, God), and 2 Corinthians 13:13 (the Lord Jesus, God, the Holy Spirit). None of these allow us to say here that the Spirit is nothing but the "I" of one of the other two, or of both.

Benjamin Warfield has pointed out that emphasis is laid upon the unity of God and the identity of the Spirit with the God who gives him, but a distinction is also made between God and his Spirit. At least this occurs in the sense that a distinction is made between God *over* all and God *in* all, between the Giver and the given One, between the Source and the Executor of the moral law. This distinction comes to the fore already in Genesis 1:2, and becomes gradually more visible in the Old Testament. It is prominent in the fixed expressions mentioning, on the one hand, God as the One who sends, lays, places, pours out, his Spirit on people, and on the other hand, the Spirit as the One who comes, rests, and descends on people. In both cases there is a kind of objectification of the Spirit in relation to God. In the former case, God separates the Spirit from himself by sending him out; in the latter case, the Spirit appears almost as a separate person, acting on his own behalf.[30]

3.4 The Perfect Deity of the Holy Spirit
3.4.1 Divine Attributes

If the Holy Spirit is a distinct person, the next question is whether he is a non-eternal and thus created person—possibly the highest angel—or an eternal and thus uncreated person, who therefore is ontically equal to the Father and the Son. Hebrews 9:14 is a good starting point for answering this question, for this passage speaks of "the eternal Spirit." And although I am not aware of direct hints of the Spirit's uncreatedness, there *are* such hints of his perfect deity.[31]

Consider Acts 5:3-4, where lying to the Holy Spirit is evidently the same as lying to God. In Romans 8:9-10, the

---
30. Warfield (1929, 126).
31. Cf. Bavinck (*RD* 2.277–79).

fact that the Spirit of God, or of Christ, dwells in a person is equated to, or at least connected with, Christ dwelling in that person. This does not mean that the Holy Spirit and Christ are identical—for the distinction between them is evident from other passages—but they are co-equal. Similarly, saying that the temple, that is, the church of God, is God's temple amounts to saying that the Spirit of God dwells in it (1 Cor. 3:16; cf. Eph. 2:22). People are baptized equally in the name of the Holy Spirit and in the name of the Father and the Son (Matt. 28:19); it is through him that people pray (Rom. 8:15, 26-27). And in particular, we find that he can be blasphemed (Matt. 12:31-32), something that strictly speaking can be said only of a divine person (see §6.5.2).

In 2 Corinthians 3:17 it is said of the Spirit that he is "Lord," which, though it concerns Christ here, is clearly a title of YHWH (cf. v. 16, where we must primarily think of YHWH; see also §3.4.3). The Spirit speaks in the New Testament just as God spoke to believers in the Old Testament (Acts 8:29; 10:19; 11:12). Stephen could say that Israel always resisted the Holy Spirit (Acts 7:51), just as the Old Testament often says that the people rebelled against God (e.g., Ps. 78:8, 17, 40, 56; 106:7, 43; 107:11). Hebrews 9:8 implies that the Holy Spirit was responsible for the arrangement of the tabernacle, just as the Old Testament ascribes this to God.

Moreover, to the Holy Spirit the same divine attributes are ascribed as to the Father and the Son:[32]

(a) *Eternal existence* (Heb. 9:14; cf. Rom. 16:26).

(b) *Majesty* (Matt. 12:31; cf. Rev. 13:6).

(c) *Omnipresence* (Ps. 139:7-10; 1 Cor. 6:19; cf. Wisdom 1:7; 7:23; 12:1).[33]

---

32. Cf. Chafer (1983, 1.304–305, 340–42, 401–402).
33. Chafer (1983, 1.410) distinguishes between *omnipresence* as the way the Spirit was present in the world before Pentecost (Acts 2) and *residence* (in the sense of dwelling in a given place) as the way the Spirit is present in the world after Pentecost (cf. 1 Cor. 3:16; 6:19). This is rather misleading because it seems to suggest that the Holy Spirit is not omnipresent in the present

(d) *Omniscience* (1 Cor. 2:11; cf. Ps. 139:1–4; also see Zech. 3:9; 4:10b, where the Lord's all-seeing seven eyes, which in Rev. 5:6 are linked with the Holy Spirit, are witnesses to God's omniscience).

(e) *Omnipotence, creative power* (Ps. 104:30; Rom. 15:19; cf. Wisdom 7:23; 8:1; Rev. 4:8).

(f) *Sovereignty* (John 3:8; 1 Cor. 12:11).

(g) *Life* (John 6:63; Rom. 8:2, 6; 2 Cor. 3:6; cf. Acts 14:15).

(h) *Love* (Rom. 15:30; cf. Gal. 5:22; Col. 1:8; 1 John 4:8, 16).

(i) *Grace* (Zech. 12:10 KJV; others: "a spirit of grace").

(j) *Righteousness* ("Paraclete" [a legal concept: advocate]: John 14:16, 26; 15:26; 16:7).

(k) *Holiness* (cf. the name *Holy* Spirit or "Spirit of holiness," Rom. 1:4).

(l) *Truth(fulness)* (John 14:17; 16:13; 1 John 5:6; cf. v. 20).

3.4.2 Involved in God's Works

The deity of the Holy Spirit also comes to manifestation in his involvement in all the works of the Godhead. As the early church put it: the works of the Trinity on [or toward] the outside are indivisible (Lat. *opera trinitatis ad extra sunt indivisa*). That is, in their activities, the three persons of the Godhead always act together.[34]

(a) *Creation* (§5.1.1). The Spirit hovering over the waters was involved in the work of creation (Gen. 1:2). By God's *ruach* ("breath, Spirit") the host of the heavens was made (Ps. 33:6; cf. 104:30). Elihu said, "The Spirit of God has made me" (Job 33:4).

(b) *Inspiration of Scripture*. It was the Spirit of Christ who

---

era. The Holy Spirit was and is always omnipresent, and this agrees entirely with his dwelling in a given place, so that the Spirit's *omnipresence* and the Spirit's *residence* are not proper alternatives.

34. Cf. Chafer (1983, 1.305–308). Since Gregory of Nazianzus, some speak of the perichoresis (Gk. *perichorēsis*; Lat. *circumincessio*) of the three divine persons: each does everything in relation to the other two because each indwells the other two (see more extensively, §10.3.2).

THE ETERNAL SPIRIT: GOD LIVING IN US

spoke in (or through) the Old Testament prophets (1 Pet. 1:10–11): "[M]en spoke from God as they were carried along by the Holy Spirit" (2 Pet. 1:21).

(c) *Incarnation* (§6.1). As a human being, the Son was born of the Virgin Mary by the power of the Holy Spirit (Luke 1:35; cf. Matt. 1:18, 20).

(d) *Jesus' baptism* (§6.1.3). The Father expressed the pleasure he took in his beloved Son, and the Spirit of God descended on him in the form of a dove (Matt. 3:16–17; Luke 3:21–22; John 1:32–34).

(e) *Jesus' sacrifice* (§6.3): "Christ, who through the eternal Spirit offered himself without blemish to God . . ." (Heb. 9:14).

(f) *Jesus' resurrection* (§6.4): "Christ . . . being put to death in the flesh but made alive by the Spirit" (1 Pet. 3:18 NKJV; NIV: "in the Spirit"; others: "in the [i.e., his] spirit"; also see Rom. 1:4).

(g) *Regeneration* (§8.2): "[U]nless one is born of water and the Spirit, he cannot enter the kingdom of God" (John 3:5); "he saved us, . . . by the washing of regeneration and renewal of the Holy Spirit" (Titus 3:5).

(h) *Indwelling believers* (§8.4.2). Christ dwells in their hearts (Eph. 3:17) but so does the Spirit (Gal. 4:6); their bodies are temples of the Holy Spirit within them (1 Cor. 6:19).

(i) *Anointing of believers* (§4.5). God anoints us in Christ (2 Cor. 1:21; cf. 1 John 2:20, 27) with the Holy Spirit (cf. Acts 10:38).

(j) *Sanctification* (§8.2.4). Believers are "sanctified [other manuscripts: loved] by God the Father" (Jude 1:1 NKJV), by Christ (Eph. 5:26; Heb. 2:11), and by the Spirit of God (1 Cor. 6:11).

(k) *Christian ministry* (§§10.4.1; 11.3.3; 12.1). The Holy Spirit places overseers over God's flock (Acts 20:28); in the diversity of gifts, ministries, and activities we discern one Spirit, one Lord, one God; it is the Spirit "who apportions to each one individually as he wills" (1 Cor. 12:4–11).

The Person of the Spirit

(l) *Preserving believers* (§4.8.1): "[Y]ou ... were sealed with the promised Holy Spirit, who is the guarantee of our inheritance until we acquire possession of it" (Eph. 1:13-14; cf. 4:30).

(m) *The church* (§§10.1-10.5). It is "a holy temple in the Lord ... a dwelling place for God by [or, in] the Spirit" (Eph. 2:21-22). "Do you not know that you are God's temple and that God's Spirit dwells in you?" (1 Cor. 3:16; cf. 2 Cor. 6:16).

(n) *Resurrection of believers.* "If the Spirit of him who raised Jesus from the dead dwells in you, he who raised Christ Jesus from the dead will also give life to your mortal bodies through his Spirit who dwells in you" (Rom. 8:11).

3.4.3 The Spirit and YHWH

It is quite remarkable to see that the Holy Spirit is not simply God. Such a designation might be understood to mean "a god," "divine," but not as divine as the Father and the Son; in other words, the name "god" could involve only "divinity," but not "deity." But the Spirit is not simply God, he is YHWH; that is, the name YHWH designates not simply God the Father, but also God the Son and God the Holy Spirit. Let me mention four examples of the latter.

(a) In Psalm 95:7-11 YHWH is speaking (see vv. 1 and 6). But in Hebrews 3:7-11 the Holy Spirit is said to be speaking here.

(b) In Isaiah 6:9 again YHWH speaking (cf. vv. 3 and 5). But in Acts 28:25 the Holy Spirit is said to be speaking here.

(c) In Isaiah 64:1 it is said to YHWH: "Oh that you would rend the heavens and come down, that the mountains might quake at your presence," an expression almost identical to Mark 1:10, "[I]mmediately he saw the heavens being torn open and the Spirit descending on him like a dove."

(d) In Jeremiah 31:33 it is YHWH, but in the quotation in Hebrews 10:15-17 it is again the Holy Spirit speaking.

Apparently, for the New Testament writers it makes no difference to say that YHWH or the Holy Spirit is speaking. This goes beyond the idea that it is simply "the Spirit of YHWH" (see Judg. 3:10; 6:34; 11:29; 13:25; 14:6, 19; 15:14; 1 Sam. 10:6; 16:13-14; 2 Sam. 23:2; 1 Kings 18:12; 22:24; 2 Kings 2:16; 2 Chron. 18:23; 20:14; Isa. 11:2; 40:13; 61:1; 63:14; Ezek. 11:5; Micah 3:8) because the New Testament speaks of the Spirit as an independent identity (which, of course, never means *ontically* independent).

Let us beware, though, of wishing to prove more than the Bible passages allow. Thus, Lewis Sperry Chafer said, "In the Old Testament, the Spirit is spoken of as Jehovah (Isa. 61:1)."[35] I do believe that the Spirit is Jehovah (more correctly, YHWH), but I do not believe that Isaiah 61:1 ("The Spirit of the LORD God is upon me, because the LORD has anointed me") is proof of this. This verse says that YHWH has anointed the Messiah with the Spirit, a fact that implies a distinction between the two. The mere fact that the Spirit is called the "Spirit of YHWH" does not at all prove that he is YHWH — even though he *is* — just as the expression the "city of YHWH" (Ps. 48:8) does not at all prove that the city *is* YHWH.

3.5 Prayer and Worship to the Spirit
3.5.1 Six Hints

Many Christians wonder whether they are allowed to pray to the Holy Spirit, or whether they are allowed, or obliged, to worship the Spirit. Some of them argue that the Spirit's servant form (Gk. *kenosis*) since he was poured out upon the church (Acts 2; cf. the parallel in Phil. 2:7) directs all attention away from him to Christ. Some claim that for this reason, we never find in the New Testament any example of praying to the Spirit or of worshiping him; instead, he is the power *through* which we worship God (cf. Phil. 3:3). Yet I believe that praying to and worshiping the Holy Spirit are not contrary to the spirit of Scripture.

First, in Ezekiel 37:9 the prophet is explicitly exhorted to invoke the Holy Spirit: "Prophesy to the *ruach* [breath, but in vv. 1 and 14 God's Spirit]; prophesy, son of man, and say

---

35. Chafer (1983, 1.399).

The Person of the Spirit

to the *ruach*, 'Thus says the Lord God: "Come from the four winds, O *ruach*, and breathe on these slain, that they may live."'" This is the basis for the ninth-century hymn "Come, Creator Spirit" (Lat. *Veni, Creator Spiritus*; see §3.5.2).

Second, we have established that the Holy Spirit is a divine person, equal to and of the same being as the Father and the Son. This means that whenever Christians pray to *God*, they pray to the Father, the Son, as well as the Holy Spirit. Many Christians who pray "Lord," especially those raised in Old Testament language, are in fact referring to YHWH as we know him from the Old Testament, and in practice think of the Father only. However, as we have seen, YHWH is Father *and* Son *and* Holy Spirit. And if the Spirit is God, and Scripture appeals to God's people to worship God (Matt. 4:10; Rev. 19:10; 22:9), then this implies that the Holy Spirit must be worshiped too.

Third, should Christians pray to the Father (e.g., Matt. 6:9) but not to the Spirit of the Father (10:20)? Can the Father be severed from his Spirit? Should Christians pray to the Son (e.g., Acts 7:59) but not to the Spirit of the Son (Gal. 4:6)? Can the Son be severed from his Spirit?

Fourth, pronouncing a blessing is in fact an implicit prayer for God's benefits. In the verse, "Then the priests and the Levites arose and *blessed* the people, and their voice was heard, and their *prayer* came to his holy habitation in heaven" (2 Chron. 30:27), blessing is explicitly described as a form of prayer. "The Lord may bless you" has the same force as "Lord, bless them." If therefore the apostle Paul pronounces the following blessing: "The grace of the Lord Jesus Christ and the love of God and the fellowship of the Holy Spirit be with you all" (2 Cor. 13:14), this has the same force as this prayer: "Lord Jesus, grant these people your grace, Father, grant them your love, and Holy Spirit, grant them your fellowship."

Fifth, in Psalm 95 God says, "[D]o not harden your hearts, as at Meribah, as on the day at Massah in the wilderness, when your fathers put me to the test and put me to the proof, though they had seen my work" (vv. 8–9). In Hebrews 3:7 these words are placed on the lips of the Holy Spirit. If therefore Psalm 95 begins with this appeal: "Oh come, let us sing to the LORD; let us make a joyful noise to the rock of our salvation! Let us come into his presence with thanksgiving; let us make a joyful noise to him with songs of praise!" (vv. 1–2), this necessarily includes an appeal to worship the Holy Spirit.

Sixth, in Isaiah 6:9 it is again YHWH speaking, while John 12:41 says it was Christ's glory being exhibited, and Acts 28:25 says it was the Holy Spirit speaking. Again, YHWH is the Triune God! If therefore the seraphim exclaim: "Holy, holy, holy is the LORD of hosts; the whole earth is full of his glory!" (v. 3), this includes glorifying the Father as well as the Son as well as the Holy Spirit.

3.5.2 Historical Examples

In conclusion, we can hardly be astonished about the fact that early Christians prayed to the Holy Spirit and worshiped him. Polycarp, the pupil of the apostle John, prayed just before he was burned as a martyr: "I praise you, [Father,] I bless you, I glorify you, through the eternal heavenly high priest Jesus Christ, your beloved child, through whom be glory to you, with him and the Holy Spirit, now and for the ages to come. Amen."[36] This reminds us of words common in the Latin Eucharist: "Glory to the Father, and to the Son, and to the Holy Spirit, as it was in the beginning, and now, and always, and in the ages of ages. Amen" (Lat. *Gloria Patri et Filio et Spiritui Sancto, sicut erat in principio, et nunc et semper et in saecula saeculorum. Amen*), or these words: "You alone are most high, Jesus Christ, with the Holy Spirit, in the glory of God the Father. Amen" (Lat. *Tu solus altissimus, Jesu Christe, cum Sancto Spiritu, in gloria Dei Patris. Amen*).

An early Christian hymn has these words: "We praise the

---

36. http://justus.anglican.org/resources/bio/108.html.

Father and the Son and the Holy Spirit of God."[37] From the ninth century we know the famous hymn "Come, Creator Spirit" (Lat. *Veni, Creator Spiritus*), presumably written by Rabanus Maurus. In the Roman Catholic Church the hymn is sung on Pentecost and other occasions.[38] Its opening stanza says:

> *Come, Holy Ghost, Creator, come*
> *from thy bright heav'nly throne;*
> *come, take possession of our souls,*
> *and make them all thine own.*

A similar hymn is *Veni, Sancte Spiritus*, presumably written by Pope Innocent III or by Cardinal Stephen Langton, the archbishop of Canterbury. It begins this way:

> *Come, Holy Spirit,*
> *send forth the heavenly*
> *radiance of your light.*

From the Eastern Orthodox Symeon the New Theologian we know this beautiful supplication:

> *Come, true light.*
> *Come, life eternal.*
> *Come, hidden mystery.*
> *Come, treasure without name.*
> *Come, reality beyond all words. . . .*
> *Come, for you are yourself the desire that is within me.*
> *Come, my breath and my life.*
> *Come, the consolation of my humble soul.*
> *Come, my joy, my glory, my endless delight.*[39]

There are many such examples. Throughout the centuries, hymns have been composed in which the Father, the Son, and the Spirit are worshiped, as in the well-known hymn by

---

37. Roberts and Donaldson (1995, 298).
38. See Congar (1997, 1.108–110).
39. http://full-of-grace-and-truth.blogspot.nl/2011/06/st-symeon-new-theologians-invocation-to.html; quoted also in Congar (1997, 2.112).

Horatius Bonar:

> *Glory be to God the Father,*
> *Glory be to God the Son,*
> *Glory be to God the Spirit:*
> *Great Jehovah, Three in One!*
> *Glory, glory*
> *While eternal ages run!*

Of course, such hymns by themselves do not prove that we are allowed to pray to the Spirit and to worship him. But they do prove at least that throughout the ages many Christians saw no problem in doing so.

3.6 Names of the Holy Spirit
3.6.1 References to Persons

The ways in which the Holy Spirit is described are numerous. Here follow the names that refer to the Godhead or to other divine persons.

A. *The Godhead:* the Spirit of God (Gen. 1:2; Matt. 3:16), the Spirit of our God (1 Cor. 6:11), the Spirit of the living God (2 Cor. 3:3).

The Spirit of YHWH (Judg. 3:10), the Spirit of Adonai YHWH (ESV: the LORD God; Isa. 61:1).

My Spirit (Gen. 6:3; Matt. 12:28; Acts 2:17), your Spirit (Neh. 9:30; Ps. 104:30; 139:7), his Spirit (Num. 11:29; Ps. 106:33; Isa. 48:16; Zech. 7:12).

B. *Father and Son:* the Spirit of your Father (Matt. 10:20; cf. Eph. 3:14, 16: "the Father ... his Spirit").

The Spirit of his Son (Gal. 4:6).

The Spirit of Jesus (Acts 16:7), the Spirit of Christ (Rom. 8:9; 1 Pet. 1:11), the Spirit of Jesus Christ (Phil. 1:19), the Spirit of [the] Lord (Acts 5:9; 2 Cor. 3:17; cf. v. 18). It is debatable whether the expression "of [the] Lord" in Acts 5:9 refers to YHWH (as in Judg. 3:10 LXX), or to the Man Jesus Christ (as in 2 Cor. 3:17).

The only designation that is almost entirely unique to the Holy Spirit (but see 1 John 2:1, where it refers to Jesus) is *Paraklētos* (AMP: "Helper, Comforter, Advocate, Intercessor-Counselor, Strengthener, Standby"; CEB: "Companion"; OJB: "Helper in Court") in John 14:16, 26; 15:26; 16:7 (see §6.7).

3.6.2 References to Attributes

A. *Numerals:* one Spirit (Eph. 4:4), seven Spirits (Rev. 1:4; 3:1; 4:5; 5:6; cf. the sevenfold description of the Spirit in Isa. 11:2). There is difference of opinion about whether the "seven Spirits" indeed refer to the Holy Spirit. At least the expression does not seem to refer to the Spirit as a person but as the perfect fullness (indicated by the number seven) of divine power, namely, the power by which he will carry out judgment (cf. the "seven torches of fire" in Rev. 4:5).

Some want to translate this as "spirits" and see this as referring to angels (cf. Heb. 1:7, 14; and also Rev. 8:2, "the seven angels who stand before God"). One objection against this exegesis is that in Revelation 1:4 the seven Spirits seem to be placed on the same level with God and with Jesus Christ as the source of grace and peace. However, in Luke 9:26, the glory of the Son, that of the Father, and that of the angels are mentioned in one breath (cf. 1 Tim. 5:21). The seven spirits are also before God's throne, which seems to indicate a position of subordination; no person in the Godhead as such ever stands before the throne.[40] Jewish tradition speaks of seven archangels: Uriel, Rafael, Raguel, Michael, Sarakael, Gabriel and Remiel.[41] Other expositors maintain that the Holy Spirit is intended;[42] still others leave the matter undecided.[43]

On the basis of these and other passages, Karl Barth conjectured that there is a deeper connection between angels and

---

40. See extensively, Smith (1961, 314–19).
41. 1 Henoch 20:1-8; cf. Dan. 10:13, "Michael, one of the chief [angelic] princes" (cf. CEV, GNT).
42. Tenney (1985, 46); Johnson (1981, 420).
43. Walvoord (1966, 37); Mounce (1977, 69–70).

the Holy Spirit.[44] Interestingly, in Islam the "Holy Spirit" (*ruh al-Qudus*) is another name for the archangel Gabriel (Jibrayil), the mediator between Allah and Mohammed.[45] In Luke 1:35, the angel Gabriel speaks about the Holy Spirit, and thus, according to some, about himself.

B. *Adjectives:* the Holy Spirit (Ps. 51:11; Isa. 63:10-11; Matt. 1:20), your good Spirit (Ps. 143:10; Neh. 9:20), the eternal Spirit (Heb. 9:14).

C. *Genitives*

* The s/Spirit of wisdom (Exod. 28:3; Deut. 34:9; Isa. 11:2, the Spirit of wisdom and understanding; Eph. 1:17, the s/Spirit of wisdom and of revelation). Translations that write "spirit" apparently understand the term to refer to (a certain state of) the human spirit, which does not exclude the illumination by the Holy Spirit, of course.

* The Spirit of counsel and might (Isa. 11:2).

* The Spirit of knowledge and the fear of the LORD (Isa. 11:2).

* The s/Spirit of judgment (Isa. 28:6; few translations have here the uppercase S, though; see §4.3.1).

* The Spirit of truth (John 14:17; 15:26; 16:13; 1 John 4:6).

* The Spirit of holiness (Rom. 1:4; the expression may be a Hebraism, meaning "Holy Spirit"; cf. "mountains of holiness," i.e., "holy mountains" in Ps. 87:1).

* The Spirit of life (Rom. 8:2).

* The Spirit of adoption (Rom. 8:15; the Spirit producing, or characterizing, the believer's sonship).

* The Spirit of gentleness (1 Cor. 4:21; Gal. 6:1; hardly anyone defends here the uppercase S, although it is certainly true that a spirit of gentleness is a fruit of the Holy Spirit; cf. Gal. 5:22).

* The Spirit of faith (2 Cor. 4:13; BRG, CJB, JUB, OJB: uppercase

---

44. Barth (*CD* III/3=18, §51.1:113; cf. §51.2:154-55).
45. Sura 16:102.

S).

* The Holy Spirit of promise (i.e., the promised Holy Spirit; Eph. 1:13; cf. Gal. 3:14; Acts 2:33).

* The s/Spirit of power and love and self-control (2 Tim. 1:7).

* The Spirit of grace (Heb. 10:29; cf. Zech. 12:10 JUB: the Spirit of grace and of prayer). "Grace" (Heb. *chen*) and "prayer" (*tachanumim*) come from the same root; it is the Spirit that leads the people to entreat God, and they will find grace in his sight, says Rashi.[46]

* The Spirit of glory and of God (1 Pet. 4:14; some manuscripts: of glory and of power and of God).

* The s/Spirit of prophecy (Rev. 19:10).

3.7 The Maternal Metaphor
3.7.1 The Feminine Spirit

The maternal metaphor is one of the most remarkable metaphors for the Holy Spirit, which, out of fear of Gnosticism and today of feminist theology, has often been neglected. Conversely, however, we may argue that precisely through feminist theology the Holy Spirit has received more of the biblical attention that he deserves.[47] More recent pneumatologists were not only feminists, though; Van de Beek points to the example of Nikolaus von Zinzendorf, who pleaded for the maternal character of the Spirit.[48]

When speaking of the maternal metaphor, we must begin with stating that the Bible does not contain a divine Mother figure in the proper sense of the term. Insofar as a parental term is applied to God, in the Bible this is always Father, never Mother. Therefore, it is understandable that the Bible uses masculine pronouns for God, and never feminine pronouns, in contrast to what many feminist theologians seem to desire. We have seen that, in the New Testament, the Greek word for

---
46. Cohen (1980, 321).
47. Van de Beek (1987, 174–78).
48. Ibid., 176; see also Meyer (1983).

"Spirit," *pneuma*, is neuter, and that John 15–16 nevertheless speaks of the Spirit with a masculine pronoun (Gk. *ekeinos*; though perhaps this is because the noun with which it is used, *Paraklētos*, is masculine; see §3.3.1). This does not mean that the Bible ascribes a gender to the Spirit. None of the divine persons has a gender, neither the Father, *nor the Son*; only in his quality as a human being is Jesus a Man, but as the eternal Son he has no gender identity.

Interestingly, the Hebrew word *ruach* is grammatically usually feminine, and this too has consequences. For instance, where in the Old Testament the Spirit is the subject of a sentence, the verb is usually in the feminine form, as fits the grammatical gender of *ruach* (Judg. 3:10; 11:29; 13:25; 14:6, 19; exceptions: Gen. 6:3; Job 4:15). Another example are the feminine pronouns with regard to *ruach*, for instance: the (human) *ruach* "returns to God who gave *her*" (Eccl. 12:7). Thus, the person who knows Hebrew "hears" a feminine element in connection with the person and work of the Spirit. Clark Pinnock has argued that, if the Hebrew language had been used for the New Testament, perhaps the feminine pronoun might have been used.[49] Perhaps it was God's arrangement that Hebrew *ruach* is feminine, Greek *pneuma* is neuter, and Latin *spiritus* (just like the Germanic word *ghost/Geist/geest*) is masculine.[50]

The feminine gender of *ruach* makes it clearer how the Holy Spirit in Genesis 1:2 is pictured as a mother bird "hovering" over the waters just like a bird over its young (§§4.1.2 and 4.7.2). "To hover" in Hebrew is *r-ch-ph*, "to hover, soar, move gently, quaver" (cf. Deut. 22:6, "the mother [bird] sitting on the young or on the eggs"). We also know in Scripture the image of those who in distress hide with God just as young birds hide under the wings of the mother bird: "[H]ide me in the shadow of your wings" (Ps. 17:8; cf. 36:7; 57:1; 61:4; 63:7; 91:4; Exod. 19:4; Deut. 32:11; Ruth 2:12; 3:9; Mal. 4:2).

---

49. Pinnock (1996, 15).
50. Ibid., 15–16.

Thus, the Syrian Christian author Aphrahat could write: "[I]n the same hour that the priest [during baptism] invokes the Spirit, She opens the heavens and descends and hovers over the waters, and those who are baptized, put her on [as a garment]."[51] But also mystics in the Latin tradition, such as Teresa of Ávila and John of the Cross, freely used various feminine metaphors. For instance, they spoke of the soul feeding at God's breasts, and receiving nourishment from his/her spiritual milk. As to the breasts, there is a rabbinical tradition that has explained the word *shaddai* in the name *El Shaddai* (a name of God traditionally rendered "God the Almighty") as "my breasts."[52] The patriarch Jacob seemed to allude to this when he said about Joseph: ". . . the Almighty [*Shaddai*] who will bless you with . . . blessings of the breasts [*shaddaim*] and of the womb [*racham*]" (Gen. 49:25).[53]

Notice the latter Hebrew word, *racham* (common form: *rechem*), which means "mother's womb" (e.g., in Ps. 22:10). It is remarkable that one of the terms for God's mercy is *rachamim* (e.g., in Isa. 63:7, 15), a word derived from *rechem*. When God has mercy on a certain person, this always suggests that he is filled with motherly compassion toward that person, in order to encompass him/her just as the womb safely encompasses the infant: "Is Ephraim my dear son? Is he my darling child? For as often as I speak against him, I do remember him still. Therefore my heart [lit., *bowels*] yearns for him; I will surely have mercy [*rachēm*] on him" (Jer. 31:20).

3.7.2 Other Feminine Characteristics

In spite of the feminine gender of *ruach*, we may never ascribe to the Holy Spirit an ontic feminine gender, just as the masculine terms "Father" and "Son" do not imply that these divine persons are ontically masculine. No matter how anthropo-

---

51. *Demonstration* 6, 16 (the Syriac word for "spirit" is also a feminine word); see http://www.academia.edu/24856498/The_Mother-Spirit_in_the_Syrian_Tradition_Aphrahat_and_Ephrem.
52. See http://www.rabbimaller.com/biblical-insights/names-of-god.
53. Pinnock (1996, 16).

morphic the Bible often speaks of God and his "body parts" (eyes, ears, mouth, nostrils, hands, feet, and even womb), they never imply an ontic gender for God.[54]

Traditionally, it has been emphasized that God is neither masculine nor feminine. However, we could just as well argue that both the masculine and the feminine find their primordial image within God himself.[55] It reminds us of an ancient rabbinical tradition, namely, that the original human (created after the likeness of God!), called Adam Kadmon (i.e., Adam of the primordial era), was an ambisexual being, which was afterwards split into two: the masculine part finds its counterpart in the Messiah, the feminine part in the Holy Spirit.[56]

It must indeed strike us that God's love is compared not only to that of a father (e.g., Ps. 103:13; Isa. 63:16; 64:8; Mal. 1:6; 2:10), but several times also to that of a mother. Thus, God has "begotten" his people like a father (cf. Christ: "begotten of the Holy Spirit," Matt. 1:20 YLT; cf. Luke 1:35), and God also "gave them birth" like a mother. In Deuteronomy 32:18 we have both thoughts together: God "fathered" Israel, and God "gave them birth" (cf. the very same verbs in Jer. 16:3, "the mothers who bore them and the fathers who fathered them"). In Isaiah 42:14 God says, "I will cry out like a woman in labor; I will gasp and pant."

Believers were "born of [the] Spirit" (Gk. *gennēthēi e[k] pneumatos*, John 3:5); this expression is entirely analogous with this one about Christ: "born of woman" (Gk. *genomenon ek gynaikos*, Gal. 4:4; cf. John 16:21). It sounds as if the Holy Spirit is a "woman" from whom believers are born, in contrast with their earthly mother (John 3:4). John 1:13 says that believers are "born of God" (Gk. *ek theou egennēthēsan*), which is the same expression. The Greek verb that is used, *ginomai*, can mean both "to beget (to father)" by a man and "to bear (to

---

54. See Henry (1982, 159–60).
55. For a discussion of this by feminist theologians, see Halkes (1984, 51–81) and references there; even more extensively, Johnson (2002).
56. Ferguson (1979, 145); see more extensively, Ouweneel (1998, §§3.2–3.3).

give birth to)" by a woman. The expression "not of the will of man" in John 1:13 could almost point to a kind of virgin birth: believers are born of their "mother" the Spirit without the intervention of a man! See James 1 as well, where verse 17 speaks of God as "Father," but verse 18 says, "he brought us forth"; this is the same verb *apokyeō* as in verse 15b, which there refers to the motherly task of "giving birth." So here again we find that God has "borne" us (has given birth to us).

"Giving birth" is a feminine task *par excellence*. But housekeeping and family care, which traditionally are also viewed as typical women's work, are sometimes ascribed to God:[57] God "knits" (ESV) or "weaves" (NASB) each child in their mother's womb (Ps. 139:13). God is also the midwife who helps the baby to be born and lays the child at the mother's breast (Ps. 22:9-10). God is also the laundress, who washes out dirty stains (Ps. 51:7; Isa. 4:4).

Both fatherly love and motherly love find their perfect model in God.[58] Therefore, Isaiah says both of these: "Can a woman forget her nursing child, that she should have no compassion on the son of her womb? Even these may forget, yet I will not forget you" (49:15); and: "As one whom his mother comforts, so I will comfort you" (66:13). In both passages, God compares his love—which is the love of the Holy Spirit (cf. Rom. 15:30)—to that of a mother. Whoever touches God's children, touches the "Mother." Therefore, God says of the wicked, "I will encounter them like a *bear* [a she-bear!] robbed of *her* cubs, and I will tear open their chests; there I will also devour them like a *lioness*" (Hos. 13:8 NASB).

David compares the peace that he finds with God to the rest of a "weaned child with its mother" (Ps. 131:2)—weaned, yet still exceedingly dependent on the mother. In Revelation 7:17 and 21:4, the lovely picture of God wiping the tears from believers' eyes reminds us of the mother wiping the tears from the eyes of her sad children (cf. Isa. 66:13 again). Here, we

---

57. Johnson (2002, 83, 101, 130–31, 136, 138).
58. Groothuis (1986, 139–40).

remember the fact that one of the meanings of *Paraklētos* — a designation of the Holy Spirit — is "Comforter."[59]

3.8 Chokmah and Shekhinah
3.8.1 Wisdom Literature and the Kabbalah

Elsewhere, I have discussed extensively how in paganism the concept of the "goddess" came to development as a feminine hypostasizing of a certain, ever-changing divine attribute.[60] First and foremost this attribute is the wisdom (Heb. *chokmah*) of God. The Holy Spirit grants wisdom, *is* the Spirit of wisdom (cf. Gen. 41:38-39; Exod. 31:3-4; Deut. 34:9; Job 32:7-10; Isa. 11:2; cf. Eph. 1:17). Lady Wisdom (see the contrast between Prov. 9:1 and 13 Voice) pours out her "spirit" (1:23), but in a sense *is* the Spirit of God. In passages such as Luke 11:48, the wisdom (Gk. *sophia*) of God is more or less synonymous with the Holy Spirit, and in James 1:5-8 (cf. Luke 11:13) and 3:13-17, wisdom functions more or less as the Spirit functions in Paul's writings.[61] As Yves Congar remarked, in Jewish Wisdom literature, Wisdom is viewed so closely with the Spirit that the two realities are almost identified, at least when they are viewed in their acting.[62] This is the clearest in the deuterocanonical book Wisdom of Solomon: Wisdom possesses a spirit (7:22b), or is a spirit (1:6). It acts in the form of a spirit (7:7b). It possesses the strength and functions that in the Old Testament are ascribed to the Holy Spirit.

At the same time, Wisdom is also closely connected with the Word, whether this is Christ as the Word of God (compare the link between Prov. 8:22-31 and John 1:18), or the Torah as the Word of God.[63] If we wish to connect Wisdom and Spirit, it may be the Spirit of Christ; if we connect the Wisdom of Proverbs 8:22-31 with the Logos in John 1:1-3, 14, it is Christ

---

59. Comblin (1989, 39); Bermejo (1989, 114–15); Hilberath (1992, 536–38); Kärkkäinen (2002, 166).
60. Ouweneel (1998, chapter 2).
61. Hildebrandt (1995, 44).
62. Congar (1997, 1.9; see 9–11).
63. See extensively, Ouweneel (1998, §§2.3 and 2.4).

himself. We are dealing here with the deeper connection between Word and Spirit, to which I will return in §5.3.1.

In later rabbinical Judaism, one can discern the tendency to hypostasize the Sophia/Chokmah to such an extent that it almost becomes a goddess. If some rabbis called Torah/Chokmah the "daughter of God,"[64] what else is this than a would-be-goddess? The Kabbalah speaks of the two "faces," or also the two "souls," of God, which refer to the masculine and the feminine. *The* holy book of the Kabbalah, the *Sefer ha-Zohar* ("Book of Splendor" or "of Radiance"), probably written at the end of the thirteenth century by Moses de Léon, argues that only those spiritual images in which the masculine and the feminine have been united are of a heavenly character. God himself is supposedly the highest example of this.

Another important expression is the *Shekhinah*, that is, the glory of God. This rabbinical expression, which does not occur in the Bible, literally means Dwelling (from Heb. sh-k-n, "to dwell"[65]). It is the Presence of God, the personification and hypostasizing of the "indwelling" or "presence" of God in the world.[66] It is quite remarkable, too, that the Kabbalah discerns in this *Shekhinah* the symbol of the Sophia, the eternal-feminine.[67] She is the queen, the daughter, as well as the bride of God, the mother of each individual Israelite. The Kabbalah views the Shekhinah as the first of all God's creatures, precisely like the canonical and deuterocanonical Wisdom literature says of Sophia, and like the Kabbalah says of the Holy Spirit (see §3.9).

In the *Sefer ha-Zohar*, the Shekhinah is designated with names that we find elsewhere for Sophia: queen, daughter,

---

64. Ouweneel (1998, 54–55).
65. For instance, the Hebrew noun for "tabernacle," *mishkan* ("dwelling [place]"), is a cognate of this verb.
66. Scholem (1977, 136).
67. See extensively, ibid., 135–91; also see Schipflinger (1988, 239–42). The term "the eternal-feminine" (German: *das Ewig-Weibliche*) has been immortalized by the great German poet Johann Wolfgang von Goethe in his play *Faust II*, and was put to music by Gustav Mahler (*Eighth Symphony*).

mother, sister of God, and so on. The Kabbalah also associates her with the bride in the Song of Solomon, and it calls the Israelites the "members" of the Shekhinah. The latter is also the "world soul" in the neo-Platonic sense (see §3.9.2), "the most high Lady" (*ha isha ha elyona*), the "woman of light," in whose secret all that is feminine in the world is rooted.

3.8.2 Early Christian Traditions

Both in the Jewish tradition and in the Christian tradition, people have tried time and again to read the idea of the divine-feminine, or the Primordial Lady (or Mother, or Daughter), into the Bible itself. In addition to Proverbs 8:22-31, they referred to the Lady of Revelation 12:1, who supposedly represents Sophia (see §3.9.1). People have tried to view in the sun, moon and stars mentioned there, (especially) according to the Egyptian example, to refer to the human spirit, soul, and body, or the Father, the ("feminine"!) Spirit, and the Son. Thus, Sophia, the divine Lady, supposedly refers, respectively, to the (macro)cosmos, to humanity (as a microcosmos) and to the Triune God.[68] Sophia allegedly shows us God who is revealed in his wisdom within the cosmos and humanity, and shows us cosmos and humanity as hidden in God.[69] Sophia is the feminine counterpart of the divine mystery. When people refer to "God" they especially think of nearness, strength, consolation, that is, of the Spirit/Sophia, the maternal aspect in God.[70]

Early Syriac Christians, until the church father Ephrem, presented the Spirit as the feminine member of the Trinity. In this view, the Trinity is a real family, Father, Mother, and Son.[71] A famous Syriac initiation prayer in the Acts of Thomas runs like this:

---

68. Tiessen (1996, 39, 199–200); cf. Schipflinger (1988, 213, 329–31).
69. Schult (1986).
70. Johnson (2002, 86–100, 127–41).
71. This is quite different from the suggestion by Pinnock (1996, 38) that one could view the Spirit as a child of the Father and the Son.

> *Come, holy name of Christ, which is above every name.*
> *Come, power of the highest and perfect compassion.*
> *Come, highest gift of grace.*
> *Come, merciful Mother.*
> *Come, consort of the male [principle].*
> *Come, revealer [a feminine word!] of hidden mysteries.*
> *Come, Mother of the seven houses,*
> > *so that your rest might be in the eighth house. . . .*
> *Come, Spirit of holiness, cleanse their minds and hearts, and seal them*
> > *in the name of the Father, Son and Holy Spirit.*

In the Gnostic-Christian (second century?) *Odes of Solomon*, the Spirit is the feminine dove,[72] who descended on Jesus at his baptism (Ode 24; see §4.7.2). The text also says (Ode 19): "The Holy Spirit opened Her bosom, and mixed the milk of the two breasts of the Father."[73] In a similar sense, the Armenian writer Nerses Snorhali compared drinking the living water of the Spirit with a child drinking from its mother's breast (cf. §3.9.1).[74] In the gnostic Gospel of the Hebrews, Jesus speaks of "my Mother, the Holy Spirit." In the equally Gnostic Gospel of Thomas, Jesus contrasts his earthly mother and father with his heavenly Mother and Father. The Syrian Aphrahat said, "As long as a man has not taken a wife, he loves and reveres God his father and the Holy Spirit his mother, and he has no other love."[75]

3.8.3 The Shekhinah and the Spirit

There is an unmistakable parallel between the Shekhinah and the Holy Spirit.[76] Take for instance the Greek term *episkiazō*, "to overshadow." We find this word in Exodus 40:29 (LXX; cf.

---

72. The Gk. word *peristera* ("dove") in Luke 3:22 is a feminine word.
73. http://gnosis.org/library/odes.htm.
74. Burgess (1989, 6–7, 172–73); a similar image is found with Catherine of Siena; see Burgess (1997, 114).
75. http://www.academia.edu/24856498/The_Mother-Spirit_in_the_Syrian_Tradition_Aphrahat_and_Ephrem.
76. See Ouweneel (1994, §4.3).

the Hebrew text: v. 35): "Moses was not able to enter the tent of meeting because the cloud settled on [Gk. *epeskiazen*, overshadowed] it, and the glory of the LORD filled the tabernacle." The cloud was the visible sign of YHWH's glory (Exod. 16:10; cf. 24:16; 34:5; 40:34; Num. 12:5), it pointed out the way to Israel (Exod. 13:21-22), it was stationed between Israel and the persecuting Egyptians (14:20), enveloped the summit of Sinai (19:9; 24:15-18; Deut. 5:22), descended on the first "tent of meeting" (Exod. 33:9-10), and afterward on the tabernacle (40:34-38), and dwelt on the mercy seat (the lid on the ark of the covenant; Lev. 16:2). The cloud led the people through the wilderness (Num. 9:15-22; 10:11-12, 34; 14:14; Deut. 1:33; Ps. 78:14; see §9.1.1). From the cloud, the Lord spoke to Moses (Exod. 20:18-22; Num. 11:25; 12:5; Deut. 31:15-16; Ps. 99:7). The same cloud of God's glory afterward filled the temple of Solomon (1 Kings 8:10-11; 2 Chron. 5:13-14).

In the deuterocanonical book of Wisdom 10:15-21, it is Wisdom (Chokmah/Sophia) who delivered Israel from Egypt, and led them through the wilderness, and thereby turns out to be identical with the Shekhinah: "[S]he [i.e., Wisdom] was to them for a covert by day, and for the light of stars by night" (v. 17; cf. Exod. 13:21-22; Ps. 105:39). And if 1 Corinthians 10:2 says, "[A]ll [Israelites] in Moses were baptized, in the cloud, and in the sea," it is conceivable that, in connection with the baptism in the cloud — the Shekhinah — Paul is thinking of a type of Spirit baptism, and that, in connection with the baptism in the sea, he is thinking of a type of water baptism.[77]

During the time when the cloud had disappeared from the temple, it nonetheless descended occasionally. In connection with the New Testament, we think first of the transfiguration on the mount, where a cloud is mentioned as well (Matt. 17:5; Mark 9:7; Luke 9:34). The idea that this involves the Shekhinah follows from the fact that God's voice was heard from this cloud; as Peter put it: ". . . the voice came to him from

---

77. Prince (1995, 290-93).

the Excellent Glory" (*hypo tēs megaloprepous doxēs*, 2 Pet. 1:17 NKJV). Again we find here in the Gospels the Greek verb *episkiazō* ("to overshadow"), mentioned above. Since Gregory of Nazianzus, the white or radiating cloud in this event has been interpreted as a manifestation of the presence of the divine Spirit. John Chrysostom argued that all those who strive for unification with God are safely kept under this "cloud of the Spirit."[78]

Second, I mention Luke 1:35, where the angel Gabriel tells Mary, "The Holy Spirit will come upon you, and the power of the Most High will overshadow you; therefore the child to be born will be called holy — the Son of God." Here we find the same remarkable technical Greek term *episkiazō* that was used at Jesus' transfiguration. In other words, we are allowed to say that the Shekhinah descended upon Mary, the cloud overshadowed her, in order to beget Jesus in her. However, rather than reading of the cloud we hear about the Holy Spirit and the power of the Most High, or simply the power of the Holy Spirit. This is the new meaning that the Shekhinah acquires in the New Testament: the power and glory of the Holy Spirit, who is called the "Spirit of glory" (1 Pet. 4:14).

During Christ's life on earth, namely, from his baptism by John, the Shekhinah rested upon him, or dwelt in him: "Destroy this temple, and in three days I will raise it up" (John 2:19); his body, *not* Herod's temple, was the true temple in which the Shekhinah dwelt in those days. John says literally that the incarnated Word "tabernacled" (Gk. *eskēnōsen*, John 1:14) here on earth; that is, his human flesh was a tabernacle in which the Shekhinah (read: the Holy Spirit) dwelt (cf. Luke 3:21-22; 4:1, 14; John 1:33), just as it had formerly dwelt on the ark in the tabernacle and in the temple (cf., e.g., Num. 7:89; Ps. 80:1).

Third, we must consider Jesus' condemnation by the priests. He told the Jewish Sanhedrin: "I tell you, from now on

---

78. Burgess (1989, 7).

you will see the Son of Man seated at the right hand of Power and coming on the clouds of heaven" (Matt. 26:64). Basically, this was saying, again, that the Shekhinah did not dwell in the temple of Herod but in *him*, Jesus, and together with him would leave this earth and ascend to heaven. Being seated at the right hand of the power (cf. Ps. 110:1) was like the Shekhinah dwelling on the mercy seat in God's sanctuary. In the eyes of the Jewish judges, such a claim was temple sacrilege, a trespass that was thought to deserve the death penalty (cf. Acts 6:13-14).

3.8.4 The Shekhinah and the Church

Just as the Shekhinah first filled the tabernacle, later the temple of Solomon, and will fill the eschatological temple of Ezekiel as well (Ezek. 43:1-5), so today it fills the temple of God, that is, the church. We can make a direct comparison between Acts 2 and Exodus 20, 1 Kings 8 and Ezekiel 43 (§10.1). As on earlier occasions, there were visible signs connected with the outpouring of the Spirit: a "sound like a mighty rushing wind," "divided tongues as of fire," speaking "in other tongues." Thus the Holy Spirit was sent down from heaven (cf. John 14:26; 15:26) just as the Shekhinah had formerly been sent down. He came to dwell in the church (see 1 Cor. 3:16; Eph. 2:21-22; cf. 2 Cor. 6:16) just as the Shekhinah had dwelt among God's people. Just as the cloud had filled God's house (Exod. 40:34; 1 Kings 8:10-11; 2 Chron. 5:13-14; cf. Ezek. 10:3-4), the Holy Spirit now fills the church (cf. Acts 2:2; cf. Eph. 5:18), which is the house of God (1 Tim. 3:15; cf. 2 Tim. 2:20; 1 Pet. 4:17).

The connection between the Shekhinah and the Holy Spirit (and [the Spirit of] Christ) sheds a special light on Matthew 18:20, where Jesus promises: "[W]here two or three are gathered in my name, there am I among them." Some expositors have linked this statement with passages in the Talmud, which go back to the post-exilic Malachi 3:16, "Then those who feared the LORD spoke with one another. The LORD

The Person of the Spirit

paid attention and heard them, and a book of remembrance was written before him of those who feared the LORD and esteemed his name." First, we find here the "two or three" (the text literally says, "a man to his neighbor"), and second, the remembrance of the Lord's name—two elements that are also part of Matthew 18:20. One Talmud passage says,[79] "[When] two sit together and there are words of Torah [spoken] between them, the Shekhinah abides among them," followed by the quotation from Malachi 3:16.

In another Talmud passage we read: "[H]ow do you know that if two are sitting and studying the Torah together the Divine Presence is with them? For it is said"—followed again by the quotation from Malachi 3:16.[80] In both passages two persons are sitting together to ponder the Torah, the Word of God, and in both cases the saying from Malachi is quoted to prove that the Shekhinah is between them.[81] Elsewhere, I have argued extensively why Jesus may be called the "eternal Torah."[82] The rabbis said, where two who remember the Lord's name have the Torah in their midst, there the Shekhinah is in their midst. Jesus said (to listeners who may have known this rabbinical exegesis), where two or three remember my name, I will be in their midst, that is, in the Spirit, that is, the Spirit of Jesus Christ.

This makes the church so wonderful. Where two or three (or two or three thousand) are together in Jesus' name, to celebrate his name, and where they ponder the Word of God, there Jesus is personally present through the Spirit of Christ. There, people may fall on their face before the glory of God, and they confess that God is really among his people (1 Cor. 14:25). The Shekhinah may be so palpably present that those who are present experience what is described in Acts 4:31, "And when they had prayed, the place in which they were

---

79. Aboth iii.2.
80. Berakoth 6a.
81. Edersheim (1971, 2.124).
82. Ouweneel (2017b, especially chapter 3).

gathered together was shaken, and they were all filled with the Holy Spirit and continued to speak the word of God with boldness." Or they experience what happened in John 20, when the risen Lord appeared in the midst of his gathered disciples: "Then the disciples were glad when they saw the Lord," and later told Thomas: "We have seen the Lord" (John 20:20, 25).

Please note that the disciples not only saw the risen *Man*, but his *divine* glory was present as it had been in the Shekhinah: it was he who, as the Creator of the new creation, "breathed" on his disciples (v. 22; cf. Gen. 2:7; see §6.10.2), and it was he whom Thomas confessed as "My Lord and my God" (v. 28). In the same way, the prophet Ezekiel fell down before the Shekhinah when he beheld the glory of the Lord (Ezek. 43:3-5; 44:4).

3.9 "Lady Spirit"
3.9.1 Women in Revelation

Erich Neumann, the great Jewish interpreter of Carl G. Jung's psychoanalytical studies on the archetype of the Primordial Mother, identified the Sophia (§3.8.1) also with "the Spirit and the Bride" (Rev. 22:17; cf. 19:7; 21:2, 9).[83] The application of this expression is strange, because Spirit and Bride are clearly distinct in Revelation (notice the plural Gk. verb *legousin* in 22:17; cf. for the Spirit 2:7; 14:13). If Neumann were right, we would have here a hendiadys (the Spiritual Bride, or, the Spirit as Bride[84]), or an explicative use of "and" (Gk. *kai*), to read: "the Spirit, namely, the Bride."[85]

Neumann's explanation becomes more understandable when we consider that Gnosticism has put so much emphasis on the femininity of the Spirit. One of the most important representatives of this tradition in the Netherlands, G. Quispel

---
83. Neumann (1955, 329).
84. Cf. "the power and coming" (2 Pet. 1:16) = "the powerful coming"; "with the Holy Spirit and with power" (Acts 10:38) = "with the power of the Holy Spirit."
85. Cf. John 1:16, where *kai* ("and") means as much as "namely."

(member of the Dutch Reformed Church, professor of church history, d. 2006), wrote about Revelation 22:17:

> The Spirit . . . is the *mater* ("mother") who pervades what is material (*mater*-ial) and sanctifies it.
>
> Just as Jewish belief asserts that the Shekinah will one day return from its exile to Jerusalem, so does John assert that the Holy Spirit will return to Jerusalem at the end.
>
> The bride—i.e., the New Jerusalem and the Daughter of Zion—has previously [21:3] been mentioned under the figure of the "tabernacle of God which is with men," in other words the Shekinah. Now the Lady [of 12:1] has bifurcated into "Mother and Daughter." At the very end of his visions, John is initiated into the vision of the two women, the Holy Spirit and the Daugh[t]er of Zion. The *epoptai* (i.e., the spectators of the mysteries of Eleusis) were also initiated into the mysteries of the Mother and the Daughter (Demeter and Kore). The woman has now descended into the depths of earthly reality. God now dwells completely among men [Rev. 21:3].[86]

In this (in my view, highly speculative) exposition, we find all the female figures that we have been discussing placed together: the Holy Spirit, the Shekhinah, the woman of Revelation 12, the bride of chapter 21, the daughter of Zion. All of these are supposedly names for the Chokmah/Sophia, and in fact for (the feminine aspect of) God himself. About the woman of Revelation 12:1 Quispel says, "[T]he mother is the Holy Spirit, the child is the Messiah; . . . ." Regarding the "crown of twelve stars" he notes,

> These are the twelve signs of the zodiac.[87] In the Syriac Acts of Thomas (Chapter 6) [see §3.8.2],[88] the Holy Spirit (in other words, Divine Wisdom) is praised in song: her garments are like the fragrant flowers of spring; with her feet, she dances for joy and her mouth is open wide. She is surrounded by seven

---

86. Quispel (1979, 119).
87. See Ouweneel (1998, Excursus 4).
88. http://gnosis.org/library/actthom.htm.

groomsmen (i.e., the planets[89]) and she has twelve attendants (i.e., the twelve signs of the zodiac). The Holy Spirit is a creative spirit, or *creator spiritus* [see §3.5.2], who gives birth to the *cosmos* and pervades everything. She is a kind of world-soul.[90]

About the woman of Revelation 21 Quispel says,

> Properly speaking, she is the Lady: i.e., the Holy Spirit. All Jewish Christians used to regard the Holy Spirit as both a lady and a mother, especially the Mother of Jesus. According to a fragment of the Jewish-Christian Gospel of the Hebrews, Jesus said this himself: "My mother the Holy Spirit." (Logion 5).[91]

As we saw, generally speaking, Syrian pneumatology in the third and fourth century referred to the Holy Spirit as "mother."[92]

On the basis of internal arguments, I cannot agree with any of Quispel's interpretations. His knowledge of Gnosticism is enormous, but this does not justify reading it into the book of Revelation. Incidentally, the woman of Revelation 12 has been interpreted in many ways. Gnostics see her as the Holy Spirit, Roman Catholics see her as the Virgin Mary, traditional Protestants see her as the church, Evangelicals rejecting supersessionism see her as Israel, the "mother" of the Messiah. However, in Revelation 19–22 the bride is not Israel but the New Testament church of Christ.[93]

3.9.2 The World Soul

In some way or another, every *hypostasizing* of God's maternal side always goes back to neo-Platonism. In this very last ancient pagan school of thought, the idea of the "world soul" was developed, which plays a great role in Sophiology as

---

89. In the ancient view, these seven "planets" (lit., wandering objects, because they move with respect to the fixed stars) are the sun, the moon, Mercury, Venus, Mars, Jupiter, and Saturn.
90. Ibid., 76; cf. Comblin (1989, 49).
91. Quispel (1979, 77).
92. Hilberath (1992, 1.512–13).
93. See extensively, Ouweneel (2012a, especially chapters 7 and 13).

well. One of the meanings ascribed to the rabbinical-gnostic Sophia/Shekhinah is that of the "world soul." The designer of neo-Platonism, Plotinus, distinguished between three transcendent substances: God, the mind (Gk. *nous*), and the world soul. According to him, God is "the One" (Gk. *to hen*, neuter!), which lies behind all experience. From this one primordial substance all beings (things-that-are) emanate, just as light and warmth flow from the sun without the latter losing anything of its substance, or as water flows from a source that yet remains inexhaustible.

The first thing that emanated was the mind (reason, spirit, Gk. *nous*), which includes the entire Platonic world of ideas. From the *nous* emanated the *world soul*, the "intermediate being" between the spiritual and the material (bodily) world. On the basis of the divine ideas, this world soul forms empirical things from matter. Between the world soul and matter are the individual souls, each of which is a reflection of the total world soul. According to Plotinus, the world soul in its entirety is present in every human soul, in the sense as described by pan*en*theism.

Early Christians were quite attracted to the idea of the world soul, that is, the idea of a "medium" between God and the cosmos. If this issue is viewed superficially, the New Testament seems to offer room for a certain panentheism by speaking of "him who fills all in all" (Eph. 1:23; cf. 4:10; Acts 17:28). The world soul was identified with the Holy Spirit or the Shekhinah/Sophia. This concerns emphatically a *feminine* mediatorship, in which the Shekhinah/Sophia itself is not divine, but created. At the same time, it fits with the feminine aspect of God.[94] Therefore, the boundary between, on the one hand, the idea of a goddess and, on the other hand, the representation of the Holy Spirit or Shekhinah as given here is paper-thin, if it exists at all.

Thomas Schipflinger has shown how these and similar

---

94. Tholens (1987, 63).

Christianized views influenced a great mystic like Hildegard of Bingen.[95] She wrote about the Chokmah/Shekhinah as co-operator at creation, mother and soul of the world, incarnated in the Virgin Mary, bride of Christ, and mother of the church. Schipflinger also wrote about the Lutheran philosopher and mystic Jakob Boehme, who distinguished within "the Absolute" the movement of two forces: a masculine creative principle (Logos) and a feminine animating principle (Sophia). The created Sophia is the image of God's own wisdom. Boehme, too, believed that Sophia had clothed herself with matter, in order to be able, in the person of Mary, to give flesh and blood to the divine Son. Mary is the incarnated Sophia.[96]

Roman Catholic theologian and natural scientist Pierre Teilhard de Chardin also played a role in the development of these ideas.[97] He saw in Sophia the "eternal feminine," which, because it was incarnated in Mary, can be the world soul between God and the cosmos. As such it carries us to the Logos (the Son), and from there to the Father. According to Teilhard, the Sophia is identical with the feminine figure that is venerated in many forms by the wise and the pious of the world religions, as the Great Mother (Isis, Ishtar, Artemis).

Today, the age-old assumption of this relationship between Sophia and Mary, studied in what is called Sophiology, has largely disappeared. During a visit to the Aya Sophia in Istanbul I surprised my (Islamic) guide with the insight that Sophia churches (such as those in Kiev and Novgorod) are in fact Mary churches. Or when you visit the Sistine Chapel in Rome, watch Michelangelo's painting of the creation of Adam, ask your guide about the young lady who lies in God's left arm. (By now, you might realize that she is Sophia/Chok-

---

95. Schipflinger (1988, 78–91); also see Tiessen (1996, 203–204); Cunneen (1996, 160–69).
96. Schipflinger (1988, 121–37); also see Tiessen (1996, 204–205).
97. Teilhard de Chardin (1999); see Schipflinger (1988, 199–206); also see Tiessen (1996, 188–89, 214–16).

mah.) Or when you visit the St. Bavo's Cathedral in Ghent (Belgium), study the world famous altarpiece by Hubert and Jan van Eyck (*The Lamb of God*), and ask your guide why a saying from the deuterocanonical book of Wisdom is placed above the painting of Mary (7:29, "[S]he is more beautiful than the sun, and above all the order of the stars: being compared with the light, she is found before it"). Or when you visit the cathedral of Seville (Spain), find the image of Mary, and reflect on its caption: *Per me reges regnant* ("By me kings reign," said by Lady Wisdom in Prov. 8:15). And realize that throughout church history all the attributes pertaining to the Holy Spirit have been gradually transferred to Mary: guide, inspirer, comforter, intercessor, mediator, advocate, defender, counselor.[98]

This limited anthology of thoughts developed within Christianity concerning Queen Sophia and her supposed relationships to the Shekhinah, to the Holy Spirit, and even to the Virgin Mary. The *uncreated* Sophia has been viewed as the feminine aspect of God himself, God's feminine self-revelation, reflection of the eternal Light, God's "Doppelgänger," God's intimate counselor and creating partner, architect of the universe, God's lover and bride (think again of Michelangelo's painting), mother of the cosmos, identical with the Holy Spirit and with the Shekhinah.

The *created* Sophia is the daughter, God's firstling; and if the term "created" in the neo-Platonic sense is understood as "emanated," then she is the fullness of God's creative ideas, or the World Soul. With these ideas, which though speculative have played a tremendous role in church history, we are far removed from the pure speech of Scripture. But in this tangle of religious fantasy we do discover a kernel of truth: the deep coherence of the divine Wisdom (Chokmah, Sophia), the divine Presence (Shekhinah), and the Holy Spirit.

---

98. Congar (1997, 1.163–64); Johnson (2002, 86, 129–30); see extensively, Ouweneel (1998, especially chapter 6).

Chapter 4
The Power of the Spirit

I am filled with power,
  with the Spirit of the L$_{\text{ORD}}$.

Micah 3:8

[Y]ou will receive power
  when the Holy Spirit has come upon you,
and you will be my witnesses in Jerusalem
  and in all Judea and Samaria,
  and to the end of the earth.

Acts 1:8

May the God of hope fill you
  with all joy and peace in believing,
so that by the power of the Holy Spirit
  you may abound in hope. . . .
I will not venture to speak of anything
  except what Christ has accomplished through me
to bring the Gentiles to obedience —
  by word and deed,
  by the power of signs and wonders,

by the power of the Spirit of God.
Romans 15:13, 18–19

Summary: *Of the three persons of the Holy Trinity, the Holy Spirit is the most difficult to describe. In this, we can begin to describe his fullness with the help of many metaphors. The basic metaphors are those of air (breath, wind), water, and fire (three of the four ancient elements). These help us to understand the Spirit as a "force" (which itself is just as much a metaphor as "person"). Oil is an important metaphor to understand the anointing with the Spirit, and wine represents the euphoria of the Spirit. As a person the Holy Spirit dwells in believers, but considering the Spirit as a force helps us understand how believers can have very little or very much of it (they should be "filled" with the Spirit). Other metaphors that are not similarly quantitative are, for instance, the Spirit as a dove, as a seal, as a hand or finger.*

4.1 Basic Metaphors of the Spirit
4.1.1 Air, Water, and Fire

THE PRINCIPAL OBJECTIONS levelled against the idea of the personality and the deity of the Holy Spirit are based upon those Bible passages that speak of the Spirit in a very *impersonal* manner. I refer especially to those passages in which the Spirit is compared in a figurative way to air (breath, wind), water, or fire, which, incidentally, are three of the four classic elements of the universe. The fourth element, *earth*, is never used figuratively for the Spirit, as far as I am aware. On the contrary, earth is the element that receives the rain, the water of the Spirit (Isa. 32:15, "the Spirit is poured out . . . the wilderness becomes a fruitful field"; 44:3-4, "I will pour water on the thirsty land . . . I will pour my Spirit upon your offspring"), and that produces the "fruit of the Spirit" (Gal. 5:22; 6:8).[1]

The objections referred to must be not only refuted (the negative aspect) but transformed into positive arguments. I refer to the fact that Scripture presents the Holy Spirit not only

---
1. Cf. Pseudo-Macarius, quoted by Burgess (1989, 146).

as a *person* but also as a *force*. The Spirit not only *has* power but *is* power, just like wind, water, and fire are powers. Take this example, in which all three metaphors occur: God's "tongue is like a devouring fire; his breath [Heb. *ruach*] is like an overflowing stream" (Isa. 30:27-28). Compare John the Baptist's *water* baptism, followed by the "baptism with the Holy Spirit [*pneuma*] and fire" (Matt. 3:11; Luke 3:16); after the water comes the wind, and the fire. See our discussion of Isaiah 4:4 in §4.3.1 below.

Two of the three elements occur in Isaiah 59:19, where we read that the Lord "will come like a rushing stream, which the wind [Heb. *ruach*] of the LORD drives." Walther Eichrodt has called the thunderstorm, in which storm (wind) and fire (lightning)—as well as the rain water!—occur together, the most significant Old Testament manifestation of God's glory.[2] Psalm 18 is an example of this: God appears in (stormy) wind (v. 10 Heb. *ruach*; cf. v. 15, the "blast" [Heb. *neshamah*] of the "breath [Heb. *ruach*] of your nostrils"), in fire, thunder, and lightning (vv. 8, 13-14), and in waters (v. 11; cf. v. 16). Consider also Psalm 29 (but see our discussion of 1 Kings 19:11-12 in §4.1.3).

I call the metaphors of air (wind, breath), water, and fire "basic" metaphors because all three are used in Scripture to express the presence of God's glory, as we will see. This cannot be said of the additional metaphors to be discussed later. God may manifest himself in stormy winds (and sometimes in the gentle breeze!), in the mighty waters (or in the gentle rain), and in the blazing fire. We will indeed find examples of *literal* winds, waters, and fires that represent God's glorious presence, while wind, water, and fire at the same time are *images* of this glory.

4.1.2 Breath, Wind: Old Testament

For "breath" the Hebrew uses both the word *nephesh* (usually "soul") and the word *ruach* (usually "spirit"). On rare occa-

---
2. Eichrodt (1967, 16).

sions, the Old Testament uses *nephesh* for God, as in Isaiah 1:14; 42:1; and Jeremiah 5:9, 29; 6:8; 9:9; 15:1; 32:41. Here, God speaks of "my soul" (see KJV), which usually amounts to saying "I." More often it is *ruach* that is used for God, in the sense of "Spirit" (see "my Spirit" in Gen. 6:3; Isa. 42:1; 44:3; 59:21; Ezek. 36:27; 37:14; 39:29; Joel 2:28–29; Hag. 2:5; Zech. 4:6; 6:8), and sometimes of "Holy Spirit" (Heb. *ruach qodesh*, Ps. 51:13 "your Holy Spirit"; Isa. 63:10–11 "his Holy Spirit")

The basic meaning of *ruach* is "moving air," which is either breath (e.g., Isa. 42:5) or wind (e.g., Gen. 8:1); the latter meaning appears in approximately one-third of the Old Testament occurrences.[3] Consequently, some passages speak of the Holy Spirit in such a way that the translator/expositor hesitates between choosing "breath" or "spirit/Spirit." A very early example is Genesis 1:2 (KJV: Spirit; CEB: wind; Voice: spirit-wind; see also §5.1). The combination of *ruach* with "hovering" (*r-ch-ph*) suggests to me the rendering "Spirit" rather than "wind."[4] This combination occurs in Deuteronomy 32:11 as well (NIV: "like an eagle that stirs up its nest and hovers over its young"; cf. §4.7).

In Job 33:4, the *ruach* of God is parallel with the *neshamah* of the Almighty, which suggests that *ruach* also means "breath" here, or that, in general, God's *ruach* is nothing but his (figurative) "breath," or an emanation in the broader sense (cf. 26:13, "By his *ruach* [NIV: "breath"; ESV: "wind"; KJV: "spirit"; KJ21: "Spirit"] the heavens were made fair"). Thus, Job 4:9 literally speaks of the "*ruach* of his nostrils," that is, his anger: "By the blast [*neshamah*] of God they perish, and by the breath [*ruach*] of his nostrils are they consumed" (KJV). (Cf. Zech. 6:8, "[they] have set my Spirit at rest," ICB: "calmed the Lord's anger.") Similarly, Psalm 33:6 speaks of the *ruach* of God's "mouth,"

---

3. Kamlah (1976, 690); for the meanings of *ruach* see extensively, Hildebrandt (1995, 1–27).
4. Kroeze (1962, 45–51); Gispen (1974, 43); Hamilton (1990, 114–15); Hildebrandt (1995, 32–36); Westermann arrives at a mixed judgment (1974, 148–50).

which makes it difficult to translate "spirit" here (but see WYC). However, Psalm 104:30 says, in a context very similar to that of Psalm 33, that God "sends forth" his *ruach*, where the translation "breath" seems less appropriate (but see CJB, NLT).

Interestingly, the "LORD's anointed" is identified as "the *ruach* of our nostrils," that is, "our life-breath" (Lam. 4:20 CJB) (cf. Exod. 15:8, "... at the *ruach* of your [i.e., God's] nostrils"). Numbers 11:31 speaks of a "*ruach* from the LORD," which was a literal wind; but in Isaiah 40:7, the "*ruach* of the LORD," blowing on the grass, may be a wind (CJB), or God's breath (ESV), or God's spirit (KJV) or God's Spirit (GNV). In Ezekiel 1:4, *ruach se'arah* clearly refers to a "stormy wind," but in verse 12 "spirit" or "Spirit" is the best rendering. In chapter 37:1–14, the meanings are more intermingled, namely, "breath" (especially vv. 5–6, "Thus says the Lord GOD to these bones: 'Behold, I will cause breath to enter you, and you shall live...'"), "wind" (especially v. 9, "Come from the four winds [*ruchot*], O breath [*ruach*], and breathe on these slain, that they may live"), and "Spirit" (especially v. 14, "I will put my Spirit within you"). God will make his *ruach* (wind) blow on the bones, so that *ruach* (breath) will enter the dead, which means that God's *ruach* (Spirit) will be put within his converted people again.

4.1.3 Breath, Wind: New Testament

The New Testament provides us a similar picture. The Greek *pneuma* (from *pneuō*, "to blow") means first and foremost "breath" (2 Thess. 2:8, "the *pneuma* of his mouth"). It also means "wind," like in John 3:8, where a parallel with the Spirit is implied: "The *pneuma* [wind] blows where it wishes.... So it is with everyone who is born of the *pneuma* [Spirit]."

In Matthew 27:50 ("Jesus ... yielded up [Gk. *aphēken*] the *pneuma*") we could render *pneuma* as "spirit" but also as "breath (of life)"; the sense is: "breathe one's last." However, in John 19:30 ("he bowed his head and gave up [Gk. *paredōken*] his *pneuma*") such a rendering is less possible (cf. CJB: "delivered"; ISV: "released"; TLB: "dismissed his spirit"; *not* simply "he died," as many have it). Consider also Luke 23:46, "'Father, into your hands I commit [Gk. *paratithemai*] my *pneuma*!' And having said this he breathed his last [Gk. *exepneusen*]." Notice the important difference between the active *paredōken* and the passive *exepneusen*. Animals and humans, including the Son of Man, "breathe their last" — only the Son of God could actively "deliver/release/dismiss" his spirit, as he had announced earlier: "For this reason the Father loves me, because I *lay down* [Gk. *tithēmi*] my life that I may take it up again. No one takes it from me, but I *lay it down* [Gk. *tithēmi*] of my own accord. I have authority to *lay it down* [Gk. *theinai*], and I have authority to take it up again" (John 10:17-18).

In John 20:22 (Jesus "breathed [Gk. *enephysēsen*] on them and said to them, "Receive the Holy *pneuma*") it is clearly the Holy Spirit that is intended, but the metaphor of blowing, breath, and wind is still present (§6.10.2).

Ethiopian Christians compared the Son and the Spirit to a river of light and a river of wind, respectively, going forth from the throne of God. The Armenians Gregory of Narek and Nerses Snorhali compared the wind of the Spirit to the gentle, refreshing breeze blowing into Christ's garden.[5] This metaphor ties in with Song of Solomon 4:16, "Awake, O north wind, and come, O south wind! Blow upon my garden, let its spices flow." A second parallel is Genesis 3:8, "in the cool [lit., wind] of the day," (Heb. *leruach hayyom*), that is, the cooler breeze after the heat of the day. Rabbi Nachmanides rendered it as "in the wind of the day," and thought, parallel with 1 Kings 19:11, of a strong wind.[6] Ephrem of Syria compared the Spirit to a wind that, during winnowing, separates the chaff from the wheat (cf. Matt. 3:12).[7]

The wind metaphor is present in Acts 2 as well: at the outpouring of the Holy Spirit, "suddenly there came from heaven a sound like a mighty rushing wind [Gk. *pnoē*], and it filled

---

5. Burgess (1989, 6, 127, 133).
6. Cohen (1983, 14).
7. *Hymns of the Faith* 38.12; see Burgess (1989, 186).

the entire house where they were sitting" (v. 2). The expression "carried along by the Holy Spirit" (2 Pet. 1:21) also suggests the wind metaphor: the prophets were like leaves driven by the wind. Sometimes, God's servants look as though they were literally driven by the Spirit as by a stormy wind, such as Elijah (1 Kings 18:12; 2 Chron. 2:16), Ezekiel (Ezek. 3:12, 14; 8:3; 11:1, 24; 43:5), and Philip (Acts 8:39).[8]

Several times in the Old Testament, wind was a sign of God's presence: "Then a wind [YLT: spirit] from the LORD sprang up" (Num. 11:31); "the sound of marching in the tops of the balsam trees" (2 Sam. 5:24). "He rode on a cherub and flew; he came swiftly on the wings of the wind" (Ps. 18:10; cf. 104:3). "As I looked, behold, a stormy wind came out of the north, and a great cloud, with brightness around it, and fire flashing forth continually, and in the midst of the fire, as it were gleaming metal" (Ezek. 1:4).

Please note that the God of Israel is never *identified* with any such natural phenomenon, whether (stormy) wind, or water, or fire. Thus, the passages just mentioned exhibit an important contrast with 1 Kings 19: "[B]ehold, the LORD passed by, and a great and strong wind tore the mountains and broke in pieces the rocks before the LORD, but *the LORD was not in the wind*. And after the wind an earthquake, but the LORD was not in the earthquake. And after the earthquake a fire, but *the LORD was not in the fire*. And after the fire the sound of a low whisper" — in which the LORD apparently was present (vv. 11–12).

Making such a forbidden identification with natural phenomena was the mistake of the Syrians, who said to their king, "Their [i.e., Israel's] gods are gods of the hills [GNT: mountain gods], and so they were stronger than we. But let us fight against them in the plain, and surely we shall be stronger than they" (1 Kings 20:23). This was quite offensive to the LORD: "Thus says the LORD, 'Because the Syrians have said,

---

8. Green (1975, 20).

"The LORD is a god of the hills but he is not a god of the valleys," therefore I will give all this great multitude into your hand, and you shall know that I am the LORD'" (v. 28). God is just as much the God of the mountains as he is the God of the valleys—the God of the storms and the God of the "low whispers"; the God of the blazing fire and of the little sparks; the God of the floods and of the droplets. Yet, being *filled* with the Holy Spirit is experiencing (figuratively speaking) the stormy winds, the blazing fires, and the mighty waters. *Not* being filled with the Spirit is experiencing only quiet breezes (here meant in the negative sense), trickling droplets, and inconspicuous sparks.

Here, an important question arises. If the Holy Spirit is actually nothing but the "breath" of God's, or Christ's, mouth—no matter how figuratively we take this—how can he be a separate entity or a distinct person? I will return to this question in §4.4.

4.2 Water
4.2.1 Outpouring of the Spirit

Although the terms *ruach* or *pneuma* themselves never mean "water," the terms that are connected with the Holy Spirit are often dealt with as though they do refer to water. This is no wonder: the first reason for the profound inner connection between breath and water is that both express the biotic principle of life. There is no (biotic) life without oxygen, and there is no (biotic) life without water. This is clearer in the Hebrew word *nephesh* ("soul"): in Job 41:21 it means breath ("His breath kindles coals"). Elsewhere it is identical with blood (Lev. 17:14 JUB: "the *nephesh* of every creature is its blood"; cf. Deut. 12:23, "the blood is the *nephesh*"). In 2 Samuel 14:14, this life is compared to water poured out ("We must all die; we are like water spilled on the ground, which cannot be gathered up again. But God will not take away *nephesh*").

We find something similar with regard to the land: the water makes the land fertile. The *ruach* of God is the wind that carries the rain clouds with it, bringing fertility to the land. Therefore, it is not strange to say that the Spirit is "poured out" like water on God's people: ". . . the Spirit is poured upon us from on high, and the wilderness becomes a fruitful field, and the fruitful field is deemed a forest" (Isa. 32:15). Notice here the parallelism in Isaiah 44:3: "I will *pour water* on the thirsty land, and *streams* on the dry ground; I will *pour my Spirit* upon your offspring, and my blessing on your descendants."

The idea of the Spirit's "outpouring" is found in several Old Testament passages: "I pour out my Spirit upon the house of Israel" (Ezek. 39:29; cf. 36:25-27). "And it shall come to pass afterward, that I will pour out my Spirit on all flesh; your sons and your daughters shall prophesy, your old men shall dream dreams, and your young men shall see visions. Even on the male and female servants in those days I will pour out my Spirit" (Joel 2:28-29; cf. Acts 2:17-18). "I will pour on the house of David and on the inhabitants of Jerusalem the Spirit of grace and supplication; then they will look on Me whom they pierced" (Zech. 12:10 NKJV).

In the New Testament we find the same thought: "Being therefore exalted at the right hand of God, and having received from the Father the promise of the Holy Spirit, he has poured out this that you yourselves are seeing and hearing" (Acts 2:33; cf. 10:45, "the gift of the Holy Spirit was poured out even on the Gentiles"). God "saved us, not because of works done by us in righteousness, but according to his own mercy, by the washing of regeneration and renewal of the Holy Spirit, whom[9] he poured out on us richly through Jesus Christ our Savior" (Titus 3:5-6; cf. also Rom. 5:5, "God's love has been poured into our hearts through the Holy Spirit who has been given to us").

Quite remarkable is also Jesus' statement on the last day

---

9. In this expression, the rendering "whom" can appropriately be replaced with "which" (as is done in many translations), because here the Spirit is being viewed not as a person, but as a substance (recall that the terms "person" and "substance" are themselves metaphors; cf. §4.4.2).

of the Feast of Booths (the day of the "water scooping," as a prayer for new rain): "'If anyone thirsts, let him come to me and drink. Whoever believes in me, as the Scripture has said, "Out of his heart will flow rivers of living water."' Now this he said about the Spirit. . ." (John 7:37–39; cf. §§6.6.2, 6.6.3). Similar images can be found in Ezekiel 47:1–12 (the river flowing from the temple), Zechariah (14:8, the living water flowing out from Jerusalem), and Revelation 22:1 ("the river of the water of life, bright as crystal, flowing from the throne of God and of the Lamb"). All of these can be related to the Holy Spirit.

4.2.2 Dew, Rain, Wells, Rivers

In the Bible, just like the wind, water is sometimes a sign of God's presence: "[W]hen they [i.e., the living creatures] went, I heard the sound of their wings like the sound of many waters, like the sound of the Almighty, a sound of tumult like the sound of an army" (Ezek. 1:24). "And behold, the glory of the God of Israel was coming from the east. And the sound of his coming was like the sound of many waters, and the earth shone with his glory" (43:2; cf. Ps. 93:4). The Son of Man's "feet were like burnished bronze, refined in a furnace, and his voice was like the roar of many waters" (Rev. 1:15). "And I heard a voice from heaven like the roar of many waters and like the sound of loud thunder" (14:2; cf. 19:6).

When representing the Holy Spirit, the metaphor of water can include the dew: ". . . It is like the dew of Hermon, which falls on the mountains of Zion" (Ps. 133:2). "I [i.e., God] will be like the dew to Israel" (Hos. 14:5). Such passages may be associated with the Holy Spirit, particularly in parallelism with rain: "May my teaching drop as the *rain*, my speech distill as the *dew*, like gentle rain upon the tender grass, and like showers upon the herb" (Deut. 32:2). "Then the remnant of Jacob shall be in the midst of many peoples like *dew* from the LORD, like *showers* on the grass" (Micah 5:7).

In other passages the rain is emphasized: "And I will

make them and the places all around my hill a blessing, and I will send down the showers in their season; they shall be showers of blessing" (Ezek. 34:26). "Let us know; let us press on to know the LORD; his going out is sure as the dawn; he will come to us as the showers, as the spring rains that water the earth" (Hos. 6:3). "Be glad, O children of Zion, and rejoice in the LORD your God, for he has given the early rain for your vindication; he has poured down for you abundant rain, the early and the latter rain, as before" (Joel 2:23; cf. vv. 28–29). "Ask rain from the LORD in the season of the spring rain, from the LORD who makes the storm clouds, and he will give them showers of rain, to everyone the vegetation in the field" (Zech. 10:1).

We find the same metaphor in connection with wells ("With joy you will draw water from the wells of salvation," Isa. 12:3; cf. 41:18), fountains (God himself is the "fountain of living waters," Jer. 2:13; 17:13; cf. Joel 3:18; Zech. 13:1), and rivers ("I will open rivers on the bare heights, and fountains in the midst of the valleys. I will make the wilderness a pool of water, and the dry land springs of water," Isa. 41:18; 43:19; 66:12).

The Armenians Gregory the Illuminator (or Enlightener) and Gregory of Narek compared the Holy Spirit to a mighty flood of water, while John Cassian and the Armenian Nerses Snorhali likened him to a lovely dew that brings the human mind and senses into harmony.[10] In an Armenian liturgical hymn, believers sing of a "fiery rain" that was poured out upon the apostles in the upper room.[11]

4.2.3 Cleansing

Water in not only the principle of life and fertility, but it is also a symbol of spiritual cleansing. The first extensive biblical description of this symbol appears in Numbers 8, which speaks of the cleansing of the Levites: "Thus you shall do to

---
10. Burgess (1989, 7, 128, 133).
11. Ibid., 113.

them to cleanse them: sprinkle the *water of purification* [ERV: the special water from the sin offering; lit., water of sin *or* water of sin offering, water to take away sin; cf. CEV, GW, NABRE, NLV] upon them, and let them go with a razor over all their body, and wash their clothes and cleanse themselves" (v. 7).

The second description appears in Numbers 19:

> And a man who is clean shall gather up the ashes of the heifer and deposit them outside the camp in a clean place. And they shall be kept for the *water for impurity* [KJV: water of separation] for the congregation of the people of Israel; it is a sin offering. ... Whoever touches the dead body of any person shall be unclean seven days. He shall cleanse himself with the water on the third day and on the seventh day, and so be clean (vv. 9, 11–12; cf. also 31:23).

The final Old Testament description appears in Zechariah 13:1, "On that day there shall be a fountain opened for the house of David and the inhabitants of Jerusalem, to cleanse them from sin and uncleanness." Perhaps this is the way we should read John 3:5, "[U]nless one is born of water and the Spirit, he cannot enter the kingdom of God." In light of what was said in §3.9.1 about the hendiadys and the explicative use of the Greek word *kai* ("and"), I suggest that we read this to say: "Unless one is born of the water of the Spirit," or, "of water, namely, the Spirit" (see §8.2). This points to the inner coherence of Word and Spirit, for the metaphor of the cleansing water is also applied to the Word: ". . . the washing of water with [or, through] the word" (Eph. 5:26) (see more extensively, §§5.3.1 and 8.2.1). Believers have been cleansed by the Word of God applied to their hearts and consciences by the Spirit of God.

4.3   Fire
4.3.1   Old Testament Passages
The Holy Spirit is also compared to fire, in at least four different ways: a destroying fire, a purifying fire, the fire of

God's radiant glory, and fire that ecstatically "sets on fire." Of course, these four may overlap extensively.

In the Old Testament, fire sometimes points to the presence of God's glory: "[T]he angel of the Lord appeared to him in a flame of fire out of the midst of a bush" (Exod. 3:2–5; cf. Deut. 33:16). "And the Lord went before them by day in a pillar of cloud to lead them along the way, and by night in a pillar of fire to give them light, that they might travel by day and by night" (13:21). "Mount Sinai was wrapped in smoke because the Lord had descended on it in fire" (19:18; cf. 24:17). "[T]he cloud of the Lord was on the tabernacle by day, and fire was in it by night, in the sight of all the house of Israel throughout all their journeys" (40:38). "As I looked, behold, a stormy wind came out of the north, and a great cloud, with brightness around it, and fire flashing forth continually, and in the midst of the fire, as it were gleaming metal. . . . As for the likeness of the living creatures, their appearance was like burning coals of fire, like the appearance of torches moving to and fro among the living creatures. And the fire was bright, and out of the fire went forth lightning. . . . Such was the appearance of the likeness of the glory of the Lord" (Ezek. 1:4, 13, 28). "[T]hrones were placed, and the Ancient of Days took his seat; his clothing was white as snow, and the hair of his head like pure wool; his throne was fiery flames; its wheels were burning fire. A stream of fire issued and came out from before him" (Dan. 7:9–10). "[W]ho can endure the day of his coming, and who can stand when he appears? For he is like a refiner's fire and like fullers' soap" (Mal. 3:2).

At several decisive moments in redemptive history, God confirmed his work by fire from heaven: when the tabernacle was erected (Lev. 9:24), when the construction of the temple was finished (2 Chron. 7:1), at the repentance of Israel through the prophet Elijah (1 Kings 18:38), as well as on the Day of Pentecost (Acts 2): we hear not only about the "mighty rushing wind" (v. 2), but also about the "divided tongues as of fire" appearing to the gathered believers and resting on each one of them (v. 3). Pope Gregory the Great said that, in this chapter, God revealed himself in fire because he himself is an immaterial and indescribable fire (Heb. 12:29), in order to kindle cold and "matter-oriented" hearts and fill them with the love of God.[12] The purifying and sanctifying work of the Spirit is "like a refiner's fire" (Mal. 3:2, although the Spirit is only implied here). Where Scripture speaks of the "fire of the LORD" (Num. 11:1, 3; 1 Kings 18:38) we are reminded of the LORD's *ruach* ("breath" or "wind," but also "Spirit"), which has a similar effect.

Isaiah 4:4 is an extraordinary and complicated text: ". . . when the LORD shall have washed away the filth of the daughters of Zion and cleansed the bloodstains of Jerusalem [water metaphor] from its midst by the *ruach* of judgment and by the *ruach* of burning." Some translations see this as referring to God's "wind" (e.g., CEB: "a wind of judgment and a searing wind"; CJB: "a blast of searing judgment"), while others leave *ruach* untranslated (e.g., NIRV: "He will judge those who spilled that blood. His burning anger will blaze out at them").[13] Several older translations relate the phrase to the Holy Spirit (cf. BRG, EXB: "the Spirit of judgment . . . the Spirit of burning [fire]"), where the Holy Spirit is seen as the "Ruach Ba'er (Spirit of Burning)" (OJB), that is, the Spirit as a purifying fire.[14]

4.3.2 New Testament Passages

According to some New Testament accounts, we read that John the Baptist speaks of a baptism "with (or, in[15]) [the] Holy Spirit and fire" (Gk. *en pneumatic hagiōi kai pyri*; Matt. 3:11; Luke 3:16). Here, fire is a picture of judgment (cf. the next verse in Luke 3, "His winnowing fork is in his hand, to

---

12. Burgess (1997, 14).
13. Cf. Oswalt (1986, 148).
14. Hildebrandt (1995, 86–87).
15. If baptizing is understood as synonymous with immersing, then "baptizing with" is linguistic nonsense; a person is immersed *in* (water, the Spirit, fire) (cf. ASV, CJB, ERV, JUB, TLV, WEB, WYC).

clear his threshing floor and to gather the wheat into his barn, but the chaff he will burn with unquenchable fire.") Various expositors explain this to mean that some will be baptized (immersed) in the Holy Spirit, and others in fire.[16] Other expositors explain the text to mean that some are baptized (immersed) in the Holy Spirit *as well as* in fire, where fire is understood in its purifying sense.[17] An important argument for this second view is the lack of the preposition "in" (*en*) before "fire" (*pyri*), so that the expression could be read as a hendiadys: immersed "in the fire of the Holy Spirit" (see further §7.1). The parallel between water and Spirit baptism is that in water baptism it is the human body that is literally immersed in (and purified by) water, and in Spirit immersion it is the human spirit that is figuratively immersed in (and purified by) the Holy Spirit.

In Romans 12:11, the exhortation to "[B]e fervent in spirit" can also be related to the Holy Spirit: "[B]e fervent in the Spirit" (CEB: "[B]e on fire in the Spirit"; cf. ISV). Similarly, in Acts 18:25 we have the same alternative: Apollos was either "fervent in spirit"[18] or "fervent in the Spirit"[19] (cf. OJB: "on fire in the Ruach Hakodesh [i.e. Holy Spirit]").

1 Thessalonians 5:19, "Do not quench the Spirit," clearly implies the metaphor of fire (cf. ISV, NOG: "Do not put out the Spirit's fire"; cf. Mark 9:48), or possibly of a lamp (cf. Matt. 25:8). 1 Clement 21:1-2 interprets Proverbs 20:27 ("The spirit of man is the lamp of the LORD, searching all his innermost parts") as referring to the Spirit of the Lord within a person (cf. Job 32:8; 1 Cor. 2:11).[20] Thus, here the lamp would be a metaphor for the Holy Spirit, directly parallel with the Word

---

16. Kelly (1896, 65–66); Gaebelein (1910, 71–73); Floor (1982, 14–15).
17. Grosheide (1954, 47–48); Dunn (1992, 695); Bruce (1979, 84, 483–84); Geldenhuys (1983, 140); Carson (1984, 105); Liefeld (1984, 856–57).
18. So Longenecker (1981, 490).
19. So Bruce (1988, 359).
20. Derek Prince (1995, 369) interpreted Prov. 20:27 to mean that the burning lamp is a symbol of the spirit of the Spirit-filled believer, intended to burn and shine by the fire of the indwelling Spirit.

(cf. Heb. 4:12). Similarly, the lamp in Luke 15:8 can be taken to represent either the Word of God, or the Holy Spirit as applying this Word; thus, in Luke 15 the first parable may be placing the Son in the foreground (as the good shepherd), the second parable the Spirit, and the third parable the Father.

In Revelation 4:5, the "seven Spirits" — if they refer to the Holy Spirit (see §3.6.2) — are compared to "seven torches of fire" burning "before the throne." In 5:6 these "seven spirits of God" are the "seven eyes" of the Lamb, which are sent out into all the earth, an idea adopted from Zechariah 4:10b, "These seven are the eyes of the LORD, which range through the whole earth" (cf. 3:9). Thinking of a lamp, of course we also think of oil (see §4.5), and hence of Zechariah 4, to which we will return in §5.7.2.

Isaiah 11:4 says of the Messiah, "[W]ith the breath of his lips he shall kill the wicked" (cf. 33:11, "your breath [*ruach*; GNT: spirit] is a fire that will consume you"; 2 Thess. 2:8, "the lawless one . . . whom the Lord Jesus will kill with the breath of his mouth"). This sounds like the igneous breath of a dragon, as it is said of the Leviathan, "Out of his mouth go flaming torches; sparks of fire leap forth," Job 41:19). In the great battle between the Lamb and the dragon, which runs like a thread through the book of Revelation, the Lamb is the igneous one — so to speak — not the dragon. When the dragon and the beast assemble the powers of the earth against the Lamb (16:12-16), the book says, "They will go to war against the Lamb, but the Lamb will defeat them, because he is Lord of lords and King of kings" (17:14 CJB).

4.3.3 Historical Comparisons

In §3.8 and 4.3.1, I discussed the parallels between the Shekhinah and the Holy Spirit. The Shekhinah is the "glory of the LORD," which appeared to Israel as a cloud, sometimes together with fire (Exod. 13:21-22; 14:24; 24:17; 40:38; cf. 16:10). Ethiopian Christians were acquainted with the metaphor of the Father as sun, the Son as sun, and the Spirit as sun, that is, all three as fire. Or this triad: the Father as sun, the Son as light, and the Spirit as warmth. Or yet another triad: the Father as fire, the Son as flame, and the Spirit as red hot coal; thus also Ephrem of Syria. The latter spoke of the divine warmth of the Spirit, defrosting all that is frozen, thawing the freezing bond of sin, leading all things to maturity, and bringing springtime to the church. According to him and many Eastern Christian authors after him, during the Eucharist the fire of the Spirit is granted to all participants to sanctify them.

According to John Cassian (ca. 400), during prayer the fire of the Spirit kindles the human spirit while the Spirit is pleading with groanings that cannot be uttered (cf. Rom. 8:26). According to Severus of Antioch (ca. 500), the fire of the Spirit consumes the thorns that Adam's sin had planted (cf. Gen. 3:18). The heretical cult of the Messalians (fourth century) spoke of a fiery Spirit baptism. Pseudo-Macarius, perhaps a Messalian too, compared the Holy Spirit to a divine torch in the heart, and to the pillar of cloud and the pillar of fire. The Armenian Nerses Snorhali said it was the light of the Holy Spirit that glowed toward Moses from the cleft in the rock, so that his face shone (Exod. 33:21-23; 34:29).[21]

In Western Christianity, Bonaventura was known to compare the Holy Spirit to fire. He connected the phrase: "From on high he sent fire; into my bones he made it descend" (Lam. 1:13) with Acts 2:1-4, but also with the incarnation of the Logos, worked by the Spirit, within the womb of Mary. He called the Spirit the fire of grace: clear in appearance, warm in effect, quick in movement, supplying light to the eyes for insight. There is nobody who longs for God who has not been kindled by the fire of the Spirit.[22]

4.4 Evaluation
4.4.1 The Use of Metaphors
Throughout history, the Pneumatomachians, that is, those

---
21. Burgess (1989, 6, 8, 132, 145, 165–66, 179).
22. Burgess (1997, 72; cf. 92: Hildegard of Bingen).

who deny that the Holy Spirit is a divine person, have used the passages mentioned to argue that the Spirit is consistently presented as an emanation, or an influence, or a force, or a gift of God. According to them, the few passages presenting the Spirit as a person must be viewed as exceptional personifications of this force or influence. They have also argued that the name of God is never directly ascribed to the Holy Spirit, and that Scripture nowhere speaks of praying to or worshiping of the Holy Spirit (though on the latter point, see §3.5 above).

In opposition to this, I reject the assertion that minimal biblical data exists concerning the personality and deity of the Spirit, and his being a person distinct from the Father and the Son. In §§3.3 and 3.4, we have found the opposite. In light of this, the metaphors of air (breath, wind), water, and fire cannot be taken as an argument against the personhood of the Spirit. To be sure, his personhood may be presented less clearly than that of the Father and the Son. The name that he bears—Holy Spirit—may not explicitly express his personality, as do the names Father and Son.[23] He may be a vital force within us rather than a person outside of us, with whom we might have communion. He may be the force through which we can have fellowship with the Father and the Son (cf. 2 Cor. 13:14, "the fellowship *of* [i.e., through, in the power of; not *with*[24]] the Holy Spirit [Gk. *hē koinōnia tou hagiou pneumatos*]." However, none of these points can diminish the force of the clear biblical testimony concerning the personality and deity of the Spirit. The Holy Spirit not only *is* the power or the wisdom of God, but he is a divine person who also *has* power and wisdom.

The Pneumatomachians cling to the passages that speak of the Spirit as a force, and neglect those speaking of him as a person. The converse danger consists in clinging to the passages that speak of the Spirit as a person, and neglecting those speaking of him as a force. Thus, Kenneth Wuest warned us

---

23. Cf. Bavinck (*RD* 2.311).
24. Cf. Wuest (1973a, 100–101).

not to take the filling with the Spirit too literally *because* the Spirit is not a substance but a person. He ignores the metaphor of force applied to the Spirit, and thus the actual meaning of being filled.[25]

Another example is Benjamin Warfield, who claimed that, throughout the Old Testament, the Spirit of God is presented as a person; in no passage he is viewed otherwise than as personal, as a free, willing, intelligent being.[26] This is just as one-sided as the Pneumatomachians' claim. I do not doubt that the Holy Spirit is a divine person; but I do doubt that each Old Testament passage where he is mentioned clearly presents him as a person. On the contrary, we may wonder whether five of those Old Testament passages present the Holy Spirit unequivocally as a divine person. Only in the New Testament does the personality of the Spirit clearly come to light. We may observe here that, on the basis of the Old Testament, no Jewish scholar viewed the Holy Spirit as a distinct person. On the one hand, this might be partly a reaction to Christian pneumatology, though. Thus, the Soncino Commentary reduced the outpouring of the Spirit in Joel 2:28 to a prophetic ecstasy (cf. Num. 11:25; 1 Sam. 10:6), and elsewhere as "vitality" (Ps. 104:30) and "mental capacity" (Exod. 35:31).[27] On the other hand, some rabbis gradually developed the idea of the Spirit as a distinct, independent personality, who sometimes even speaks *to* God.[28]

We have to realize here that, in the end, the term "person" is a metaphor, too. In this term, we try to enclose similarities that we notice between, on the one hand, Father, Son, and Spirit, and, on the other hand, human beings (and angels). However, at the same time, Father, Son, and Spirit surpass everything that human beings are as persons. Humans have *intellect*, but "my thoughts are not your thoughts. . . . For as

---

25. Wuest (1973a, 104; cf. 108, 111); thus also F. F. Bruce in §4.6.3.
26. Warfield (1929, 124).
27. Cohen (1980, 72).
28. Sjöberg (1968, 387–88).

the heavens are higher than the earth, so ... my thoughts than your thoughts" (Isa. 55:8–9). Humans have a *will*, but only God's will is perfectly sovereign (cf. John 3:8; 1 Cor. 12:11). The metaphor of personality says something essential about the Holy Spirit, but so do the metaphors of air, water, and fire. In other words, in my view, it is equally biblical to say that the Holy Spirit is a *person* (who has power) and to say that he is a *force*. We will investigate this in the following sections.

4.4.2 Person As Well As Force

Claiming that one may describe the Holy Spirit with the metaphor of force just as properly as with the metaphor of person is saying something much more than that the person of the Spirit is powerful or has power (cf. Acts 1:8). The latter is self-evident. No, the Holy Spirit, who is a powerful person, *is* also force, power, strength. *He* is "the power at work within us" (Eph. 3:20). Perhaps this is nowhere more evident than in the fact that the Spirit is *quantifiable*, so to speak. What else does it mean that we read in John 3:34 that God "does not give the Spirit in limited measure" (ISV; CJB: "in limited degree")? If the Spirit is only a person, how could he be described in terms of some measure? Many translations render the phrase in a positive way: "he gives the Spirit without measure" (ESV) or "without limit" (NIV). How could a person be given without limit?

There are more examples. God says in Numbers 11:17, "I will take some of the Spirit that is on you [i.e., Moses] and put it on them [i.e., the elders of Israel]." Elisha asks for a "double portion" of the Spirit (capital S: BRG, GNV) that was on Elijah (2 Kings 2:9). 1 John 4:13 says that "he has given us *of* [Gk. *ek*] his Spirit" (CEB: "a measure of his Spirit"; Phillips: "a share of his own Spirit"). English translations have an extra problem here, one that does not appear in the original texts and in many other languages (cf. note 9); this involves using the personal or impersonal pronouns in reference to the Holy Spirit — "the Spirit who" (e.g., John 6:63; Rom. 5:5; 8:11), or "the Spirit that" and "the Spirit, which" (e.g., Num. 11:17, 25; Isa. 59:21; Titus 3:5–6). In Romans 5:5, for example, one may wonder whether the metaphor of person or of force is being employed (cf. the various translations).

It does not help to argue that such quantitative speaking must be understood metaphorically, since speaking of the Spirit either as a person or as a force is equally metaphorical. We can do *nothing other* than speak metaphorically here; the issue involves what metaphor best fits with biblical parlance.

"Person" and "force" would be contradictory as logical concepts, but not as metaphors. Thus, the Holy Spirit is a person who comes to dwell *in* the believers, collectively and individually (Rom. 8:9, 11; 1 Cor. 3:16; 6:19; 2 Tim. 1:14; cf. John 14:17). As such, one cannot have "more" or "less" of him; he dwells in a believer, or he does not. However, the Holy Spirit is also a power that, to some degree, comes *upon* or *over* a person, or with which (not whom!) one is invested. Thus, the risen Lord said, "[Y]ou will receive power when the Holy Spirit has come *upon* you" (Acts 1:8; cf. 10:38, "with [the] Holy Spirit and power"). Or also: "I am sending the promise of my Father [i.e., the promised Spirit; Acts 1:4–5] *upon* you. But stay in the city until you are *clothed* with *power* from on high" (Luke 24:49). Or compare the Messianic prophets: "Behold my servant, whom I uphold, my chosen, in whom my soul delights; I have put my Spirit *upon* him" (Isa. 42:1). "The Spirit of the Lord GOD is *upon* me, because the LORD has anointed me" (61:1).

Precisely because the Holy Spirit is not only a person (a "he") but also a force (an "it"), believers definitely can possess this force to a lesser or higher degree. They can be "full" (Luke 4:1; Acts 6:3, 5; 7:55; 11:24) or "filled" with the Spirit (Luke 1:15, 41, 67; Acts 2:4; 4:8, 31; 9:17; 13:9, 52; Eph. 5:18), but also possess a minimum of it. They can even "quench" the Spirit (1 Thess. 5:19). A person cannot be "quenched," a force (in this case, a fire) can be quenched. This must not be confused with the way one may be "full" of a person, as when, for instance, people are in love. This expression cannot be quantified—but, apparently, the Holy Spirit is a power the quantity of which there can be much or little.

In the latter case one can ask for the Spirit, that is, pray for a greater measure of it: "If you then, who are evil, know how to give good gifts to your children, how much more will the heavenly Father give the Holy Spirit to those who ask him!" (Luke 11:13). This is not a one-time request; a son does not ask his father for food only once in his life, but many times (cf. vv. 11-12). Time and again, a believer experiencing a spiritual emptiness in one's life may ask for the Spirit. Since the Holy Spirit already dwells in that believer, and does so incessantly (cf. John 14:16), this must mean: praying for the fullness, the abundance of the Spirit. This is possible only if both metaphors of person and force are applicable to the Holy Spirit.

In an analogous way, David's prayer, "take not your Holy Spirit from me" (Ps. 51:11), does not imply some indwelling of the person of the Holy Spirit; such New Testament ideas may not be read back into the Old Testament. Thus, David's concern cannot have been that the *person* of the Spirit might no longer dwell in him, but that the *power* of the Spirit might no longer be upon him, especially in view of his prophetic ministry; as he said, "The Spirit of the LORD speaks by me; his word is on my tongue" (2 Sam. 23:2). David was afraid that he would lose his prophetic anointing (see §4.5).

Of King Saul we do indeed read: "[T]he Spirit of the LORD departed from Saul" (1 Sam. 16:14). Here, the power of the Spirit had left Saul, and had passed from him to his successor, David (v. 13), just as—in a *positive* context—it had passed from Moses to Joshua (Deut. 34:9), and from Elijah to Elisha (2 Kings 2:9, 15). Saul lost this power when it passed to David; Moses and Elijah did not lose this power when it passed to their successors. None of these cases involves the person of the Spirit dwelling in people, but the power of the Spirit resting *upon* people.

4.5 Oil[29]
4.5.1 Medicine or Sacrament?

The metaphors relating to force involve more than the three already mentioned — air, water, and fire — which I have called "basic metaphors" because all three are used in Scripture to express the presence of God's glory, as we have seen. In this and the following sections I deal with two other metaphors relating to force, namely, oil and wine, which are also quantifiable (i.e., you can have much or little of them), and three metaphors that are not quantifiable: dove, seal, and hand/finger.

In the parable of the Good Samaritan, we read that the latter poured oil and wine on the victim's wounds (Luke 10:34). In my view, here both oil and wine are metaphors of the Holy Spirit. In Luke 10, oil functions as a medicine. As such, the passage may be compared with Mark 6:13: the disciples "anointed with oil many who were sick and healed them." Think also of James 5:14–15, "Is anyone among you sick? Let him call for the elders of the church, and let them pray over him, anointing him with oil in the name of the Lord. And the prayer of faith will save the one who is sick, and the Lord will raise him up." Is oil here an ancient medicine (cf. Isa. 1:6; Luke 10:34), a tonic or refreshment (cf. Ps. 23:5b), or is it a sacred ("sacramental") means, possibly referring to the Holy Spirit (Isa. 61:1, "The Spirit of the Lord GOD is upon me, because the LORD has anointed me")? Or is this contrast impermissible, since Scripture knows no contrast between "natural" medicine and the "supernatural" panacea?

Minimally we must ask: If oil were a common medicine, a kind of remedy for every disease, then why is a prayer for the sick person needed? In James 5 it is obviously not the oil itself that heals, but the "prayer of faith." Thus, the meaning of the oil merges into a higher, spiritual meaning. As Mart-

---

29. See Ouweneel (2004, §4.1–4.2 and 2005a, §10.1).

Jan Paul put it, anointing with oil in Mark 6 and James 5 may symbolize dedicating the patient to God and to the work of the Holy Spirit.[30]

4.5.2 Old Testament Passages

In §4.4.2 we saw that the power of the Holy Spirit comes *upon* or *over* the believer. This reminds us immediately of what the Bible says about the anointing with the Spirit. Through a literal anointing the special oil comes *upon* a person, and in abundant quantity, the oil runs down from the head. As we read in Psalm 133:2, "It is like the precious oil on the head, running down on the beard, on the beard of Aaron, running down on the collar of his robes." This probably refers to Aaron's collar, not his skirts (cf. KJV). But with the latter, the anointing would be even more abundant: "It is like fine oil poured on the head which flows down the beard — Aaron's beard, and then flows down his garments" (NET). The point is: just as a person can be anointed with much oil or with little oil, so too a person may receive much or little of the Spirit when anointed.

Very special is the use of oil during a leper's cleansing, which many see as a clear type of the sinner's cleansing. First, the priest puts the blood of the guilt offering on the lobe of the person's right ear, the right thumb and the right big toe, through which the person's hearing (and obeying), acting, and walking are atoned (Lev. 14:14). After this, the priest puts oil on the same spots, on top of the blood, and also on the head (vv. 17–18), which points to the sanctification by the Spirit of the obedience, acting, and walking of the reconciled sinner.[31]

In the Old Testament, kings,[32] priests,[33] and some prophets

---

30. Paul (1997, 109).
31. Grant (1890, 330); Mackintosh (n.d., ad loc.).
32. Judg. 9:8; 1 Sam. 9:16; 10:1; 15:1, 17; 16:3, 12–13; 2 Sam. 2:4, 7; 5:3; 19:10, 21; 23:1; 1 Kings 1:34, 39, 45; 19:15–16; 2 Kings 9:3, 6, 12; 11:12; 23:30; 1 Chron. 11:3; 29:22; 2 Chron. 22:7; 23:11; Ps. 18:50; 89:20; Isa. 45:1; Dan. 9:25–26.
33. Exod. 28:41; 29:7, 21, 29; 30:30; 40:13, 15; Lev. 6:22; 7:36; 8:12, 30; 16:32; 21:10, 12; Num. 3:3; 35:25. In Zech. 4:14, the Davidic Zerubbabel and Aar-

were anointed with oil (1 Kings 19:16b). In 1 Chronicles 16:22 (= Ps. 105:15), the patriarchs are called both "anointed ones" and "prophets" (cf. Gen. 20:7). In Isaiah 61:1, the "anointed one" is typologically Christ speaking (Luke 4:16–21), but primarily he is the prophetic author. Similarly, just as in the Old Testament these kings, priests, and prophets were anointed with oil, the New Testament kings/priests (Heb. 13:15; 1 Pet. 2:5, 9; Rev. 1:6; 5:9–10; 20:4, 6; 22:5) and prophets (1 Cor. 14:24) are anointed with the Holy Spirit (2 Cor. 1:21–22; 1 John 2:20, 27; cf. Acts 10:38).

One Old Testament king, David, was anointed no fewer than three times: once among his brothers (1 Sam. 16:13), a second time by his own tribe, Judah (2 Sam. 2:4), and a third time by the elders of the entire nation (5:3). One might say: this man of God received abundant anointing. This was true in the spiritual sense as well: immediately after his first anointing, "the Spirit of the LORD rushed upon David from that day forward" (1 Sam. 16:13). And at the end of his life we read, "The oracle of David, the son of Jesse, the oracle of the man who was raised on high, the anointed of the God of Jacob, the sweet psalmist of Israel: 'The Spirit of the LORD speaks by me; his word is on my tongue'" (2 Sam. 23:1–2).

Already in the Old Testament, anointing with oil and anointing with the Spirit are closely connected. The prophets realized that the former was only a symbol of the latter. When Zechariah asked what the oil featured in his vision meant, the angel answered: "Not by might, nor by power, but by my Spirit, says the LORD of hosts" (Zech. 4:1–6; see more extensively, §5.7.2). Elisha was the only Old Testament prophet of whom we read that he was to be anointed (1 Kings 19:16) — and on him was a "double portion" of the Spirit (capital S; cf. BRG, GNV) that had been on Elijah (2 Kings 2:9, 15).[34]

---

onic high priest Joshua are typologically the "two anointed ones" (lit., "two sons of fresh oil," AMP).

34. Cf. Sirach 48:12 (DRA), "Elias [i.e., Elijah] was indeed covered with the whirlwind, and his spirit was filled up in Eliseus [i.e., Elisha]," that is (in my

Of the Messiah we read, "The Spirit of the Lord GOD is upon me, because [better: as a consequence of the fact that] the LORD has anointed me" (Isa. 61:1). The fact that it is YHWH who anoints the Messiah (from Heb. *mashiah*, "anointed one") is not new. Of David, too, God says, although Samuel was the instrument in his hand: "*I* have anointed you king over Israel" (2 Sam. 12:7), and: "I have found David, my servant; with my holy oil *I* have anointed him" (Ps. 89:20). What is new is that Isaiah 61:1 is the only Old Testament passage that speaks unequivocally of an anointing with the Holy Spirit.

4.5.3 New Testament Passages

The apostle Paul says, "[I]t is God who establishes us with you in Christ, and has *anointed* us, and who has also put his seal on us and given us his Spirit in our hearts as a guarantee" (2 Cor. 1:21–22). And the apostle John writes: "[Y]ou have been *anointed* by the Holy One, and you all have knowledge [of the truth] [another reading: you know everything]. . . . But the *anointing* that you received from him abides in you, and you have no need that anyone should teach you. But as his *anointing* teaches you about everything, and is true, and is no lie—just as it has taught you, abide in him" (1 John 2:20, 27). Here, the emphasis lies especially on the fact that being anointed with the Spirit gives *insight* into the entire truth of God. It does not grant omniscience, as a superficial reading of the text might suggest, but it does grant understanding of *everything* that believers must know in view of the spiritual warfare in which they live.

This aspect of the anointing with the Spirit—insight, wisdom, understanding—reminds us of Isaiah 11:2, "And the Spirit of the LORD shall rest upon him, the Spirit of wisdom and understanding, the Spirit of counsel and might, the Spirit of knowledge and the fear of the LORD." The apostle Paul prays "that the God of our Lord Jesus Christ, the Father of glory, may give you the Spirit of wisdom and of revelation in

---

view), Elisha was filled with the Spirit that had been in Elijah.

the knowledge of him" (Eph. 1:17).

In other passages, oil refers more to the *power* that the believer needs in this spiritual warfare. The great example of this is Christ himself. His name means "anointed (one)," and the apostle Peter said of him: "God anointed Jesus of Nazareth with the Holy Spirit and with power.[35] He went about doing good and healing all who were oppressed by the devil, for God was with him" (Acts 10:38). Here we see the effect of the anointing: in its power Jesus went through the land and freed those "imprisoned" people—the sick and the possessed—from the power of the devil. This is what Isaiah had said, "The Spirit of the Lord GOD is upon me, because the LORD has anointed me . . . to proclaim liberty to the captives, and the opening of the prison to those who are bound" (Isa. 61:1). Jesus read these words aloud in the synagogue of Nazareth, and applied them to himself (Luke 4:16-21).

The anointing of the Holy Spirit has the same effect upon believers: "[T]hese signs will accompany those who believe: in my name they will cast out demons; they will speak in new tongues; they will pick up serpents with their hands; and if they drink any deadly poison, it will not hurt them; they will lay their hands on the sick, and they will recover" (Mark 16:17-18). Here, in a fivefold effect, we find the enormous power of God's Spirit that the anointing involves. This is what Jesus said (John 14:12), "[W]hoever believes in me will also do the works that I do; and greater works than these will he do, because I am going to the Father"; that is, such people will be my successors in God's work on earth, and to this end they will receive the same anointing that I possessed.

4.5.4 The Elect Messiah

The anointing of the Holy Spirit is no longer destined for only a small elite, like the kings, priests, and prophets in the Old

---

35. Literally, "with Holy Spirit and power," that is, "with the power of the Holy Spirit" (cf. 1 Thess. 1:5; also see 2 Pet. 1:16, "the power and coming of our Lord Jesus Christ," i.e., "the powerful coming . . .").

Testament, but for *all* regenerate and dedicated Messianic confessors (cf. Joel 2:28, "*all* flesh," i.e., all the people of God). This does not imply a degradation of the anointing itself, but rather an elevation of New Covenant believers. Their anointing is evidence of God's esteem for them. God does not anoint just any people, but only people whom he specifically elects for this. David is a beautiful example of this, for the Lord says of him, "I have granted help to one who is mighty; I have exalted one *chosen* from the people. I have found David, my servant; with my holy oil I have *anointed* him, so that my hand shall be established with him; my arm also shall strengthen him" (Ps. 89:19–21). And of the Messiah, Isaiah says prophetically, "Behold my servant, whom I uphold, my *chosen*, in whom my soul delights; I have put *my Spirit* upon him; he will bring forth justice to the nations" (Isa. 42:1). Both passages show that it is *chosen* (specially elected) people whom God anoints.

Being chosen, or elected, in whatever form, is emphatically not only a matter of divine sovereignty. God had chosen David, not only on the basis of his own sovereign decision but also because of the kind of person David was: "The LORD has sought out a man *after his own heart*" (1 Sam. 13:14; cf. Acts 13:22). One might say that the good within David had been worked in him by God's grace, but these good things were also a matter of David's own responsibility. To be sure, God chose David, and *as a consequence* David became a person on whom God's pleasure could rest in a very practical way. However, the reverse is equally true: God found his pleasure in David because of the type of person that young David was, and the life he led, and *therefore* God chose him to be king of Israel. God's sovereignty and human responsibility must not be played off against each other.[36]

We see this in the clearest way in the Messiah himself. From eternity the Father had been well pleased with his Son.

---

36. On this important but complicated matter, see extensively, Ouweneel (*RT* III/1).

But when Jesus was baptized, the Father expressed his pleasure in him because of all he had found in him during the thirty years that the Son had lived on the earth as Man (Matt. 3:17). We certainly cannot say that God chose Jesus Christ on the basis of a sovereign decision as if he could just as well have chosen another. No, he did so both because Jesus was the Father's eternal Son, and because of the joy and satisfaction that the Father found in the Son during the latter's life on earth. I just quoted from Isaiah 42:1: "Behold my servant, whom I uphold, my *chosen*, in whom my soul delights." God chose Jesus *because* Jesus was the Son of his good pleasure.

In the story of the transfiguration on the mount, one Gospel writer quotes the Father as follows: "This is my Son, my *Chosen One*" (Luke 9:35); another Gospel writer says, "This is my *beloved* Son, with whom I am well pleased; listen to him" (Matt. 17:5; cf. Mark 9:7). The chosen One is chosen because he is the beloved One — the beloved One is beloved because he is the chosen One. Psalm 45:7 (cf. Heb. 1:9) says of the King-Messiah (cf. vv. 1, 5–6): "[Y]ou have loved righteousness and hated wickedness. *Therefore* God, your God, has anointed you with the oil of gladness beyond your companions."[37] Jesus was chosen not only because of his eternal position as the Son with the Father but also because, as the Messiah on earth, he loved righteousness and hated wickedness. The Father delighted in his eternal Son — and he delighted in Jesus, the perfect Man on earth.

4.5.5 Elect Believers

The situation of believers is similar to that of Christ. By God's sovereign decision he "chose us [i.e., believers] in him [i.e., Christ] before the foundation of the world, that we should be holy and blameless before him" (Eph. 1:4). By God's sov-

---

37. Ps. 45 does not identify the "companions," but the New Testament letter of Heb. identifies them as Jesus-believers (compare Gk. *metochoi* in 1:9 with 3:14). In the anointing, Christ occupies the first place among them, but in Isa. 61:3 the "oil of gladness" is also for those who have gone through mourning and oppression; see Ouweneel (1982, 1.28).

ereign grace he justifies wicked humans (Rom. 4:5). However, when these *had been* justified, he viewed them in Christ, clothed with Christ, as "conformed to the image of his Son" (Rom. 8:29), with the "new self . . . renewed in knowledge after the image of its creator" (Col. 3:10), and thus "favored" in the Beloved (Eph. 1:6 HCSB). To the extent that believers live according to this image, God's good pleasure rests on them as well, not only because of God's eternal election but also because of their Christian walk. They surely need God's grace for such a walk, but at the same time this walk is entirely their own responsibility.

When Christ was baptized, God anointed him with the power of the Holy Spirit because he could say of him, "This is my beloved Son, with whom I am well pleased" (Matt. 3:17; cf. Mark 1:11; Luke 3:22). God anoints his children with the power of the Spirit because he can say of them as well, "These are my beloved sons and daughters, with whom I am well pleased." God says, "The one who conquers will have this heritage, and [*as a consequence*] I will be his God and he will be my son" (Rev. 21:7). And elsewhere, "'Therefore go out from their midst, and be separate from them,' says the Lord, 'and touch no unclean thing; then [*as a consequence*] I will welcome you, and I will be a father to you, and you shall be sons and daughters to me,' says the Lord Almighty" (2 Cor. 6:17-18).

These sons and daughters themselves will always say — and rightly so — that only God's grace causes any divine pleasure to rest on them. A practical example of this relationship between divine grace and human responsibility is found in Genesis 6:8-9, "Noah found favor in the eyes of the LORD. . . . Noah was a righteous man, blameless in his generation. Noah walked with God." It is useless to ask whether Noah found favor in God's eyes because he was righteous, or whether he was righteous because he had found favor in God's eyes. In a sense, both statements are true, like two sides of the same coin.

Sometimes the Lord disciplines his children *because* he delights in them: "[T]he LORD reproves him whom he loves, as a father the son in whom he delights" (Prov. 3:12). He disciplines them because not everything in them is a delight for him (Heb. 12:6, where Prov. 3:12 is quoted). This shows how strongly they still depend on grace. However, it is equally sure that the Lord of the servants in whom the anointing has become visible will be able to say (as we hear in the parable), "Well done, good and faithful servant. You have been faithful over a little; I will set you over much. Enter into the joy of your master" (Matt. 25:21, 23). This is just as true as this other saying of Jesus (Luke 17:10): "[W]hen you have done all that you were commanded, say, 'We are unworthy servants; we have only done what was our duty.'"

In summary, we notice that anointing implies consecration and dedication. First, it is the anointed person who henceforth will always be there for God, just as, second, God in the anointing testifies that he will always be there for the anointed person. The former is consecration (of the person to God), the latter is blessing (from God to the person). "[Y]our name is oil poured out" (Song 1:3), and: "So shall they put my name upon the people of Israel, and I will bless them" (Num. 6:27). At the anointing, God's name, which involves glory and power, is placed upon the person who is anointed, who is consecrated to the Lord, and in turn, is blessed by the Lord.

4.6   Wine[38]
4.6.1   "Drunk" with the Spirit

There is a contrast between "do not get drunk with wine, for that is debauchery" and "be filled with the Spirit" (Eph. 5:18).[39] We find a similar contrast with John the Baptist, who was not to drink wine or strong drink, but would be filled

---
38. Cf. Ouweneel (2005a, 280, 327, 334, 343).
39. The Gk. phrase *en pneumati* might be read here as "in the spirit" (YLT), but in 2:33, 3:5, and 6:18, the same expression refers to the Holy Spirit. The Gk. construction *plēroō* with *en* is unusual but not unknown; we find it also in Col. 4:12 (Received Text; see KJV).

with the Holy Spirit (Luke 1:15).[40] Such contrasts make sense only if there is also a certain parallelism: Do not drench your mind with the spirit[41] of the alcohol, but drench your mind with the Holy Spirit. Or even: do not get drunk with wine, but get drunk with the Spirit. The contrast is that with wine comes debauchery, which makes one lose self-control, whereas self-control is the very fruit of the Spirit (Gal. 5:22; cf. 1 Cor. 14:32, "the spirits of prophets are subject to prophets").[42] Yet, Paul apparently sees a genuine similarity. Acts 2:13 shows that those who are *filled* with the Spirit, speaking in tongues and worshiping God, may make the impression on bystanders of being "*filled* with new wine." To the superficial observer, there may be little difference between the ecstatic intoxication with wine, and the ecstatic intoxication with the Holy Spirit (see §11.1.2).

Some Old Testament persons, who were very close to God, sometimes made the impression of being drunk:

> As she [i.e., Hannah] continued praying before the LORD, Eli observed her mouth. Hannah was speaking in her heart; only her lips moved, and her voice was not heard. Therefore Eli took her to be a drunken woman. And Eli said to her, "How long will you go on being drunk? Put your wine away from you." But Hannah answered, "No, my lord, I am a woman troubled in spirit. I have drunk neither wine nor strong drink, but I have been pouring out my soul before the LORD" (1 Sam. 1:12-15).

Jeremiah tells us how the prophetic word in his heart became "as it were a burning fire shut up in my bones, and I am weary with holding it in, and I cannot" (20:9), and: "My heart is broken within me; all my bones shake; I am like a drunken man, like a man overcome by wine, because of the

---

40. Cf. Liefeld (1984, 827).
41. Cf. expressions such as "spirit of wine," "(methylated) spirit," "spirits" (strong drink).
42. Stott (2006, 54–60).

LORD and because of his holy words" (23:9).[43] Similarly, David said, "My heart became hot within me. As I mused, the fire burned" (Ps. 39:3). These things possibly happened to the judges when the Spirit of the Lord came upon them, filled them, and drove them (see §5.4), and to David, when "the Spirit of the LORD rushed upon" him (1 Sam. 16:13), and to Ezekiel, as God's Spirit lifted him up and fell upon him (3:12, 14; 8:3; 11:1, 5, 24; 43:5).

Today as well, people who are filled with the Spirit sometimes exhibit phenomena that remind us of drunkenness:[44] they are characterized by euphoria, a feeling of heaviness, falling and not being able to stand up, walking waveringly, talking in a mixed tongue. And in particular a Bacchian euphoria, as in Acts 13:52, "[T]he disciples were filled with joy and with the Holy Spirit." Or this: "[B]e filled with the Spirit, *addressing* one another in psalms and hymns and spiritual songs, *singing* and *making melody* to the Lord with your heart, *giving thanks* always and for everything to God the Father in the name of our Lord Jesus Christ." All three gerunds depend on being "filled with the Spirit." That is, those who are filled with the Spirit begin to address others with blessing (cf. Col. 3:16), will sing, make melody, and give thanks.

4.6.2 Historical References

The Egyptian (?) Pseudo-Macarius (late fourth century?) compared the Spirit-filled believer to someone who with euphoric joy sits at a royal banquet, or with someone who is drunk with strong drink, ecstatic and intoxicated by the Spirit, and thus experiences the latter's divine, spiritual mysteries.[45] Also the

---

43. Elihu's words: "I am full of words; the spirit within me constrains me. Behold, my belly is like wine that has no vent; like new wineskins ready to burst" (Job 32:18–19) are also applicable if we would read "Spirit" here (as does GW), which, however, is an unlikely rendering. More acceptable is this rendering: "the wind [Heb. *ruach*] swells my belly"—see Smick (1988, 1003)—so that *ruach* and fermenting wine have the same effect here: they dilate the belly.
44. Wimber and Springer (1986, 227).
45. Burgess (1989, 147).

Assyrian Nestorians, Isaac of Nineveh and Abdisho Hazzaya, spoke of the Spirit-filled person whose mind is intoxicated as by wine. Just as a person who, on a day of sorrow, drinks wine, becomes intoxicated, and forgets to mourn his sorrow (cf. Prov. 31:6), so one who is intoxicated with the love of God forgets all their pain and sadness in this world, and becomes impervious to all their sinful passions.[46]

According to the Armenian Gregory the Illuminator (or Enlightener), the apostles were given to drink from the "cup of the Spirit" (Acts 2; cf. 1 Cor. 12:13, we all "were made to drink of one Spirit"), and became "cupbearers" throughout the world in order to distribute the wine of the Spirit to the spiritually thirsty at the wedding banquet of God's kingdom.[47] Bonaventure described how Francis of Assisi was sometimes drunk with the Spirit, especially when taking part in the Eucharist.[48] The Spanish mystic, John of the Cross, compared the Holy Spirit to a spicy wine of sweet, delicious, and powerful love, with which God sometimes gets the "advanced" souls "drunk" in the sense of Psalm 36:8–9, "They feast [AMP, MEV, NASB: drink their fill] on the abundance of your house, and you give them drink from the river [i.e., the Holy Spirit] of your delights. For with you is the fountain of life."[49]

With regard to God we find this remarkable statement: "Then the Lord awoke as from sleep, as a warrior wakes from the stupor of wine" (Ps. 78:65 NIV). The picture seems to be that of a warrior who imbibes courage, and thus defeats his adversaries (v. 66).

Evangelist Rodney Howard-Browne described his baptism in the Holy Spirit as the fire of God falling suddenly upon him. It began at his head, and went straight to his feet. His power burned in his body, and this lasted for three days. From his inner parts, a river of living water began to flow. He

---

46. Ibid., 98, 105.
47. Burgess (1989, 122).
48. Burgess (1997, 74).
49. Ibid., 196.

began to laugh in an uncontrollable way, then he began to cry, and then to speak in new tongues. He was so drunk with the new wine of the Holy Spirit that he was literally out of his senses.[50]

4.6.3 Quantification

F. F. Bruce commented about Ephesians 5:18: "The antithesis between wine and the Spirit does not suggest that the Spirit is a sort of fluid with which one may be filled, any more than the collocation of baptism in water with baptism in the Spirit suggests that the Spirit is a sort of fluid in which one may be dipped," and in a note he adds: "Or which may be poured out on one, as in Acts 2:17-18, 33; Tit. 3:6 (Gk. *ekcheō*); cf. 1 Cor. 12b (Gk. *potizō*). The verbs which are used primarily in reference to liquids have figurative force when they are used of the Spirit."[51]

This, in my view, is quite a confusing argument. Every reader understands that verbs such as "to fill," "to baptize," and "to pour out," with respect to the Spirit are meant in a metaphorical way. However, they are not *more* "figurative" (or less "literal") than terms such as "person" and "to dwell" with regard to the Spirit. But in one breath Bruce seems to eviscerate this metaphorical meaning. It is of great significance that, in the *metaphorical* sense, the Holy Spirit definitely *is* a "fluid" (a) with which one can be "filled" like a vessel is filled with water, or (b) in which one can be "baptized" (dipped, immersed) like a thing (or a person during water baptism) is immersed in water, or (c) which can be "poured out" on a person like one can pour out a bowl of water on him. These metaphors underscore the fact that we can speak of the Holy Spirit in the *quantitative* sense (see §4.4.2). This is true for all five metaphors discussed so far.

(1) The image of *air* (*breath*, *wind*) (§4.1) illustrates how, in the believer's life, the Spirit can be like the "sound of a low

---

50. Howard-Browne (1994, 94).
51. Bruce (1984, 380n60).

whisper" (1 Kings 19:12; cf. Gen. 3:8), but also a "sound like a mighty rushing wind" (Acts 2:2). The gentle breeze can be a positive metaphor for the calm work of the Spirit under certain circumstances. As a negative metaphor, the breeze stands for a *small* effect of the Spirit. Being "filled" with the Spirit is then stirring up the breeze until it becomes a strong wind, so that even the dead come to life: "Come from the four winds [Heb. *ruchot*], O breath [Heb. *ruach*], and breathe on these slain, that they may live" (Ezek. 37:9).

(2) The image of *water* (§4.2) shows how, in the Christian life, the Spirit can be like a languid brook, but also like an overflowing river (Deut. 8:7; Ps. 78:16; Isa. 30:25; Joel 3:18), or "a spring of water welling up to eternal life" (John 4:14): "'Out of his heart will flow rivers of living water.' Now this he [i.e., Jesus] said about the Spirit, whom those who believed in him were to receive" (7:38–39; see §§6.6.2–6.6.3).

(3) The image of *fire* (§4.3) illustrates how the activity of the Spirit in a believer's life can be as weak as a spark under the ashes (cf. Isa. 1:31), but also as strong as a flaming fire (cf. Ps. 104:4; 105:32; Dan. 7:9; Rev. 1:14–15). It may almost be quenched (1 Thess. 5:19), but also be stirred up, like the smith "blows the fire of coals" (cf. Isa. 54:16); as Paul says, "be on fire in the Spirit" (Rom. 12:11 CEB, ISV).

(4) The image of *oil* (§4.5) shows that there can be a small anointing and an abundant anointing upon a believer. Aaron was anointed so abundantly that the "precious oil" on his head was "running down" on his beard and "on the collar of his robes" (Ps. 133:2). David was figuratively anointed so abundantly that "the Spirit of the LORD rushed upon David from that day forward" (1 Sam. 16:13). Jesus had been anointed with "Holy Spirit and power" to such an extent that he "went about doing good and healing all who were oppressed by the devil, for God was with him" (Acts 10:38). But even in him the anointing was not always manifested to the same degree. In Luke 5:17, the power of the anointing was evidently

present: "[T]he power of the Lord was with him to heal." But in Mark 6:4–6 it was equally evident that, at a certain moment, this power was *not* available: "[H]e could do no mighty work there, except that he laid his hands on a few sick people and healed them. And he marveled because of their unbelief."

(5) The image of *wine* (§4.6) is very illustrative; I read Ephesians 5:18 in such a way that Paulus almost seems to say: become full (or even drunk) with the wine of the Spirit, or let your mind be intoxicated with the Spirit. I have described the Bacchian euphoria of the Spirit with words like exuberant joy, euphoria, ecstasy, being out of one's senses. In opposition to this, there is a *good* soberness (e.g., 1 Cor. 15:34; 1 Thess. 5:6, 8; 2 Tim. 4:5; 1 Pet. 1:13; 4:7; 5:8), but also a *wrong* soberness, which is nothing but spiritual complacence and lethargy. The apostle Paul knew both the ecstasy and the good soberness: "[I]f we are beside ourselves [*exestēmen*, related to *ecstasy*], it is for God; if we are in our right mind, it is for you" (2 Cor. 5:13). But to those who are sober in the wrong sense he says, "Awake, O sleeper, and arise from the dead, and Christ will shine on you" (Eph. 5:14).

4.7 Dove
4.7.1 The Dove On the Lamb

When Jesus was baptized in the Jordan by John the Baptist, the Holy Spirit descended upon him from heaven "in bodily form, like a dove," or even, "in the form of a dove" (Luke 3:22 CEV; cf. Matt. 3:16; Mark 1:10; John 1:32). As Jesus was "coming up" (Gk. *anabainōn*) out of the water, the Spirit was "descending" (Gk. *katabainon*) on him (Mark 1:10). The addition "in bodily form," which we find in Luke only, suggests that a visible dove descended on Jesus.[52] The literal bird represented the Holy Spirit, who *with* the dove descended on Jesus, but then invisibly. Similarly, the "sound of a mighty rushing wind" in Acts 2:2 represented the Holy Spirit, who *with* the sound of the wind came upon the disciples, but then invisibly.

---

52. Cf. Grosheide (1954, 51); Greeven (1968, 68); *contra* Dods (1979, 697).

The dove/Spirit not only descended but "remained [Gk. *emeinen*] on him" (John 1:32), like the Shekhinah had descended on Israel, and remained on (with, among) the people. The same verb (Gk. *menō*) is used in 14:17, ". . . the Spirit of truth, whom the world cannot receive, because it neither sees him nor knows him. You know him, for he dwells [or, remains; Gk. *menei*] with you and will be in you." Although Scripture does not literally say so, we may conclude that the "dove" descends on believers as well, in order to dwell with them. There is a dove sitting on their heads or their shoulders!

In John 1, John the Baptist spoke of Jesus as the Lamb of God (v. 29), so that we have here the interesting figure of the dove descending on the Lamb: "Behold, the Lamb of God . . . I saw the Spirit descend from heaven like a dove."

The event exhibits a remarkable parallel with the first exodus (from Egypt) and the second one (from Babylon).[53] At the former event, Israel was "baptized into Moses in the cloud [i.e., the Shekhinah] and in the sea [i.e., the Red Sea]" (1 Cor. 10:2), after which the Shekhinah accompanied them (on the parallel between the Shekhinah and the Holy Spirit, see §3.8). At that occasion God "put in the midst of [or within (N) KJV] them his Holy Spirit" (Isa. 63:11). After they had washed themselves again at Mount Sinai,[54] the Shekhinah came down on the mountain (Exod. 19:11, 16, 18), and afterward on the tabernacle (40:34-35, 38), and then traveled with them (vv. 36-37; Num. 9:15-23). At the second exodus (from Babylon), Israel was again led out into the wilderness (Isa. 40:3; 43:19-20; 48:20-21; 49:10) with the promise of the Spirit who would descend upon renewed Israel (32:15; 44:3; cf. 63:10-14).[55]

At his baptism, Jesus was called "Son of God" for the first

---

53. Lane (1979, 56).
54. They not only washed their clothes (Exod. 19:10) but they were also sprinkled (24:8), which, to the Jewish mind, is inconceivable without ritual washing of the body (the *mikveh*—see Jemavoth 46b and cf. Shulam (1998, 214)—analogous to baptism; see Ouweneel (2001a, 199).
55. Cf. Buse (1956).

time, just like Israel was at the exodus ("son": Exod. 4:22-23; Deut. 1:31; 8:5; Hos. 11:1-3; "sons": Deut. 14:1; cf. Rom. 9:26 "sonship"), and just like the eschatological Israel (Hos. 1:10 "sons"). The Shekhinah (the Spirit) descended on Jesus, too, and he too was led by the Shekhinah into the wilderness (Mark 1:12), on his way to the "promised land" (cf. Heb. 12:2).

4.7.2 Ancient Parallels

In the ancient Near Eastern world, the dove was considered to be a holy bird; the hovering dove symbolized the warmth of nature.[56] It was the emblem of the goddess of love; some have explained the Greek word for "dove," *peristera*, as a Semitic loanword, supposedly derived from *perach-Ishtar*, "bird of Ishtar" (the Babylonian counterpart of Aphrodite/Venus).[57] Similarly, the Holy Spirit is closely linked with love (Rom. 5:5; 15:30; Col. 1:8, and the parallel between 1 John 4:12, 16, and 13; also see Wisdom 1:6 [GNT], "Wisdom is a spirit that is friendly to people"). Thus, the dove also represents gentleness, a "tender force,"[58] and this is exactly what the Holy Spirit is: both feminine-tender (§3.8) and masculine-strong.

The rabbis sometimes thought of a dove in connection with Genesis 1:2, where the Spirit (Heb. *ruach*, a feminine word) hovered over the waters like a mother dove hovers over its young.[59] As the "dove" hovered over the first creation, the Spirit as a dove descended on Jesus, the beginning (Gk. *archē*) of the (new) creation of God (Rev. 3:14). Philo viewed the dove as an allegory for *Sophia* (see §3.8 on the parallels between Sophia and the Holy Spirit). The Armenian Gregory of Narek compared the Spirit to the spiritual spring, when "the voice of

---

56. Dods (1979, 697).
57. Greeven (1968, 64).
58. Aeppli (1984, 378).
59. Ben Zoma, Chagigah 15a (but see the comment by Edersheim, 1979, 1.287, who suggests that Ben Zoma was under Christian influence); see also Gen. Rabbah 2.4, where the *ruach* of Gen. 1:2 is identified with the spirit of the Messiah because it says, "And the Spirit of the LORD shall rest upon him" (Isa. 11:2); see further, Yalkut on Gen. 1:2.

the turtledove is heard in our land" (Song 2:12). Many other Eastern Orthodox authors have used the dove metaphor;[60] at times they described it as hovering over the waters, at other times as descending as a sign of a new era emerging for humanity and the cosmos.[61] On icons, the dove was and is *the* symbol of the Holy Spirit. In the West, Gregory the Great deduced from the fact that the Spirit is presented both as a dove and as a fire that neither innocence (harmlessness, simplicity; Matt. 10:16) nor fiery fervor alone are pleasant to God; the believer must both be holy *like* the Spirit and exhibit fervor *through* the Spirit.[62]

In the story of Noah's flood, the clean dove (clean in the cultic sense; cf. Lev. 1:14) appears in contrast to the unclean raven (cf. Lev. 11:15; Deut. 14:14), as the Spirit stands over against the flesh: "At the end of forty days Noah . . . sent forth a raven. It went to and fro until the waters were dried up from the earth. Then he sent forth a dove from him, to see if the waters had subsided from the face of the ground. But the dove found no place to set her foot, and she returned to him to the ark, for the waters were still on the face of the whole earth. . . . He waited another seven days, and again he sent forth the dove out of the ark. And the dove came back to him in the evening, and behold, in her mouth was a freshly plucked olive leaf" (Gen. 8:6–11). As the Spirit of God like a dove hovered over the earth at creation, thus he hovered over the earth at the re-creation after the flood; the Midrash suggests an even deeper link between creation and post-flood recreation by claiming that the olive leaf in the dove's beak came from the Garden of Eden.[63] As the dove brought news of a new creation to the ark, so the Holy Spirit proclaims that the world will be renewed, beginning with the baptism of Jesus.[64]

---

60. The Odes of Solomon, Gregory the Illuminator, Ephrem of Syria, Pseudo-Macarius, Narsai, Gregorius of Narek, and Nerses Snorhali.
61. Burgess (1989, 8, 121, 133, 147).
62. Burgess (1997, 15).
63. Cohen (1983, 41).
64. McDonnell (1996); see also Edersheim (1979, 1.284); Hildebrandt (1995,

As the dove represents the Holy Spirit, the unclean raven represents the flesh, which feels at home in a world that lies under judgment, says Frederick Grant. The contrast in Galatians 5:16-25 is between Spirit and flesh. In a world that lies under judgment, the dove can find no rest. Thus, in the Bible, the dove is a type of divine love (cf. Song 1:15; 2:14; 4:1; 5:2, 12; 6:9; for the rabbis, the dove here was Israel; cf. Ezek. 7:16) but also of human sorrow (cf. Ps. 55:4-8; Isa. 38:14; cf. also Matt. 10:16, "innocent as doves"). However, after Noah had sent forth the dove the second time, it returned with the olive leaf—the assurance of fertility and a completed judgment. The third time, by not returning, the dove indirectly led Noah and his family to take possession of the new earth.[65]

4.8 Other Images
4.8.1 Seal[66]

The apostle Paul wrote, "In him [i.e., Christ] you also, when you heard the word of truth, the gospel of your salvation, and believed in him, were sealed with the promised Holy Spirit, who is the guarantee of our inheritance until we acquire possession of it, to the praise of his glory" (Eph. 1:13-14). "[I]t is God who establishes us with you in Christ, and has anointed us, and who has also put his seal on us and given us his Spirit in our hearts as a guarantee" (2 Cor. 1:21-22). By giving the Spirit to believers, God seals or stamps them as his own possession.[67]

The Spirit is called the "Holy Spirit of promise" (NKJV), which might mean the "promised Holy Spirit" (ESV; cf. Acts 2:23), but it could also refer to the promise that has been, or will be, realized in (the power of) the Holy Spirit.[68] In the light of what follows in the text the meaning rather seems to be:

---

38); Keener (1997, 60) refers to the Jewish literature.
65. Grant (1890, 44).
66. See extensively, Lampe (1951), though he follows an early Christian interpretation that identifies the seal with water baptism.
67. Bruce (1984, 265).
68. Wood (1978, 27).

the Holy Spirit that involves a promise. He is a "guarantee," as Paul says elsewhere: "God . . . has given us the Spirit as a guarantee" (2 Cor. 5:5; lit., ". . . given us the guarantee of the Spirit"; MEV).[69] The Spirit is a "guarantee" (or a "pledge," NASB), which soon, when the inheritance will be received and the "purchased possession" will be "redeemed" (NKJV), will be realized, and the promise fulfilled. Thus it is also expressed in Ephesians 4:30, ". . . the Holy Spirit of God, by whom you were sealed for the day of redemption." The Spirit is a "down payment" (ESV alternate reading; cf. "firstfruits of the Spirit," Rom. 8:23), while in the coming glory the complete payment will follow (cf. 2 Cor. 1:22 ERV, "Yes, he put his Spirit in our hearts as the first payment that guarantees all that he will give us").

In the New Testament, the verb "to seal" (Gk. *sphragizō*) has many different meanings, which can all be related to Ephesians 1:13.[70] Thus, sealing is a confirmation of authenticity (John 3:33; 6:26; cf. Gk. *sphragis*, "seal," in Rom. 4:11; 1 Cor. 9:2; 2 Tim. 2:19), and hence also of protection (Rev. 7:2–8; 9:4). It is stamping a thing as one's own possession, or as destined for someone else (Rev. 8:3–8; cf. 2 Tim. 3:4; Rev. 9:4). It involves keeping something safe (Matt. 27:66), or in safe custody (Rev. 20:3). And it involves secrecy as well (Rev. 10:4; 22:10; cf. Gk. *sphragis* in 5:1–2, 5, 9; and 6:1).

The person who, when coming to faith, is "sealed" with the Holy Spirit, thus receives from God first a confirmation of authenticity: "I acknowledge this person as a genuine child of mine." God puts his seal on the person's saving faith, and thus stamps the person as his inalienable child and possession. Therefore, this person is protected once and for all against the powers that wish to snatch the believer out of God's hand (cf. John 10:28–29). Just like the imperial seal on Jesus' tombstone (Matt. 27:66), this seal is a warning: do not touch this sealed object, do not dare to damage or break it, and do not violate

---

69. For the various meanings of "guarantee," see Floor (1982, 148–50).
70. Salmond (1979, 268); Floor (1982, 150–54).

what has been sealed.

Sealing as a means of secrecy is also applicable here: the outsider does recognize the Christian, and may discern the effects of the Spirit dwelling in the believer, but does not know the believer's future: the outsider is unaware of the inheritance awaiting, and of the possession that has already been acquired but must still be redeemed. What has been sealed is known to believers but to the world it is a secret: "Beloved, we are God's children now, and what we will be has not yet appeared [to the world]; but *we* know that when he appears we shall be like him, because we shall see him as he is" (1 John 3:2). God is "making known to us the mystery of his will, according to his purpose, which he set forth in Christ as a plan for the fullness of time, to unite all things in him, things in heaven and things on earth" (Eph. 1:9–10).

4.8.2 Hand and Finger

In Ezekiel, we read several times that "the hand of the LORD" rested on the prophet in a way that reminds us of the activity of the Holy Spirit.[71] The two are mentioned together in 3:14: "The Spirit lifted me up and took me away, and I went in bitterness in the heat of my spirit, the hand of the LORD being strong upon me." In 1 Chronicles 28 there is a clear parallel between the Spirit and the hand of God: David gave Solomon "the plans of all that the Spirit had put in his mind" (v. 12 NIV), and: "All this he [i.e., God] made clear to me [i.e., David] in writing from the hand of the LORD, all the work to be done according to the plan" (v. 19). Apparently, saying that David's plans came from God's Spirit is the same as saying that they came from God's hand.

Quite remarkable is the parallel between Matthew 12:28, "[I]f it is by the *Spirit* of God that I cast out demons, then the kingdom of God has come upon you," and Luke 11:20, "[I]f it is by the *finger* of God that I cast out demons, then the king-

---

71. Ezek. 1:3; 3:22; 33:22; 37:1; 40:1. The Spirit mentioned also in 3:12; 8:3; 11:1, 5, 24; 36:27; 37:14; 39:29; and 43:5.

dom of God has come upon you." Apparently, the "finger of God" represents the Holy Spirit. The same metaphor is found with the two stone tablets of the law. On these tablets the Decalogue had been written "with the finger of God" (Exod. 31:18; Deut. 9:10); Paul draws a parallel with the "fleshy tables of the heart," on which we read an "epistle of Christ," written "with the Spirit of the living God" (2 Cor. 3:3 KJV). Again, the finger represents the Spirit.

This sheds light on Exodus 8:19, where the magicians of Egypt say, "This is the finger of God." Gnats had come forth from inanimate matter; the magic skill of these savants was insufficient for reproducing this phenomenon. The finger of God is the power of God's Spirit: The statement, "When I look at your heavens, the work of your fingers, the moon and the stars, which you have set in place . . . " (Ps. 8:3) is materially identical to the statement, "By the word of the LORD the heavens were made, and by the breath [Heb. *ruach*] of his mouth all their host" (Ps. 33:6; cf. 104:30).[72] Here again, the image of a hand can also refer to God's power (Josh. 4:24), particularly in his judgment (Exod. 9:3; 16:3; Deut. 2:15; Judg. 2:15; 1 Sam. 5:6, 9; cf. also Dan. 5:5), but also in his blessings (Num. 11:23; 2 Sam. 24:14; 1 Kings 18:46; Ps. 109:27).[73]

The link with the Holy Spirit is very clear in 2 Kings 3:15, where the "hand of the LORD" came upon Elisha, so that he began to prophesy. There is no material difference between this hand and the Spirit of God, who stirs the prophets to prophesying (2 Pet. 1:21; cf. 1 Kings 18:46; Isa. 8:11; Jer. 15:17). Remarkable also is Acts 4, where God's hand makes decisions (v. 28), and where he stretches out his hand to heal (v. 30). Again, this is no different from God acting through his Holy Spirit.[74]

Severus of Antioch and others described the Spirit as the

---

72. Cf. Kaiser (1990, 354).
73. The finger as a sign of God's creative power is marvelously depicted in Michelangelo's creation of Adam in the Sistene Chapel at the Vatican.
74. Hildebrandt (1995, 146–48, 182, 189–90, 207).

non-corporal finger of God. In the view of these Eastern Orthodox writers, it is this finger that moves over water: the primordial waters of Genesis 1, the waters of the Red Sea, the watery womb of Mary, the waters of baptism, or the "sea of glass" in Revelation 4:6 and 15:2.[75] Irenaeus called the Spirit together with the Son the "two hands" with which God creates and perfects (§§5.2.2, 5.8.1).[76] They constitute a double mission, in which the one is not greater than the other: on the one hand, the Son as a Man on earth did nothing apart from the power of the Spirit; on the other hand, the glorified Son sent the Spirit to the earth. On the one hand, the humiliated Jesus in the Gospels is, so to speak, a gift of the Spirit to God's people; on the other hand, in the book of Acts the Spirit is a gift from the glorified Jesus to God's people.

4.8.3 Ear, Pearl, Key, Milk, Honey

Christian literature contains quite a few other metaphors for the Holy Spirit, which only indirectly relate to biblical metaphors. Thus, the Syrian church father Ephrem compared the Father to the root, the Son to the stem, and the Spirit to the ear of grain (cf. Gal. 6:8, "the one who sows to the Spirit will from the Spirit reap eternal life"), or he spoke of the root, the tree, and the fruit, respectively (cf. Gal. 5:22).[77]

According to ancient mythology, a pearl is produced by a flash of lightning hitting an oyster in the sea. According to Ephrem, the Holy Spirit is the lightning flash that hits the "oyster," and in this way produces Christ, the "pearl of great value" of Matthew 13:46. Pearl divers undergo the same process as people who are to be baptized: they remove their clothes, are oiled ("anointed"), and dive into the water to find this pearl. Ephrem extended the imagery to the extent that for him, even the piercing of the pearl, to be worn in a necklace,

---

75. Burgess (1989, 7, 207).
76. Adv. Haer. 4.20.1.
77. Burgess (1989, 6, 179).

refers to the sufferings of Christ.[78]

According to the late fourth-century Egyptian Ammonas, the "pearl of great value" is not Christ but the Holy Spirit himself, who comes to adorn the house of faithful believers. In Ammonas' view, the "treasure hidden in a field, which a man found and covered up" (v. 44) is the Holy Spirit as well, because of the joy that he produces (cf. Acts 13:52; Rom. 14:17; Gal. 5:22; 1 Thess. 1:6).[79]

Symeon the New Theologian compared the Holy Spirit to a key: if Jesus is the door (John 10:7, 9), then the Spirit is the key to this door, and the Father's house is the dwelling place to which the door gives entrance.[80] "No one comes to the Father except through me" (John 14:6) — but no one comes to Jesus except through the Holy Spirit (cf. John 3:5; Titus 3:5).

In addition to the common images of wind or breath, water, fire and wine, John of Ávila also referred to the Holy Spirit with the images of milk and honey, the well-known metaphors describing the riches of the promised land (Exod. 3:8, 17). Milk refers to the mother metaphor: the Holy Spirit nourishes the soul like a mother nourishes her baby (cf. 1 Pet. 2:2, and §3.8). Honey refers to the sweetness of life in the Spirit (in Ps. 19:10 and 119:103 honey is an image of the Torah, which, however, is made alive by the Spirit; see §5.8). By comparison to this sweetness, according to John of Ávila, the perfume of the Spirit makes all other perfumes seem more bitter than gall.[81]

---

78. Burgess (1989, 181–82).
79. Ibid., 153–54.
80. Congar (1997, 1.97; 3.4).
81. Burgess (1997, 185).

Chapter 5
The Earlier Work of the Spirit

> ... *But they rebelled*
> *and grieved his Holy Spirit;*
> *therefore he turned to be their enemy,*
> *and himself fought against them....*
> *Where is he who brought them up out of the sea*
> *with the shepherds of his flock?*
> *Where is he who put in the midst of them his Holy Spirit,*
> *who caused his glorious arm to go at the right hand of Moses?*
>
> Isaiah 63:10–12

Summary: *In the Old Testament era, the Holy Spirit was active at creation, before and after the Flood, and at the exodus from Egypt; during these three episodes the Spirit was opposing the powers of chaos (Heb. tohu wabohu, tehom). The Spirit journeyed with Israel through the wilderness, was active in the days of the judges, of Samuel, in the lives of Israel's and Judah's kings (especially Saul, David, and Solomon must be mentioned), and of the prophets, with the Messiah-Prophet as the highlight. The Spirit is mentioned prominently in connection with the First Temple, but minimally with the*

Second Temple. Word and Spirit are closely related (although it is not always clear whether we should read Spirit or spirit). Finally, the question is dealt with whether the Holy Spirit dwelt in Old Testament believers the same way he dwells in New Testament believers. The clear differences between the two situations are identified.

5.1 Creation
5.1.1 Tohu Wabohu

IN §3.4.2 WE HAVE SEEN that all three persons within the Godhead are involved in all the works that God performs toward the external world (Lat. *opera ad extra*). This is different from God's works within the Trinity, such as: the Father generates the Son, the Father sends the Son, and Father and Son send the Spirit. Let us now consider the Holy Spirit's role in God's external works in the Old Testament. We will see that the Holy Spirit is closely involved in the work of creation as well as in that of re-creation, and that this work forms a model for *all* of the Spirit's life-giving work. This is presented, for example, in his work described in Ezekiel 36 (the work of regeneration) and 37 (the work of renewal and restoration).

In this chapter, we will consider the great biblical truths that God desires to dwell with humans, that he does so through the Spirit, and that his coming to dwell is always connected with conflict (see, e.g., Gen. 1:1–3 and Exod. 15:1–18). From Genesis 1:2 until the consummation of time, the Holy Spirit performs his life-giving and renewing work amid warfare against the hostile powers. On a small scale, this warfare occurs in the believer's life as well (Rom. 8:4–26; Gal. 5:13–26; Eph. 6:12).

Already on the first page of the Bible, we encounter the Holy Spirit as the One who brings life and order into every form of "waste and emptiness" (Heb. *tohu wabohu*), in all dryness, dullness, and darkness. This is his nature: "It is the Spirit who gives life" (John 6:63). In 1 Corinthians 15:45 the risen Lord, as the "last Adam," is a "life-giving s/Spirit." In Ezekiel 37, the Spirit awakens dry bones to life, and in Romans 8:11 he gives life to mortal bodies. Jeremiah describes the condition of Israel in his day with the same words appearing in Genesis 1:2: "I looked on the earth, and behold, it was without form and void [Heb. *tohu wabohu*]; and to the heavens, and they had no light" (Gen. 4:23). Israel needed the same activity as the entire earth in Genesis 1: the life and the light of God's Spirit.

The Spirit of God hovering over the waters of the primordial flood was obviously involved in the work of creation (Gen. 1:2). I have argued before (§4.1.2) that I prefer the rendering "Spirit" to "wind." The verse expresses God's care for the created world, a topic that must now be elaborated. This care is compared to that of the mother bird—some have thought of the dove (§4.7.2)—"hovering" over its young (cf. Deut. 32:11). Or the Spirit was hovering over the globe like an egg that must be incubated and hatched, so that order would sprout from chaos (cf. "brooding" instead of "hovering" in TLB; cf. AMP; MSG: "God's Spirit brooded like a bird above the watery abyss").

The parallel with Deuteronomy 32 is all the more striking, because in verse 10 we find the same word we found in Genesis 1:2 ("waste and emptiness", Heb. *tohu wabohu*): ". . . the LORD's portion is his people, Jacob his allotted heritage. He found him in a desert land, and in the howling waste [*tohu*] of the wilderness; he encircled him, he cared for him, he kept him as the apple of his eye." Just as God's Spirit was with the earth as it was still waste, so God's Spirit was with his people while they still wandered in the waste of the wilderness.[1] And if Genesis 1:2 reminds us of a bird hovering over the waste places, this reminds us of Israel being taken out of Egypt and carried by God through the wilderness: "You yourselves have seen what I did to the Egyptians, and how I bore you on eagles' wings and brought you to myself" (Exod. 19:4).

---

1. Neve (1972, 70); Hildebrandt (1995, 31, 36).

Kline argued that Psalm 104 ties in with Genesis 1:2, presenting God as making the clouds his chariot and riding on the wings of the wind (Heb. *ruach*).² The medieval Jewish scholar Rashi (acronym for Rabbi Shlomo Itzhaki) saw in Genesis 1:2 the Throne of Glory, hanging in the air, hovering over the waters, supported by God's breath (Heb. *ruach*), as a dove hovering over its nest.³ In the deuterocanonical book of Jesus Sirach, something similar is said about wisdom: "I made my home in highest heaven, my throne on a pillar of cloud" (Sirach 24:4 GNT).

5.1.2 Creator Spirit

The Holy Spirit's involvement in the work of creation is mentioned several times, in various ways. With reference to Genesis 1, Psalm 33:6 says, "By the word of the LORD the heavens were made, and by the breath [or Spirit; Heb. *ruach*] of his mouth all their host." This connection between Word and Spirit (see more extensively in §5.8) is based upon the fact that speaking the word occurs through the breath of the mouth. God's breath (Heb. *ruach*) is not just breathing, it is also speaking, as is expressed, for instance, in the parallelism of Isaiah 34:16, "[T]he mouth of the LORD has commanded, and his breath [Heb. *ruach*] has gathered them." The tenfold "And God said" in Genesis 1 is the breath of his mouth: "For he spoke, and it came to be; he commanded, and it stood firm" (Ps. 33:9; cf. 148:5, "he commanded and they were created").⁴

Psalm 104:30 says of God's creatures, "When you send forth your Spirit, they are created." Elihu says, "The Spirit of God has made me" (Job 33:4). In connection with the work of creation the prophet asks, "Who has directed the Spirit of the LORD, or [as] His counselor has taught Him?" (Isa. 40:13 NKJV). The Spirit did not need any human counsel; he is himself the "Spirit of counsel" (11:2). Or perhaps we should pre-

---

2. Kline (1980, 15).
3. Cohen (1983, 1).
4. Hildebrandt (1995, 42).

fer this rendering: "[W]ho has measured [ESV; ISV: fathomed] the Spirit of the LORD?" The Septuagint renders *ruach* here as *nous* (mind) which is followed by the apostle Paul in Romans 11:34, "For who has known the mind [or thoughts; *nous*] of the Lord, or who has been his counselor?" The same occurs in 1 Corinthians 2:16, "'For who has understood the mind [*nous*] of the Lord so as to instruct him?' But we have the mind [*nous*] of Christ," that is, we are to think, to reason, to deliberate like Christ.

In the deuterocanonical book of Judith, she sings in her final hymn of the Creator-Spirit (the *Creator Spiritus* of the medieval poets): "Let all thy creatures serve thee, for thou didst speak, and they were made [cf. Ps. 33:9]. Thou didst send forth thy Spirit [cf. Ps. 104:30], and it formed them; there is none that can resist thy voice" (Judith 16:14 RSV)."

5.1.3 *Tehom*

Elsewhere I have argued that, in Genesis 1:2, the Holy Spirit appears in contrast to the chaos powers.[5] The "deep" (or "abyss," "world ocean") in this verse is the Hebrew word *tehom* (NABRE: "abyss"; AMP: "primeval ocean") (cf., e.g., Gen. 7:11; 8:2; 49:25; Deut. 33:13; Job 28:14; 38:16, 30; 41:31; Ps. 33:7; 42:8; 104:6; Prov. 8:27-28; Isa. 51:10; Ezek. 26:19; Amos 7:4; Jonah 2:6; Hab. 3:10). Hermann Gunkel linked the Hebrew word *tehom* with the chaos monster Tiamat of Babylonian mythology.[6] This power was thought to be related in turn to the Rahab.[7] Rahab is primarily the name of the chaos angel, the angelic prince of the worldwide, impetuous *tehom* (the word *rahab* means "impetuous"). We meet the Rahab in Job 26:12 (cf. 9:13), where it is parallel with "the sea," and apparently is identified with it. In verse 13 it must recoil before God's breath (*ruach*).

---

5. Ouweneel (2003, 51–55, 221; cf. 327–31); see also Scheepers (1960, 246–60); Kroeze (1962).
6. However, see Gispen (1974, 42–43).
7. On this subject, see Kroeze (1962, 5–10).

In the Talmud and Midrash, this and other verses (see also Ps. 89:10; Isa. 51:9) suggest that Rahab is the name for the angelic prince of the ocean or the *tehom*. More generally, Rahab is the chaos angel, the angelic prince of the original condition of *tohu wabohu*, and especially of the worldwide, impetuous *tehom*. This angelic prince functions under the control of God's power (Job 26:12; cf. 38:8–11); in Genesis 1 this is more specifically the "Spirit of God," whose "hovering" over the earth reminds us of the bird that protects its young against threats (here, the chaos powers). Through the Holy Spirit, the powers must retreat, and the earth is prepared for human habitation: God "formed the earth and made it (he established it; he did not create it empty [*tohu*!], he formed it to be inhabited!)" (Isa. 45:18). The condition of the world began "without form and void" (Heb. *tohu wabohu*), but God did not intend it to remain this way: the Spirit triumphed over the chaos powers, so that humanity could dwell on the earth.

Thus the Bible begins with the greatest powers that threaten God's people: in the material world the chaos, the primeval flood, and the darkness, and in the spiritual world the demonic powers. In this twofold world, the Holy Spirit begins to work, and he continues working until the great final goal is reached, described on the last pages of the Bible. No more chaos, but the perfect order of the New Jerusalem. No more primeval flood, for the sea will be no more (Rev. 21:1; the "sea" represents the chaotic world of the nations; cf. Isa. 8:7; 17:13; Rev. 17:15). No more darkness, "for the glory of God gives it light, and its lamp is the Lamb" (Rev. 21:23). No more demonic powers, for the devil and his angels are cast into the everlasting fire (Matt. 25:41; Rev. 20:10). From Genesis 1 to Revelation 22, the work of redemption is the work of the Spirit, as the close companion of the Father and the Son.

5.2   After Creation
5.2.1   Providential Upholding
The Christian knows the cosmic order revealed by God to be

a *creational* order; that is, an orderly system that is explained by the creational power and will of God (cf. Rev. 4:11). God's creatures obey his word, his ordinances, his appointments, his commands, his decrees, sometimes called his covenant, or covenantal faithfulness (Job 38:33; Ps. 89:2–3, 5, 37; 104; 119:89, 91; 147:15, 18; 148:6, 8; Isa. 45:12; Jer. 31:35; 33:20, 25). These ordinances must never be understood in some deistic sense, that is, as fixed laws that God instituted at creation once and for all, which since then function in an autonomic way, independently of God. Creation is not a giant automaton; it is continually dependent on God's work of *sustenance*: "[I]n him [i.e., Christ] all things hold together" (Col. 1:17). God's "Son . . . upholds the universe by the word of his power" (Heb. 1:2–3).

In the latter passages, the emphasis is on the Second Person in the Godhead. However, the fact that he does nothing apart from the power of the Holy Spirit is expressed in various poetic words, in which the various meanings of "breath" and "Spirit" (*ruach*) are very close: "By his wind [*ruach*] the heavens are cleared" (Job 26:13 NASB), that is, "By his wind/breath the sky clears" (cf. ERV, ISV). "Then the channels of the sea were seen, and the foundations of the world were laid bare at your rebuke, O LORD, at the blast of the breath [*ruach*] of your nostrils" (Ps. 18:15). "When you send forth your Spirit [or breath; *ruach*], they [i.e., God's creatures] are created, and you renew the face of the ground" (Ps. 104:30). God's "breath [*ruach*] is like an overflowing stream that reaches up to the neck, to sift the nations with the sieve of destruction" (Isa. 30:28). "The grass withers, the flower fades when the breath [*ruach*] of the LORD blows on it" (40:7). "So they shall fear the name of the LORD from the west, and his glory from the rising of the sun; for he will come like a rushing stream, which the wind [*ruach*] of the LORD drives" (59:19).

The work of God's providential upholding involves not only inanimate nature, plants, and animals, but also humanity: "[T]here is in humans a Spirit, the breath of the Almighty, that gives them understanding" (Job 32:8 GW). Nothing in the text limits these words to the regenerate. In all cultures, there are "those who by patience in well-doing seek for glory and honor and immortality" (Rom. 2:7). This can be authentic only through the Holy Spirit (and never apart from Christ). God "gives *to all mankind* life and breath and everything. And he made from one man every nation of mankind . . . that they should seek God, and perhaps feel their way toward him and find him. Yet he is actually not far from each one of us, for 'In him we live and move and have our being'; as even some of your own poets[8] have said, 'For we are indeed his offspring'"—and according to Paul this is true for *all* people (Acts 17:25-28). People can truly and sincerely "grope" for God (NKJV) only through the Spirit (see extensively §10.9).

Again we find here the deep connection between Word and Spirit (see more extensively §5.8). Scripture speaks both of God's *Word* as creational ordinances *for*, and of God's *Spirit* acting *in*, cosmic reality (including culture and history; see next §). God reveals *himself*, or rather, something *of* himself, in reality. The creational ordinances, that is, the law-order *for* reality, are parallel with God's Spirit working *in* nature. In Genesis 1, the Spirit of God hovering over the waters, and the voice of God calling forth his creatures, almost coincide. To express it in the terms of Herman Dooyeweerd: God's *Word* is found on the law-side of reality, God's *Spirit* on the subject side (or factual side) of reality.[9]

5.2.2 History and Culture

The work of God's providential upholding in the power of the Holy Spirit pertains both to nature and to human history and culture.[10]

(a) In every wondrous work of *nature* we find God's creational revelation, which is the same as saying: the miraculous power of his Spirit. We behold his majesty in the greatness of

---

8. Cf. Aratus, *Phaenomena* 1-5; Cleanthes, *Hymn to Zeus*.
9. See extensively, Ouweneel (2014).
10. Cf. Berkhof (1986, 68–72).

the celestial bodies (Ps. 19:1-6), and his faithfulness in their constancy (Ps. 89:1-5, 28-29, 36-37). We hear the voice of his Spirit in the thunder (Ps. 29); we feel the power of his Spirit in the mountains and forests, in the vegetative and animal kingdom (Ps. 104, 147).

(b) Concerning *history*, J. Dengerink[11] argued that the "reality event" is constant, though not static or rigid but dynamic. In this dynamic, both the subject side (where the Spirit is at work) and the law-side (where the Word is at work) reach further disclosure. In history, we are dealing with the actions of humans, including all their errors, uncertainties, and wavering. However, history is also the action of God's Spirit, and as such it is a manifestation of God. In the broadest sense of the word, *all* history is redemptive history because all historic events, in some way or another, are related to the realization of God's salvation in history. No matter how difficult it may be to *interpret* history, yet, from the beginning to the end, history is the manifestation of God in that he embeds traces of himself throughout history on its way to the consummation of time, in a manner that is discernible by believers who recognize God's hand (i.e., his Spirit; see §4.8.2) in history.

(c) In a certain sense, God manifests himself in *cultural products* as well: in this painting or that machine we admire God's creational power. We are dealing here with cultural creations that humans have produced through their God-given ability to discover creational laws, and to properly and adequately apply them.[12] These laws belong to the law-side of cultural reality; God's Spirit, who manifests himself also in these cultural creations, belongs to the subject side. Culture is nothing but the creative unfolding of the creational potentialities that God has embedded in nature. No matter how corrupt a culture may be, it always contains good elements, which were not brought about apart from the operation of God's Spirit.[13]

---

11. Dengerink (1986, 226).
12. Smit (1980, 177).
13. The difference between Bezalel, who was "filled with the Spirit of God"

And where corrupt cultural products *conflict* with God's law-word, they can do so only because God's law-word exists and is also valid for such products. God is never responsible for such corruptions, yet they are possible only due to the operation of God's Word and God's permissive Spirit.[14]

Calvin stated that not only natural laws but *all* laws, including (*contra* Descartes) the laws of logic, are valid only as long as they are maintained by the Creator—more concretely, by God's Spirit—because of his covenant, in which Jesus Christ functions as Mediator (cf. Deut. 31:9; Ps. 78:10; 89:2–3, 6, 9, 29–30, 37–38; Jer. 33:20, 25).[15] In this, the deep connection between God's creational work and God's redemptive work is brought to expression (see further in §10.10).

5.3 Flood and Exodus
5.3.1 The Noahic Flood

In Genesis 6:3 God said to himself, "My Spirit shall not abide in [or, strive/contend with[16]] man forever, for he is flesh." The reason for this serious judgment is the "flesh": the incorrigible sinfulness of humanity before the Noahic Flood (6:5), and, incidentally, also after the Flood (8:21).

It is uncertain whether the Holy Spirit is intended in this verse; see, for instance, the CEV: "I won't let my life-giving breath [cf. 2:7] remain in anyone forever." Or the MSG: "I'm not going to breathe life into men and women endlessly." Related to this is the question concerning the last part of the verse: "[H]is days shall be 120 years." Those who interpret *ruach* as the human "breath" usually think of the maximal age of humans:[17] "No one will live for more than one hundred twenty years" (CEV). Some who translate "my Spirit" also think of the

---

    (Exod. 31:2–3; 35:31–32; 36:1–2), and *each* authentic creator of culture is at most one of degree.
14. Troost (1982, 191–92).
15. Quoted by Stafleu (1987, 256).
16. Both renderings are possible; the Hebrew word *yadon* is uncertain; see Hamilton (1990, 266n13); Sailhamer (1990, 78n3).
17. Cf. Gispen (1974, 224); Sailhamer (1990, 77); Hildebrandt (1995, 83–84).

human lifespan: "I will not let my Spirit be troubled by them forever. I will let them live only 120 years" (ERV). Some Targums, along with Jewish scholars (Rashi, Obadiah ben Jacob) and Christian scholars (Augustine, Luther, Calvin), not only saw in the verse the Holy Spirit but also interpreted the last part of the verse as referring to the time (until the Flood) that God afforded humanity to repent.[18]

After the Flood, God made a new beginning with the earth. Thus, it is no wonder that there are many parallels between the creation story and the Flood story. Here are a few that are relevant to our discussion.

(a) We already found the parallel between Genesis 1:2 and 6:3: where the Spirit is "hovering," a check is kept on chaos, and a certain order is maintained. Before the Flood, where the Spirit is withdrawn, the chaos powers are given free rein.[19]

(b) Just as in Genesis 1:2 the Spirit hovered over the primeval waters like a bird (often considered to be the dove, §4.7) in order to set it free from the grip of the chaos powers, so too in 8:8–12 the dove flew out over the primeval waters to find out to what extent the earth had been set free from the grip of the chaos powers (§4.7.2). (Please note that we find the ominous term *tehom* both in Genesis 1:2 and in 7:11.)

(c) Just as the work of creation culminated in God's resting (Gen. 2:2–3), so too he looked with favor upon the post-Flood earth because of the "savor of rest" (Heb. *nihoah*, from *n-w-h*, "to rest")[20] of the burnt offering (Gen. 8:21 GNV, JUB).

(d) Just as, after creation, the first man (Adam) fell in the garden (the Garden of Eden) by abusing the fruit of the tree of the knowledge of good and evil (Gen. 3:6), so too, after the Flood, the first man (Noah) fell in a new garden, a vineyard, by abusing the fruit of the vine (9:21).

(e) In both cases, the consequences of this double fall

---

18. Cohen (1983, 25–26); Hamilton (1990, 269).
19. Hamilton (1990, 267).
20. Noah's name is derived from this as well (cf. Gen. 5:29).

strongly affected the progeny of Adam and Noah, respectively (Gen. 3:15-16; 9:25).

5.3.2 The Exodus from Egypt

Not only the parallels between creation and the Flood, but also those between creation and Israel's exodus from Egypt are strong. Among other things, this is because in both cases the same chaos powers were involved. Consider Psalm 89:9-10, "You rule the raging of the sea; when its waves ruse, you still them. You crushed Rahab like a carcass; you scattered your enemies with your mighty arm." The context seems to point to creation (cf. v. 12) but many believe the text is referring to the exodus. Indeed, besides being, in a general way, the angelic prince of the ocean (cf. Job 26:12; see §5.1.3), Rahab has a special reference to Egypt; sometimes it is even simply a name for Egypt (Ps. 87:4; Isa. 30:7).

In Isaiah 51:9-10, Rahab is specifically the angelic prince of Egypt: "Was it not you [i.e., God] who cut Rahab in pieces, who pierced the dragon [Heb. *tannin*]? Was it not you who dried up the sea, the waters of the great deep [Heb. *tehom*], who made the depths of the sea a way for the redeemed to pass over?" Because Pharaoh represented or even embodied this angelic prince, he himself could be called a "dragon": "Behold, I am against you, Pharaoh king of Egypt, the great dragon [Heb. *tannin*] that lies in the midst of his streams" (Ezek. 29:3). The "dragon," Rahab, refers primarily to the angelic prince of the Red Sea.

In rabbinic literature, this idea of the angelic prince of the Red Sea is well-known. Rabbah ben Mari taught: "... the Holy One, blessed be He, ordered the Prince of the [Red] Sea, 'Spue them forth on to the dry land'.... Straightway he spued them forth on to the dry land, and Israel came and saw them [i.e., the Egyptian army], as it is said, *and Israel saw the Egyptians dead on the sea-shore* [Exod. 14:30]."[21]

Psalm 74:13-14 is another relevant passage: "You divided

---

21. Pesahim 118b; cf. Arakin 15a for a slightly different version.

the sea by your might; you broke the heads of the sea monsters [one Heb. word: *tanninim*] on the waters. You crushed the heads of Leviathan; you gave him as food for the creatures of the wilderness." This is presumably another reference to the exodus from Egypt (cf. vv. 15-16). It may also be that, just like in Psalm 89:10 and Isaiah 51:9-10, the idea here is that the chaos powers of Genesis 1:2, once resisted and subjected by God's Spirit, at the exodus of Israel again raised their monstrous heads in order to be defeated again.

Such a link is also suggested by the Hebrew term *tehomot* (plural of *tehom*) in Exodus 15:4-5, 8: "Pharaoh's chariots and his host he cast into the sea, and his chosen officers were sunk in the Red Sea. The floods [Heb. *tehomot*] covered them; they went down into the depths [*metsolot*] like a stone. . . . At the blast [*ruach*] of your nostrils the waters piled up; the floods [*nozlim*] stood up in a heap; the deeps [*tehomot*] congealed in the heart of the sea." Verses 8 and 10 show that, also at the exodus, it was God's *ruach* that withstood the *tehomot*. This reminds us of Psalm 104: God makes his angels *ruchot* (v. 4), in connection with the *tehom* (v. 6) and the waters that flee at God's rebuke (v. 7). Thinking of the chaos powers, we are reminded of this key verse, in which God says, "[O]n all the gods of Egypt I will execute judgments" (Exod. 12:12). The Egyptians knew the chaos powers as "gods," an expression that God adopts here. But in his own terminology, these "gods" are nothing but monsters (dragons).

5.3.3 The Spirit Journeying with Israel

Just as the Spirit of God hovered over the earth in confrontation with the chaos powers (Gen. 1:2), so too, at the exodus from Egypt, God sent his Holy Spirit to be in the midst of Israel to watch over them and protect them against the powers. This is what we read in Isaiah 63, perhaps the Old Testament passage in which the Holy Spirit is most clearly presented as a person. Some have even discerned trinitarian references in the text: the Father in verse 16 ("you are our Father"), the pre-incarnate Christ in verse 9 ("the angel of his presence"), and the Holy Spirit: "But they rebelled and grieved his Holy Spirit [cf. Eph. 4:30]; therefore he turned to be their enemy, and himself fought against them. Then he remembered the days of old, of Moses and his people. Where is he who brought them up out of the sea with the shepherds of his flock? Where is he who put in the midst of them[22] his Holy Spirit . . . ?" (vv. 10-12).[23]

In the second part of this quotation, the prophet refers back to the exodus. The "shepherds of his [i.e., God's] flock" (v. 11) were Moses and Aaron, who as the shepherds of Israel, together with the entire nation, had been "brought up" by God out of the Red Sea. He gave the people his Holy Spirit, who journeyed with them, in their midst. We are reminded here of the parallel with the Shekhinah (the pillar of the cloud) that found its dwelling place in the midst of Israel (in the tabernacle), and journeyed with them: "For the cloud of the LORD was on the tabernacle by day, and fire was in it by night, in the sight of all the house of Israel throughout all their journeys" (Exod. 40:38; cf. vv. 34-35). God sent his Holy Spirit to be in the midst of Israel, that is *in concreto*, to Moses and the elders of Israel (Num. 11:17, 25-26, 29).

The passage quoted continues as follows: the Lord ". . . who divided the waters [of the Red Sea and of the Jordan] before them to make for himself an everlasting name, who led them through the depths. . . . Like a horse in the desert, they did not stumble. Like livestock that go down into the valley, the Spirit of the LORD gave them rest. So you led your people, to make for yourself a glorious name" (vv. 10-14). Like livestock going down into the valley, Israel went down from the mountains of Moab to the valley of the Jordan. Just as the work of creation and the Flood culminated in rest, so too here: ". . . the Spirit of the LORD gave them rest," as Moses had prophesied: ". . . you go over the Jordan and live in the

---

22. Better than "within him" (KJV), i.e., in the people's hearts; cf. Hag. 2:5, "My Spirit remains in your midst."
23. Young (1972, 482); Bultema (1981, 606–607); Grogan (1986, 342).

land that the LORD your God is giving you to inherit, and . . . he gives you rest from all your enemies around, so that you live in safety" (Deut. 12:10; cf. Josh. 21:44, "And the LORD gave them rest on every side just as he had sworn to their fathers"). Nowhere did this rest come to expression more clearly than in the Sabbaths, the weekly day of rest, which constituted the sign of the Sinaitic covenant (Exod. 31:13, 17; Ezek. 20:12, 20).[24]

5.3.4 The New Garden

The work of creation culminated in the Garden of Eden, and the Flood culminated in Noah's vineyard. Similarly, the exodus involved a garden, in the sense that Israel itself was the "vine brought out of Egypt; you [i.e., the Lord] drove out the nations and planted it. You cleared the ground for it; it took deep root and filled the land" (Ps. 80:8–9; cf. Hos. 10:1, "Israel is a luxuriant vine that yields its fruit"). "You will bring them in and plant them on your own mountain" (Exod. 15:17). Israel is compared to both a vine and a vineyard: Israel was "a vineyard on a very fertile hill. . . . For the vineyard of the LORD of hosts is the house of Israel, and the men of Judah are his pleasant planting," of which the Lord expected good "grapes" (Isa. 5:1–2, 7).

In a certain sense, the Garden of Eden was a sanctuary, in which God dwelt (Gen. 3:8). In this respect, Eden pointed forward to Solomon's temple with its clearly paradisal motifs (see §5.6.2).[25] In the tabernacle, which functioned as God's sanctuary during Israel's wilderness journey, we find paradisal motifs in the golden lampstand with "its base, its stem, its cups, its calyxes, and its flowers" (Exod. 25:31–36; 37:17–22). Just as the entire creation is the work of God's Spirit (§5.1), so too the tabernacle is the work of God's Spirit (Exod. 31:3; 35:31). In addition, after the construction of the tabernacle, the

---

24. See Ouweneel (2017b, Appendix 3).
25. Hildebrandt (1995, 46–48, 71), who also points out (46) that sometimes the entire universe is compared to a tabernacle: the skies are like a tent spread out (Job 9:8; Ps. 104:2; Isa. 40:22).

Spirit's dwelling place was determined precisely: after Exodus 40:34-38, the Holy Spirit, that is, the Shekhinah, dwelt in the tabernacle,[26] namely, between the cherubim on the mercy seat (Exod. 25:22; Num. 7:89; 1 Sam. 4:4; 2 Kings 19:15; Ps. 80:1; 99:1).

Adam fell in the Garden of Eden, and Noah fell in his vineyard. Similarly, Israel, who itself was a "vineyard," fell. This occurred already in the wilderness: "[T]hey rebelled and grieved his Holy Spirit; therefore he turned to be their enemy, and himself fought against them" (Isa. 63:10). Both the creation and the Flood culminated in rest, a rest that was disturbed by the sin of Adam and Noah, respectively. Israel's wilderness journey should have culminated in rest as well. But instead, God complained about his people: "For forty years I loathed that generation and said, 'They are a people who go astray in their heart, and they have not known my ways.' Therefore I swore in my wrath, 'They shall not enter my rest'" (Ps. 95:10-11; cf. Heb. 3:10-11; 4:3, 5).

5.4 The Spirit in the Pentateuch and Judges
5.4.1 The Pentateuch

At many places in the Old Testament, the Holy Spirit is implicitly yet unmistakably involved. How this Spirit rests on people, and works in or through them, is described in various ways. Take, for instance, Genesis 41:38, where Pharaoh says that the Spirit of God was in Joseph (but perhaps he only meant "the spirit of the gods"). Similarly, it is said of Daniel, because of the same prophetic[27] wisdom, that the "spirit of the holy gods" *or* the "Spirit of the holy God" was in him (Dan. 4:8-9, 18; 5:11, 14). It is not a good idea to translate the verb here as "dwells" (ISV in 5:11), since this specific term is reserved for the New Testament era (see §5.9).

---

26. Hildebrandt (1995, 75-76).
27. It is amazing that the rabbis never acknowledged Daniel as a prophet (his book belongs to the *Ketubim*, not to the *Nabiim*); Jesus, though, called him the "prophet Daniel" (Matt. 24:15).

About Bezalel God said to Moses, "I have filled him with the Spirit of God, with ability and intelligence, with knowledge and all craftsmanship, to devise artistic designs, to work in gold, silver, and bronze, in cutting stones for setting, and in carving wood, to work in every craft" (Exod. 31:2-5; cf. 35:31). In this way, this man received the capacity to perform his work on the tabernacle and its utensils. Some see a similar connection between Zechariah 4:6 ("Not by might, nor by power, but by my Spirit") and the construction of the Second Temple (see §5.7.2).[28] The prophet Micah uses the term "filled": "But as for me, I am filled with power, with the Spirit of the Lord, and with justice and might, to declare to Jacob his transgression and to Israel his sin" (Micah 3:8). In the New Testament, we will find the phrases "filled with the Spirit" (Luke 1:15, 41, 67; Acts 2:4; 4:8, 31; 5:3; 9:17; 13:9; Eph. 5:18) and "full of the Spirit" (Luke 4:1; Acts 6:3; 6:5; 7:55; 11:24) several times.

5.4.2 The Book of Judges

The expression used for the judge Gideon is rather unusual: "[T]he Spirit of the LORD clothed Gideon" (Judg. 6:34), that is, the Spirit placed himself as a coat on Gideon, and thus empowered him (cf. AMP, NABRE).[29] However, even more unusual is this possible reading: "[T]he Spirit of the LORD clothed himself in Gideon" (JUB), that is, the Spirit put Gideon on like a man puts on a coat, or a soldier puts on a uniform. Thus, Gideon became an instrument used by the Spirit.[30] As Soltau put it, the Spirit turned Gideon into a coat in order to realize through him God's purposes. As a man wears his coat wherever he goes, so the Spirit carried Gideon along and made him invincible and triumphant.[31] We find the same expression for Amasai: it is either "the Spirit clothed Amasai," *or*, "the Spirit clothed himself in Amasai" (JUB) (1 Chron. 12:18). Similarly, "the Spirit of God clothed Zechariah," or "the Spirit of God

---

28. Cohen (1980, 284); Erickson (1983, 867); Hildebrandt (1995, 101).
29. Cf. Hildebrandt (1995, 115).
30. Goslinga (1951, 130).
31. Soltau (n.d., 65).

clothed himself in Zechariah" (JUB) (2 Chron. 24:20). Either the Spirit was a coat on these people, or they themselves formed a coat for the Spirit!

It is in many different ways that the Holy Spirit comes over God's servants, sometimes with strength, almost violence (cf. "the Spirit of the LORD *fell* upon me," Ezek. 11:5), as in the case of Samson: "[T]he Spirit of the LORD began to stir [or rouse, excite] him," or "rushed upon [or, took control of] him" (Judg. 13:25; 14:6, 19; 15:14), and the future kings Saul (1 Sam. 10:6, 10; 11:6;[32] 19:23 [see below]; cf. 16:14) and David (16:13).

Sometimes the Spirit comes in a more quiet way, as in the case of the judge Othniel: "The Spirit of the LORD came [or was,[33] Heb. *wattehi*] upon him" (Judg. 3:10). Here, the Targum reads the "spirit of prophecy," which Cohen explains as follows: "It signifies a sudden and powerful emanation from God which took possession of the individual and endowed him with gifts transcending the ordinary limits of human power."[34] The expression of the Spirit "coming" (or "being") upon God's servant is found many times; I mention Jephthah (Judg. 11:29), Azariah (2 Chron. 15:1), and Jahaziel (20:14); also compare Balaam (Num. 24:2), Simeon (Luke 2:25, 27), and the messengers of Saul (1 Sam. 19:20; see below).

During the period before Israel had kings, and the elders and priests provided political and religious leadership, the judges were in fact charismatic leaders (i.e., leaders by force of character rather than by appointment).[35] They were sent by God, and driven by their faith: "And what more shall I

---

32. Goldmann (1983, 60) interprets this as the God-given determination and mental power of Saul, not as the Holy Spirit.
33. Here the ESV has the rendering "was," but in many similar passages where it renders this verb as "came," it occasionally offers in a marginal note the alternative rendering of "was."
34. Cohen (1982, 178; cf. 214 [an "accession of overwhelming vigour and courage"], 268 [an "irresistible impulse accompanied by unusual physical strength"]).
35. Hildebrandt (1995, 112–13); very extensively, (from a pneumatologiccal viewpoint): Welker (1992, 52–74).

say? For time would fail me to tell of Gideon, Barak, Samson, Jephthah, of David and Samuel and the prophets—who through faith conquered kingdoms, enforced justice, obtained promises, stopped the mouths of lions, . . ." (Heb. 11:32–38).

Their being driven by God's Spirit showed that their mission was of divine origin. This is all the more remarkable when we consider Gideon's original fear, Jephthah's rash vow, and especially (to use a Pauline phrase) Samson's carnal rage. While on his way to a bride who would never enjoy the approval of the Lord, he met a lion, and "the Spirit of the LORD rushed upon him, and although he had nothing in his hand, he tore the lion in pieces as one tears a young goat" (Judg. 14:6). He was too friendly with the Philistines—but when they began to bother him, "the Spirit of the LORD rushed upon him," again (v. 19). His strength seemed to be purely physical (he has always been depicted as a bodybuilder), but in fact his was a Spirit-given strength that ultimately surpassed the physical, which remained with him in spite of his sinful actions. To use New Testament terms, his struggle was the typical Spirit-versus-flesh struggle that was later described in Romans 8 and Galatians 5. God's Spirit did not give up on him, no matter how many un-Spirit-like motives often drove him.

5.5 The Prophets
5.5.1 Samuel and David

After the judges came the prophets. Samuel was the last judge (1 Sam. 7:6, 15), if we ignore his sons (8:1) and King Saul, who was demanded by the people to "judge" Israel (v. 6). Samuel was also the first of a new series of prophets; as Paul said, God gave Israel "judges until Samuel the prophet" (Acts 13:30). Indeed, "all Israel from Dan to Beersheba knew that Samuel was established as a prophet of the LORD" (1 Sam. 3:20; cf. 9:6–9; 2 Chron. 35:18; Acts 3:24).

From Samuel's career stem the most remarkable Old Testament examples of the Spirit working in people, namely, in connection with Saul.[36] Thus we read:

> "After that you [i.e., Saul] shall come to Gibeath-elohim. . . . And there, as soon as you come to the city, you will meet a group of prophets coming down from the high place with harp, tambourine, flute, and lyre before them, prophesying. Then the Spirit of the LORD will rush upon you, and you will prophesy with them and be turned into another man." . . . When he turned his back to leave Samuel, God gave him another heart.[37] And all these signs came to pass that day. When they came to Gibeah, behold, a group of prophets met him, and the Spirit of God rushed upon him, and he prophesied among them" (1 Sam. 10:5-6, 9-10).

The verb "to prophesy" has been well rendered as "being caught up in a prophetic frenzy" (CEB, NRSV) or "prophetic ecstasy" (NABRE, VOICE). (Compare "trance" in Acts 10:10, 11:5, and 22:17, and "Spirit-inspired trance" in Rev. 1:10 CEB.)

1 Samuel 19:20-24 is especially interesting:

> Saul sent messengers to take David, and when they saw the company of the prophets prophesying, and Samuel standing as head over them, the Spirit of God came upon the messengers of Saul, and they also prophesied. When it was told Saul, he sent other messengers, and they also prophesied. And Saul sent messengers again the third time, and they also prophesied. Then he himself went to Ramah and came to the great well that is in Secu. And he asked, "Where are Samuel and David?" And one said, "Behold, they are at Naioth in Ramah." And he went there to Naioth in Ramah. And the Spirit of God came upon him also, and as he went he prophesied until he came to Naioth in Ramah. And he too stripped off his clothes, and he too prophe-

---

36. Ashley (1993, 213-14); Welker (1992, 74-80). Goslinga (1968, 226; cf. 360-62) says of these passages: "What is at stake in [1 Sam.] 10 and 19 . . . has its own distinct character, goes out from Jahweh, and is worked by his Spirit."
37. Rashi made a distinction between the other "heart" in 1 Sam. 10:9 (i.e., the spirit of royal strength) and the "spirit of prophecy" in v. 10; see Goldman (1983, 54).

sied before Samuel and lay naked all that day and all that night. Thus it is said, "Is Saul also among the prophets?"

1 Samuel 10 deals with the beginning of Saul's kingship, but in chapter 19 much has changed: God's Spirit has come upon David, and has departed from Saul (16:13-16). Saul and his men are prevented from taking David captive because, once more, God's Spirit comes upon them. As beautiful and full of promises as Saul's ecstatic behavior was in chapter 10, so sad and pitiful is it in chapter 19.[38] Already before he encountered the company of prophets, the Spirit rushed upon him (19:23); because he rebelled against God's Spirit he had to experience the latter's influence even more strongly than his servants did.[39]

Concerning Saul's successor, David, we read so many better things. In addition to the references to the Spirit's work within him (see §5.6.1), I mention 1 Chronicles 28:11-12 (NKJV): "Then David gave Solomon his son . . . the plans for all that he had by the Spirit, of the courts of the house of the LORD. . . ." The plans for the temple, which were to be implemented by his son Solomon, had been revealed to David by the Spirit of God (although I do realize that others rather translate: "the plan of all that he had in mind for the courts of the house of the LORD").

5.5.2 Messiah-Prophet

Of special interest are the prophecies concerning the Holy Spirit about the coming Messiah (see §6.1): "There shall come forth a shoot from the stump of Jesse, and a branch from his roots shall bear fruit. And the Spirit of the LORD shall rest upon him, the Spirit of wisdom and understanding, the Spirit of counsel and might, the Spirit of knowledge and the fear of the LORD" (Isa. 11:1-2). "Behold my servant, whom I uphold, my chosen, in whom my soul delights; I have put my Spirit upon him; he will bring forth justice to the nations" (42:1).

---
38. Hildebrandt (1995, 171-72).
39. Goldman (1983, 120).

"[N]ow the Lord GOD has sent me, and his Spirit" (48:16). "My Spirit that is upon you, and my words that I have put in your mouth, shall not depart out of your mouth, or out of the mouth of your offspring, or out of the mouth of your children's offspring . . . from this time forth and forevermore" (59:21). "The Spirit of the Lord GOD is upon me, because the LORD has anointed me to bring good news to the poor; he has sent me to bind up the brokenhearted, to proclaim liberty to the captives, and the opening of the prison to those who are bound" (61:1).

The Messiah himself is here the prophet, the first among equals (*primus inter pares*) among the prophets; he is one of them, and at the same time the chief one (cf. Deut. 18:15, 18–19; John 1:45; 4:44; 6:14; 7:40; Acts 3:22; 7:37). It was characteristic for the prophets that God spoke through them by means of his Holy Spirit (Neh. 9:30; Zech. 7:12; cf. Isa. 48:16; Ezek. 11:5; cf. false prophets: 1 Kings 22:24; 2 Chron. 18:23), and this was true of Jesus as well. See particularly how he applied Isaiah 61:1 to himself; after having quoted this verse, he told the people of Nazareth, "Today this Scripture has been fulfilled in your hearing" (Luke 4:16–21).

At the same time, there is a contrast: "Long ago, at many times and in many ways, God spoke to our fathers by the prophets, but in these last days he has spoken to us by his Son" (Heb. 1:1–2). However, the word "but" in the ESV suggests *too much* contrast; compare the NKJV: "God, who at various times and in various ways spoke in time past to the fathers by the prophets, has in these last days spoken to us by [His] Son." Here we have a culmination rather than a contrast: in these last days the best prophet of all has come: God's own Son.

In the context of the Spirit's operating through the prophets it is interesting to consider Wisdom 7:27 (GNT): "Even though Wisdom acts alone, she can do anything. She makes everything new, although she herself never changes. From generation to generation she enters the souls of holy people, and makes them God's friends and prophets."[40] Here wisdom is closely connected with the Holy Spirit (cf. §§3.8 and 5.8); so in 9:17 (GNT) we read, "No one has ever learned your will, unless you first gave him Wisdom, and sent your holy spirit down to him." In this book, Sophia/Spirit is like love itself, which comes to live in the "souls of holy people," and makes them "friends of God," such as were Abraham (2 Chron. 20:7; Isa. 41:8; James 2:23) and Moses (Exod. 33:11). And it makes them "prophets," as, in addition to Abraham (Gen. 20:7; Ps. 105:9–15) and Moses (Deut. 18:15; 34:10), were so many in the Old Testament. Incidentally, in ancient and modern languages the words for "friend" and "love" are often related etymologically,[41] so that the Sophia/Spirit here also is the love of God, poured out into holy souls (cf. Rom. 5:5).

No book in the Old Testament mentions the Holy Spirit more often than Ezekiel. To give a few examples: "[A]s he spoke to me, the Spirit entered into me and set me on my feet" (2:2; cf. 3:24). "Then the Spirit lifted me up, and I heard behind me the voice of a great earthquake" (3:12; cf. v. 14; 8:3; 11:1, 24; 43:5). "And the Spirit of the LORD fell upon me" (11:15). "[H]e brought me out in the Spirit of the LORD" (37:1). Little wonder that Ezekiel has been called the prophet of the Spirit,[42] just as Isaiah has been called the prophet of the Son, and Jeremiah the prophet of the Father.[43]

Because God's Spirit was present in Israel, especially with the leaders, the expression "they rebelled against God's Spirit" (Ps. 106:33 marginal reading) may mean the same as "against God," but also against the Spirit as he worked in Moses.[44] Here, Nehemiah 9:20 must be noted, where we read

---

40. Cf. Johnson (2002, 144, 235).
41. Cf. Heb. *oheb'-h-b*, Greek *philos/phileō*, Lat. *amicus/amo*, Eng. *friend* from root *pri-*, "to love."
42. Block (1989).
43. See www.biblebelievers.com/Bible_Survey.html#ezekiel; the latter point is debatable because God as "my Father" in Jer. (3:4, 19) is the Triune God of Israel, not the eternal Father of the eternal Son.
44. Some think of Moses' "spirit," but "rebellion" is always against God (cf. Isa.

concerning Israel's wilderness journey: "You gave your good Spirit to instruct them and did not withhold your manna from their mouth and gave them water for their thirst." This must have been the Spirit as he worked through Moses (see how manna and the Spirit appear together in Num. 11).

Under the name "good Spirit," the Holy Spirit is mentioned in Psalm 143:10, "Let your good Spirit lead me on level ground!" Only to a limited extent can the expression "*good* Spirit" be placed in opposition to the "*evil* spirit of God" in 1 Samuel 16:15, for in the latter case we are dealing with an "evil spirit *from* the LORD" (v. 14; an evil angel or demon; cf. Judg. 9:23; 1 Kings 22:19-22; 2 Chron. 18:18-21). In New Testament language, the "good Spirit" is God the Spirit, one of the three persons within the Godhead; the "evil spirit" is explicitly distinguished from God (cf. Num. 11:31, a "wind [*ruach*] from the LORD").[45]

5.5.3 Prophetesses

I am unaware of any women in the Old Testament who were explicitly described as being filled with, or led by, the Holy Spirit. But of course, this does not mean that such women did not exist. Deborah was a prophetess and a judge, as well as a singer, and as such she certainly belonged to the category of Spirit-inspired women (Judg. 4:4; 5:1). Miriam, Moses' sister, was called a "prophetess" (Exod. 15:20), and she too was a singer (v. 21). Both her song and Hannah's song (1 Sam. 2:1-10), which is so similar to Mary's song (Luke 1:46-55), were of course Spirit-inspired.

Interestingly, we are told that both Elizabeth (1:41) and Zechariah (1:67) were "filled with the Holy Spirit" as they spoke their prophetic words—but this is not said about Mary (v. 46). I believe that this was not to esteem her words as lower than those of Elizabeth and Zechariah, but rather to empha-

---

63:10–11; Ridderbos [1958, 511]).
45. See more extensively, Noordtzij (1957, 223); Goslinga (1968, 318); Green (1975, 35); and Welker (1992, 84–95).

size that Mary belonged to a Spirit-led class of her own, if I may put it this way. Her song exhibited a Spirit-led character unlike the words of Elizabeth and Zechariah.

If we limit ourselves to the Old Testament for now, other examples of prophetesses besides Miriam and Deborah were Huldah (2 Kings 22:14; 2 Chron. 34:22) and the wife of Isaiah (Isa. 8:3; although perhaps she was called a "prophetess" only because she was the wife of a prophet). (Noadiah in Neh. 6:14 was a false prophetess, just like the New Testament "Jezebel" of Rev. 2:20.)

Of unusual interest is Joel 2:28–29, "And it shall come to pass afterward, that I will pour out my Spirit on all flesh; your sons *and your daughters* shall prophesy, your old men [GNT: old people] shall dream dreams, and your young men [GNT: young people] shall see visions. Even on the male *and female* servants in those days I will pour out my Spirit." Incidentally, the point made in these verses is not so much that, in the last days, not only the men but also the women will receive the outpouring of the Spirit. Rather, the emphasis is on the fact that the Spirit will be poured out not only on kings and priests but on *all* members of God's people, both men and women, old and young.

5.6 The Temple of Solomon
5.6.1 David the Man of God

Just as the Holy Spirit was explicitly associated with Moses (Num. 11:17; Isa. 63:11–12), so too in the new phase beginning with David, the Spirit was with *this* man of God (cf. Deut. 33:1; Ps. 90:1 resp. Neh. 12:24, 36). When confessing his sins, David said, "Cast me not away from your presence, and take not your Holy Spirit from me" (Ps. 51:11). This passage is unusual because of the adjective "holy," which is connected with the Spirit elsewhere in the Old Testament only in Isaiah 63:10–11.

David was anointed with oil, but this anointing was directly coupled with the work of the Spirit: "Then Samuel took the horn of oil and anointed him in the midst of his brothers.

And the Spirit of the LORD rushed upon David from that day forward" (1 Sam. 16:13). David himself implicitly connected his anointing with the activity of the Spirit: "The oracle of David, the son of Jesse, the oracle of the man who was raised on high, the anointed of the God of Jacob, the sweet psalmist of Israel: 'The Spirit of the LORD speaks by me; his word is on my tongue'" (2 Sam. 23:1-2; cf. Acts 1:16; 4:25).

In the Old Testament, there was no question of any indwelling of the *person* of the Spirit, as we know this from the New Testament (e.g., 1 Cor. 3:16; 6:19; see §5.9). David possessed the Spirit as a *force* in view of his royal and prophetic ministry.[46] Therefore the Spirit could indeed depart from him if he were to become unfaithful to his calling.[47] Presumably he had before him the frightening example of Saul, from whom the "Spirit of the LORD" had indeed departed because of his unfaithfulness (1 Sam. 16:14).[48]

Just as the crossing of the Red Sea was crowned with the song of Moses, which described how the blast (*ruach*) of God's nostrils had defeated Israel's enemies (Exod. 15:8, 10), so too David's warfare against his enemies was crowned with *his* song. We find this song in 2 Samuel 22 and the parallel Psalm 18.[49] Again we hear about the breath (*ruach*) of God's nostrils (2 Sam. 22:16; Ps. 18:15); we hear also of God soaring on the "wings of the wind [*ruach*]" (2 Sam. 22:11; Ps. 18:10). These wings remind us of the dove that hovered over the earth at the time of creation and after the Flood, and of the eagle to which God compared himself at the exodus (Exod. 19:4; Deut. 32:11-12).

There are more parallels between Moses' song and David's song. Thus, we find in the former song (Exod. 15:8): "At the blast [*ruach*] of your nostrils the waters piled up; the floods stood up in a heap; the deeps congealed in the heart of the

---

46. Ridderbos (1958, 93).
47. Hildebrandt (1995, 82, 126–27).
48. Wolston (1926, 16).
49. Hildebrandt (1995, 77–80).

sea." This means that the waters of the sea heaped up in such a way that the bed of the sea became visible. In David's song we read (2 Sam. 22:16-17; Ps. 18:15-16): "Then the channels [or, beds] of the sea were seen; the foundations of the world were laid bare, at the rebuke of the LORD, at the blast of the breath [*ruach*] of his nostrils. He sent from on high, he took me; he drew me out of many waters."

5.6.2 Building the Temple

David's son Solomon oversaw the building of the temple that David himself had entirely prepared (1 Chron. 28-29). We call it the First Temple, though we do not ignore the building that had stood near the tabernacle at Shiloh during the time of Eli the priest. This building had room to sleep (1 Sam. 3:3), and had doors (v. 15). It was called the "house of the LORD" (1:7, 24; 3:15), and even the "temple of the LORD" (1:9; 3:3). After the ark had been captured by the Philistines (4:11), this temple was destroyed (Ps. 78:60-61; Jer. 7:12, 14), although perhaps some of it remained (cf. 1 Sam. 14:3). Somewhat later, the tabernacle came to be located at Nob (21:1, 6), and again a little later at Gibeon (1 Chron. 16:39; 21:29; 1 Kings 3:4-5).

Disregarding the first "temple of the LORD," Jewish tradition calls Solomon's temple the First Temple. It stood at the location that God had revealed to David (2 Chron. 3:1; cf. 1 Chron. 21:18-30). Just as the tabernacle had been prepared through the Spirit of God, so too the temple of Solomon: "For the Holy Spirit had given David all these plans" (1 Chron. 28:12 TLB). Even more: as the cloud, the Shekhinah (i.e., the Holy Spirit) had rested upon the tabernacle, it came to rest upon Solomon's temple (1 Kings 8:10-11; 2 Chron. 5:13-14).

The term "rest" is appropriate here; as David said, "I had it in my heart to build a house of rest for the ark of the covenant of the LORD and for the footstool of our God" (1 Chron. 28:2), and as God said, "This is my resting place forever; here I will dwell, for I have desired it" (Ps. 132:14; cf. v. 8). However, here again the rest was not to endure. Just as the first humans had been driven out of Eden, just as the mass of Israel had never entered the rest of the promised land (Ps. 95:11), so too Israel was driven from its country, and its temple was destroyed by the Babylonians. The LORD said of this, "[Y]ou have burdened me [KJV: made me serve] with your sins; you have wearied me with your iniquities" (Isa. 43:24). Where there is servitude, labor, and weariness, there cannot be the rest of the Sabbath. One of the purposes of the Babylonian exile was to give the land of Israel its rest, which it had not enjoyed for centuries because Israel had not kept the Sabbath years (2 Chron. 36:20-21; cf. Lev. 25:1-7).

The First Temple contained true paradisal motifs. What does this mean? The Garden of Eden was paradise (Gen. 2:8; LXX: *paradeisos*); a paradise is a "garden locked . . . , a spring locked . . . an orchard [Heb. *pardes*, related to *paradeisos*] of pomegranates with all choicest fruits, henna with nard" (Song 4:12-13), in short: a garden of (fruit) trees and other precious plants, and of lovely waters. Eden's paradise, too, was characterized by (fruit) trees and rivers (Gen. 2:9-13). Solomon's temple contained carvings in the form of gourds and open flowers, palm trees, pomegranates, lily-work (1 Kings 6:18, 29, 32, 35; 7:18, 20, 22, 24; cf. Ezek. 41:18-20). With the First Temple there is no mention of a river, but rivers are mentioned in the eschatological temples of Ezekiel (47:1-12) and John (Rev. 22:1).[50] However, in a figurative sense, the First Temple did have a river of life: "How precious is your steadfast love, O God! The children of mankind take refuge in the shadow of your wings. They feast on the abundance of your house, and you give them drink from the river of your delights. For with you is the fountain of life; in your light do we see light" (Ps. 36:7-9; cf. Jer. 17:13).

The Talmud tells us that Rabbi Hosea said, "When Solomon built the Sanctuary, he planted therein all sorts of pre-

---

50. Hildebrandt (1995, 47). The Messianic kingdom is described pervasively in terms of paradisal images (see especially Isa. 29:17; 32:15-18; 35:1-2; 41:18-20; 51:3; 55:12-13; cf. also 11:6-10; 65:17-25).

cious golden trees, which brought forth fruit in their season."[51]

As with Adam, Noah, and Israel under Moses, so too David's life experienced a fall. After the sin with the golden calf, Moses entreated: "If your presence will not go with me, do not bring us up from here. For how shall it be known that I have found favor in your sight, I and your people? Is it not in your going with us?" (Exod. 33:15–16). Without the Shekhinah — that is, the Holy Spirit — it was useless for Israel to continue its journey to the promised land. Similarly, David prayed, "Cast me not away from your presence, and take not your Holy Spirit from me" (Ps. 51:11). Without the Holy Spirit, it was useless for David to continue his ministry.[52]

The conclusion is important: the Holy Spirit graciously continued to abide with God's people, after Adam's fall, after Noah's Flood, after Israel's fall at Sinai, and after David's fall. And we may add: he has also graciously continued to abide with the church after so many falls on the part of Christians — including collective falls — throughout the centuries.

5.7 The Second Temple
5.7.1 Haggai

After the Babylonian exile and the return to the land of Israel, the Second Temple was built. Remarkably enough, this time no mention is made of the Shekhinah coming to rest on the temple in the form of the pillar of the cloud. Ezekiel had viewed the Shekhinah withdrawing from the First Temple (Ezek. 9–11), and its return is mentioned (43:1–4) only in connection with the end time — that is, the time of the Messiah. In the Second Temple, there is no mention of paradisal motifs either.

At best we may assume that the prayer of the exiles in Isaiah 51:9–11 was fulfilled:

Awake, awake, put on strength, O arm of the Lord; awake, as

---

51. Yoma 39b; cf. Rabbi Oshaia in Yoma 21b.
52. Hildebrandt (1995, 82).

in days of old, the generations of long ago. Was it not you who cut Rahab in pieces, who pierced the dragon? Was it not you who dried up the sea, the waters of the great deep, who made the depths of the sea a way for the redeemed to pass over? And the ransomed of the LORD shall return [from Babylon] and come to Zion with singing; everlasting joy shall be upon their heads; they shall obtain gladness and joy, and sorrow and sighing shall flee away.

Here we find all the Exodus motifs: once again we encounter a dragon, a battle, a victory, a glorious exodus, and a glorious entrance into the promised land. Isaiah sheds light on various parallels between the exodus from Egypt and the exodus from Babylon (35:6-7; 41:18; 43:16-21; 48:20-21; 51:9-11).

The Second Temple looked quite meager compared with the first one; there was no pillar of the cloud, and no ark of the covenant (cf. Jer. 3:16). Yet, the prophet Haggai spoke boldly of the parallel with the exodus from Egypt, and thus also of the Holy Spirit:

> Who is left among you who saw this house in its former glory [viz., that of the First Temple]? How do you see it now? Is it not as nothing in your eyes?[53] Yet now be strong, O Zerubbabel, declares the LORD. Be strong, O Joshua, son of Jehozadak, the high priest. Be strong, all you people of the land, declares the LORD. Work, for I am with you, declares the LORD of hosts, according to the covenant that I made with you when you came out of Egypt. *My Spirit remains in your midst.* Fear not (Hag. 2:3-5).

The parallel is obvious—though we should not suggest that this Spirit of God "filled" the temple with the presence of God.[54] I prefer to follow the rabbinic tradition, which, in line with the Old Testament, states that the Shekhinah, the

---

53. Cf. Ezra 3:12, "[M]any of the priests and Levites and heads of fathers' houses, old men who had seen the first house, wept with a loud voice when they saw the foundation of this house being laid, though many shouted aloud for joy."
54. *Contra* Hildebrandt (1995, 48–49).

equivalent of the Holy Spirit, was not present in the Second Temple. For instance, Rabbi Samuel ben Inia said

> that in five things the first Sanctuary differed from the second [i.e., these five were in the first, but not in the Second Temple]: in the ark, the ark-cover [i.e., the mercy seat], the Cherubim [on the mercy seat; these three form one unit], the fire [that came down from heaven], the *Shekhinah*, the Holy Spirit [of prophecy], and the *Urim and Thummim* [in the high priest's breastpiece].[55]

Of course, we must not minimize Haggai's words: "*I am with you,*" says the LORD, *just like* I was with you at the exodus from Egypt, when God's Spirit dwelt among the people (cf. Isa. 63:11). However, it is an exaggeration to claim that the Lord again dwelt in Jerusalem; there is no evidence for this. In Ezra 1:3 it is debatable whether we should translate: "the house of the LORD God of Israel (He [is] God), which [is] in Jerusalem" (NKJV), or: "the house of the LORD, the God of Israel—he is the God who is in Jerusalem" (ESV). On the basis of Ezra 1:4-5 and 2:68, I prefer the former rendering; but the latter rendering does not necessarily imply that God dwelt in the Second Temple as he had in the First. Since the beginning of the Babylonian exile, God is rather the "God of heaven"—a biblical expression that is almost exclusively exilic and post-exilic (Ezra 1:2; Neh. 1:4-5; Dan. 2:18-19, 37).

5.7.2 Zechariah

For understanding the relationship between the Holy Spirit and the construction of the Second Temple, Zechariah 4 is of essential importance. In a vision, the prophet saw "a lampstand all of gold, with a bowl on the top of it, and seven lamps on it, with seven lips [or, pipes, tubes, spouts] on each of the lamps that are on the top of it" (v. 2). This is a total of forty-nine burning spouts. In addition to the lampstand, he saw two olive trees with two branches, from which the golden oil

---

55. Talmud: Yoma 21b.

flowed through two golden pipes to the bowl (the oil container) (vv. 3, 12). The meaning of the oil (cf. §4.5) is here twofold: enlightening and anointing. On the one hand, the purpose of the oil lamps is to spread light. On the other hand, the two olive trees or branches are interpreted as two persons anointed with oil, namely, the king's son Zerubbabel and the high priest Joshua, who together formed a double type of the Messiah, Israel's ultimate Priest-King (vv. 12-14; cf. 6:12-13).

In Revelation 11:4, we find again two figurative olive trees, which are described as two "witnesses," just as Zerubbabel and Joshua had formed an illuminating double witness in Israel. The power for this witnessing lay in the Holy Spirit: "This is the word of the LORD to Zerubbabel: 'Not by might, nor by power, but by my Spirit,' says the LORD of hosts" (Zech. 4:6). Only in this power could the temple at Jerusalem be rebuilt. Just as there was a continual flow of oil (vv. 2-3, 12), so too there would be a continual flow of Spirit power, necessary for both rebuilding the temple and renewing the people (vv. 9-10).[56] Zechariah 4 is one of the Old Testament passages where oil (or anointing) and the Holy Spirit are most closely linked (see further 1 Sam. 16:13; 2 Sam. 23:1-2; Isa. 61:1).

There is another (indirect) hint of the Holy Spirit in Zechariah 4, namely, in verse 10b: "These seven are the eyes of the LORD, which range through the whole earth" (cf. 3:9; 2 Chron. 16:9). Some expositors refer these words to verse 2, so that the seven eyes would then be identical with the seven lamps.[57] Others connect them with chapter 3:9, where we hear about "the stone that I [i.e., God] have set before Joshua, . . . a single stone with seven eyes"; in the latter case, there would be a direct link between Zechariah 4:7-9 and verse 10b.[58] Others again accept neither connection but translate: ". . . these seven, namely, the eyes of the LORD, which run to and fro through-

---

56. Barker (1985, 629).
57. See Haller (1925, ad loc.), Sellin (1930, ad loc.).
58. Ridderbos (1935, 84-86).

out the earth."⁵⁹ We find these seven "eyes" again in Revelation 5:6, where we read: "I saw a Lamb standing, as though it had been slain, with seven horns and with seven eyes, which are the seven spirits [KJV: Spirits] of God sent out into all the earth." With its seven eyes, the "stone" (corner stone? crowning stone?) of the rebuilt temple would point to the fullness of the Holy Spirit, a fullness that would later belong to the Messiah as well.

5.8 Word and Spirit
5.8.1 Wisdom, Torah, Logos

In the Old Testament we find a special connection between Word and Spirit, which is repeated in the New Testament, for instance, in this: "[T]ake . . . the sword of the Spirit, which is the word of God" (Eph. 6:17). In §3.8 we have dealt with this connection when we discussed the Chokmah/Sophia (Wisdom) of God.

On the one hand, in the Old Testament and subsequent Jewish literature, Lady Wisdom is often viewed as almost identical with the Holy Spirit. Lady Wisdom says, "If you turn at my reproof, behold, I will pour out my spirit [*ruach*] to you; I will make my words known to you" (Prov. 1:23) — reminding us that the Holy Spirit grants wisdom (e.g., Deut. 34:9; Isa. 11:2; Eph. 1:17). Lady Wisdom *is* the creative Spirit of God: "The LORD by wisdom founded the earth" (Prov. 3:19). "Wisdom, the artisan of all, taught me" (Wisdom 7:22 NABRE).

On the other hand, Lady Wisdom is also closely connected with the Word, both in the sense of the Torah,⁶⁰ and in the sense of the Logos as John speaks of it (John 1:1, 14), which is Christ (see extensively the connection between Prov. 8:22-41 and John 1:1-18). As to the former connection: in Sirach 24, Lady Wisdom says, "Then the creator of all things gave me a command; the one who created me pitched my tent and said, 'Make your dwelling in Jacob, and let Israel receive your

---
59. Barker (1985, 630, 632), following E. W. Hengstenberg and C. F. Keil.
60. See extensively, Ouweneel (1998, §§2.3 and 2.4).

inheritance.' Before the ages, from the beginning, he created me, and till eternity I will never fail. I ministered before him in the holy tent, and so I was established in Zion" (vv. 8–12 CEB). Thus, Wisdom is found in "the covenant scroll of the Most High God, the Law that Moses commanded us" (v. 23). God gave wisdom "to his child Jacob, to Israel, whom he loved. After this, she appeared on the earth and lived among humans. She is the scroll containing God's commandments, the Law that exists forever. All who hold on to her will live, but those who desert her will die" (Baruch 3:36–4:1 CEB)

Many more parallels between Word and Spirit are found in both the Old and the New Testaments. Thus, it is not only the Spirit who gives life (Ps. 104:30; John 6:63) but also the Word (Deut. 32:46–47; John 1:4). And what is true of life is also true of light: "Your word is a lamp to my feet and a light to my path" (Ps. 119:105; cf. v. 130; 56:13; Prov. 16:23); "In him was life, and the life was the light of men" (John 1:4). However, the lamp, fueled with oil, also refers to the Holy Spirit: "Seven lamps [Gk. *lampades*] of fire [were] burning before the throne, which are the seven Spirits of God" (Rev. 4:5).

It is the Spirit who brings healing (Acts 10:38), but the Word does this too (Ps. 107:20; Prov. 4:20–22; Matt. 8:8).[61] Paul says with equal emphasis that the Word dwells in believers (Col. 3:16) and that the Spirit dwells in them (Rom. 8:11; 1 Cor. 3:16; 2 Tim. 1:14). Sometimes the Spirit inspires the prophet (Isa. 42:1; 48:16; 61:1; Ezek. 11:5; Micah 3:8), and sometimes the Word comes to him (Isa. 9:8; 38:4; Jer. 1:2, 4, 11, 13; Ezek. 1:3 etc.; Hos. 1:1). There is little substantial difference between the two. Sometimes we find them together: when Israel left Egypt, God was with them "[according to] the word that I covenanted with you when you came out of Egypt, so My Spirit remains among you" (Hag. 2:5 NKJV).[62] "My Spirit that is

---

61. See Suurmond (1995, 37–41); he refers to Irenaeus, who called Word and Spirit the two creative hands of God (41) (§4.8.2).
62. Many translations omit rendering the Heb. *dabar*, "word," and the GNT even omits rendering the Heb. *weruachi*, "and my Spirit."

upon you, and my words that I have put in your mouth, shall not depart out of your mouth, or out of the mouth of your offspring, or out of the mouth of your children's offspring . . . from this time forth and forevermore" (Isa. 59:21).

5.8.2 More Parallels

In the thunderstorm, the thunder as God's voice (the Word! Ps. 29), the lightning as the fire of the Spirit (§4.3.1), and the fertile rain, together pointing to both the Word and the Spirit, merge into one metaphor. Indeed, with its characteristic of fertility, rain points not only to the Spirit but sometimes also to the Word: "For as the rain and the snow come down from heaven and do not return there but water the earth, making it bring forth and sprout, giving seed to the sower and bread to the eater, so shall my word be that goes out from my mouth; it shall not return to me empty, but it shall accomplish that which I purpose, and shall succeed in the thing for which I sent it" (Isa. 55:10–11).

Further, we have considered the fact that, as a symbol of cleansing, water points to both the Word and the Spirit (§4.2). On the one hand, the metaphor of cleansing water is applied to the Word: "You are already clean through the word which I have spoken to you" (John 15:3 MEV); ". . . having cleansed her [i.e., the church] by the washing of water with the word [Gk. *en rhēmati*]" (Eph. 5:26).[63] Regeneration is being "born again, not of perishable seed but of imperishable, through the living and abiding word [*logos*] of God" (1 Pet. 1:23). On the other hand, water cleansing and regeneration are linked with the Spirit: the word "washing" just mentioned (Gk. *loutron*) occurs elsewhere only in Titus 3:5, where Paul speaks of the "washing of regeneration and renewal of the Holy Spirit." Perhaps this is also the way we should read John 3:5, "[U]

---

63. The Gk. phrase *en rhēmati* is here either "with a word" from the mouth of believers (so Bruce [1984, 388–89]); or in the sense of the baptismal formula (so Wood [1978, 77]); or "through the Word" as what brings about the cleansing (so Wuest [1953, 132]); Salmond (1979, 368).

nless one is born of the water of the Spirit. . . ," or "of water, namely, the Spirit," or "of water [i.e., the Word] and the Spirit" (see §8.2.1).

In the New Testament, we encounter the Pauline idea of the Spirit's dwelling in believers (Gk. *oikeō* [Rom. 8:9, 11a; 1 Cor. 3:16], *enoikeō* [Rom. 8:11b; 2 Cor. 6:16; 2 Tim. 1:14], *katoikētērion* [Eph. 2:22]). We are familiar also with the Johannine idea of the Spirit's abiding in/on believers (Gk. *menō*, John 1:33; 14:17; 1 John 3:24; 4:13). In the Old Testament, such notions are associated with the Shekhinah, especially when they refer to the tabernacle or the First Temple. Indeed, the Spirit's dwelling in the New Testament temple (1 Cor. 3:16; 2 Cor. 6:16; Eph. 2:22) is parallel to the dwelling of the Shekhinah in the First Temple (see §3.8.3).

The term Shekhinah does not occur in the Bible but is parallel with the Old Testament expression "the glory of the LORD" (Heb. *kabod* YHWH) and related expressions.[64] It is true, in Ezekiel 43:5 the Spirit and the glory are distinguished: "[T]he Spirit lifted me up and brought me into the inner court; and behold, the glory of the LORD filled the temple." Yet, the parallels should not be overlooked: just as God's glory filled the Old Testament tabernacle and temple, so too God's Spirit fills the New Testament temple. Indeed, the Holy Spirit is the "Spirit of glory" (1 Pet. 4:14).

5.8.3 Spirit: Uppercase or Lowercase S?

In the Old Testament, it is often easy to see whether the text speaks of the (human) spirit or of the (divine) Spirit. Thus, David clearly knew the difference between "renew a right spirit [heb. *ruach nakon*] within me" and "take not your Holy Spirit [Heb. *ruach qodsheka*] from me" (Ps. 51:10-11). And Isaiah dis-

---

64. See Exod. 16:7, 10; 24:16, 19; 29:43; 33:18, 22; 40:34–35; Lev. 9:6, 23; Num. 14:10, 21–22; 16:19, 42; 20:6; Deut. 5:24; 1 Kings 8:11; 2 Chron. 5:14; 7:1–3; Ps. 26:8; 57:6,12; 63:2; 102:15–16; 145:11–12; Isa. 3:8; 6:3; 24:23; 35:2; 40:5; 58:8; 59:19; 60:2; 66:5, 18–19; Ezek. 1:28; 3:12, 23; 8:4; 9:3; 10:4, 18–19; 11:22–23; 39:21; 43:2, 4–5; 44:4; Hab. 2:14; Hag. 2:4, 8, 10; Zech. 2:5, 8.

tinguished between the "Spirit of the Lord YHWH" (Heb. *ruach adonai* YHWH, Isa. 61:1) and the "faint spirit" (Heb. *ruach kēha*, v. 3).

However, in some cases it is hard to distinguish whether the text is speaking of the human spirit strengthened by God, or of the Holy Spirit working on or in a person.[65] This is the case, for instance, in Numbers 11:17, 25-26, and 29, where "some of the s/Spirit" that was on Moses is placed on the seventy elders. Ashley argued that, of the approximately forty times in the Old Testament where *ruach* is used with the preposition *al* ('[up]on"), twenty-five clearly refer to God's Spirit, seven refer to other "spirits" that come from God (Gen. 8:1, "wind"; 1 Sam. 16:16, 23, a "harmful spirit from God"; Isa. 11:2, in my view the Holy Spirit), and six refer to the human spirit.[66] To my mind, in the case of Numbers 11, particularly verse 29 makes clear that God's Spirit is intended: "Would that all the LORD's people were prophets, that the LORD would put *his* Spirit [Heb. *rucho*] on them!" — a desire expressed in Joel 2:28-29 and fulfilled in Acts 2.

The event in 2 Kings 2 seems to be parallel with this, where Elisha asks the departing Elijah: "Please let there be a double portion of your spirit [*ruach*] on me" (v. 9). Afterward, the prophets of Jericho stated, "The spirit [*ruach*] of Elijah rests on Elisha" (v. 15), and apparently distinguished this spirit from the "Spirit [*ruach*] of the LORD" (v. 16). However, Luther was convinced that Elisha was asking Elijah for a double portion of the Holy Spirit,[67] an interpretation that has sometimes been connected with the fact that twice as many miracles are reported of Elisha as of Elijah. Others believe that Elisha was not asking for anything more than the right of succession. Vonk explained that Elisha was asking "if he could be [treated as] Elijah's eldest son, so that according to the biblical right of the firstborn, he might receive a double portion of Elijah's

---

65. Cf. Welker (1992, 101-107).
66. Ashley (1993, 211).
67. Quoted by Patterson and Austel (1988, 178).

Spirit-gifts."[68] In a sense, John the Baptist was also a successor of Elisha (cf. Matt. 17:10-13), so that we might perhaps read "Spirit" in Luke 1:17, "he [i.e., John] shall go before him [i.e., God] in the Spirit and power of Elias" (BRG).

In Deuteronomy 34:9 (cf. Num. 27:18) we have a similar problem. Some translations read, "Joshua . . . was full of the Spirit of wisdom" (BRG, CJB, GW, JUB),[69] while many others read "spirit" ([N]KJV, NIV, NASB, ESV). In Exodus 28:3 (cf. 31:3; 35:31) most translations have "spirit of wisdom [or, skill]" (except JUB: "Spirit of wisdom"; OJB: *Ruach Chochmah*), whereas many have "Spirit of wisdom" in Isaiah 11:2; interestingly, some translations have "The Spirit of the Lord . . . the spirit of wisdom" (ASV, CEB, NASB). In Ephesians 1:17, some translations read "the Spirit of wisdom," others read "the [or, a] spirit of wisdom." It is hard to find uniformity in some translations. No wonder, since in each of these passages both renderings can be defended, because the notions of the human spirit enlightened by the Holy Spirit and the Holy Spirit enlightening the human spirit are not far apart.

Another example is Job 32:18, where Elihu says, "I am full of words; the spirit [*ruach*] within me constrains me." Most have "spirit" here, but see the GW and NOG (*Ruach*). Word and Spirit (see §5.8.1) have filled his mind, permeate his spirit, and burst forth (vv. 19-20). After the lifeless explanations of the older three friends, who adhere to a simplistic world order — the "established order" (cf. §2.1.1) — Elihu comes, driven by the Spirit, not to accuse Job of hidden evil, but to prepare him for a personal, existential encounter with God (cf. 42:5-6).

Generally speaking, the implicit activity of the Holy Spirit is present much more often than we might expect at first glance. Stephen told the spiritual leaders of his day, "You

---

68. Vonk (1977, 623). If a man had two sons, his inheritance would be divided into three portions, and the eldest son would receive two portions, a double portion, of the inheritance.
69. Cf. Ridderbos (1984, 317): ". . . the Spirit of the Lord who gives Joshua this wisdom."

stiff-necked people, uncircumcised in heart and ears, you always resist the Holy Spirit. As your fathers did, so do you" (Acts 7:51). He said this after having shown how the forefathers had dealt with Joseph (v. 9) and Moses (vv. 27, 35, 39). According to Stephen, resisting these earlier men of God had amounted to resisting the Holy Spirit. In the case of Moses this is obvious (cf. §5.3.2), but it is remarkable that, according to Stephen, this was also true in the case of Joseph. If resisting Joseph was the same as resisting the Holy Spirit, then the Spirit must also have worked in and through Joseph. Interestingly, no one other than Pharaoh acknowledged this because of Joseph's prophetic wisdom: "Can we find a man like this, in whom is the Spirit of God?" (Gen. 41:38). (Incidentally, translators are here again divided between rendering this as "spirit [of the gods]" and "Spirit [of God].")

5.9 Dwelling in People?
5.9.1 Three Differences

Can we say that, in the Old Testament, the Holy Spirit dwelt in believers as he dwells in New Testament believers? It is hard to assume this *a priori*, because John 7:39b says, "[A]s yet the Spirit had not been given, because Jesus was not yet glorified" (see §6.6.3). I cannot doubt that this is also the idea of Acts 19:2; not, "[W]e have not even heard that there is a Holy Spirit," but "[W]e did not so much as hear whether the Holy Spirit was [given]" (ASV; cf. DLNT), or "We did not even hear if [the] Holy Spirit was [come]" (Darby) (see §6.6.3). Because those who were speaking here were disciples of John the Baptist, it is hard to believe they had never heard of the Holy Spirit (cf. Matt. 3:11, 16; John 1:32–33). Their point was rather, it seems to me, that they did not know whether Spirit baptism had already arrived, that is, whether the person of the Spirit himself had already come to earth to dwell personally in people.

Indeed, what significance would the outpouring of the Holy Spirit have had if, already before the Day of Pentecost, the Spirit had dwelt and worked on earth in the same way as he did afterward? (I will discuss John 20:22 in §6.10.2.) Although the disciples were born again (cf., e.g., John 15:3), they were told to wait until they would receive the Holy Spirit (being born again *by* [the power of] the Spirit is very different from having the *person* of the Spirit dwelling within oneself, as we will see). Jesus said, "[B]ehold, I am sending the promise of my Father [i.e., the Holy Spirit; cf. Acts 1:4; 2:33] upon you. But stay in the city until you are clothed with power from on high" (Luke 24:49). "[W]hile staying with them [i.e., the disciples] he [i.e., Jesus] ordered them not to depart from Jerusalem, but to wait for the promise of the Father, which, he said, 'you heard from me; for John baptized with water, but you will be baptized with [or, in] the Holy Spirit not many days from now'" (Acts 1:4–5).

The difference was not only that in the Old Testament, only special servants of God possessed the Holy Spirit, whereas in the New Testament all believers do. Nor is the point that, in the Old Testament, believers received only a portion of the Spirit, whereas in the New Testament they may receive him fully. No, I see at least three *essential* differences.

(a) It is never said of Old Testament believers that the Holy Spirit dwelt in them, as Paul says this of New Testament believers: "You . . . are not in the flesh but in the Spirit, if in fact the Spirit of God *dwells* in you . . . his Spirit who *dwells* in you" (Rom. 8:9, 11); "God's Spirit *dwells* in you" (1 Cor. 3:16; cf. 6:19, "your body is a temple of the Holy Spirit within you"); "the Holy Spirit who *dwells* within us" (2 Tim. 1:14). The *power* of the Holy Spirit was upon quite a few Old Testament believers; but dwelling presupposes the *person* of the Spirit coming down to this earth, and taking his abode in believers.

(b) It is never said of Old Testament believers that they possessed the Holy Spirit permanently; on the contrary, David could pray, "[T]ake not your Holy Spirit from me" (Ps.

51:11).[70] But Jesus told his disciples, "And I will ask the Father, and he will give you another Advocate, *to be with you forever*. This is the Spirit of truth, whom the world cannot receive, because it neither sees him nor knows him. You know him, because he abides with you [Gk. *par' humin menei*],[71] and he will be in you" (John 14:14-17 NRSV). The *power* of the Spirit may vary, also within New Testament believers — but the *person* of the Spirit has come to dwell in them uninterruptedly.

(c) In the Old Testament there was no *collective*, no unified community consisting exclusively of true believers, in which the Holy Spirit could dwell (see the next §). In the New Testament there *is* such a collective: the body of Christ, which is the "temple" in which the Holy Spirit "dwells" (1 Cor. 3:16; Eph. 2:21-22). The Old Testament temple was only a metaphor for the church of God; the dwelling of the Shekhinah in this temple was only a metaphor for the Spirit's dwelling in the church (see the next § as well as §10.2).

5.9.2 Dwelling and Working

Isaiah 63:11 says that God put his Holy Spirit in the midst of the Israelites. This is not the same as saying that the Holy Spirit *dwelt* in Israel, that is, in the hearts or bodies of the individual Israelites. In fact, the Spirit could be found as having come upon only Moses and the elders (Num. 11:16-30), and afterward Joshua, the judges (seven times: Judg. 3:10; 6:34; 11:29; 13:25; 14:6, 19; 15:14) and the prophets (from Samuel to Malachi, David included; 2 Sam. 23:1-2). The Shekhinah did not dwell on or in the Israelites, but in their midst, in the inaccessible sanctuary, in "thick darkness" (1 Kings 8:12; 2 Chron.

---

70. Practically speaking, though, New Testament believers may pray this in a sense that is opposite to that of Luke 11:13 ("... will the heavenly Father give the Holy Spirit to those who ask him"); that is, do not take away, or grant me, the *fullness* of your Spirit (cf. §5.9.3).
71. It is crucial to observe that here the verb "abide" (Gk. *menō*) is used, which many translations render mistakenly as "dwell" (ESV; KJV; NKJV; RSV) or "live" (NIV; TNIV), but which the ASV and NASB render correctly as "abide." As we shall see, the Gk. verb *oikeō* is correctly translated as "dwell, live, inhabit."

6:1).

This is not surprising; Israel was *not* "a holy congregation and gathering of true Christian believers," or simply "true YHWH believers" (cf. the Belgic Confession Art. 27), as the church is.[72] Israel was a mixture of believers and unbelievers. On the one hand, not all Israelites were true believers; on the other hand, there were true believers outside Israel, such as Job and his friends (Job 1-2), Rahab (Josh. 2), Jael the Kenite (Judg. 4), Naaman (2 Kings 5), the Rechabites (Jer. 35), and Ebed-melech (Jer. 38). In the Old Testament, no collective of true believers existed; one of the essential purposes of Christ's coming was to bring together the "scattered children of God" and make them one (John 11:52 NIV); this unified entity is called the church of God. Before this, there was no collective in which the Holy Spirit could have dwelt — for the time such an indwelling had not yet arrived. We remember here John 7:39, "[A]s yet the Spirit had not been given, *because Jesus was not yet glorified.*" The glorified Christ, qualified with this exaltation, sent us the Holy Spirit from the Father (John 15:26).

The Spirit is omnipresent, and of course, as such he worked among people long before Acts 2. At the very beginning of history, he was "hovering over the face of the waters" (Gen. 1:2). However, a person may live at one place, and work at many other places. The Holy Spirit worked on earth throughout Old Testament times, but there was no such phenomenon as the permanent "dwelling" (Gk. *oikeō*) of the Spirit as there is now in the (New Testament) church of God (1 Cor. 3:16; cf. 2 Cor. 6:16; Eph. 2:21-22) as well as in the individual believer (Rom. 8:9, 11; 1 Cor. 6:19). Solomon said of the First Temple, "[W]ill God indeed dwell on the earth? Behold, heaven and the highest heaven cannot contain you; how much less this house that I have built" (1 Kings 8:27), adding that heaven was God's "dwelling place" (vv. 30, 39, 43, 49). But now we

---

72. I am speaking here of the church as the holy gathering of true Christians—not of the church in its outward appearance, which may be a "great house" containing vessels for honor *and* for dishonor (2 Tim. 2:20 NKJV).

can say that indeed God—that is, God the Holy Spirit—does dwell on earth, namely, in the church of the living God.

It is typically Jewish to say, "The heavens are the LORD's heavens, but the earth he has given to the children of man" (Ps. 115:16); that is, God's place is in heaven, humanity's place is on earth. Christians may agree with this, but they may add that, at present, we have a glorified *Man* seated at God's right hand, and we have *God* the Holy Spirit, dwelling on earth in the church.

In the Old Testament, we have no more than some temporary activity of Spirit: filling, coming upon, falling upon, rushing upon, and speaking through people. What seems to come closest to any notion of dwelling is Genesis 6:3, "My Spirit shall not abide in [*katameinēi* LXX; or remain in; according to others: strive with] man forever." First, we have the problem of the correct translation here (abiding in or striving with). Second, "abiding in" is a rather strong rendering; more prudent would be "remaining with" (AMP, HCSB, ISV, TLV). There is no question here of any dwelling within believers, collectively or individually (*contra* AMPC, WYC). And the very idea of "*not* remaining" shows that we do not have here any form of permanent indwelling.

5.9.3 Temporary Anointing

We do have some statements of Gentile kings, declaring about certain men of God that the Spirit of God (or, of the gods!) was in them. Pharaoh said about Joseph: "Can we find a man like this, in whom is the Spirit of God [or, the gods]?" (Gen. 41:38). Nebuchadnezzar said about Daniel, ". . . in whom is the spirit of the holy gods [or, Spirit of the holy God]" (Dan. 4:8; cf. Belshazzar in 5:11, 14). But, first, we should not conclude too much from such pagan testimonies. Second, in such cases we are always dealing with a special work of the Spirit, manifested at certain moments in men of God. This is no evidence for a permanent indwelling of the Spirit in any Old Testament believer. Thus, we discussed earlier David and his prayer: "[T]ake not your Holy Spirit from me" (Ps. 51:11). In complete agreement with the scope of Old Testament revelation, David was not thinking here of a divine *person* who might have dwelt in him earlier. He was thinking of the *power* of the anointing he had received, especially his prophetic ministry, and this power might possibly depart from him (cf. 2 Sam. 23:2; see §§4.4.2 and 4.5).

Incidentally, New Testament believers, who do have the Holy Spirit indwelling in them, can still pray for "Holy Spirit" (without the article) in the sense of the power of the Spirit, or a renewal of this power (Luke 11:13; see note 69 and §6.5.3). Similarly, after committing heinous sins, they may pray that the anointing that they had received for their ministry will not be taken away from them. But this must be distinguished from the *person* of the Spirit dwelling permanently in them.

The temporary character of the Spirit's working in or upon people also explains why the Spirit could descend upon persons who were not truly godly, such as Balaam: "Balaam lifted up his eyes and saw Israel camping tribe by tribe. And the Spirit of God came upon him" (Num. 24:2; for an evaluation of who Balaam really was, see 2 Pet. 2:15, Jude 1:11, and Rev. 2:14).[73] Of others we can only say that they were probably not true believers (such as King Saul), although the Spirit descended on them (cf. 1 Sam. 10:6, 10; 11:6; 19:23).

In fact, this was the situation until the Day of Pentecost. Thus, all twelve disciples received "authority over unclean spirits, to cast them out, and to heal every disease and every affliction," *including Judas* (Matt. 10:1-4), although Jesus later called him a "devil" (John 6:70-71).[74] To this end, they needed the power of the Holy Spirit, although this is not mentioned. Thus, the Spirit also worked through Judas, although he never possessed the Spirit by way of indwelling. Such people belong to those of whom Jesus said, "On that day many will say

---

73. See Welker (1992, 96-98).
74. This does not imply that the disciples at that time already possessed the Holy Spirit permanently; *contra* Congar (1997, 1.51).

to me, 'Lord, Lord, did we not prophesy in your name, and cast out demons in your name, and do many mighty works in your name?' And then will I declare to them, 'I never knew you; depart from me, you workers of lawlessness'" (Matt. 7:22-23). They have "shared in the Holy Spirit" (cf. Heb. 6:4; see §8.5.3), but only in some outward sense.

There has been much discussion about the question to what extent possessing the Spirit differed in the Old Testament and the New Testament.[75] In this respect, the Greek church fathers and some Latin fathers made a fundamental distinction between the Old and the New Testament. They believed that before the coming of Christ gifts of the Spirit but not the person of the Spirit had been granted, and that the Holy Spirit did not personally dwell in believers. However, the large majority of Latin fathers and later Western theologians believed that, because of their faith in the coming Christ, the Old Testament righteous possessed the same status of being children of God as well as a personal indwelling of the Holy Spirit. The incarnation of the Son and the outpouring of the Spirit brought about only a fuller abundance of this grace and this presence of the Spirit.

In this respect, evangelical, especially dispensational, theologians are often more in line with the Eastern theologians. The boundary between the Old and the New Testament depicted perhaps nowhere more clearly than in these words by Jesus: "I tell you, among those born of women none is greater than John. Yet the one who is least in the kingdom of God is greater than he" (Luke 7:28; cf. Matt. 11:11) — because, as I see it, John belonged to the old dispensation, not to the kingdom of God.[76] "The Law and the Prophets were until John; since then the good news of the kingdom of God is preached" (Luke 16:16). The apostle John says, "[T]he law was given through Moses; grace and truth came through Jesus Christ' (John 1:17). And Paul: "Now before faith came, we

---

75. Congar (1997, 1.74–77).
76. Ibid., 1.73.

were held captive under the law, imprisoned until the coming faith would be revealed. So then, the law was our guardian until Christ came, in order that we might be justified by faith" (Gal. 3:23–24). Here, the era of the law is followed by the era of faith, or of Christ.

As long as Jesus had not been glorified (exalted at God's right hand), "as yet the Spirit had not been given" (John 7:39; see §6.6.3). The sporadic exceptions to this rule are dwarfed by the fullness with which the Spirit has broken through on the Day of Pentecost. It is only with Acts 2 that, in God's redemptive history, an entirely new situation arrives on earth, the significance of which we cannot overestimate. We will deal with this extensively in chapter 7; but first we must see how the Holy Spirit worked upon and in the person of Jesus Christ (chapter 6).

Chapter 6
Christ and the Holy Spirit

God anointed Jesus of Nazareth
   with the Holy Spirit and with power.
He went about doing good
   and healing all who were oppressed by the devil,
      for God was with him.
                                    Acts 10:38

Jesus returned in the power of the Spirit to Galilee,
   and a report about him went out
   through all the surrounding country.
And he taught in their synagogues,
   being glorified by all.
                                    Luke 4:14–15

Summary: *This chapter investigates how the Holy Spirit was involved in Jesus' incarnation and birth, how such relationships were announced in Isaiah, how the Holy Spirit was involved in Jesus' death (here the "exodus" metaphor is examined) and in his resurrection. The Holy Spirit played a great role in supporting Jesus'* *ministry, but also constituted a major subject in his teaching. Much attention is given to what is said about the Holy Spirit especially in John's Gospel. The similarity between John 4 and 7 is studied, and the meaning of the Holy Spirit as Paraclete (John 14–16) is investigated. The link between the Spirit's witnessing mentioned in John 15 and his witnessing mentioned in 1 John 5:6–8 is considered. The importance of Jesus' ascension as a condition for the Spirit's descent is stressed, as are the benefits of this descent for Jesus' followers. Finally, how does John 19:30 relate to the Holy Spirit, and how does John 20:22 relate to Acts 2?*

6.1 Jesus' Beginnings in This World
6.1.1 The Incarnation of the Word

IN THIS CHAPTER, we deal with the enormous significance of the Holy Spirit in the person and work of Jesus Christ, and with the announcement of the Spirit who would descend to dwell in God's people. Christ is the incarnated Logos ("the Word became flesh," John 1:14), and as such, Christians confess him as perfect God and perfect Man in one person.[1] In this quality he was begotten by God, through the Holy Spirit, from the Virgin Mary. In opposition to those who attacked Jesus' deity, the church has always strongly emphasized that Jesus is the incarnated *Logos* ("the Word was God," John 1:1). In opposition to those who attacked Jesus' humanity the church has always strongly emphasized that Jesus is the *incarnated* Logos.

In order to understand the ministry of Christ we must emphasize that, to be sure, he could accomplish the work only because he was God. Yet he did not accomplish this work in his own divine power but as a humble, dependent Man on earth, in obedience to the Father and in the power of the Holy Spirit. Clark Pinnock pointed out that the Spirit is more central in the history of Jesus than theology has usually acknowledged. Through the Spirit Jesus was conceived, anointed, empowered, sent, led, and raised.[2] (The biblical referenc-

---

1. See extensively, Ouweneel (2007b).
2. Pinnock (1996, 81–82; see extensively, his entire chapter 3).

es to underscore this will arise for discussion throughout the present chapter.) Thus, in order to understand the work *of* the Spirit in him, his incarnation *by* the Spirit and his anointing *with* the Spirit are of fundamental significance.

According to Jewish tradition, the Holy Spirit departed from Israel after the three final prophets: Haggai, Zechariah, and Malachi. Thereafter Israel enjoyed only the "echo" (*bat qol*) of heavenly messages, which was nothing but a vague surrogate of God's voice.[3] Already the believers in exile complained: "We do not see our signs; there is no longer any prophet, and there is none among us who knows how long" (Ps. 74:9). Moreover, Jewish tradition acknowledged that—as we can already conclude from the Old Testament itself—the Shekhinah, the equivalent of the Holy Spirit, was not present in the Second Temple (§5.7). When the First Temple was about to be destroyed, the Holy Spirit returned to heaven.[4] It is all the more remarkable that Jesus was born of the Holy Spirit, and then about thirty years later was anointed with the Spirit. In connection with his birth, the Holy Spirit was active in various godly people (Luke 1:15, 35, 41, 67; 2:25-27) in such a way that the rabbinic statements were simply proven false.

Back in §3.8.3 I briefly discussed Luke 1:35 within the context of the relationship between the Shekhinah and the Holy Spirit (cf. Matt. 1:18, 20). The angel[5] Gabriel told Mary, "The Holy Spirit will come upon you, and the power of the Most High will overshadow you; therefore the child to be born will be called holy—the Son of God." The first two phrases, separated by "and," resemble Hebrew poetic parallelism, or a song.[6] That is, the Holy Spirit and the power of the Most High are here essentially identical. The power of the Spirit

---

3. Tosefta on the Talmud tract Sota 13:2; cf. idem on tract Sanhedrin 11:1; see more extensively, Edersheim (1979, 1.285–86); Keener (1997, 13–16).
4. Midrash Rabbah on Eccl. 12:7.
5. Nowhere in the Bible is Gabriel called an archangel, although he is recognized as such by Jews, Christians, and Muslims.
6. Godet (1978, ad loc.).

would come upon the Virgin Mary and rest upon her — as the Shekhinah once rested on the tabernacle and the First Temple — so that she would become pregnant.

The assumption that this involved the power rather than the person of the Spirit is supported by the absence of the article before the name "Holy Spirit" (*pneuma hagion*) as well as before the word "power" (Gk. *dynamis*). Similarly we read in Matthew 1:18, 20 that Jesus was conceived "from [the] Holy Spirit" (Gk. *ek pneumatos hagiou*). The result of this conception by God through the *Holy* Spirit was a *holy* thing (*to hagion* in Luke 1:35 is neuter; so the KJV and the ASV), not so much a holy *person* (Gk. *ho hagios*).[7] Perhaps we should add "child" (in Gk. the neuter noun is *teknon*), and translate along with the ESV and others: "the child to be born will be called holy."[8] The child is just as holy as the Spirit through whose power he was conceived. In opposition to the very unholy explanation of Mary's pregnancy that occupied Joseph's mind stands the most holy explanation: she was pregnant "from [the] *Holy* Spirit" (Matt. 1:18).[9]

6.1.2 The Virgin Birth

On a superficial level, the conception of Jesus reminds us of the mythological stories concerning the conception and birth of divine sons, where gods in human form consort with earthly women. However, there is also sharp contrast.[10] In Matthew 1 and Luke 1, there is no speculation about exactly what occurred in Mary's womb. *How*, at the conception of the Messiah, the divine was united with the human (Mary)

---

7. Geldenhuys (1983, 77) reads without any comments *the Holy One* (so the NIV), which in Greek would have been *ho hagios*, as in Mark 1:24, John 6:69, Acts 3:14, 1 John 2:20, and Rev. 3:7. Bruce (1979, 464) is correct: *the holy thing–holy product of a holy agency*; he does not translate the verb as "born" but "begotten," and thus explains the neuter form from the fact that an embryo was involved here.
8. Cf. Liefeld (1984, 833).
9. Bruce (1979, 67).
10. See literature in Grundmann (1964, 300n55).

is only suggested by the Greek verbal forms *epeleusetai* (from *eperchomai*, "to come over") and *episkiasei* (from *episkiazō*, "to overshadow").[11]

Grundmann suggested that Jesus is not the Son of God because his birth is miraculous, but his birth is miraculous because he is the Son of God.[12] I would say that both are true: as the *eternal* Son of God he existed from eternity before his human birth, and as such a miraculous birth was fitting for him. However, Luke 1:35 seems to emphasize instead that also in his *humanity* he is Son of God, namely, because of his miraculous birth. In the New Testament we find three aspects of Jesus' Sonship: (1) He is the Logos who became flesh (cf. John 1:14 with v. 18), but (2) he is also a Man conceived by the Holy Spirit, and for this reason too he is Son of God; and (3) because of his resurrection he was "declared to be the Son of God in power" (Rom. 1:4).

In the Old Testament, people received the title "son of God" because of their election for a certain office — especially the royal one — where having been "begotten" was identical with this election (Ps. 2:7; cf. Rom. 9:17). Something similar could perhaps be said of the angels who, because of their having been created by God, are called "sons of God" (Job 1:6; 2:1; 38:7; also Gen. 6:4?). However, in their case this does not mean anything more than "belonging to the divine world."[13] By contrast, in Luke 1:35 we encounter a work of the Holy Spirit, through which the Second Person's eternal deity was united with his newly generated human nature.[14] He is the eternal Son of the Father, but also as a human he is the Son of God, namely, through a genuine begetting "from the Holy

---

11. Rabbinic tradition in general does not speak of a divine generation of the Messiah, but Qumran theology does seem to be familiar with this idea; see Schulz (1971, 400n4).
12. Grundmann (1964, 300n56).
13. Schneemelcher (1972, 396).
14. We speak here of the hypostatic union of his two natures. Each form of adoptionism ("Jesus was adopted to be son of God") must be avoided here; see Congar (1997, 3.171).

Spirit."

6.1.3 Jesus' Baptism

It had been announced by the Old Testament prophets that the Holy Spirit would rest on the Messiah (Isa. 11:1-12; 42:1; 61:1; see §6.2). In connection with the dove metaphor for the Holy Spirit (§4.7), we discussed Jesus' baptism and the Holy Spirit's descent upon him (Matt. 3:16-17; Mark 1:10-11; Luke 3:21-22; John 1:32-33). This is the place to add some more thoughts on this subject.

The first point requiring our attention is the distinction between Jesus' conception by the Holy Spirit (Luke 1:35; §6.1.1) and his anointing with the Spirit about thirty years later (3:23).[15] In his conception by the Spirit he differs fundamentally from all other humans, who in all cases have been fathered by a man. The exception is Adam, of whom it is said that he was a "son . . . of God" (3:23, 38); in this respect, as the first Adam, he exhibited a certain parallel with Jesus as the last Adam (1 Cor. 15:45): Adam had been begotten as it were by the divine breath (Heb. *neshamah*, Gen. 2:7), as Jesus was begotten by the divine Spirit (*ruach*); in their meanings these two Hebrew words are closely related (§3.1.3).

Incidentally, there *is* a remarkable parallel between Jesus' conception and that of — not natural humans but — *believers*: they are "born of the Spirit" (Gk. *gennēthē ek pneumatos*, John 3:5; cf.1:12, "born of God," *ek theou egennēthēsan*). This is entirely analogous to the expression: "born of a woman" (Gk. *gegomenon ek gynaikos*, Gal. 4:4; cf. John 16:21) as applied to Jesus. He was born of a woman, but through the Holy Spirit; believers are reborn through the Holy Spirit. As I said in §3.7.2, the expression "not of the will of man" (John 1:13) could almost be taken as pointing to a virgin birth: just like Jesus, believers have been born of the Spirit without the intervention of any man.

---

15. *Contra* Pinnock, who stated that Jesus was anointed with the Spirit as Christ already in Mary' womb (1996, 86), and Congar (1997, 1.16).

In receiving the Spirit there is also a parallel between Jesus and every believer, except that the latter receives the Spirit only after conversion and regeneration (see §8.3). It is all the more remarkable that Ambrose, Cyril, and Bede connected Jesus' anointing in Acts 10:38 with the Word's incarnation. In contrast to this, Athanasius rightly associated it with Jesus' baptism.[16] Jesus was the Son from eternity, and he became a human being at his incarnation, but strictly speaking, he formally became Christ (the Anointed One) at his baptism when he received the Spirit.[17]

Yet another difference between Jesus and the believer receiving the Spirit is the voice from heaven. John proclaimed "a baptism of repentance for the forgiveness of sins" (Mark 1:4). Because of Jesus being baptized, people might have thought that he was a penitent sinner just like the others who were baptized; so the heavens were "torn open" (v. 10), and "a voice came from heaven, 'You are my beloved Son; with you I am well pleased'" (v.11; Luke 3:22). Jesus united himself to the people, but at the same time the opened heaven declared his absolute uniqueness as the Father's beloved Son. Believers are sons by adoption,[18] Jesus is Son both from eternity in the Father's bosom (John 1:18), and through his virgin birth from Mary (Luke 1:35; see §6.1.2). In the same way, the Father declared the Son's uniqueness precisely when Peter equated him with Moses and Elijah (Matt. 17:4-5; Mark 9:5, 7; Luke 9:33, 35).

The fundamental idea calls to mind 1 Timothy 3:16, which states that Jesus was (literally) "justified in [the] Spirit," in the sense of "vindicated by the Spirit." We find this sense of the Greek verb *dikaioō* ("to declare or confirm [defend] the righteousness of something or someone") also, for instance, in Psalm 51:4 (Septuagint, quoted in Rom. 3:4, "you [i.e., God]

---

16. Knowling (1979, 260).
17. See extensively, Pinnock (1996, 80–93).
18. The Gk. noun is *huiothesia*, "adoption," lit. "being made son," being given the status of a son: Rom. 8:15, 23; Gal. 4:5; Eph. 1:4 (see §8.4.3 note 49).

may be justified in your words") and Luke 7:29 ("they justified God," i.e., "they declared God just/righteous"). In 1 Timothy 3 it is not the Father, but the power of the Holy Spirit through which Jesus' person, and after his baptism also his entire work, is openly declared to be "just/righteous," that is, answering to the justice/righteousness of God. Jesus turned out to be in all things the Righteous One (Gk. *dikaios*; in Heb.: the true *tsaddiq*), as he is often called (Acts 3:14; 7:52; 22:14; 1 Pet. 3:18; 1 John 2:1; perhaps James 5:6). This seems to be related to what is said below (§6.9.2) about "righteousness" in John 16:10.

As a final remark on the relationship between Jesus' conception and his anointing, I mention a consideration for those who (as I do) appreciate typology. Of the five basic types of sacrifices in Leviticus 1–7, four refer to Christ's bloody offering, and one to his holy life preceding his death: the grain offering. This consisted of unleavened loaves or wafers of fine flour about which we are told two things: they were "mixed with oil" and/or "smeared [lit., anointed, KJV] with oil" (Lev. 2:4). The former, fine flour mingled with oil, reminds us of Jesus' conception, in which his divine nature (the oil) was united to his human nature (the flour). The latter, the "anointing" with oil, reminds us of the Spirit descending on Jesus at his baptism.[19]

6.2 Jesus and the Spirit in Isaiah
6.2.1 Isaiah 11

In the book of Isaiah, there are three special promises concerning the Spirit who would rest upon the Messiah, and the meaning of the Spirit for Messiah's ministry. The first promise is chapter 11:1–2, "There shall come forth a shoot from the stump of Jesse, and a branch from his roots shall bear fruit. And the Spirit of the LORD shall rest upon him, the Spirit of wisdom and understanding, the Spirit of counsel and might, the Spirit of knowledge and the fear of the LORD."

---

19. Grant (1890, 281–82); Mackintosh (n.d., ad loc.).

The text ties in directly with Isaiah 10:33-34, where the destruction of the Assyrian empire is announced: ". . . the great in height will be hewn down, and the lofty will be brought low. He will cut down the thickets of the forest with an axe. . . ." In contrast to this we see another tree, this one a mere stump, the house of David, here named after Jesse, David's father. Jesse was a farmer as plain as that stump would have become by the time that the Messiah would be born. The Messiah, whose Davidic origin had been mentioned earlier (Isa. 7:13-14; 9:6-7; cf. 16:5; 22:22; 55:3-4), is merely a shoot from a stump, a branch from his (or its) roots (cf. the Branch in 4:2; Jer. 23:5; 33:15; Zech. 3:8; 6:12).[20]

As the king of Assyria relied on his own wisdom and power (10:8-14), the Messiah would rely on the Holy Spirit. As the Spirit of YHWH had rested upon Besalel, judges, kings, and prophets (§§5.4 and 5.5), so the Spirit rested on the One who, since his baptism (§6.1.3), was king and prophet in Israel. This Spirit is described here by a sevenfold name. Malbim (acronym for Rabbi Meir Loeb ben Jehiel Michael) identified the three conceptual pairs, following mention of the "Spirit of the LORD," with Messiah's intellectual, administrative, and spiritual attributes, respectively.[21] Rupert of Deutz divided the history between Jesus' first and second coming into seven stages according to these seven aspects of the Spirit; he discovered these aspects in reverse order in the seven letters of Revelation 2 and 3.[22]

Here is a brief summary of these seven aspects of the Spirit.[23]

(a) *The Spirit of the LORD:* the Spirit of YHWH, the Spirit who goes out from him and in whom his being is manifested.

(b) *Wisdom* (Heb. *chokmah*): practical experience and insight about how to apply knowledge (also see [f]); in Ephe-

---

20. Cf. Oswalt (1986, 278-79); Grogan (1986, 87).
21. Slotki (1983, 56).
22. Burgess (1997, 38-39).
23. Cf. Congar (1997, 2.134-41).

sians 1:17 we also hear of "the Spirit of wisdom and of revelation"; this is the Spirit who makes one wise concerning the revealed things of God.[24]

(c) *Understanding* (Heb. *binah*), or insight (so, e.g., in Prov. 2:3a; 3:5; 8:14; 9:10), especially in governmental tasks (cf. 1 Kings 4:29, "God gave Solomon wisdom and understanding [Heb. *tebunah*, related to *binah*] beyond measure, and breadth of mind like the sand on the seashore").

(d) *Counsel* (Heb. 'ētsah): advice, plan, design (cf. the related *yo'ēts*, "Counselor," Isa. 9:6), that is, the capacity of arriving at the right decisions.

(e) *Might* (Heb. *geburah*): strength (cf. the related *el gibbor*, "mighty God," Isa. 9:6), needed to carry out decisions.

(f) *Knowledge* (Heb. *da'at*): see Proverbs 1:4, 7, 22, 29; here especially the intimate fellowship with God (Jer. 31:34; Hos. 6:6; Heb. 2:14).

(g) *The fear of the* LORD (Heb. *yir'at* YHWH): this is connected with *chokmah* (Ps. 111:10; Prov. 9:10; 15:33), *binah* (Job 28:28), and *da'at* (Prov. 1:7, 29; 2:5).

According to his *divine* nature, Christ possesses in himself all wisdom, understanding, counsel, might, and knowledge; these qualities belong not only to the Spirit but also to the Son (and the Father) in person. We have here, then, a link with Isaiah 9:6, and in my view also with Proverbs 8:22-31. However, as *Man*, who is an example to all humanity, Jesus possesses his wisdom, understanding, counsel, might, and knowledge, as well as the fear of YHWH, by the power of the Holy Spirit. Please note that Solomon, as son of David, seemed to be *the* example of wisdom, but he lacked the requisite "fear of YHWH," which is mentioned here of the Messiah, not only in Isaiah 11:2 but also in verse 3 ("his delight shall be in the fear of the LORD").

---

24. The uppercase spelling of "Spirit" is defended by Wood (1978, 22) and Salmond (1979, 274); the lowercase "spirit," is defended by Bruce (1984, 269–70).

This description has obviously been connected with the expression "the seven Spirits of God" who are before the throne of God (Rev. 1:4; 3:1; 4:5; 5:6). This is a probable reference to the Holy Spirit, not as a divine person but as the Spirit of power, by which God will execute the judgments from his throne. Here the number seven points to the diversity and perfection with which Christ will carry out those judgments (see §§3.6.2, 4.3.2, 5.7.2, 5.8.1).

One of the consequences of the Spirit's operation within the Messiah will be that he will judge and rule in a righteous way (Isa. 11:3-5). When, in the Messianic kingdom, the Spirit will be poured out on all the people of God, the consequences will be similar:[25] one day "the Spirit is poured upon us from on high, and the wilderness becomes a fruitful field, and the fruitful field is deemed a forest. Then justice will dwell in the wilderness, and righteousness abide in the fruitful field" (32:15-16; cf. also the "s/Spirit of judgment" in 4:4 and 28:6, which is ascribed to the Messiah).

6.2.2 Isaiah 42

Isaiah 42:1-9 is the first of the four well-known prophecies concerning the Servant of YHWH. It begins as follows: "Behold my servant, whom I uphold, my chosen, in whom my soul delights; I have put my Spirit upon him; he will bring forth justice to the nations" (v. 1; on this verse, see §§4.4.2 and 4.5.4 above). I see a direct causal relationship between the first and the second halves of the verse: *because* the Messiah is the chosen one of YHWH, in whom his soul delights (cf. Matt. 3:17; 17:5), he has put his Spirit upon him.

This corresponds with Psalm 89, where God said of David, "I have granted help to one who is mighty; I have exalted one chosen from the people. I have found David, my servant; with my holy oil I have anointed him" (vv. 19-20). Though this involves an anointing with oil, not with the Spirit, the basic idea is the same: it is the chosen one, the elect person in

---

25. Grogan (1986, 207).

whom God is well pleased, whom he anoints with the Spirit, or with holy oil, respectively, the oil being an image of the Spirit (see §§4.5, 5.9.3, and 7.2.2).

Just as in Isaiah 11:1–5 and 32:15–16, the consequence of this anointing is that, according to Isaiah 42, the Messiah "will bring forth justice [Heb. *mishpat*] to the nations" (v. 1b; cf. 3b, "he will faithfully bring forth justice [*mishpat*]"), and "the coastlands wait for his law [Heb. *torah*, or teaching]" (v. 4b).

Whether the text refers primarily to Israel or to the Messiah is a matter requiring extensive discussion.[26] The short answer is: in a sense it refers to both. Isaiah 49:3 unequivocally says that the Lord's servant is Israel. However, in chapters 52–53 the characteristics of the s/Servant come more and more to describe the Messiah. The two are closely linked, though: the Messiah has been described as the true personification of Israel.[27] What happened to them happened to him.

6.2.3 Isaiah 61

As we saw, Jesus is not only the anointed King but also the anointed Prophet (cf. Isa. 61:1–3). The Judaism of his day, which viewed the Holy Spirit especially as the Spirit of prophecy, believed that this Spirit had departed from Israel after the last prophet of Israel, Malachi (although they believed the divine voice from heaven [Heb. *bat qol*] was still heard occasionally; §6.1.1).[28] Therefore, it was quite significant that Jesus openly applied the prophecy of Isaiah 61 to himself (Luke 4:16–21), and implicitly presented himself as the Prophet promised in Deuteronomy 18:15, 18 (cf. Matt. 13:57; Luke 13:33; cf. Matt. 21:11; Luke 24:19; John 1:45; 4:25; 6:14; 7:40; Acts 3:20–26; 7:37). He was thereby indicating that the Spirit of prophecy had also returned to Israel.[29]

Actually, this return had begun already with John the

---

26. Ouweneel (2000a, chapter 2).
27. De Graaff (1987).
28. Talmud: Sotah 48b.
29. Kärkkäinen (2002, 29–30).

Baptist (cf. Matt. 11:9; Luke 1:15), if not with Elizabeth (Luke 1:41), Zechariah (v. 67), Simeon (2:25-32), and Anna (v. 36). With reference to Simeon, the Holy Spirit is mentioned three times: "Now there was a man in Jerusalem, whose name was Simeon, and this man was righteous and devout, waiting for the consolation of Israel, and *the Holy Spirit was upon him*. And it had been revealed to him *by the Holy Spirit* that he would not see death before he had seen the Lord's Christ. And he came *in the Spirit* into the temple" (vv. 25-27).

Isaiah 61:1-3 is special because it is the only Old Testament passage in which anointing is directly linked with the Holy Spirit: "The Spirit of the Lord GOD is upon me, because the LORD has anointed me." Some take the causal order as follows: "The Spirit of *Adonai* is upon me; therefore he has anointed me" (CJB, cf. DRA). But in my view the "because" (Luke 4:18, Gk. *hoy heineken*) literally indicates the cause: the anointing is the cause of the Spirit of Adonai YHWH being upon the Prophet. It had been the same with David: first there was the anointing, then the Spirit rushed upon him (1 Sam. 16:13). This is also what Peter expressed in Acts 10:38, "God anointed Jesus of Nazareth with the Holy Spirit and with power."

Those in the Old Testament who are special types of the Messiah were often granted the Holy Spirit or were called "anointed." Thus, in Psalm 105:15 the latter expression is applied to the patriarchs (cf. vv. 9-10): "Touch not my anointed ones, do my prophets no harm!" Of the three, certainly Isaac, and to some extent also Jacob, were Messianic types. So too were Moses (Num. 11:17, 25; cf. Ps. 90:1; 105:26; 106:23), Aaron (Exod. 29:7; Lev. 8:12; Ps. 105:23; 106:16), and David (1 Sam. 16:13; 2 Sam. 23:1-2; Ps. 89:19-21).[30] Just as these were types of Christ, so too New Testament believers are followers and representatives of Christ, continuing the ministry of Isaiah 61:1-3.

In Luke 4:14, Jesus came to Galilee "in the power of the

---

30. Ouweneel (2005a, 170).

Spirit." This emphasis on Jesus' walk in the Spirit is typical of Luke's Gospel: "Jesus, full of the Holy Spirit, returned from the Jordan and was led by the Spirit in the wilderness for forty days, being tempted by the devil" (vv. 1-2). "[H]e rejoiced in the Holy Spirit and said, 'I thank you, Father'" (10:21). And in the application to believers: ". . . how much more will the heavenly Father give the Holy Spirit to those who ask him!" (11:13); ". . . the Holy Spirit will teach you in that very hour what you ought to say" (12:12).

After arriving in Galilee, Jesus read in the synagogue of Nazareth the passage in Isaiah 61. He plainly added, "Today this Scripture has been fulfilled in your hearing" (v. 21). His ministry referred specifically to:[31]

(a) The *poor* (or afflicted; KJV: meek): these may be those who are economically poor (cf. Luke 6:20; 7:22; 14:13, 21; 16:20, 22; 18:22; 19:8; 21:2-3), but also those who are spiritually poor and afflicted (cf. Ps. 40:17; 72:12-14; Zeph. 3:12; Matt. 5:3, "the poor in spirit").

(b) The *brokenhearted*: compare Isaiah 57:15, "I dwell in the high and holy place, and also with him who is of a contrite and lowly spirit, to revive the spirit of the lowly, and to revive the heart of the contrite" (cf. Matt. 5:4, "Blessed are those who mourn, for they shall be comforted").

(c) The *captives* and *those who are bound* or *oppressed*: these were primarily the exiles of Judah in Babylon (cf. Isa. 42:22, "they are all of them trapped in holes and hidden in prisons"; 49:9; 51:14; cf. 35:10; 43:3-4; 51:11), but of Jesus' ministry on earth we are told, "God anointed Jesus of Nazareth with the Holy Spirit and with power. He went about doing good and healing all who were *oppressed by the devil*" (Acts 10:38).

(d) Speaking of the sick, we notice that the quotation in Luke 4 has this addition: "recovering of sight to the blind," which is lacking in the Masoretic text. Apparently, this addition echoes the Targum (the Aramaic paraphrase of the Old

---

31. Grogan (1986, 333).

Testament).[32]

In summary, Jesus confronted the evil powers by the Holy Spirit, namely, with the Word of God (Luke 4:1-13). He walked in the power of the Spirit (4:1, 14), he healed the sick, and set the possessed free by the Spirit (Matt. 12:28; Acts 10:38); even his inner feelings were directed by the power of the Spirit (Luke 10:21). He was God, and as God he forgave sins (Matt. 9:1-6), accepted worship (Matt. 8:2; 9:18; 14:33; 15:25; 20:20), and took up his own human life in resurrection (John 10:17-18). However, when he preached the Word or performed miracles, he did so as the anointed Man in the power of the Holy Spirit. Only in this way could he set an example for his followers (cf. John 14:12).

6.3 The Holy Spirit and Jesus' Death
6.3.1 Exodus and Baptism

In §4.7.1 we have investigated a number of biblical indications that suggest a parallel between Jesus' baptism and Israel's exodus. But there is a deeper significance in Jesus' "exodus," as there is also a deeper significance in his "baptism": "I have a baptism to be baptized with, and how great is my distress until it is accomplished" (Luke 12:50). Here, the term "baptism" refers to his death, and it is similar in Luke 9:31, where, on the mount of transfiguration, Moses and Elijah spoke with Jesus "of his *exodus* [i.e., departure], which he was about to accomplish at Jerusalem." This was not simply his "death" but his *atoning* death. What he was going to "accomplish" (in 12:50, Gk. *teleō*) was what he declared on the cross: *Tetelestai*, "It is accomplished" (John 19:30 CJB, MOUNCE). His "exodus" was a "baptism," as Israel's exodus had been a "baptism" (1 Cor. 10:1-4) in the sense of a passing through the waters, the chaos, the darkness. The Jewish Passover, which was closely related to Israel's exodus, was the basis for the Lord's Supper, in which "the Lord's death" is proclaimed (1 Cor. 11:26).

In Hebrews 9:14 we hear about the involvement of the

---
32. G. Dalman, quoted by Geldenhuys (1983, 167).

Holy Spirit in this work of atonement: ". . . Christ, who through the eternal Spirit [Gk. *dia pneumatos aiōniou*] offered himself without blemish to God." We are tempted to view this passage in terms of the Trinity; yet, I feel this would be arbitrary. The term "God" cannot be simply equated with "the Father"; "God" is the Triune God. Of course, "Christ" is the Son of the Father, but here the emphasis is not on his being a divine person but on his being the Man Christ Jesus. As this Man he brought to the holy and righteous God — who in fact is the Triune God — the sacrifice of himself for all those who would believe in him.

As a comparison, I mention another passage in which we find the complicated relationship between the *Man* Christ Jesus — who in his own being *is* the Son of God — and the Trinity: "in him [i.e., Christ] all the fullness [of God] was pleased to dwell" (Col. 1:19; the ESV is correct here if the words "of God" are placed within brackets; cf. 2:9). The picture is ruined if we follow the KJV: "It pleased the Father that in him should all fullness dwell," for the passage does not deal with the Father and the Son as such, but with the Trinity and the Man Jesus: in this *Man* dwelt the fullness of the Trinity — in the very person who himself was at the same time God the Son. The fact that his humanity is in view here is even clearer in 2:9, "[I]n him [i.e., Christ] the whole fullness of deity dwells [present tense!] *bodily*"; that is to say, in the glorified body of the Man Christ Jesus, seated at the right hand of God, dwells the whole Trinity — in him who at the same time *is* himself in his own person the Son of the Father.[33]

6.3.2 "The Eternal Spirit"

To return to Hebrews 9: here we read first of *God*, that is basically, the "fullness of deity" (cf. Col. 2:9), the Triune God. Second, we read of *Christ*, not viewed here primarily as the Son of the Father but as the Man Jesus who died on the cross (of course, he is both, but in many Bible passages we must de-

---

33. See extensively, Ouweneel (2007b, chapters 8 and 9).

termine what is more prominent: his deity or his humanity). Third, we read of the "eternal Spirit," but this is not primarily the *person* of the Holy Spirit, as, for instance, in verse 8 ("the Holy Spirit indicates"), but the *power* of the Spirit through which Christ has accomplished his sacrifice. If I am right, such an exegesis (as in more cases, e.g., John 20:22; see §6.10.2) is underscored by the lack of the article before *pneuma*. Yet, of course, what Jesus accomplished cannot be severed from the person of the Holy Spirit. Perhaps the author is thinking here of the sacrificial terminology of Isaiah 53, which deals with the suffering Servant of YHWH, of whom 42:1 says, "I have put my Spirit upon him."[34]

Obviously redemption could not be accomplished apart from the other two persons of the Godhead, but this is not the crucial point here. Perhaps we could say that here the power of the Spirit is a power in Christ himself, so that the verse alludes to the miracle of the perfect humanity and deity of Christ.[35] It is true: the Man Christ who brought the sacrifice of himself is at the same time the eternal Son: in the power of the eternal Spirit, who is the Spirit of God's Son (Gal. 4:6), he offered himself. This was a *Man* who offered himself, but who *could* do so because from eternity he was and is God. However, within the present context, should we not say that Jesus is first the dependent Man who accomplishes all his works, not in his own divine power, but in the power of the Holy Spirit? Just as he survived the devil's temptations only in the power of the Spirit (Luke 4:1, 14), so too, at the cross, he overcame the devil in the same power of the Spirit.

Clark Pinnock warned against any form of Logos Christology. This is a Christology that emphasizes Christ being the Logos to such an extent that it robs the self-emptying of the Son (Phil. 2:7) of its radical character, and thereby jeopardizes his true humanity. In fact we are dealing here with the danger of Docetism. However, Pinnock also rejected liberalism, which

---

34. Bruce (1964, 205).
35. Grosheide (1955, 209–10).

views the Spirit *only* as the divine element in Jesus, and not as the third person of the Godhead, who dwelt in the God-Man Jesus.[36] Pinnock called the cross "an intertrinitarian drama":[37] the drama of the Father, "who did not spare his own Son but gave him up for us all" (Rom. 8:32; cf. John 3:16), and of the Son, "who through the eternal Spirit offered himself without blemish to God" (Heb. 9:14).

6.4 The Holy Spirit and Jesus' Resurrection
6.4.1 1 Peter 3:18

Jesus' resurrection belongs as much to his work of redemption as does his death. When he said at the cross, "It is finished" (John 19:30), he anticipated and included his resurrection within three days. For, "if Christ has not been raised, your faith is futile and you are still in your sins" (1 Cor. 15:17). The "gospel by which you are being saved" (vv. 1–2; cf. Eph. 1:13) is not only "that Christ died for our sins in accordance with the Scriptures," but also "that he was buried, that he was raised on the third day in accordance with the Scriptures" (1 Cor. 14:3-4). God raised Jesus from the dead, for he was not only "delivered up for our trespasses" but also "raised for our justification" (Rom. 4:24-25). Christ not only "through the eternal Spirit offered himself without blemish to God" (Heb. 9:14) but he was also "made alive in [or by] the Spirit" (so many translators of 1 Pet. 3:18; see below). Here again we could speak of an "intertrinitarian event": the Son "was raised from the dead by the glory of the Father" (Rom. 6:4) and in the power of the Spirit. Paul speaks of "the Spirit of him who raised Jesus from the dead" (8:11).

Peter says of Jesus: ". . . having been put to death in the flesh, but made alive in the Spirit" (1 Pet. 3:18). The juxtaposition flesh–Spirit is well known (e.g., Matt. 26:41; John 6:63;

---

36. Pinnock (1996, 90–92); cf. Suurmond (1995, 44–48), who rejected both the early church Logos Christology and the Pentecostal Spirit Christology, and believed that only a Wisdom Christology can do justice to the person of Jesus (cf. §3.8).
37. Pinnock (1996, 104).

Rom. 1:3-4; 8:1-14; Gal. 5:16-25; 1 Tim. 3:16) but it is not always easy to indicate the precise intention of this contrast. For 1 Peter 3:18 at least three different interpretations have been proposed.[38]

(a) Jesus died in the physical sense but he lived on as a spirit, whether before or after his resurrection (cf. 1 Cor. 15:45b); the latter addition is necessary because of verses 19-20, which many understand as describing how between his death and resurrection Jesus descended into the realm of death (see below).

(b) Jesus died in a physical body but came alive in a spiritual body (cf. 1 Cor. 15:44).

(c) Jesus died to the natural human existence but was raised in view of the glorified human existence.

Interpretation (a) reads a Greek body-spirit dualism into the text, which is quite inappropriate here because Jesus was "flesh" also after his resurrection (Luke 24:39). Given the way the word "flesh" is used in verse 21 it seems to refer most clearly to natural human existence, which in ordinary humans is characterized by the sinful flesh, for which Jesus died (cf. Rom. 8:3). In opposition to this, the new mode of being, that of the resurrection, is spiritual in nature, that is, characterized by the Holy Spirit.

It is not very obvious to interpret the Greek word *pneumati* ("in [the] Spirit") here in the sense of "by [the] Spirit" (as does [N]KJV) because then a dative of existence (Gk. *sarki*, "in [the] flesh") is placed in juxtaposition with a dative of cause or instrument.[39] A consistent exegesis understands that Christ died to the sphere or mode of existence of the flesh, and was made alive (by the Father, Rom. 6:4) in the sphere or mode of existence of the Spirit.

---

38. Davids (1990, 136-37, including n 22).
39. Blum (1981a, 242).

6.4.2 1 Peter 3:19-20

The interpretation of 1 Peter 3:18 is strongly determined by the exegesis of verses 19-20, a notorious *crux* in the New Testament, into which we can enter here only briefly. The "prison" (Gk. *phylakē*) is no doubt a negative concept; indeed, this place contains those who "formerly did not obey." This leaves us with basically two options:[40] "the spirits" are (1) the souls of those who perished in Noah's Flood, or (2) the fallen angels of Genesis 6:1-4 in their "prison,"[41] or their descendants, who also perished in the Flood.

The "proclaiming in the Spirit of Christ" occurred either in the days of Noah, or between Christ's death and resurrection, or after his resurrection. In the first case, verses 19-20 are read as follows: ". . . in which [Spirit] he [*in those days of Noah*] went and proclaimed to the [*people whose*] spirits [*are now*] in prison, because they formerly did not obey, when God's patience waited in the days of Noah. . . ." Indeed, Genesis 6:3 refers to the Spirit through which God had then spoken and acted. F. Spitta thinks here of the fallen angels of Genesis 6:1-4 who heard the announcement of their judgment.[42] Others think of the wicked in the days of Noah, to whom the Spirit preached through Noah in vain.[43]

Those who see verse 19 as referring to an event between Jesus' death and resurrection assume that Jesus' resurrection is not in view before verse 21c, whereas verse 18c speaks of his existence as a bodiless spirit.[44] This interpretation is hardly possible because the phrase "made alive" (v. 18) cannot refer to a phase or event before the resurrection (cf. 1 Cor. 15:22; note that in Eph. 2:5-6, the believers' spiritual "being made

---

40. See the surveys in ibid., 241, and Davids (1990, 138–42).
41. Cf. Gk. *tartaōsas* ("being cast into the Tartarus [i.e., a divine place of judgment]") in 2 Pet. 2:4; also see Jude 6.
42. Spitta (1890, ad loc.).
43. Augustine; Darby (n.d., ad loc.); Grant (1902, 161–63); Kelly (1923, 200–205); "many Reformed" according to Greijdanus (1931, 62); more recently extensively, Grudem (1988, 157–61, 203–39).
44. So Hart (1979, 68).

alive" presupposes their spiritual "resurrection"). Therefore, in my view, the text gives no indication of some descent of Christ into *Hades*, let alone into "hell" (*Gehenna*), between his death and resurrection.

Space prevents our discussion of the phrase in the Apostles' Creed, "he descended into hell" or "into the realm of the dead" (Lat. *descendit ad infernos*). These words are troublesome in themselves, placed as they are between the phrases "buried" (Lat. *sepultus*) and "rose again" (Lat. *resurrexit*).

If one insists that 1 Peter 3 is referring to an event that occurred during Jesus' time on earth, perhaps we should rather think of the ascension of the risen Christ (cf. v. 22), whereby he proclaimed his triumph over the fallen angels,[45] or over the deceased wicked, including Noah's contemporaries, who are supposedly mentioned here in an exemplary way.[46]

6.4.3 Romans 1:3-4

The flesh-Spirit juxtaposition in 1 Peter 3:18 is encountered in Romans 1:3-4 as well. This passage speaks of God's Son, "who was descended from David according to the flesh and was declared to be the Son of God in power according to the Spirit of holiness by his resurrection from the dead, Jesus Christ our Lord." Just as with 1 Peter 3, one question to be answered is whether the reference is to two "sides" of the person of Christ—the human side (his flesh) and his divine side (the Spirit in him)—or to two consecutive phases in his earthy history: from his birth to his resurrection, and then after his resurrection. Although the former interpretation is quite ancient (e.g., John Calvin, Johann Albrecht Bengel, Charles Hodge), newer exegetes prefer the latter one.[47]

This means that, according to his human nature (the flesh), Christ was born of David's family, but through his resurrec-

---

45. So Blum (1981a, 241-43).
46. So Greijdanus (1931, 62-64); Hommes et al. (1946, 489).
47. Moule (1893, 16-17); Ridderbos (1959, 25); Murray (1968, 6-12, including n 5); Denney (1979, 586).

tion from the dead[48] he was "declared" (or AMP: "designated"; CEB: "identified"; CJB: "demonstrated") to be God's Son *in power*. In his resurrection, his Sonship was revealed in the fullness of the divine power attached to it. And this occurred "according to the Spirit of holiness," that is, the Holy Spirit.[49] His new status as the Son of God risen in power is closely related with the Holy Spirit;[50] therefore, it can be said that since his resurrection he is a life-giving s/Spirit (1 Cor. 15:45), and that the Lord is the Spirit (2 Cor. 3:17).

By way of summary, I observe that, from all eternity, Christ was the Son of God, one with the Father and the Spirit, and that within time the efficacy (Lat. *virtus*) of the Spirit can be seen in him in three ways:[51]

(a) He became Son of God in human form by being conceived by the Spirit of the Virgin Mary (Luke 1:35).

(b) He was acknowledged as Son by the Father when the Holy Spirit descended upon him (Luke 3:21-22).

(c) After his resurrection, he was declared to be God's Son in power, and this power is that of the Holy Spirit (Rom. 1:4).

6.5 The Holy Spirit in the Synoptic Gospels
6.5.1 Matthew 10:19-20; Mark 13:11; Luke 12:11-12

In the four Gospels we read that Jesus announced the coming of the Holy Spirit several times. In each Gospel this is done in accordance with the book's own character. Interestingly, in the synoptic Gospels it is Jesus who is sent in the power of the Spirit, while in John's Gospel it is Jesus who himself promises to send the Spirit. The church fathers as well as the medieval

---

48. The Gk. phrase is *ex anastaseōs nekrōn*, lit., "through resurrection of dead [ones]": his resurrection provided a model for that of the other dead (cf. Rom. 8:11; 1 Cor. 15:20–21).
49. The expression "Spirit of holiness" is usually viewed as a Hebraism; cf. Ps. 87:1, "holy mountains," lit. "mountains of holiness" (JUB) (see §3.6.2).
50. Cf. Rabbi Pinehas ben Jair: ". . . fear of sin leads to holiness, holiness leads to the [possession of] the Holy Spirit, the Holy Spirit leads to the resurrection of the dead" (Talmud: Abodah Zarah 20b).
51. Cf. Congar (1997, 3.171).

theologians emphasized that as God Jesus *gave* the Spirit (this fits John's Gospel) but as Man he *received* the Spirit (this fits more the synoptic Gospels).[52]

It is typical of Matthew to tell us that the Jesus on whom the Spirit has descended was foretold by the prophets (12:17-18), that in the Spirit's power the war was fought against the evil powers (v. 28), and that the baptismal formula involves the Father, the Son, and the Holy Spirit (28:19). Typical of Mark is the promise of the Spirit spoken in the eschatological sermon (13:11). Typical of Luke is the great emphasis on the Spirit in the story of Jesus' youth (1:15, 35, 41, 67; 2:25-27) and of his walk (4:1, 14, 18; 10:21), and the promise of the Spirit for those who ask for him (11:13).

In anticipation of the outpouring of the Spirit that was to occur on the Day of Pentecost, Jesus promised the special power and wisdom that the Spirit would grant his followers at the right time: "When they deliver you over, do not be anxious how you are to speak or what you are to say, for what you are to say will be given to you in that hour. For it is not you who speak, but the Spirit of your Father speaking through you" (Matt. 10:19-20; cf. Mark 13:11), or: "[W]hen they bring you before the synagogues and the rulers and the authorities, do not be anxious about how you should defend yourself or what you should say, for the Holy Spirit will teach you in that very hour what you ought to say" (Luke 12:11-12).

This word is not an excuse for lazy preachers,[53] but a promise that, when witnesses of Jesus would stand before Jewish councils or Roman magistrates, they would be granted a supernatural wisdom, which would put to shame the rhetorical tricks of their prosecutors (cf. Acts 24:1). The book of Acts gives us examples of this promised reality (4:8; 13:9; cf. Exod. 4:12; Jer. 1:9), but church history is replete with it, including the present century.

---

52. Congar (1997, 3.169).
53. Carson (1984, 249).

The expression "not you . . . but the Spirit" in Matthew 10:20 must not be taken as a sharp contrast. It is a Hebraism, as we find it, for instance, in Genesis 45:8 ("not you . . . but God") and Exodus 16:8 ("not against us but against the LORD").[54] Luke 12:12 says that "you" have to speak, but that it is the Holy Spirit who will assist "you" in this. In other circumstances, too, it is true that, when we do not know anymore what to do, the Spirit is our Assistant: "[T]he Spirit helps us in our weakness. For we do not know what to pray for as we ought, but the Spirit himself intercedes for us with groanings too deep for words" (Rom. 8:26).[55] Actually the entire Trinity is involved in this work of assistance: in Matthew 10 it is the "Spirit of your Father," and in 2 Timothy 4:17 it is "the Lord" (Jesus) who assists the Christian who stands before an earthly judge as Jesus' witness.

There are many reasons why, on the Day of Pentecost, the Holy Spirit was poured out on the believers, but this witnessing is of prime significance. The most general and fundamental reason for the Spirit's outpouring is to glorify Christ in and through Christians (John 16:14-15). But this occurs in many more ways than just worship (cf. Eph. 5:18-20). According to the New Testament, one of the most important ways in which Christ is glorified is by proclaiming his name "to the end of the earth"; the Holy Spirit has come to give believers the power for this worldwide testimony (Acts 1:8).[56]

Nowhere is the Great Commission stated in more universal terms than in Mark: "Go into all the world and proclaim the gospel to the *whole creation*" (16:15) — and in Mark there is only one reference to the Spirit's connection with believers, namely, to give them the power and wisdom for this proclamation (13:11).[57] We may say, though, that the Spirit is implicitly present in the well-known final words (if these are

---

54. Ibid.
55. Grosheide (1954, 164).
56. Keener (1997, 192).
57. Cf. Green (1975, 58–59).

authentic[58]):

> "[T]hese signs will accompany those who believe: in my name they will cast out demons; they will speak in new tongues; they will pick up serpents with their hands; and if they drink any deadly poison, it will not hurt them; they will lay their hands on the sick, and they will recover." So then the Lord Jesus, after he had spoken to them, was taken up into heaven and sat down at the right hand of God. And they went out and preached everywhere, while the Lord worked with them and confirmed the message by accompanying signs (Mark 16:17–20).[59]

6.5.2 Matthew 12:28, 31–32; Mark 3:29

Since his baptism by John, when Jesus had received the Holy Spirit, he was conscious of being led by the Spirit (cf. Luke 3:22; 4:1, 14, 18; 10:21; 11:13). In one of his most intense controversies with the Pharisees this guidance played a great role. They accused him of casting out the demons by "Beelzebul [i.e., Satan[60]], the prince of demons" (Matt. 12:24; Mark 3:22; Luke 11:15). Jesus refuted this foolish statement extensively, making this pivotal statement: "But if it is by the Spirit of God that I cast out demons, then the kingdom of God has come upon you" (Matt. 12:28; interestingly, the parallel text Luke 11:20 reads "finger" instead of "Spirit"; see §4.8.2).

"If" (Gk. *ei*, followed by the present tense) is not conditional here, but states a fact: "It being the case that by the Spirit of God I cast out demons. . . ." As surely as Jesus cast out demons, namely, by the power of God's Spirit, so surely had the kingdom of God come in his person to the people; this amounted to saying that he himself was the anointed King, the Messiah. Not every exorcism occurred with the same sov-

---

58. See on this Metzger (1975, 122–26).
59. See more extensively, Ouweneel (2005a, §4.2).
60. From Hebrew *Baʿal-Zebul*, "Lord of the house," originally a Philistine idol (see 2 Kings 1:2); here in the form of a nickname: *Baʿal-Zebub*, "Lord of the flies"; in Matt. 10:25 and 12:24, 27, some manuscripts read the former (ESV), others read the latter (KJV).

ereign authority as it occurred with Jesus (the Pharisees' sons cast out demons as well; Matt. 12:27; Luke 11:19; cf. also Acts 19:13-16). In his case, the authority and power were so great and so evident that his casting out of demons could serve as a proof that God's kingdom had arrived, *and* his being accused of casting out demons by Beelzebul could be designated as an unpardonable blasphemy against the Holy Spirit (Matt. 12:31-32; Mark 3:29; Luke 12:10).[61]

Scripture does not contain the expression "the sin against the Holy Spirit," although it is an oft used phrase that has confused many Christians. In a certain sense, *every* sin is a sin against the Holy Spirit, for the Holy Spirit is God, and therefore sinning against the Triune God involves sinning against the Spirit.[62] Impurity is a sin against the Spirit (1 Thess. 4:7-8), as are the sins of lying to and testing the Spirit (Acts 5:3, 9), resisting the Spirit (7:51), grieving the Spirit (Eph. 4:30), quenching the Spirit (1 Thess. 5:19), and outraging the Spirit of grace (Heb. 10:29).[63] However, Matthew 12 and its parallel passages deal with a very specific sin: *blasphemy* against the Holy Spirit. This is speaking evil of the Spirit, and doing so on purpose, deliberately, consciously. In the present case, the Pharisees knew that Jesus cast out demons by the Holy Spirit, yet they claimed that he did so by Beelzebul.

Now the remarkable point is that Matthew 12:32a and Luke 12:10a tell us that blasphemy against the Son of Man, and all blasphemies (which is primarily blasphemy against God; Mark 3:28) are forgiven, but not the blasphemy against the Holy Spirit. Why this is so is a question that has occupied many Christians.[64] Augustine spoke of a "great secret" (*grande*

---

61. Dunn (1997, 44–49; 1992, 696); also see the comments on Dunn's view by Carson (1984, 289).
62. Therefore it is incorrect when Siebesma writes in a heading: "A believer commits no sin against the Holy Spirit" (Doornenbal and Siebesma [2005], 227). My reply: the believer does indeed—every day, I am afraid.
63. Cf. Duffield and Van Cleave (1996, 344–46).
64. See extensively, Bavinck (*RD* 3.155–57); Berkouwer (1971, 323–53). Pinnock (1996, 89) feels that it underscores the central role of the Spirit in Jesus'

secretum). Some have sought the solution of the problem in passages like Acts 5:3-5 (Ananias' death after his lying to the Holy Spirit), 1 John 5:16 (KJV: "sin unto death"), and in Hebrews 10:20; the latter text deals with apostate Christians (cf. 4:4-6): "How much worse punishment, do you think, will be deserved by the one who has trampled underfoot the Son of God, and has profaned the blood of the covenant by which he was sanctified, and has outraged the Spirit of grace?" However, outraging the Spirit is coupled here with trampling underfoot the Son of God — so perhaps we must make a distinction here between the Son of Man in his humiliation and the Son of God in his exaltation. In other words, people might be mistaken as to the true nature of the humble Man Jesus — and this sin could therefore be repented and forgiven, as in the case of Saul (1 Tim. 1:13) — but people could *not* be mistaken as to the evident work of the Holy Spirit.

It is important to note that in Scripture, forgivable sins have been committed in ignorance (Luke 23:34; Acts 3:17; 17:30; 1 Tim. 1:13; Heb. 5:2; 1 Pet. 1:14), whereas unforgivable sins have been committed "with a high hand" (Num. 15:30; cf. Luke 12:47-48), that is, in conscious rebellion. Blasphemy against the Holy Spirit implies a deliberate, calculated, rebellious, malign slandering. It proceeds from the evil spirit that calls light darkness, love hate, and life death (cf. 2 Cor. 6:16): "Woe to those who call evil good and good evil, who put darkness for light and light for darkness, who put bitter for sweet and sweet for bitter" (Isa. 5:20). A. B. Bruce argued that the *content* of such slander is less important than the *motive* of this slander: slandering out of ignorance, misunderstanding, or half-knowledge is forgivable, but slandering out of malice, a deeply rooted abhorrence of the good, or a selfish preference of evil for one's own benefit, is unforgivable.[65]

The unforgivable blasphemy against the Holy Spirit involves an act that is committed not flippantly, but deliberate-

---

ministry.
65. Bruce (1979, 189).

ly, as was the case with the malignant and irremediable Pharisees. Those who worry whether they might have committed "the sin against the Holy Spirit" are the very ones who, by their fear and repentance, demonstrate that they do not belong to this category. It is unthinkable that a person would come to God with sincere contrition concerning whatever sin, and would still be refused: "[W]hoever comes to me I will never cast out" (John 6:37). To the rule, "If we confess our sins, he is faithful and just to forgive us our sins and to cleanse us from all unrighteousness" (1 John 1:9), no exceptions are mentioned. As John C. Ryle put it, there is indeed sin that is never forgiven. But those who are concerned about it are the least likely to have committed it.[66]

Blasphemy against the Holy Spirit is an "eternal sin" (Mark 3:29) — not a sin that repeats itself eternally, but a sin for which there is no forgiveness in eternity. In fact, this is because it is not repented in eternity either, although the expression itself does not say this.[67]

Other than in Matthew and Mark, the blasphemy against the Spirit in Luke 12 stands in the context of the Spirit's works in the Christian witnesses (see vv. 10 and 12). This is an encouragement to his followers: the blasphemy against the Spirit *who speaks through them* is far worse in God's sight than the blasphemy of the prejudiced Pharisees against the Son of Man.[68]

6.5.3 Luke 11:13

In Luke's Gospel the Greek word *pneuma* occurs no fewer than thirty-six times, in Acts seventy times, but only nineteen times in Matthew, twenty-three in Mark, and twenty-four in John; in the great majority of cases this word refers to the Holy Spirit.

In Luke's Gospel we are struck by this peculiar statement

---

66. Ryle (1993, 59).
67. Bruce (1979, 362).
68. Ibid., 556.

in 11:13, "If you then, who are evil, know how to give good gifts to your children, how much more will the heavenly Father give the Holy Spirit to those who ask him!" Much of the pericope (vv. 1–11) is found in Matthew 6:9–15 and 7:7–11, but this saying is in Luke alone. The parallel text resembling it most closely is Matthew 7:11, where we find "good things" (or "good [gifts]") instead of "the Holy Spirit." Apparently, the connection is not that one who receives good gifts from God in this way also receives the Holy Spirit, but that the Holy Spirit is the greatest of all God's good gifts, the most desirable for all true followers of Jesus.

Far-fetched is the interpretation by S. Greijdanus, who, because the words "for it" ("those who ask him for it") are lacking, suggests that the Lord may have intended that God gives the Holy Spirit not only to those who ask him for this Spirit but to everyone who sincerely prays to him.[69] This is both theologically and exegetically incorrect: the parallel with the earthly father, who gives his son a fish or an egg when the latter asks for a fish or an egg (vv. 11–12), makes clear that the text refers to those who *ask for the Holy Spirit*.

At face value, one might be inclined to think that this asking for the Spirit could refer only to Acts 1, where one hundred twenty believers were praying as they waited for the Spirit whom the Lord had promised (cf. vv. 5, 8, 14; Luke 24:49; John 15:26). However, such an interpretation of Luke 11:13 would be far too limited.[70] Nor would it be relevant to point out that, in Luke 11, the Spirit had not yet been given (John 7:39), so that verse 13 could not have been realized before Acts 2.[71] We need only think of John the Baptist and his parents, Elizabeth and Zechariah, as well as Simeon, who, permanently or occasionally, were filled with or led by the Holy Spirit (Luke 1:15, 41, 67; 2:25–27).

Moreover, how often does a child ask their parents for

---

69. Greijdanus (1955, 294).
70. *Contra* Liefeld (1984, 949).
71. *Contra* Grant (1897, 403).

food ([N]KJV: bread, fish, an egg; vv. 11–12)? Not just once in its lifetime but each time the child is hungry. Could it be different with the believer? For instance, when the believer stands before an earthly judge as a Christian witness, will the believer not pray for the Lord's promise, namely, the guidance and power of the Holy Spirit (12:12)? Luke 11:13 does not deal with one single prayer for the indwelling of the *person* of the Holy Spirit but with the frequent prayer for the guidance and power of the Spirit. If a child is hungry the child asks their father for food. If God's child is spiritually hungry, they ask their heavenly Father for the filling with the Holy Spirit.

In this connection, it is interesting that in Luke 11:2, some manuscripts plus Marcion and Gregory of Nyssa, knew a version of the Lord's prayer in which, instead of "your kingdom come," we read: "[Y]our Holy Spirit come over us and cleanse us." Such a prayer underscores the possibility that the believer may come to the Father with this prayer at any given moment (see §§7.2.2, 7.8.2).

6.6 The Holy Spirit in John 4[72] and 7
6.6.1 John 4:10, 14

During his encounter with the Samaritan woman, Jesus said, "If you knew the gift of God, and who it is that is saying to you, 'Give me a drink,' you would have asked him, and he would have given you living water" (John 4:10). To the woman's question where she might obtain this "living water" he responded, "[W]hoever drinks of the water that I will give him will never be thirsty again. The water that I will give him will become in him a spring of water welling up to eternal life" (v. 14).

In this passage, the Holy Spirit is not explicitly mentioned. However, because of the rather obvious relationship with John 7:37–39 (see §6.6.2), many have thought here of the Spirit. But in what sense? Is the "gift of God" the Holy Spirit? Is the "living water" the Holy Spirit? Because in verse 10 it is the

---

72. John 4:23–24 is discussed in §10.6.1.

living water that is "given" we may assume that this water is identical with the "gift of God." Because of John 7:37–39, we have reason to assume that, here too, this living water is the Holy Spirit. However, Jesus does not say so, and the question may be raised how the woman could have presumed that he was referring to the Spirit.

"Living water" was a well-known concept among Samaritan writers,[73] in close connection with the Old Testament: "The teaching of the wise is a fountain of life" (Prov. 13:14); God himself is "the fountain of living water(s)" (Jer. 2:13; 17:13; cf. Ps. 36:9, "with you is the fountain of life"). According to the rabbis, God is the "fountain (spring, well)," and his instruction in general, and more specifically his Torah, is the living water (cf. Eph. 5:26). Sometimes the living water is the Spirit who speaks through the Torah.[74] In connection with John 7, it may be best to say that the living water in John 4 is either the Word of God made alive by the Holy Spirit,[75] or the Holy Spirit himself working through the Word.[76] Materially this makes little difference.

The work of the Spirit in regeneration (John 3:5) is fundamentally different from the *gift* of the Spirit of which John 4 speaks (see more extensively §§8.1.1 and 8.2.1–8.2.2). What the Holy Spirit works in us must be distinguished from his coming in person to dwell within us. Through regeneration, a person receives life from God. But when the Holy Spirit comes to dwell in the believer, that person becomes a fountain of water "welling up to eternal life." That is, the Holy Spirit leads us into the fullness of the divine life, the "abundance" of life (John 10:10), the life that involves fellowship with the Father and the Son (1 John 1:1–3; cf. John 17:3), the life that, in the end, is nothing but Christ himself (1 John 5:20; cf. Col. 3:4).

---

73. Macdonald (1964, 425).
74. Morris (1971, 260–61 including notes 29–32).
75. Ibid., 260–61; Grant (1897, 501–02).
76. Cf. Kelly (n.d.-b, 27–52); Wolston (1926, 47–68); Bouma (1927, 62); Chafer (1983, 6.51).

John 4 shows us that the one force that can rise to God — the Spirit who as a fountain wells up to eternal life — is a force that originally descended from God himself. Nothing can exalt itself to the divine level that did not first descend from that level, as Congar put it.[77] In a wider context, this also means that no one "can come to me [i.e., Christ] unless the Father who sent me draws him" (John 6:44). The Son himself can ascend to heaven only because he is the One who descended from heaven (3:13). And believers can ascend to heaven only because they bear the image of the "man of heaven," that is, the "second man," who is "from heaven" (1 Cor. 15:47-49).

6.6.2 John 7:37-38

The apostle John speaks of the Holy Spirit many times; some passages have been discussed already, others will be discussed later. Some passages will not be discussed because they do not actually deal with the Holy Spirit (*contra* certain expositors and some translations) but with the human spirit of Christ (11:33; 13:21; 19:30). Some passages related to the descent of the Holy Spirit on the Day of Pentecost will be discussed now. First, there is John 7:37-39, "On the last day of the feast [i.e., the Feast of Booths], the great day, Jesus stood up and cried out,[78] 'If anyone thirsts, let him come to me and drink. Whoever believes in me, as the Scripture has said, "Out of his heart will flow rivers of living water."' Now this he said about the Spirit, whom those who believed in him were to receive, for as yet the Spirit had not been given, because Jesus was not yet glorified" (cf. §6.6.1 on 4:14).

John 7 is the only place in the New Testament where the Feast of Booths is explicitly mentioned.[79] On each of the seven days of the feast, a long line of priests, carrying jars in their

---

77. Congar (1997, 2.108), referring to the metaphor of communicating vessels.
78. Jesus' "crying out" (Gk. *krazō* and *kraugazō*) often announces important, perhaps also emotional, proclamations (7:28; 11:43; 12:44); Morris (1971, 413, 422).
79. See Ouweneel (2001b, 180–81). The book of Revelation seems to contain allusions to the Feast of Booths (7:9, 15; 21:3).

hands and surrounded by an exulting crowd, descended to the bath water of Siloam. There they filled their jars with the last water remaining after the dry summer, and carried it to the inner temple court, through the Watergate and through the Court of the Gentiles and the Court of the Women.[80] The water was solemnly poured out into a bowl next to the ornamented altar, from where it flowed through a tube to the foot of the altar. The ceremony was a token of gratitude for the rain that had made the harvest possible. During the rite, the words of Isaiah 12:3 were sung: "With joy you will draw water from the wells of salvation." Presumably Jesus was referring to this when he said, ". . . as the Scripture has said" (other passages suggested: Exod. 17:6; Num. 21:16-18; Ps. 105:41; Isa. 55:1; 58:11; Ezek. 47:1; Joel 3:18; Zech. 13:1; 14:8). In Jesus' quotation from Scripture, the phrase "his heart" might be referring to that of the Messiah,[81] but the context suggests the heart of the believer.[82]

In John 7 we find Jesus at the last and most important of all the festivals explained in Leviticus 23, namely, on "the last day of the feast, the great day,"[83] when the temple square was full of people, praying for a new time of rain in autumn as a condition for a new harvest. And there, Jesus' voice reverberated across the temple square as he spoke the quoted words.

The application that he made here is quite remarkable. The ceremony of drawing the water alludes to Isaiah 12:3, but also to the "rivers of living water" that one day, during the Messianic kingdom, will flow from Jerusalem, both the heavenly and the earthly Jerusalem (Ezek. 47:1-12; Zech. 14:8; Rev. 22:1-2; cf. 7:17; 21:6; 22:17). Jesus is saying, as it were, just like the waters of life will *one day* flow from *Jerusalem* as a blessing for the entire surroundings, so too, *already now*, they may flow

---

80. See Talmud: Sukkah IV (48a–50a).
81. See Congar (1997, 1.50).
82. Morris (1971, 423–24); Tenney (1981, 86).
83. I leave aside here the complex discussion about whether this is the seventh or the eighth day of the Feast of Booths; cf. Morris (1971, 421n74).

from the heart of each believer. One day, Jerusalem will be the center of the entire earth, and will moisten the earth with its water of blessing. But already now, those who have "drunk" this "living water" — that is, all believers — become themselves fountains from which the Spirit's waters of life flow to bless others around them.[84] In John 4:14 the (implied) Holy Spirit is Jesus' gift to the believer; in 7:38 the Spirit is Jesus' gift *through* the believers to others.

The Spirit's waters of life flow from the believer's heart, or literally, his "belly" (KJV; Gk. *koilia*)[85] — not his head. The belly, or the intestines (bowels), is/are the seat of compassion. The Greek word *esplanchnisthē* ("he had compassion") was derived from *splanchna*, which means "bowels (intestines)" (see Acts 1:18).[86] It is from the "bowels" of God and believers, respectively, that is, from the seat of compassion and affection, that the blessings of the Holy Spirit flow out to others.[87] We have seen in §3.7.1 that we might even think here of God's very "womb."

6.6.3 John 7:39

Of great interest is John's own comment in verse 39. First, he explains that the "living water" refers to the Holy Spirit. Second, he adds that "as yet the Spirit had not been given, because Jesus was not yet glorified." Literally the text says that "[the] Spirit was not yet" (Darby), which of course does not mean that the Spirit did not yet *exist*. A similar difficulty is found in Acts 19:2, where, in my view, the translation should not be: "[W]e have not even heard that there is a Holy Spirit"

---

84. Cf. the Midrash Sifrē on Deut. 11:22: "The disciple who begins is like a well that can only give the water that it has received; the more advanced disciple is a well that gives living water."
85. See extensively, Morris (1971, 425–26n84).
86. In Luke 1:78 the Gk. phrase *splanchna eleous* ("tender mercy") literally means "bowels of mercy" (DRA). In 2 Cor. 7:15, Phil. 1:8, and 2:1, the Gk. word *splanchna* has been translated as "affection," and in Philem. 1:7, 20 and 1 John 3:17 as "heart" (ESV).
87. In the Old Testament, see also 1 Kings 3:26, Isa. 16:11, 63:15, and Jer. 31:20.

(thus most translations) but: "We did not even hear if [the] Holy Spirit is [here]" (Gk. *ei pneuma hagion estin*)[88] (see §5.9.1). The Holy Spirit is eternal and omnipresent; but before the Day of Pentecost he did not yet *dwell* (Gk. *oikeō*) on this earth (cf. Rom. 8:9, 11; 1 Cor. 3:16; 6:19; Eph. 2:22; and 2 Tim. 1:14).

In both John 7:39 and Acts 19:2 the idea is that there was a time when the Holy Spirit was not yet on earth, at least not in the special way that is announced in John 14-16 and is fulfilled in Acts 2. John 7 stipulates precisely the primary condition for this dwelling by the Spirit on earth: the glorification of Jesus, which would be the border between the era of the law and that of the Spirit (cf. John 1:17; Gal. 3:23-25).[89] This glorification here refers especially to Jesus' ascension, although in other passages it also comprises his miraculous works (John 8:54; 11:4), sufferings, death, and resurrection (12:16, 23-24; 13:31-32; 17:1, 5; also see 16:14; 17:10).

In Acts 2:33 the same connection is made between the glorification of Christ and the coming of the Holy Spirit: "Being therefore exalted at the right hand of God, and having received from the Father the promise of the Holy Spirit, he has poured out this that you yourselves are seeing and hearing." There could be no descent of *God* the Holy Spirit on *earth* before the ascent of the *Man* Christ Jesus to *heaven*. Nor could the Spirit descend upon believers until the Spirit had dwelt perfectly in Jesus, who is the example for all those who would receive the Spirit after him and through this Spirit would continue his works (John 14:12).[90]

In summary, the Holy Spirit performed *work* on earth during the Old Testament era, in and through believers, but with these differences.

(a) He does not work in the same *mighty* way as he has since the Day of Pentecost.

(b) He works in a *broad* way, for now the Spirit rests no

---

88. See Kelly (1966, 164).
89. Tenney (1981, 87); cf. Ouweneel (1997, 222–27).
90. Dods (1979, 768).

longer on just a few privileged persons, but on "all flesh," that is, all the people of God (Joel 2:28; Acts 2:17).

(c) Since Acts 2, the Spirit not only *works* on earth but he also *dwells* on earth, both in individual believers (Rom. 8:9, 11; 1 Cor. 6:16; 2 Tim. 1:14) and in the church as a whole (1 Cor. 3:16; 2 Cor. 6:16; Eph. 2:22).

(d) The Spirit could come only after Jesus' ascension, first, because he replaced Jesus as Paraclete here on earth (John 14:16-17; 16:7; see the next sections).

(e) The Spirit could come only after Jesus' ascension, second, because he has come to witness of the glorified Christ (16:14-15).

6.7 The Holy Spirit in John 14
6.7.1 The "Advocate"

The conversations that Jesus had with his disciples in the upper room (Mark 14:15; Luke 22:12) belong to the highlights in John's Gospel. It has been said that John 1-12 figuratively leads us into the temple's court, John 13 to the "laver of brass" (see vv. 1-11), John 14-16 into the Holy Place, and John 17 into the Most Holy Place.[91] In John 14-16 the announcements of the coming and work of the Holy Spirit belong to the most important subjects. He is simply referred to as "Holy Spirit" (14:26) but also as the Paraclete (Gk. *Paraklētos*, Helper, Comforter, Advocate, Intercessor, Counselor, Strengthener, Standby, Companion, 14:16, 26; 15:26; 16:7),[92] and as the "Spirit of truth" (14:17; 15:26; 16:13).

In John 14:16-20 and 25-26 we read, "I will ask the Father, and he will give you another Helper, to be with you forever, even the Spirit of truth, whom the world cannot receive, because it neither sees him nor knows him. You know him, for he dwells with you and will be in you. I will not leave you as orphans; I will come to you. Yet a little while and the world will see me no more, but you will see me. Because I live, you

---
91. Meyer (n.d., 7-8).
92. For the possible origin of this concept, see Floor (1982, 70-71).

also will live. In that day you will know that I am in my Father, and you in me, and I in you.... These things I have spoken to you while I am still with you. But the Helper, the Holy Spirit, whom the Father will send in my name, he will teach you all things and bring to your remembrance all that I have said to you."

The Holy Spirit is the "other" (Gk. *allos*, another of the same kind; not *heteros*, another of a different kind[93]) Paraclete (14:16), that is, either "another One, namely, the Paraclete" (in this case, Jesus himself is not a Paraclete), or the "other Paraclete," the new One after the Paraclete Jesus. Indeed, Jesus is called Paraclete in 1 John 2:1, but this is in connection with the ministry that he performs *at present* at the right hand of the Father.

Although the Greek verb *parakaleō* can mean "to comfort" (Matt. 5:4; Luke 16:25; Acts 15:31–32; 20:12; 2 Cor. 1:4, 6; 2:7), the *Paraklētos* is much more than a "Comforter" (in spite of the traditional translations). The Vulgate avoids the translation problem by the rendering *Paraclitus*. The early Protestant translations (Luther: *Tröster*; KJV: "Comforter") seem to go back especially to Wycliffe's rendering of "comforter," but this word must be understood in its original meaning (*con*, with + *fortis*, strong): "Strengthener" (cf. his *comfortith* in Phil. 4:13, "strengthens").

The Greek term *paraklētos* is a technical term for what in Latin is *advocatus*, "called to be together with," that is, called to assist a person in legal affairs. An advocate is a person who legally defends and pleads the cause of another person; hence we get such translations of *Paraklētos* as Advocate, Intercessor, Counselor, Defender, Standby.[94] Yves Congar argued that it is best to retain the translation Paraclete, as the rabbis also did (*p'raqlit*),[95] because no translation can contain all the nuances

---

93. Morris (1971, 648–49n42).
94. In addition to the lexica, see extensively, Morris (1971, 649, 662–66).
95. Exod. R. 18 (80b).

of the term.⁹⁶

The Paraclete functions primarily not to bring comfort and consolation, but, as especially 1 John 2:1 underscores, to serve in a legal context. Compare Romans 8:26 and 34 as well, where both the Spirit within believers and Christ in heaven intercede for them (Gk. *[hyper]entynchanō*), which again refers to a legal function. The Holy Spirit is a lawyer—unlike the kind we know in society, people who, for a lot of money, try to get the best for their clients insofar as the loopholes and the fine print in the law allow them, but a lawyer who performs his task in a *holy* (14:26) and a *truthful* way (14:17; 15:26; 16:13). An example is Acts 9:31b, "[W]alking in the fear of the Lord and in the comfort [Gk. *paraklēsei*, encouragement, help, strengthening] of the Holy Spirit, it [i.e., the church] multiplied," where we may think of the interceding and assisting work of the Paraclete.

6.7.2 The "Other Paraclete"

The Holy Spirit is really "another" (a new) Paraclete, a substitute for Jesus, since what he does is to some extent the same as what Jesus did for his disciples. As the Spirit was transferred from Moses to Joshua (Deut. 34:9), and from Elijah to Elisha (2 Kings 2:9-10, 15), thus the Spirit was transferred from Jesus to the disciples in order to do in them what he had done in Jesus (cf. John 14:12).⁹⁷ Jesus "abode" in them (6:56; 14:20, 25; 15:3-5; 1 John 3:24), as does the Spirit (John 14:17;⁹⁸ 1 John 4:12-13). He taught them (John 6:59; 7:14, 28; 8:2, 20; 13:13 "Teacher") as does the Spirit (14:26; 16:13). He witnessed (3:11, 32; 8:14, 18), as does the Spirit (15:26). He speaks what he hears (3:32;

---

96. Congar (1997, 1.53).
97. Brown (1970, ad loc.).
98. The rendering "to dwell in," as many translate, is confusing here; the Gk. phrase is *menō para*, "to abide with," not *oikeō en*, "to dwell in," the term reserved for the Spirit's post-Pentecost dwelling in the church. There is a tension here between the present and the future: the Spirit "abides [present tense] with you and will be [future] in you"; but some translations read "is in you" (cf. GNT).

8:26, 40; 15:15), as does the Spirit (16:13). The world could not receive Jesus (1:11) as it cannot receive the Spirit (14:17). The believers know Jesus (17:3) as they know the Spirit (14:17). Jesus was sent by the Father (14:24; 15:21; 16:5), as the Spirit was sent by the Father (14:26).[99]

Actually, it is striking that none of these meanings really fits with the idea of an advocate—an idea that we encounter much more clearly in 1 John 2:1, which describes Jesus as our Advocate with the Father in view of our sins. In John 14–16 there is no mention of sins and weaknesses. Therefore, it seems to be preferable to think here of the more general meaning of helper, or even companion, friend—more specifically, a legal friend who, in the widest sense, handles one's affairs, and looks after one's interests in a court of justice.

The Paraclete comes in answer to the Son's prayer (14:16). He is given, or sent, by the Father (14:16, 26), or sent by the Son from the Father (15:26; 16:7). The Paraclete "abides" with believers eternally, which means in Pauline terms: the church remains eternally the temple of the Holy Spirit (1 Cor. 3:16; 2 Cor. 6:16; Eph. 2:22), and (the bodies of) individual believers remain such temples too (Rom. 8:9, 11; 1 Cor. 6:19; 2 Tim. 1:14). He would "abide" with them—for he already *was* with them because Jesus was with them—but from the Day of Pentecost he would be "*in* them" (John 14:17c).

6.7.3 Other Aspects

The Spirit is the "Spirit of truth," both because he is perfectly truthful, and because he guides believers into all the truth (John 16:13). This is the truth that "the world"—here, the evil world characterized by sin and Satan (cf. 12:31; 14:30; 16:8–9, 11)—does not know and cannot know (14:17), a truth embodied in Jesus himself (14:6). The world "saw" Jesus in the flesh,

---

[99]. See the survey by Congar (1997, 1.55–56). Paul, too, notes many parallels between Christ and the Holy Spirit; see the survey by Congar (1997, 1.37–38). Regarding both Jesus and the Spirit being sent, and the consequences thereof, see Congar (1997, 2.7–12, 42–43).

but did not perceive him in his true spiritual significance (1:10 [cf. v. 14]; 14:17; 1 John 3:1).

Jesus did not leave his disciples behind as "orphans" in the world, that is, as children who, because of their parents' death, have, as it were, been left to their destiny by these parents. Jesus assured his followers that he would not abandon them, and did so through the promise "I will come to you" (v. 18b). But what does this mean? There are basically four possibilities, and each has its own problems.

(a) "I will come to you in the person of the Holy Spirit" (thus many older and newer expositors);[100] however, nowhere else does Jesus identify himself in such a way with the Holy Spirit (but cf. Acts 16:7; Rom. 8:9; 2 Cor. 3:17; Gal. 4:6; Phil. 1:19).

(b) "I will come to you immediately after my resurrection" (cf. 16:16, 22; 20:14, 19);[101] however, soon after his resurrection he did leave them again; in fact, the disciples became orphans only at Jesus' ascension.

(c) "I will come to you spiritually, invisibly, if you are sincerely devoted to me" (cf. 14:23; Eph. 3:17; Col. 1:27);[102] however, Jesus made his promise not just to intensely devoted believers but to all believers.

(d) "I will come to you when I will receive you in my Father's house" (cf. 14:1-3);[103] however, if Jesus was thinking here of his return from heaven, he would indeed leave his own as orphans for many centuries, and the twelve disciples would never have experienced the fulfillment of this promise.

Personally, I prefer (a) in combination with (c) because of the link with verse 23 ("If anyone loves me, he will keep my word, and my Father will love him, and we will *come* to him

---

100. Kelly (1966, 295); Green (1975, 43); Dods (1979, 825). Congar (1997, 2.101) quotes extensively Cyril of Alexandria.
101. Morris (1971, 651–52), who adduces v. 19 as an argument (cf. 16:16–19); Tenney (1981, 147).
102. Grant (1897, 580 notes); Gaebelein (1980, 286).
103. Bouma (1927, 183) following Augustine, Bede, Ryle, and others.

and make our home with him"), for the "coming" of the Father and the Son here is possible only in the power of the Holy Spirit.

The Holy Spirit would "teach you [i.e., Jesus' followers] all things and bring to your remembrance all that I have said to you" (14:26). By the power of the Holy Spirit, they would not only remember all the teachings of Jesus, but also *understand* them. Therefore, Jesus told Peter, "What I am doing you do not understand now, but afterward [i.e., after Acts 2] you will understand" (13:7), and he told all the disciples: "I still have many things to say to you, but you cannot bear them now" (16:12). We need only remind ourselves of the disciples' doubts, questions, and incomprehension (13:6, 22, 28, 36–37; 14:5, 8; 16:5, 19, 29–30) to grasp this statement of Jesus. All his teachings had to be brought back to their memory, but thanks to the indwelling Holy Spirit they would not only remember but also understand them.

6.8 The Holy Spirit in John 15
6.8.1 John 15:26–27

In John 15:26–27 Jesus says, "But when the Helper comes, whom I will send to you from the Father, the Spirit of truth, who proceeds from the Father, he will bear witness [Gk. *martyreō*] about me. And you also will bear witness [Gk. *martyreō*], because you have been with me from the beginning"; compare 1 John 5:6 as well, "[T]he Spirit is the one who testifies [Gk. *martyreō*], because the Spirit is the truth."

After all that has been said in §6.7 about the "Helper" and the "Spirit of truth," and in §1.6 about the "procession" of the Spirit, the only point remaining to be discussed is the subject of the "witnessing" by the Spirit.[104] In John there are no fewer than nine "witnesses" to Jesus:[105] the Father (5:31–32, 34, 37;

---

104. Cf., in a very different context, Paul's statement: "[M]y conscience bears me witness in the Holy Spirit" (Rom. 9:1), where his conscience—in itself not always a reliable criterion—functions in the power of the Holy Spirit.
105. Cf. Morris (1971, 90).

8:18), the Son himself (8:14, 18; cf. 3:11, 32; 8:37), the Holy Spirit (15:26; cf. 16:14), Jesus' works (5:36; 10:25; cf. 14:11; 15:24), the Scriptures (5:39; cf. vv. 45–47), John the Baptist (1:7), the Samaritan woman (4:39), the crowd (12:17), and the disciples (15:27; 19:35; 21:24).

There is a seeming contrast in the text between the witness of the Spirit (v. 26) and that of the disciples (v. 27) — "not only the Spirit, but you also" — which is often overlooked.[106] Here, the specific basis for the disciples' witness is not that they would receive the Holy Spirit, but that they had been with Jesus from the beginning of his ministry (cf. Acts 1:21–22, ". . . the men who have accompanied us during all the time that the Lord Jesus went in and out among us, beginning from the baptism of John until the day when he was taken up from us"). No doubt they needed the power of the Holy Spirit for this witnessing, but that is not the point here. The point is that they could and would witness concerning what *they* had seen and heard from Jesus during his time on earth. They could not do more than that; they were not witnesses of the glorified Christ in heaven.

This seems to be the precise point of verse 26. We are dealing here with the Spirit's own testimony, not about Jesus' words and works during his earthly ministry but about his glorification (John 16:13–15; see §6.9). In other words, the testimony of the Holy Spirit, who was sent by the *glorified* Lord, and which was about him, must be distinguished from the testimony of the twelve disciples, who were sent by the Lord in his state of *humiliation*, and which was about him.[107] The disciples could bear witness concerning the Jesus they had known on earth; but the Spirit has his own testimony concerning Jesus as he is now, glorified with the Father. Of course, this testimony, too, comes to expression in the ministry of humans, especially in New Testament letters (see, e.g., the references to Jesus at the right hand of God: Rom. 8:34; Eph. 1:20; Col. 3:1; Heb. 1:3, 13;

---

106. Ibid., 684.
107. Kelly (1966, 323–24).

8:1; 10:12; 12:2; 1 Pet. 3:22).

6.8.2 Comparison with 1 John 5:6–8

The witnessing by the Spirit in John 15:26 reminds us of 1 John 5:6–8, which speaks of such witnessing (testifying) as well: "This is he who came by water and blood—Jesus Christ; not by the water only but by the water and the blood. And the Spirit is the one who testifies, because the Spirit is the truth. For there are three that testify: the Spirit and the water and the blood; and these three agree."[108] In addition to the Spirit, who is "the truth" (v. 6; cf. 4:6; John 14:17; 15:26; 16:13), we find "the water" and "the blood" personified as witnesses. With respect to what "water" and "blood" mean here, there are at least four interpretations.

(a) Especially in verse 8, water and blood refer here to the two sacraments, baptism and the Lord's Supper, respectively (Luther, Calvin).[109] This exegesis goes back to what I see as a sacramental misunderstanding of John 3:5 (see §8.2) and 6:51–56; moreover, it does not find any point of connection within the context of 1 John.[110] Usually this interpretation also implies that water and blood in 1 John 5:8 mean something else than in verse 6, which is quite unlikely.

(b) In John's argument, the three witnesses are being adduced in opposition to docetism, which denied "Jesus as come in the flesh" (4:2–3; cf. 2 John 1:7). The idea, then, would be that Jesus did come "by the water," namely, his baptism by John, but not "by the blood," namely, his atoning death. But not so, John supposedly argues, for Jesus came "not by the

---

108. It is generally agreed today, except by contemporary defenders of the Byzantine Text, that the part in italics in the following quotation is a gloss from a much later date—see Marshall (1978, 236); Lalleman (2005, 207); *contra* Greijdanus (1934, 118–19): "There are three that bear witness *in heaven: the Father, the Word, and the Holy Spirit; and these three are one. And there are three that bear witness on earth*: the Spirit, the water, and the blood" (NKJV).
109. So Green (1975, 78, 112); Congar (1997, 1.57–58).
110. So Lalleman (2005, 206); *contra* Barker (1981, 353).

water [of his baptism] only but by the water and the blood [of his atoning death]" (so Tertullian), to which was supposedly added the confirming testimony of the Holy Spirit.[111]

(c) It has been argued that the notion of Jesus' baptism lies far outside the scope of John's thinking in this passage. If "Jesus as come in the flesh" refers to the incarnation, then "water" might refer to amniotic fluid or male sperm (cf. §8.2.1), and "blood" to the blood of birth.[112]

(d) Water and blood refer to Jesus' death on the cross because of John 19:34, "But one of the soldiers pierced his side with a spear, and at once there came out blood and water" (so Augustine). John supposedly refers to the water and the blood because of their purifying and atoning significance, respectively.[113]

Because of the remarkable terminological connection between John 19 and 1 John 5, I think the last interpretation (d) leaves us with the fewest exegetical problems. Jesus' "having come" is then not just a reference to his incarnation but to his entire life and death and resurrection on earth. His "having come" is his character; he is the "coming One" (Gk. *ho erchomenos*, Rev. 1:4, 8; 4:8).

6.9 The Holy Spirit in John 16
6.9.1 To the Disciples' Benefit

In John 16:7–15 Jesus says, "Nevertheless, I tell you the truth: it is to your advantage that I go away, for if I do not go away, the Helper will not come to you. But if I go, I will send him to you. And when he comes, he will convict the world concerning sin and righteousness and judgment: concerning sin, because they do not believe in me; concerning righteousness, because I go to the Father, and you will see me no longer; concerning judgment, because the ruler of this world is judged. I

---

111. Greijdanus (1934, 116–17, 119); Marshall (1978, 231–34); Smith (1979, 195); Barker (1981, 351).
112. Lalleman (2005, 204–06).
113. So Plummer (1894, ad loc.); Candlish (1973, ad loc.).

still have many things to say to you, but you cannot bear them now. When the Spirit of truth comes, he will guide you into all the truth, for he will not speak on his own authority, but whatever he hears he will speak, and he will declare to you the things that are to come. He will glorify me, for he will take what is mine and declare it to you. All that the Father has is mine; therefore I said that he will take what is mine and declare it to you."

It was to the advantage (or benefit) of the disciples that Jesus would go away, that is, would suffer, die, rise, and ascend to heaven. At least five reasons for this advantage can be mentioned.

(a) In John 7:38-39 Jesus said that the Paraclete could come only after he had been glorified. This was the very reason why the Holy Spirit would come: to testify of the glorified Christ (16:14-15), and this was to the benefit of the disciples.

(b) As we have seen, Jesus told his disciples many things that they did not understand, and which they would understand only if and when the Holy Spirit came to dwell in them (§6.7.3).

(c) Another advantage would be that the disciples would no longer depend on the physical presence of Jesus (vv. 24-27). Imagine that all Christians today would have to travel to the Holy Land to consult Jesus! Since the Day of Pentecost, they can consult the Holy Spirit, who is always near them.

(d) The Holy Spirit would become the disciples' source of spiritual power. Unfortunately, the divine person whom they had had *with* them—the Son of God—turned out to be no hindrance to their fleeing, betraying, and denying him. However, due to the divine person whom they would have *within* them—the Holy Spirit—they, "filled with the Holy Spirit," "continued to speak the word of God with boldness" (Acts 4:31), and they rejoiced each time when they are "counted worthy to suffer dishonor for the name" (5:41).[114]

---

114. Morris (1971, 697).

(e) Moreover, the Holy Spirit would "convict the world concerning sin and righteousness and judgment" (John 16:8) (see the next section).

6.9.2 Threefold Legal Proof

Taken out of their context, the words of John 16:8 are often applied to the preaching of the gospel.[115] "Convicting concerning sin" would then mean touching the sinner in his heart and conscience, so that he acknowledges his sinfulness and repents. However, the text gives a very different, at first sight rather mysterious explanation: ". . . concerning sin, because they do not believe in me." In his quality as counselor, the Holy Spirit acts here not as the lawyer toward future believers, but as the prosecutor toward "the world" (viewed as the system of sin and Satan).[116] As such, before the divine tribunal, as it were, he presents the legal and convincing evidence of what really constitutes sin, righteousness, and judgment.

This is all the more striking because, during the very night that Jesus spoke these words, the world in turn tried to present convincing evidence that Jesus was a sinner (John 9:24), and thus that it—the world itself—was righteous (Luke 18:9), and that it would pronounce its judgment concerning Jesus (Matt. 26:65-66).[117]

In opposition to this we have this threefold legal evidence that is presented by the Holy Spirit, and that, as it were, entails a kind of "review" of the case of Jesus:[118]

(a) More than any moralistic argument, the fact that the world did not wish to believe in him who is the Son of God, the sent One of the Father, constitutes convincing evidence of its sinfulness (John 16:9; cf. 3:18-19, 36; 15:22). Of course, secondarily this also implies that, if an unbeliever acknowledges his sinfulness through the power of the Holy Spirit, he may

---

115. See Chafer (1983, 6.95-98).
116. Johnson (2002, 137); Kärkkäinen (2002, 35).
117. Westcott (1966, ad loc.).
118. M. F. Berrouard, quoted by Congar (1997, 2.122).

repent; but this is clearly not the first meaning of the text.

(b) The fact that Jesus would return to the Father — with the initially saddening side-effect that the disciples would see him no longer — constitutes convincing evidence concerning righteousness (John 16:10). This can be taken as referring either to Jesus' own righteousness that he had displayed on earth, or to God's righteousness who recompensed him for this by glorifying him in heaven (cf. "righteous Father," John 17:25). It is not easy to say which interpretation is correct. As to the former interpretation: in my view, the issue here is not how a person may be justified, or may receive righteousness from God, but rather what constitutes true righteousness. Just as the world needs proof of what constitutes sin, it needs proof of what a righteous life entails, a life that is radically opposed to sin.

Therefore, together with others,[119] I favor the latter interpretation, because the main subject here is not Jesus' life on earth but his return to, and glorification by, the Father. After Jesus had accomplished his wonderful work in a perfect way (John 19:30), his glorification would be a righteous act of God, one that Jesus himself asked for: "I glorified you on earth, having accomplished the work that you gave me to do. And now, Father, [as a consequence] glorify me in your own presence with the glory that I had with you before the world existed" (John 17:4-5). God demonstrated his righteousness in that on the One who had been cast out by the world he would heap the highest glory (cf. Acts 3:14-15).

(c) The fact that, through the work on the cross, the definitive verdict on Satan, the ruler of this world, has been executed, is the convincing evidence of God's righteous judgment: ". . . concerning judgment, because the ruler of this world is judged" (John 16:11). "Now is the judgment of this world; now will the ruler of this world be cast out" (John 12:31). In military terms, Jesus would overcome the world (John 16:33),

---

119. Grant (1897, 592–93); Kelly (1966, 332); Gaebelein (1980, 307–08).

and thus also the ruler of this world (John 12:31; 14:30; 16:11). In legal terms, Satan would be sentenced and executed (Rev. 20:10).

6.9.3 Guiding Into the Truth

The things just said were all rather difficult for the disciples to understand (v. 12); this was precisely why they would need the indwelling Spirit *in order to* understand them (cf. 13:7). The Holy Spirit would "guide" them "*into* all the truth"; not guide them around within it, but introduce them to it. The truth is like a *terra incognita*, an unknown territory, of which they had seen so far only small parts, without even grasping them. But now they would learn them in their entirety (including the "things that are to come") as well as understand (insofar as it is given to creatures to perceive the divine truth). The Holy Spirit would tell the disciples whatever he himself would hear; as a servant he would obediently pass on only what he would be commanded to do, just as Jesus himself had done (3:32; 8:26, 40; 15:15).

Of course, this does not mean that each believer receives all instruction directly from the Holy Spirit. It was primarily the apostles (Matthew, John, Peter, Paul, James) and the men from the immediate apostolic circle (Mark, Luke, Jude, the author of Hebrews) who received this teaching, and wrote it down for us in the New Testament:

(1) "[T]he Holy Spirit . . . will teach you all things and bring to your remembrance all that I have said to you" (John 14:26); this we find in the Gospels.

(2) "[W]hen the Helper comes, whom I will send to you from the Father, the Spirit of truth, who proceeds from the Father, he will bear witness about me" (John 15:26); this we find especially in the book of Acts.

(3) "When the Spirit of truth comes, he will guide you into all the truth" (16:13a); this we find especially in the New Testament letters.

(4) "[H]e will declare to you the things that are to come" (16:13b); this we find especially in the book of Revelation.

It is through these Scriptures, as well as through the teachers who, by the anointing of the Spirit, expound the Scriptures to us (Acts 13:1; 1 Cor. 12:28; Eph. 4:11–13), that the Holy Spirit unfolds and confirms "all the truth" to the hearts of the believers.

In all respects, the teaching of the Spirit would be Christocentric, with the *glorified* Christ as the center of this teaching: "He [i.e., the Spirit} will glorify me, for he will take what is mine and declare it to you. All that the Father has is mine; therefore I said that he will take what is mine and declare it to you" (vv. 14–15). The word "mine' refers to all that would have to do with the glorified Christ, and to what he would possess (cf. 13:3; 17:5, 10, 24). The Spirit could not come before Jesus was glorified (7:39), precisely because it is his most exalted task to glorify here on earth the One who is glorified in heaven, in and through the words and deeds of his followers.

6.10 The Holy Spirit in John 19 and 20
6.10.1 John 19:30

In §6.3 we have seen in what way the Holy Spirit was involved in Jesus' sacrificial death: Christ "through the eternal Spirit offered himself without blemish to God" (Heb. 9:14). It is by the power of the Spirit that Jesus has accomplished his atoning work. This spiritual power is here a power in Christ himself, so that the verse seems to allude especially to the wonder of his perfect humanity and deity. The Man Christ who brought the sacrifice is at the same time the eternal Son: he offered himself in the power of the eternal Spirit, who is the Spirit of God's Son (Gal. 4:6). It was a *Man* offering himself, who *could* do so because from eternity he was and is God.

It is remarkable that some, especially Roman Catholic expositors,[120] have thought of the Holy Spirit in John 19:30 as

---

120. E.g., Congar (1997, 1.51–52).

well.[121] We read here, "[H]e gave up his spirit [Gk. *paredōken to pneuma*]." Hoskyns believes that, on the basis of 1 John 5:8 ("The Spirit and the water and the blood"), we cannot read our verse in any other way than as referring to the Holy Spirit.[122] If in John 19:34 "blood and water" are mentioned so emphatically, the Holy Spirit must be referred to in this passage as well, and this would be the case in verse 30. However, not all expositors are convinced of this connection between John 19:34 and 1 John 5:8 (see §6.8.2).

If John 19:30 refers to the Holy Spirit, the meaning might be that, in his dying, Jesus transferred the Spirit to the disciples who stood near the cross (cf. 7:37-39). However, with Morris I believe that the text gives us no basis for such an interpretation.[123] Although there is a clear difference with Matthew 27:50 ("yielded his spirit," Gk. *aphēken to pneuma*) and Mark 15:37; Luke 23:46 ("breathed his last," Gk. *exepneusen*), there is no basis for reading the word *pneuma* in these three passages differently from the way we read it in John. The distinction is rather that, in John 19, Jesus does not "breath his last" (or "expire") as a human who is at the end of his strength, but actively "gives up" his spirit in the sense of John 10:17-18, "For this reason the Father loves me, because I lay down my life [Gk. *psychē*] that I may take it up again. No one takes it from me, but I lay it down of my own accord. I have authority to lay it down, and I have authority to take it up again." In the end, *each* human "expires"; and many believers have, at the end of their lives, committed their spirit into the Father's hands (cf. Luke 23:46 with Ps. 31:5; Acts 7:59). However, only Jesus was capable of "laying down" his human life in order to "take it up" again in his resurrection.[124] It was *human* life that he "laid down" and "took up" again — but he *could* do so only because he was God.

---

121. Brown (1970, 931).
122. Hoskyns (1947, ad loc.).
123. Morris (1971, 816).
124. Darby (*CW* 33.298); Kelly (1966, 398-99).

6.10.2 John 20:22

After his resurrection, Jesus spoke words to his disciples that have often caused astonishment: "'Peace be with you. As the Father has sent me, even so I am sending you.' And when he had said this, he breathed [on them][125] and said to them, 'Receive [the] Holy Spirit. If you forgive the sins of any, they are forgiven them; if you withhold forgiveness from any, it is withheld'" (John 20:21-23).

Again, after John 17:18, Jesus speaks of "sending" (Gk. *apostellō*) into this world his *apostles* ("sent ones") as his substitutes. After giving this commission he breathes on (in, over) them (Darby, MSG: into). The word for "breathe" reminds us of the fundamental meaning of the Greek word *pneuma*: "air flow" (breath, wind; cf. John 3:8 and §4.1). The Greek verb *emphysaō* is the same as in Gen. 2:7 (Septuagint): "[T]hen the LORD God formed the man of dust from the ground and breathed [Gk. *enephysēsen*] into his nostrils the breath of life, and the man became a living creature" (cf. Job 27:3). Thus began the old creation. The renewal of it, at least as far as Israel is concerned, is found in Ezekiel 37:9, where the same verb occurs (Septuagint): "Come from the four winds, O breath, and breathe [Gk. *emphysēson*] on these slain, that they may live."

In John 20 we find the demonstration of Paul's statement: "Thus it is written, 'The first man Adam became a living being' [Gen. 2:7]; the last Adam became a life-giving spirit" (1 Cor. 15:45). The first Adam *received* life, namely, natural life;[126] the last Adam *grants* life, namely, the life that is characterized by the Holy Spirit. He *is* Spirit (cf. 2 Cor. 3:17), just as Scripture speaks elsewhere of the Spirit of Christ (Rom. 8:9; Phil. 1:19) and the Spirit of God's Son (Gal. 4:6). He is the model of

---

125. The words "on them" do not belong to the text; the textual testimony for these words is so weak that Nestle-Aland does not even mention it. However, the Gk. verb *emphysaō* does mean "to breathe on" or "in," so that an object must be added to complete the meaning.
126. It is strange that John Owen (1680) supposed that in Gen. 2:7 we are reading that God breathed the Holy Spirit into Adam; quoted by Pink (1970, 23), who agrees.

the spiritual (Spirit-led) Christian (1 Cor. 2:15-16) but also the source of the Christian's new, Spirit-worked life.

The astonishing point in John 20:22 is that Jesus grants the Holy Spirit to his disciples before the outpouring of the Spirit on the Day of Pentecost. To distinguish between the two, some have spoken here of the "Johannine Pentecost." This is all the more remarkable because other passages clearly imply that Jesus would send the Spirit after his return to the Father (John 7:39; 14:16, 26; 15:26; 16:7, 13).[127] Some solutions to the problem are that Jesus either *announces* here symbolically the coming of the Spirit[128] — this hardly seems to do justice to Jesus' special breathing — or is here giving an *advance* of the Spirit.[129] Personally I feel the lack of the article before the word for "Spirit" is meaningful here: Jesus grants some power of the Spirit even before the *person* of the Spirit has come,[130] or he grants them his own resurrection life in the power of the Spirit.[131]

Yves Congar suggests that here Jesus is transferring the Holy Spirit to them, but does not yet send them the Paraclete, whom he had promised in John 14 and 16. He too points out that the Spirit is given here not as a person (there is no article before the Greek phrase *pneuma hagion*) but as a force that corresponds with the mission that is being transferred.[132] Indeed, verse 23 makes clear for what purpose the Holy Spirit will be needed (among other things): he will give guidance and power to the young church in order the it may accomplish its task in this world for which it is sent (v. 21).

Indeed, it is important that the words "Receive [the] Holy Spirit" are immediately followed by the words: "If you forgive the sins of any, they are forgiven them; if you withhold forgiveness from any, it is withheld" (v. 23). Roman Catho-

---

127. Hoskyns (1947, ad loc.). On John 14:17 see n94.
128. Cf. Dunn (1970, 178); Tenney (1981, 193): initial announcement.
129. See Floor (1982, 79–80), who discusses the various possibilities.
130. *Contra* Morris (1971, 846n54).
131. Cf. Kelly (1966, 427); Darby (*CW* 25.307; cf. 33.304).
132. Congar (1997, 1.53).

lics and Eastern Orthodox Christians have derived from this a formal ecclesiastical authority to absolve (grant forgiveness for) sins.[133] However, we must notice that these words were not addressed specifically to the eleven apostles but to all the gathered disciples (vv. 19-20; cf. Luke 24:33-49; cf. also the one hundred twenty of Acts 1:15). Thus, we cannot derive from this some special authority for a certain class (apostles, overseers, pastors); this involves the authority of believers as a whole (the local church). Also notice the Greek perfect tense of the words "forgiven" (Gk. *apheōntai*) and "withheld" (Gk. *kekratēntai*): strictly speaking the church does not forgive but only formally confirms to whom forgiveness *has already been* divinely given, or from whom it *has already been* divinely withheld. The church does so in the power of the Holy Spirit that has been given to it,[134] whether (I would add) in its pastoral work or in church discipline.[135]

---

133. Cf. Congar (1997, 2.123–24; 3.269).
134. Morris (1971, 847–50).
135. Cf. Ouweneel (2006, chapter 3).

Chapter 7
The Coming of the Spirit

I baptize you with water,
   but he who is mightier than I is coming,
   the strap of whose sandals I am not worthy to untie.
He will baptize you with the Holy Spirit and fire.

                              Luke 3:16

When the day of Pentecost arrived,
   they were all together in one place.
And suddenly there came from heaven a sound like a mighty rushing wind,
   and it filled the entire house where they were sitting.
And divided tongues as of fire appeared to them
   and rested on each one of them.
And they were all filled with the Holy Spirit
   and began to speak in other tongues
   as the Spirit gave them utterance.

                              Acts 2:1–4

Summary: *Spirit baptism (i.e., the figurative submersion of the human spirit into the Holy Spirit) was first announced by John the Baptist (in contrast to his own water baptism), then by Jesus himself. Jesus' preparation by the Spirit and then his baptism in the Spirit form a sequence that occurred in the early church. The Day of Pentecost commemorates the lawgiving at Sinai – a parallel to the Spirit-giving on Zion, just as there are parallels between the Torah and the Holy Spirit themselves. After the one hundred twenty disciples had been baptized in the Spirit, three thousand new converts were added to the church, in whom conversion, water baptism, and Spirit baptism virtually coincided. Among the Samaritans (Acts 8) things occurred differently: after they had received water baptism, the apostles had to travel to them in order to facilitate their Spirit baptism. In fact, no cases in Acts are the same: God dealt differently with the Ethiopian eunuch, with Saul of Tarsus, with Cornelius and his friends, and with the Ephesian disciples of Acts 19. All these cases are analyzed in this chapter, which closes with some key terms in connection with the Holy Spirit: the kingdom of God, the phenomena of witnessing and of signs and wonders produced by the Spirit.*

7.1 Spirit Baptism Announced
7.1.1 By John the Baptist (Synoptic Gospels)

ALL OF THE SYNOPTIC GOSPELS describe how John the Baptist announced the baptism with the Holy Spirit: "I baptize you with water for repentance, but he who is coming after me is mightier than I, whose sandals I am not worthy to carry. He will baptize you with the Holy Spirit [Gk. *en pneumati hagiōi*] and fire" (Matt. 3:11; cf. Mark 1:7-8; Luke 3:16). In §4.3.2 I referred to the remarkable addition in Matthew and Luke of the Greek phrase *kai pyri*, "and fire," which means here: immersion into the purifying fire of the Holy Spirit.[1] An important argument for this interpretation is the absence of the article before the Greek word *pyri*, so that the expression can

---

1. Grosheide (1954, 47–48); Dunn (1992, 695); Bruce (1979, 84, 483–84); Geldenhuys (1983, 140); Carson (1984, 105); Liefeld (1984, 856–57).

be read as a hendiadys (two nouns joined with "and" can be interpreted as modifying one another): "in the fire of the Holy Spirit." Compare the statement "anointed with the Holy Spirit and power," which can be rendered as "... with the power of the Holy Spirit" (Acts 10:38; thus Phillips); or the statement "in demonstration of the Spirit and of power," rendered as "... the power of the Spirit" (1 Cor. 2:4; thus CJB[2]); or "in power and in the Holy Spirit," rendered as "in the power of the Holy Spirit" (1 Thess. 1:5; thus Phillips).

It is important to consider the prepositions here. We read of a "baptism with water" where "with (or in) water" translates a noun in the dative case with no preposition (Gk. *hudati*, Mark 1:8; Luke 3:16; Acts 1:5), or with a preposition, as in the Greek phrase *en hudati* (Matt. 3:11; John 1:26), which is either locative ("in[to] water"), or instrumental ("with [the means of] water"). It is the same with the Spirit: in all relevant passages, the expression "baptizing with the Spirit" is the Greek phrase *en pneumati*, which is either locative ("in[to] the Spirit"), or instrumental ("with [the means of] the Spirit"). Because of the parallel with the Greek noun *hudati* (three times without a preposition), it seems more obvious to view the Greek phrase *en pneumati* as instrumental rather than as locative, that is, "with the Spirit" rather than "in[to] the Spirit."[3] However, because of the original meaning of the Greek verb *baptizō*, "to immerse" or "submerge," the locative meaning cannot be excluded: just as the human body is literally baptized (immersed, submerged) in water, the human spirit is figuratively submerged in the Holy Spirit, or even, in the "fire" of the Spirit.

No doubt John the Baptist was a true prophet of judgment (cf. Matt. 3:7–10; Luke 3:7–9). He came indeed "in the spirit and the power of Elijah" (Luke 1:17), who was *the* example of an Old Testament prophet of judgment (1 Kings 17:1; 18:17; 21:20–24; 2 Kings 1:9–12). Yet, this does not mean that

---

2. Fee (1987, 95).
3. So Grosheide (1954, 46).

the Spirit baptism announced by John would be a baptism of judgment only, even if the Greek noun *puri* ("and [with] fire") may suggest this. John's water baptism was a "baptism of repentance for the forgiveness of sins" (Mark 1:4), and in this latter expression it is eschatological salvation that reverberates. His message concerned not only the chaff that had to be burned, but also the wheat that had to be gathered into the barn (Matt. 3:12; cf. 13:30). Those who accepted John's water baptism were thus prepared for the Messiah's blessed Spirit baptism.

John meant this partly as a contrast, for he could baptize only the outside, whereas the Messiah would baptize the inside as well. However, he was pointing also to the surpassing power and effect:[4] the Messiah would give more than John himself would ever be able to give, just as the Messiah's glory was so much greater than John's. John's water baptism led to the blessing of the forgiveness of sins and to the encounter with the Messiah; the latter's Spirit baptism would lead to the full blessing of the Messianic kingdom.

The point is not what John himself may have understood in this regard,[5] but what the Spirit baptism means in the whole of New Testament revelation. Through the Holy Spirit himself (cf. Luke 1:15), John's words reached further than he himself might have been aware of (cf. a similar situation in 1 Pet. 1:10-11). Luke Johnson linked John's statement with that of Jesus in Luke 12:49: "I came to cast fire on the earth, and would that it were already kindled!" He (perhaps rightly) commented that this statement is deliberately obscure because it has two referents: both the coming judgment by the Son of man and the eschatological gift of the Holy Spirit (Acts

---

4. Notice the Gr. particle *de* in Matt. 3:11, which can mean "but," "and even," or "yes, what is more": "I baptize with water, my Successor still more with the Spirit."
5. *Contra* Bruce (1979, 84), who wished to see the Spirit baptism announced by John as a baptism of judgment only (but see 483–84, where he supposes that Luke himself read an "evangelical" meaning into John's words).

2:3).⁶

7.1.2 By John the Baptist (Gospel of John)

The apostle John has transmitted the words of John the Baptist in his own way:

> John answered them, "I baptize with water, but among you stands one you do not know, even he who comes after me, the strap of whose sandal I am not worthy to untie." . . . I myself did not know him, but for this purpose I came baptizing with water, that he might be revealed to Israel. . . . "I saw the Spirit descend from heaven like a dove, and it remained on him. I myself did not know him, but he who sent me to baptize with water said to me, 'He on whom you see the Spirit descend and remain, this is he who baptizes with the Holy Spirit.' And I have seen and have borne witness that this is the Son of God" (John 1:26-27, 31-34).

Here the Baptist is emphasizing how his water baptism led people to Christ, and—just as in the synoptic Gospels—how much greater the latter would be than he himself: even greater than a master with respect to a slave (". . . the strap of whose sandal I am not worthy to untie"). It was not only the bystanders who did not know the Messiah, that is, did not know who he was (v. 26), but John himself did not really know him either (vv. 31, 33), in spite of his important task of revealing him to Israel. This "not knowing" must not be taken in the most absolute sense, for the two men were related (Luke 1:36); and when Jesus came to John to be baptized—that is, before the Spirit descended upon him—John protested (Matt. 3:14); he must therefore have known with whom he was dealing. Yet, he needed a divine sign in order to recognize Jesus as the Messiah: this Jesus would be the One on whom John would see the Spirit descend. This did not involve a vision, but rather he would see the Spirit descending upon Jesus in the form of a dove (see §4.7).

---

6. Johnson (1991, 209).

A feature present in all four Gospels is the Baptist's emphasis that the Messiah would come *in order to* baptize with the Holy Spirit. We could mention many reasons why Christ came into this world; but if one would have asked John the Baptist, he might have replied: He will come in order to grant people the Holy Spirit, or even, he comes in order to fulfill Ezekiel 36 and Joel 2. John the Baptist prepared the way of the Messiah, the anointed King of Israel, but the Messiah would prepare the way of the Holy Spirit, just as the Holy Spirit would prepare the way of the Messianic kingdom.

There is another remarkable feature in John's Gospel that is worth mentioning: the metaphor of baptism suggested that the Holy Spirit would be available in abundance.[7] Therefore John adds in 3:33, "[H]e [i.e., Jesus] gives the Spirit without measure." Jesus would come with the fullness of the Spirit (cf. Rom. 15:29, "in the fullness of the blessing of Christ"; cf. also John 10:10, "life abundantly"). To understand this, we must remember that the New Testament speaks of the Spirit not only as a person (of whom one cannot have "more" or "less") but also as a power, a stream (or wind, or fire) of blessing, of which one *can* indeed have much or little (see extensively, chapter 4 above).

7.1.3 By Jesus Himself

Jesus, too, foretold the baptism with the Holy Spirit. After his resurrection, he said to his followers (Luke 24:49), "And behold, I am sending the promise of my Father upon you. But stay in the city until you are clothed with power from on high." Here, the Spirit is not explicitly mentioned but, in light of the parallel in Acts 1:8 ("you will receive power when the Holy Spirit has come upon you"), the gift of the Spirit is clearly intended here. The "promise of my Father" (also see Acts 1:4-5) is what my Father has promised: the Holy Spirit, who had been announced already by the Old Testament prophets (Isa. 32:15; 44:3; Ezek. 36:27; 37:14; Joel 2:28-29).

---

7. Morris (1971, 153).

The metaphor of being "clothed" or "invested" with "power" fits the presentation of the Holy Spirit as a power that comes *upon* or *over* the believer (cf. Isa. 42:1; 61:1; Acts 1:8) (cf. §4.4). This power comes "from on high" (Gk. *ex hupsous*), that is, from God (cf. Luke 1:78), who himself is the Most High (Gk. *hupsistos*). Just as Jesus had been begotten by the "power of the Most High" (Gk. *dynamis hupsistou*, 1:35), his followers would be clothed with "power from on high" (Gk. *ex hupsous dynamis*).

In Acts 1:4-5, 8, the risen Lord continued speaking about this subject:

> And while staying[8] with them he ordered them not to depart from Jerusalem, but to wait for the promise of the Father, which, he said, "you heard from me; for John baptized with water, but you will be baptized with [or in] the Holy Spirit not many days from now." . . . "[Y]ou will receive power when the Holy Spirit has come upon you, and you will be my witnesses in Jerusalem and in all Judea and Samaria, and to the end of the earth" (cf. 11:16).

As we just saw, the "promise of the Father" is the Holy Spirit as he had been promised by God the Father, or by Jesus as a Spirit coming from the Father (John 14:26; 15:26; 16:7). Just as Jesus himself had been anointed at his water baptism with the Holy Spirit "and with power" (Acts 10:38), his followers would be baptized with the Holy Spirit and in this way "receive power." In this passage, this is especially the power to bear witness, first in Jerusalem, then in the other parts of the land of Israel, and afterward in the rest of the world (see Acts 1:22; 2:32; 3:15; 5:32; 10:39, 41; 13:31; 22:15, 18, 20; 23:11; 26:16, 22).

Commentators have often pointed out that, with this geographical description, an outline of the entire book of Acts is provided: the phrase "in Jerusalem" comprises Acts 1-7, "in

---

8. Or "eating"; Gr. *synalizomenos* (cf. Vulgate, NIV, and Acts 10:41; Luke 24:42–43).

all Judea and Samaria" comprises Acts 8 to 11:18, and "to the end of the earth" comprises the rest of the book.[9] One could also put it this way: in Acts 2:37-41 the first *Semites* are converted, in Acts 8:26-39 the first *Hamite* (the Cushite eunuch; cf. Gen. 10:6), and in Acts 10:44-46 the first *Japhethites* (the Roman Cornelius and his friends). This entire worldwide testimony was based on this mandate given by the risen Lord himself, and occurred through the power that he himself was going to grant, namely, "not many days from now," that is, only a few days later. To be precise, it was ten days later: the difference between the forty days that Jesus stayed with them (Acts 1:3), and the fifty days between the Sunday in the Passover week and the Day of Pentecost (Lev. 23:15-16; Deut. 16:9).[10] In light of these things, it is no wonder that various expositors have spoken of this book as reporting the Acts, not so much of the apostles, but rather of the Holy Spirit.[11]

Presumably, the disciples' question in verse 6 — "Lord, will you at this time restore the kingdom to Israel?" — was inspired by Jesus' words in verses 4 and 5.[12] The reason is that, for the Jews, the gift of the Holy Spirit was indissolubly connected with the eschatological restoration of Israel and the establishment of the Messianic kingdom (Isa. 32:15; 44:3; Ezek. 36:27; 37:14; Joel 2:28-29). Jesus separated this gift from the *eschaton*, as it were, and promised the coming of the Holy Spirit only for "this time" (vv. 7-8). Nonetheless, we must say that, in a certain sense, the end times *had* arrived: already with his coming into this world, "these last days" (Heb. 1:2), and the "last hour" (1 John 2:18), and "the ends of the ages" have come upon God's people (1 Cor. 10:11 NKJV).

It seems clear that Jesus' disciples had received John's baptism; at any rate, some of them had first been disciples of

---

9. Bruce (1988, 36–37); in ancient sources, Rome is "the end of the earth," that is, precisely where the book of Acts ends (Knowling [1979, 57]).
10. See Ouweneel (2001b, 110–114).
11. See the book titles by Pierson (1996) and Wagner (2000).
12. Knowling (1979, 56); Longenecker (1981, 256).

John the Baptist (John 1:35-40). However, it is said nowhere that the risen Lord administered Christian baptism to his disciples. In contrast to the disciples of whom we read in Acts 19:2-7, John's baptism as well as the Spirit baptism of Acts 2 were apparently sufficient to equip them.[13] In this respect, they resembled their Lord, who also had received both John's baptism and the baptism with the Holy Spirit. Obviously, nobody could have administered Christian baptism to him.

7.2 Parallels Between Jesus and the Church
7.2.1 Preparation

It has often been noticed that, in Luke's two writings, his Gospel and the book of Acts, he suggests clear parallels between the beginning of Jesus' ministry, that is, his baptism by John and his anointing with the Spirit, and the beginning of the Christian church's history. I mention some remarkable points, the first being the preparation for Jesus' ministry and the church's ministry, respectively (for other points, see the next sections).

Jesus' entire life until his baptism, his first thirty years (cf. Luke 3:23), was one of spiritual preparation for the ministry that he would conduct. During those years, he did not preach or perform any miracles, unless we would give credence to the apocryphal "Gospels" about Jesus' youth, which appeared in the second century, and which tell us several stories about miracles that Jesus allegedly performed during his youth. For instance, the infancy Gospel of Thomas (II.3-5) tells us that Jesus fashioned birds of clay, and then brought them to life.[14] The New Testament does not contain such stories, and I think for a good reason. By his divine power, Jesus may have been able to perform such miracles as a youth. However, God wished Jesus' ministry to be based not upon his own divine power but entirely upon the power of the Holy Spirit, which

---
13. Bruce (1988, 36n30).
14. http://www.gnosis.org/library/inftoma.htm; the story has become famous because the Quran (5:110) also contains a version of this story.

he had not received before he was thirty years old. Only in this way could he become a true example for his followers.

The most important event that Luke narrates about this time of preparation (apart from Luke 2:40, 52) is Jesus' visit to the temple. Many render Luke 2:49 as follows, "Did you not know that I must be in my Father's house?" The Greek simply has *en tois tou patros mou dei einai me*, which can also be rendered as ". . . my Father's business. . ." ([N]KJV), or "the things of my Father" (YLT). Whatever rendering we adopt, from his thirteenth year onward, Jesus must have visited the temple at least three times each year (cf. Deut. 16:16).

After Jesus' ascension, his followers, too, had to prepare themselves for the outpouring of the Holy Spirit, which would grant them the power for their ministry (Luke 24:49; Acts 1:4–5, 8, 13–14). They, too, did so in the temple (Luke 24:53), which Jesus himself had called "my Father's house" (John 2:16; incidentally, he also called the heavenly temple "my Father's house," 14:2). Luke's Gospel begins with a mute priest in the temple (1:20–22), and it ends with a crowd of worshiping, joyful, God-blessing disciples in the very same temple (24:52–53).

7.2.2 The Anointing With the Spirit

A second parallel between the beginning of Jesus' ministry and that of the Christian church is this. When Jesus was baptized, the Holy Spirit descended upon him. This was his anointing, as we know from Acts 4:27 and 10:38, which granted him the power for his ministry. Just like Moses, Jesus did not receive any anointing with oil, for in both cases there was no person on earth who could have been qualified to do this. His anointing—which made him the Messiah (Heb. *Mashiach*, "Anointed One")—was a spiritual one: not with oil but with the Spirit.

Similarly, the early Christians were not anointed with oil but with the Holy Spirit. When, on the Day of Pentecost, the disciples were baptized with, and filled with, the Holy Spirit, this indeed entailed an anointing for them as well (2 Cor. 1:21-22; 1 John 2:20, 27), through which they received the power for *their* ministry (cf. Luke 24:49; Acts 1:8).

A third parallel is *prayer*. It is remarkable to see what role, according to Luke, prayer played in this preparation, both in the case of Jesus (Luke 3:21), and in the cases of the one hundred twenty disciples (Acts 1:14), of Saul of Tarsus (9:11), and of Cornelius (10:1-4, 30). It reminds us of Luke 11:13, ". . . how much more will the heavenly Father give the Holy Spirit to those who ask him!" Jesus himself, as well as the apostles, Saul, and Cornelius, received the Holy Spirit prayerfully.

The Spirit came upon Jesus to "remain" (Gk. *menō*) on him (John 1:32). Similarly, Jesus promised that in the same way the Spirit would "remain" (Gk. *menō*) on his followers (John 14:17 GNT; cf. 1 John 3:24). (The translations do not consistently distinguish between "to remain," "to dwell," and "to abide," each of which can be a legitimate rendering of the Gk. verb *menō*.)

After Jesus had received the Holy Spirit, for the rest of his earthly life he himself was led by the Spirit (Matt. 4:1; Luke 4:1, 14; 10:21). Spiritual Christians, too, are led by the Spirit (Rom. 8:14; Gal. 5:18; cf. Ps. 143:10; 1 Cor. 2:15-16; see §9.1.2).

Jesus had been announced as the One who would baptize with the Holy Spirit, and he began to perform this in Acts 2. The apostles in turn became those through whose ministry Jesus granted the Spirit baptism to others as well (for this point see especially Acts 11:16-17).

7.2.3 The Works of the Spirit

A fourth parallel between Jesus' ministry and that of the Christian church is this. Just as clearly as Jesus was the prophet of Israel, and indeed uttered prophetic words (Deut. 18:15-18; Luke 4:17-21; John 6:14; Acts 3:22-23; 7:37), so clear was the thoroughly prophetic character of the early church (Acts 2:17-18; 11:27-28; 13:1; 15:32; 19:6; 21:9-10; cf. 1 Cor. 14:24, 31). Moses' desire was finally fulfilled: "Would that all the LORD's people were prophets, that the Lord would put his Spirit on them!" (Num. 11:29). In the Old Testament only a few were prophets, and only these (and a few others) were filled with the Holy Spirit. In the New Testament, all believers receive the Spirit, and in a certain sense have a prophetic character (apart from the specific prophetic office; 1 Cor. 12:28–29; Eph. 4:11), as we see in 1 Corinthians 12:10 and 14:24, 31.

In Jesus, the power of the received Spirit immediately began to be manifested in signs and wonders, that is, in healing the sick and casting out demons (Luke 4:31–41). These miracles were closely related to his preaching the kingdom of God: "[H]e went throughout all Galilee, teaching in their synagogues and proclaiming the gospel of the kingdom and healing every disease and every affliction among the people" (Matt. 4:23; cf. 9:35). The reason is that in the fulfilled kingdom of God there would no longer be any diseases (Isa. 33:24; cf. 29:18; 35:5–6).

In the early church, the same thing occurred as in Jesus' ministry. The first evidence of this is in Acts 2:43, "And awe came upon every soul, and many wonders and signs were being done through the apostles" (cf. the connection with v. 22; see also 3:1–11, 4:30, and 5:12–16). Here again, there was often a clear connection between preaching the kingdom and performing miracles:

> [T]he crowds with one accord paid attention to what was being said by Philip, when they heard him and saw the signs that he did. For unclean spirits, crying out with a loud voice, came out of many who had them, and many who were paralyzed or lame were healed. . . . Philip . . . preached good news about the kingdom of God and the name of Jesus Christ . . . signs and great miracles [being] performed (8:6–7, 12–13).

A fifth parallel is the following. As soon as Jesus had received the Holy Spirit, the Spirit drove him to confront the evil powers in the wilderness (Luke 4:1–2). As soon as his followers had received the Holy Spirit, they too had to confront these powers, as is clear from their prayer:

> "Why did the Gentiles rage, and the peoples plot in vain? The kings of the earth set themselves, and the rulers were gathered together, against the Lord and against his Anointed" — for truly in this city there were gathered together against your holy servant Jesus, whom you anointed, both Herod and Pontius Pilate, along with the Gentiles and the peoples of Israel, to do whatever your hand and your plan had predestined to take place (Acts 4:25-28; cf. Ps. 2:1-2).

We remember in this connection that hidden behind the powers of "flesh and blood" (Herod, Pilate) are the "rulers," the "authorities," the "cosmic powers over this present darkness," the "spiritual forces of evil in the heavenly places" (Eph. 6:12).

7.3 The First Outpouring
7.3.1 Sinai and Zion

In the book of Acts we find at least six, and (if we accept the Western text of Acts 8:39; see §7.6.1) perhaps seven, examples of granting the Spirit to early Christians, the first two of them found in Acts 2.

In Acts 2:1 the Day of Pentecost dawns, literally the day of the "fiftieth" (Gk. *pentēkostē*) because of the seven weeks between the "day of the firstfruits" (Heb. *Yom habBikkurim*, the presentation of the firstfruits of the barley harvest; Lev. 23:10-14) and the Feast of Weeks, or Pentecost (Heb. *Shavu'ot*, lit. "sevens").[15] After the destruction of Jerusalem and the temple, when Israel was dispersed among the nations, the harvest aspect of *Shavu'ot* lost its significance. The only remaining feature related to harvest is that the Jewish houses and synagogues are abundantly ornamented with flowers; *Shavu'ot* has become a real flower festival. But it is also possible that the flowers are meant as a festival ornament for the Torah, the Law that God gave Israel at Mount Sinai. This brings us

---

15. About this feast, see Ouweneel (2001b, §4.2).

to the entirely new significance of *Shavu'ot* in Israel, a meaning that can be demonstrated as early as the second century, in the Diaspora, but which is probably centuries older than that. It has become the "time of the giving of our Law" (Heb. *zeman mattan Toratenu*), the festival of the lawgiving at Sinai. It is a festive time during which the Torah-loving Jew studies the Torah even more intensively than usual; some spend the entire night of Pentecost studying God's Law.

The connection between *Shavu'ot* and the law-giving at Sinai is based on the fact that *Shavu'ot* is celebrated on the same day (the sixth day of the third month) as that on which, according to the rabbis, the Law was given. However, whereas at *Shavu'ot* Israel thinks of the Sinaitic lawgiving (Exod. 20), Christians think of the outpouring of the Holy Spirit during that festival (Acts 2). At the *first* Pentecost festival in history, Israel was born as the covenant people of God, and at the *first* Pentecost festival after Messiah's death and resurrection, the New Testament church was born. At Mount Sinai, God's relationship began with the Old Testament collective people of God,[16] when he gave them the Torah, just as on Mount Zion his relationship with the New Testament people of God began, when God gave them the Spirit.[17]

On both occasions, at Mount Sinai in Exodus 19-20 and on Mount Zion in Acts 2, many "voices" were heard (thus literally in both Exod. 19:16 [Heb. *qolot*] and Acts 2:4 [Gk. *glōssai*]). At Sinai, there was first a "sound," which changed into a "fire," which the people understood as a "language" — according to Philo the three signs of God's presence.[18] Similar phenomena appeared in Acts 2:2-4 and 6.[19] Fire was observed at Sinai (Exod. 19:18), and in Acts 2:3 we read about "tongues

---

16. Of course, long before this, God had entertained relationships with chosen individuals, from Adam to Moses, but not yet with a chosen nation.
17. The Venerable Bede (ca. 700) pointed to this parallel; see Burgess (1997, 22-23).
18. Philo, *De Decalogo* 33.
19. Longenecker (1981, 270).

as of fire" (Gk. *glōssai hōsei puros*). Interestingly, the Torah, or God's Word, is compared to both fire (Jer. 23:29) and water (Eph. 5:26; cf. John 15:3), just as the Spirit is compared to both fire and water (cf. §§4.2 and 4.3 above).[20]

7.3.2 Torah and Spirit

The connections and parallels between the law-giving and the outpouring of the Spirit, between the Torah and the Holy Spirit, are numerous. Giving the Torah is like giving the Holy Spirit, just as grieving God by breaking the Torah (Ps. 78:39-41) is like grieving the Spirit (Isa. 63:20-21; cf. Eph. 4:30). Under the new covenant the Spirit of the living God writes Christ upon the believers' hearts (2 Cor. 3:3), which is virtually the same as saying that the Torah is written upon their hearts (Jer. 31:33; Heb. 8:10).

Living by the Spirit is living under the law of Christ, and no longer living under the flesh (Gal. 5:13-6:2). This is true freedom, for the law is the "law of freedom" (James 1:25; 2:12; cf. 2 Cor. 3:17). Just as the Torah (i.e., "instruction") led and taught God's people, the Spirit leads and teaches God's people (John 14:26; 16:13; Rom. 8:14). Just as the Torah makes alive and illuminates the eyes (Ps. 119:93; 19:9), the Spirit makes alive and illuminates the heart's eyes (2 Cor. 3:6; Eph. 1:17-18). The Torah was written "with the finger of God" (Exod. 31:18; Deut. 9:10), while Jesus acted "by the finger of God" (Luke 11:20), that is, by the Spirit of God (see §4.8.2). True sons of God are those who keep the Torah, that is, are led by the Spirit (Deut. 8:5-6; Rom. 8:14). Both the Torah and the Spirit convict people of sin, of righteousness, and of judgment (cf. Rom. 3:20; 5:20; 7:7-11; Gal. 3:19 with John 16:8). Rejecting the Torah belongs to the same category as resisting the Holy Spirit (Acts 7:38-51). Through the power of the Holy Spirit, the righteousness (Gk. *dikaiōma*, "righteous demand") of the Torah is fulfilled in

---

20. According to Gregory of Narek (ca. 1000), the Spirit manifested himself at Sinai through an earthquake, a strong wind, and a consuming fire; see Burgess (1989, 127).

believers (Rom. 8:4).

In §3.8 we examined the relationships between wisdom (Heb. *chokmah*) and the Spirit, whereas here we are referring to the relationships between the Torah and the Spirit. To close the circle, I remind the reader of the relationships between Chokmah and Torah, the Wisdom of God and the Law of God. In Jewish tradition, Jesus Sirach had Wisdom declare (24:3–11),

> I am the word spoken by the Most High. I covered the earth like a mist. I made my home in highest heaven, my throne on a pillar of cloud. Alone I walked around the circle of the sky and walked through the ocean beneath the earth. I ruled over all the earth and the ocean waves, over every nation, over every people. I looked everywhere for a place to settle, some part of the world to make my home. Then my Creator, who created the universe, told me where I was to live. Make your home in Israel, he said. The descendants of Jacob will be your people. He created me in eternity, before time began, and I will exist for all eternity to come.[21] I served him in the Sacred Tent and then made my home on Mount Zion. He settled me in the Beloved City and gave me authority over Jerusalem.

In this chapter, Sophia is entirely identical with Torah, for Sirach makes Sophia explain how a place was allotted to her among the people of Israel in the form of the covenant book of Sinai. The Torah is presented here as having existed from before the foundation of the world. Sirach says that all things have been created through the wisdom of the Torah, through which all human life is upheld, and that she has received a place within temporal reality in her Sinaitic form.

Similarly, the apocryphal book of the Wisdom of Solomon says in 7:22a, 25–26:

---

21. In the Middle Ages, this phrase, and also Prov. 8:22–23, were applied to the Virgin Mary, who was viewed as the incarnation of Sophia; see Cunneen (1996, 150).

The Coming of the Spirit

Wisdom, who gave shape to everything that exists, was my teacher. . . . She is a breath of God's power [cf. the Spirit!] — a pure and radiant stream of glory from the Almighty. Nothing that is defiled can ever steal its way into Wisdom. She is a reflection of eternal light, a perfect mirror of God's activity and goodness (cf. also 8:3-4; 9:4, 9-10a).

In the book of Baruch the Hebrew words *torah* and *chokmah* are used almost identically. To abandon the Torah is to abandon the source of wisdom (3:9, 12). Baruch, too, explains that the *eternal* Chokmah of God has appeared on earth in the *material* form of the book of his commandments, the Law that lasts forever (3:37-4:1). In summary, Jewish tradition views Chokmah and Torah as basically identical, and the New Testament closely links both of these with the Holy Spirit.

7.3.3 The One Hundred Twenty

Acts 1:15 tells us about some one hundred twenty believers waiting together for the coming of the Holy Spirit. They were the twelve apostles (Matthias having replaced Judas; vv. 16-26) plus a number of other followers, including Mary, Jesus' mother. The house where they were staying (2:2) probably included the upper room mentioned in 1:13. Others have thought of the temple (cf. Luke 24:53), which would explain more easily how Peter in Acts 2 could address such a large crowd, namely, in the temple square (cf. also v. 46).

One of the Bible passages traditionally read at *Shavu'ot* is Ezekiel 1. If this was the case already in New Testament times, one can imagine how the disciples in Acts 2 were impressed with the words: "As I looked, behold, a *stormy wind* came out of the north, and a great cloud, with brightness around it, and *fire* flashing forth continually, and in the midst of the fire, as it were gleaming metal" (Ezek. 1:4). This would have been so especially because some moments later they experienced similar things: "And suddenly there came from heaven a sound like a mighty rushing *wind*, and it filled the entire house where they were sitting. And divided tongues as of *fire* appeared to them and rested on each one of them" (Acts 2:2-3).

For the meaning of "wind" and "fire" as metaphors, see §§4.1 and 4.3 above. John the Baptist had announced a baptism "with holy wind and fire" (Gk. *en pneumati hagiōi kai pyri*), and this seems to be how it occurred. Incidentally, note Luke's careful language: "a sound *like* a . . . wind," "tongues *as* of fire," which describes their form and radiance.[22] The word "divided" in verse 3 may mean the tongues as of fire appeared initially as a single entity and then divided into individual tongues above the people who were present. Interestingly, verse 3 speaks of "tongues [Gk. *glōssai*] as of fire," while in verse 4 the early Christians began to speak in "other tongues [Gk. *glōssais*]." The fire of the Spirit was visible on them through the tongues as of fire that appeared above them, and was audible through the spoken tongues in which they expressed themselves.[23] According to Gregory the Great (ca. 600), the Holy Spirit appeared in tongues as of fire because the Spirit brings about in all those whom he fills a burning as well as a speaking.[24]

The church fathers viewed this speaking in tongues as a reversal of the confusion of tongues at Babel (Gen. 11:1-9).[25] It was closely connected with prophesying (cf. 19:6) by both the men and the women among the one hundred twenty.[26] This was underscored by Peter quoting Joel's statement: "[Y]our sons and your daughters shall prophesy" (2:17), thus confirming what the bystanders had already observed. We see the same effect occurring among the elders of Israel on whom the Holy Spirit came: the Lord "took some of the Spirit that

---

22. 1 Enoch 14:8-25 describes God's celestial court as "surrounded by tongues of fire."
23. In v. 11 the Gk. word is also *glōssa*, but in v. 6 it is *dialektos*, "language" (cf. 1:19).
24. Burgess (1997, 14).
25. Congar (1997, 1.44 and 48n5).
26. In the Septuagint, the Gk. verb *apophthengesthai* ("to give utterance," v. 4; "to address," v. 14, "to speak," 26:25) is used often to characterize the prophets' speaking (1 Chron. 25:1; Ezek. 13:9, 19; Micah 5:11; Zech. 10:2).

was on him [i.e., Moses] and put it on the seventy elders. And as soon as the Spirit rested on them, they prophesied" (Num. 11:25; see further §11.1.2 on "ecstasy").

According to Luke, what happened on the Day of Pentecost was the fulfillment of Jesus' statement in Acts 1:5 concerning the baptism with (or in) the Holy Spirit (cf. 11:16–17), though in 2:4 he uses a different word: ". . . they were all *filled* with the Holy Spirit." We will come back to the connection between being "baptized" and "being filled" with the Holy Spirit (see §§8.6 and 8.7 below). Jesus was baptized with water by John, and at this event he was anointed with the Holy Spirit, which constituted the basis for his entire ministry. Similarly, the one hundred twenty were baptized and anointed with the Holy Spirit by Jesus, an event that constituted the basis for *their* entire ministry (§7.2).[27]

7.4 The Three Thousand
7.4.1 Peter's Sermon

After the Holy Spirit had been poured out on the one hundred twenty followers of Jesus, the Jews who had gathered in the city for the Feast of Pentecost flocked to them, having heard the sound mentioned in verse 2. They were astonished that they were hearing the disciples speaking in the languages of the nations where these Pentecostal pilgrims lived (vv. 6–12). Peter stood up, together with the other apostles, and gave the crowd an explanation based on the prophecy of Joel 2:28–32, with which all these Jews must have been familiar.

The question has been asked regarding to what extent Peter himself realized that these events could involve only a pre-fulfillment of this prophecy. Perhaps he purposely expressed himself in a prudent way by saying, "this is what was uttered through the prophet Joel" (Acts 2:16), rather than using more explicit expressions such as "the Scripture had to be fulfilled" (1:16) and "what God foretold by the mouth of all the prophets, that his Christ would suffer, he thus fulfilled"

---

27. Longenecker (1981, 268–69).

(3:18).

At any rate, the way in which Peter presented the quotation from Joel is what the rabbis call *pesher*; this interpretative technique focuses on the general line of the fulfillment, without focusing on various details (see other examples in Acts 4:11; 13:33-34; 15:15-18). If we do focus on the details, we notice that, from the Day of Pentecost until today, the Holy Spirit has *not* been poured out on "all flesh" (KJV; so also 2:17), that is, on the *entire* people of God (Gentile but also Jewish); this will not occur until the end of the present age (cf. Isa. 45:25; 60:21; Ezek. 36:27; 37:14; Rom. 11:26).[28] Nor was much of the rest of the prophecy fulfilled in Acts 2; see the words quoted by Peter as well: "I will show wonders in the heavens and on the earth, blood and fire and columns of smoke. The sun shall be turned to darkness, and the moon to blood, before the great and awesome day of the LORD comes" (vv. 30-31; cf. Matt. 24:29; Luke 21:11, 25; Rev. 6:12),[29] and actually also what follows in Joel 3.

The pivotal point is that the events that were foretold *could not* have been fulfilled in Acts 2 because they belong to the *coming* "day of the LORD" (v. 20), the day of judgment and consummation (Joel 1:15; 2:1, 11, 31; 3:14); that is, they are linked with Christ's second coming rather than with his first coming (1 Cor. 5:5; 2 Cor. 1:14; 1 Thess. 5:2; 2 Thess. 2:2; 2 Pet. 3:10).[30] It seems that Peter wished to underscore this future complete fulfillment by replacing the words "after this" in the Masoretic Text and the Septuagint with the words "in the last days" (v. 17; cf. 2 Pet. 3:3, where for Peter the expression "in the last of the days" is still future).

Subsequently, Peter quoted other prophecies in order to explain both the resurrection of the Christ who had died, and his glorification (vv. 22-35). By way of summary, he closed

---

28. Cf. Duffield and Van Cleave (1996, 325).
29. In my view, such Bible references make clear that Bruce's claim (1988, 61–62) that Joel 2:31 refers to Good Friday must be rejected.
30. Knowling (1979, 80); Patterson (1985, 255–57).

as follows: "Let all the house of Israel therefore know for certain that God has made him both Lord and Christ, this Jesus whom you crucified" (v. 36). With these words, Peter pointed out the remarkable relationship between Jesus' ascension and glorification, on the one hand, and the descent of the Holy Spirit, on the other. The outpouring of the Holy Spirit constituted for the apostles, and for all those who wished to hear it, the certain proof *that* Jesus had indeed been glorified at the right hand of God. It was like a person asking, at the departure of a beloved one, that they would send a message back after their safe arrival.[31] The disciples had seen the Lord leaving the earth (Mark 16:19; Luke 24:51; Acts 1:9), but they were not able to observe what had happened to him after this. Now that the Holy Spirit had come, they knew with certainty that Jesus had been glorified, and had taken his place at the Father's right hand, as he himself had foretold (Matt. 22:44; 26:64 and parallels).

7.4.2 The People's Response

As they listened to Peter, many Jews were "cut to the heart" (v. 37), and asked Peter to point out to them the way of salvation. Peter answered, "Repent and be baptized every one of you in the name of Jesus Christ for the forgiveness of your sins, and you will receive the gift of the Holy Spirit. For the promise is for you and for your children and for all who are far off.... Save yourselves from this crooked generation" (vv. 38–40). The result of these words was phenomenal: "So those who received his word were baptized, and there were added that day about three thousand souls" (v. 41).

Peter's call for repentance and baptism connected with that given earlier by John the Baptist (Matt. 3:2, 6; Mark 1:4; Luke 3:3). One might get the impression that, now that John's water baptism had been replaced by Christ's Spirit baptism, water baptism had become redundant. However, the baptism to which Peter invited the people was not the continuation of

---

31. Prince (1995, 319–21).

John's baptism but quite a different one. The correspondence between the two baptisms was that they were both introductory rites for converted people who needed forgiveness of sins. However, they introduced people to different companies, so to speak. John's baptism introduced people to the company of repentant people who prepared themselves to receive the imminent Messiah. Christian baptism introduces people to the kingdom of God that exists under the rule of the risen and glorified Christ seated at God's right hand.

It was this Christian baptism that the risen Lord had urged his apostles to administer: "All authority in heaven and on earth has been given to me. Go *therefore* [i.e., in the light of my universal kingship] and make disciples of all nations, baptizing them in [or unto] the name of the Father and of the Son and of the Holy Spirit" (Matt. 28:18-19). Like that of John, this baptism is "for the forgiveness of sins," but with at least three new characteristics.[32]

(a) This Christian baptism is explicitly founded upon Jesus' atoning sacrifice (cf. Matt. 26:28, ". . . this is my blood of the covenant, which is poured out for many for the forgiveness of sins").

(b) It is a baptism in the name of the Triune God, but also specifically "in the name of [*the glorified Man*] Jesus Christ" (Acts 2:38; cf. 8:16; 10:48; 19:5; cf. 22:16; 1 Cor. 1:13, 15).

(c) Christian baptism is unbreakably connected with the "gift of the Holy Spirit" (Acts 2:38): as we will see, all those who received water baptism also received Spirit baptism (sometimes in the reverse order, 10:44-46).

The words of verses 38-39 have given rise to much discussion, among other things as to the chronology of the events mentioned: conversion - water baptism - Spirit baptism. We will return to this matter below, but at this point I wish to state that, in my view, instead of hammering on the proper order, it is more fruitful to stress that the three events belong

---

32. See extensively, Ouweneel (2005b).

The Coming of the Spirit

together, and in some ideal sense coincide (cf. Rom. 8:9; 1 Cor. 6:11). Conversion and water baptism are so closely knit together that the phrase "for the forgiveness of your sins" must be linked with both. Thus, notice the links between conversion and forgiveness in 3:19, and between water baptism and salvation in Mark 16:17 and 1 Peter 3:21. Water baptism and Spirit baptism, too, are so closely connected that the latter can be described as an inward work in the heart, and the former has now become the outward sign of it.[33] There cannot be a proper Christian water baptism without the concomitant Spirit baptism.

7.4.3 Gift and Gifts

Of course, the "gift" (Gk. *dōrea*) of the Spirit in Acts 2:38 (cf. 8:20; 10:45; 11:17) must be sharply distinguished from the "gifts" (Gk. *charismata*, lit. "portions of grace") of the Spirit in 1 Corinthians 12:4 (cf. also the "spiritual gifts" in v. 1 and 14:1). In the former case, the Spirit is passive: it is he himself who is given to God's people. In the latter case, the Spirit is active: it is he who gives gifts to God's people (see chapter 12). It is impractical to use the words "gift" and "gifts," because they are so similar, whereas their meanings are so different. In the rest of this book I will generally use the word *charismata* instead of "gifts."

On the one hand, the giving of the Spirit himself is linked with regeneration (John 3:5; Titus 3:5), with forgiveness (Acts 2:38), and with anointing and sealing (2 Cor. 1:21–22; Eph. 1:13) (see chapter 8 below). On the other hand, the *charismata* consist of various effects of the Spirit's activity in the lives of believers. The gift of the Spirit cannot be substantively distinguished here from Spirit baptism, and from being filled with the Spirit (Acts 1:5; 2:4). The result of this gift (Gk. *dōrea*) are the gifts (Gk. *charismata*), of which the book of Acts mentions glossolalia, gifts of healing, working of miracles, prophecy (e.g., 19:6), faith (e.g., 3:16), the ability to distinguish between

---

33. Bruce (1988, 70).

spirits (16:16-18); elsewhere clear hints are given of other *charismata* (1 Cor. 12:8-10), such as utterances of wisdom (e.g., 6:2-4) and utterances of knowledge (e.g., 5:1-10) (see further in chapter 12 below).

In contrast with Acts 8:17, 9:17, and 19:6, we are not told either in Acts 2:38-39 or 10:44-48 that the Spirit was granted to the new converts by the laying on of hands. On the one hand, one might argue that such laying on of hands was self-evident;[34] on the other hand that, if it had been done, Luke would certainly have reported such an important thing.[35] Such matters are closely related to the biases of the expositor; we will examine this point more closely in §§8.6-8.8 below.

The appeal given in verse 38 is further explained in verse 39: "For the promise is for you and for your children and for all who are far off, everyone whom the Lord our God calls to himself." This elicits various questions.

First, what is meant here by "the promise"? Is this the promise of the gospel?[36] Or the promise of the forgiveness of sins and the gift of the Holy Spirit?[37] It is amazing how the prejudices of covenant theology have guided the Reformed liturgical "Form for the Baptism of Infants" as well as various Reformed Bible commentators[38] to read into this text the Abrahamic promise of Genesis 17:7, apparently inspired to do so especially because of the reference to children.[39] Within the context of Acts 2, however, there is not the slightest reason to do this; "the promise" refers here not to the Abrahamic promise, but to "the promise of the Holy Spirit" (v. 33; cf. 1:4).

Second, what does the expression "your children" entail? Does it refer to the (little) children among Peter's listeners?[40]

---

34. Longenecker (1981, 284).
35. Bruce (1988, 70).
36. Ibid., 71.
37. Longenecker (1981, 285).
38. Grosheide (1962, 1.43-44).
39. See more extensively, Ouweneel (*RT* IV/2, §§8.3.1, 8.4.3).
40. Bruce (1988, 71).

In my view, within the context of Acts 2, Peter seems to be thinking instead of the future generations who would one day share in the Messianic kingdom (cf. Isa. 49:25; 54:1; 59:21; 60:9; Jer. 30:20; 31:17; Ezek. 37:25; Zech. 10:7, 9).[41]

Third, who are "all who are far off"? Does this refer to only the Jews in the Diaspora? Or also to the Gentile nations? Even if Peter himself were thinking especially of the former group, the Gentiles cannot be excluded here (cf. Eph. 2:13, 17, a quotation from Isa. 57:19), as is shown by what follows in the book of Acts (cf. 22:21, "Go, for I will send you far away to the Gentiles").[42]

7.5 The Samaritans
7.5.1 The Gospel in Samaria

In Acts 6:5-6, a certain Philip is mentioned, not to be confused with the apostle Philip (John 1:43-48; Acts 1:13). The Philip of Acts 6, a Greek speaking Jew, was chosen to be (what we might call) a deacon, but he gradually came to function more like an evangelist (21:8). He went from Jerusalem to Samaria, and preached Christ to the Samaritans — a preaching for which Jesus himself had laid the foundation (John 4:40-42). It had an enormous effect: "And the crowds with one accord paid attention to what was being said by Philip, when they heard him and saw the signs that he did. For unclean spirits, crying out with a loud voice, came out of many who had them, and many who were paralyzed or lame were healed. So there was much joy in that city" (Acts 8:5-8).

The Samaritans had been quite impressed by a man whom we know today as Simon Magus (the man who had once practiced magic, Acts 8:9-11). He is known as the first heretic of the church. The Gnostic sect of the Simonians (second century) claimed him as their founder, and as a god in human form. In Acts 8, we hear about the confrontation between him and Philip. When the latter came, the Samaritans heard an

---
41. Longenecker (1981, 285).
42. Knowling (1979, 92).

even better message than they had received from Simon: "[W]hen they believed Philip as he preached good news about the kingdom of God and the name of Jesus Christ, they were baptized, both men and women" (v. 12). Even Simon "believed" (whatever this may have entailed) and was baptized.

Philip not only preached the gospel to the Samaritans but did not hesitate to baptize them as well. This is remarkable because in Matthew 10:5-6 Jesus had commanded the twelve: "Go nowhere among the Gentiles and enter no town of the Samaritans, but go rather to the lost sheep of the house of Israel," apparently reckoning the Samaritans to be Gentiles rather than Israelite descendants.[43] However, in Acts 1:8 the risen Lord had sent his disciples explicitly to Samaria as well. Of course, this commission was not limited to the one hundred twenty. We do not know whether the prospective evangelist Philip belonged to the one hundred twenty — the *apostle* Philip did (v. 13) — but the Lord's commission was valid for *any* of his servants who knew themselves to be called to go to Samaria.

In my view, this baptizing by Philip is an important argument against those who claim that the Samaritan converts received their Spirit baptism only later, arguing that before this baptism by Philip, their faith had not been genuine but only a form of mass emotion, based on the signs.[44] Green and Floor have rightly argued that the context does not allow us to draw such a conclusion;[45] this is not the way to solve the "riddle of Samaria" (so Dunn). The riddle is this: many Samaritans truly repented and were born again. This was apparently recognized by Philip because he baptized them. Yet, they had not received the Holy Spirit; this happened later for the first time (see the next section).

---

43. *Contra* Bruce (1988, 167).
44. Dunn (1970, 64–65); Versteeg (1979, 183–88).
45. Green (1975, 138); Floor (1982, 90–92); Prince (1995, 239).

7.5.2 Spirit Baptism for the Samaritans

> Now when the apostles at Jerusalem heard that Samaria had received the word of God, they sent to them Peter and John, who came down and prayed for them that they might receive the Holy Spirit, for he had not yet fallen on any of them, but they had only been baptized in the name of the Lord Jesus. Then they laid their hands on them and they received the Holy Spirit (Acts 8:14-17).

It is remarkable that Philip felt free to baptize the Samaritan converts, but it is equally remarkable that he did not take the initiative to lay hands on the baptized Samaritans so that they would receive the Holy Spirit. Nor did the converts automatically receive the Spirit baptism at the moment of their water baptism (cf. the three thousand in 2:38-41), nor even at the moment of their conversion (cf. Cornelius and his friends in 10:44-46). Rather, the apostles in Jerusalem took the initiative to send a team to Samaria, presumably to inspect Philip's work: Peter and John, who had labored together earlier (Acts 3:1-11; cf. John 20:3-10). It is interesting that John is mentioned here, the very disciple who, with his brother James, had wished fire to come down from heaven to destroy a certain Samaritan village (Luke 9:52-54).

Only after Peter and John had laid hands on the Samaritan converts did the latter receive the Holy Spirit. Various reasons lead us to assume that one consequence of this laying on of hands was that these believers spoke in tongues and prophesied, even if this is not explicitly mentioned (as it *is* mentioned in Acts 2:4, 17; 10:45-46; 19:6). The first reason is that, in verse 16, the people involved *knew* that the Spirit had not yet been granted to them because the outward signs were lacking.

Second, in Acts 10:44, 46, and 11:15 the verb "to fall" of 8:16 is linked with outward phenomena (speaking in tongues, prophesying; cf. "came on them" in 19:6, where the effect is again speaking in tongues and prophesying).[46] Why would this have been different in chapter 8?

Third, Simon *saw* that through the apostles' laying on of hands the Holy Spirit was given, and was very impressed by this (v. 18). Perhaps this is the most convincing argument: how could we explain Simon's amazement and thrill if receiving the Holy Spirit had not been accompanied with quite impressive outward phenomena? Similarly, Paul could assume that the Galatian Christians would remember their receiving the Holy Spirit (Gal. 3:2). How *could* they remember this if there had been no outward signs? The only immediate signs mentioned in the book of Acts (apart from the sound of wind and the tongues as of fire in 2:2-3) are speaking in tongues and prophesying.

7.5.3 False Inferences

From the order of the events in Acts 8—conversion, water baptism, Spirit baptism—at least two far-fetched conclusions have been drawn. First, on the basis of this text, Episcopalian circles (in the broad sense of the term, including Roman Catholics) have created a distinction, also temporally, between water baptism and what they call "confirmation," and have derived an argument from it that confirmation can be performed only by someone standing in the line of apostolic succession. Second, on the basis of the same text, Pentecostal and Charismatic circles have postulated a distinction—also temporally—between conversion and receiving the Holy Spirit by the laying on of hands.[47]

I see at least three objections to such arguments.

(a) In all such claims we are dealing with the typical hermeneutical error of deriving *norms* from historical *events*: there and then it happened thus and so, and therefore it must always happen thus and so. The church in Troas apparently celebrated the Lord's Supper every week (Acts 20:7), so *we*

---

46. Knowling (1979, 216).
47. Longenecker (1981, 284–85, 358–59); Bruce (1988, 168–70).

The Coming of the Spirit

must celebrate it every week (but what about 2:46?). Each church in Revelation 2 and 3 had its own "angel," so *we* must have a pastor in every church (as if the Greek word *angelos* could not have other meanings here). And a recent one: early Christians continued to celebrate the Jewish festivals (e.g., Acts 20:16; 1 Cor. 16:8), so *we* must celebrate the Jewish festivals (as if what *Jewish* Christians did was also obligatory for *Gentile* Christians; cf. the contrast in Acts 15:1–21).

(b) If the distinction between baptism and confirmation, or between conversion and Spirit baptism, were really so important, we would certainly have expected that the New Testament letters would have further explained and emphasized this matter. This is not the case at all. On the contrary, from Ephesians 1:13 we instead get the impression that coming to faith and receiving the Spirit coincide. Romans 8:9 teaches that those who do not have the Spirit of Christ do not belong to him, so how could a person be a true believer without having received the Spirit? And if, as I believe, 1 Corinthians 12:13 refers to Spirit baptism (see §8.6 below), no one can be a member of Christ's body without Spirit baptism. In other words, how could a person be called a member of Christ's body, the church, without having received the Holy Spirit? (See further in §§8.6–8.8 below.)

(c) Of the six or seven times in the book of Acts when the Holy Spirit was conferred, only the special cases of Acts 8:17 and 19:6 entailed a conferring of the Spirit through the laying on of hands. In Acts 2:4 and 38, there was no question of the laying on of hands, nor in 9:17 either, where Ananias laid his hands on Saul, but spoke of being filled with the Spirit as a future event. In 10:44, receiving the Spirit occurred before the converts had received water baptism. In fact, no two cases in the book of Acts seem to be exactly the same, as we will see when we consider the other times in Acts when the Spirit was conferred. This makes it impossible to derive general norms from these events (see [a] above). Moreover, the New Testament generally assumes that genuine believers have received the Holy Spirit (see [b] above). Later I will argue that receiving the Spirit and being baptized with the Spirit are identical events (chapter 8).

7.5.4 The Meaning of the Samaritan Events

In fact, it is not difficult to find a plausible explanation of the exceptional course of events in Acts 8.[48] It was certainly wise, if not indispensable, that the apostles personally confirmed the reception of the Samaritans, who before had been so strongly despised, into the young Christian church (cf. 1 Cor. 12:13, Spirit baptism makes one a member of Christ's body; see §8.6). It was unacceptable that a separation between Jewish and Samaritan Christians would arise or would continue. Through the ministry of Peter and John, the ministry of Philip in Samaria was validated and extended.

There is another factor to be mentioned. It was Peter who had received the keys of the kingdom of God (Matt. 16:19). This did not exclude the role of the other apostles (cf. 18:18), but Peter certainly received a special position. In the book of Acts this comes to light in the prominent role that he played in admitting into the newly begun church of God, first, Jewish believers (Acts 2), second, Samaritan believers (Acts 8), and third, Roman believers (Acts 10).

This does not mean that the laying on of hands can be performed only by people standing in the line of apostolic succession. In Acts 9:12, 17 an ordinary disciple in Damascus, Ananias, laid hands on Saul of Tarsus, who would become the great apostle Paul. In Acts 13:1–3 the prophets and teachers of Antioch laid hands on the apostles (14:4, 14) Paul and Barnabas. Neither Ananias nor the Antiochian prophets and teachers are known to stand in the line of apostolic succession. Moreover, in both cases the person lower in position laid hands on the person higher in (future) position. Therefore it is incorrect to suggest that only higher officials administered

---

48. See Green (1975, 137–38), who also refers to Conzelmann (1987) and Lampe (1969).

the laying on of hands.[49]

This is entirely parallel with water baptism: in Acts 2, many more than the twelve apostles must have baptized all three thousand Jewish converts in one day. The Samaritan converts and the Ethiopian eunuch were baptized by the deacon Philip (8:12, 38). Saul of Tarsus was baptized by an anonymous person, perhaps the ordinary disciple Ananias (22:16). Cornelius and his friends were baptized by anonymous companions of Peter, *not* by Peter himself (10:48). Notice also Paul's reluctance to personally baptize people (1 Cor. 1:13–17).

It has been pointed out several times that the events in Samaria (Acts 8) were not simply a continuation of Acts 2. G. E. Ladd spoke of a "Jewish Pentecost" (Acts 2), a "Samaritan Pentecost" (Acts 8), and a "Gentile Pentecost" (Acts 10).[50] Entirely in line with Acts 1:8, the gospel extended in concentric circles: the step forward in Acts 2 was as equally significant as the one in Acts 8, and as the essentially new step in Acts 10. Every new "Pentecost" had its own specific characteristics, which cannot simply be transferred to believers today. On the contrary, the three "Pentecostal events" were unique and unrepeatable. As I said before, we must be very careful deriving norms from historical events.

7.6 Two Individuals
7.6.1 The Ethiopian Eunuch

In the remainder of Acts 8 we find the story of the eunuch, the Ethiopian court official, who came to faith through the ministry of Philip the evangelist. When they came to some water, the eunuch asked, "See, here is water! What prevents me from being baptized?" (v. 36). There was no impediment, and therefore "they both went down into the water, Philip and the eunuch, and he baptized him. And when they came up out of the water, the Spirit of the Lord carried Philip away, and the eunuch saw him no more, and went on his way rejoic-

---

49. Knowling (1979, 217).
50. Ladd (1975, 346).

ing" (vv. 38-39).

The Western family of New Testament manuscripts is represented mainly by the Codex Bezae Cantabrigiensis (whose siglum is D), a few papyri, a few ancient translations (Syriac and Latin), and quotations from Cyprian, Augustine, and Ephraemi. This text type is often longer than the Alexandrian text type, the latter considered by many textual critics to be the superior text type. Instead of "the Spirit of the Lord carried Philip away," the Western text (supported by a correction in the Codex Alexandrinus and by Jerome; D at this location is illegible) reads in Acts 8:39, ". . . the Holy Spirit fell on the eunuch, and an angel of the Lord carried Philip away."

This longer reading, which, though presumably not authentic, may yet be reliable, suggests that the eunuch's water baptism was followed by his Spirit baptism. Those who view this Western reading as the original one, suggest that perhaps the shorter reading arose erroneously, or by deliberate omission, because the longer reading seemed to conflict with verses 15-18: if the Spirit could be conferred *there* only by the intervention of the apostles, why not *here* as well?[51] Those who prefer the shorter reading do so on the basis of the strong textual testimony, as well as on the basis that the words of the longer reading were added later (a) to make explicit that the eunuch's water baptism was followed by his Spirit baptism, and (b) to bring what is said about Philip's departure into agreement with his commission (viz., by an angel of the Lord, v. 26).[52]

Quite apart from the longer reading of the Greek text, there can be no doubt that the eunuch received the Holy Spirit. Thus, the fact that he continued his journey with joy (v. 39) cannot be reasonably explained other than from the gift of the Holy Spirit (cf. 13:52; Rom. 14:17; Gal. 5:22; 1 Thess. 1:6). The text does not tell us whether Philip had laid his hands on the eunuch, but it is quite possible. Notice the sequence

---

51. So also Adolf B. C. Hilgenfeld, quoted by Knowling (1979, 227).
52. Metzger (1975, 360-61).

The Coming of the Spirit

in the Western reading: the Holy Spirit fell on the eunuch, and only then an angel of the Lord carried Philip away. There was time enough to lay his hands on the eunuch. However, both the Western and the Alexandrian readings are silent on this point, so that neither Charismatics nor anti-Charismatics should claim the verse for their point of view.

7.6.2 Saul of Tarsus

In Acts 9 we find the account of the conversion of Saul of Tarsus, which contains this passage:

> Ananias departed and entered the house. And laying his hands on him he said, "Brother Saul, the Lord Jesus who appeared to you on the road by which you came has sent me so that you may regain your sight and be filled with the Holy Spirit." And immediately something like scales fell from his eyes, and he regained his sight. Then he rose and was baptized (vv. 17-18).

As stated earlier (§7.5.4), an ordinary disciple from Damascus was chosen by the Lord to lay his hands on Saul (cf. vv. 10-16). As he did so, the Lord worked two things: he healed Saul from the blindness with which he had been struck three days earlier, and he filled him with the Holy Spirit. Just as the Spirit baptism in 2:4 ("they were all filled with the Holy Spirit") entailed equipping the one hundred twenty for their ministry (1:8), so too the Spirit baptism of Saul formed the necessary preparation for *his* ministry, as the Lord himself indicated (vv. 15-16; 22:14-15).

Here we find a remarkable similarity between the preparation of John the Baptist ("he will be filled with the Holy Spirit, even from his mother's womb," Luke 1:15) and that of Saul (cf. Gal. 1:15, "God, who had set me apart before I was born, and who called me by his grace..."). The two remind us of Jeremiah: "Before I formed you in the womb I knew you, and before you were born I consecrated you; I appointed you a prophet to the nations" (Jer. 1:5; cf. Ps. 22:9-10).

Immediately after Saul received the laying on of hands,

he underwent water baptism (cf. 22:16, "Rise and be baptized and wash away your sins, calling on his name"). It is not clear in what order Spirit baptism and water baptism occurred here. In Acts 9:17 we read that Ananias did lay his hands on him, but Ananias spoke about Saul's being filled with the Holy Spirit as a future occurrence. Perhaps we should not bother too much about the proper order: it is quite conceivable that Ananias baptized Saul immediately after having laid his hands on him, so that water baptism and Spirit baptism more or less coincided.

We do not hear whether, at his Spirit baptism, Saul spoke in tongues. At any rate we know that he spoke in tongues later, and did so more often than other believers: "I thank God that I speak in tongues more than all of you" (1 Cor. 14:18). It therefore seems obvious that, as happened in other cases (2:4; 10:46; 19:6), Paul received this *charisma* when he was filled with the Holy Spirit. However, Luke's emphasis lies elsewhere: the power of the Spirit was manifested in Saul primarily in his preaching, which he began right away: "And immediately he proclaimed Jesus in the synagogues, saying, 'He is the Son of God.' . . . Saul increased all the more in strength, and confounded the Jews who lived in Damascus by proving that Jesus was the Christ" (vv. 20, 22).

7.7 A Gentile Pentecost
7.7.1 Cornelius and His Friends

In Acts 10, the apostle Peter was prepared by the Holy Spirit to go preach the gospel in the house of a Gentile. He was invited by the centurion Cornelius in Caesarea, "a devout man who feared God with all his household, gave alms generously to the people, and prayed continually to God," and "an upright and God-fearing man, who is well spoken of by the whole Jewish nation" (vv. 2, 22). Peter addressed Cornelius along with "his relatives and close friends" (v. 24), and proclaimed to them the good news of Christ.

At a given moment Peter made the key statement: "[E]

veryone who believes in him receives forgiveness of sins through his name" (v. 43), which apparently impressed the company. The result of this enormous impact was visible right away:

> While Peter was still saying these things, the Holy Spirit fell on all who heard the word. And the believers from among the circumcised who had come with Peter were amazed, because the gift of the Holy Spirit was poured out also on the Gentiles. For they were hearing them speaking in tongues and extolling God. Then Peter declared, "Can anyone withhold water for baptizing these people, who have received the Holy Spirit just as we have?" And he commanded them to be baptized in the name of Jesus Christ (vv. 44–48).

F. H. Chase has called this the "Pentecost of the Gentile world,"[53] and Richard J. Knowling spoke of the "Gentile Pentecost,"[54] as I also quoted from George E. Ladd.[55] This is not surprising; Peter himself reported:

> "As I began to speak, the Holy Spirit fell on them *just as on us at the beginning*. And I remembered the word of the Lord, how he said, 'John baptized with water, but you will be baptized with the Holy Spirit.' If then God gave the same gift to them as he gave to us when we believed in the Lord Jesus Christ, who was I that I could stand in God's way?" When the other apostles heard these things they fell silent. And they glorified God, saying, "Then to the Gentiles also God has granted repentance that leads to life" (11:15–18).

Of course, in the literal sense there can be only one Pentecost. The person of the Holy Spirit can descend from heaven only once, and the New Testament church can be constituted only once. There was only one beginning of the church as the body of Christ, the temple of God, and the bride of the Lamb.

---

53. Chase (1902, 79).
54. Knowling (1979, 262).
55. Ladd (1975, 346).

Yet, apart from the admission into the church of the Ethiopian eunuch in Acts 8, who formed an isolated case, the admission into the church of Gentile—namely, Roman—believers in Acts 10 constituted a tremendous development in early church history (cf. §8.6).

7.7.2 The Sequence of Events

The particular point of Acts 10 is the unique order of the events. First, the conversion occurred, which is not mentioned in 10:44 but follows from 11:17, "... the same gift ... as he gave to us when we believed in the Lord Jesus Christ" (cf. 15:8–9). Second, the Spirit was given, and only in the third place was water baptism administered. In 2:41 (the three thousand) and 8:38–39 (the Ethiopian eunuch) the order was reversed; therefore, Peter does not compare the event of 10:44–46 with the conversion of the three thousand but with the Pentecost experience of the one hundred twenty (11:15; 15:8). While the matter of laying on hands is unclear in 2:41 and 8:38–39, it is clear that Cornelius and his friends received the Holy Spirit *without* the laying on of hands. This fact must be a warning to all those who make such a laying on of hands a condition for receiving the Spirit.

However, here again, as with the events of Acts 8:14–17, we should not turn this into a universal norm. Just as the apostles had to come to Samaria in order to confirm Philip's ministry, so too Peter and his companions were wisely brought here for a specific reason.[56] Without this obvious, sovereign intervention of God, the apostle might not have found the boldness to baptize these Gentile, that is, uncircumcised, believers (recall that circumcision was always a prerequisite for the Jewish baptism of male proselytes). And if Peter had done so apart from divine confirmation, he might have met with heavy opposition from Jerusalem[57] (see Peter's report in Acts 11:1–18).

---

56. Bruce (1988, 217–18).
57. Jews have said, "The Holy Spirit never fell on a Gentile," according to an anonymous quotation cited by Knowling (1979, 262).

Peter emphasizes here the connection and agreement between Acts 2 and 10: not only chapter 2 but also chapter 10 was a fulfillment of the word of Jesus (1:5). Despite the unique character of Acts 2, what occurred in Acts 10 was just as much a Spirit baptism as in Acts 2. God himself, without any human intervention, and without any public confession of faith from these Gentile believers, had granted them the (greater) Spirit baptism. After this, Peter and his companions could do nothing else than administer to them also the (lesser) water baptism. In Acts 15:8-10, this sovereign act of God is an argument in Peter's discourse to impose no other conditions on the believers from the Gentiles: if their faith was enough for their Spirit baptism, to what other conditions would one wish to bind them *afterward*?

The comparison between Acts 2:38, 8:12-17, and 10:44-46 makes clear that the sequence of water baptism and Spirit baptism is not essential. Or perhaps it is more accurate to say that conversion, water baptism, and Spirit baptism in some ideal sense coincide, as stated earlier. Water baptism is an outward, Spirit baptism an inward, aspect of conversion and coming to faith. All of this together forms a single entity, in which it is of secondary importance whether the outward sign precedes the inward Spirit baptism, or follows upon it.

7.7.3 The Disciples at Ephesus

And it happened that . . . Paul . . . came to Ephesus. There he found some disciples. And he said to them, "Did you receive the Holy Spirit when you believed?" And they said, "No, we have not even heard that there is a Holy Spirit." And he said, "Into what then were you baptized?" They said, "Into John's baptism." And Paul said, "John baptized with the baptism of repentance, telling the people to believe in the one who was to come after him, that is, Jesus." On hearing this, they were baptized in the name of the Lord Jesus. And when Paul had laid his hands on them, the Holy Spirit came on them, and they began speaking in tongues and prophesying. There were about twelve men in all (Acts 19:1-7).

These Ephesian disciples, approximately twelve in number, have often been referred to as disciples of John the Baptist, but this claim is doubtful. When Luke speaks of "disciples," he always means followers of Jesus (Acts 6:1-2, 7; 9:1, 10, 19, 25-26, 36, 38; 11:26, 29; 13:52; 14:20-22, 28; 15:10; 16:1; 18:23, 27; 19:9, 30; 20:1, 30; 21:4, 16). Moreover, Paul observes in verse 2 that these men had come to faith, and this can mean only that they were followers of Jesus, no matter how limited their knowledge of the gospel may have been.[58] However, when Paul met them, he found that they lacked something: the Holy Spirit. This is very important because it shows that although people have confessed their sins and know Jesus as the only way of salvation, they may have been born again without having yet received the Holy Spirit. This is either because they do not really *know* the full "gospel of their salvation" (cf. Eph. 1:13; Rom. 1:16; 1 Cor. 15:1-3), or they do not dare to *apply* it to themselves (see more extensively §§8.7-8.8 below). Both are usually consequences of deficient (e.g., hyper-Calvinist) preaching.

In the case of the Ephesian disciples, it is obvious that certain things must have been lacking in their faith, or in their knowledge of the gospel, for they did not know the Holy Spirit. Moreover, it should strike us that Paul immediately *noticed* that they did not possess the Holy Spirit, because certain effects were absent. To understand this we remember that, in Acts 8:17-18 and 10:44-46, it was immediately obvious to bystanders that certain other persons did possess the Holy Spirit because the latter spoke in tongues and prophesied — as did the Ephesian disciples *after* they had received the Holy Spirit (19:6).

As I pointed out earlier, I judge that many translations render the Ephesian disciples' reply incorrectly: "[W]e have

---

58. *Contra* Green (1975, 135), who claimed that it is crystal clear that these disciples could in no respect be called Christians.

not even heard that there is a Holy Spirit" (ESV; cf. NKJV, NIV, NASB, RSV, and others). It seems unlikely to me that men who had been baptized with John's baptism would have known so little of John's teaching.[59] Would they never have heard that John baptized with water but that, as he had announced, Another would come who would baptize in the Holy Spirit? Correct renderings, in my view, are these: "[W]e did not so much as hear whether the Holy Spirit was [given]" (ASV). "We did not even hear if [the] Holy Spirit was [come]" (Darby). "But we did not even hear if [the] Holy Spirit is [given]" (DLNT). Such a translation is fully in line with John 7:39, "[A]s yet the Spirit had not been given, because Jesus was not yet glorified." Apparently, the Ephesian twelve had not understood that the Spirit baptism by Jesus had already occurred.

To Paul it was very strange that any baptized person would not have received the Holy Spirit; therefore he asked his question about their baptism. Presumably these people had made less progress than Apollos, who, "though he knew only the baptism of John," "had been instructed in the way of the Lord. And being fervent in spirit [or rather, in the Spirit], he spoke and taught accurately the things concerning Jesus" (Acts 18:25).

Perhaps we must assume that a disciple of John had announced the gospel to these twelve men in Ephesus to the best of his own knowledge of it. As a consequence, these men had come to faith in Jesus, whereas this preacher did not know anything more than the baptism of John. Therefore he did not know that, since the Day of Pentecost, this baptism was no more applicable, as Paul explained (v. 4). This is why the twelve men still had to undergo Christian baptism. This is the only case of "re-baptism" in the Bible, though this term is not really correct because they were being baptized now for the first time "in the name of the Lord Jesus." However, this water baptism did not automatically bring the Holy Spir-

---

59. Kelly (1952, 275).

it upon them. Just as Peter and John had done with the Samaritan believers (Acts 8:17), here as well Paul laid his hands on the Ephesian disciples. And now the effect became visible that Paul had missed in verse 2: "[T]he Holy Spirit came on them, and they began speaking in tongues and prophesying" (19:6).[60]

7.8 The Holy Spirit and Some Key Terms
7.8.1 The Kingdom of God

The proclamation of the kingdom of God plays a great role in the book of Acts, and not seldom in direct connection with the coming of the Holy Spirit. Thus, we learn that the risen Lord "presented himself alive to them [i.e., to his disciples] after his suffering by many proofs, appearing to them during forty days and speaking about the kingdom of God" (1:3). This is quite astonishing; all the subjects that the Lord dealt with could be summarized under this one heading: the kingdom of God. One of these subjects was the imminent descent of the Holy Spirit (vv. 4–5, 8). Conversely, in this same context the disciples asked him, "Lord, will you at this time restore the kingdom to Israel?" (v. 6). The Lord's answer to this legitimate question does not concern us right now; the pivotal point is the connection between the Holy Spirit and the kingdom of God (see vv. 7–8).

Similarly, the gospel that Philip preached in Samaria was the "good news about the kingdom of God and the name of Jesus Christ" (8:12). Those who accepted this gospel received the Holy Spirit (v. 17). We read that only after the Ephesian disciples had been baptized and had received the Holy Spirit, Paul "entered the synagogue and for three months spoke boldly, reasoning and persuading them about the kingdom of God" (19:8). This preaching was part of his usual ministry: ". . . you among whom I have gone about proclaiming the king-

---

60. The imperfect tense of the verbs used here suggests that this did not occur only once (then we would have rather expected the aorist tense), but that this was something ongoing (Knowling 1979, 403).

dom" (20:25). "From morning till evening" Paul was "testifying to the kingdom of God" (28:23); he "welcomed all who came to him, proclaiming the kingdom of God and teaching about the Lord Jesus Christ with all boldness and without hindrance" (vv. 30-31).

A special connection is made in Romans 14:17, "For the kingdom of God is not a matter of eating and drinking but of righteousness and peace and joy in the Holy Spirit." What matters in the kingdom of God—the rule of Christ, now specifically over Christians, eventually over all people—is not a tug-of-war concerning theological idiosyncrasies: what we may or may not eat and drink, or what special days must we observe (vv. 2, 5-6). Rather, the first thing that matters is righteousness: doing justice to each other, the weak toward the strong, and especially the strong toward the weak (vv. 10-13). As a consequence, there will also be peace and joy, which belong to the fruit of the Spirit (Gal. 5:22). Seeking God's righteousness in his kingdom is the Master's commission to his followers (Matt. 6:31-33).

Righteousness is characteristic of the Messianic kingdom as it will be manifestly realized in the last days:

> For to us a child is born, to us a son is given; and the government shall be upon his shoulder. . . . Of the increase of his government and of peace there will be no end, on the throne of David and over his kingdom, to establish it and to uphold it with justice and with righteousness from this time forth and forevermore (Isa. 9:6-7).

> There shall come forth a shoot from the stump of Jesse, and a branch from his roots shall bear fruit. And the *Spirit of the* LORD *shall rest upon him*. . . . He shall not judge by what his eyes see, or decide disputes by what his ears hear, but with righteousness he shall judge the poor, and decide with equity for the meek of the earth. . . . Righteousness shall be the belt of his waist, and faithfulness the belt of his loins (11:1-5).

Behold, a king will reign in righteousness, and princes will rule in justice . . . *until the Spirit is poured upon us from on high*. . . . Then justice will dwell in the wilderness, and righteousness abide in the fruitful field. And the effect of righteousness will be peace, and the result of righteousness, quietness and trust forever (32:1, 15-17).

"I will put my Spirit within you and cause you to walk in my commandments, and ye shall keep my rights [Heb. *mishpatay*], and do them" (Ezek. 36:27 ISV).

In both Isaiah 11 and 32, the righteousness of God's kingdom is linked with God's Spirit, just as in Romans 14:17. Here I refer again (see §6.5.3) to the striking variant reading of Luke 11:2, where, instead of "your kingdom come," we read, "[Y]our Holy Spirit come over us and cleanse us." Various church fathers preferred this reading because they were convinced that the kingdom of God had arrived on the Day of Pentecost with the coming of the Holy Spirit[61] — which in a certain sense is perfectly correct, of course. Symeon the New Theologian put it this way: "In fact the kingdom of God is a sharing in the Holy Spirit [cf. Heb. 6:4]. He it is of whom it is said, 'The kingdom of God is in the midst of you'[62] (Luke 17:21), so that we must apply ourselves to the task of receiving and possessing the Holy Spirit."[63] I find the latter interpretation less likely (see below); in my view, Jesus was not referring to the Holy Spirit, who had not yet been poured out, but to himself. But the former point is well taken: being in the kingdom of God and sharing in the Holy Spirit are more or less identical.

There are two kinds of "sons of the kingdom," as Jesus himself already pointed out: the false ones and the genuine ones (compare interestingly Matt. 8:12 with 13:38). There are those who say, "Lord, Lord," but do not enter the kingdom

---

61. Congar (1997, 2.69).
62. In order to make the connection with the indwelling Spirit, Symeon probably read: "is within you" ([N]KJV and many others).
63. Congar (1997, 2.70, 121).

(7:21-22; cf. 25:11-12; Luke 6:46), and there are those who witness in the power of the Spirit that "Jesus is Lord" (1 Cor. 12:3), and thus show that they belong to the kingdom (cf. 4:20; 6:9-10; 15:24, 50). Only the presence and possession of the Spirit constitute the difference between the former and the latter group.

One of the most remarkable passages concerning the kingdom of God is Luke 17:21b just quoted: ". . . the kingdom of God is in the midst of you [Gk. *entos humōn*]" (ESV, NIV), or "among you" (CJB, AMP), or "within you" ([N]KJV, GNT). Indeed, the Greek phrase *entos humōn* can be understood in various ways. The rendering "within you" would be quite fitting if this were a statement by Jesus to his own disciples, but is rather unlikely given the fact that he was addressing unbelievers.[64] Another possible rendering is "within your reach," which is defended by Tertullian, who translated it with the Latin phrase *in manu* ("in your hand, in your power").

The rendering of the ESV, the NIV, and others suggests that the kingdom was present in the person of the king himself, Jesus, who was standing in the midst of his listeners; the kingdom was manifest in the works he did (cf. 11:20).[65] As we saw, the expression has also been applied to the Holy Spirit: wherever the Holy Spirit is active, the kingdom of God becomes manifest (cf. Matt. 12:28). Walter Kasper sees the kingdom of God wherever people trust in God and his love, whether or not they speak explicitly of God or Jesus (cf. Matt. 25:35-40).[66] And what Paul Evdokimov says of the church is rather true of the kingdom: we know where the kingdom is, but it is not up to us to judge and to say where it is not—for the Holy Spirit works everywhere.[67]

---

64. Greijdanus (1941, 105); Bruce (1979, 594); Liefeld (1984, 997).
65. So Geldenhuys (1983, 440); Bruce (1979, 594); in the latter's view, an objection to this rendering is that in Gk. the phrase "in the midst of you" would instead be *en mesōi humōn* (cf. John 1:26).
66. Kasper (1974).
67. Evdokimov (1959, 343).

7.8.2 Witnessing

The nouns "witness" (Gk. *martys*) and "testimony" (Gk. *martyrion*), and the verb "to witness/testify" (Gk. *[dia]martyreō, -omai*) are key terms in the book of Acts, and are closely linked with the work of the Holy Spirit. In Acts 1:8, despite the word "and" (a Hebraism), there is a clearly causal or consecutive connection: "[Y]ou will receive power when the Holy Spirit has come upon you, and you will be my witnesses" means either "... *for* you will be ..." (causative), or "*so that* you will be my witnesses" (consecutive).

The apostles had been eye- and ear-witnesses of all that Jesus had done and said (cf. Luke 1:2). They were "men who have accompanied us during all the time that the Lord Jesus went in and out among us, beginning from the baptism of John until the day when he was taken up from us" (Acts 1:21-22). As such they could testify to that "which was from the beginning, which we have heard, which we have seen with our eyes, which we looked upon and have touched with our hands, concerning the word of life" (1 John 1:1). From a superficial point of view, no special power seems needed for such a testimony, just as ordinary witnesses before an earthly tribunal need no such power; a good memory, honesty, and accuracy suffice. However, for their witnessing the apostles and other servants of the Lord did need the power of the Holy Spirit in order to render their testimony spiritually effective.

Jesus made this clear in Luke 24, after his resurrection. First he said, "You are witnesses of these things" (v. 48). But this did not mean that they could begin witnessing immediately: "And behold, I am sending the promise of my Father [i.e., the Holy Spirit] upon you. But *stay* in the city *until* you are clothed with power from on high" (v. 49). Before they went out to testify, they had to "*wait* for the promise of the Father" (Acts 1:4). They could not be true witnesses without the power of the Holy Spirit for at least three reasons.

(a) To be able to properly witness to what the Lord had

said and done, the witnesses needed *insight* into Jesus' words and deeds, and only the Spirit could grant them this insight (John 14:26; 16:13; cf. 13:7).

(b) The Holy Spirit would also give them the *courage* for this testimony; see the difference between John 20:19 (the doors locked out of fear) and Acts 2:14 (Peter standing up and publicly witnessing).[68] The apostles spoke with "confidence" or "boldness" (Gk. *parrēsia*; 2:29; 4:13, 29), which sometimes was explicitly a consequence of being filled with the Spirit: "[T]hey were all filled with the Holy Spirit and [read: so that they] continued to speak the word of God with boldness" (4:31; cf. v. 8).

(c) The Holy Spirit would place in their mouths the right *words* for their testimony: "[S]ay whatever is given you in that hour, for it is not you who speak, but the Holy Spirit" (Mark 13:11; cf. Matt. 10:19-20; Luke 12:11-12 [cf. 21:15]).

Especially at the beginning of Acts, the testimony concerning Jesus' resurrection was prominent (1:22; 2:32; 3:15; 4:33; 10:39, 41; 13:31). In 5:32 this was placed alongside the testimony of the Holy Spirit: "[W]e are witnesses to these things, and so is the Holy Spirit, whom God has given to those who obey him." This double testimony seems similar to the one we found in John 15:26-17, "But when the Helper comes, . . . he will bear witness about me. And you also will bear witness, because you have been with me from the beginning" (see §6.8.1). Perhaps the two testimonies in Acts 5 are more similar: Knowling explained the first testimony—that of the apostles—as the historical testimony concerning the redemptive facts, and the second testimony—that of the Holy Spirit—as the inner testimony of the Holy Spirit within the listeners (cf. Rom. 8:16).[69] In Grosheide's view, the intention of the text is that "the Spirit confirms the testimony of the apostles, 1 Cor. 2:4; Heb. 2:4."[70]

---

68. This distinction struck Gregory the Great (ca. 600) (Burgess 1997, 15).
69. Knowling (1979, 155).
70. Grosheide (1962, 1.87).

A testimony in the power of the Holy Spirit can have a tremendous effect.[71] The apostles testified "with great power" to the resurrection of Christ (Acts 4:33). They "filled" Jerusalem with their teaching (5:28). Philip's testimony brought "much joy" to the city of Samaria (8:8). After the testimony of Paul and Barnabas, the "next Sabbath almost the whole city [i.e., Antioch in Pisidia] gathered to hear the word of the Lord" (13:44). Paul and Silas "disturbed" the city of Philippi, and in Thessalonica they were accused of having "turned the world upside down" (17:6). There was no limit to what God's Spirit could do. Through the apostolic testimony, the city of Ephesus was filled with "confusion" (19:29).

Paul wrote, "[M]y speech and my message were not in plausible words of wisdom, but in demonstration of the Spirit and of power, so that your faith might not rest in the wisdom of men but in the power of God" (1 Cor. 2:4-5). The testimony of God's servants, given in the power of the Spirit, always accomplishes something tremendous. That today such testimony often does *not* have this effect is due not simply to our living in a different epoch and culture. It is due especially to the frequent absence of the power of the Holy Spirit. Usually this is due in turn not to the Spirit himself but to the witnesses—though we must recognize that the Spirit remains sovereign in all his work.

7.8.3 Signs and Wonders

Again, notice that in the book of Acts the Spirit's testimony always accomplished something tremendous, whether it was revival or resurgence, which basically consists of opposing the evil powers.[72] In Acts 8, as the Spirit worked wonders through Philip, he was opposing the dark powers that Simon Magus was exercising, and the Spirit triumphed over them. In 16:16-18, the Holy Spirit worked through Paul to triumph over a woman who had a "spirit of Python" (thus literally; see

---

71. Prince (1995, 317–18).
72. See more extensively, Ouweneel (2005b, 91–96).

DRA), which means that she was a servant of the pagan god Apollo. In Acts 19, the Spirit's testimony triumphed over the servants of the pagan goddess Artemis (twin sister of Apollo). In 28:4–6, the healing power of the Spirit triumphed over the pagan goddess of avenging, Nemesis (so Darby; or "the goddess Justice"; so NIV). All these gods and goddesses were nothing but servants of Satan;[73] the book of Acts testifies that the Holy Spirit is stronger than Satan.

The signs and wonders described in Acts were the work of the Holy Spirit, as explained in Hebrews 2:4, "God also bore witness by signs and wonders and various miracles and by gifts of the Holy Spirit distributed according to his will." This corroborative testimony given by God himself accompanied testimony given by believers concerning the Lord and his word (v. 3). Elsewhere we read that the glorified Lord confirmed the apostles' words with his testimony consisting of signs and wonders: "[T]hey went out and preached everywhere, while the Lord worked with them and confirmed the message by accompanying signs" (Mark 16:20); ". . . the Lord, who bore witness to the word of his grace, granting signs and wonders to be done by their hands" (Acts 14:3).

In both Acts 8 and 19, preaching the gospel was linked with great signs and wonders:

> And the crowds with one accord paid attention to what was being said by Philip, when they heard him and saw the signs that he did. For unclean spirits, crying out with a loud voice, came out of many who had them, and many who were paralyzed or lame were healed . . . signs and great miracles [were] performed (8:6–7, 13).

> [A]ll the residents of Asia heard the word of the Lord, both Jews and Greeks. And God was doing extraordinary miracles by the hands of Paul, so that even handkerchiefs or aprons that had touched his skin were carried away to the sick, and their dis-

---

73. See extensively, Ouweneel (2003).

eases left them and the evil spirits came out of them (19:10–12).

On the one hand, in the book of Acts entering the kingdom of God (see §7.8.1) was linked with sufferings, persecution, and oppression. The apostles warned believers "that through many tribulations we must enter the kingdom of God" (14:22b); that is, they would follow in the footsteps of Jesus who had *suffered* here on earth. On the other hand, the kingdom of God is a place where the *risen* and *glorified* Lord manifests himself in the power of the Holy Spirit (cf. Mark 16:20): "For the kingdom of God does not consist in [idle] talk but in power," that is, the power of the Holy Spirit (1 Cor. 4:20).

About Stephen we read that he was "a man full of faith and of the Holy Spirit," and as one "full of grace and power, [he] was doing great wonders and signs among the people" (Acts 6:5, 8). Paul conducted his ministry "by the power of signs and wonders, by the power of the Spirit of God" (Rom. 15:19). He speaks to the Galatian Christians about the twofold blessing of him "who supplies the Spirit to you and works miracles among you" (Gal. 3:5).

Chapter 8
Believing Through the Holy Spirit

> [U]nless one is born of water and the Spirit,
>   he cannot enter the kingdom of God.
> That which is born of the flesh is flesh,
>   and that which is born of the Spirit is spirit.
>
> John 3:5–6

> In him you also,
>   when you heard the word of truth, the gospel of your salvation,
> and believed in him,
>   were sealed with the promised Holy Spirit,
> who is the guarantee of our inheritance
>   until we acquire possession of it,
> to the praise of his glory."
>
> Ephesians 1:13–14

Summary: *This chapter is governed by two important distinctions. The first is between the work of the Spirit in the soul (regeneration, coming to faith) and the indwelling of the Spirit. Not only are these* *two matters distinct, but the latter does not follow automatically upon the former. Aspects of the former are confession of sins, rebirth, being made alive, sanctification, and justification, spiritual circumcision, and so on. Aspects of the latter are being set free from the "law of sin and death," indwelling, adoption as sons, conformity to Christ, and so on.*

The second distinction is between receiving the Spirit (being sealed and anointed with the Spirit, his indwelling) and experiencing the fullness of the Spirit (being filled with the Spirit, power in ministry, and the gifts of the Spirit). The question is discussed whether Spirit baptism refers to the former (as most Christians think), or to the latter event as a "second blessing" (as many Pentecostals and Charismatics believe). Important passages are investigated (Rom. 7 and 8; 1 Cor. 12:13; Eph. 1:13-14). Our conclusion is that the terminology used is far less important than experiencing the Spirit's power and gifts.

8.1 Introduction
8.1.1 A Twofold Work of the Spirit

WHEN A PERSON IS REGENERATED and comes to faith in Christ, there are two activities of the Holy Spirit that must be sharply distinguished.[1] The first is the Holy Spirit regenerating a person (known also as rebirth, making alive, spiritual circumcision), and the second is the Holy Spirit personally dwelling in the converted man or woman. These two activities are not necessarily connected.[2] For instance, Old Testament believers possessed life from God, which must necessarily have been produced within them by the Holy Spirit, but they did *not* possess the Spirit personally dwelling in them. For this reason, D. M. Lloyd-Jones did not accept the identification of rebirth and Spirit baptism because, in that case, before the Day

---

1. *Contra* Calvin, *Institutes* 4.16.25, who identifies rebirth and Spirit baptism, which is followed by many Reformed theologians (e.g., Floor [1982, 161] and Runia [2000, 105]).
2. This lack of connection is not seen by Nathan and Wilson (1995, 210–11), although I do agree with their conclusion (no second blessing; see §§8.7–8.8), but this lack of connection *is* seen by Duffield and Van Cleave (1996, 324).

of Pentecost the disciples and apostles could not have been born again—in his view an untenable claim. He believed this would also imply that no Old Testament saint had eternal life, and also that the Samaritan believers were not regenerated before Peter and John had laid their hands on them (Acts 8).[3]

I think Lloyd-Jones was correct about this. The distinction between the Holy Spirit regenerating and indwelling is clearly made in Ezekiel 36. First, we find here what in the New Testament is called rebirth (new birth, regeneration, spiritual cleansing, creating a new heart): "I will sprinkle clean water on you, and you shall be clean from all your uncleannesses, and from all your idols I will cleanse you. And I will give you a new heart, and a new spirit I will put within you. And I will remove the heart of stone from your flesh and give you a heart of flesh" (vv. 25-26; cf. 11:19; 18:31). Second, we read that the indwelling of the Spirit is a clearly distinct matter: "I will put my Spirit within you" (v. 27; cf. 37:14).

The point is the difference between God renewing the human spirit (by the Spirit!) and God granting his Spirit. The contractor who refurbishes a house is not necessarily the same as the new inhabitant of the house. The Spirit is both the One who renews a person and the One who comes to dwell within the renewed person; but the latter does not occur automatically at the time of the former. In other words, rebirth through the Spirit never automatically entails the indwelling of the Spirit. David, who in view of his ministry had been anointed with the Holy Spirit (cf. 2 Sam. 23:1-3), knew this distinction: "renew a right spirit [Heb. *ruach*] within me" is another matter than "take not your Holy Spirit [Heb. *ruach*] from me" (Ps. 51:10-11).

The gospel comes to people "not only in word, but also in power and in the Holy Spirit" (1 Thess. 1:5), and the person who has come to faith has "received the word . . . with the joy of the Holy Spirit" (v. 6). Rebirth is "[out] of the Spirit" (John

---

3. Lloyd-Jones (1997, 237).

3:5), the renewal of a person is "of the Holy Spirit" (Titus 3:5; cf. Rom. 7:6). "It is the Spirit who gives life" (John 6:63; cf. Eph. 2:5; Col. 2:13). This is all by the *power* of the Holy Spirit (§§8.2 and 8.3). But, I repeat, this is something very different from the *person* of the Holy Spirit coming to *dwell* in the converted, regenerated, renewed, living person (§§8.4 and 8.5). In the Old Testament, too, a person could come to faith only by the power of the Spirit, as stated implicitly in Ezekiel 36. However, before the Day of Pentecost this faith was not *sealed* with the Holy Spirit in any of those believers (cf. 2 Cor. 1:22; Eph. 1:13; 4:30). It was not yet the time that had been foretold by Joel 2:28 (Acts 2:17): the time when God would pour out his Spirit on all his people.

Here a "seal" is a divine sign, a token (cf. Rom. 4:11; 1 Cor. 9:2), especially of divine ownership (cf. 2 Cor. 1:22; Rev. 5:1–9) and of the confirmation of the truth of a matter (cf. John 3:33; 6:27; 2 Tim. 2:19); it may also be a divine protection against evildoers (cf. Matt. 27:66; Rev. 7:3; 9:4). All these aspects are applicable to the sealed believers.

8.1.2 Even Today No Automatism

Thus, in the Old Testament there was regeneration; there were those who had "a new life through the Spirit" (1 Pet. 4:6 ERV; see §8.2.3). There was also faith (significant passages are Gen. 15:6; Hab. 2:4b). But there was no sealing with the Spirit, no personal indwelling of the Spirit in believers. In those days, there was only the *anointing* with (the power of) the Holy Spirit for *a few* believers in view of a specific ministry. This means that, in our thinking, rebirth *by* the Spirit and indwelling *of* the Spirit ought not to be automatically linked. When we come to see this, we will also understand that, also after Acts 2, there is not necessarily such an automatic link. In summary:

(a) In the Old Testament there was rebirth and faith; but because salvation—Christ's death, burial, and resurrection (1 Cor. 15:1–3)—had not yet been accomplished, there was not yet faith in the gospel of *this* salvation that could be sealed with the Holy Spirit (Eph. 1:13; 4:30).

(b) After Acts 2, rebirth can occur in conjunction with sincere confession of sins and the forgiveness of sins (1 John 1:9). However, due to defective preaching, a person may not know the gospel of salvation sufficiently, or may not feel free to accept this gospel and apply it personally. In this case, too, there is not yet that faith in the gospel of salvation that can be sealed with the Holy Spirit.

(c) By contrast, in *each* regenerated person who in faith has accepted this gospel of salvation, this faith is sealed with the Holy Spirit. I am not aware of any exceptions in the present epoch. This event, with all its theological nuances, is basically identical with the baptism *in/with* the Spirit, the anointing *with* the Spirit, the indwelling *of* the Spirit, and so on.

(d) However, here again, because of defective preaching, the sealed believer does not always experience the *power* of, or the being *filled* with, the Spirit immediately. If this does happen at a later stage, this is sometimes falsely called "Spirit baptism."

We will return more extensively to these important points in the second half of the present chapter.

8.1.3 Aspects of Conversion

Without developing a full-blown soteriology here,[4] we state that conversion is a matter of human responsibility; therefore we hear the frequent appeal to human conscience: "Repent!" (in the New Testament from Matt. 3:2 to Rev. 2:5). However, its counterpart, rebirth (regeneration, new birth), is a matter of God's sovereign grace and the work of the Holy Spirit. Paul beautifully juxtaposes the two: "[W]ork out your own salvation with fear and trembling, for it is God who works in you, both to will and to work for his good pleasure" (Phil. 2:12–13). The former is the aspect of human responsibility (hence the

---

4. See more extensively RT III/4 (*Eternal Life*).

imperative), the latter is the aspect of God's sovereign grace. Scripture never plays these two aspects off against each other, which has unfortunately happened all too often in church history.

This work of God's Spirit in a person's soul has various aspects, of which I will enumerate ten.

(1) The natural person is *lost* (John 3:15-16; 1 Cor. 1:18; 2 Cor. 2:15; 4:3; 2 Thess. 2:10; 2 Pet. 3:9), and therefore needs *salvation*, like a person drowning needs rescue (John 3:17; 12:47; Acts 4:12; 16:31; Rom. 1:16; 10:9-10; 1 Cor. 1:18; 15:1-2; Eph. 2:5, 8; 1 Tim. 1:15; 2:3-4; 2 Tim. 1:9; Titus 3:4-5; Heb. 5:9; 1 Pet. 1:9; Jude 1:3).

(2) The natural person is *imprisoned* in the power of sin, death, and Satan, and therefore needs *redemption* (Rom. 3:24; 1 Cor. 1:30; Eph. 1:7; Col. 1:14; Heb. 2:15; 9:12; 1 Pet. 1:18; Rev. 1:5); the New Testament also speaks of *release* (Rom. 7:6), or *being set free* (8:1-2; cf. John 8:32, 36; 2 Cor. 3:17). The underlying metaphor is that of captivity.

(3) The natural person has a corrupt nature: "Can the Ethiopian change his skin or the leopard his spots? Then also you can do good who are accustomed to do evil" (Jer. 13:23). In the New Testament, this is called the *flesh*. The person needs a "new nature," which is called *spirit*; one receives this in *rebirth* (new birth, regeneration) (John 3:5-6).

(4) One's natural state is called the *old self* (Rom. 6:6; Eph. 4:22; Col. 3:9; older translations: *old man*), and therefore needs *renewal* (Rom. 7:6; 12:2; Titus 3:5-6) to a *new self* (Eph. 4:23-24; Col. 3:10; *new man*). "And I will give them one heart, and a new spirit I will put within them. I will remove the heart of stone from their flesh and give them a heart of flesh" (Ezek. 11:19; cf. 36:26).

(5) One's natural state is called (spiritual) *uncircumcision*, and therefore one needs (spiritual) *circumcision* (Rom. 2:29; Col. 2:11). "Circumcise therefore the foreskin of your heart, and be no longer stubborn" (Deut. 10:16; 30:6; Jer. 4:4).

(6) The natural person is *dead* in trespasses and sins, and therefore needs to be *made alive* (Eph. 2:1, 5; Col. 2:13; KJV and others: *quickened*). "Thus says the Lord GOD to these bones: 'Behold, I will cause breath to enter you, and you shall live. And I will lay sinews upon you, and will cause flesh to come upon you, and cover you with skin, and put breath in you, and you shall live, and you shall know that I am the LORD'" (Ezek. 37:5–6).

(7) The natural person has committed many *sins*, and therefore needs *forgiveness* (Matt. 26:28; Eph. 1:7; 4:32; Col. 1:14; 2:13; 1 John 1:9) and *cleansing* (John 13:10; 1 Cor. 6:11; Eph. 5:26; Heb. 9:14; 1 John 1:7). "Wash me thoroughly from my iniquity, and cleanse me from my sin!" (Ps. 51:2).

(8) By nature the natural person is an *enemy* of God, and therefore needs *reconciliation* with God (Rom. 5:10–11). "And you, who once were alienated and hostile in mind, doing evil deeds, he has now reconciled in his body of flesh by his death, in order to present you holy and blameless and above reproach before him" (Col. 1:21–22).

(9) By nature the natural person is *unjust* (even wicked), and therefore needs *justification* (Rom. 3–8; Gal. 3; James 2). "In the LORD all the offspring of Israel shall be justified and shall glory" (Isa. 45:25).

(10) By nature the natural person is *unholy*, and therefore needs *sanctification* (i.e., to be made holy; 1 Cor. 1:2; 6:11; 2 Thess. 2:13; Heb. 10:10, 14; 1 Pet. 1:2). "[Y]ou shall be to me a kingdom of priests and a holy nation" (Exod. 19:6; cf. 1 Pet. 2:9).

More points could be mentioned, but these are the most important ones, which also include the facets that in the New Testament are explicitly linked with the work of the Holy Spirit (see §8.2).

8.2 The Holy Spirit and Rebirth
8.2.1 John 3

By night rabbi Nicodemus, a Pharisee, a "ruler of the Jews" (i.e., member of the Sanhedrin, the Jewish council), and even "*the* teacher of Israel" (John 3:1, 10), came to see Jesus. When he introduced himself with the claim "we know," Jesus countered this with the words: "[U]nless one is born again he cannot see the kingdom of God" (v. 3) — not only "cannot enter" (v. 5) but "cannot perceive" or "discern." In the vertical dimension, the not (yet) reborn person, no matter how learned according to human standards, knows nothing. By contrast, the anointed believer, no matter how unlearned, knows everything (1 John 2:20 alternate reading). Because of his sinfulness, even the Jew, a member of God's chosen people, needs a new birth in order to participate in the Messianic kingdom (see Ezek. 36:25-26). Nicodemus did not understand this, or appeared not to understand it, whereupon Jesus added, "Truly, truly, I say to you, unless one is born of water and Spirit [Gk. *ex hudatos kai pneumatos*], he cannot enter the kingdom of God" (John 3:5).

In verses 6 and 8 we hear only of the Spirit; why is water mentioned in verse 5?[5] Many have thought of Christian baptism here,[6] but (a) an outward ritual, such as water baptism, with or without the Spirit, can never grant new life, and (b) Christian baptism was unknown to Nicodemus; how could Jesus blame him for not understanding these things (v. 10)?[7]

---

5. We leave aside here the unnecessary speculation of Rudolf Bultmann that the phrase "of water and" (Gk. *hudatos kai*) is a gloss. Congar (1997, 1.49 and 2.191) suggests that these words *must* be a gloss because Christian baptism was not yet known in Nicodemus' time—a striking example of the fallacy of begging the question.
6. It is remarkable how easily Green (1975, 111) and Pannenberg (1991, 1:225-26, 233, 246, 264) accept this traditional interpretation without any argument for it.
7. Expositors of John's Gospel can be divided generally into two groups: those who interpret John (especially chapters 3 and 6) either sacramentally or non-sacramentally (Keener 1997, 136-37, 149-51 including notes).

In my view, we must instead understand water here as a symbol for cleansing (cf. 2:6; but also see §§3.9.1 and 4.2.3). If, according to Jesus, Nicodemus should indeed have been familiar with the idea of a spiritual cleansing through water, then we think immediately of Ezekiel 36:25, "I will sprinkle clean water on you, and you shall be clean from all your uncleannesses." Such a cleansing occurs through the Word of God, empowered by the Spirit of God. In the same Gospel Jesus says to his disciples, "Already you are clean because of [Gk. *dia* + accusative; "through" KJV, "by" RSV, NRSV][8] the word that I have spoken to you" (15:3). Paul says that Christ has "cleansed" his body — that is, the church — "by the washing of water with[9] the word" (Eph. 5:26). In 1 Peter 1:23 the rebirth is "through[10] the living and abiding word of God."

The baptism of John, with which Nicodemus was of course familiar (John 1:25–33), had a similar meaning; it was "a baptism of repentance for the forgiveness of sins" (Mark 1:4; cf. "purification" in John 3:25). Insofar as Jesus was alluding to any baptism at all, this could have been none other than John's baptism. It is conceivable, though in my view unlikely, that Jesus wanted to say: You became acquainted with a ministry of water, which symbolically cleansed from sins, and in connection with which Another was announced who would baptize in the Spirit; without these two, cleansing by water and rebirth through the Spirit, you cannot enter the kingdom of God.[11]

On the basis of many rabbinical sources, Hugo Odeberg suggested that here water could refer to male sperm.[12] This is worth considering since in other passages rebirth is connected with the notion of "seed": "[Y]ou have been born again, not of

---

8. The Gk. *dia* + accusative means "because of," but sometimes is hardly distinguishable from the meaning of the Gk. *dia* + genitive: "through" or "by."
9. Gk. *en*, locative: "in," or instrumental: "by."
10. Gk. *dia* + genitive: "through" (cf. note 8 above).
11. G. Campbell Morgan, quoted by Morris (1971, 216n27).
12. Odeberg (1929, 48–71).

perishable seed [Gk. *spora*] but of imperishable, through the living and abiding word of God" (1 Pet. 1:23; cf. Luke 8:11, "The seed [Gk. *sporos*] is the word of God"). "No one born of God makes a practice of sinning, for God's seed [Gk. *sperma*] abides in him; and he cannot keep on sinning, because he has been born of God" (1 John 3:9). Here, "God's seed" is either the Holy Spirit, or the Word of God, or the new nature that through the Spirit has been produced in the regenerated person.[13] In John 3:5, the meaning could then be: "born of water, namely, the Spirit." Indeed, an additional argument for this is that water refers to the Spirit in 7:38-39 as well (cf. 4:14; §6.6).[14]

8.2.2 A New Nature

Of course, the notions of being (spiritually) born again and being made (spiritually) alive are closely related; yet they are not the same. In John 3, the emphasis is not so much on the new *life* that is received but on what is commonly referred to as the believer's new *nature*. Thus, we read in verse 6, "That which is born of the flesh is flesh, and that which is born of the Spirit is spirit." In other words, that which is "flesh" (and "the flesh profits nothing," 6:63 NKJV) can never become "Spirit," even if a person were born of his mother a thousand times, or of another sinful person. The new nature that a person needs is "spirit (out) of Spirit." A person must not be born for the second (or the thousandth) time of the same origin, but born again of a new origin: the Greek word *anōthen* means either "from above" (from heaven) or "again"; it does not mean "for the second time" (which requires the Gk. *deuteron*, v. 4), but

---

13. For a summary of all the proposed meanings of "seed," see Lalleman (2005, 175). Following Thomas Aquinas, Congar (1997, 2.100) explains the "seed" as the Holy Spirit, but a bit later (102) as the Word of God.
14. Dunn (1970, 192), Wuest (1973b, 56–57), and Keener (1997, 150) choose this exegesis (explicative use of *kai*). In a Qumran text (1QS 3.7–9), the Holy Spirit is referred to as the means by which cleansing and atonement occur: the person's flesh will be cleansed when sprinkled with water of purification (cf. Num. 19); see Shulam (1998, 284).

in a new way.[15]

The way this is accomplished cannot be grasped by ordinary humans, says verse 8: "The wind [Gk. *pneuma*] blows where it wishes, and you hear its sound, but you do not know where it comes from or where it goes. So it is with everyone who is born of the Spirit [Gk. *pneuma*]." If we cannot follow the traces and movements of the wind, even less can we follow those of the Holy Spirit in the work of rebirth. "As you do not know the way the spirit comes to the bones in the womb of a woman with child, so you do not know the work of God who makes everything" (Eccl. 11:5). If David said of his body, "I praise you, for I am fearfully and wonderfully made" (Ps. 139:14a), how much more this can be said of a person's renewed spirit.

John 3:5 may be compared with Titus 3:4–6, ". . . God our Savior . . . saved us, . . . by the washing of regeneration and renewal of the Holy Spirit, whom he poured out on us richly through Jesus Christ our Savior." The points of similarity are that, first, here too, "regeneration"[16] is a "washing" (Gk. *loutron*),[17] that is, a cleansing from sin; and second, it is linked with the renewing work of the Holy Spirit. Another point of similarity is that, here too, many expositors understand the Greek word *loutron* to refer to baptism.[18] Our objection here is the same: it is inconceivable that a material means would be an indispensable condition for a spiritual result.[19] Regeneration itself is not brought about by water but by that to which water refers: the Word of God (see above) as empowered by

---

15. See Morris (1971, 213n13).
16. The Gk. word used here is *palingenesia*, which appears elsewhere only in Matt. 19:28, a verse dealing with the "regeneration" of the world at Christ's second coming.
17. The translation "washing" is preferable to "bath" (NABRE); so Hiebert (1978, 445).
18. Bouma (1937, 222), who denies the implication that regeneration would be brought about by baptism; Ridderbos (1967, 289); White (1979, 198).
19. Hiebert (1978, 445) sees this as problematic in light of Matt. 15:1–20, Rom. 2:25–29, and Gal. 5:6.

the Holy Spirit. Thus, the two phrases in verse 5b essentially express the same thing ('regenerated" and "renewed"), as in Semitic poetic parallelism.

There are two ways to read verse 5b (Gk. *dia loutrou palingenesias kai anakainōseōs*): "by [the] washing of regeneration and [by the] renewal..." (KJ21), or "by [the] washing of regeneration and [of] renewal" of the Holy Spirit (ESV). In the latter case, "regeneration" and "renewal" are both dependent on "washing"; so, for instance, the Vulgate: *per lavacrum regenerationis et renovationis Spiritus sancti*. The last phrase of the verse (Gk. *pneumatos hagiou*) can also be linked with "regeneration": the "washing" consists in the (one-time) "regeneration/renewal by the Holy Spirit." We could also read: "the (one-time) washing of regeneration and the (continual) renewal by the Holy Spirit" (cf. Rom. 12:2; Eph. 4:23; 5:26-27). This would thus present a parallel with natural life: first there is birth, then the development toward adulthood.[20] Both are the work of the Holy Spirit in the believer.

Verse 6, "... the Holy Spirit, whom he poured out on us richly through Jesus Christ our Savior," does *not* imply an ongoing process: the aorist form of the verb (Gk. *execheen*) points to a one-time event. This may be a reference to the outpouring of the Spirit in Acts 2, but I think it is instead a reference to the person's individual sharing in the Spirit at the moment of Spirit baptism. This outpouring is effectuated by "God our Savior" (v. 4), "through Jesus Christ our Savior" (v. 6).

8.2.3 Made Alive by the Spirit

We have just looked at regeneration as an event in which a new nature replaces an old, corrupted nature (the "flesh"). A different description of regeneration is that of life invading and permeating a state of death. This, too, is the work of the Holy Spirit *par excellence* (cf. Gen. 1:2; Ezek. 37:9-10, 14): "It is the Spirit who gives life; the flesh is no help at all. The words that I have spoken to you are s/Spirit and life" (John 6:63).

---

20. White (1979, 199).

This is comparable to what Paul writes, "[T]he letter kills, but the Spirit gives life" (2 Cor. 3:6).

Jesus' words in John 6:63 are understandable only to those who rise above their natural ("carnal") state (living "in the flesh"), and know the life worked by the Spirit (cf. 1 Cor. 2:14–16). These words are of a spiritual nature; they are life for those who, by the Spirit, have already been made alive (the ancient term is "quickened"). Or, by the power of the Holy Spirit these words *bring* life to those who have been opened up to it. The effect of Jesus' words (Gk. *rhēmata*) is produced by the Spirit; in an analogous way, Paul speaks of "the sword of the Spirit, which is the word [Gk. *rhēma*] of God" (Eph. 6:17).

The idea of a person being made alive is elaborated by Paul, though without explicitly referring to the Spirit: "God, being rich in mercy, because of the great love with which he loved us, even when we were dead in our trespasses, made us alive together with Christ" (Eph. 2:4–5). "And you, who were dead in your trespasses and the uncircumcision of your flesh, God made alive together with him, having forgiven us all our trespasses" (Col. 2:13).

Peter makes the following statement, which has proven perplexing and difficult for expositors: "For this reason the gospel was preached also to those who are dead, that they might be judged according to men in the flesh, but live according to God in the spirit [or, Spirit]" (1 Pet. 4:6 NKJV). Some see those "living in [the] Spirit" (Gk. *pneumati*) as (a) Old Testament believers.[21] Others see them as (b) all the people who died before Jesus' death, addressed by him between his death and resurrection, in order that they may still believe.[22] Still others see them as (c) those who were spiritually dead in Peter's day, in order that they might believe; and others see them as (d) Christians who passed away.[23]

---

21. Wolston (1893, 310); Kelly (1923, 219–20).
22. Hart (1979, 72).
23. W. J. Dalton, J. N. D. Kelly, J. Moffatt, E. G. Selwyn, according to Blum

Because of my interpretation of 1 Peter 3:19–20 (see §6.4.2 above), I reject (b), all the more because such a second chance after death to believe is unknown in the Bible. In my view, interpretation (c) is unacceptable because it explains the "dead" in verse 6 differently from the "dead" in verse 5. Whether one chooses (a) or (d), in both cases the text speaks of believers who, during their earthly existence, received spiritual life from God, or were led in their earthly lives by the Spirit of God.

8.2.4 Sanctification and Justification by the Spirit

In 1 Corinthians 6:11, Paul told the believers in Corinth: "But you were washed, you were sanctified, you were justified in the name of [Gk. *en tōi onomati*, "in the power of"] the Lord Jesus Christ and by [Gk. *en*, "in the power of"] the Spirit of our God." Here again, the washing has often been linked with baptism, but this is no more necessary, and no more obvious, than it is in John 3:5, Titus 3:5–6 (§8.2.2), and Ephesians 5:26. Not every spiritual reference to water in the New Testament necessarily involves baptism.

Here Paul is referring to spiritual cleansing, which is produced in a person at the moment of rebirth. The aorist tense emphasizes the instantaneous character of the event: at the very moment when the Corinthians came to faith, they were cleansed of their sins, and they were declared by God to be holy and righteous. One could discern here a certain "order of salvation": the convert is first cleansed of personal unrighteousness, and then God sets apart the convert for himself (sanctification), and once in this special position God declares this person to be righteous in Christ who has died and risen.[24]

God does so because of (or in the power of) (a) the name of Jesus Christ, and (b) the Holy Spirit. The former constitutes the *foundation*: sanctification and justification occur on the ba-

---

(1981a, 245) and Blum himself; see also Greijdanus (1931, 70–71); Davids (1990, 153–55).
24. See extensively, Ouweneel (*RT* III/2).

sis of the person and the work of Christ. The latter constitutes the *means*: sanctification and justification occur through the Holy Spirit. We find something similar in Romans 15:16, ". . . so that the offering of the Gentiles [i.e., believing Gentiles, who are presented as a sacrifice to God] may be acceptable, sanctified by [Gk. *en*, in the power of] the Holy Spirit." This is substantially the same as "through sanctification by [lit., of] the Spirit [Gk. *en hagiasmōi pneumatos*]" (2 Thess. 2:13; in 1 Pet. 1:2 the identical Greek expression is rendered "in the sanctification of the Spirit").

The only other passage that speaks of justification "in [the] Spirit [Gk. *en pneumati*]" is 1 Timothy 3:16, which says that Christ was "justified in [the] Spirit" (see §6.1.3). There is both similarity and difference here. In the former passage, the Greek verb *dikaioō* means especially "*make* (a person) righteous," while in the latter case it means "*confirm* (a person's) righteousness." The common basic meaning is "to *declare* righteous," either a person who was not like this before (i.e., the wicked; Rom. 4:5), or a person who *was* righteous before (God, Christ, or the believer *after* conversion).[25]

In Galatians 5:5, we find this remarkable expression: "For through the Spirit [Gk. *pneumati*], by faith [Gk. *ek pisteōs*], we ourselves eagerly wait for the hope of righteousness." A person is justified through the Spirit (not through the flesh; 3:3) and by faith (not by the law; 5:4); similarly, through the same Spirit and by the same faith, the person once justified waits for the "hope of righteousness." This is probably not the righteousness that is hoped for, but the righteousness that hopes.[26] Due to justification by faith, righteousness is the believers' present possession. However, in this righteousness there is a dimension of hope: through the Spirit they wait for the complete salvation (cf. Rom. 5:9-10; 10:9-10), including the redemption of their bodies (Rom. 8:23-25), the perfect enjoyment of eternal life (cf. Gal. 6:8; Rom. 5:18b), the everlast-

---

25. See extensively, ibid., §§1.4 and 1.5.
26. Ouweneel (1997, 317).

ing glory of God (cf. Rom. 5:1-2; 8:30); in short: eternal bliss in and with Christ.

H. Berkhof described justification and sanctification as two of the three works that occur in rebirth, and wished to add a third one to them: being filled with the Spirit: "The Spirit in justification occupies the center of ourselves; in sanctification, the whole circle of our human nature; and in filling us, he occupies our individuality, the special mark which I and I alone bear, the special contribution which I have to make to the whole of life. He takes it up for the whole of the Kingdom of God."[27] Such a view is acceptable as long as we retain the distinction discussed in §8.1: justification and sanctification are based upon what the Spirit does in a person, apart from the question whether the Spirit comes to dwell in this person, whereas, since Acts 2, being filled with the Spirit presupposes this very indwelling of the Spirit. Later in this chapter I will deal with this subject more extensively.

8.3 Related Expressions
8.3.1 Obedience, Circumcision

According to Acts 5:32, the Holy Spirit is he "whom God has given to those who obey him." Here, faith is viewed as an act of obedience; compare the contrast in John 3:36, "Whoever *believes* in the Son has eternal life; whoever does not *obey* the Son shall not see life, but the wrath of God remains on him."[28] A similar contrast is found in 1 Peter 2:7-8, namely, those who believe versus those who "disobey the word." Compare also God's command to repent in Acts 17:30, a command that must be obeyed.[29] On the one hand, the gift of the Spirit proceeds from the sovereign will of God, but on the other hand it arises in connection with people's obedience of faith.

Quite remarkable is the following expression in Romans

---

27. Berkhof (1964, 90).
28. Murray (1888, 69–77).
29. In Rom. 1:5 and 16:26, Paul speaks of the "obedience of faith," which either means the obedience that leads to faith, or the obedience that is the result of faith.

2:29, "But a Jew is one inwardly, and circumcision is a matter of the heart, by the Spirit, not by the letter." This verse does *not* say that everyone who is circumcised in heart is a Jew, although it has often been understood this way.[30] The assertion that all A is B does not entail that all B is A (all dogs are animals, but not all animals are dogs). But apart from this, we have Philippians 3:3 and Colossians 2:11 to show that (Jewish and Gentile) Christians, too, can be called true Christians only if they are circumcised in their *hearts* (cf. Deut. 10:16; 30:6; Jer. 4:4; 9:25-26). Such a spiritual circumcision does not make them Jews (in any sense of the word), but it does make them born-again believers.

I mention Romans 2:29 especially because Paul adds here, "by the Spirit, not by the letter," that is, not on the basis of the Mosaic Law—which prescribes the circumcision of the flesh—but by the power of the Holy Spirit (cf. 7:7; 2 Cor. 3:6). Basically, the spiritually circumcised heart is identical with the "new heart" or the "heart of flesh" in Ezekiel 36:26, which is the fruit of what in John 3:5 is called rebirth (§8.2.1). In the Odes of Solomon (second century?) the poet says, "[T]he Most High circumcised me by his Holy Spirit, then he uncovered my inward being towards him, and filled me with his love. And his circumcising became my salvation, and I ran in the way, in his peace, in the way of truth" (Ode 11.2).[31]

Please note the use of the word "flesh," which is sometimes confusing. Ezekiel 44:7 speaks of people "uncircumcised in heart and flesh," where "flesh" simply means "body." In John 3:6, "flesh" is a description of the old (sinful, corrupt) nature. But in Ezekiel 11:19 and 36:26, the "heart of flesh" is a description of the new nature, which is the opposite of the "heart of stone."

---

30. See Moo (1996, 175).
31. http://gnosis.org/library/odes.htm; cf. Burgess (1989, 174); Shulam (1998, 275).

8.3.2 Released, Set Free

The expression "by the Spirit, not by the letter" in Romans 2:29 (see previous section) is similar to the expression in chapter 7:6, where Paul speaks of being *released* from the law: "[N]ow we are released [Gk. *katargeō*] from the law, having died to that which held us captive, so that we serve in the new way of the Spirit and not in the old way of the written code [lit., of the letter]." This means that one is set free from every obligation to acquire righteousness by keeping the Torah in one's own strength. In short: one is *not* released from any form of "law" (cf., e.g., Gal. 6:2), but released from *legalism*.[32]

The result of this is serving God either "in newness of spirit" (KJV), that is, with a renewed (human) spirit, or "in the newness of the Spirit" (NKJV), that is, in a lifestyle that has been renewed (cf. 6:4, "newness of life") by the power of the Holy Spirit. The similarity to 2:29 ("Spirit—letter," that is, the Holy Spirit versus the written law) makes the latter rendering more likely.

In Romans 8:1-2 this *release* is more strongly connected with the Spirit: "There is therefore now no condemnation for those who are in Christ Jesus. For the law of the Spirit of life has *set* you *free* [Gk. *eleutheroō*] in Christ Jesus from the law of sin and death" (cf. John 8:36, "[I]f the Son sets you free [Gk. *eleutheroō*], you will be free indeed"). It is an interesting question whether the first "law" (Gk. *nomos*) in verse 2 simply means "principle," just as in the second case (cf. 7:21-26), or whether it means the "law of Christ" (1 Cor. 9:21; Gal. 6:2), that is, the "law of freedom" (James 2:12; cf. 1:25).[33]

In either case, here being "set free" (liberated), not only from guilt but also from the power of sin (cf. Rom. 8:3b, 4), is the work of the Holy Spirit. He is referred to as the "Spirit of life," that is, the Spirit who works true life in people: this is

---

32. Ouweneel (2001a, 74; *RT* III/2).
33. Cf. Stern (1992, 380–81); Ouweneel (2001a, 130, 145); see Reinmuth (1985) on the connection between Spirit and Torah.

life in Christ Jesus.³⁴ Paul no longer speaks only of what has been accomplished *for* the believer (atonement of guilt), but also of what is being accomplished *in* the believer by the Holy Spirit, viz., deliverance from the principle or rule of sin and death. Believers can still sin, but they do not have to sin; they are no longer under the *power* of sin (cf. 6:7, 13, 22, "set free from sin").

Elsewhere, Paul speaks of "God, who has made us sufficient to be ministers of a new covenant, not of the letter [i.e., the written law] but of the Spirit. For the letter kills, but the Spirit gives life . . . where the Spirit of the Lord is, there is freedom" (2 Cor. 3:5-6, 17). "[T]he law is holy, and the commandment is holy and righteous and good" (Rom. 7:12) — but a law that one tries to fulfill in one's own strength, without the Holy Spirit, can bring only death and condemnation upon that person (2 Cor. 3:7, 9; see further in §8.4.4)

8.3.3 The Spirit of Faith

In 2 Corinthians 4:13 we find the expression "spirit of faith" (Gk. *pneuma tēs pisteōs*). Although most translations use the lowercase "s" here (except BRG, CJB, JUB), most older expositors see a direct reference here to the Holy Spirit. Charles Hodge³⁵ pointed out that the Spirit is often identified in terms of his effects: Spirit of life (Rom. 8:2), Spirit of sonship (v. 15), the Spirit of wisdom and revelation (Eph. 1:17), the Spirit of grace and supplications (Zech. 12:10; cf. Heb. 10:29), the Spirit of glory (1 Pet. 4:14) (if at least in all or most of these instances the uppercase "S" is intended). Thus, in 2 Corinthians 4:13 the Holy Spirit is the Spirit working and maintaining faith in people, both in Old and in New Testament believers. Even if one prefers the rendering "spirit of faith," we may still see here an indirect reference to the Holy Spirit. "[T]hat which is born of the Spirit is spirit" (John 3:6) means that the spirit (mentality,

---

34. The phrase "in Christ Jesus" belongs either to the "Spirit of life" or to "set free."
35. Quoted by Hughes (1962, 147).

attitude) of faith in the believer is the product of, and is empowered by, the Holy Spirit.

There are good reasons to read "spirit" here, also because of similar expressions such as "spirit of gentleness" (1 Cor. 4:21; Gal. 6:1). Compare also this ambiguous statement: "God gave us a spirit not of fear but [a Spirit?] of power and love and self-control" (2 Tim. 1:7; see also §8.4.3 on the expression "s/Spirit of sonship"). But even the believer's "spirit [mentality, attitude] of gentleness" or "spirit of power, love and self-control" can never be severed from the Holy Spirit. Findley formulated a general principle in this respect, namely, that the thought of the Holy Spirit is latent in every biblical reference to the "spirit" of the believer.[36] This is the case in 1 Corinthians 4:21, but also in 5:3-4 ("I am present in spirit. . .") and 14:15-16 ("I will pray [or sing praise] with my spirit") (see §11.8.2). Any "spirit of gentleness" or "spirit of power, love, and self-control" within the believer is inconceivable without the empowering work of the Holy Spirit.

We found in Galatians 5:5-6 how the Spirit is related to *hope* (cf. also Eph. 1:17-18) and to *faith*, and in 2 Corinthians 4:13 again to *faith*. In Romans 15:30 ("the love of the Spirit") and Colossians 1:8 ("your love in the Spirit"), the Spirit is related to *love*. In 1 Corinthians 12, the *charismata* are manifestations of the Spirit (vv. 7, 11), but love is the attitude of the believer enabling one to use these *charismata* properly (v. 31; this is the main subject of 1 Cor. 13). "So now faith, hope, and love abide, these three; but the greatest of these is love" (1 Cor. 13:13) — and all three function properly only in the power of the Holy Spirit.

8.4 Receiving the Spirit at Conversion
8.4.1 General Remarks

The person believing in Christ and possessing the assurance of personal salvation is not only born again (made alive, sanctified, justified, spiritually circumcised) through (the pow-

---

36. Findley (1979, 806).

er of) the Holy Spirit (§8.2), but the *person* of the Holy Spirit dwells within that person. This is described in various ways. The Spirit is "supplied" (Gal. 3:5) or "given" (Acts 5:32; 11:17; 1 Thess. 4:8) to a person, or "God's love has been poured into our hearts through the Holy Spirit who has been given to us" (Rom. 5:5), and "we know that he [i.e., God] abides in us, by the Spirit whom he has given us" (1 John 3:24).

1 John 4:13 says that God "has given us of [Gk. *ek*, out of] his Spirit," which is not exactly the same as in 3:24. This is explained by the renderings of the CEB ("a measure of his Spirit") and the EXB (alternate reading: "we share in his Spirit").[37] Indeed, the Greek preposition *ek* suggests the idea of sharing with believers. It reminds us of John 3:34b (God "gives the Spirit without measure") and Numbers 11:17 (even though the context is very different): "I will take some of the Spirit that is on you [i.e., Moses] and put it on them [i.e., the elders]" (cf. v. 25). Such sharing reminds us also of the key term "fellowship" (Gk. *koinōnia*, having things in common) in 1 John 1:3, 6-7, so that we might read in 4:13, "God has made us to share in his Spirit."[38]

In juxtaposition with the God who gives the Spirit we find the person who receives the Spirit: "Did you receive the Spirit by works of the law or by hearing with faith? Are you so foolish? Having begun by the Spirit, are you now being perfected by the flesh?" (Gal. 3:2-3). "Christ redeemed us from the curse of the law by becoming a curse for us . . . so that in Christ Jesus the blessing of Abraham might come to the Gentiles, so that we might receive the promised Spirit [lit., the promise of the Spirit] through faith" (vv. 13-14). Please note that the activity introduced by the latter "so that" does not depend on the activity introduced by the former one;[39] in other words, the gift of the Holy Spirit *never* belonged to the "blessing of

---

37. *Contra* Lalleman (2005, 193–94). Cf. renderings that entirely erase the distinction (ERV, GNT: "he gave us his Spirit").
38. Medema (1993, 172); cf. Kelly (1970, 309–10).
39. Ouweneel (1997, 193–94).

Abraham" in any form. He himself did not receive the person of the Holy Spirit dwelling in him—he did not receive the *promise* of the Spirit—as do New Testament believers. Thus, the "promise of the Spirit" surpasses the promise of Abraham. This is what many Reformed expositors ought to have realized with regard to Acts 2:39, where Peter is referring not at all to the promise of Abraham, but to the promise of the Spirit (v. 33)—two very different matters.[40]

Just to be clear: please note that I am *not* denying that the Spirit worked in Abraham. Abraham is called a "prophet" (Gen. 20:7) and one of God's "anointed" (Ps. 105:9-15), and though he never received any anointing *oil*, we do not exaggerate when we say that a certain anointing of the Spirit was upon him. However, what I do deny is that the *person* of the Spirit ever *dwelt* in him. This is exclusively a post-Pentecost blessing. The Spirit may have worked in and through John the Baptist far more powerfully than in many Christians—but he never shared in this post-Pentecost blessing. This may be one of the reasons why "the one who is least in the kingdom of heaven is greater than he" (Matt. 11:11).

Finally, what has been given to a person, and what one has received, one possesses: "I think that I too have the Spirit of God," says Paul (1 Cor. 7:40b; cf. 6:19). Jude writes about "natural" [Gk. *psychikoi*] people "not having the Spirit" (v. 19 GNV). Paul, too, uses this Greek word *psychikos* (1 Cor. 2:14): "The natural person [Gk. *psychikos anthrōpos*] does not accept the things of the Spirit of God"—because such a person does not *have* the Spirit. These "natural" people (living in terms of

---

40. Cf. the Christian Reformed Church's liturgical "Form for the Holy Baptism of Infants and Young Children (2016)," (Option 3): "In baptism God seals the promises he gave when he made his covenant with us, calling us and our children to put our trust for life and death in Christ our Savior, deny ourselves, take up our cross, and follow him in obedience and love. God graciously includes our children in his covenant, and all his promises are for them as well as us (Gen. 17:7; Acts 2:39)" (available at https://www.crcna.org/resources/church-resources/liturgical-forms-resources/baptism-children/form-holy-baptism-infants-and-young-children-2016).

the *psychē*) must be clearly distinguished from the "carnal" (Gk. *sarkinoi* or *sarkikoi*) people of chapter 3:1, 3. In my view, the latter group does have the Spirit—they are believers—but they do not live by his power. The "spiritual [person]" (Gk. *pneumatikos*) of 2:15 constitutes a third category: this person not only has the Spirit but lives by the power of the Spirit. In summary (using the Greek adjectives):

(a) The *psychikos* is not a believer, and so does not have the Spirit.

(b) The *sarkikos* is a believer, has the Spirit, but lives by the flesh.

(c) The *pneumatikos* is a believer, has the Spirit, and lives by the Spirit.

There is one expression that in fact belongs to this section §8.4 as well, namely, being anointed with the Holy Spirit (2 Cor. 1:21; cf. Acts 4:27; 10:38; 1 John 2:20, 27; Isa. 61:1). This subject has been touched upon in §4.5, and will be dealt with more extensively in chapter 11.

8.4.2 The Indwelling of the Spirit

Obviously, the indwelling of the Holy Spirit is a metaphor. He is a person dwelling in a spiritual house like a human being lives in a literal house. The Holy Spirit dwells in the church as a whole; to explain this, the church is compared to a house or a temple (1 Cor. 3:16; cf. Eph. 2:20-22). We will deal with this subject in chapter 10. Let us now deal with the Spirit dwelling in individual believers.

In 2 Timothy 1:14 Paul tells his pupil, "By [Gk. *dia*, by means of) the Holy Spirit who dwells within us, guard the good deposit entrusted to you." To the Roman believers he mentions that "the Spirit of God dwells in you" (Rom. 8:9). And to the Corinthian Christians he writes in the framework of his warnings concerning fornication: "Or do you not know that your body is a temple of the Holy Spirit within you, whom you have from God?" (1 Cor. 6:19). Not only has the human *spirit* been baptized (submerged) in the Holy Spirit, but the *entire* person, spirit as well as body, is a dwelling place of the Spirit. Consider John 2:19-21, where Jesus compares his body to a temple, apparently because God, or the Shekhinah, dwelt in him (cf. Col. 1:19; 2:9). In 1 Corinthians 6:19, the term "body" can represent the entire person, as it does elsewhere (". . . present your bodies as a living sacrifice," Rom. 12:1). However, in connection with fornication we may expect the bodily aspect to come more to the fore here than the spirit aspect.[41]

In other passages, the emphasis is on the Spirit dwelling in the human heart as the pivotal and concentration point of the entire human existence (cf. Prov. 4:23, "from [the heart] flow the springs of life"). "God has sent the Spirit of his Son into our hearts" (Gal. 4:6). The text underscores that this is the Spirit of God's *Son*, whereas in Ephesians 3:14-17 this is the Spirit of the *Father*—the same Holy Spirit—who effectuates the Son's dwelling in the believer's heart: "For this reason I bow my knees before the *Father* . . . that . . . he may grant you to be strengthened with power through *his* Spirit in your inner being, so that Christ may dwell in your hearts through faith."

James, too, speaks of the Spirit dwelling in believers: "Or do you suppose it is to no purpose that the Scripture says, 'He yearns jealously over the spirit that he has made to dwell in us'?" (4:5; cf. very differently, the ASV, "Or think ye that the scripture speaketh in vain? Doth the spirit which he made to dwell in us long unto envying?"). Again, the translations vary with regard to the lowercase "s" and the uppercase "S" (the latter is found in the NKJV). Oesterley prefers the uppercase: it is the Holy Spirit who has an envious yearning toward us (cf. the ERV, "The Spirit God made to live in us wants us only for

---

41. Cf. the Armenian Gregory of Narek (ca. 1000), who called his body a "tabernacle," and prayed God to cast out all the evildoers from it, so that God's "good Spirit" could rest in it; see Burgess (1989, 128).

himself").⁴² Some renderings omit translating the Greek word *pneuma* altogether: "And do you suppose God doesn't care? The proverb has it that 'he's a fiercely jealous lover'" (MSG). This is quite understandable because the question is whether the passage is really referring to the Holy Spirit.

Burdick prefers the NIV (cf. the ESV): "Or do you think Scripture says without reason that he jealously longs for the spirit he has caused to dwell in us?" as fitting the context best.⁴³ Consider as well the alternate reading in the NIV: ". . . that the Spirit he caused to dwell in us longs jealously."⁴⁴ *Both* renderings seem fitting because both amount to saying that God (the Holy Spirit), who disapproves of spiritual adultery (v. 4), lays claim to the inner being of believers. The greatest problem here is thinking that "jealousy" (Gk. *phthonos*) always seems to entail malice, and thus cannot be ascribed to the Spirit.⁴⁵ Therefore, Adamson restricts this to the human spirit, which cherishes jealous desires.⁴⁶ However, the problem with *this* explanation is the idea that the human spirit dwells within a person. Therefore, one could use the uppercase "S," but the rendering of the text would then be: "Is it the *Spirit* dwelling in us who jealously desires?" — or is this not rather the person's own wicked heart?⁴⁷

8.4.3 The Spirit of Sonship

Paul tells the Roman believers, "For you did not receive the spirit of slavery to fall back into fear, but you have received the Spirit of adoption as sons, by whom we cry, 'Abba! Father!' The Spirit himself bears witness with our spirit that we are children of God" (Rom. 8:15-16). Our first question is whether in verse 15 we must read "spirit" or "Spirit" of

---

42. Oesterley (1979, 459).
43. Burdick (1981, 193–94); Greijdanus (1950, 52, 56) has something similar.
44. So Wuest (1973a, 81–82).
45. Oesterley (1979, 459) ignores this objection and thinks this refers to the Holy Spirit.
46. Adamson (1976, 171–72).
47. Cf. Grant (1902, 211); Ouweneel (1981, 74).

adoption. The situation seems similar to that in 2 Timothy 1:7, "God gave us a spirit not of fear but of power and love and self-control," where the Greek word *pneuma* is not repeated, so that in both phrases we must presumably think of the person's spirit or spiritual state of mind (cf. Rom. 11:8; 1 Cor. 4:21; Gal. 6:1). Yet, we are inclined to understand this as the "*Spirit* of power and love and self-control" (§8.3.2). Similarly, we wonder if we should not read "*Spirit* of sonship (or, of adoption as sons)," as does the ESV and others. At first glance, it seems rather forced to understand the word "spirit" in the phrase "spirit of slavery" differently than in the phrase "spirit of sonship."

However, there is a strong parallel with Galatians 4:5-6, ". . . so that we might receive adoption as sons. And because you are sons, God has sent the Spirit of his Son into our hearts, crying, 'Abba! Father!'" This is an important reason why many expositors prefer the reading "Spirit [not spirit] of sonship" in Romans 8:15.[48] Not only do believers possess the "position of sons"[49] because of the Spirit dwelling in them, but it is also the Spirit who stirs up the feelings proper to their sonship, so that they exclaim, "Abba! Father!" (cf. Mark 14:36). It is also the Spirit who gives them the inner confirmation within their spirits that they are children of God (v. 16). Through Christ, all believers "have access in one Spirit to the Father" (Eph. 2:18).

---

48. Murray (1968, 295–96); Harrison (1976, 92–93), in the line of Calvin, Alford, Hodge, Haldane, Godet, and others.
49. The Gk. noun *huiothesia* means "put into the position of sons" (from the Gk. words *huios*, "son," and *tithēmi*, "to place, to put"); hence the term "adoption" in many Eng. translations. The term denotes something more than a merely legal status: believers *are really* sons of God; the Spirit of sonship resides in the *heart* (Gal. 4:6). Unfortunately, many translations render this as "children" instead of "sons," thereby failing to respect the theological difference between being "child" (Gk. *teknon*) and being a "son" (Gk. *huios*); the CEV has "children" three times in Rom. 8:14–16, although the Gk. has *huioi*, *huiothesia*, and *tekna*, respectively. The term "sons" denotes the believers' new *position*, whereas the term "child" denotes their *feelings*; see Denney (1979, 648).

The Spirit of God's Son within the believer directs the heart of the person now adopted as son toward the Father of *the* Son, who is now also *the believer's* Father. If we wish to do justice to the parallel between the double usage of the Greek word *pneuma* in Romans 8:15, we might freely render: "You did not receive the Holy Spirit as a Spirit of slavery [cf. 2 Cor. 3:17], but as a Spirit of sonship."[50]

Through the Spirit of sonship we cry, "Abba! Father!" In a wider sense, through the Holy Spirit we learn to speak things that *can* be spoken only through the Spirit. 1 Corinthians 12:3 gives a striking example of this, which this time concerns not the Father but the Son: "Therefore I want you to understand that no one speaking in the Spirit of God ever says 'Jesus is accursed!' and no one can say 'Jesus is Lord' except in the Holy Spirit." In opposition to the imperial cult of that time, in which the emperor was venerated as "Lord and God" (Lat. *dominus et deus*), the confession of Jesus as "Lord" was an acknowledgement not only of his rule but also of his deity. The statement that Jesus is God is not only a theological conclusion, but a genuine faith confession, as well as an act of worship, which is possible only through the Holy Spirit. This was true before the Day of Pentecost: Thomas worshiped Jesus by saying, "My Lord and my God!" (John 20:28). To Peter's confession ("You are the Christ, the Son of the living God") Jesus responded, "Blessed are you, Simon Bar-Jonah! For flesh and blood has not revealed this to you, but my Father who is in heaven." This is substantially the same as saying, ". . . but the Holy Spirit," or "the Spirit of my Father" has revealed this to you.

8.4.4 The Ministry of the Spirit

At the announcement of the new covenant, God said that he would put his Torah within the Israelites, and would "write it on their hearts" (Jer. 31:33; cf. also Heb. 8:10). In the new covenant, we are dealing with the Torah in its completeness

---

50. Murray (1968, 296–97); Denney (1979, 648).

and fullness, its richest, deepest sense, as it has obtained form in the person of Christ.[51] There is here no longer any essential difference between the ideas that God's *Torah* is written on the believer's heart, or that God's *love* has been poured into the believer's heart (Rom. 5:5; cf. 13:8–10 with v. 14), or that God's *Spirit* has been sent into the believer's heart (Gal. 4:6), or that *Christ* dwells in the believer's heart through faith (Eph. 3:17). Therefore, when applying to Christians this teaching concerning the new covenant, Paul can freely replace the word "Torah" with the word "Christ" (2 Cor. 3:3 NKJV): "[C]learly you are an epistle of *Christ*, ministered by us [i.e., as ministers of the *new* covenant, v. 6], written not with ink but by the Spirit of the living God, not on tablets of stone [like the Torah in the *old* covenant] but on tablets of flesh, [that is,] of the heart." The Torah in its fullest and deepest sense, as meant by Jeremiah, coincides with Christ, as meant by Paul, written in (or on) believers' hearts. Both the Torah and Christ are the perfect expression of God's being and will toward humanity.

Paul calls his spiritual work here a "ministry": in verse 3 he uses the Greek verb *diakoneō* ("to minister"), in verse 6 the Greek noun *diakonos* ("minister"), and after this he uses several times the Greek noun *diakonia* ("ministry"):

> Now if the *ministry of death*, carved in letters on stone, came with such glory that the Israelites could not gaze at Moses' face because of its glory, which was being brought to an end, will not the *ministry of the Spirit* have even more glory? For if there was glory in the *ministry of condemnation*, the *ministry of righteousness* must far exceed it in glory (2 Cor. 3:7–9).

Four ministries are mentioned here; two of them are negative: the ministry of death and of condemnation, and two are positive: the ministry of the Spirit and of righteousness. In its effect on corrupt people, the Mosaic Torah entailed a "ministry of death" and "of condemnation" because it condemns to death all those who trespass it. In opposition to this, we find

---

51. Ouweneel (2001a, 130).

the ministry of the new covenant (cf. v. 6), which consists of the "ministry of the Spirit" and "of righteousness."

Paul implies that the ministry of the new covenant consists of two parts: righteousness and the Spirit. The former part is expressed in these words (part of the promise of the new covenant): "I will forgive their iniquity, and I will remember their sin no more" (Jer. 31:34). The latter part is expressed in these words: "I will put my law within them, and I will write it on their hearts" (v. 33). In light of 2 Corinthians 3:3 this latter phrase envisions writing *Christ* on the hearts of God's people through the Holy Spirit. The Decalogue was written on tablets of stone; what we may now read on "tablets of flesh" in the heart is a "letter of Christ" — in my view not so much a letter *from* Christ (*contra* ESV, NIV) but a letter *about* Christ (Phillips). In brief: it is *Christ* who is read on the hearts of the believers.

The new covenant is "not of the letter but of the Spirit. For the letter kills, but the Spirit gives life" (v. 6). As usual, it is difficult to determine whether "spirit" (KJV, ASV, DRA) is intended, or "Spirit" (NKJV and most others; cf. Rom. 2:29; 7:6).[52] Together with many older expositors[53] I think here of the Holy Spirit, especially because of the close of the verse: ". . . the Spirit gives life" (cf. §8.2.3).

8.5 Firstfruits and Measures
8.5.1 Firstfruits of the Spirit

In Romans 8:23 Paul speaks of those "who have the firstfruits of the Spirit." "Firstfruits" (Gk. *aparchē*) is actually singular: "the first crop of the harvest" (CEB). Paul's intention is to present the Holy Spirit himself as the "first fruit," that is, "the first part of God's promise" (ERV), "the first of God's gifts" (GNT). This is similar to the expression "the earnest of the Spirit" (2 Cor. 1:22; 5:5; Eph. 1:13–14 KJV), in which the Spirit himself is this earnest (i.e., pledge, down payment). In a freer render-

---

52. When Bernard (1979, 54) claims that Paul never contrasts "spirit" (Gk. *pneuma*) with "letter" (Gk. *gramma*), he is mistaken.
53. And joined by Harris (1976, 335); *contra* Hughes (1962, 101).

ing: God has "given us his Spirit in our hearts as a guarantee [or down payment, deposit]" (ESV, NKJV, NIV). What Paul says is that believers have received the Holy Spirit as a pledge, a down payment, a guarantee, a deposit in view of the full blessing that they will receive in the eschaton.

The metaphor has been derived from the Mosaic Torah. Two of Israel's festivals were feasts of firstfruits. On the day after the Sabbath in the Passover week (Heb. *Yom habBikkurim*), the Israelites brought a sheaf of the firstfruits of the barley harvest to the priest, who waved it before the Lord. Seven weeks later, at the Feast of Weeks or Pentecost (Heb. *Shavu'ot*), every Israelite brought two loaves of bread from the wheat harvest as firstfruits to the Lord (Exod. 23:16; 34:22; Lev. 23:10, 17, 20; Num. 28:26; Deut. 16:9-10; also see Lev. 2:12; Num. 15:20-21; 18:13; Deut. 12:17; 18:4; 26:2, 10).

Strictly speaking, there is a difference between a pledge and a down payment. An engagement ring is a pledge ("I promise that I will marry you"), not a down payment. The Holy Spirit is a pledge, a promise, in view of the full blessing; it is also a down payment, a first portion of this blessing, until the moment when the fullness of the Spirit will be granted.[54] Harrison rejected this interpretation, but for the wrong reason: he argued that, if the Spirit is a person, he cannot be given "more" in the future than he is given now.[55] This consideration overlooks the fact that Scripture speaks of the Spirit also as a power, of which the believer can have more at one time and less at another time, during his walk of faith (see §§4.1 and 4.4; see also the next section).

Yet, it is true that the idea of the New Testament believers having received a "part" of the Spirit, and receiving the

---

54. Murray (1968, 306–307 including n 38) prefers the latter interpretation (taking the genitive as a partitive genitive), whereas Denney (1979, 650) and Floor (1982, 143–44), agreeing with S. Greijdanus, J. C. Coetzee, and A. Nygren, all prefer the former interpretation (taking the genitive as an explicative genitive). Floor points out that J. Behm offers the latter (*TDNT* 1.475), and G. Delling, eleven pages later, offers the former interpretation.
55. Harrison (1976, 94).

"full" Spirit in resurrection, finds no support in Scripture. This is why I too prefer the former interpretation: the Spirit is a pledge rather than a down payment. Taking the full context into account, we conclude that Paul says that now we have received "only" the Holy Spirit, but at the resurrection ("the redemption of our bodies," Rom. 8:23b) we will receive the full blessing of God. Although believers' current bodies are already temples of the Holy Spirit (1 Cor. 6:19), the full blessing of God is associated with their resurrection bodies. At present, the believers' spirits have been baptized (submerged) into the Holy Spirit, who is the "Spirit of sonship" (Rom. 8:15). Soon they will receive the full realization of this sonship, which is the redemption of their bodies (v. 23).

8.5.2 Four "Measures" of the Spirit

Taking everything together, we may distinguish four "measures" of the Spirit, so to speak. For this expression, compare passages like these: "Who has measured the Spirit of the LORD?" (Isa. 40:13), and: "For he whom God has sent utters the words of God, for he gives the Spirit without measure," that is, he gives the Spirit in his fullness (John 3:34). These are the four "measures," four "degrees" in the way the Holy Spirit functions in people.

(a) In the Old Testament, the Spirit was given only to some individuals, and never in the form of some permanent indwelling (cf. 1 Sam. 16:14; Ps. 51:11), but only as the power for a certain ministry. As such, it could work in persons who presumably were not believers, such as Balaam and King Saul (see next section).

(b) Since the Day of Pentecost (Acts 2), the Spirit has been given to all true believers; to be precise, it is their *faith* on which God places the seal of his Spirit (Eph. 1:13; 4:30). The Holy Spirit comes to dwell in them personally, uninterruptedly, and forever (John 14:16, ". . . another Helper, to be with you forever"; 1 Cor. 6:19, "your body is a temple of the Holy Spirit within you").

(c) When we say that the believer not only has the Spirit but ought to be filled with it, the emphasis is on the Spirit not as a person but as a power, of which he can have much or little. The believer is supposed to know the Spirit in its fullness already within one's earthly life. This is a constant calling (Eph. 5:18, "be filled with the Spirit"; cf. Acts 2:4; 4:8, 31; 9:17; 13:9, 52).

(d) Yet, the Spirit is only a pledge, only a firstfruit. The Spirit was promised, but is himself also a promise in view of God's full blessing in the eschaton. Believers will not experience the full effects of the Spirit both in their own existence and in the entire cosmos before the resurrection of their bodies.

8.5.3 Partakers of the Spirit

There is one more expression that demands our attention when it comes to the meaning of the Holy Spirit within the individual Christian's life. Hebrews 6:4–6 speaks of "those who have once been enlightened, who have tasted the heavenly gift, and have *shared in* [many other versions read: were made *partakers of*] *the Holy Spirit*, and have tasted the goodness of the word of God and the powers of the age to come," but have fallen away (see also 10:26–29). The pivotal question here is whether this description can be true only for people who are born again, or whether it can apply to people who shared in the blessings of the Holy Spirit only outwardly.[56]

It is remarkable that the stronger Greek word *koinōnios* is not used here, as in 10:33 ("partners"), but the Greek word *metochos*, as in 1:9 ("companions") and 3:1, 14 ("share in"). The Greek verb *metechō*, "to share," means to take or receive a share in a matter from the outside. Nominal Christians have a share in the "house of God" viewed from the standpoint of human responsibility (1 Cor. 3:12-15; 1 Tim. 3:15-4:3; 2 Tim. 2:16-22). That is, by being members of a local congregation they are part of a place where the Holy Spirit dwells,

---

56. See Ouweneel (1982, 1.78).

works, and blesses, and in this (limited) sense they "share in," or "partake of," the Holy Spirit.[57] When the rain of the Spirit falls, they too get wet. However, at best they have tasted the rainwater but they have never drunk from it (cf. Heb. 6:4-5, "tasted [not eaten] the heavenly gift, . . . tasted [not eaten] the goodness of the word of God").

An important example of such sharing in the Spirit is the Christian family. It makes a tremendous difference whether children grow up in "the world," or in the blessed atmosphere that Christian parents create around themselves and their children. Such children may be called "enlightened," they "taste the heavenly gift," they "share in the Holy Spirit," they "taste the goodness of the word of God and the powers of the age to come." However, if they never respond to the light, if they only taste and never eat, if they are under the blessed influence of the Holy Spirit but never open their hearts to him, all of this will be of no avail. They will be like the children of the world, but in fact they are worse: their privileges were so immense that their responsibilities are correspondingly many more than those of children from non-Christian families. "For it would have been better for them never to have known the way of righteousness than after knowing it to turn back from the holy commandment delivered to them" (2 Pet. 2:21).

As we have seen, the Bible describes various people in whom this "sharing in" or "partakership of" the Spirit went to such an extent that, by the power of this Spirit, they did great things (probably) without having been born again: Balaam (Num. 24:2, "the Spirit of God came upon him," and v. 4, "the oracle of him who hears the words of God, who sees the vision of the Almighty"), King Saul (1 Sam. 10:6, 10: "the Spirit of God rushed upon him," but also 16:14, "the Spirit of the LORD departed from Saul"), and Judas (Matt. 10:4, 7, 20: "For it is not you who speak, but the Spirit of your Father speaking through you," a promise that apparently applied to Judas) (cf.

---

57. Wuest (1973a, 95).

also Simon Magus, Acts 8:13, 18-24).

8.6 "Baptism" in 1 Corinthians 12
8.6.1 Which Baptism?

We have already dealt with Spirit baptism in §7.1, where we discussed the relevant passages in the Gospels and Acts. Only once in the New Testament letters do we find a (debatable) reference to Spirit baptism, namely, in 1 Corinthians 12:13, "For in one Spirit we were all baptized into one body — Jews or Greeks, slaves or free — and all were made to drink of one Spirit."

This is one of several New Testament passages where it is not immediately clear whether the text is speaking either of a spiritual cleansing, or of water baptism, or of Spirit baptism.

(a) *Neither baptism.* Passages such as John 3:5, 1 Corinthians 6:11, Ephesians 5:26, and Titus 3:5, which speak of water, or of cleansing or washing, have all been related to water baptism without — in my view — sufficient exegetical grounds. In my view, Jesus or Paul is referring simply to the spiritual cleansing of the heart.

(b) *Both baptisms.* There are passages such as Ephesians 4:5 where some expositors have thought of both water and Spirit baptism.[58]

(c) *Not Spirit baptism but water baptism.* Passages such as Mark 16:16, Romans 6:3-4, Galatians 3:27, Colossians 2:12, and 1 Peter 3:21 have been thought by several expositors to refer to Spirit baptism,[59] whereas, in my view, they all refer to water baptism.[60]

(d) *Not water baptism but Spirit baptism.* Conversely, many expositors claim that 1 Corinthians 12:13 does not speak of Spirit baptism but of water baptism.[61] Other expositors have

---

58. Kraan (1978, 56–58) and Bruce (1984, 336–37) think of water and Spirit baptism together.
59. Unger (1944, 497–99); Chafer (1983, 6.138–61).
60. See extensively, Ouweneel (2005b).
61. Van Veldhuizen (1922, 101); Grosheide (1957, 330); Ridderbos (1975, 372–

great difficulty with this[62] — and in my view for good reasons.

A key word is the Greek preposition *en*, which is rendered either "in" (ESV, ASV) or "by" ([N]KJV, NIV). Those who choose the rendering "by" must without exception have thought of water baptism here. However, the first and primary meaning of the Greek preposition *en* "in," is locative. It is the common presupposition indicating "that in which" a person is baptized. At water baptism a person's body is baptized "in[to]" water (see, e.g., Matt. 3:6, "in the river Jordan"; Acts 8:38, "they both went down into the water"; Matt. 3:11 ASV, JUB, WEB, "baptize in water"), and at Spirit baptism a person's spirit is baptized "in[to]" the Holy Spirit.

Very enlightening here is the contrast in Matthew 3:11 (CJB), "It's true that I am immersing you *in* water . . . but the one coming after me . . . will immerse you *in* the Holy Spirit [Heb. *Ruach HaKodesh*] and in fire" (see likewise in Acts 1:5). This is entirely parallel to what Paul writes in 1 Corinthians 12:13, "in one Spirit we were all baptized." The result (indicated by the Gk. preposition *eis*) of the fact that this has occurred to *all* believers is that they form "one body," a community of people who have all been baptized in the Holy Spirit. In my view, it is hardly defensible to explain baptizing "in the Spirit" (Gk. *en pneumati*) as referring to Spirit baptism in Matthew 3:11, and to water baptism in 1 Corinthians 12:13.[63]

If the Greek preposition *en* is viewed here as instrumental, that is, as referring to the means by which people are baptized,

---

73); Findlay (1979, 890); Welker (1992, 23); Pinnock (1996, 124, 167); and many older exegetes (including Augustine and Calvin). In connection with 1 Cor. 12:13, "we all were made to drink of one Spirit," the Armenian Gregory the Illuminator (ca. 300) believed that Israel at *its* "water baptism" (cf. 1 Cor. 10:2) was made to drink the "cup of the Spirit" in the midst of the Red Sea, and as a consequence rejoiced and sang; see Burgess (1989, 121).

62. Kelly (n.d.-a, 205–208); Grant (1901, 510); Mare (1976, 264); Fee (1987, 604–606); Medema (1989, 190–92); Runia (2000, 94–95).

63. For Baptists, the matter is quite important because 1 Cor. 12:13 is the only verse from which they seek to prove that by water baptism a person is added to the body of Christ, and thus to a local congregation.

even then one cannot possibly say that, at water baptism, people are baptized "through" the Holy Spirit (*contra* ERV). With even less warrant can we understand the Greek preposition *en* as if it were equivalent to the Greek preposition *hupo* ("by") in the sense that the Spirit would be the One who performs the water baptism (*contra* [N]KJV, NIV).[64] This is incorrect both exegetically and theologically; Scripture knows nothing of a baptism in which the Holy Spirit is the acting person. It is not the Spirit who baptizes, but people are baptizing other people in(to) the Spirit.

Therefore, I fail to see how water baptism could possibly be read into 1 Corinthians 12:13. In my view, the verse refers unambiguously to Spirit baptism. Through repentance and faith, a person is baptized in, and sealed with, the Holy Spirit, and thus becomes a member of the body of Christ. In summary, we may make the following distinction: water baptism introduces a person into the kingdom of God (cf. Matt. 28:18–20),[65] while Spirit baptism introduces this person into the body of Christ.

8.6.2 Unity Through Spirit Baptism

The two quoted lines in 1 Corinthians 12:13 seem to fit together as in a Semitic poetic parallelism:

> we were all baptized in one Spirit (Gk. *en heni pneumati*)
> we were all made to drink of one Spirit (Gk. *hen pneuma*).

Both metaphors (baptizing, making to drink) lead to the same result: the believer's spirit is submerged into the Spirit, and is drenched with the Spirit, just as a sponge that is submerged into water is drenched with the water. The sponge is put into the water, and the water is put into the sponge. A believer is immersed into Holy Spirit, and the Spirit is placed within that person.

What appears here to be parenthetical thought, "into one

---

64. Prince (1995, 225); *contra* Schep (1972, 21); Floor (1982, 106).
65. See extensively, Ouweneel (*RT* IV/2, especially Appendix 1).

body" (Gk. *eis hen sōma*), is the actual core around which Paul's argument turns. He argues in 1 Corinthians 12 that, in spite of the great diversity of *charismata* (vv. 4–11) and of ethnic and social classes (v. 13, "Jews or Greeks, slaves or free"), there is only one Holy Spirit (and also one Lord and one God, vv. 5–6). There is a contrast here with the many spirits to which the Corinthian believers had been accustomed when they were still pagans (cf. v. 2, "You know that when you were pagans you were led astray to mute idols, however you were led").

Thus, Paul's point is not just the fact of having been baptized in the Spirit, and having been made to drink of the Spirit, but the result of these: a community of people who, with regard to descent, status, and spiritual capacities, are very different and yet by the one Spirit have been forged into a supernatural unity (cf. vv. 12, 25–27). This is of great practical importance. Neither in 1 Corinthians 12, nor elsewhere, does the significance of Spirit baptism primarily entail that individuals receive certain *charismata*, but rather that they become aware of belonging to the same body of Christ.[66] Spirit baptism does not primarily refer to the believer's personal blessings but to the believer's connection with millions of other believers, to whatever race or social class (and I add, to whatever denominational fellowship) they may belong.

Of course, in principle this Spirit baptism occurred on the Day of Pentecost (Acts 2), for it was there and then that the New Testament church *had its origin*. However, by saying "we all," Paul includes the personal experience of each individual believer. In Acts 2, through Spirit baptism the individual believers have been joined into one body, and through each subsequent Spirit baptism new members have been added to this body. Thus, Paul is not referring to a particular historical event, in this case the Pentecost event, but to what his readers had personally experienced, and to which he therefore could appeal in his argument. How did the Corinthian Christians

---

66. See Lloyd-Jones (1997, 268).

know that, in spite of all their diversity, they were a unity? How could they, each of them personally, make this true in their hearts? By realizing that each of them, no matter how much each differed from the others, had shared in the one Spirit baptism.[67]

In short, Paul is not referring primarily to what had its origin in Jerusalem on the Day of Pentecost, but to what had its origin in *Corinth*: "[Y]ou [the church of God in Corinth] are the body of Christ and individually members of it" (v. 27). Everything that the worldwide body of Christ entails is represented among you in Corinth. And you are personally and practically aware of this because of your Spirit baptism.

8.7 A "Second Blessing"?
8.7.1 Believing and Sealing

Having investigated all the passages on Spirit baptism, we must now face the question at what moment in a person's spiritual development Spirit baptism occurs. That is, does Spirit baptism coincide in time with the moment of repentance and faith in the Lord Jesus Christ (which is the traditional view)? Or does Spirit baptism, as a so-called "second blessing," usually occur at a later time, either with or without the laying on of hands (as many Pentecostal and Charismatic theologians believe)?[68]

In support of the traditional view, passages have been adduced such as Romans 8:9b, "Anyone who does not have the Spirit of Christ does not belong to him," and 1 Corinthians 12:13, "[I]n one Spirit we were all baptized into one body." In other words, it seems impossible to assume that a person belongs to Christ by faith, or to the body of Christ, without yet having received the Spirit. However, we should not conclude from such verses more than they actually say. Every prodigal son is converted at the moment he arises to go to the Father,

---

67. Fee (1987, 605–606).
68. Not all these theologians accept the *term* "second blessing," though; see Duffield and Van Cleave (1996, 323).

and thus he has all the rights that belong to sonship. Yet, he is not aware of this before he enjoys the embrace of the Father (Luke 15:20).[69] A person who spiritually exists in this state between having arisen to return home and being in the Father's embrace, but who dies, is not lost. But such a person has never known the position and the rights of a son; that believer has never learned to say "Abba! Father!" (see §8.7.2 on Romans 7). In other words, that believer was not yet in a state upon which God could place the Spirit's seal (Eph. 1:13; 4:30). One does not receive the Holy Spirit when one arises to go to the Father (this is regeneration), but when one enjoys the Father's embrace (this is the moment when one receives the assurance of salvation).

As we saw at the beginning of this chapter, regeneration and receiving the Holy Spirit must never be identified. Rebirth is a work of the Spirit within a person, but this does not entail that the Spirit (immediately) comes to dwell personally within the reborn person. These two events *might* coincide in time, as they did in Acts 10:44–46, but in most other cases in the book of Acts they did not. The Spirit's indwelling is not automatically entailed in rebirth. Experience teaches us as well that often some time elapses between rebirth and the assurance of salvation (see §8.7).

Ephesians 1:13 says, "In him [i.e., Christ] you also, when you heard the word of truth, the gospel of your salvation, and believed in him, were sealed with the promised Holy Spirit" (cf. 4:30, ". . . the Holy Spirit of God, by whom you were sealed for the day of redemption"). The phrase "when you believed" is an aorist participle in Greek, *pisteusantes*, which can be rendered in various ways: "after ye believed" (KJ21), "because you believed" (CEB), "when you believed" (NIV). Expositors have evaluated the temporal relationships in various ways. Some have emphasized that the aorist participle refers to an action that precedes that of the main verb, that is, first

---

69. Darby (*CW* 31.276).

faith, then sealing.⁷⁰ Others see here, and in Acts 19:2, where we find the same construction ("Did you receive the Holy Spirit when you believed?"), what is called a "coincident" aorist ("when" = "at the moment that").⁷¹ Hearing, faith, and being saved are accompanied by the sealing with the Holy Spirit: at the moment that the Ephesian Christians had believed, they had received the Holy Spirit.⁷² Regardless of the rendering chosen, Ephesians 1 does not teach that a period of time elapses between believing and sealing.

8.7.2 Romans 7 and 8

In the present context, it is fascinating to investigate Romans 7 and 8. The interpretations of especially Romans 7:14–24 are numerous. In terms of the person and work of the Holy Spirit, the main interpretations are these.

(a) The "I" is unregenerate, and thus does not possess the Holy Spirit.⁷³

(b) The "I" is regenerate, but does not yet possess the Holy Spirit.⁷⁴

(c) The "I" is regenerate, and also possesses the Holy Spirit, but experiences the common difficulties of Christian life.⁷⁵

(d) The "I" is regenerate, and also possesses the Holy Spirit, but does not yet know the power of the Holy Spirit, as that power is described in Romans 8. This is the view that I wish to defend.

---

70. Grosheide (1960, 24); Salmond (1979, 268); Prince (1995, 241).
71. Cf. Bruce (1984, 265n94); Van 't Spijker (1991, 30–32).
72. Wood (1978, 27).
73. So the Greek church fathers, and more recently W. Kümmel, R. Bultmann, P. Althaus, and others; see Murray (1968, 256–57n19); Harrison (1976, 83–84).
74. Darby (*CW* 31.270) argued that the person of Rom. 7:15–24 cannot be sealed because that person is still a captive of the law of sin, and where the Spirit of the Lord is, there is freedom (2 Cor. 3:17). In Rom. 8 this person is set free, and this person is no longer in the flesh.
75. So Augustine and many Western theologians after him, including the Reformers; this view has been combated, in my view rightly, by J. A. Bengel, F. B. Meyer, F. Godet, J. Denney, and many others; see Murray (1968, 257n20).

To me it seems clear, *contra* (a), that the person of Romans 7:14-24 is born again, and *knows* they are born again:[76] "So now it is no longer I who do it, but sin that dwells within me" (v. 17), and, "I delight in the law of God, in my inner being" (v. 22). However, this person lacks any power of the Spirit (who is not mentioned at all in this passage): ". . . I am of the flesh, sold under sin. For . . . I do not do what I want, but I do the very thing I hate. . . . I have the desire to do what is right, but not the ability to carry it out. For I do not do the good I want, but the evil I do not want is what I keep on doing" (vv. 14-19). Believing that this is the common experience of the Christian is to ignore the life of victory by the Spirit as described in Romans 8, as we read in verse 37: in all things "we are *more than conquerors* through him who loved us" (*contra* [c]).

At the same time, this self-knowledge of the regenerate person shows that such a person possesses the assurance of salvation. That person is a believer in the sense of Ephesians 1:13, and therefore possesses the Holy Spirit (*contra* [b]). So we are dealing here with a *born again* person, who possesses the assurance of faith, and thus possesses the Holy Spirit as well. The person's problem lies elsewhere: *that person is not free*. The "I" is indeed renewed, but forced to experience its powerlessness.[77] It is the *regenerate* person who says here, "Wretched man that I am! Who will deliver me from this body of death?" (v. 24). It is the *liberated* person who replies: "Thanks be to God through Jesus Christ our Lord! . . . There is therefore now no condemnation for those who are in Christ Jesus. For the law of the Spirit of life has set you free in Christ Jesus from the law of sin and death" (7:25-8:2).

The person of 7:14-24 is regenerated *by* the Spirit, but does not know the *power* of the Spirit, even though the Spirit dwells in such a person. As Everett Harrison excellently expresses it: "[T]he experience pictured here . . . [demonstrates] what would indeed be the situation if one who is faced with the

---

76. Cf. Murray (1968, 257–59).
77. Kelly (1869, 326).

demands of the law and the power of sin in his life were to attempt to solve his problem independently of the power of Christ and the enablement of the Spirit."[78]

Thus, Romans 7:14-24 must be clearly distinguished from Galatians 5:16-18. In Romans 7, the regenerate "I" experiences defeat after defeat in the struggle against the flesh because the Spirit is totally absent from the picture. In Galatians 5, however, just as in Romans 8:5-14, the regenerate "I" triumphs over the flesh by the power of the Spirit.[79] Romans 7 is dealing not with the difficulty of the believer still having the sinful nature within, but rather with the fact that the *law* of sin still rules over the believer (7:21, 23, 26; 8:2). This is *not* the normal state of a Christian, but the state of a Christian who has not yet been set free. If "the law of the Spirit of life" has set a person "free in Christ Jesus from the law of sin and death" (8:2), sin still dwells within this person, but that person is no longer dominated by the *law* of sin.[80]

Already before chapter 7, Paul had said, ". . . [O]ne who has died has been *set free* [Gk. *dedikaiōtai*] from sin. . . . [H]aving been *set free* [Gk. *eleutherōthentes*] from sin, [you] have become slaves of righteousness. . . . [Y]ou have been *set free* [Gk. *eleutherōthentes*] from sin and have become slaves of God" (6:7, 18, 22). The Spirit who grants the life that the believer possesses in Christ Jesus is a new and spiritual breath of life (cf. Gen. 2:7), which gives power to live free from the law of sin and death. This means not that the believer will never sin again (cf. 1 John 1:8), but that the believer is no longer *dominated* by the power of sin.

8.8   Time Between Rebirth and Spirit baptism
8.8.1   Five Cases

The fact that there may be a period of time between conversion/rebirth and Spirit baptism is evident from certain pas-

---

78. Harrison (1976, 84).
79. Ouweneel (1997, 346n6).
80. Grant (1901, 242).

sages in the book of Acts, which have been discussed in the previous chapter.

(a) The one hundred twenty disciples in Acts 1 and 2 had been born again long before they received the Holy Spirit (Matt. 5:13-14; see especially about the twelve, Luke 10:20; John 15:3; 17:6-19). This point does not carry much weight because the Spirit was not poured out before Acts 2. However, it does illustrate that rebirth itself (as all Old Testament believers had also experienced it) does not entail enjoying the indwelling of the person of the Holy Spirit.

(b) The three thousand new converts of Acts 2:38-41 experienced saving faith, water baptism, and Spirit baptism almost simultaneously, as did the Ethiopian eunuch (8:39 Western text) and the Ephesian disciples (19:5-6). Yet a period of time lay between these phenomena, no matter how small: first there was conversion, then water baptism, then Spirit baptism.

(c) In the case of the Samaritans, there was a substantial period of time between conversion/water baptism and Spirit baptism. We have taken note of the redemptive-historical reason for this,[81] but such a reason does not alter the fundamental fact that, even after the Day of Pentecost a period of time *may*, but not necessarily *does*, occur between conversion and Spirit baptism.

(d) In the case of Saul of Tarsus, three days elapsed between his conversion and his water/Spirit baptism (Acts 9:9, 17-18; 22:12-16). Weget gives the strong impression that Saul received assurance of salvation only when Ananias addressed him as "brother," and told him what the Lord would do to him (9:17). Saul repented and converted on the road to Damascus (see his questions in 22:8, 10); but what basis do we have for asserting that, already there and then, he possessed the saving faith, the faith of which Ephesians 1:13 speaks and which is sealed with the Holy Spirit? He received life at the

---

81. For this and the following points, see Longenecker (1981, 284-85).

moment of repentance; he received salvation, and thus the Spirit, three days later. Again, this illustrates the difference between rebirth *by* the Spirit and the gift *of* the Spirit.[82] "[F]or three days he was without sight, and neither ate nor drank" (Acts 9:9); he was experiencing both physical and spiritual darkness. Both forms of darkness departed at the same moment when Ananias laid his hands on him.

(e) In the case of Cornelius and his friends, there is no question of a period of time passing: they believed, and as a consequence the Holy Spirit fell on them immediately, even before their water baptism (Acts 10:44-48). If we wished to find criteria in Acts for the normal sequence, we would find them here, in the case of Gentiles coming to faith: when you believe, you receive the Holy Spirit. However, in practice, many people hear only a defective gospel: not the "gospel of your salvation" (Eph. 1:13), that is, "the gospel . . . by which you are being saved . . . that Christ died for our sins in accordance with the Scriptures, that he was buried, that he was raised on the third day in accordance with the Scriptures" (1 Cor. 15:1-4). In other words, such people do not know the full gospel,[83] as Peter preached it in Acts 10:34-43, and as Paul did in Romans 4:24-5:1: we "believe in him who raised from the dead Jesus our Lord, who was *delivered up* for our trespasses and *raised* for our justification. Therefore, since we have been justified by faith, we have *peace with God* through our Lord Jesus Christ." As a consequence of deficient preaching, people may indeed be born again, but they will receive assurance of salvation only when they have accepted the gospel of their salvation.

8.8.2 Again: Rebirth and Spirit Baptism

It is worth emphasizing again that the work of the Holy Spirit in the soul to produce repentance and faith must be clear-

---

82. Kelly (1952, 131-32).
83. Of course, I do not mean this in the sense intended by the Full Gospel movement.

ly distinguished from receiving the Holy Spirit. In Acts 2:37, the Spirit had already been working in the souls of the three thousand, but they had not yet received the Spirit. The latter always necessarily *follows upon* the former; it is an additional blessing, a privilege founded on the faith that is already actively at work in the heart.[84] *First* the Spirit brings about rebirth and faith, *then* he comes to dwell personally in the reborn and believing heart.

Thus, strictly speaking, regeneration and receiving the Spirit can never coincide; the latter necessarily follows the former, even if only by an instant, as in Acts 10:43–46. Sometimes it is three days, as in the case of Saul of Tarsus (9:9). And in certain hyper-Calvinist circles, it may take decades before a regenerated soul finds assurance of faith, and then receives the Holy Spirit. Apart from these situations, we distinguish another problem: *when* the Spirit has come to dwell in a regenerated and believing person, it may take an instant, or many years, before the power source of the Spirit is activated, and the believer experiences being *filled* with the Spirit.

Thus, we find three distinct experiences: (a) rebirth through the Spirit, (b) assurance of faith and sealing with the Spirit, and (c) being filled with the Spirit. In the ideal situation, these three situations follow immediately upon each other. In practice, however, a considerable period of time can occur between (a) and (b), as well as between (b) and (c). In both cases, the cause is usually deficient biblical teaching. For instance, the period of time between (a) and (b) may be due to hyper-Calvinist preaching, which emphasizes a unilateral predestination, and thus makes it hard for the regenerated to appropriate salvation for themselves (which appropriation is a suspect notion in such circles).[85] The period of time between (b) and (c) is often due to traditional preaching that is afraid of anything "charismatic." In this way, believers are hindered in experiencing being filled with the Holy Spirit, and enjoying

---

84. Kelly (n.d.-b, 161).
85. See extensively, Ouweneel (*RT* III/1).

the power and gifts of the Holy Spirit.

Symeon the New Theologian believed that Christians receive the full possession of the Spirit only later in their Christian life. The gift of the Spirit emerges gradually, and enters our conscious awareness later, when it is kindled anew. This is related to the believer's own spiritual development, as well as to the ecclesiastical context in which the believer has been raised and lives.[86]

8.9 The Fullness of the Spirit
8.9.1 Five Groups

We have seen that, on the one hand, the claims that Spirit baptism can occur only through the laying on of hands by an authorized person is an exaggeration (for this claim contradicts Acts 2:2-3, 41 and 10:44-46), and that Spirit baptism can be genuine only if it is immediately followed by glossolalia (for this is not mentioned in Acts 2:41; 8:17, 39; and 9:17-19). On the other hand, we noticed that the laying on of hands did occur often (at least in Acts 8:17; 9:17; 19:6), and that glossolalia did occur often (2:4, 11; 10:46; 19:6). In Acts 8 as well, the gift of the Spirit must have been accompanied by outward manifestations (see §7.5 above), that is, prophecy and especially glossolalia. We know that Paul, too, spoken in tongues (1 Cor. 14:18). In fact, only in Acts 2:41-47 do we find no outward manifestations; but it is quite unlikely that the three thousand Jews would have received less than the Samaritans in Acts 8 and the Romans in Acts 10. Therefore, it is at least quite *plausible* that, in all cases of Spirit baptism in Acts, glossolalia occurred.[87]

Today we may observe that many Christians apparently do not know the *characteristics* of Spirit baptism. Let me, by way of summary, distinguish five different groups of Christians in relation to this aspect.

(1) Due to the work of the Holy Spirit, the first group has

---
86. Pinnock (1996, 168).
87. Prince (1995, 232-34, 247-55).

an awakened conscience but is not yet regenerated. Presumably Nicodemus (John 3) was an example of this. Perhaps Cornelius (Acts 10:1-2, 22), too, but it seems more likely that, before Peter's visit, he belonged to group (2).

(2) The second group consists of people who, again due to the work of the Holy Spirit, have sincerely confessed their sins before God, and thus, as 1 John 1:9 teaches us, have received the forgiveness of their sins. We therefore cannot call them anything other than born again, even though they do not wish or dare to say this of themselves because they have not yet accepted in faith the gospel of their salvation. This is either because they do not yet know the gospel (see Cornelius, in [1] above), or because they do not dare to accept this gospel. This is because of an overwhelming sense of guilt, or because of imbalanced doctrine (e.g., an extreme doctrine of predestination). It seems to me that Saul of Tarsus, during the three days after his conversion, was in this state—born again but having no assurance of salvation—because of the devastating awareness of his sins. Such persons have *not* received the Holy Spirit because they have not yet believed the gospel of their salvation (cf. Eph. 1:13), either because they do not know it, or because they do not dare to appropriate it.[88]

(3) The third group contains persons who are born again, and know it; they have believed the gospel, and have thus received the Holy Spirit. But they are still weighed down by the "law of sin," and live in the midst of the experiences of Romans 7:15-24 (see §8.6.2). *Positionally*, they possess peace with God (Rom. 5:1-11), but *practically* they do not experience this, nor do they experience walking in the Spirit (Rom. 8:1-17; Gal. 5:16-26). They do possess the "Spirit of adoption as sons" (Rom. 8:15; Gal. 4:6), but they hardly dare to say, "Abba! Father!" Nor do they experience the *power* of the Holy Spirit in prayer (Acts 4:31; how could we say of a person who

---

88. It is strange that Pinnock (1996, 275n32) did not distinguish between the preparatory work of the Spirit in the (as yet) unbelieving person and the possession of the Spirit by the believer.

does not experience this power that he prays "in the Spirit"? Eph. 6:18; Jude 1:20; cf. 1 Cor. 14:14-15), or in worship (Acts 16:25-26), in prophetic words, in witnessing, in glossolalia, in experiencing miraculous works in their own ministry (Acts 4:31; Rom. 15:19; Gal. 3:5; Heb. 2:4).[89] Perhaps the difference between the basic regenerated life and living by the power of the Holy Spirit can be summarized in the well-known statement by Jesus: "I came that they may have life and *have it abundantly*" (John 10:10).[90]

(4) The fourth group of people has the assurance of salvation *and* knows the power of the Holy Spirit by their own experience, but must mature further in this, that is, grow to adulthood in Christ (1 Cor. 14:20; Eph. 4:13-16; Col. 1:10; 2:19; Heb. 5:12-14; 1 Pet. 2:2; 2 Pet. 3:18). As to the Holy Spirit, this means a growing personal experience of the fullness of the Holy Spirit, especially with respect to the great diversity of the *charismata* (see §§12.1-12.5 below).

(5) The fifth group consists of the "fathers in Christ": "I am writing to you, fathers, because you know him who is from the beginning. . . . I write to you, fathers, because you know him who is from the beginning" (1 John 2:13a, 14a), that is, Christ (1:1-3) together with all the riches that can be found in him (cf. Col. 1:27-28; 2:2-3), including the treasures of the Spirit.

8.9.2 Evaluation

Let us now look a little more closely at these five groups described in the previous section. The *first* group must come to true repentance and confession of sins. The *second* group needs the preaching of the "gospel of your salvation" (see §§8.6.1 and 8.7.1), through which, if they accept it in faith, they will receive assurance of salvation and peace with God, and begin to walk in the Spirit (see on this §§9.2 and 9.3). The

---

89. Cf. Duffield and Van Cleave (1996, 339-42); see more extensively, §§11.3-11.5 below.
90. Prince (1995, 342).

third and the *fourth* groups need faith in, and a longing for, the fullness of the Spirit, and must continually pray for this fullness (Luke 11:13; cf. vv. 5-10; 18:1-8). They need to develop a walk in obedience, and to break with hindrances in their spiritual lives.[91] In response to such a radical and receptive attitude of mind, the Holy Spirit will absolutely breakthrough in his full power. Experience teaches us that the laying on of hands may play a useful role in this, although it is not an absolute condition.

This breakthrough may also come at the moment when such believers are particularly touched by the Holy Spirit during their personal devotional time, or during a church service, or through a conversation with a competent minister. Seraphim of Sarov mentioned still other means, which are somewhat foreign to Western views of Christian life but are worth mentioning: prayer, fasting, alms, charity, and other good works, performed in the name of Christ, are means by which we come to experience the fullness of the divine Spirit. He identified the true *goal* of our Christian life to be that we are overwhelmed by the Holy Spirit.[92]

This was no doubt the way in which Mother Teresa experienced the fullness of the Spirit. A little different again was the approach by Symeon the New Theologian. He argued that no person, leaving the state of darkness of the soul, will behold the light of the Most Holy Spirit without trials, efforts, sweat, violence, and persecution.[93] This was and is the path along which the martyrs experience the fullness of the Spirit. This is what the apostle Peter means: "If you are insulted for the name of Christ, you are blessed, because the Spirit of glory [some manuscripts insert: and of power] and of God rests upon you" (1 Pet. 4:14).

In such a view, in addition to the responsibility and ac-

---

91. See more extensively, Torrey (1910, 118–46); Duffield and Van Cleave (1996, 331–38).
92. Quoted by Congar (1997, 2.69).
93. Ibid., 2.70.

tivity of believers, the sovereignty of the Holy Spirit remains guaranteed: he breaks through at the moment when *they* open themselves to him, and *he* is willing to do so. In this context, Suurmond spoke of a "critical-organic" interpretation of Spirit baptism. He placed this in opposition to the narrow approach of both Charismatics, who tie it too closely to the laying on of hands and to glossolalia, and traditional Catholics and Protestants, who link it too much to sacramental moments (infant baptism, Catholic and Lutheran confirmation, Protestant profession of faith).[94] The Spirit *may* use these means to break through, but he is not bound to them.

8.10 Terminological Confusion
8.10.1 Second Blessing? Baptized? Filled?

I think it is a theological error to call the filling of the Spirit that I have described a "Spirit baptism." What the book of Acts calls being filled with the Spirit (2:4; 4:8, 31; 9:17; 13:9, 52) has been confused with Spirit baptism by many authors. This is not surprising: two times we read that people who received Spirit baptism were "filled" with the Spirit: the one hundred twenty in Acts 2:4, and Saul of Tarsus in 9:17. But it is a logical error to turn this statement around, and claim that each filling with the Spirit is a (new) Spirit baptism. This mistake is made, for instance, by Duffield and Van Cleave,[95] and much earlier by Reuben A. Torrey.[96] The latter stated several times[97] that a person can have the Spirit dwelling within without having been baptized with the Spirit;[98] he apparently means "filled" instead of "baptized."

This kind of confusion occurs quite often, but this should not lead us to ignore the real issue: the most important thing is *that* believers receive the power of the Holy Spirit in their spiritual lives in view of their ministry — no matter what theo-

---

94. Suurmond (1995, 99–100).
95. Duffield and Van Cleave (1996, 322–44).
96. Torrey (n.d., 82–154).
97. Ibid., 87–90.
98. Ibid., 109.

logical name they attach to this receiving. Being born again and having a theological diploma is not enough for being a pastor: the person needs the power of the Holy Spirit. Even Jesus did not begin his ministry before he had been anointed with the power of the Holy Spirit (Acts 10:38). For the twelve apostles exactly the same was true: they *waited* for the "promise of the Father" (Acts 1:4–5; cf. Luke 24:49). This requisite waiting is all the more relevant for ordinary servants of the Lord today.[99]

What I have described here is also the viewpoint of, for instance, Michael Green, who spoke of a mistaken name for a valid experience.[100] Clark Pinnock emphasized the close connection between water baptism and Spirit baptism, without identifying them. He too argued that the term—second blessing, Spirit baptism, filled with the Spirit—is not the point. No matter what we call it, it is important that the fullness of baptismal blessing is realized within us, in whatever way. The Pentecost reality is far more important than the terminology. Pinnock suggested that it is perhaps best to describe spiritual breakthroughs as actualizations of one's initiation, that is, one's water baptism. Conversion itself all too often does not give power, and does not grant the experience of a life change. There may be, and often is, a period of time between water baptism and the blossoming of what that baptism involves. Indeed, if the Spirit is not present in a person's life with power, this situation must be corrected. God gives the Spirit in abundance, and it is important that we receive this power, experience it, and walk in it. The point is not the terminology, and the question is not *when* but *whether* one has experienced the power of the Spirit personally. Whether we call it Spirit baptism is unimportant compared with the problem that so many Christians do not practically experience the power of the Spirit. Believers must know God experientially, not only with the intellect. They need to be empowered for

---
99. Ibid., 106–107.
100. Green (1975, 142–47).

mission, delivered from fear, capable of testifying, and full of praises.[101]

The summary of the previous argument is this: It does not matter what you call it—make sure you possess it! Thomas Smail wrote something similar to the above in the tenth chapter of his book, *The Glory of God*.[102] Charismatic renewal does not depend on a correct theology concerning terms like second blessing, Spirit baptism, and being filled with the Spirit. Smail argued that there are two dangers. On the one hand, Pentecostals must not insist on a single expression, namely, Spirit baptism, as the only adequate description of the spiritual experience that they would like to see restored in the entire church. On the other hand, non-Pentecostals must not think that, if they can point out the theological shortcomings in the theology of Spirit baptism, they can thus discard the entire charismatic challenge.[103] The notion of a second blessing might be fundamentally mistaken, but the challenge remains: "Be filled with the Spirit" (Eph. 5:18).

8.10.2 John Wimber

John Wimber, founder of the Vineyard Movement, had his own approach to this terminological as well as existential matter.[104] He stated that the experience of Pentecostals is better than their own interpretation of it. In other words, endeavor to receive the same experience as theirs without necessarily adopting their theology of it. It is best to reserve the term "Spirit baptism" for what happens when a person comes to the assurance of faith: the person is sealed with the Spirit (Eph. 1:13; 4:30). Every *subsequent* interaction between the person and the Holy Spirit is not a baptism but a filling with the Spirit, Wimber argued. Such fillings can occur repeatedly; they are intended both for the beginning of our Christian life

---

101. Pinnock (1996, 169–70).
102. Smail (n.d., 137); cf. Smail et al. (1993).
103. Smail (n.d., 138–39).
104. Wimber and Springer (1986, 165–68); cf. Phypers (1973, 140–45).

and for many subsequent repetitions.

Let me give two examples from the Bible of what Wimber is saying here. First, Peter received Spirit baptism once (see Acts 2:4), together with the other apostles, as a fulfillment of the Lord's prediction (1:8). But at special times *afterward* he experienced being filled with the Spirit, as in 4:8 (cf. v. 31), namely, every time he needed it, whether preaching or witnessing or otherwise. Second, Saul of Tarsus received Spirit baptism once, too (see Acts 9:17). But at special times *afterward* he experienced being filled with the Spirit, as in 13:9 (cf. v. 52), namely, every time he needed it, whether preaching or witnessing or otherwise. Now the terminological confusion is this: in neither Acts 2:4 nor 9:17 is the term "(Spirit) baptism" used; it says "filled" here. Only by taking all the Scriptural data together do I feel free to say that what occurred at these times was Spirit baptism, and what occurred at those events reported in 4:8 and 13:9 was *not*. At Spirit baptism one is filled with the Spirit for the first time, but conversely, every filling with the Spirit is not a baptism. *Spirit baptism occurs only once; filling may occur many times.*

Whether we use the phrase "baptized in the Spirit" or "filled with the Spirit," in both cases there is an experience of the *power* of the Spirit, and this is what matters—not the correct theological phrase. Wimber said that, when speaking with evangelical Christians about the Holy Spirit, he asked them if they received the Holy Spirit when they believed (cf. Acts 19:2). If they said "yes"—and of course, this is what they all should say—Wimber told them that they need only to *actualize* what the Spirit gave them, that is, allow room for the gifts of the Spirit.[105]

I myself would ask such Christians how they *know* that they have received the Spirit. Is it because they can cite Bible verses that tell them so? In other words, is it only a *theoretical* knowing? Or do they know *by experience* the *power* of the Spirit

---

105. See previous note.

in whatever form? What can they say about experiencing this power? Do I know there is electricity in my house because I have read so in my contract with the power company? Or do I know this because I have turned on the lights, or have used electricity-powered devices, like my computer?

Pentecostal Christians have caused confusion by telling other Christians that the latter should receive (or be baptized in/with) the Holy Spirit. This is a mistake: the latter have already received the Spirit when they came to faith. When Pentecostals become aware of this, they sometimes make a distinction between "having" the Spirit and being "baptized" in/with the Spirit (for instance, with a mistaken appeal to John 20:23) — a distinction that is totally unknown in the New Testament. What Pentecostals should ask other Christians instead is this: Do you know what it is to be *filled* with the Spirit? Do you know the *power* of the Spirit? And if so, how?

If those other Christians cannot satisfactorily answer such questions, our Pentecostal friends may help them to develop the enormous potentialities of the Spirit *who is already dwelling in such Christians*. In this way, Pentecostals may be a blessing to other Christians. But they are *not* a blessing by stressing their ideas of a second blessing and of Spirit baptism, which can only create havoc. Genuine Christians do not need to receive the Spirit at all because they already have him. What we all need is to release the *power* of the Spirit within us, that is, to give room and opportunity to the Spirit to fill more areas of our lives, and through us to reach out to the world (to paraphrase Wimber once more).

8.10.3 Luke Versus Paul?

In recent discussions about Spirit baptism, one of the arguments that has played a role is that we must clearly distinguish the pneumatologies of the various New Testament authors.[106] In 1970, Howard Marshall stated that Luke was not

---

106. Menzies and Menzies (2005, chapters 3, 5, and 14).

only a historian but also a theologian[107] (if we can use this term *avant la lettre*). Along the same line, Roger Stronstad argued that Luke's pneumatology differed essentially from that of Paul, without contradicting it; the latter is more soteriological, that of Luke more charismatic.[108] In other words, Paul deals more with the work of the Spirit in connection with obtaining salvation and enjoying its effects in Christian living. Luke deals more with the Spirit as the One who grants power for the believer's ministry.[109] Thus, the theory can be defended that, according to Paul, a person receives the indwelling of the Spirit at conversion, whereas, according to Luke, a person receives the power of the Spirit *later*, at Spirit baptism.

My first difficulty with this view is that Luke does not theologize at all; he is only describing historical facts, and nowhere sets these within a theological framework. And, as said before, facts may never be elevated to norms, as if what happened at a specific time and in a specific way in the history of salvation requires that it should *always* happen in the same way in the life of the church.[110] Therefore, Berkhof rightly saw as a fundamental mistake of the Pentecostal movement that it wishes to interpret Paul the theologian in the light of Luke the historian, instead of the reverse.[111]

My second difficulty with this view is that Paul also speaks of Spirit baptism, and does so in the very framework of the functioning of the *charismata*. According to 1 Corinthians 12:13, a person cannot be called a member of the body of Christ if he or she has not received Spirit baptism (§8.5). Conversely, in Luke's writing as well, Spirit baptism occurs within a soteriological context (Acts 2:38; 10:43–44). While it is

---

107. Marshall (1970).
108. Stronstad (1984, 12).
109. Wuest (1973a, 81) saw that today the Spirit is given to the believer for ministry (as in Old Testament times) but also for sanctification. However, he did not identify these two elements as belonging to a Lucan and a Pauline pneumatology, respectively.
110. Cf. Green (1975, 133–34); Floor (1982, 114); Runia (2000, 93, 97).
111. Berkhof (1964, 88, 90); cf. Phypers (1973, 111); Floor (1982, 115).

true that the two authors have different emphases, we cannot seriously claim that, according to Paul, certain people already have the Spirit, whereas according to Luke they do *not* yet have him. Such a far-reaching claim requires separate, independent evidence.[112]

Thus, I honor the differences claimed between the pneumatology of Paul and that of Luke, but these differences do not justify the distinction between receiving the Spirit at conversion (Paul) and a *subsequent* Spirit baptism (Luke). For me, the significance of this entire discussion lies only in the fact that the believer must *learn to know* the Spirit whom one receives when one accepts the gospel of personal salvation also as the Spirit who is the source of power for one's ministry. It is fine, though not necessary, if the laying on of hands is a means by which the power of the Spirit is released. A person does not *receive* the Spirit (baptism) when hands are laid upon that person, but the power of the Spirit is activated. In the former view, the lamp is connected to the power grid. In the latter view, the lamp *has already been* connected, but the light must be switched on. The effect is the same: the lamp begins to shine.

---

112. In this respect, I agree with Dunn (1993; cf. Runia [2000, 93–94]), despite the attempt by R. Menzies to refute Dunn's objections (2005, chapter 5).

Chapter 9
Walking By the Holy Spirit

[A]ll who are led by the Spirit of God
> are sons of God.

For you did not receive the spirit of slavery
> to fall back into fear,

but you have received the Spirit of adoption as sons,
> by whom we cry, "Abba! Father!"

The Spirit himself bears witness with our spirit
> that we are children of God.
>> Romans 8:14–16

[W]alk by the Spirit,
> and you will not gratify the desires of the flesh.

For the desires of the flesh are against the Spirit,
> and the desires of the Spirit are against the flesh,

for these are opposed to each other,
> to keep you from doing the things you

> *want to do.*
> *But if you are led by the Spirit,*
> *you are not under the law.*
>
> Galatians 5:16–18

Summary: *The first major topic of this chapter is the guidance of (the "being led by") the Spirit, in Israel, in the book of Acts, in church history (one Bible but very different applications), and also in the history of theological exegesis (including recent hermeneutical developments). Second, for the subject of guidance, Romans 8 is of special importance: believers are led by the Spirit or by the flesh. In this light, attention is paid to the Eastern Orthodox notion of* theosis *in connection with the typically Protestant subject of justification. The third part of this chapter is devoted to Galatians 5, especially to the "fruit of the Spirit." The elements of this fruit are analyzed and compared with the works of the flesh and the demands of the law. In the fourth and last part, the issue of positional and practical sanctification is dealt with, as well as "praying in the Spirit."*

9.1 Guidance By the Spirit
9.1.1 The Pillar of the Cloud

IN §3.8 WE CONSIDERED the parallels between the pillar of cloud (the Shekhinah) that accompanied Israel, and the Holy Spirit. One of the characteristics of the pillar of cloud was that it led Israel through the wilderness—a type pointing to the guidance by the Spirit as we know it especially from the New Testament. At the exodus from Egypt, before Israel's passage through the Red Sea, we hear that "the LORD went before them by day in a pillar of cloud to lead them along the way, and by night in a pillar of fire to give them light, that they might travel by day and by night. The pillar of cloud by day and the pillar of fire by night did not depart from before the people" (Exod. 13:21–22).

In the book of Numbers we read several times how the

Walking By the Holy Spirit

"cloud" led the people through the wilderness. The most significant passage is chapter 9:17-22,

> And whenever the cloud lifted from over the tent [of meeting], after that the people of Israel set out, and in the place where the cloud settled down, there the people of Israel camped. At the command of the LORD the people of Israel set out, and at the command of the LORD they camped. As long as the cloud rested over the tabernacle, they remained in camp. Even when the cloud continued over the tabernacle many days, the people of Israel kept the charge of the LORD and did not set out. Sometimes the cloud was a few days over the tabernacle, and according to the command of the LORD they remained in camp; then according to the command of the LORD they set out. And sometimes the cloud remained from evening until morning. And when the cloud lifted in the morning, they set out, or if it continued for a day and a night, when the cloud lifted they set out. Whether it was two days, or a month, or a longer time, that the cloud continued over the tabernacle, abiding there, the people of Israel remained in camp and did not set out, but when it lifted they set out.

Concrete examples of such guidance by the cloud are found in the following chapters:

> In the second year, in the second month, on the twentieth day of the month, the cloud lifted from over the tabernacle of the testimony, and the people of Israel set out by stages from the wilderness of Sinai. And the cloud settled down in the wilderness of Paran. . . . And the cloud of the LORD was over them by day, whenever they set out from the camp (Num. 10:11-12, 34).

In Numbers 14:14, Moses said to God, "[Y]our cloud stands over them and you go before them, in a pillar of cloud by day and in a pillar of fire by night." In retrospect, God spoke of God "who went before you in the way to seek you out a place to pitch your tents, in fire by night and in the cloud by day, to show you by what way you should go" (Deut. 1:33). Asaph said afterward, "In the daytime he led them with a cloud, and all the night with a fiery light" (Ps. 78:14). "In the pillar of the cloud he spoke to them; they kept his testimonies and the statute that he gave them" (99:7).

"Leading" is not just "pointing the way." This is what a signpost does, which points in a direction but itself remains stationary. No, the Shekhinah, or the Holy Spirit, is a guide, a leader, One who points the way and at the same time accompanies the travelers. He goes ahead of them, and empowers his travel companions for the journey. At the same time, the journey remains the believers' own walk. *They* walk, *they* take every step with their own feet, *they* are responsible for every step they make. But the *Spirit* points them toward the right path, as the Shekhinah did in the wilderness; *he* supports the believers when they are discouraged and feeble. The Spirit is their guarantee that they will safely reach their destination. "He spread a cloud for a covering, / and fire to give light by night" (Ps. 105:39).

In cases of weakness, the Lord may even carry his people: "The LORD your God who goes before you will himself fight for you, just as he did for you in Egypt before your eyes, and in the wilderness, where you have seen how the Lord your God carried you, as a man carries his son, all the way that you went until you came to this place" (Deut. 1:30-31). Compare Psalm 28:9, "Oh, save your people and bless your heritage! / Be their shepherd and carry them forever" (cf. Isa. 40:11; 46:3-4; 63:9).

The route of God's New Testament people is also a path through the wilderness, a metaphor used in 1 Corinthians 10:1-11 and Hebrews 3:7-19. As Jesus was led by the Spirit in the wilderness (Luke 4:1), so too is the church. They never enjoy permanent rest; they never reach a point — not even during the Reformation or any other later revival — when they could say: We will camp here until Christ comes back. Each time the Holy Spirit is on the move, the church needs to be on the move, too. Woe to those who then argue: Our fathers found rest at this wonderful campsite, so why can't we? It was an appropriate place of rest when the Spirit brought God's people there, but it is no longer suitable when the Spirit is on the move. If, however, the Spirit continues camping at a certain site, woe to those who want to be on the move; the Spirit is not with them. The Holy Spirit alone is the safe guide, who keeps God's people from both conservatism ("stay where you are") and progressivism ("stay always on the move"). Until the eschaton, the refrain of Revelation 2 and 3 remains applicable: "He who has an ear, let him hear what the Spirit says to the churches."

9.1.2 Guidance in the Book of Acts

After the Holy Spirit had been poured out (Acts 2), and the New Testament church had been formed, we find in the book of Acts several examples of the ways in which believers were *led* by the Spirit. Philip the evangelist is such an example. He was led by the Spirit, a fact that in Acts 8 does not differ substantially from the guidance by an angel of the Lord. In verse 26 ("an angel of the Lord said to Philip"), it was an angel who appeared to him, while in verse 29 ("the Spirit said to Philip") the Spirit presumably spoke in his heart (cf. also v. 39, "the Spirit of the Lord carried Philip away").[1] We find a similar distinction in the case of Peter: first, the Lord spoke to him through a vision—while an angel spoke to Cornelius in a vision—and then he heard the inner voice of the Spirit (Acts 10:3, 14, 19).[2]

In Acts 15:28 we see how the Holy Spirit leads or guides not only individual believers but also an entire company of believers: "For it has seemed good to the Holy Spirit and to us...." Of course, this does not mean that the apostles and elders were placing themselves on the same level as the Holy Spirit. It does mean that, on the one hand, they explicitly stat-

---

1. Cf. Knowling (1979, 221, 223).
2. Cf. Longenecker (1981, 389).

ed that their decision was due to the guiding of the Holy Spirit, and on the other hand, that they agreed with it according to their very own responsibility.³ In other words, through their own deliberations *they* had arrived at a decision, but they had recognized the guiding of the Spirit in this process.

In Acts 13:1–4 we read,

> Now there were in the church at Antioch prophets and teachers. . . . While they were worshiping the Lord and fasting, the Holy Spirit said, "Set apart for me Barnabas and Saul for the work to which I have called them." Then after fasting and praying they laid their hands on them and sent them off [Gk. *apelysan*]. So, being sent out [Gk. *ekpemphthentes*] by the Holy Spirit, they went down to Seleucia, ...

Luke seldom tells us how this guiding of the Spirit worked, whether through prophetic statements by certain believers, through an inner voice or inspiration, or through external circumstances. In this case, the voice was so important and far-reaching that it was possibly heard at the same time by all the gathered prophets and teachers; or it was a prophetic statement by one person, but then one with great prophetic authority.

Notice the "they" in verse 3; all five men fasted and prayed, and subsequently the other three "prophets and teachers," Simeon, Lucius, and Manaen, laid hands on Barnabas and Saul. The three were not the men who sent out the other two; this sending (Gk. *ekpempō*) was the work of the Holy Spirit (the "sent off" [Gk. *apoluō*] in v. 3 does not mean anything more than "let them go," GNV). But the three united themselves with this work of the Spirit by laying hands on the two men. We should then be careful with our language when we speak of churches "sending out" missionaries. It is the Spirit who sends out, and the church unites with the Spirit's work.

In Acts 16:6–7, we see the Spirit guiding throughout the

---

3. Knowling (1979, 328).

ministry of Paul and of his co-workers: "And they went through the region of Phrygia and Galatia, having been forbidden by the Holy Spirit to speak the word in Asia. And when they had come up to Mysia, they attempted to go into Bithynia, but the Spirit of Jesus did not allow them." I repeat, Luke seldom tells us how this guiding of the Spirit worked. Perhaps the expression "Spirit of Jesus" in verse 7 suggests that some prophet in Paul's company made a statement in the name of Jesus.[4] The important thing is that Paul recognized this as a word from the Lord; he knew how to distinguish between the *Spirit* not allowing them, and *Satan* hindering them (for the latter, see 1 Thess. 2:18).

It was of extraordinary significance that Paul and his companions followed the guiding of the Holy Spirit in Acts 16. In this way, through the wisdom of God, the gospel was planted on the European continent at such an early stage. Not only this; in Acts 16:6 Paul was prevented from preaching the gospel in Asia, but in Acts 19 he arrived there after all—however, at God's time, under his blessing, so that a great revival occurred in the region. If Paul had visited Asia too early, before the Spirit led him there, he might have easily stood in the way of this later, powerful movement of God's Spirit.[5]

9.1.3 Paul's Visit to Jerusalem

The most complicated exegetical question surrounding this matter of being led by the Spirit concerns Paul's going up to Jerusalem at the end of his third missionary journey. It begins in Acts 19:21, "Now after these events Paul resolved in the Spirit to pass through Macedonia and Achaia and go to Jerusalem." There is no possessive pronoun here; the text does not say "in his spirit," *contra* the MEV and others. So the Greek expression *en tōi pneumati* means "in the spirit" (KJV, DRA) or "in the Spirit" (NKJV, ESV).[6] Several expositors have argued for the

---

4. Knowling (1979, 341); Bruce (1988, 306–307).
5. Prince (1995, 339).
6. Some modern translations eliminate the problem by omitting the word "s/

latter rendering.⁷ The translational choice partially depends on the interpretation of these following passages.

Acts 20:22-23 offers a new piece of the jigsaw puzzle: "And now, behold, I am going to Jerusalem, constrained by the Spirit, not knowing what will happen to me there, except that the Holy Spirit testifies to me in every city that imprisonment and afflictions await me." Again the question arises how we have to read the Greek phrase *tōi pneumati* in verse 22. Some translations render it as "the Spirit" (ESV, NIV, NASB), as do several expositors.⁸ Others render it as "the spirit" (KJV, ASV, DRA; Kelly⁹), a reference to Paul's own spirit. The reason for the latter rendering is obvious: the text seems to contain a contradiction. Does the Holy Spirit urge Paul to go to Jerusalem (v. 22), and does the same Spirit then warn him *not* to go (v. 23)? However, the text does not say the latter; it is rather a warning about what awaits Paul. It is not inconceivable that Paul was being both urged and warned by the same Spirit.

But what about Acts 21:4, where friends tell Paul "through [Gk. *dia*] the Spirit . . . not to go on to Jerusalem"? If I have understood 19:21 and 20:22 correctly, this cannot mean that the Spirit would *here* forbid Paul to go to Jerusalem. I presume that the Spirit warns Paul again, and that the *friends* therefore beg Paul not to go.¹⁰ Verse 11 seems to agree with this, where we read that the prophet Agabus tells Paul, "Thus says the Holy Spirit, 'This is how the Jews at Jerusalem will bind the man who owns this belt and deliver him into the hands of the Gentiles.'" In these words, Paul does not receive a prohibition from the Spirit; rather, it is predicted that he *will* go, but that

---

Spirit" altogether (NIV, ERV, GW).
7. Longenecker (1981, 500); Bruce (1988, 371); *contra* Kelly (1952, 288). Grosheide (1963, 2.95) says, "It does not say that the apostle received a special indication from the Holy Spirit."
8. Grosheide (1963, 2.112); Longenecker (1981, 512); Knowling (1979, 431–32); Bruce (1988, 390).
9. Kelly (1952, 304).
10. Cf. Grosheide (1963, 2.121); Knowling (1979, 442–43); Longenecker (1981, 516); Bruce (1988, 398).

he will have much to endure in the city. This is followed by a new attempt by Paul's friends to stop him: "When we heard this, we and the people there urged him not to go up to Jerusalem" (v. 12), but here the Holy Spirit is not mentioned. Grosheide understands this to have been a "temptation by the devil,"[11] which is rather far-fetched seeing that among those trying to keep Paul from traveling to Jerusalem is Luke, the author of Acts (see the "we" in v. 12).

In my view, it was perfectly correct that Paul did not allow himself to be stopped by his well-intentioned friends. Back when he was called to be an apostle, he was shown how much he would have to suffer for the name of Jesus (9:16). Following him through the chapters of Acts, I cannot doubt that he was led by the Holy Spirit, even though the same Spirit showed him "in every city" — possibly through various prophets living in these cities (cf. 2 Kings 2:3, 5) — that "imprisonment and afflictions" awaited him (20:23). Indeed, the Spirit both urged and warned him.

9.2 Guidance in Church History
9.2.1 Earlier Centuries

Today the Spirit speaks in a way different from before. Scripture remains the same, but the manner in which the Spirit speaks through the one Word changes in every generation. Each epoch, and every ecclesiastical and theological community, must listen to what the Spirit says to the churches *here and now* (cf. Rev. 2:7). As Clark Pinnock put it, a theology that does not ask God's will for the present may be orthodox, but does not really listen to him. Doctrines must testify of the present time, and not be timeless abstractions. Theologians must read the Bible, and also listen to what the Spirit says. In this way we grow as hearers of the Word of God.[12] Even with a completed and closed canon in hand, and with full theological libraries at our disposal, the word of Jesus is still valid:

---

11. Grosheide (1963, 2.123).
12. Pinnock (1996, 215–16).

the "Spirit of truth . . . will guide you into all the truth" (John 16:13).

A few examples may clarify my point. The Tanakh gave no instruction about what the early, Spirit-filled Jewish church was supposed to do with thousands of newly converted Gentiles: was the church to impose the Mosaic Torah on them or not? But the church did have the Holy Spirit. In Acts 15 the Spirit guided the spiritual leaders to the right decision about what commandments remained in force for Gentile believers. Of course, such guiding continued *after* the time of Acts. Thus, the Spirit guided the church in formally establishing the canon of both the Old and the New Testaments. In this way, the boundaries of future theological discussions were also being established, for these boundaries were formed by the boundaries of the books accepted as Holy Scripture.[13]

In the fourth century, the unity of, and the relationship between, the three divine persons, and the unity of, and the relationship between, the two natures of Christ, were high on the agenda of the Holy Spirit. Most Christians gratefully accept from the hand of the Spirit the results of the discussions, set forth in the Nicene Creed and the Formula of Chalcedon. At the same time, however, the great ecumenical councils were also infected with a good deal of carnality, when we think, for instance, of the stringent measures taken against the Jews (already at Nicaea), but also against other Christians (Nestorians, Monophysites). Think as well of the carnal "Robber Council" (449), which was repudiated by the Council of Chalcedon two years later. Moreover, the Trinitarian and Christological discussions divided the Eastern church so seriously that, in the seventh century, Islam overran it like a plague, and shook Christians like ripe apples from their various sectarian trees. In other words, it is a tremendous task to discern between the Spirit and the flesh during such debates. God's Word is perfect, and the Spirit is perfect — but the church is not.

---

13. In the present time, the New Testament canon is under debate again because of the popularity of the Gnostic "gospels"; see Green (2005).

In the Reformation (beginning of the sixteenth century), understandably the doctrine of justification by faith alone occupied the central place because the Reformers were opposing the Roman Catholic doctrinal developments of the Middle Ages. However, those who are saying today that this doctrine must still occupy the central place in the church's apologetic, or even that this doctrine is central to the New Testament, are thinking ahistorically, and are living outside theological reality.[14] In the doctrinal development within the New Testament, this doctrine is only one of many, and not even the most prominent one. By overemphasizing the doctrine of justification, other New Testament doctrines have been badly neglected. Let me mention four rather painful examples of such neglect.

(1) The subject of the baptism in/with the Holy Spirit, being filled with the Spirit, the gifts of the Spirit (see the present volume).

(2) The subject of the kingdom of God — perhaps the most pivotal subject in the entire Scripture — in its present and eschatological significance.[15]

(3) The place of Israel in the ways and promises of God, from a covenantal,[16] an ecclesiological,[17] and an eschatological[18] point of view.

(4) The subject of the present significance of eternal life, and the spiritual growth of believers according to God's image in Christ, that is, what Eastern Orthodox Christians call *theosis*.[19]

In the eighteenth century, "world missions" for the first time became an issue. Imagine that Jesus had said that the "gospel of the kingdom will be proclaimed throughout the

---

14. See extensively, Ouweneel (*RT* III/2).
15. See extensively, Ouweneel (*RT* III/1).
16. See extensively, Ouweneel (2017b; *RT* IV/2).
17. See extensively, Ouweneel (2010a; 2010b).
18. See extensively, Ouweneel (2012a).
19. See extensively, Ouweneel (2009b).

whole world as a testimony to all nations, and then the end will come" (Matt. 24:14). First, most Western Christians had no idea what the "gospel of the kingdom," as distinct from the gospel of God's grace for poor sinners, could possibly entail. Second, Christianity was mainly limited to Europe, and to regions where European immigrants had settled. However, in 1727 a new outpouring of the Holy Spirit was granted to the Moravian Community in Herrnhut (Saxony, Germany); sixty-five years later, this small community had sent three hundred missionaries to the ends of the earth.

9.2.2 Recent Centuries

In the nineteenth century, because of the many divisions within the Reformed world, and especially because of the rise of a great plurality of Evangelical denominations, the church question began to occupy a central place. What is a biblical church or congregation, as distinct from other, less biblical churches and congregations? Today, with the decline of established denominations and the rise of the global "house church" movement, which involves many millions of Christians, very different answers to these questions are given than were given 150 to 200 years ago. I firmly believe that the Holy Spirit was present in the answers given both at that time and today (which does not mean that everything in those past and present answers is of the Spirit).

Another matter, high on the agenda of the Holy Spirit during the nineteenth century, was the study of biblical prophecies. During the early decades, this issue arose and spread among many denominations simultaneously. The Reformers had paid hardly any attention to the prophecies, except in a spiritualized form, in their practical application to the church. Apart from a small handful of Puritan theologians and of Dutch theologians of the Second Reformation, real interest in Israel and the nations as the subject of biblical prophecy did not arise until the nineteenth century. Bible scholars refuted supersessionism (replacement theology), and predicted that the Jews would return to their country and build their own state there—despite the fact that, during the still dominant Ottoman Empire, this seemed virtually impossible.

Just as the Holy Spirit had worked powerfully in the soteriological issues of the sixteenth century, in early Puritanism, Pietism, and the Dutch Second Reformation of the seventeenth century, in the missionary issues of the eighteenth century, in the ecclesiological and prophetic issues of the nineteenth century, so too he worked powerfully in the pneumatological issues of the twentieth century. In the Pentecostal and Charismatic revival, the Holy Spirit with his fullness and gifts was central. This time the Holy Spirit had placed *himself* on the ecclesiastical and theological agenda, if we may reverently put it this way. During the Pentecostal revival (beginning of the century), all attention was focused on Spirit baptism, viewed as a second blessing. I see this revival as a work of the Spirit, even though today we cannot view Spirit baptism anymore as the early Pentecostals did, as I am showing in the present book. The Charismatic movement was a correction of the Pentecostal revival, just as the Third Wave was a correction of the Charismatic movement. This is as it always has been: the Spirit was working, revealing new aspects from Scripture that had formerly been neglected, but this work was mixed with human weakness, and sometimes with the sinful flesh, a mixture that had to be exposed by subsequent generations.[20]

For Christians at the present time, all the issues mentioned are still important: justification by faith, reformation of the heart, the church's missionary task, the biblical structuring of churches and congregations, the meaning of the biblical prophecies, the relationship between Israel and the church, the meaning of the kingdom of God and of the Holy Spirit, and so forth. However, we must realize that in the meantime, the Spirit is "on the move" again. What does the Spirit wish to say to the churches of *today*? To refer to the imagery of Num-

---

20. Cf. Ouweneel (2010b, §2.3.5): the Reformation was a work of God's Spirit, whereas Protestantism was and is the work of humans.

bers 9:15-22 again: conservative Reformed Christians are in danger of becoming firmly settled in their sixteenth-century campsite, overlooking the fact that the "pillar of the cloud" has since long "set out" to new campsites. Conservative secessionists (traditional Protestants and free church Evangelicals) can become firmly settled in their nineteenth-century campsite (as is the case with parts of the Brethren movement, from which I myself came). Conservative Pentecostals are firmly settled in a campsite built in the early twentieth century.

Those who become settled in these ways are always suspicious of those who move on. Catholics were (and are) suspicious of Protestants, traditional Protestants were (and are) suspicious of free church Evangelicals, traditional Evangelicals were (and are) suspicious of Pentecostals, traditional Pentecostals were (and are) suspicious of Charismatics, and so on. Partial suspicion is always warranted: at their beginnings, the new movements all made mistakes, and sometimes even committed grave errors. But this cannot be an excuse for remaining spiritually, emotionally, and theologically settled in the century when a movement began. Wittenberg (1517, beginning of the Lutheran Reformation) had the answers for that time, but not for the entire remainder of church history. The same holds for the Synod of Dordt (1618-1619), for the Westminster divines (ca. 1647), for Herrnhut (1727, the Moravian revival), for Dublin (1828, beginning of the Brethren movement), for Ulrum (1834, beginning of the Reformed secession in the Netherlands), or for Azuza Street (1906, beginning of the Pentecostal movement), and so forth.

9.2.3 Same Bible, Different Applications

The point is not only that we need, as it were, all of church history in order to extract to the surface all the treasures of the Bible.[21] Such an idea presupposes in turn the notion of some timeless exegesis that simply needs yet to be perfected (see more extensively §9.3). But this is not what I mean.

---

21. So Pinnock (1996, 219, 222-23).

The point is that, from the *same* Bible, the Holy Spirit spoke in the sixteenth century in a way different than he speaks in the twenty-first century. From the same letter to the Romans, the Spirit spoke differently to Augustine (think of his *tolle, lege*; fifth century),[22] to Anselm of Canterbury (think of his forensic theory of justification; eleventh century),[23] to Martin Luther (think of his *sola fide*; sixteenth century),[24] to John N. Darby[25] (nineteenth century), to Karl Barth (early twentieth century),[26] and to Messianic Jewish theologian Joseph Shulam (late twentieth century).[27]

Only a naïve literalism believes that Scripture speaks univocally, making the same sounds and accents down through the centuries, so that one only has to draw upon tradition to recognize, learn, and interpret these sounds and accents. This view betrays ignorance with respect not only to Scripture, *but especially with respect to the guiding of the Holy Spirit.*

Of course, I am not pleading for the opposite kind of naiveté, sometimes found especially among Charismatics, namely, listening to Scripture without any knowledge of the theological tradition of twenty centuries, making an ahistorical appeal to the direct enlightenment of the Spirit. This kind of biblicism seeks to reinvent the wheel within theology, without wishing to learn from both the wisdom and the errors of earlier generations. To the former (traditionalist) group (firmly settled in their respective campsites) we respond, "Say not, 'Why were the former days better than these?' For it is not from wisdom that you ask this" (Eccl. 7:10). To the latter (biblicist) group we respond, "Is there a thing of which it is said, 'See, this is new'? It has been already in the ages before us" (1:10).

---

22. He was converted by Romans 13:14–15; see his *Confessions* VIII.12.27–28.
23. Cf. his forensic approach to Romans in his *Cur Deus Homo*.
24. As reflected in his *Lectures* on Romans in 1515–1516.
25. Darby (*CW* 7 and 10, and various writings).
26. Barth (1933), which caused an upheaval in Western theology.
27. Shulam (1998); his approach to Rom. can be summarized in the question: "How do I become a *tsaddiq* [righteous person]?"

It would be foolish not to listen to Nicaea and Chalcedon, to Calvin, Wesley, and Darby, as if wisdom had begun with *our* heroes. However, insofar as we accept their views, we do so not because they are invested with the formal authority of popes, councils, synods, creeds, or academic institutions, or because of the moral authority of their own personality and godliness. We accept them only *insofar* as they (a) agree with Scripture, and (b) have been worked by the Holy Spirit: the Spirit himself bears witness with our spirit that some of their insights are good approximations of the *truth*. To evaluate (a) properly, a theological training is quite helpful; to evaluate (b) properly, an intimate life with the God of the Bible is indispensable.

Notice the words "we," "us," and "our": the Spirit's witness in our spirits is given not only to the individual, even though Protestantism strongly (and rightly) emphasizes the responsibility of the individual. Rather, this testimony is given to the *community* of Christians (in practice often on a local level). No individual Christian, no matter how admired by their followers, has a monopoly on the truth, or even on some aspect or detail of the truth. It is typically sectarian[28] to think otherwise. It is only "with all the saints" that we understand the truth of God (Eph. 3:18), just as it is only as we stand on the shoulders of the apostles, prophets, evangelists, shepherds, and teachers of the past (4:11-14) that we grasp the truth. This is not primarily a theological (i.e., logical-analytical) understanding (although the latter is not excluded from it), but a spiritual, existential grasping with the heart (cf. 1:17-18). This understanding is not solidified in univocal, permanent formulas and theories, but is always flexible, according to time, location, and need. As long as God's thoughts are higher than our thoughts (Isa. 55:9), no human written formulations can ever be imposed on other people for evermore.[29] Even the most renowned creeds and confessions re-

---

28. See Ouweneel (2010a, chapters 13–14) on this important term.
29. Here is a simple example: the word "person" in translations of the Athanasian

main defective human work. Only Scripture is inspired, and thus forever divinely authoritative and trustworthy.

9.2.4 Different Times, Different Views

"For everything there is a season, and a time for every matter under heaven" (Eccl. 3:1). The apostle Paul spoke about how masters and slaves had to behave in the given situation of slavery, but he did not speak about the abolition of slavery. In his *Bezwaren tegen den geest der eeuw* ("Objections to the Spirit of the Age," 1823), Jewish Christian Isaac da Costa, a main figure in the Dutch "Revival" (*Reveil*) of the first half of the nineteenth century, still defended the enslavement of blacks with an appeal to the curse of Genesis 9:25,[30] as did so many Christian authors at the time. However, William Wilberforce prayerfully understood the call of the Spirit, and knew that in his day the moment had come to abolish slavery. Today, it would be difficult to find a responsible author who would defend slavery and the traditional appeal to the curse of Ham.

A second example: for centuries, Christians defended rule by absolute monarchy; they would have rejected the notion of democracy with indignation. At the time of the French Revolution (1789) and afterward, many Christians still rejected the idea of popular sovereignty. However, American Christians during the American Revolutionary War (1775-1783), and afterward many Christians in other parts of the world, understood the leading of the Spirit, and began to see that democracy is actually the least bad form of government, that it can definitely be combined with the notion of divine sovereignty, and that its benefits overcome so much oppression.[31] England

---

Creed can no longer be used effectively, because, for us, the term "person" means something very different than it did for early and medieval Christians; see Ouweneel (2007, §2.3.2).

30. Da Costa (1968, 143).
31. Guillaume Groen van Prinsterer, in his *Unbelief and Revolution* (2018), has done pioneer's work here, though he himself was cautious regarding the idea of democracy. Only "after the devastations of the Nazi dictatorship" did Pope Pius XII acknowledge "with little enthusiasm the good right of a democratic

was saved from a bloody revolt like the French Revolution, according to some because the Spirit-filled John Wesley, the founder of Methodism, had brought about a tremendous renewal of English society. It is no wonder that the early leaders of the British unions and of the Labour Party were for the most part Methodists.[32]

A third example: our sexual morality differs in some essential respects from the biblical morality in that our society is no longer patriarchal, marriage (as a goal in itself) is less strongly associated with procreation, and marriage is no longer a social-economic necessity for women. We would not want it otherwise. Herein, too, we prayerfully seek to understand the call of the Holy Spirit *in the present time*, without surrendering certain timeless biblical principles, such as the institution of marriage itself, and the limitation of sexual intercourse to the sphere of marriage between one man and one woman.[33] We see similar developments when it comes to the position of women, the functioning of church offices, the functioning of the gifts of the Spirit, and so on. With the unique, one-time, invariable speaking of Scripture, the Holy Spirit speaks to us differently today than he did in past centuries.

It is very important to understand the "signs of the times." When many Christians hear this expression, they are accustomed to thinking of the end times, whereas the only passage where the phrase occurs (Matt. 16:3) refers to the life, death, and resurrection of Jesus (v. 4; 12:39-40). In the parallel passage, Jesus asks, ". . . why do you not know how to interpret the present time?" (Luke 12:56; cf. the interesting Issacharites "who had understanding of the times, to know what Israel ought to do," 1 Chron. 12:32). This question of understanding one's time echoes throughout the centuries, in every genera-

---

form of state"; see Suurmond (1995, 69).
32. Suurmond (1995, 72). I add that it is just as remarkable that many pioneers in French socialism were not Catholics but Protestants (which means: Reformed), who themselves had been oppressed for centuries.
33. Ouweneel (2006, 21-23).

tion, until our own. In the last document of Vatican II, *Gaudium et spes* ("Joy and Hope") we read, "To carry out such a task, the Church has always had the duty of scrutinizing the signs of the times and of interpreting them in the light of the Gospel. . . . The People of God believes that it is led by the Lord's Spirit, Who fills the earth. Motivated by this faith, it labors to decipher authentic signs of God's presence and purpose in the happenings, needs and desires in which this People has a part along with other men of our age."[34]

9.3 Exegesis and the Spirit's Guidance
9.3.1 Hermeneutical Developments

In past times, it was so simple. Theologians learned the trade of grammatical-historical exegesis, did their "objective" work, and were confident that the result had been produced by the Holy Spirit. However, no one could determine, for the practitioners of such a noble, solid linguistic craft, whether it would have made any difference if the Spirit had indeed led them. No problem: it was the "professional" result that counted. In those days, theology was still simply about the cognitive-propositional contents of the Bible. Just as the liberals appealed to "religious experience," the conservatives appealed to the "biblical facts." For them, theological knowledge was the result of the logical-analytical study of the "biblical data" by a trained, objective theologian.[35]

Today, nothing about this picture is viewed as correct. "The" biblical facts no longer exist because our observations of these so-called facts are determined primarily not by our

---

34. http://www.vatican.va/archive/hist_councils/ii_vatican_council/documents/vat-ii_const_19651207_gaudium-et-spes_en.html, points 4 and 11.
35. According to Hodge (1872, 18), it is the task of theology to systematize "the facts of the Bible," and to establish the principles or general truths that these "facts" entail. According to Griffith Thomas (1930, xxi), it is the task of theology to investigate "all the spiritual facts of revelation," to determine their value, and to organize them into a doctrinal system. Pinnock (1996, 225) rightly commented that, after someone like Hodge had collected the data, there would not be much left for later theologians to do.

learnedness nor even by the Holy Spirit, but by our context (our language, culture, history, communities, traditions). In the formation of this context, the Holy Spirit was, and is, certainly present in a directive way, but so too are our sinful flesh and our human defects. Moreover, as this context is constantly changing, both "the" facts and "the" theologians change, and so does theology itself.[36]

To me, this seems to be a fortunate situation because now there is *real* room for asking if it makes any difference whether the expositor is led by the Holy Spirit or not. The real issue comes down to who establishes whether theological interpretations come from the Spirit, and if so, which ones? A council or synod? And individually: the theologian's learnedness or intuition? But all of these are determined by their social, historical, and cultural contexts. The Holy Spirit is not absent from these contexts—but who will determine how much comes from the Spirit, and how much comes from these (rather arbitrary) contextual factors? By what criteria?

French Protestant philosopher Paul Ricoeur has presented a "hermeneutics of suspicion," that is, suspicion with regard to the easiness with which the human mind deceives itself. Many traditional theologians were convinced that, despite their weaknesses, they were led by the Holy Spirit, for this was their deepest intention. In reality, says the new hermeneutics, they were manipulated at least partially by historical, social, and unconscious factors (Did they live in the sixteenth century or the twenty-first century? Were they European or American?[37] First World or Third World? Eastern Orthodox, Catholic, or Protestant? Traditional Protestant or free church Evangelical? Male or female? White collar or blue collar? Was theirs urban theology or rural theology? And so on.). As Merold Westphal stated, not only secular thinkers like Karl Marx,

---

36. For these sections, see Ouweneel (2000b, 497–503; 2002; 2006b; 2007, §13.4).
37. In Ouweneel (2017a) I have tried to show how differently average American and European orthodox Christians view the notion of Christian politics.

Friedrich Nietzsche, and Sigmund Freud (called by Ricoeur the "masters of suspicion"), but also Martin Luther and Karl Barth, have strongly protested against false piety. This piety reduces God (and the Bible) to a means or instrument for realizing one's own human aims by an appeal to the Holy Spirit.[38] Such aims, I add, can include preserving one's own academic position, or the status of one's own denomination, or glorifying the great predecessors of one's own theological tradition, including their creeds and synodical decisions.

The Holy Spirit can never be packaged or contained in past creeds and decrees, no matter how much such a claim may serve the interests of our own denomination or academic position. No, the Spirit works in a *developmental* and *organic* way when he steers and drives the historical process, of which we are just a tiny part. I say this without belittling, on the one hand, the great things the Holy Spirit has done in the past, and on the other hand, human responsibility, in which also the sinful flesh is actively present.

9.3.2 Is There Meaning In the Text?

Ricoeur's "suspicion" does not entail any skepticism in the classical sense, for skeptics doubt the *contents* of our convictions. However, the "masters of suspicion" throw doubt on the *motives* behind, and on the *functions* of, our views. They point out the danger that, in fact, we are really interested not in the truth, even if we say (and think) so, but rather in the attractiveness of our views, in what they can do for us, in their usefulness. There are questions to be asked that some of us might not like to hear, such as: what social circumstances, what power games,[39] what preconceived opinions and motives — which are anything but of the Spirit — play a role in our exposition of Scripture?

It seemed that this critical hermeneutic asked the most critical questions conceivable. However, the French Jewish

---
38. Westphal (1993, 6).
39. Cf. Bönker and Wintels (2004).

philosopher Jacques Derrida went one step further with his *deconstructionism*.[40] All scientific and scholarly (including philosophical and theological) theories are pieces of literature, of rhetoric. According to Derrida, there are no good or bad theories, and no criteria for good or bad theories; there are only preferred and non-preferred theories. No one can look with the eyes of God (from a "God's-Eye Point of View," as American philosopher Hilary Putnam liked to say[41]) to establish what interpretations of "texts" — such as the Bible, books in general, fields of research, the world as a whole — are better or worse. Those who feel they can interpret "objectively" should try to observe or interpret *themselves* "objectively." We do not stand above or outside reality, but in the midst of it; we are part of it.

God alone is beyond (created) reality, we are not. When God reveals himself to us, he necessarily makes use of a creaturely *medium*, which presents itself as "text," whether nature or Scripture. We do indeed *believe* that God has revealed himself; in this respect, Christian thinkers differ from many modern philosophers and linguistic theorists. Therefore, Kevin J. Vanhoozer answered the question asked in the title of his significant study, *Is There a Meaning in This Text?*, in the affirmative.[42] There *is* meaning in the various texts mentioned, and it *is* our task to interpret these texts in order to understand them, and thus to understand the voice of their Author, the Holy Spirit, in them. However, this does not mean that the interpreter — in the past or today — always understands the texts properly, or that his interpretation (theory) is the only correct one, or is even an approximation of the true meaning of the text in question.

9.3.3 The New Hermeneutics and the Spirit

An appeal to the Holy Spirit without any critical self-reflec-

---

40. See Lacoue-Labarthe and Nancy (1981); Mallet (1993).
41. See Putnam (1990).
42. Vanhoozer (1998).

Walking By the Holy Spirit

tion is nothing but self-deception. In this regard, we must listen to the penetrating questions raised by post-modern critics in recent decades. Many theologians have either ignored post-modern thought, or have responded to it in a very negative way. Other Evangelical theologians have faced post-modern criticism in a much more open way, and without embracing post-modern*ism* (with its relativism and pluralism), have seen positive opportunities in the post-modern challenge. I think especially of A. McGrath, and A. C. Thiselton, K. J. Vanhoozer, S. J. Grenz, and J. K. A. Smith (though each in a different measure).[43]

We do not have to agree with Derrida's philosophy in order nevertheless to listen to his warnings and those of his collaborator, Jean-François Lyotard.[44] All too often, theologians have spoken in the name of the Holy Spirit, just as secular philosophers spoke in the name of "sacred" Reason. In both cases, the impression was given that opponents were viewed either as idiots or as heretics. They were burned at the stake, figuratively, but in the past often literally. In this context, Lyotard has pointed to the function of the "grand narratives" (*grands récits*), especially metaphysical thought systems, but also religions, ideologies, scientific paradigms, and the like. In his view, the time of such "grand narratives" is over. This is not true of stories in general; on the contrary, reality has been replaced by texts, stories, and narratives. Never before has the narrative character of the Bible been so heavily emphasized.[45] No, what Lyotard refers to are those "narratives," such as theological theories (dogmas, decrees), which in the past have always led to the abuse of power (terror) because they were presented as the only true image of "objective reality."

Scholarly (e.g., theological) models are "texts," "literature," products of human creativity, full of the same rhetor-

---

43. McGrath (1992; 1996); Thiselton (1992; 1995); Vanhoozer (1998; 2002); Grenz and Franke (2000); Smith (2006).
44. Lyotard (1979; 1983).
45. See Green and Pasquarello (2003).

ical, metaphorical, and related strategies that are so characteristic of *all* forms of literature. There is nothing wrong with this; on the contrary, it may help theologians to see that they do not automatically, or perhaps do not at all, proclaim "truths." Through our faith in divine revelation we *know* with our hearts that there *is* meaning in both nature and Scripture, for the Holy Spirit himself put it there. However, more than ever before, we realize today that this meaning is not disclosed "objectively" to any given reader. Only gradually does meaning disclose itself through a cumbersome and intensive *interaction* between the "horizon" of the "text" (nature or Scripture) and the reader's own "horizon" (the reader's context as determined by language, culture, history, community, and tradition).

In this process, both the Holy Spirit and human weakness and sinful flesh are present, both in the origin of this context and in the interaction mentioned. As Pinnock put it, the inspiration of Scripture and the illumination of the reader, both wrought by the Holy Spirit, together demand a style of interpreting that takes seriously both the ancient text and the modern horizon. If we disown the earlier inspiration, we may fall into the snare of heresy. If we disown the present "inspiration" — Pinnock should have said illumination! — we may fall into the snare of dead orthodoxy by neglecting what is crucial and actual.[46] At moments in the past, the Holy Spirit inspired the Scriptures. At moments in the present, he gives light to understand the Scriptures *for our time*.

9.3.4 Self-Reflection

"Contextual hermeneutics," as I have very briefly tried to summarize it, seems to me to be very helpful in breaking away from the audacious truth claims that came to us from earlier theology under the pretext of coming from the Holy Spirit. Christians ought to maintain the absolute truth of God as that is contained in Holy Scripture; but they should be cautious

---

46. Pinnock (1996, 230).

with regard to all alleged representations or restatements of this truth in human-deficient theological models. In a lot of so-called "orthodoxy" there is less of the Spirit, and a lot more of scholastic rationalism and confidence in human thought systems, as well as confessionalism and denominationalism, than many Christians seem to realize. There *are* no "objective (biblical) data" that are simply waiting to be "ordered" by the intellect of the theologian.[47] As Pinnock put it, the Bible is not a box full of pieces for the theological jigsaw puzzle; it offers little or no truth that can be expressed in an abstract, non-contextual way.[48] During the twentieth century, philosophers of science have made it more and more evident that there are no "objective" empirical data, including "biblical data."

Unfortunately, G. Spykman was forced to conclude that some systematic theologians reject all philosophical reflection as if it were a secular temptation that is inappropriate for "sacred" theology.[49] It would be like—if I understand these theologians—a serious Christian young man dating a beautiful atheist girl. Such traditionalist theologians often do not see, or see only insufficiently, that they too have been influenced by exactly those factors that have been exposed by post-modern thinkers. Thus, M. Oeming maintained that *each* form of biblical interpretation is necessarily linked with certain more or less conscious philosophical presuppositions. Therefore, it is the task of each biblical hermeneutic to account for these foundations and implications rooted in the expositor's worldview.[50] And A. Troost argued that certain orthodox theologians' short-sighted and unscholarly hostility toward philosophers causes theology to be entrenched in conservatism, or the opposite: to move it in a more or less modernistic direction. This is because the correct theoretical resistance to *both*

---

47. *Contra* Schilder (n.d., 37).
48. Pinnock (1996, 225).
49. Spykman (1988, 138).
50. Oeming (1998, 3).

tendencies is lacking.[51]

God's self-revelation is absolute — but all our theoretizing about it is, and remains, fallible human work, and thus relative. As Y. Congar put it, no matter how true and venerable the forms we know may be, they are not the last word concerning the ultimate realities that they express. Dogmas (and we may add, creeds, confessions, decrees, models, and theories) are not yet perfect.[52] This is a fundamental insight: the divine truth is transcendent and infinite — the forms in which theologians try to express these truths are immanent and finite. This should make us careful not to appeal to the guidance of the Spirit too quickly, too naïvely. By maintaining the absolute, transcendent starting point of all believing theology we are kept from post-modern relativism. At the same time, by always mistrusting our own hearts (cf. Rev. 2:23), and thus relativizing all our theological models, we are kept from confessionalism, theologism, and denominationalism, which is sectarianism.[53] Only then, when theology will become truly modest again, there can be room for the renewing work of the Holy Spirit.

9.4 Spirit Guidance in Romans 8
9.4.1 Flesh and Spirit

It is evident that Luke and Paul have different emphases in their description of the work of the Holy Spirit (cf. §8.10.3).[54] While both of them have written about the charismatic aspects of this work of the Spirit, Luke referred less to the soteriological dimension of the Spirit's word, that is, the significance of the Spirit in receiving and working out redemption in the life of a person. With Paul, it is this very aspect that occupies center stage.

Two passages are of special importance when it comes to

---

51. Troost (2005, 223).
52. Congar (1997, 2.34).
53. See Ouweneel (2010a, chapters 13–14).
54. Kärkkäinen (2003, 32).

the Christian's walking in the power of the Holy Spirit: Romans 8 (§9.4) and Galatians 5 (§§9.6–9.8). In the former passage, Paul says,

> ... us, who walk not according to the flesh but according to the Spirit. For those who live according to the flesh set their minds on the things of the flesh, but those who live according to the Spirit set their minds on the things of the Spirit. For to set the mind on the flesh is death, but to set the mind on the Spirit is life and peace. For the mind that is set on the flesh is hostile to God, for it does not submit to God's law; indeed, it cannot. Those who are in the flesh cannot please God. You, however, are not in the flesh but in the Spirit. . . . So then, brothers, we are debtors, not to the flesh, to live according to the flesh. For if you live according to the flesh you will die, but if by the Spirit you put to death the deeds of the body, you will live. For all who are led by the Spirit of God are sons of God (vv. 4–9a, 12–14; cf. 6:12–14 and 7:6).

In Romans 8, two "states" are placed in opposition to each other:

(a) Living "according to the flesh" (v. 5, Gk. *kata sarka*; cf. v. 8, "in the flesh," Gk. *en sarki*), that is, the being dominated by the sinful nature, or being oriented toward the desires of sin. This state is characterized by *death* (i.e., here, being separated or estranged from God) (v. 6; cf. v. 13a), *hostility* toward God (v. 7), and *powerlessness* (v. 8).

(b) Living "according to the Spirit" (v. 5, Gk. *kata pneuma*), that is, being dominated by the Holy Spirit, or being oriented toward the desires of the Spirit (cf. the NIV).[55] This state is characterized by *life* (i.e., life from God by the Spirit; cf. 5:17–18, 21; 6:4; 8:13b), *peace* (v. 6, viz., with God, 5:1), and *power* (cf. v.

---

55. Cf. a similar expression (with a different meaning): "him who was born according to the Spirit" (Gal. 4:29), i.e., Isaac, the "son of promise" (vv. 23, 28), but a promise that could be fulfilled only by the Holy Spirit; see Ouweneel (1997, 300).

13).[56]

In principle, with respect to their position before God, all believers are "people of the Spirit."[57] Therefore, strictly speaking, Romans 8:5-8, differently than 7:5-24, refers to the people's unregenerated condition; compare verse 9: "You, however, are not in the flesh but in the Spirit." Yet, here Paul is addressing believers; his warning implies that the same sinful flesh can be active in the regenerated person as well. Therefore he says "you" in verse 13: "For if you live according to the flesh you will die, but if by the Spirit you put to death the deeds of the body, you will live." Here, eternal death is opposed to eternal life (5:21; 6:22-23).

We may make the same type of claim with regard to the "spiritual" (Gk. *pneumatikos*) person (1 Cor. 2:15; 3:1; Gal. 6:1). The latter differs essentially from the "natural person" (Gk. *psychikos anthrōpos*), who is not born again (1 Cor. 2:14). No matter how brilliant the mind of the "natural person" may be, such a person is governed by the *psychē*, the animal life.[58] The "spiritual person" is not necessarily governed by an excellent spirit but by the Holy Spirit. In principle every believer is a "spiritual person" (Gk. *pneumatikos*), for such a person has received the Spirit (Gk. *pneuma*).[59] However, in practice believers, too, can be carnal (1 Cor. 3:1-3, from Latin *caro*, "flesh"), that is, people who are led not by the Spirit but by the (sinful) flesh.[60]

---

56. Cf. a similar contrast in Isa. 31:3, where Israel is called upon to trust not in man/flesh but in God/Spirit (Heb. *ruach*).
57. In Hos. 9:7 (YLT) it is especially the prophet who is the "man of the Spirit" (Heb. *ish haruach*).
58. Usually, these are people who believe that they are nothing but evolved animal beings anyway.
59. Cf. the contrast in Jude 1:19 (DLNT), "natural [ones], not having [the] Spirit." 1 Cor. 2:14 in the ERV reads "natural people" to mean "people who do not have God's Spirit"; the term "unspiritual" (CEB, RSV) is confusing because believers, too, can be unspiritual (i.e., carnal, living according to the flesh) (cf. 3:1–3).
60. 1 Cor. 3:1 and 3 use two different words: Gk. *sarkinos* (v. 1, referring to the material of which something is composed; "fleshy" in 2 Cor. 3:3 KJV) and Gk.

9.4.2 Mortifying Evil Actions

In Romans 8:13-14 we find three characteristics of the believer that inseparably belong to the Christian position.

(1) By the Spirit the believer puts to death the deeds of the body (which means the activities of the flesh, manifested through the members of the body).

(2) The believer is led by the Holy Spirit, which means that one not only possesses the Spirit but is guided and dominated by him.

(3) The believer is a son of God, that is, adopted by God to be his son (this includes female believers).

At the same time, there is not only a positional but also a moral aspect here, similar to Colossians 3:5, "Put to death therefore what is earthly in you [lit., your members that are on the earth]: sexual immorality, impurity, passion, evil desire, and covetousness, which is idolatry." "Put to death" here is an imperative. This practical aspect is not absent in Romans 8:13-14, though, for verse 14 does not say simply, "all who *have* the Spirit," but "all who *are led by* the Spirit." As a matter of principle, we may expect those who have the Spirit to be led by the Spirit; yet, this must become practically true.

This subject is linked with the essence of believers' adoption as sons. God predestined them "to himself" for his own "good pleasure" (Eph. 1:5 NKJV), which is very practical. Therefore in practice God is not satisfied with his sons unless they are *led* by the Spirit. We see this elsewhere: "'Therefore go out from their midst, and be separate from them,' says the Lord, 'and touch no unclean thing; then[61] I will welcome you, and I will be a father to you, and you shall be sons and daughters to me,' says the Lord Almighty" (2 Cor. 6:17-18). "The one who *conquers* will have this heritage, and I will be his God and he will be my son" (Rev. 21:7). The latter verse is reminiscent of

---

sarkikos (v. 3, in the material [1 Cor. 9:11] or the moral sense [2 Cor. 1:12]).
61. Gk. *kai*, lit. "and," here with the sense of "then," "on this condition" (a Hebraism).

2 Samuel 7:14, where God says of Solomon, "I will be to him a father, and he shall be to me a son. When he commits iniquity, I will discipline him with the rod of men, with the stripes of the sons of men." The father disciplines the son in order that the son also practically will be a pleasure to him: "[T]he LORD reproves him whom he loves, as a father the son in whom he delights" (Prov. 3:12).

We are reminded here of him who was the Son of the Father's delight *par excellence*, who as such never needed any discipline, and who was continually led by the Holy Spirit: "'You are my beloved Son; with you I am well pleased.' . . . And Jesus, full of the Holy Spirit, returned from the Jordan and was *led by the Spirit* in the wilderness. . . . And Jesus returned in the *power* of the Spirit to Galilee" (Luke 3:22; 4:1, 14). Also after his resurrection, Jesus as a Man still acted "through [Gk. *dia*] the Holy Spirit" (Acts 1:2).

Another example of such guidance by the Spirit, before Acts 2, is found in Simeon: ". . . this man was righteous and devout, waiting for the consolation of Israel, and the Holy Spirit was upon him. And it had been revealed to him by the Holy Spirit that he would not see death before he had seen the Lord's Christ. And he came in the Spirit into the temple" (Luke 2:25–27). Notice that in verse 25 there is no article before "Holy Spirit"; one could almost translate: "there was Holy Spirit on him," remembering that at this time no believer had the person of the Spirit dwelling within one's heart.

In verse 26, the Greek preposition ("by") before "the Holy Spirit" is *hupo*, suitable to the Greek passive form *kechrēmatismenon*, and the article is present before "Holy Spirit": it was the person of the Spirit who had revealed to him that he would not die before he had seen the Messiah (cf. Matt. 2:12, 22: "in a dream"; Acts 10:22, "by a holy angel").

In verse 27, we find the phrase "in the Spirit" (Gk. *en tōi pneumati*), that is, in the power that the person of the Holy Spirit granted Simeon.

9.4.3 Other Pauline Passages

The exhortation in Ephesians 5:18, "be filled with the Spirit," is often connected with the metaphor of wine (§4.6), or with the fullness of the Spirit (see §11.2.5), or with the baptism in the Spirit (§§8.6–8.8). However, interestingly enough, the immediate context in which we find this commandment involves learning the Lord's will very practically: "Look carefully then how you walk, not as unwise but as wise, making the best use of the time, because the days are evil. Therefore do not be foolish, but understand what the will of the Lord is" (vv. 15–17). Then follows immediately the exhortation that believers should not "get drunk with wine, for that is debauchery, but be filled with the Spirit" (v. 18). Wine is what "gladdens the heart of man" (Ps. 104:15), but the Holy Spirit gives far greater joy (cf. Luke 10:21, "rejoiced in the Holy Spirit'; Acts 13:52, "filled with joy and with the Holy Spirit"; 1 Thess. 1:6, "the joy of the Holy Spirit"). This joy is linked with gratitude, which is inconceivable without the readiness to submit wholeheartedly to the Lord's will.[62]

We find something similar in Colossians 1. The believers at Colossae were not characterized just by love, but by "love in the Spirit" (v. 8), that is, a love characterized, governed, and directed by the Holy Spirit.[63] This emboldens the apostle to pray that the Colossian Christians "may be filled with the knowledge of his will in all spiritual wisdom and understanding, so as to walk in a manner worthy of the Lord, fully pleasing to him: bearing fruit in every good work and increasing in the knowledge of God" (vv. 9–10).

This being filled, this spiritual increase, this process of inward transformation, always occurs through the power of the Holy Spirit: "Now the Lord is the Spirit, and where the Spirit of the Lord is, there is freedom. And we all, with unveiled

---

62. Green (1975, 152–53).
63. Interestingly, this is the only reference to the Holy Spirit in Col.; all the emphasis in this letter is on Christ, whereas the Spirit is mentioned twelve times in Eph.

face, beholding the glory of the Lord, are being transformed into the same image from one degree of glory to another. For this comes from the Lord who is the Spirit" (2 Cor. 3:17-18). Of course, this basic notion comes to light also in passages where the Spirit is not explicitly mentioned: "Do not be conformed to this world but [by the power of the Spirit!] be transformed by the renewal of your mind, that by testing you may discern what is the will of God, what is good and acceptable and perfect" (Rom. 12:2); "... until we all [by the power of the Spirit!] attain to the unity of the faith and of the knowledge of the Son of God, to mature manhood, to the measure of the stature of the fullness of Christ" (Eph. 4:13). Believers "have put on the new self, which [by the power of the Spirit!] is being renewed in knowledge after the image of its creator" (Col. 3:10). "[By the power of the Spirit!] grow in the grace and knowledge of our Lord and Savior Jesus Christ" (2 Pet. 3:18). And so forth.

9.5 Theosis
9.5.1 A Step Beyond Justification

All the Bible passages just mentioned are related to what Eastern Orthodox Christians since Athanasius refer to as the highest goal in Christian life, namely, *theosis* (from Gk. *theos*, "g/God"), that is, deification (from Lat. *deus*, "g/God"). This is related particularly to a notion embedded in the verb "transform" in 2 Corinthians 3:18 and Romans 12:2, where we find the Greek verb *metamorphoō*, from which the English noun "metamorphosis" is derived. In my view, this is one of the most appropriate terms relating to the idea of *theosis*, because the Christian's inner metamorphosis — the word corresponds with Latin *transformatio* — entails a realization of the image of God in Christ.

Theosis is emphatically *not* sharing or participating in the *being* of God; in other words, it is not a version of Satan's lie: "[Y]ou will be like God" (Gen. 3:5). *Theosis* is a growing up toward the *image* of God. This is the only plausible way to understand 2 Peter 1:3-4, God "called us to his own glory and excellence, by which he has granted to us his precious and very great promises, so that through them you may become partakers of the divine nature [Gk. *theias koinōnoi physeōs*]." To "partake" in the divine nature is a very strong expression (cf. ERV, "share in being like God"; MSG, "participation in the life of God"; Phillips: "share in God's essential nature" — here you can see that the theological boundary is easily crossed).

With regard to the emphasis on *theosis*, a deeper connection exists between Eastern Orthodox and Evangelical thinking. As central as the doctrine of justification has been in Lutheran and Calvinist theology (§9.2.1), just as strongly is the emphasis on what comes *after* justification in Eastern Orthodox and Evangelical theology — blessings that are clearly identified by Greek terms such as *metamorphōsis* ("transformation"), or *theōsis* ("deification"), or *plērōma* ("fullness," see §9.5.2), or *teleiōsis* ("perfection").

K. Hutten characterized most sects (his term) that originated after the Reformation as going a step beyond justification.[64] He viewed this as being dissatisfied with the Reformation's *sola gratia* ("by grace alone") and *sola fide* ("by faith alone"). Also to J. Hoek, spirituality is nothing but "the justification of the wicked by faith in Christ alone"; he asked with regard to "Evangelical spirituality": "Is justification here not too much a transitional stage in a process of growth?"[65] He hit the nail on the head: justification is a transitional stage in a process of growth; I could not have said it better. But, to reassure Hoek and other Reformed theologians, I hasten to add that every "step beyond justification" is taken by grace alone, by faith alone, and by the Holy Spirit. Just as with conversion, however, a person must actively open oneself to the grace of God and the work of the Spirit.[66]

To justification Paul adds peace with God and the hope of the glory of God (Rom. 5:1–2). This is not just a future aim, for

---

64. Hutten (1957).
65. Hoek (2006).
66. See Ouweneel (2004, 20).

he says in 8:29-30 that believers have been "predestined to be conformed to the image of his Son, in order that he might be the firstborn among many brothers. And those whom he predestined he also called, and those whom he called he also justified, and those whom he justified he also glorified." The ultimate aim of predestination is not justification but glorification. Being conformed to the image of God's Son coincides more or less with being glorified: in the full sense, both are future (cf. Phil. 3:20-21), but at the same time they are a matter that to some extent must be realized already in *this* life.

This can occur only in the power of the Holy Spirit, for Paul says that "hope does not put us to shame, because God's love has been poured into our hearts through the Holy Spirit who has been given to us" (Rom. 5:5). Therefore, we could perhaps put the matter this way: traditional Protestant theology does not move us beyond what the Spirit does *in* us, namely, justification. Evangelical theology begins with the *indwelling* of the Spirit in the believer, and proceeds to emphasize the great consequence of this, spiritual transformation.

9.5.2 The Fullness of God

Another aspect of *theosis* is found in Ephesians 3:14-19,

> For this reason I bow my knees before the Father, . . . that according to the riches of his glory he may grant you to be strengthened with power through his Spirit in your inner being, so that Christ may dwell in your hearts through faith—that you, being rooted and grounded in love, may have strength to comprehend with all the saints what is the breadth and length and height and depth, and to know the love of Christ that surpasses knowledge, that you may be filled with [better: (un)to, Gk. *eis*] all the fullness of God.

Here I observe no fewer than six "steps beyond justification," in which each step follows upon, and flows from, the previous step.

(1) The inner being is "strengthened with power through

his [i.e. here, the Father's] Spirit."

(2) Christ dwells in believers' hearts through faith.

(3) Believers are "rooted and grounded in love."

(4) They have "strength to comprehend with all the saints what is the breadth and length and height and depth."[67]

(5) They "know the love of Christ," which at the same time "surpasses knowledge."

(6) They are "filled unto all the fullness of God," that is, they receive a fullness that ultimately touches upon God's fullness itself.[68] In my view, no other verse in Paul's writings is more profound, and expresses better than this one what *theosis* is (v. 19).

We may immediately compare the latter claim with the important word play in Colossians 2:9-10, "For in him [i.e., Christ] the whole fullness [Gk. *plērōma*] of deity dwells bodily, and you have been filled [Gk. *peplērōmenoi*, brought to fullness] in him." Believers come to fullness in him in whom is all the fullness of God. The Man in whom the Triune God reveals his fullness is the Man in whom a believer finds personal fullness as well. "What more do you need?," is Paul's argument to the Colossian Christians, who were in danger of falling into the snare of "philosophy and empty deceit, according to human tradition, according to the elemental spirits of the world, and not according to Christ" (v. 8).

Compare here John's typical way of expression: "Whoever confesses that Jesus is the Son of God, *God abides in him, and he in God*" (1 John 4:15). Jesus prayed that believers "may be one even as we [i.e., the Father and the Son] are one, *I in them and you* [Father] *in me*, that they may become perfectly one, ... that the love with which you have loved me may be *in them, and I in them*" (John 17:22-23, 26). The aim of Christian living is to become like Jesus, like God: "You therefore must be per-

---

67. I prefer the interpretation that relates these four dimensions to the "mystery" (vv. 3, 9); see Zerwick (1969, 93).

68. Cf. Bruce (1984, 329–30).

fect, as your heavenly Father is perfect" (Matt. 5:48). "Be merciful, even as your Father is merciful" (Luke 6:36). "Therefore be imitators of God, as beloved children. And walk in love, as Christ loved us and gave himself up for us, a fragrant offering and sacrifice to God" (Eph. 5:1-2).

To put it differently, *theosis* is the route to the ultimate pure bliss. Therefore, 1 Timothy 1:11 speaks of the "gospel of the glory of the blessed [Gk. *makarios*, "blissful"[69]] God," in which the goal of all preaching is indicated: divine glory and bliss. Pinnock, too, has referred here to what has always been the emphasis in Eastern Orthodoxy: believers' identity is found in relation with God. The aim is submersion in the riches of divine life. *Theosis* is the source of what C. S. Lewis has called the inconsolable longing in Christians. Ecstasy is awaiting them. They not only have been forgiven, but they are being transformed, and exalted toward the divine. Christ is being formed in them (Gal. 4:19).[70]

Clark Pinnock, in his analysis of the *theosis*, did push it a little too far: in my view we definitely cannot say that the Son shares his divine sonship with us, or that we are invited into the Trinity as co-heirs of Christ.[71] However, Pinnock seemed to be in good company when quoting Irenaeus (154): "God became Man, in order that Man would become God."[72] Pinnock clarified that this entails being united with God without becoming God; this union is personal union, not ontological.[73]

---

69. Scarcely any English translation has provided a better rendering than "blessed," which actually translates the Gk. term *eulogētos* (2 Cor. 1:3; Eph. 1:3; 1 Pet. 1:3). "Glorious and wonderful" (CEV), "great" (MSG), and "honored" (NLT) are honorable attempts; the Gk. *makarios* is rendered in Lat. as *beatus* (not *benedictus*), which means "beatific, merry, cheerful, delighted, enchanted, enraptured, blissful."
70. Pinnock (1996, 151 including note 4 with many references).
71. Ibid., 153.
72. Ibid., 154; *Adv. Haer.* 3.19.1; cf. Athanasius (*On the Incarnation* 2.54); see Lossky (1985, chapter 5).
73. Pinnock (1996, 154, cf. 181–82).

9.6 The Conflict Between Flesh and Spirit[74]
9.6.1 Receiving and Walking

In Galatians 5:16–25 Paul says,

> But I say, walk by the Spirit, and you will not gratify the desires of the flesh. For the desires of the flesh are against the Spirit, and the desires of the Spirit are against the flesh, for these are opposed to each other, to keep you from doing the things you want to do. But if you are led by the Spirit, you are not under the law. . . . [T]he fruit of the Spirit is love, joy, peace, patience, kindness, goodness, faithfulness, gentleness, self-control; against such things there is no law. And those who belong to Christ Jesus have crucified the flesh with its passions and desires. If we live by the Spirit, let us also keep in step with the Spirit.

Before this, the apostle had written, "Are you so foolish? Having begun by the Spirit, are you now being perfected by the flesh?" (3:3). In chapter 5 this subject of the Spirit is elaborated.[75] The Christian's new nature itself has no power; if the believer did not have the Spirit, or did not open up to the Spirit's working (cf. Rom. 7:15–24; see §8.7.2), the flesh could again become dominant all too easily, and choke the believer's new life. However, the believer did receive the Spirit, who constitutes a source of internal power by which one can live according to God's will. But it is not enough to have *received* the Spirit; the believer is responsible for truly *walking* in the power of the Spirit. One does so by staying close to God, close to Christ in prayer, by allowing the Word to speak personally, and by developing a spirit of dependence and obedience.

The person walking by (or in) the power of the Spirit, orienting the course of one's life to the Spirit's guidance, simply no longer has room for the works of the flesh. The "you will" in verse 16 is an ordinary future tense, not an imperative. One who is filled with Christ no longer has any room for the de-

---
74. See extensively, Mauerhofer (1980, especially §§3.1 and 3.2).
75. Ouweneel (1997, 339–65).

sires of the flesh. The first part of verse 16 is a command, the second part is a promise that will be realized if the believer carries out the command. Pour oil in a glass filled with alcohol, and the heavier oil ("of the Spirit") will expel the alcohol ("for that is debauchery") from the glass. Wait for spring, and the tender young leaves of the oak (the "fruit of the Spirit," v. 22) will cause the autumn leaves that still hang at the tree to fall away. The formal command in Christian living is to let the Spirit work, with *theosis* as one's aim.

To be sure, the Greek term *pneuma* in verse 16 does not refer to the human spirit, for this knows the desires of the flesh just as much as the soul and the body. Rather, this is the Holy Spirit, just as in 3:3, 6:8, and Romans 8:4–9, 12–14.[76] Each time the context is decisive; thus, in 1 Corinthians 5:5 and Hebrews 12:9 the flesh does oppose the human spirit (cf. also 2 Cor. 7:1).

9.6.2 Two Antagonists

Galatians 5:17 says, "For the flesh lusts against the Spirit, and the Spirit against the flesh" (NKJV). The word "and" renders the Greek word *de*, which sometimes indicates a certain expansion: "yes, what is more" (cf. Gk. *de* in Titus 1:1): "For the flesh lusts against the Spirit, yes, the Spirit against the flesh." These two powers are mutual antagonists. Our sinful flesh (the "old nature") and the Holy Spirit within us "lust" (or "desire"; see Luke 22:15; Phil. 1:23) against each other. That is, within a person the flesh tries to prevail over the Spirit, and the Spirit in turn tries to gain the upper hand over the flesh. This leads to genuine warfare in the believer's heart; Peter speaks of "the passions of the flesh, which wage war against your soul" (1 Pet. 2:11). Both antagonists attempt to gain dominance.

The purpose of this battle is "to keep you from doing the things you want to do."[77] Verse 17 seems to suggest that the

---

76. *Contra* O'Neill and Windisch, quoted by Fung (1988, 249).
77. Gal. 5 differs fundamentally from Rom. 7 (see § 8.7.2); *contra* Ridderbos

person's Ego is a will-less instrument, a plaything tossed to and fro between the flesh and the Spirit. However, the believer possesses not only the flesh (the old, sinful nature) and the indwelling Holy Spirit, but also the new nature (the regenerated Ego). This is the renewed "I" of Romans 7:17 and 20, which knows how to distinguish itself from "sin that dwells within me." "That which . . . is born of the Spirit is spirit" (John 3:6): this is the new nature, which exhibits the characteristics of the Spirit from whom it issued. The "new nature" is the nature (character) of the "new man" (Gk. *kainos anthrōpos*; Eph. 2:15; 4:24; Col. 3:10–11; or translated as "new person," and less accurately as "new self"). This is the person redeemed by Christ, the regenerated, believing person, who longs to serve and obey God.

Please note, the Spirit *is* not the new nature, but he is the divine person who dwells in the believer, and grants the latter's new nature a power that the person does not have inherently. Romans 8 and Galatians 5 describe the "new person," who not only longs to do good, but who by the power of the Holy Spirit also concretely performs good. The new nature *wishes* to do the will of God, but *cannot* do this on its own, and therefore *allows* the Spirit to work within, and the Spirit performs this good in and through the "new person." This is the same as saying that the "new person" performs this good in the power of the Holy Spirit. Being led by the Spirit means restraining the old, sinful nature in the power of the Spirit, and accomplishing God's commandments with a joyful heart.

The "new person" is not a passive plaything being tossed between the flesh and the Spirit, but that person actively *sides* with the Spirit. The believer's new nature hates the works of the flesh, and longs to produce the fruit of the Spirit (cf. vv. 19–22). Therefore, verse 18 says, "But if you are led by the Spirit. . . ." The new nature would like nothing more; being

---

(1959, 204) and Boice (1976, 495). Gal. 5 involves the flesh against the Spirit; Rom. 7 involves the flesh against the regenerated "I" who does not yet experience the power of the Spirit.

led by the Spirit is the natural characteristic of true sons of God (Rom. 8:14; see §9.4). This *being* led therefore does not suggest passivity, but an active longing by the "new person," who consciously opens oneself to the guidance of the Spirit. Thus, Paul says in this verse in a comforting way, Don't worry about this inner warfare between flesh and Spirit, for if you allow yourself simply to be led by the Spirit, you will automatically produce the fruit of the Spirit. In this way, being led by the Spirit does not differ essentially from walking by the Spirit (v. 16). The new nature decides whether to be led by the Spirit or by the flesh—and we do realize that such a decision is itself dependent on the Spirit, "for it is God who works in you, both to will and to work for his good pleasure" (Phil. 2:13).

9.6.3   A Fine Balance

This sensitive equilibrium between the Spirit's guiding and the person's responsibility ought not to be disturbed in either direction. On the one hand, if believers go astray, they themselves are to be blamed; at best one might say that God *allows* this in order to teach his children a necessary lesson. If they ignore God's counsel, they cannot blame *him* for this. On the other hand, if they safely reach the finish line, it is due to *his* grace. This is true even though he credits the believers for it; otherwise something like "rewards" could not exist (Matt. 5:12; 6:4, 6, 18; 1 Cor. 3:14; 9:17–18; Col. 3:24; Heb. 10:34; 2 John 1:8; Rev. 11:18; 22:12). Yet, if they joyfully walk down the right path, they can never take personal credit for doing so (cf. 1 Pet. 4:18, "the righteous is scarcely saved"). Jesus said to his disciples, "So you also, when you have done all that you were commanded, say, 'We are unworthy servants; we have only done what was our duty'" (Luke 17:10). But he also says to the faithful servants, "Well done, good servant!" (19:17).

The final line in Galatians 5:18 is quite remarkable. Paul says, "[I]f you are led by the Spirit, you are not under the law." Thereby Paul is showing that the conflict between faith and law (see Gal. 3 and 4) is closely related to that between Spirit and flesh. The Pharisaic observance of the law is not the best protection against the works of the flesh, because a person does not have inherent power to accomplish the law. Pharisaic observance of the law *is* typically something *of* the flesh (cf. Phil. 3:1-6, especially v. 3), and enhances rather than subdues the activity of the flesh (Rom. 7:5, 8-11). This is not because the law is not good (on the contrary, Rom. 7:12), but because humans are not good. When we combine Galatians 5:16 ("walk by the Spirit, and you will not gratify the desires of the flesh") and 18 ("if you are led by the Spirit, you are not under the law"), we see that being under the law and gratifying the desires of the flesh belong together.

Of course, I am referring here to the Mosaic Torah, and the attempts of the flesh to observe it. In opposition to this, there is a deep coherence between fulfilling the law *of Christ* (Gal. 6:2) and being led by the Spirit.[78] The pathway for the Christian is *not* one of fulfilling the Mosaic Law in *one's own* (supposed) strength, but of fulfilling the law of Christ in *the Spirit's* strength. There are two differences here: two forms of the Law, and two sources of strength. The former pathway (that of the Mosaic Law and one's own strength) enhances the works of the flesh (v. 19), the latter pathway (that of the law of Christ and the Spirit's strength) produces the fruit of the Spirit (v. 22).

Paul says, as it were, If you are led by the Spirit, you show in this way that you belong to a very different order of things than that of the Mosaic Torah, namely, that of faith in Christ. The person who is led by the Spirit no longer has anything to do with the works of the flesh *as well as* with that order of things that does not suppress but rather advances the works of the flesh. The Holy Spirit fulfills in us the righteous requirement of the law (Rom. 8:4)—though *we* are no longer under the law but under the Spirit, which is the same as being "un-

---

78. See extensively, Ouweneel (2017b).

der grace" (6:14-15).

Insofar as we are bound to a law it is the "law of the Spirit of life" (Rom. 8:2), the "law of Christ" (Gal. 6:2; 1 Cor. 9:21), the "law of liberty" (James 1:25; 2:12), the "commandments" of Jesus (John 13:34; 14:15, 21; 15:10, 12), and this is the liberty of the Spirit (2 Cor. 3:17). As Thomas Aquinas put it, a person who avoids evil, not because it is evil but because of a law of the Lord, is not free. On the other hand, the person who avoids evil because it is evil, is free. It is here that the Holy Spirit works, inwardly perfecting our spirit by communicating to it a new dynamic, and this functions so well that the person refrains from evil out of love, as if the divine law commanded him to do so.[79]

9.7 The Fruit of the Spirit
9.7.1 Introduction

In Galatians 5:19-22, Paul again places the flesh in opposition to the Spirit. First he enumerates fifteen or sixteen[80] "works of the flesh," then the nine-fold "fruit of the Spirit." He who lives by the flesh cannot have a share in the kingdom of God; but he who has "crucified" the flesh, and lives by the Spirit as well as walks by the Spirit, can have such a share. Paul's list of the "works of the flesh" contains a number of *sexual* sins (sexual immorality, impurity, sensuality), *religious* sins (idolatry, sorcery), and *social* sins (enmity, strife, jealousy, fits of anger), party spirit (rivalries, dissensions, divisions), hatred (envy, [murder]), and excess (drunkenness, orgies).

In opposition to the works of the flesh, Paul places the fruit of the Spirit (vv. 22-23). The term "works" (plural) suggest concrete acts, although these cannot be severed from the inner attitude, present especially in works like enmity or envy. The term "fruit" (singular) suggests the inner attitude

---

79. Quoted in Congar (1997, 2.125).
80. The exact number depends on whether "murders" (Gk. *phonoi*) belongs to v. 21; see Metzger (1975, 597-98). For those fascinated with numbers: in comparison with the ninefold fruit of the Spirit, the number fifteen is appropriate (3×5 corresponds to 3×3), as is sixteen (4^2 corresponds to 3^2).

of the heart, although this cannot be severed from the concrete actions issuing from the heart: the *demonstration* of love, joy, peace, and so on, in concrete attitudes and deeds.[81] Many works of the flesh can be enumerated, which can differ, and are not all manifested in the same person. However, in a sense there is only one fruit of the Spirit; the nine aspects of it are not available separately. A believer may be very loving and glad, but if one is not patient or faithful, in fact the entire fruit is spoiled. The nine aspects belong to an inseparable whole: they are, to employ a metaphor,[82] not nine oranges but nine segments of one orange.

There is another difference: the "works of the flesh" are works by people themselves because, even though these are "works of the law" (2:16; 3:2, 5, 10), it is one's own flesh (sinful nature) that performs these works. However, the fruit is the fruit of the Holy Spirit, which he produces in and through believers. This certainly involves their own responsibility and active participation (cf. 2 Pet. 1:5-7), yet the Spirit produces the fruit. It is produced not by the observance of the law in one's own strength, for legalism itself is a work of the flesh. It is produced not even by the new nature in its own strength, for the latter *has* no strength in itself. The entire fruit must come from the Spirit. Insofar as the law has anything to do with it (see v. 23 and 6:2), it is the Spirit who fulfills in the believer the righteous requirement of the law (Rom. 8:4).

The nine segments of the one fruit of the Spirit must not be confused with the nine *charismata* of the Spirit (see §12.2). For instance, among these *charismata* we find faith (1 Cor. 12:9), which occurs in Galatians 5:22 as well (Gk. *pistis* can mean both "faith" and "faithfulness"). However, the relationships between the Holy Spirit and *pistis* are at least threefold:

---

[81]. Gregory the Great argued that, just as we cannot see the sun but we can see its shining upon the landscape, so we cannot see the Holy Spirit but we can see the Spirit's fruits and wondrous works in the lives of holy people; see Burgess (1997a, 16).

[82]. Of course, the term "fruit" itself is a metaphor.

(1) *Saving* faith is a gift that all believers have received through the Holy Spirit: "For by grace you have been saved through faith. And this is not your own doing; it is the gift of God" (Eph. 2:8).

(2) In Galatians 5:22 the Greek word *pistis* has the sense of "faithfulness" (although KJV and many later translations [not NKJV] have "faith"); here it is one of the Spirit-worked aspects of common Christian living.

(3) In 1 Corinthians 12:9, faith is a special gift, granted at a certain moment when the believer needs it in a special way, and reaches out for it (see §12.4.1). This is the faith that moves mountains (Matt. 17:20; 21:21; 1 Cor. 13:2). Some believers receive this act of great faith (Gk. *pistis*) at a particular moment—whereas all believers should exhibit faithfulness (the other use of *pistis*) all the time.

Please note that here we are not dealing with aspects that are given automatically when the Spirit is granted to a person. Manifesting the fruit of the Spirit is a matter of practical spiritual growth and sanctification of life. Unfortunately, it is possible to have received the Spirit, and yet be so carnal,[83] that is, manifesting so many works of the flesh, that the fruit of the Spirit becomes hardly visible (cf. "carnal," being "of the flesh," in Rom. 7:14, 1 Cor. 3:1, 3, and 1 Pet. 2:11; cf. also "grieving" and "quenching" the Spirit, in Eph. 4:30 and 1 Thess. 5:19).

Speaking of the fruit of the Spirit, it is remarkable that in 2 Corinthians 6:6 (". . . by purity, knowledge, patience, kindness, [the] Holy Spirit, genuine love") the Holy Spirit *himself* seems to be one of the fruits of the Spirit. Perhaps by way of exception, here the expression means "in a holy spirit,"[84] or it is in apposition to "kindness"; the Greek *en chrēstotēti en pneumatic hagiōi* could then mean "by kindness in [the power of] the Holy Spirit."

---

83. The term "carnal" (from Lat. *caro*, "flesh") is rather outdated; cf. KJV and modern translations in the passages mentioned.
84. DLNT; NRSV; Hughes (1962, 228–29); Harris (1976, 357).

9.7.2 Inner Excellency

I am now going to arrange the nine segments of the Spirit's fruit into three groups of three. This arrangement must not be applied too rigidly; a strict division is impossible. The three groups overlap because, for instance, love and gentleness, too, involve people's relationships with their neighbors. Only the first group can be easily distinguished from the other six elements. The well-known arrangement according to one's relationship to God (1-3), to the neighbor (4-6), and to oneself (7-9) is hardly tenable, because love (first category), and even self-control (second category), cannot be severed from one's relationship to the neighbor. Rendall suggested that *all* nine elements involve one's relationships to one's neighbors.[85] Hendriksen saw in the first category fundamental moral features, in the second category relationships to fellow-believers, and in the last category relationships to God, to all people, and to oneself, respectively.[86]

In his upper room discourses, Jesus connected the first group of virtues with each other. He spoke of "my love" (John 15:9-10), "my joy" (v. 11), and "my peace" (14:17) (apart from "my glory" in 17:24). Paul connected the three directly with the Holy Spirit in Romans 5:5 ("God's love has been poured into our hearts through the Holy Spirit who has been given to us") and 14:17 ("the kingdom of God is . . . a matter of . . . righteousness and peace and joy in the Holy Spirit"). All true love, joy and peace, insofar as they surpass mere human emotions, are a fruit of the Spirit.

(1) *Love* (Gk. *agapē*). Since Paul placed so much emphasis on love earlier in the chapter (vv. 13-14), it is understandable that he opened the list with this virtue. In Colossians 3:12-14 love is the "bond of perfection" (NKJV) that encompasses all previous virtues. Love is the nature of God himself (1 John 4:8, 16), but he has poured it out in believers' hearts through the Holy Spirit (Rom. 5:5). If there is one virtue that should char-

---
85. Rendall (1979, 188).
86. Hendriksen (1968, ad loc.).

acterize Christian living, it is love (see in Paul's letters, e.g., Rom. 14:15; 1 Cor. 8:1, 13; 12:31; 13:13; 16:14, 24; 2 Cor. 2:4, 7–8; Eph. 1:15; 4:15; 5:2; Col. 2:2): "love of the Spirit" (Rom. 15:30); "love in the Spirit" (Col. 1:8). It might even be presumed that *the* fruit of the Spirit is love, and that joy, peace, patience, kindness, goodness, faithfulness, gentleness, and self-control are nothing but special aspects and effects of love.

(2) *Joy* (Gk. *chara*; cf. the old term: *charity* from Latin *caritas*). This term does not refer here to the common human (natural) joy in earthly things themselves (e.g., Eccl. 9:7), although there is nothing wrong with this kind of joy. Rather it refers to joy "in the Lord" (Phil. 3:1; 4:4; cf. Neh. 8:10, "the joy of the Lord is your strength"). The believer can experience this joy when earthly circumstances give rise only to sadness (2 Cor. 6:10; 8:2; 1 Thess. 5:16; cf. Phil. 2:27–28 with 3:1). Real joy is "joy in the Holy Spirit," that is, worked by the Spirit, or in the power of the Spirit (Rom. 14:17, the kingdom of God is a matter of "righteousness and peace and joy in the Holy Spirit"; cf. Luke 10:21, Jesus "rejoiced in the Holy Spirit"; 1 Thess. 1:6, "the joy of the Holy Spirit").

(3) *Peace* (Gk. *eirēnē*). This virtue entails an inner state of rest, calm, and harmony (cf. 1 Cor. 14:33, "God is not a God of confusion but of peace"). The equivalent Hebrew term *shalom* implies wholeness, health, prosperity, well-being, safety, not only for oneself, but particularly in relationships with other people (Rom. 12:18, "live peaceably with all") and with God, both positionally (Rom. 5:1, "since we have been justified by faith, we have peace with God") and practically (Phil. 4:6–7, "the peace of God . . . will guard your hearts and your minds in Christ Jesus"). Peace, too, involves the Spirit directly, for the "unity of the Spirit" is maintained "in the bond of peace." In Romans 14:17 and 15:13, peace is related to the Spirit, but then coupled with joy. God himself is called the "God of peace" (Rom. 16:20; 1 Cor. 14:33; 2 Cor. 13:11, "the God of love and peace"; Phil. 4:9; 1 Thess. 5:23; Heb. 13:20).

9.7.3 Benevolence Toward Others

The next three features all involve a patient, kind, benevolent attitude toward other people. In 1 Corinthians 13:4-6 ("Love is patient and kind; love does not envy or boast; it is not arrogant or rude. It does not insist on its own way; it is not irritable or resentful; it does not rejoice at wrongdoing, but rejoices with the truth"), we find patience, kindness, and tolerance as characteristics of love. This corroborates the idea that the actual fruit of the Spirit is love, and that the next eight virtues are simply particular aspects of love. 2 Corinthians 6:6 and 10 ("... patience, kindness, the Holy Spirit, genuine love ... as sorrowful, yet always rejoicing ...") combines love and joy from the first category of virtues with patience and kindness from the second category.

(4) *Patience* (Gk. *makrothymia*), or longsuffering, forbearance, tolerance. We have seen that God is love, and that he is the God of peace. Similarly, being patient ("slow to anger") is an attribute of God, together with mercy, grace, and goodness (Exod. 34:6; Neh. 9:17; Ps. 86:15; 103:8; 145:8; Joel 2:13; Jonah 4:2; also see Num. 14:18; Rom. 2:4; 2 Pet. 3:9). Just like God, the Spirit-filled believer is full of patience, "slow to anger," slow with punishment and retribution (2 Cor. 6:6; Eph. 4:1; Col. 3:12; 1 Thess. 5:14), but also patient and forbearing under oppressions inflicted by others (Rom. 5:3; 12:12; 2 Cor. 1:6; 6:4; 2 Thess. 1:4; James 1:2-3).

(5) *Kindness* (Gk. *chrēstotēs*), or kindheartedness, gentleness, benignity. In some of the Old Testament passages just quoted, we find the expression "abundant (or abounding) in goodness [ESV: steadfast love, Heb. *chesed*]" (Exod. 34:6; Num. 14:18; Neh. 9:17; Ps. 86:15 [cf. v. 5]; 103:8; 145:8; Joel 2:13; Jonah 4:2; cf. Rom. 2:4). This entails a friendly, benevolent, favorable attitude toward others. Here, too, the believer is called to exhibit the image of God (cf. Eph. 5:1; regarding God's character, see Rom. 11:22; Eph. 2:7; Titus 3:4; regarding the believer's character, see Luke 6:35; 2 Cor. 6:6; Eph. 4:32; Col. 3:12; and in

a more general sense: 1 Cor. 3:4).

The Greek term *chrēstotēs* comes from *chrēstos*, "good, generous, benevolent." Some ancient writers referred to Christ (Gk. *Christos*, "Anointed One") as Chrestos ("Good, Kind One"), presumably as a mistaken spelling.[87] The inhabitants of Antioch, too, confused the names Christos and Chrestos; in Acts 11:26 some manuscripts read not *christianoi* ("Christians") but *chrēstianoi*. The problem was exacerbated when, in the second century, the Greek vowels *i* and *ē* began to be pronounced alike (so-called iotacism).

(6) *Goodness* (Gk. *agathōsynē*), or benevolence, generosity. The passages just mentioned that contain the phrase "abounding in goodness" could be connected just as easily, or more easily, with this term *agathōsynē*. The term *agathos* ("good") is sometimes linked with *dikaios* ("just, righteous") (Rom. 5:7; Eph. 5:9), giving to others what is just and fair. Compare here Matthew 20:4, 13, 15, where the goodness of the master consists in his generosity (in v. 15 the ESV has "generosity" where the Greek says *agathos*; see the alternate reading). This goodness is opposed to the "bad eye" (cf. the KJV: "Is thine eye evil, because I am good?") of the first laborers, who begrudge the last laborers their wages.

9.7.4 Other Moral Features

The following characteristics, too, basically concern a person's relationships to others, even the characteristic of self-control. In fact, it is interesting to notice that the New Testament never deals with what we might call a purely individualistic "character building" or "self-actualization,"[88] but always with the neighbor's well-being.

(7) *Faithfulness* (Gk. *pistis*), or faith, fidelity. It is true, of course, that saving faith is produced in the person's heart by the Holy Spirit (cf. Eph. 2:8). Elsewhere in Galatians, the Greek

---

87. Suetonius (*Life of Claudius* 25.4).
88. The term was coined by Goldstein (1995); the notion itself is important enough.

term *pistis* is indeed always rendered as "faith." However, in the present verse we are dealing with a fruit of the Spirit that is produced in practical Christian living, and which, like all the other character aspects, primarily involves the believer's relationship to other people. Therefore, most translations and expositors suppose that here the Greek term *pistis* means "faithfulness," "reliability," "trustworthiness," "loyalty." Note as well that the Greek adjective *pistos* in the New Testament is the common word for "faithful" (loyal, reliable). In Matthew 23:23, Jesus mentions "faithfulness" (Gk. *pistis*) along with "justice [Gk. *krisis*, judgment] and mercy [Gk. *eleos*]" as being the "weightier matters" of the Mosaic Torah (also see "merciful and faithful" together in Heb. 2:19). Romans 3:3 speaks of the "faithfulness [KJV: faith] of God." 2 Thessalonians 3:2 says that "not all have faith," where one might expect that at least some English translations would have "faithfulness"; the TLV comes closest: "not all are trustworthy." In Titus 2:10, "showing all good faith" can also be rendered as "showing all good fidelity" (KJV) or "faithfulness" (GNV), or "proving themselves trustworthy" (AMP). The Greek noun *pistis* can mean "trust in God"; but as a fruit of the Spirit it means that the *believer personally* can be trusted.

(8) *Gentleness* (Gk. *pra-ytēs*[89]), or meekness, humility, mildness, lowliness. This is not "gentle" or "meek" in the sense of soft, weak, languid, cowardly, which in fact means characterless. Rather, the term refers to kindness, compliance, indulgence, peacefulness, tolerance, the capacity of "giving in" when necessary or advisable, but always presupposing inner strength. We see this most clearly in Jesus; he was "gentle [Gk. *pra-ys*] and lowly [Gk. *tapeinos*] of heart" (Matt. 11:29), "humble [Gk. *pra-ys*]" (21:5). Yet, the same Matthew tells us that "Jesus entered the temple and drove out all who sold and bought in the temple, and he overturned the tables of the money-changers and the seats of those who sold pigeons"

---

89. In this word, the *a* (as in car) and the *y* (as in lynch) must be pronounced as two distinct syllables.

(21:12). On another occasion, Jesus expressed the combination of anger and sadness: "[H]e looked around at them with anger, grieved at their hardness of heart" (Mark 3:5). In Paul, too, we see a combination of gentleness and severity: "Shall I come to you with a rod, or with love in a spirit of gentleness [Gk. *pra-ytēs*]?" (1 Cor. 4:21). "I, Paul, . . . by the meekness [Gk. *pra-ytēs*] and gentleness [Gk. *epeikeia*] of Christ..." (2 Cor. 10:1). "Brothers, if anyone is caught in any transgression, you who are spiritual should restore him in a spirit of gentleness [Gk. *pra-ytēs*]" (Gal. 6:1). This spiritual energy, wrapped in gentleness, leads us to the last virtue.

(9) *Self-control* (Gk. *enkrateia*), or temperance, continence, self-restraint. This is the capacity of controlling oneself, one's passions, drives, and so on. This is the capacity that an athlete must learn: "Every athlete exercises self-control in all things" (1 Cor. 9:25), and that is also important for elders (Titus 1:8) and unmarried people (1 Cor. 7:9). If indeed the word refers particularly to a check upon sexual impulses, this virtue would form a counterbalance with respect to the sexual immorality, impurity, and sensuality mentioned in Galatians 5:19. At the same time, self-control does not imply some form of asceticism that would be an aim in itself, but rather a means to attain a higher goal: "Do not deprive one another, except perhaps by agreement for a limited time, that you may devote yourselves to prayer; but then come together again, so that Satan may not tempt you because of your lack of self-control" (1 Cor. 7:5; cf. 9:25–27). In short: self-control entails governing oneself with respect to others in order to fulfill God's will in one's relationship with him and with other people (cf. Acts 24:25).

9.8 The Remainder of Galatians 5
9.8.1 The Fruit and the Law

In Galatians 5:21, Paul adds the phrase "things like these," indicating that his list of works of the flesh is not exhaustive. In the same way, he speaks in verse 23 of "such things," which again implies that, in addition to the nine virtues, others could have been mentioned. Thus, we find hope, alongside faith and love (1 Cor. 13:13); righteousness and holiness (Eph. 4:24); alongside kindness, meekness, and patience we find compassionate hearts and humility (Col. 3:12). Thus, alongside faith, Peter mentions self-control and love, virtue, knowledge, steadfastness, godliness, and brotherly affection (2 Pet. 1:5–7). We might mention as well the six virtues of the Spirit in Isaiah 11:2: wisdom, understanding, counsel, might, knowledge, and the fear of the LORD (godliness) (§6.2.1). Perhaps, Paul is mentioning in Galatians 5:22–23 especially those virtues that were of particular relevance to the Galatian Christians.

In verse 23b Paul says, "[A]gainst such things [Gk. *toioutōn*] there is no law." Many translations do not read "such things" but simply "such," which could also mean "such persons." The sense is that there is no law whatsoever that could possibly turn against "such virtues" or "such virtuous people." There is no article before "law" (Gk. *nomos*); therefore, the sentence does not necessarily refer to the Mosaic Torah. No law whatsoever would prohibit anything like the fruit of the Spirit. Yet, within the context of the entire letter Paul is probably thinking especially of the Mosaic Torah; perhaps we should translate, "[The] law is not against these things" (cf. NLV). In the fruit of the Spirit the Mosaic Torah finds nothing blameworthy. On the contrary, saying that the Spirit works this fruit in believers is the same as saying that the Spirit fulfills in them the righteous requirement of the law (Rom. 8:4).

Thus, "the law is not against it" is a euphemism for saying, These are the very things that the law encourages. Anyone who demonstrates the fruit of the Spirit *fulfills* the Torah according to the *spirit* of the Torah. The law does demand, but the law itself can give me neither the right motivation, nor the proper spiritual strength. The Holy Spirit can give me both. And when he works in us, the law finds in our lives nothing to complain about. But not only that: God's very will, as it becomes manifest in the Torah, is accomplished.[90]

9.8.2 In Step With the Spirit

Paul argued that flesh and Spirit are opposed to each other, and that the flesh produces evil works, but the Spirit produces precious fruit. In Galatians 5:24 he states that believers — "those who belong to Christ Jesus" — have "crucified the flesh with its passions and desires," and thus he can conclude in verse 25 that they "live by the Spirit," and therefore: "[L]et us also keep in step with the Spirit." Please note verse 24 speaks of an accomplished fact: they *have* crucified (aorist tense) the flesh, once and for all. In coming to faith, they have once and for all acknowledged the fact that Jesus' work on the cross involved the absolute end of the power of the flesh. In the light of this, the command of verse 25 is fitting: "Keep in step with the Spirit."

Here again we encounter the well-known tension between, on the one hand, accomplished divine salvation and, on the other hand, the believer's continual responsibility to work this out in a practical way. The flesh *has been* crucified by faith — let us now walk accordingly. Paul presents the crucifixion of the flesh as a well-established redemptive fact, which at the same time is the believer's activity. Of course it is God who has nailed the "old self" to the cross of Christ, and has condemned it once and for all (cf. 2:20; Rom. 6:6). However, when a person comes to faith, that believer actively accepts this divine judgment upon the "old person," identifies personally with it, so that the believer, as it were, in faith personally executes God's sentence upon one's own flesh.

Paul argues that, as a matter of principle, believers *have* crucified the flesh when they came to faith. But where this flesh (the sinful nature) is nonetheless manifested anew, they must actively put these carnal activities to death, that is, place them under the death sentence of Christ, by the power of the Holy Spirit: "So put to death [and] deprive of power the evil

---

90. See extensively, Ouweneel (2017b).

longings of your earthly body" (Col. 3:5 AMP). Instead of such evil things, believers should endeavor to produce good fruit by the power of the Holy Spirit.

Paul includes himself in the command of verses 25–26: "If we live by the Spirit, let us also keep in step with the Spirit. Let us not become conceited, provoking one another, envying one another." Notice the two verbs: If we *live* Spirit-wise (Gk. *pneumati*), then we will *walk* Spirit-wise (Gk. *pneumati*).[91] That is, if the former is true, prove this through the latter: by our walking in the Spirit it becomes manifest that a person lives by the Spirit. The latter is taken for granted: "Where it is true that. . . ," that is, a person who by faith has received life from God, has received it through the Spirit, and lives by this Spirit (cf. 2:20). However, this must be continually realized in a practical way. This is a principle that we encounter often with Paul: realize what you are; be practically what you are positionally.

Many Christians neglect either one or the other. They emphasize either the certainty of the Christian position, without sufficiently realizing this in Christian practice (cf. James 2:14–16). Thus, they give rise to the question whether indeed they *are* in this position. Or they emphasize Christian practice, and because that is often so miserable they begin doubting their Christian position. Paul never allows us to fall into either of these extremes. He argues that, where the Spirit is the source of the new life that believers have received, the Spirit should also be the source of the deeds that they now perform as fruits of this new life. In other words, let them no longer produce the works of the flesh but rather the fruit of the Spirit.

9.8.3 The Harvest of the Spirit

Let me add a minor point here. Lucien Cerfaux prefers to

---

91. The sense is indeed "walking," but the verb is not the same as in verse 16 (Gk. *peripateō*); it is *stoicheō*, as in 6:16 (cf. Rom. 4:12; Phil. 3:16). This verb is related to the Gk. noun *stoicheia* in Gal. 4:3 and 9, and means "walking in a row," "keeping in step with." Materially, there is not much difference between "walking" and "keeping in step with," and also "being led" (v. 18).

translate the Greek noun *karpos* in Galatians 5:22 not as "fruit" but as "harvest" of the Spirit.[92] Such a rendering leads us immediately to chapter 6:7-8, "Do not be deceived: God is not mocked, for whatever one sows, that will he also reap. For the one who sows to his own flesh will from the flesh reap corruption, but the one who sows to the Spirit will from the Spirit reap eternal life." The expression "sowing to one's own flesh/to the Spirit" means developing a way of life that pleases either the (sinful) flesh or the Holy Spirit (cf. 5:16, "gratify the desires of the flesh"; v. 18, being "led by the Spirit"; v. 25, keeping "in step with the Spirit").[93]

Paul underscores the effects of both types of sowing. The former type leads to destruction, which over against eternal life must involve eternal destruction (cf. 2 Pet. 2:12b).[94] Compare the ERV: "If you live to satisfy your sinful self, the harvest you will get from that will be eternal death. But if you live to please the Spirit, your harvest from the Spirit will be eternal life." The latter type is a "sowing *to* [the pleasure of] the Spirit" who dwells in believers. Note once more the apostle's emphasis on the believer's personal responsibility.

If we view the matter from the viewpoint of God's divine grace, then by the power of this very Spirit the believer will produce a proper harvest. The believer cannot please the indwelling Spirit in any other way than by the very power of this Spirit. The harvest of such a Spirit-pleasing life is eternal life, which, for Paul, always means the eternal bliss with Christ, in connection with either heaven or the kingdom to be revealed (Rom. 2:7; 5:21; 6:22-23; 1 Tim. 1:16; Titus 1:2; 3:7). Through the same Spirit, the foretaste of this coming harvest can be enjoyed today (1 Tim. 6:12, 19).

---

92. Cerfaux (1967, 461-63).
93. Ouweneel (1997, 381-82).
94. Cf. the contrast between "eternal punishment" and "eternal life" in Matt. 25:46.

9.9 Some Remaining Aspects
9.9.1 Practical Sanctification

In §8.2.4 we dealt with sanctification and justification through the Spirit. The subject there was *positional* sanctification; in addition to this, there is *practical* sanctification.[95] We have seen that the distinction between position and practice is of vital importance. The former sanctification occurs once and for all, namely, at the moment when a person comes to faith in Christ. One is then "in Christ"; this is one's unchangeable position. Therefore, whenever the New Testament speaks of this sanctification, it does so always in terms of the past. A person *has been* sanctified (i.e., made holy) once and for all, and so one *is* holy. However, when the topic is ordinary Christian living, that is, one's *practice*, then one must still *become* holy (sanctified), that is, realize practically what one is positionally.

As far as their Christian position is concerned, believers are holy (sanctified, made *sanctus*, "holy") and righteous (justified, made *iustus*, "righteous"). This is why believers are often referred to as "saints" (holy ones), "holy brothers," or "sanctified."[96] *Practical* sanctification (becoming holy) means again, "be what you are," realize practically what you are positionally, that is, before God in Christ. *God* is holy, *you* in Christ are now holy too, therefore *behave* in a holy way.

An example of this, in which the Holy Spirit is involved, is the following: "God has not called us for impurity, but in holiness. Therefore whoever disregards this, disregards not man but God, who gives his Holy Spirit to you" (1 Thess. 4:7–8). Notice that it is not "for" (as in the case of impurity) but "in" holiness. This refers to the atmosphere or settled condition in

---
95. See Ouweneel (1999, chapters 3–5).
96. In addition to epistolary greetings, see Matt. 27:52; Acts 9:13, 32, 41; 20:32; 26:10, 17–18; Rom. 1:7; 8:27; 12:13; 15:25–26, 31; 16:2, 15; 1 Cor. 6:1–2; 14:34; 16:1, 15; 2 Cor. 8:4; 9:1, 12; 13:12; Eph. 1:15, 18; 2:19; 3:8, 18; 4:12; 5:3; 6:18; Phil. 4:22; Col. 1:4, 12, 26; 3:12; 1 Thess. 3:13; 5:27; 2 Thess. 1:10; 1 Tim. 5:10; Titus 2:3; Philem. 1:5, 7; Heb. 3:1; 6:10; 10:10, 14; 13:24; 1 Pet. 3:5; 2 Pet. 1:21; Jude 1:3; Rev. 5:8; 8:3–4; 11:18; 13:7, 10; 14:12; 16:6; 17:6; 18:20, 24; 19:8; 20:9; 22:21.

which the Christian must walk.[97] Next, it does not say "gives you [Gk. *humin*] his Spirit," but "*to* you [Gk. *eis humas*]," or even "in you": "gives His Holy Spirit to you [to dwell in you and empower you to overcome temptation]" (AMP). The passage unmistakably refers to practical sanctification, which faces the believer as a continual challenge and responsibility (see also 2 Cor. 7:1; Heb. 12:14; 1 Pet. 1:15–16 [cf. Lev. 11:44–45]; 2 Pet. 3:11). Paul emphasizes that this practical holiness can be realized only in the power of the Holy Spirit, which God has given to believers especially for this purpose. Impurity, then, is a sin against the Holy Spirit.

In this passage the adjective *holy* modifying *Spirit* has special impact, even more so because of the order of the Greek words: *to pneuma autou to hagion*, "his Spirit, the holy One." Believers must learn to live in accordance with the holy character of the Spirit who dwells in them.[98] Paul makes a similar appeal in a context that again involves a warning against immorality: "Flee from sexual immorality. . . . Or do you not know that your body is a temple of the Holy Spirit within you, whom you have from God? You are not your own, for you were bought with a price. So glorify God in your body" (1 Cor. 6:18–19; cf. 3:16–17).

It is remarkable that, in 1 Thessalonians 4:8, God is called the "Giver" of the Holy Spirit such that, as the Greek verbal form *didonta* (present participle) suggests, this "giving" is an ongoing act of God.[99] That is, he is the One who makes the power of the Holy Spirit continually available to us, so that we have no excuse for impurity.[100] He who disregards this power and surrenders to sexual immorality, thereby disregards (KJV: despiseth; NKJV: rejects) the Giver of this power.

---

97. Morris (1959, 128).
98. Without any apparent basis, Moffatt connects this with baptism (1979, 27).
99. Some manuscripts have Gk. *donta* (aorist), an apparent change by copyists who wanted to emphasize the one-time gift of the Spirit.
100. Morris (1959, 128).

9.9.2 Praying in the Spirit

The New Testament speaks twice of a "praying in the Spirit," first in the description of the "armor of God": ". . . praying at all times in the Spirit, with all prayer and supplication. To that end, keep alert with all perseverance, making supplication for all the saints" (Eph. 6:18). After having mentioned six metaphorical pieces of armor, from the belt to the helmet, Paul does not give a metaphor for the seventh piece of armor, but refers to it in straightforward language: *prayer*. Praying "in the Spirit" (Gk. *en pneumati*)[101] is praying in the power of, with the help of, according to the will of, and in communion with, the Holy Spirit, or even in the "atmosphere" of the Spirit.[102] This praying is connected with the Word of God, which is the "sword of the Spirit" (v. 17), that is, a weapon in the church's spiritual warfare, just like praying should occur "in the Spirit" as well.

This connection is stated similarly in the second passage: "But you, beloved, building yourselves up in your most holy faith and praying in the Holy Spirit, keep yourselves in the love of God, waiting for the mercy of our Lord Jesus Christ that leads to eternal life" (Jude 20-21). Here again, Word and prayer go hand in hand: praying in the Spirit is linked with "building yourselves up in your most holy faith," the latter being the entire truth of faith as contained in God's Word.[103] This truth of faith is in peril: "I found it necessary to write appealing to you to *contend* for the faith that was once for all delivered to the saints. For certain people have crept in unnoticed who long ago were designated for this condemnation, ungodly people, who pervert the grace of our God into sensuality and deny our only Master and Lord, Jesus Christ" (vv. 3-4). In their spiritual warfare against the undermining of the Christian faith, believers have as a weapon their powerful

---

101. Not the human spirit; *contra* GNV and the great Dutchmen Erasmus and Grotius, quoted by Salmond (1979, 389).
102. W. Barclay, quoted by Wood (1978, 89).
103. Blum (1981b, 395).

praying in the Holy Spirit.

We find another beautiful connection between praying and the Spirit in Philippians 1:19, "I know that through your prayers and the help of the Spirit[104] of Jesus Christ this will turn out for my deliverance." The Holy Spirit, who is the Spirit of Christ as head of his body, also dwells in the members of this body on earth.[105] Paul counts upon deliverance, first, through the prayers of the Philippian Christians, and second, through the help of the Spirit, who dwells in them as well as in him. This is not a contrast: praying in the Spirit leads to help through the same Spirit.

In 1 Thessalonians 5:17–19, too, there is possibly a connection between praying and the Spirit: "[P]ray without ceasing, give thanks in all circumstances; for this is the will of God in Christ Jesus for you. Do not quench the Spirit." In §10.4.2, I will point out a link between verse 19 and the next verses; at present I do the same between verse 19 and the preceding verse. When a Spirit-filled church surrenders to the Spirit, and does not quench the fire of the Spirit out of indifference or any other sin, then in the temple of Christ's body day and night a fire of a supernatural prayer and worship will burn, which will never extinguish.[106] Prince saw a parallel here with the supernatural fire that had been kindled on the altar of the burnt offering (Lev. 9:23–24): "The fire on the altar shall be kept burning on it; it shall not go out. . . . Fire shall be kept burning on the altar continually; it shall not go out" (6:12–13).

9.9.3 Glossolalia in Romans 8?

"Praying in the Spirit" can be important particularly in situ-

---

104. Here the Gk. phrase *tou pneumatos* is a subjective genitive; it is unclear to me how Kent (1978, 117) can find in this "objective aspects" as well.
105. Müller (1984, 58).
106. Prince (1995, 330). Note that the imperatives in 1 Thess. 5:14–22 are plural, not singular. This suggests that Paul is not commanding *individual* believers, but he is commanding the *church*. Given the liturgical practices of the Roman Catholic Church and the Orthodox Church, it is indeed possible for the church to pray without ceasing (cf. the Liturgy of the Hours).

ations in which believers no longer find the words to express themselves in prayer:

> Likewise the Spirit helps us in our weakness. For we do not know what to pray for as we ought, but the Spirit himself intercedes for us with groanings too deep for words. And he who searches hearts knows what is the mind of the Spirit, because the Spirit intercedes for the saints according to the will of God (Rom. 8:26-27).

The Spirit comes to help[107] believers in their groanings[108] (cf. vv. 18-25), and, on the church's behalf, expresses in prayer what believers cannot express themselves. This is either because believers do not, or do not sufficiently, fathom their own needs, or because they do not, or do not sufficiently, discern what exactly they require in order to satisfy their needs.

God understands this praying in the Spirit (v. 27), no matter how little believers themselves know what they ought to pray and how "deep for words" their groanings may be. God understands them because theirs is a praying "according to the will of God" (Gk. *kata theon*, "according to God," "in agreement with God"), so that he can do nothing other than grant them what they ask. This is a praying of the Spirit *for* the saints (believers), but also a praying *in* them, for the Spirit dwells in them. This is different with Christ, who also prays for believers but not *in* them; he intercedes for them at the right hand of God (v. 34; cf. Heb. 7:25). Christ is the Paraclete in heaven *for* believers (1 John 2:1), the Holy Spirit is the Paraclete on earth *in* (and for) believers. Yet, the Son is also "in" them: within them, in their hearts, and these divine persons speak with each other: the Father and the Son dwell there (John 14:23; Eph. 3:14-17), the Spirit of God's Son dwells

---

107. The verb "to help, to come to the aid of" (Gk. *synantilambanetai*) occurs only here and in Luke 10:40; it makes us understand that in Rom. 8:26 it is not only the Spirit who prays, but as a Helper he is present in the believer's prayers; see Harrison (1976, 96).

108. They are not the groanings *of* the Spirit, but they do come in the believer's heart (v. 27!) *from* the Spirit; see Murray (1968, 312).

there (Gal. 4:6), and the Father listens to him, and replies to him.

The Spirit praying in believers in a manner that involves them means the same as saying that *they* pray in the power of the Spirit. We find this same notion in Galatians 4:6, "And because you are sons, God has sent the Spirit of his Son into our hearts, crying, 'Abba! Father!'" Here it is the Spirit who cries, but this is the same as saying that *they* cry through the Spirit. Indeed, in Romans 8:15 it is believers who cry "Abba! Father!," namely, "by" (Gk. *en*, in the power of) the Spirit of the adoption as sons (§8.4.3). There is no material difference between believers crying in (i.e., through) the Spirit, and the Spirit crying in (i.e., within) believers.

Some expositors have thought that the term "praying in the Spirit" (Eph. 6:18; Jude 20) and the Spirit interceding with "groanings" (Rom. 8:26) involves praying in tongues.[109] This may be correct, but the arguments for this understanding are not very strong. This is different in 1 Corinthians 14:15, "I will pray with my spirit, but I will pray with my mind also; I will sing praise with my spirit, but I will sing with my mind also." The possessive pronouns have been added by the translators; the Greek says only *tōi pneumati* and *tōi nōi*, respectively. The pronoun "my" is suggested by verse 14 (Gk. *to pneuma mou*, "my spirit"), yet it is possible that in verse 15 the Greek phrase *tōi pneumati* means "in the [Holy] Spirit" (so indeed CEB).

Because it is clear that verse 15 speaks of glossolalia (see vv. 14 and 19), we do know that praying "in the [Holy] Spirit" (Gk. *tōi pneumati*) may imply glossolalia. Even if we translate verse 15 as "in [my/your] spirit," it is obvious that this can occur only in the power of the Holy Spirit (cf. 12:7–11; cf. AMP, "with the spirit [by the Holy Spirit that is within me]").[110] But we cannot reverse this: not all praying in the Spirit is a praying in tongues. We therefore cannot use 1 Corinthians 14 to prove that in both Ephesians 6 and Jude we are dealing with

---

109. Sanford (1966, 151–52); Käsemann (1971, 131).
110. Bruce (1984, 411n87); Fee (1987, 670n21).

glossolalia. We need the power of the Spirit just as well in ordinary prayer. Even when a believer prays and sings "with his mind" (1 Cor. 14:15), that believer needs the power of the Spirit.[111]

---

111. For more on this, see §12.5.2 below.

Chapter 10
The Dwelling Place of the Holy Spirit

Do you not know that you are God's temple
   and that God's Spirit dwells in you?
                    1 Corinthians 3:16

Or do you not know that your body
   is a temple of the Holy Spirit within you,
   whom you have from God?
                    1 Corinthians 6:19

Christ Jesus . . . , in whom the whole structure, being joined together,
   grows into a holy temple in the Lord.
In him you also are being built together
   into a dwelling place for God by the Spirit.
                    Ephesians 2:20–22

Summary: *In and through the Shekhinah, which is the Holy Spirit, God dwelt with his redeemed people from the beginning: in the* *tabernacle, in the First Temple, (not in the Second Temple?), in (the body of) Jesus, in the individual believer, in the New Testament church, which is God's "house" and "temple." The Spirit regulates the details of the church's life in the world, providing its leadership (overseers, prophets), maintaining its positional and practical unity, stimulating its worship in various forms, facilitating its worldwide testimony (note the similarities between Jesus and the church here), and fostering the administration of the sacraments (what are they, and how are we to understand their relationship to the Spirit?).*

It is important to see that, in addition to dwelling in the church, the Holy Spirit also works in the world: in touching hearts of people, but also in culture and history. To have a proper view of this, we must eliminate the age-old nature–grace dualism with its juxtaposition of creation and re-creation, church, and society, etc.

10.1   God's Dwelling Places
10.1.1 Eden, Sinai, Moriah

THE CHURCH AS TEMPLE OF GOD, in which the Holy Spirit dwells (1 Cor. 3:16; Eph. 2:20–22), constitutes a sanctuary that is part of a long series in the Bible. From the beginning, God longed for a place where he could dwell among his people in and through the Holy Spirit. In §5.3.4 we saw that, in a certain sense, the Garden of Eden already constituted a kind of sanctuary, a bordered paradise, in which God communed with the first humans (cf. Gen. 1:28–30; 2:16–17; 3:9–19). The first earthly construction in the Bible that served as a dwelling place of God was the tabernacle (Heb. *mishkan*, "habitation," from *sh-k-n*, "to dwell," from the same root as *Shekhinah*; see §3.8), built near Mount Sinai. As soon as his people had been redeemed from Egypt, God's Spirit worked in them the longing for this dwelling place:

> You have led in your steadfast love the people whom you have redeemed; you have guided them by your strength to your holy abode.[1] . . . You will bring them in and plant them on your own

---

1. Heb. *nawē*, originally "pasture-ground"; here "place, abode" (cf. 2 Sam. 15:25; Jer. 25:30).

mountain, the place, O LORD, which you have made for your abode,[2] the sanctuary, O Lord, which your hands have established (Exod. 15:13, 17).

In Exodus 15:2, we find the Hebrew word *we-anwēhu*, which is usually rendered as something like "and I will praise him." Others, however, read, "I will prepare him a habitation" (KJV). It would be rather strange if virtually the first words of the redeemed nation would have spoken of God's dwelling place that was now to be built. The Targum connects *we-anwēhu* with *nawē*, "abode" (see note 1), and therefore Rashi translated: "I will make him to dwell in a habitation," that is, in the tabernacle. Rabbi Obadiah ben Jacob Sforno translated: "I will build a habitation for his dwelling." However, the rabbis gave many other possible renderings as well.[3]

The people's longing for God's habitation, no doubt produced in them by the Holy Spirit, corresponded remarkably with God's own longing. The first time Moses ascended to him on Mount Sinai (Exod. 24:15-18), the LORD's very first words to him were these: "Speak to the people of Israel, that they take for me a contribution (viz., precious metals, tissues, wood, oil, spices, jewels].... And let them make me a sanctuary, that I may dwell in their midst. Exactly as I show you concerning the pattern of the tabernacle, and of all its furniture, so you shall make it" (Exod. 25:2, 8-9).

After Eden the first visible habitation to be built for the Most High God was the tabernacle (Exod. 25-29, 35-40), and later the First Temple was built (1 Kings 6-8; 2 Chron. 2-7) on Mount Moriah (2 Chron. 3:1). The Second Temple (Ezra 3-6; Hag. 1-2) was God's abode in only a limited sense, for we never read that the Shekhinah descended upon it (perhaps this is one of the meanings of Hag. 2:4).[4] The Shekhinah

---

2. Heb. *leshibtekha*, "for your dwelling," from *sh-b-t*, "to cease [working]" (cf. *Shabbat*), here: "to rest, to dwell."
3. Cohen (1983, 416).
4. Notice the ambiguous wording of Ezra 1:3, "... the house of the LORD God of Israel, (he is the God,) which is in Jerusalem" (KJV) or "... the house of

will return one day to the temple of the Messianic kingdom (Ezek. 43:1-12). Perhaps the main reason for the Shekhinah's absence from the Second Temple was that the Messiah himself would appear one day in this temple, whose body would be the true dwelling place of God (see next section).

10.1.2 Jesus the New Temple

When God said through Haggai, "The latter glory of this house shall be greater than the former" (Hag. 2:10), the rabbis thought of the duration of the Second Temple (from 516 BC to AD 70, i.e., 585 years) compared to that of the First Temple (410 years, said the rabbis), and the splendor with which King Herod decorated this Second Temple.[5] Christian tradition has instead understood Haggai 2:10 to refer to the Messiah, especially in light of verse 8 (ISV), "the One desired by all nations will come" (NKJV, TLB: "the Desire of All Nations"). When Jesus entered the temple, as a baby and then twelve years later (Luke 2:22-50), a glory entered that the First Temple had never seen. But it was a *hidden* glory, veiled by human flesh. Jesus' body was the new and true temple, in which the Holy Spirit dwelt: "And the Word became flesh and dwelt among us" (John 1:14a), literally, "tabernacled" (Gk. *eskēnōsen*, from *skēnoō*, related to *skēnē*, "tent, tabernacle"): "tabernacled (fixed His tent of flesh, lived awhile) among us" (AMPC; cf. EXB; OJB: "made his sukkah, his Mishkan [Tabernacle] among us"). Verse 14 continues: ". . . and we have seen his glory, glory as of the only Son from the Father, full of grace and truth." In the power of the Holy Spirit, only Jesus' believing followers could perceive his divine glory through the veil of his humanity: "That which . . . we have heard, which we have seen with our eyes, which we looked upon and have touched with our hands, concerning the word of life. . . ." (1 John 1:1).

If Jesus' body was God's true temple, and Herod's vacant and desecrated temple was not, we can understand that while

---

the LORD, the God of Israel—he is the God who is in Jerusalem" (ESV).
5. Cohen (1957, 260–61).

standing next to this building, Jesus could truly say: "'Destroy this temple, and in three days I will raise it up.' The Jews then said, 'It has taken forty-six years to build this temple, and will you raise it up in three days?' But he was speaking about the temple of his body" (John 2:19-21). The Shekhinah rested on Jesus, or dwelt in him (see more extensively §§6.1.1-6.1.2 above). Long ago, the dove had hovered over the waters at the beginning of creation, and had gone out after the Flood as a sign of what was, as it were, a new creation. Now the dove had descended upon Jesus (Luke 3:22, see §6.1.3 above) as the "beginning [Gk. *archē*] of the [new] creation of God" (Rev. 3:14). Just as the apostle Peter related water baptism to the Flood (1 Pet. 3:20-21), so Jesus' baptism, as well as the baptism of all who were baptized after him and in his name, constituted the beginning of a new world (Rom. 6:4).

After Jesus' resurrection and ascension, on the Day of Pentecost, the Holy Spirit descended from heaven. Again he was like the dove that looked for a "place to set her foot" (cf. Gen. 8:9), and found it first in Jesus (at his baptism), and afterward in the church (see §10.2). One day, the church, too, will ascend to heaven (1 Thess. 4:13-17), and be succeeded on earth by the temple of Ezekiel 40-43. This temple cannot be interpreted as a symbolic representation of the church, since it appears for the first time after the restoration of Israel, after the new outpouring of the Holy Spirit on the people (36:27; 37:14; 39:29), after the triumph over the eschatological world power, and after the arrival of the Messianic kingdom (Ezek. 34-39). All of these events will be preceded by, and will require, the second coming of Christ (cf. Ezek. 34:23-24; 37:24-25).[6]

Whether one views Ezekiel's temple as a literal temple in Israel, or as a spiritual, heavenly temple in the sense of the New Jerusalem (Rev. 21),[7] it is an eschatological dwelling place of the Holy Spirit:

---

6. See Walvoord (1991, 395-98).
7. See extensively, Ouweneel (1990, 239-41; 2012a, §3.4).

> Then he [i.e., the angelic "man" of 40:4] led me to the gate, the gate facing east. And behold, the glory [i.e., *Shekhinah*] of the God of Israel was coming from the east.[8] And the sound of his coming was like the sound of many waters, and the earth shone with his glory. . . . As the glory of the LORD entered the temple by the gate facing east, the Spirit lifted me up and brought me into the inner court; and behold, the glory of the LORD filled the temple. While the man [cf. 40:4] was standing beside me, I heard one speaking to me out of the temple, and he said to me, "Son of man, this is the place of my throne and the place of the soles of my feet, where I will dwell in the midst of the people of Israel forever. And the house of Israel shall no more defile my holy name, neither they, nor their kings, by their whoring and by the dead bodies of their kings at their high places (Ezek. 43:1–7).

10.1.3 From Garden to Garden

In §5.3.4, I pointed out that, in a certain sense, the Garden of Eden seems to continue in subsequent epochs: we find paradise motifs in the tabernacle, the First Temple, and also in the eschatological temple (Ezek. 40:16, 22, 26, 31, 34, 37; 41:18–20, 25–26; 47:1–12).

Remarkably, after Jesus' resurrection, the new epoch begins in a garden as well (John 19:41–20:17). In the first garden, the first Adam died his spiritual death—in the new garden the last Adam rose from the dead. In the Garden of Eden, the sad fallen Eve hid herself among the trees—in the garden of Joseph, the sad Mary Magdalene appeared as a new Eve.[9] In the Garden of Eden, God asked, "Where are you[10]?" (Gen. 3:9)—in the garden of Joseph, Jesus asked, "Woman, why are you weeping? Whom are you seeking?" (John 20:15). In the

---

8. The "east" is mentioned here because this is the direction the Shekhinah had gone when leaving the First Temple (cf. Ezek. 11:1, 23), at a moment just preceding the destruction of this temple by the Babylonians.
9. See Ouweneel (1998, 97–101).
10. Notice that "you" is singular here.

Garden of Eden, God revealed himself in his forgiving grace to Adam and Eve—in the garden of Joseph, the risen Lord revealed himself to Mary. After the first humans had been driven from the Garden of Eden, a cherub guarded the way back to the tree of life (Gen. 3:24). In the garden of Joseph, two angels sat in the open and empty tomb, who explained that there was no longer any reason for crying (John 20:12-13).

In §7.3 we saw the deep connection between the exodus from Egypt and the founding of the church in Acts 2. This is because of the feast of Pentecost, which refers back to the law-giving at Mount Sinai. There are more connections: in the end, the believers sing "the song of Moses, the servant of God, and the song of the Lamb" (Rev. 15:3). Israel's route through the wilderness is like the church's route through the present world, as is explicitly taught in the New Testament (1 Cor. 10:1-11; Heb. 3:7-4:11). God's warfare against Israel's spiritual adversaries (cf. Exod. 12:12; 15:3-10; Num. 33:4) continues in the New Testament church (2 Cor. 10:3-6; Eph. 6:12; Phil. 1:27-30; 1 Tim. 6:12).

Interestingly, the church itself is like a Garden of Eden, with its trees and rivers, for it produces the "fruit of the Spirit" (Gal. 5:22; cf. "reaping" in 6:8), and "rivers of living waters" are flowing from it, that is, the works of the Holy Spirit (John 7:38-39). The Lord says of her as it were, "A garden locked is my sister, my bride, a spring locked, a fountain sealed. . . . a garden fountain, a well of living water, and flowing streams from Lebanon" (Song 4:12, 15). Just as each new phase in God's ways with his people culminated in rest (§5.3), so too the church is a place of rest and peace (Rom. 5:1; Phil. 4:7; Col. 3:15). And just as every new phase ended in spiritual decline, so to with the church, if viewed from the standpoint of human responsibility. In 2 Timothy 2:20 the church is no longer the "house of God" (cf. 1 Tim. 3:15) but a "great house" with vessels to the honor as well as vessels to the dishonor of the master. Peter says, "[I]t is time for judgment to begin at the household of God" (1 Pet. 4:17).

10.2   A Holy Temple
10.2.1   Dwelling Place of the Holy Spirit

Living by the Spirit is an experience of each individual believer, but it is also a collective experience: it involves the entire church. Not only the body of the single believer (1 Cor. 6:19) but also the church as a whole is a temple of the Holy Spirit: "Do you not know that you [plural] are God's temple and that God's Spirit dwells in you? If anyone destroys God's temple, God will destroy him. For God's temple is holy, and you [plural] are that temple" (3:16-17; cf. v. 9: "You are . . . God's building").[11]

This is one of ten times in 1 Corinthians in which Paul introduces an important statement with the words, "Do you not know. . .?" (see also 1 Cor. 5:6; 6:2-3, 9, 15-16, 19; 9:13, 24; cf. Rom. 6:3,16; 7:1; 11:2). Paul's statement is not a dogmatic pronouncement but, given the wrong practices in Corinth, an exhortation. Be aware, in a very practical sense, of the fact that you are God's temple, and that he who affects it in any way affects God himself, so to speak (cf. Lev. 15:31, evildoers "die in their uncleanness by defiling my tabernacle that is in their midst"). The church as God's temple is holy in at least two respects. First, it is the Spirit of God who dwells there, that is, the *Holy* Spirit. Second, believers who together form the temple are holy (e.g., 1 Cor. 1:2, ". . . to those sanctified in Christ Jesus, called to be saints"; 6:11, "you were sanctified"). Notice here the last words of 3:17, "and such are ye" (ASV; Gk. *hoitines este humeis*) which can refer back to "temple,"[12] but also to "holy."[13]

This holy (sacred, sanctified) character of the church, both locally (here, in Corinth[14]) and universally, is mentioned also

---

11. Fee (1987, 149–50) rightly warns against the individualistic view of vv. 16–17 as if the subject here were the same as in 6:19.
12. Fee (1987, 149n21); KJV, NIV, and ESV.
13. Findlay (1979, 793); AMP, CEB, and GNV.
14. Cf. the body metaphor, applied locally as well: "you [plural] are the body of Christ and individually members of it" (1 Cor. 12:27).

in 2 Corinthians 6:14-16, though without mentioning the Holy Spirit:

> [W]hat partnership has righteousness with lawlessness? Or what fellowship has light with darkness? What accord has Christ with Belial [i.e., Satan]? Or what portion does a believer share with an unbeliever? What agreement has the temple of God with idols? For we are the temple of the living God; as God said, "I will make my dwelling among them and walk among them, and I will be their God, and they shall be my people" (for this quotation, cf. Lev. 26:11-12; Ezek. 37:27; Jer. 31:33; and Heb. 8:10).

10.2.2 Dwelling and Ministry

At least three notions are directly attached to the metaphor of the temple: the church is a place where God *dwells*, and thus a place where God's *glory* is manifested, and concomitantly a place where his people perform *priestly ministry* to express their worship. As we have seen, the first aspect is seen the very first time God referred to the tabernacle: "[L]et them make me a sanctuary, that I may dwell in their midst" (Exod. 25:8; cf. 15:17; 29:45; 1 Kings 6:12-13; Ezek. 37:26-28; 43:7-9; Rev. 21:3). In the following passage all three elements are enumerated: "There [i.e., at the entrance of the tabernacle, at the altar of burnt offering] I will meet with the people of Israel, and it shall be sanctified by my *glory*. I will consecrate the tent of meeting [i.e., the tabernacle] and the altar. Aaron also and his sons I will consecrate to serve me as *priests*. I will *dwell* among the people of Israel and will be their God" (Exod. 29:43-45).

Later, in connection with Solomon's temple, we find these three aspects again: "And when the priests came out of the Holy Place, a cloud filled the house of the LORD, so that the *priests* could not stand to minister because of the cloud, for the *glory* of the LORD filled the house of the LORD. Then Solomon said, 'The LORD has said that he would *dwell* in thick darkness'" (1 Kings 8:10-12). It will be like this in the temple of the Messianic kingdom: "[B]ehold, the *glory* of the LORD filled the temple.... [T]his is the place of my throne and the place of the soles of my feet, where I will *dwell* in the midst of the people of Israel forever.... [T]he Levitical *priests* of the family of Zadok, who draw near to me to minister to me..." (Ezek. 43:5, 7, 19).

In §3.8, I pointed to the connection and parallelism between the Shekhinah and the Holy Spirit. Although the term *Shekhinah* does not occur in the Old Testament, the notion is clearly represented by the pillar of cloud (see Exod. 40:34-38; Lev. 9:23-24; 1 Kings 8:11; 2 Chron. 5:14; 7:1-3; Isa. 6:1-5). Just as the Shekhinah, the divine Presence, once dwelt in the physical tabernacle, and later in the First Temple, so too, the Holy Spirit now dwells in the spiritual temple, that is, the church of God.[15] And whereas the priestly sons of Aaron ministered in the tabernacle and the two temples, all New Testament believers are priests: "... a spiritual house, to be a holy priesthood, to offer spiritual sacrifices acceptable to God through Jesus Christ" (1 Pet. 2:5). "Through him [i.e., Christ] then let us continually offer up a sacrifice of praise to God, that is, the fruit of lips that acknowledge his name" (Heb. 13:15; cf. Hos. 14:2b; also see Rev. 1:6; 6:10; 20:6). We will come back to this in §10.6.

In Ephesians 2:20-22, Paul introduces the same imagery: "... Christ Jesus..., in whom the whole structure,[16] being joined together, grows into a holy temple in the Lord. In him

---

15. Incidentally, the idea that God's people *themselves* are a spiritual sanctuary is not entirely foreign to the Old Testament: "When Israel went out from Egypt, ... Judah became his sanctuary" (Ps. 114:1-2). Conversely, God himself is sometimes called a "sanctuary" to his people (Isa. 8:14).
16. The best reading is the Gk. phrase *pasa oikodomē*, that is, without the article; Salmond (1979, 300-301) claims that therefore we *must* translate the phrase as "each building" (cf. ASV). Greijdanus (1925, 64) translates this as "every building" in the sense of "each kind of building." Grosheide (1960, 48n44) and Bruce (1984, 307) defend the rendering "the whole building" (NIV) or "all the building" (KJV). Wood (1978, 43) leaves the matter undecided.

you also are being built together into a dwelling place for God by [or in] the Spirit." Paul likes to combine biological and architectural language, like this: ". . . rooted and grounded in love" (3:17; cf. Col. 2:7), and ". . . makes the body grow so that it builds itself up in love" (Eph. 4:16). Similarly, he speaks in 2:21 of a "structure" (or "building") that "grows" into a temple.[17] This implies not that by this growing process the church is still *becoming* a temple, but rather that, since the outpouring of the Holy Spirit (Acts 2), it *was* a temple (cf. 1 Cor. 3:16), which at the same time goes through a process of development throughout church history. On the one hand, this temple was complete from the outset, and thus from the outset it was a suitable "dwelling place[18] for God in the Spirit." On the other hand, new building stones are being added continually (cf. 1 Pet. 2:5), such as the Ephesian believers (Eph. 2:22). The whole collection of these stones is well "joined together" (Gk. *syn[h]armologoumenē*) into a harmonious structure (v. 21).[19]

In 1 Corinthians 3:16, it is said more directly that God's Spirit dwells in the church as a temple; in Ephesians 2:22 the formulation is more indirect: it is a dwelling place of God "in [the] Spirit." This can be understood in an instrumental sense: "by the Spirit," "in the power of the Spirit," but also (preferably) in a locative sense: the Holy Spirit is the spiritual sphere in which God's dwelling place is realized.[20] In the Lord (Christ) as the foundation and principle of everything, believers are being built together into a dwelling place of God, and this is being realized through their being-together-in-the-Spirit.[21]

---

17. Bruce (1984, 306–307).
18. In the LXX the Gk. word *katoikētērion* (cf. Rev. 18:2) often refers to the divine abode, either on earth (the temple) or in heaven.
19. Of course, as a comparison Paul hints at the temple in Jerusalem, but perhaps he is also alluding to the temple of Artemis in Ephesus; thus Wood (1978, 42).
20. Ibid.
21. Salmond (1979, 301).

10.3 Dwelling "In God"
10.3.1 Four Aspects

In the writings of the apostle John we do not find the Greek term *ekklēsia* with any other meaning than a purely local meaning (3 John 1:6, 9; Rev. 1-3; 22:16). John has his own, more familial terminology to describe God's dwelling with his people, and his people's dwelling in him. Characteristic in this terminology are the Greek preposition *en* ("in") and the Greek verb *menō*, "to abide" (cf. also the related Gr. noun *monē*, "room, abode," in John 14:2, 23). There are at least four ways in which John uses these terms in order to describe divine relationships.

First, the terms are used for the Father and the Son themselves: "Do you not believe that I am in the Father and the Father is in me? The words that I say to you I do not speak on my own authority, but the Father who dwells [Gk. *menōn*] in me does his works. Believe me that I am in the Father and the Father is in me" (John 14:10-11).

Second, believers too, those who have received the Son as their life (1 John 5:11-12; cf. John 6:53-54), are involved in this Trinitarian community: "In that day [of the *eschaton*] you will know that I am in my Father, and you in me, and I in you" (John 14:20). "Abide [Gk. *meinate*] in me, and I in you" (15:4; see vv. 3-7). "If what you heard from the beginning abides in you, then you too will *abide* [Gk. *meneite*] in the Son and in the Father" (1 John 2:24). The collective (in Pauline terms: ecclesial) aspect comes to expression in the notion of "unity": "... that they may all be one, just as you, Father, are in me, and I in you, that they also may be in us, ... that they may be one even as we are one, I in them and you in me, that they may become perfectly one" (John 17:21-23).

Third, this union and communion of the Father and the Son with believers is connected with the Holy Spirit, so that it becomes a truly Trinitarian union and communion: "Whoever keeps his commandments abides in God, and God in him. And by this we know that he abides in us, by the Spirit whom he has given us" (1 John 3:24). "[I]f we love one another, God *abides* in us and his love is perfected in us. By this we know that we *abide* in him and he in us, because he has given us of his Spirit" (4:12–13). Through the Spirit, God or Christ "abides" (dwells) in us.

Fourth, in the latter passage this mutual "abiding" of God and believers in each other is connected with divine love, so that this Trinitarian communion emerges as not only a Spirit communion but also a love communion—which ultimately amounts to the same thing, of course (see in §1.2.2 how, because of this, Augustine has linked the Spirit and love). The text continues: "Whoever confesses that Jesus is the Son of God, God *abides* in him, and he in God. So we have come to know and to believe the love that God has for us. God is love, and whoever abides in love *abides* in God, and God *abides* in him" (1 John 4:15–16; cf. John 14:23; 15:9–10). To abide in God is to abide in love, and the reverse, for God is love. This is what Jesus prayed: "I made known to them your name, and I will continue to make it known, that the love with which you have loved me may be in them, and I in them" (John 17:26). And the apostle John says, "[W]hoever keeps his word, in him truly the love of God is perfected. By this we may know that we are in him: whoever says he *abides* in him ought to walk in the same way in which he walked" (1 John 2:5–6).

In summary:

(a) The Son abides in the Father, the Father abides in the Son. This is the intertrinitarian fellowship.

(b) Believers abide in the Father and in the Son, the Father and the Son abide in believers. Moreover, God abides in believers, they abide in God. This is the extratrinitarian fellowship.

10.3.2 Eternal Life

The community of the Spirit, of love, and of life, which I have just depicted, is essentially what the apostle John describes with the phrase "eternal life" (Gk. *zōē aiōnios*). This is not a quantitative expression, telling us something about the duration of this life, but a qualitative one, telling us something about the *nature*, the character, the quality of the life that the believer receives: abundance (John 10:10), intimate knowledge of divine persons (17:3), fellowship with, and joy in, divine persons (1 John 1:1-4).[22] In Jesus this eternal life has descended to humanity, as it were from the bosom of the Father (v. 2; 5:20; cf. John 1:18). To state it with an oversimplified comparison: Paul is particularly interested in the question how people can ascend to heaven—John is particularly interested in the question how heaven can descend to people.

Let me explain this. The French mystic Charles de Condren expressed the remarkable thought that the sanctuary to which believers have free access (Heb. 10:19-22) is nothing other than the bosom of the Father.[23] Actually, this emphasis is more characteristic of Paul: through the Holy Spirit believers on earth have access to the heavenly Father (Eph. 2:18), and the goal of their earthly walk is eternal life with God (cf. Rom. 6:22; 1 Tim. 6:12). John's writings emphasize more specifically that in Jesus, eternal life has descended from heaven to *us*, and in the power of the Spirit can be known and enjoyed on earth. To reformulate the comparison stated at the end of the previous paragraph: for Paul, our true life is we in Christ in heaven; for John, true life is Christ in us on earth.

Let me add a note here on what is called *perichoresis* (Gk. *perichorēsis*), a subject mentioned earlier. This term refers to the relationships between the three divine persons. It was coined by the Cappadocian church father Gregory of Nazianzus. Literally it means something close to "dance," a circling around of trinitarian life, a coming and going among the divine persons, and their movement in grace toward creation.[24] Clark Pinnock placed great emphasis on God as "pure

---

22. See more extensively, Ouweneel (2009b, chapter 4).
23. Congar (1997, 2.113).
24. Cf. Pinnock (1996, 22).

relationality," and as a "social trinity," into which humans are invited as well.[25] The term *perichoresis* refers to the divine "dance" in which humans are invited to participate, and this ties in with what was expressed in the Johannine passages just quoted. Pinnock has expressed some wonderful thoughts on these things, which I freely summarize here.

The Spirit moves humanity to personal communion and partaking in the divine nature (cf. 2 Pet. 1:4), which was God's eternal purpose.[26] God created the world for his own pleasure, and his pleasure as a triune lover was and is to invite new partners into the dance. We could think of the Holy Spirit as the choreographer for the dance of creation, analogous to what he does in the fellowship of the sublime Trinity.[27] The Trinity is an open, inviting community, and the Spirit wants the church to be the same. That is, the church should resemble life of the Trinity by exercising mutuality and by giving oneself to the other. The fellowship that we enjoy together is related to our fellowship with the Father and the Son (1 John 1:3). *Fellowship* refers both to the divine life within the Trinity *and* to the life of the community, because it is God's intention that the community should reflect the fellowship of the Trinity, which is the ontological basis of the church.[28]

United with Christ, without becoming Christ, we are also united with God without becoming God. This union is not ontic but personal, in which the distinction between Creator and creature is maintained. We enter into the dance of the Trinity not as equals but as adopted partners.[29]

I add here that it does not seem far-fetched to me, in connection with the so-called "parable of the prodigal son," to compare the father's house to the church. Becoming a Christian and being added to the church is "coming home" to the

---

25. Ibid., 22–23, 31, 34–35.
26. Ibid., 23.
27. Ibid., 56.
28. Ibid., 117.
29. Ibid., 154. "Adoption" is adoption as sons, in short: sonship (Gk. *huiothesia*).

Father. Jesus describes this house as a place of "music and dance" (Gk. *symphōnias kai chorōn*) (Luke 15:25). Here we are reminded again of the Greek term *perichorēsis*, derived from *choros*, "dance." The church is a community of people who have returned to the Father, and have been introduced by him into his Trinitarian "symphony" and "choreography": "[T]hat which we [i.e., the apostles] have seen and heard we proclaim also to you, so that you too may have fellowship with us; and indeed our fellowship is with the Father and with his Son Jesus Christ. And we are writing these things so that our joy may be complete" (1 John 1:3-4; cf. 2:24).

10.4 Spiritual Leadership in the Church
10.4.1 Overseers

We now come to a very different aspect of the Spirit's dwelling place on earth. The Spirit does dwell in the individual believer (e.g., Rom. 8:9, 11; 1 Cor. 6:19; 2 Tim. 1:14), but collectively the local church is the primary dwelling place of the Holy Spirit. Therefore, we must discuss how the Holy Spirit's work is manifested particularly in the activities of the local church leaders.

The only thing that the New Testament tells us about leadership in the local church is that it is common to have elders or overseers (Acts 11:30; 14:23; 15:2-23; 16:4; 20:17, 28; 21:18; Phil. 1:1; 1 Tim. 3:1-2; 4:14; 5:17, 19; Titus 1:5, 7; James 5:14; 1 Pet. 5:1, 5; cf. "leaders," Heb. 13:7, 17, 24). The figure of the single pastor, as *the* leader of a local congregation, is unknown in the New Testament.[30] We do read of elders "who labor in preaching and teaching" (1 Tim. 5:17). The only alleged suggestion of a single leadership is in 1 Timothy 3:1-7; Paul speaks here of deacons and women (the deacons' wives or female deacons) in the plural, but about the "overseer" in the singular (v. 2; cf. Titus 1:5 and v. 7). Yet, Reformed dogmatician Herman Bavinck had to admit that the New Testament

---

30. See Ouweneel (2010a, §8.3) for arguments why I view a plurality of leaders as more biblical.

does not know an official distinction between "overseer" (Gk. *episkopos*) and "elder" (*presbyteros*).[31] He referred to many church fathers, such as Theodoret, Chrysostom, Epiphanius, and Jerome, who had to acknowledge as well that the New Testament uses the terms interchangeably.[32]

The church has "teaching elders" (1 Tim. 5:17), but no teaching elder functions among (and over) a number of non-teaching elders. What is more striking is that the "teacher" in the New Testament (e.g., Eph. 4:11) does not have to be a leader (elder, overseer, pastor) at all; he has a teaching ministry, and this does not necessarily imply an oversight ministry. Nor does Ephesians 4:11 necessarily suggest that the shepherd and teacher are the same person (*contra* the ESV note: "Or the shepherd-teachers"). In fact, rarely is a good shepherd also a good teacher, and *vice versa*. In a time of widespread illiteracy—lasting until the nineteenth century—that a church would have one pastor was understandable, but today this practice is outdated. In many churches and congregations some people have more knowledge of Scripture, more teaching ability, and more spiritual authority to preach than the official pastor.[33]

Regardless, the local congregation is led by elders and overseers, of whom Paul says, "Pay careful attention to yourselves and to all the flock, in which the Holy Spirit has made you overseers, to care for the church of God" (Acts 20:28). The question is *how* the Holy Spirit makes overseers in the church. Perhaps this occurs through prophetic statements, as we read about in connection with Barnabas and Saul, who were set apart by the Holy Spirit through prophets and teachers (Acts 13:2-4), and in connection with Timothy: "Do not neglect the gift you have, which was given you by prophecy when the

---

31. Bavinck (*RD* 4.360).
32. Ibid.; it must be admitted, though, that elsewhere (341–43) Bavinck does distinguish between elders and overseers.
33. Cf. the refreshing self-criticism in the Reformed world expressed by Van Bruggen (1984) and Graafland (1999).

council of elders[34] laid their hands on you" (1 Tim. 4:14).[35] Some presume that the same procedure was followed here as in Acts 6:3-6: choosing "men of good repute, full of the Spirit and of wisdom," with the apostles laying their hands on them (cf. 14:23).[36] In whatever way human choice and appointment may have been involved here (cf. Acts 14:23; 1 Tim. 3:1-13; Titus 1:5-9), overseers are reminded that ultimately they owe their office to the Holy Spirit, and thus must render account primarily to God.

That the early church did not see any contradiction between, on the one hand, appointment by people and, on the other hand, appointment by the Holy Spirit is demonstrated in a report by Clement of Alexandria.[37] According to him, after his release the apostle John returned from Patmos to Ephesus, where he occupied himself with church work and chose as church leaders those "who had been appointed by the Spirit." In other words, John was following the initiative of the Holy Spirit.

I already mentioned Acts 13:1-3, "Now there were in the church at Antioch prophets and teachers, Barnabas, Simeon who was called Niger, Lucius of Cyrene, Manaen a lifelong friend of Herod the tetrarch, and Saul. While they were worshiping the Lord and fasting,[38] the Holy Spirit said, 'Set apart for me Barnabas and Saul for the work to which I have called them.' Then after fasting and praying they laid their hands on them and sent them off." There is an early fourth century Latin work from the African church that renders these verses as follows: "Now there were in the church at Antioch prophets and teachers, [namely,] Barnabas and Saul, on whom the following prophets laid their hands: Simeon. . . , Lucius. . . ,

---

34. The "council of elders" is one word in the Gk.: *presbyterion* (cf. KJV, NASB: "the presbytery").
35. Bruce (1988, 392).
36. Knowling (1979, 435).
37. *Quis dives salvetur* 208–210.
38. In Acts 10:30, too, fasting led to a divine announcement.

Manaen...; they had received an answer from the Holy Spirit. .."—presumably through a prophetic declaration of one or several of them.[39]

Overseers, elders, prophets, teachers—not to mention apostles, evangelists, shepherds (Eph. 4:11)—they all point to a wide variety of ministries within the local church. In all this diversity of *charismata*, ministries, and activities, we notice the activity of the one Spirit, the one Lord, and the one God: "it is the same God who empowers them all in everyone.... All these are empowered by one and the same Spirit, who apportions to each one individually as he wills" (1 Cor. 12:4-11). We will return to this in chapter 12.

10.4.2 Prophets

In the guidance of the Holy Spirit, prophets often seem to play an important role in the church (Acts 11:27-28; 13:1-3; 15:32; 21:9-11). Hence this important statement by Paul: "Rejoice always, pray without ceasing, give thanks in all circumstances; for this is the will of God in Christ Jesus for you. Do not quench the Spirit.[40] Do not despise prophecies, but test everything; hold fast what is good" (1 Thess. 5:16-21). In §4.3.2 we discussed this quenching (a physical metaphor): the Holy Spirit is compared to a fire that can be extinguished. This may happen when believers allow themselves to be led by the flesh, so that the power of the Spirit decreases in their practical Christian living, and they no longer display the "fruit of the Spirit" (a botanical metaphor). This fruit entails (as Paul says here): "Rejoice always, pray without ceasing, give thanks in all circumstance" (vv. 16-18).

Quenching the Spirit can happen when a congregation offers no opportunity for the special activities of the Spirit: glossolalia, prophetic utterances, but also healings and deliverances (cf. 1 Cor. 12-14). Whereas Paul had to restrain the

---

39. Bruce (1988, 244n1; 245n10).
40. The Gk. word *mē* suggests that the meaning is actually, "Stop quenching the Spirit"; so too v. 20: "Stop despising prophecies."

Corinthian believers in this respect (as today we would like to see happen in certain charismatic circles), he apparently had to encourage those in Thessalonica to provide more opportunity for this kind of manifestations (as today we would like to see happen in certain traditional Protestant circles).[41]

If we may connect 1 Thessalonians 5:20 ("Do not despise prophecies") directly with verse 19 ("Do not quench the Spirit"), this would support the thought that Paul was thinking here especially of spiritual manifestations in the church. His warning would then be not to suppress spiritual utterances such as glossolalia and prophecies in the church, or not to suppress spiritual utterances such as prophecies in the church in favor of, for instance, glossolalia. The text is so concise that it is impossible to determine with certitude the intentions of the apostle. We can see a more clear connection between verses 20 and 21, indicated by "but" or "rather" (Gk. *de*): on the one hand, believers should not despise prophecies, but on the other hand, they should not unthinkingly swallow everything either. Prophecies had to be tested, and the good elements had to be retained: "Let two or three prophets speak, and let the others [i.e., the other prophets or the other church members] weigh what is said" (1 Cor. 14:29).

One could also assume here a connection with Revelation 2:7, 11, 17, 29; 3:6, 13, 29: "He who has an ear, let him hear what the Spirit says to the churches." This is an appeal to the faithful in all seven churches in the province of Asia to give heed to what the Spirit had to say to them through the *prophet* John (cf. Rev. 1:3; 22:7, 9-10, 18-19). Here again the warning applies: Do not despise prophetic utterances.

Reformed and Presbyterian denominations recognize three offices in the congregation: the pastors (i.e., shepherds) or ministers of the Word, the overseers or elders, and the deacons.[42] It is all the more remarkable that, in the list found in

---
41. Morris (1959, 175); Thomas (1978, 292); Kärkkäinen (2002, 33).
42. Belgic Confession, articles 30 and 31. The Church Order of Dordt (art. 2, 3, 18) speaks of four offices: in addition to the three mentioned, also doctors of

1 Corinthians 12:28, the prophet appears before the teacher, and immediately after the apostle, while in Romans 12:8 he appears first.[43] This raises various questions: Why did the Reformation turn the ministry of the teacher into an office, but not that of the prophet? Why do the Reformed denominations recognize the shepherd-teacher but not the prophet? I am referring here to Ephesians 4:11 (without entering right now into the ministries of the apostles and evangelists). Is it not time for theologians to reflect anew upon the function of the prophet in today's church?

Let me mention one example. Paul says, "[T]he one who prophesies speaks to people for their upbuilding and encouragement and consolation" (1 Cor. 14:3). Two questions come to mind. First, can we reverse this thesis, claiming that everyone speaking to people for their upbuilding and encouragement and consolation is performing a prophetic ministry? The answer is no. Second, is it biblical to claim that the prophetic task is being performed today by the shepherd-teachers?[44] The answer again is no. Prophetic tasks must be performed by the prophets, pastoral tasks by the shepherds, teaching tasks by the teachers.

10.4.3 The New Testament Church "Office"

In §1.1, I described how the establishment of an ordained clergy in the church (second century) left less and less room for the free working of the Holy Spirit. At first, the hierarchical, institutional, and charismatic elements seemed to go more or less hand in hand. However, the church's severe rejection of the Montanists (see §1.4.2 above)[45] showed that the charismat-

---

theology; but this office scarcely functions in the life and practice of local congregations.
43. Cf. Reformed theologian Graafland (1999, 317; cf. 329: "Paul sees their [i.e., the prophets'] task as the most important one in the church [1 Cor. 14:1]).")
44. See extensively, Ouweneel (2010a, §9.5; chapters 9–10).
45. It is important to remember that most of what we know about this early charismatic movement comes from anti-Montanist sources, so that it is scarcely possible to obtain an objective picture of this movement; cf. Tabbernee

ic emphasis was losing ground. Unfortunately, the Reformation produced no change in this situation. Protestant churches emphasized a well-ordered clergy, together with rigorous church polity, which restricted the free working of the Spirit. The reason for this seems to have been not so much a fundamental theological conviction but rather the fear of disorder and loss of control. Some like to quote 1 Corinthians 14:23, "God is not a God of confusion" — without realizing that the same apostle wrote a few verses earlier (v. 26): "What then, brothers? When you come together, *each one* has a hymn, a lesson, a revelation, a *tongue*, or an interpretation. Let *all things* be done for building up."

Much more attention is being given today to the insight that both the church's official dimension (the overseers; §10.4.1) and the church's charismatic dimension (particularly the prophecies; §10.4.2) are correlative. If the official element gains the upper hand, the Spirit is quenched, and charismatic life is suffocated. If the charismatic element begins to prevail, beyond the superintending of the overseers, room is created for all kinds of excesses and extremism. The *charismata* need the offices, just as a tender plant needs a solid container.[46]

I actually prefer to place the word "office" between quotation marks, for the New Testament does not employ the word. Where translations do use it, it appears in expressions such as "office of overseer" (1 Tim. 3:1; cf. "office" in Acts 1:20), which is nothing but the single Greek word *episkopē*. Or we find "priestly office" (Heb. 7:5; Gk. *hierateia*). In Hebrews 7:23, the phrase "in office" is added in the ESV without any basis for this in the Greek. If in these passages the notion of "office" is somehow present, then its referent is certainly not a clerical order (from *clerus*, "clergy") distinct from the "laity" (from *laos*, "people"). The fundamental New Testament teaching of the priesthood of all believers is incompatible with any clerical class thought to mediate between God and believers, un-

---

(1997).
46. Pinnock (1996, 140).

like the functions of the priests in Old Testament Israel.

Not only the priesthood but also the *charismata* are available for all believers. In 1 Corinthians 12:28, the apostles, prophets, and teachers are mentioned together with various other ministries, without any clerical distinctions. The care by overseers for the church is not essentially different from the care by *all* believers for one another (cf. 1 Thess. 5:12-13 with v. 14: "We ask you, brothers, to respect those who labor among you and are over you in the Lord and admonish you, and to esteem them very highly in love because of their work. Be at peace among yourselves. And we urge you, brothers [and sisters], admonish the idle, encourage the fainthearted, help the weak, be patient with them all"). Paul employed his *charismata* among believers at Rome basically in the same way that each believer is supposed to employ one's gifts toward fellow believers (Rom. 1:11).[47]

10.4.4 The Correlativity of Gifts and Offices

The arguments just given do not at all diminish the need for overseers (Gk. *presbyteroi, episkopoi, hēgoumenoi*). Each local congregation has the responsibility to seek a balance between overseers and prophets. Notice that in Acts 13:1-3 the prophets apparently belonged to the group that gave spiritual guidance to the church at Antioch. The overseers are not above the prophets, and *vice versa*. The former should not seek to control (and thus easily suppress) charismatic life, but should certainly help it to proceed smoothly. They ought not to obstruct the flowing current of the Spirit, but should certainly guide it along safely. This is not in conflict with the free working of the Holy Spirit because, if things are in order, the overseers are led by the Spirit just the same. Structure, office, institution, polity, and the like should never be played off against the Spirit. The

---

47. Suurmond (1995, 189–92). He pointed out (207) that the different views of the offices formed the greatest stumbling block in the ecumenical movement, and that W. A. Visser 't Hooft presented in 1951 the charismatic model as the only possible ecumenical model.

overseers listen to the Spirit who works through the prophets (and related *charismata*), just as the prophets listen to the Spirit who works through the overseers.

Reformed theologian C. Graafland pointed to

> the organic interrelationship of the spontaneous and the organizational in performing the charismatic task. Here again, there turns out to be no question of an official separation, in which a contrast is created between the office coming from above, in an over-against position toward the congregation, *and* the believers' spontaneous works, coming up out of the congregation. They are mutually inclusive.[48]

And Catholic theologian Yves Congar, with special emphasis on the teaching aspect in the church, said that teaching without prophetism (i.e., prophetic ministry) can easily degenerate into legalism, but prophetism without teaching can become illusory.[49] In my own terms: God's Word without God's Spirit easily becomes Pharisaism, whereas God's Spirit without God's Word easily becomes fanaticism.

As surely as in traditional churches the offices have often strangled the *charismata*, just as surely in certain Charismatic circles the reverse occurs insofar as the deliberateness of the offices is played off against the spontaneity of the *charismata*. Paul makes clear that unbridled spontaneity is more at home in paganism: "Now concerning spiritual gifts, brothers, I do not want you to be uninformed. You know that when you were pagans you were led astray to mute idols, however you were led" (1 Cor. 12:1-2). In opposition to this, he soberly states: "[T]he spirits of prophets are subject to prophets" (14:32), that is: no matter how strongly the prophets may be driven by the Spirit, they always retain their self-control.

Moreover, prophets must submit themselves to the evaluation of others: "Let two or three prophets speak, and let the others weigh what is said" (v. 29). As I said, at this moment

---

48. Graafland (1999, 320).
49. Congar (1997, 2.155).

it does not matter too much how this phrase "the others" is understood,[50] for the Spirit belongs to the *entire* church. And more concretely, when Paul says, "God is not a God of confusion but of peace" (v. 33), overseers are the ones chiefly responsible for maintaining this peace. For the rest, with respect to employing the *charismata*, I refer the reader to chapter 12 below, and to §12.9 below for a discussion of 1 Corinthians 14.

10.5 The Unity of the Church
10.5.1 Body, House, Family

Let us now consider the worldwide New Testament church in its entirety, and see how the Holy Spirit manifests himself in her. It is convenient to do so with the help of the well-known metaphors that the New Testament uses for the church.

Body. It is of great practical importance to see that the Holy Spirit is a Spirit of communion and community, because believers have the Spirit *in common*.[51] "[T]he fellowship of the Holy Spirit [Gk. *koinōnia tou hagiou pneumatos*] be with you all" (2 Cor. 13:14), pointing to the fellowship *with* the Holy Spirit, or the fellowship with each other *through* the Holy Spirit, or the fellowship with each other *in (the sphere of)* the Holy Spirit.[52] Believers have been baptized in the Spirit, so that they form one communion, one body (1 Cor. 12:13). They are "standing firm in one spirit [NIV: Spirit]" (Phil. 1:27), and the *charismata* and ministries aim at building up the entire community, the entire body (Rom. 12:4-8; 1 Cor. 12:14-26; Eph. 4:11-16).[53]

House. This community is more than the sum of its individual members; it is not only the sum total of the inhabitants of God's house (Eph. 2:19, "members of the household [one

---

50. The phrase "the others" can refer to (a) other prophets, (b) other church members, or (c) overseers; see Grosheide (1957, 376), who prefers (a), and Fee (1987, 694) and Prince (1995, 373), who prefer (b) (which includes [c]).
51. Kärkkäinen (2002, 33).
52. Cf. the phrase "the fellowship of his Son" (1 Cor. 1:9), with the same possible variety of meanings.
53. Cf. extensively, Martin (1984).

Greek word: *oikeioi*] of God"), but they are also that house (Gk. *oikos*) itself (1 Tim. 3:15; Heb. 3:6; 10:21; 1 Pet. 4:17), of which the church members are the stones (1 Pet. 2:4-5). The imagery is flexible, since believers are both the building materials and the building inhabitants.

Family. In Ephesians 2:18, in the course of an argument concerning the unity of Jewish and Gentile believers within the one body of Christ, Paul says, "[T]hrough him [i.e., Christ] we both have access in one Spirit to the Father." As to their Christian position, Paul states that believers through Christ have "obtained access by faith into this grace in which we stand" (Rom. 5:2), and that in Christ "we have boldness and access with confidence through our faith in him" (Eph. 3:12; cf. Heb. 10:19-22; 1 Pet. 3:18). In Ephesians 2:18 it is both positional and practical: both kinds of believers, Jewish and Gentile, now belong to the same family of God. That is, they have the same Father, and having the one Spirit of adoption (Rom. 8:15; Gal. 4:6) in common, they can now come together to the Father, and call him "Abba! Father!" As far as their position in Christ is concerned, the difference between Jewish and Gentile believers has been removed (cf. Rom. 10:12; 1 Cor. 12:13; Gal. 3:28; Col. 3:11).[54]

Some (e.g., Anselm of Canterbury, d. 1109) translate the Greek phrase *en heni pneumati* in Ephesians 2:18 as "in one spirit." However, the connection between "one body" and "one Spirit," both here and in Ephesians 4:4,[55] suggests that the Holy Spirit is meant. Jewish and Gentile believers have been redeemed by the same Lord, they have become children of the same Father, and have access to the Father "in" the same Spirit. The latter is either instrumental ("through," "in

---

54. Please note, this is "in Christ." Just as with males and females, slaves and free, who are all "one in Christ," yet in practical living these distinctions are still quite important. The same is true of Jewish and Gentile believers; see extensively, Ouweneel (2017b, chapters 5-6).

55. Calvin and others understand Eph. 4:3 as referring to the "unity of the [human] spirit," and v. 4, regarding "one body and one spirit," as a parallel between the individual and the church.

the power of") or locative ("in the sphere of the same Spirit").[56]

10.5.2 Ephesians 4:3-6

As a follow up, we find in Ephesians 4:3-6 the appeal to be "eager to maintain the unity of the Spirit in the bond of peace. There is one body and one Spirit—just as you were called to the one hope that belongs to your call— one Lord, one faith, one baptism, one God and Father of all, who is over all and through all and in all." The "unity of the Spirit" is the very unity that Christians must maintain in a truly practical sense. This can never be *replaced* by various forms of organizational, institutional unity, although, of course, it cannot be *severed* from such forms of unity either. There can hardly be a "unity of the Spirit" without some form of organizational, institutional unity—but conversely, there *can* indeed be such forms of organizational, institutional unity that have very little to do with the "unity of the Spirit." Therefore, we must always be alert to the danger that the Spirit can be quenched (1 Thess. 5:19), and that we would be left with some form of human organization only.

The apostle is emphasizing not that there is only one Spirit, such as when we speak of the unity of God, nor that the Spirit is one. Rather, the point is that believers are not only positionally one (see 2:11-22) but must also be practically one. This is possible only through the Holy Spirit, in the "bond of peace" (cf. Col. 2:19; 3:14). The positional unity is a given; the body of Christ *is* one, despite all human division. But the church's practical unity is a continual challenge.

In Ephesians 4:3-6, just as in 2:18 (§10.5.1), the three persons of the Godhead are in view.

(a) The Ephesian believers have the same *Spirit*, here connected with the one body and the one Christian hope.

(b) They have one *Lord*, connected with the one Christian

---

56. Salmond (1979, 298).

faith (the Christian truth), and the one water baptism (which is a baptism in the name of the Lord; Acts 8:16; 19:5); all are brought under the Lord through the same "water gate," so to speak.

(c) They have one *Father* of all, referring here to all believers; he is over them all and through them all and in them all.[57]

This Trinitarian character of the believers' unity must be manifested in practice. They maintain their practical unity by moving together in the sphere of the one Spirit, serving together the one Lord, and calling together upon the one Father. I think that we may safely say that the first is the sphere of the *body* of Christ (1:23; 2:16) formed by the Spirit (1 Cor. 12:13). The second is the sphere of the *temple* of the Lord (Eph. 2:20–22). The third is the sphere of the *family* of God the Father (Eph. 2:18).

10.5.3 Philippians 2:1–5

This practical exhortation ties in with Philippians 2:1–2, "So if there is any encouragement in Christ, any comfort from love, any participation in the Spirit [Gk. *koinōnia pneumatos*], any affection and sympathy, complete my joy by being of the same mind [Gk. *to auto phronēte*], having the same love, being in full accord and of one mind [Gk. *to hen phronountes*]."

Here again, we cannot discuss every exegetical detail; I will simply refer to the mention of the Spirit here. The Greek phrase *koinōnia pneumatos* either suggests that Christians have the responsibility of demonstrating their unity and mutual fellowship in the power of the Holy Spirit (cf. NKJV), or refers to their common sharing in the Spirit (NIV) about which believers must be aware. A third suggested meaning, fellowship *with* the Spirit, seems to me less likely here.[58] A fourth suggestion has been that the passage is referring again to the human

---

57. The meaning of "all" is blurred if, without any solid basis, we read, "above all, and through all, and in *you* all" (KJV), or ". . . *us* all" (DRA).
58. *Contra* Müller (1984, 73).

spirit.[59]

I prefer to think here of the fellowship that believers have with *each other*, in the power of the Spirit, or in the sphere of the Spirit, or by sharing the same Spirit. It is through the Holy Spirit that although they may not necessarily think alike in all things, nevertheless they are *like-minded* in all things. This mind is described further in the following verses:

> Do nothing from selfish ambition or conceit, but in humility [Gk. *tapeinophrosynē*] count others more significant than yourselves. Let each of you look not only to his own interests [or things, affairs, qualities, plans; the Greek actually has no noun here], but also to the interests of others. Have this mind [Gk. *touto phroneite*] among yourselves, which is yours in Christ Jesus (Phil. 2:3–5).

Notice in verses 1–5 the four references to the Greek verb *phroneō*, which means here something like "to be minded," "to have one's mind directed upon." Being of one mind is having the minds of everyone oriented upon the same object. Verse 5 then means something like have the same mind (attitude, mentality) as Christ Jesus had, think the way Jesus thought (ERV); let the focus of your mind be the same as the focus of Jesus' mind.

10.6 Worship
10.6.1 John 4

Today there is only one temple that deserves the name "temple" in the true biblical sense, and this is the church of the living God. The physical temple at Jerusalem was, and will be, a "house of prayer" for all nations (Mark 11:17; cf. Isa. 56:7), and this is also true of the church as the spiritual temple of God. The Holy Spirit who dwells in it is a "Spirit of grace and of prayers" (Heb. *ruach chen wetachanunim*, Zech. 12:10). The same letter that calls the church of the living God the "house of God" (1 Tim. 3:15) places particular emphasis on prayer

---

59. Kent (1978, 126).

and worship (1:17; 2:1-2, 8; 4:5; 5:5; 6:16).

In John 4, in the story of the Samaritan woman, we find a passage that is of special importance for church life: "[T]he hour is coming, and is now here, when the true worshipers will worship the Father in spirit [NIV: Spirit] and truth, for the Father is seeking such people to worship him. God is spirit, and those who worship him must worship in s/Spirit and truth" (vv. 23-24). Notice the context. The woman had asked Jesus about the right place of worship: the sanctuary on Mount Gerizim, where the Samaritans worshiped, or the temple at Jerusalem, where the Jews worshiped. Jesus replies that in the new dispensation—which actually had already begun with his coming—the true worshipers would worship God the Father "in s/Spirit and truth." In Pauline language: Jesus is not necessarily saying that now God has done away with all earthly sanctuaries, but that there is today a spiritual sanctuary, composed of all true worshipers.

Jesus tells us that the Father is *seeking* such persons, that he *longs* for true worshipers. By declaring to the Father what he means to them, and how they admire his greatness, believers answer to the desires of his own heart. At the same time, the Father places a condition upon such worship: true worship must be in accordance with God's own character. God is s/Spirit, so that true worship takes place in "s/Spirit and truth." It is either "spirit" (lowercase "s"), that is, this worship is spiritual, and no longer earthly, material. Or it is "Spirit" (uppercase "S"), that is, worship worked in and through us by the Holy Spirit.

As usual, there has been much discussion about whether "spirit" or "Spirit" is the correct rendering. Leon Morris believed that "spirit" was intended, not Spirit, because worship would no longer involve a concrete, geographical place, and a corresponding outward form, but would be spiritual and truthful worship. Of course, true worship must take place in the power of the Spirit, but according to Morris this is not the point here.⁶⁰ Jesus is talking about worship in the true spirit.⁶¹

In contrast with this, Craig Keener has pleaded for the rendering of "Spirit and truth" because of the parallel with the expression "Spirit of truth" (John 14:17; 15:26; 16:13; 1 John 4:6). He supposes that "worshiping in [the power of] the Spirit" refers to ecstatic worship (1 Chron. 25:1-6; 1 Cor. 14:14-16).⁶²

William Kelly chose the rendering "spirit," but commented that believers cannot worship in spirit and truth without having the Spirit and knowing Christian truth. In addition to these two qualities, Jesus says that they must worship in the right attitude of spirit and truth. But this could not be the case if they would grieve the Spirit or dishonor the Lord.⁶³ Similarly, Arno Gaebelein argued that such worshiping of the Father with the heart (i.e., in spirit) is possible only for true believers, who are in Christ and possess the Holy Spirit, for only the Spirit makes this worship possible.⁶⁴

10.6.2 The Collective Aspect

Another verse relevant to our point is Philippians 3:3, which has the Greek phrase *hoi pneumati theou latreuontes*, which refers to those "serving [God] in/by/through [the] Spirit of God." Some manuscripts have the Greek phrase *hoi pneumati theōi latreuontes*, which means "serving God in spirit," or, "in/by/through [the] Spirit." Nevertheless, the first reading is preferred.⁶⁵ The Greek verb *latreuō* means "to serve" particularly in the sense of "rendering worship." Translations have either "to serve" or "to worship." In the letter to the Hebrews, the Greek verb *latreuō* is a technical term for the priestly ministry in the temple (8:5; 9:9; 10:2; 13:10; cf. also 9:1, 6, 14; 12:28; see further Rom. 9:4 NIV, "temple worship").

In line with John 4:23-24, Paul emphasizes in Philippians

---

60. Morris (1971, 270–71); cf. Bouma (1927, 64); Tenney (1910, 116–17).
61. Dods (1979, 728).
62. Keener (1997, 154).
63. Kelly (1966, 91–92).
64. Gaebelein (1980, 92).
65. Müller (1984, 107n4); Metzger (1975, 614).

3:3 that true worship is free of all geographical and cultic restrictions: those who serve/worship God through his Spirit, and glory in Christ Jesus, and put no confidence in the flesh, are the true "circumcision," in the spiritual sense, *not* those who cling to the literal circumcision and temple worship *without* the Spirit.[66] Here worshiping in the Spirit is being opposed to worshiping in the flesh.

Although, of course, such worship (Gk. *latreia*) can be performed individually (cf. Rom. 12:1), John 4 and Philippians 3 can also be applied collectively. Kelly wrote that, when worshipers are "sought" by the Father, they come together unto the name of the Lord (cf. Matt. 18:20) and enjoy his presence through the Spirit.[67] The collective aspect is far more important than the individual one, precisely because we are dealing here with the true, spiritual "temple worship," which is proper to the church as the temple of God. As a "spiritual house" (this is the church; cf. 1 Tim. 3:15; Heb. 3:6) believers are called to be "a holy priesthood, to offer spiritual sacrifices acceptable to God through Jesus Christ" (1 Pet. 2:5).

10.6.3 The Creative Aspect

Where the Holy Spirit is truly the leader of church worship, there we will always find creativity, for he is and remains the Creator-Spirit. Wherever creativity disappears, worship shrinks into traditional forms. Wherever the Spirit opens up new means and possibilities of worship, we invariably see more room for symbolism. According to God's creational order, humans are symbol users. Iconoclasm—destroying and eliminating symbolic forms of worship—has always impoverished the church's worship and life, and has reduced both to predominantly rational matters.[68]

One reason why some present-day Evangelical congregations feel strongly attracted to Eastern Orthodoxy—and in

---

66. Hess (1976, 550–51).
67. Kelly (1966, 91).
68. Pinnock (1996, 121–22).

some cases have even joined it—is because of this rich use of symbols. Where the Spirit becomes active, there you will find more interest in richer instrumental support of church singing, in flags and banners, in liturgical dancing and drama, in the visual arts, in clapping and lifting of hands, in shouts of joy, and the like. In §2.4.3, I quoted Ensley, who observed that from the ninth to the sixteenth centuries, spontaneous worship, improvised songs of jubilee, hand clapping, even dancing, and a kind of glossolalia, were common among saints, mystics, and many simple believers.[69] Renewed interest in incense, as well as in religious vestments and processions need not disquiet us, as long as such renewal is authentic, that is, comes from the heart, from a sincere and primary desire to please the Lord, not oneself.

Indeed, this is the criterion: if these outward forms become a goal in themselves, they will simply lead again to new, rigid, and ultimately empty traditions. Being authentic about these matters means arising from the Spirit. Both traditionalism (think of widely praised Calvinist "sobriety") and the restless yearning for novelty (as in "progressive" Evangelicalism) can easily arise from the flesh.

10.7 Jesus and the Church
10.7.1 Six Similarities

By submitting to baptism, Jesus united himself with the believing remnant in Israel that, through repentance and forgiveness of sins (Mark 1:4), had prepared itself for the coming of the Messiah. As a consequence, there are profound similarities between him and his people (who, from the Day of Pentecost, constitute the New Testament church).

(1) Jesus was born of the Spirit (Luke 1:35), the repenting person is reborn of the Spirit (John 3:5), and on the Day of Pentecost the church was born of the Spirit. The thought of a birth here is not strange if we consider that the church is a body and a bride; like Eve, she is "from man" (Gk. *ex andros*,

---

69. Ensley (1977).

1 Cor. 11:8), that is, from Christ.

(2) Jesus was "anointed with the Holy Spirit and with power" (Acts 10:38), just as this happens to all believers since the Day of Pentecost. To the "*church* of God that is at Corinth" (2 Cor. 1:1), Paul writes, "[I]t is God who establishes us with you in Christ, and has anointed us, and who has also put his seal on us and given us his Spirit in our hearts as a guarantee" (vv. 21-22; cf. 1 John 2:20, 27).)

(3) The Holy Spirit dwelled in Jesus, just as the Shekhinah had once dwelt in the tabernacle and the First Temple, and he (the Spirit/Shekhinah) now dwells in the church (1 Cor. 3:16; Eph. 2:22). This fact is manifested in power: the authority that was once upon Jesus is now upon the church (Acts 1:8; cf. John 14:12).

(4) When Jesus says of himself, "[O]n him the Father has set his seal" (John 6:27), the aorist tense of the Greek verb refers back to an event that occurred at a certain moment in the past, probably Jesus' baptism by John the Baptist.[70] By causing the Spirit to descend upon Jesus, and by declaring that Jesus was his beloved Son in whom he had found his pleasure, the Father put the seal of authenticity and authority upon him (cf. §4.8.1). Here again there is a clear similarity to the believers on whom, when they came to faith, the seal of the Spirit was put as well. In Ephesians 1:13, this is initially an individual matter, but in the course of the chapter the sum total of the sealed ones comes to refer to the church: God "put all things under his feet and gave him as head over all things to the church, which is his body, the fullness of him who fills all in all" (1:22-23).

(5) After having received the Holy Spirit, Jesus was immediately led by the Spirit into the wilderness (§6.2.3).[71] Sim-

---

70. Morris (1971, 359n71).
71. More accurately, "led up by the Spirit into the wilderness" (Gk. *anēchtē eis tēn erēmon*, Matt. 4:1) *versus* "led by the Spirit in the wilderness" (Gk. *ēgeto en tēi erēmōi*, Luke 4:1). Cf. Mark 1:12 ("The Spirit immediately drove him out into the wilderness"): Jesus was actually "driven out" by the Spirit.

ilarly, individual spiritual believers as well as the church as a whole are led by the Spirit (Rom. 8:14; Gal. 5:18; Acts 15:28), which occurs in the "wilderness" of their Christian walk (cf. 1 Cor. 10:1-11; Heb. 3:7-4:11). Both Jesus and the church are doing something similar to ancient Israel: "Now these things happened to them as an example, but they were written down for our instruction, on whom the end of the ages has come" (1 Cor. 10:11).

(6) What is remarkable here is that the presence of the Holy Spirit in Jesus' life brought him into direct and immediate contact with the powers of evil.[72] The same happened to the church; already in Acts 4, the early Christians declared, "[T]ruly in this city there were gathered together against your holy servant Jesus, whom you anointed, both Herod and Pontius Pilate, along with the Gentiles and the peoples of Israel, to do whatever your hand and your plan had predestined to take place. And now, Lord, look upon their threats and grant to your servants to continue to speak your word with all boldness, while you stretch out your hand to heal, and signs and wonders are performed through the name of your holy servant Jesus" (Acts 4:27-30).

10.7.2 Another Six Similarities

(7) Jesus was "declared to be the Son of God in power according to the Spirit of holiness by his resurrection from the dead" (Rom. 1:4). Similarly, Christians constitute a company of sons of God, who may indeed claim to be sons because they have received the "Spirit of the adoption as sons" (Rom. 8:15; cf. Gal. 4:6).

(8) Jesus had come into the world in order to testify to the truth in the power of the Spirit (John 18:37; cf. 1 Tim. 6:13); he was "the faithful (and true) witness" (Rev. 1:5; 3:14). Today, the believers must be the same: "[Y]ou will receive power when the Holy Spirit has come upon you, and you will be my witnesses in Jerusalem and in all Judea and Samaria,

---

72. Erickson (1983, 871).

and to the end of the earth" (Acts 1:8). It is the Spirit of truth who leads the church in fulfilling this task (John 14:27; 15:26; 16:13).

(9) When Jesus was on earth, he was not only the witness to, but also the embodiment of, the truth. No truth was found outside of him; he *is* the truth (14:6). In the deepest sense of the word, today no truth can be found outside the church, for it is the church that preserves the truth (in the forms of the Bible and of preaching), just as formerly Israel did the same (Rom. 3:2; but cf. also §10.9). Today, the church of the living God is the "pillar and foundation of the truth" (1 Tim. 3:15).

(10) In the power of the Spirit, the church continues the ministry that Jesus had begun on earth: "[W]hoever believes in me will also do the works that I do; and greater works than these will he do, because I am going to the Father" (John 14:12). "And these signs will accompany those who believe: in my name they will cast out demons; they will speak in new tongues; they will pick up serpents with their hands; and if they drink any deadly poison, it will not hurt them; they will lay their hands on the sick, and they will recover" (Mark 16:17-18).

(11) As Jesus testified in no other power than that of the Holy Spirit, the same is true of the church: "[W]hen they bring you to trial and deliver you over, do not be anxious beforehand what you are to say, but say whatever is given you in that hour, for it is not you who speak, but the Holy Spirit" (Mark 13:11).

(12) Just as people persecuted Jesus for his testimony, they would do this to Christians: "A servant is not greater than his master. If they persecuted me, they will also persecute you. If they kept my word, they will also keep yours" (John 15:20). In the power of the Spirit they will be able to endure the tribulations: "If you are insulted for the name of Christ, you are blessed, because the Spirit of glory [some insert: and of power] and of God rests upon you" (1 Pet. 4:14). Through many

tribulations believers must enter the kingdom of God (Acts 14:22), and the kingdom is the Holy Spirit's sphere of operation (§7.8.1).

10.7.3 Jesus as Prototype

It is understandable that Jesus has been called the "prototype of the church."[73] In biblical language: Christ is the head, the church is his body (Eph. 1:22-23; 2:16; 4:4, 12, 15-16; 5:23, 30; Col. 1:18, 24; 2:19; 3:15). The believers are in Christ (Rom. 8:1; 12:5; 2 Cor. 5:17; Gal. 1:22; 3:28; Eph. 1:1; 2:6; Col. 1:2, 28; 2:7, 10; 1 Thess. 2:14), and Christ is in them (John 6:56; 17:23, 26; Rom. 8:10; 2 Cor. 13:5; Col. 1:27). Sometimes when the New Testament says "church," it could just as well say "Christ": "For just as the body is one and has many members, . . . so it is with [not the church, as one would expect, but] Christ" (1 Cor. 12:12). Wherever the church is being persecuted, it can be said just as well that Jesus is being persecuted: "Saul, Saul, why are you persecuting *me*? . . . I am Jesus, whom you are persecuting" (Acts 9:4-5; 22:7-8; 26:14-15).

Compare this with another statement by Jesus: "Truly, I say to you, as you did it [i.e., benefits] to one of the least of these my brothers, you did it to me" (Matt. 40). So many features of Jesus' life in the world—he was begotten of, and anointed with, the Spirit, and sent into this world—now characterize the church: "As the Father has sent me, even so I am sending you" (John 20:21; cf. 17:18). In this world Jesus was the "faithful and true witness" (see above), so that now in his stead, the church has been called to give the very same testimony. This is its precious responsibility; therefore, in terms of this very quality Jesus is set in opposition to the unfaithfulness of the church at Laodicea (Rev. 3:14). In contrast to that unfaithful witness, brother Antipas (2:13) is a positive example; he was a "faithful witness" as Jesus had been.

This testimony contains an element of self-confirmation;

---

73. Pinnock (1996, 114). This is more correct than viewing Sophia/Mary as the prototype of the church (as Augustine does); see Ouweneel (1998, 253–55).

that is, the church performs this task not only out of duty but also because of the inner drive of the Holy Spirit. Wherever the power of the Spirit in the church is overflowing, the church cannot stop testifying. The only thing it has to do is to be at the disposition of the Spirit: "For out of the abundance of the heart the mouth speaks" (Matt. 12:34).[74] Therefore, spiritual revival in churches and congregations is so important, not only for their own benefit, but for the blessing of the world: "You are the salt of the earth, but if salt has lost its taste, how shall its saltiness be restored? It is no longer good for anything except to be thrown out and trampled under people's feet. You are the light of the world.[75] A city set on a hill cannot be hidden.[76] Nor do people light a lamp and put it under a basket,[77] but on a stand, and it gives light to all in the house. In the same way, let your light shine before others, so that they may see your good works and give glory to your Father who is in heaven" (Matt. 5:13–16).

10.7.4 Proper Preparation

The church's testimony in this world is not dependent primarily on believers' natural talents and appropriate education. When the Jewish leaders noticed that the apostles were "uneducated, common men," they were astonished. The point that really mattered was what we read in the sequel: first, Peter was "filled with the Holy Spirit" (Acts 4:8; cf. v. 31); second, the Jewish leaders "recognized that they [i.e., the apostles] had been with Jesus" (Acts 4:13).

These two great qualities do not exclude training, of course, for the disciples had been trained by Jesus himself for three and a half years, and before he became the apostle Paul, Saul of Tarsus had spent three years in the Arabian wilderness, to be alone with the Lord (Gal. 1:17). However, the very

---

74. Pinnock (1996, 142–43).
75. Elsewhere, Jesus testifies exactly the same about himself (John 8:12; 9:5).
76. In Rev. 21:9–10 this city is the New Jerusalem, which is illuminated by the glory of God, while the Lamb is its lamp (v. 23).
77. Or in a jar, or under the bed, or in a cellar (Luke 8:16; 11:33).

nature of this type of training makes it clear that the efficacy of the Christian testimony does not lie in academic training and degrees themselves; as Paul put it: "[M]y speech and my message were not in plausible words of wisdom, but in demonstration of the Spirit and of power" (1 Cor. 2:4). Throughout the centuries, missionary work in this world was done particularly by—often ordinary—people who were driven by the Holy Spirit: "[W]hen they bring you to trial and deliver you over, do not be anxious beforehand what you are to say, but say whatever is given you in that hour, for it is not you who speak, but the Holy Spirit" (Mark 13:11).

Of course, this is not to denigrate theological schools at all; for decades I was involved in them myself, with great pleasure. But it does say something critical about preaching and theologizing *without the power of the Spirit*. Let us never forget that academic training as such does not grant anyone this indispensable power.

Jesus gave us a striking example of this when he told the Sadducees, "You are wrong, because you know neither the Scriptures nor the power of God" (Matt. 22:29). Today, many would have great difficulty with an *ad hominem* accusation like this; they prefer theological arguments, not accusations. But Jesus knew, and knows, the hearts of his opponents. In a rational sense, the Sadducees were thoroughly familiar with the Scriptures, trained as they were by erudite rabbis. But they did not know the Scriptures in any spiritual, experiential sense because they lacked the power of the Spirit. As a consequence, fundamentally they did not understand the Scriptures even in a theological sense.

10.8 The Sacraments
10.8.1 What Are Sacraments?

Is there such a thing as a "sacrament"?[78] The etymology of the word need not occupy us now, but we do need to consider the theological sense. This is the meaning that the term has

---

78. See more extensively, Ouweneel (2010b, especially chapter 5).

gradually acquired (especially since Tertullian): a sacrament (re)presents God, who in the sacrament symbolically comes to people and blesses them. As such, the sacrament is a means of grace (of transference, of blessing), that is, a means for transferring God's grace (blessing) to the persons receiving the sacrament.[79] In the broader sense, God's Word is a means of grace or transference as well, because it confers blessing. In the narrower sense, a sacrament is traditionally understood as means of grace whereby the transference occurs with the help of material means (which, incidentally, has led to an almost continual discussion on the exact meaning of the phrase "with the help of").

These material means are the water of baptism, the bread and wine of the Lord's Supper, and the anointing oil (in the Roman Catholic Church, this oil is used in four sacraments: baptism, confirmation, consecration to the priesthood, and the anointing of the sick). In addition to this material means (Lat. *medium*, plural, *media*), there are many other means through which, by the working of the Holy Spirit, divine grace (blessing, salvation) comes to people. Occasionally these have also been referred to as "sacraments": preaching, prayer, hymn singing, benedictions, the laying on of hands, confession, the ministry of deliverance, the ministry of deacons, the pastoral interview, the fellowship of the saints, and so on.

All these means of grace have been described as the "instrumentarium of the Holy Spirit."[80] The Holy Spirit is not bound to these means, as (especially Roman Catholic) *sacramentalism* suggests, which virtually limits the working of the Spirit to the sacraments. The most extreme form regarding the material sacrament as presenting God to people is found in the doctrine of transubstantiation, according to which the bread and wine of the Eucharist are really and physically transformed into the real body and blood of Christ. But in

---

79. See Bavinck (*RD* 4.464–95); Berkhof (1986, 347–48); Van Genderen and Velema (2008, 753–57, 779–87).
80. Th. L. Haitjema, mentioned by Van Genderen and Velema (2008, 755).

fact, the extreme sacramentalist view is encountered also in the traditional doctrine according to which a person is regenerated in or through water baptism (a teaching based on an unwarranted appeal to John 3:5, "born of water and Spirit"). In both cases, the idea is that, in the administration of the sacrament, something really "happens," whether to the material symbols themselves, or at least to the persons to whom the sacrament is administered.

In opposition to this, we find the *spiritualistic* (particularly Evangelical) tendency, which severs the Spirit from the sacraments, and belittles the latter. The term "sacrament" is then strictly rejected, and water baptism and the Lord's Supper are reduced to purely symbolic acts. Baptism and the Lord's Supper "refer" to something, but they do not "do" anything to the person receiving them. This view appears not to take certain passages very seriously: in water baptism the person "puts on Christ" — not: baptism is a symbol of *having* put on Christ (Gal. 3:27); in/through baptism a person is "buried" and "raised" — not: baptism is a symbol of *having* been buried and raised with Christ (Rom. 6:4; Col. 2:12); baptism "saves" — not: baptism is a symbol of *having* been saved (1 Pet. 3:21). And regarding the Lord's Supper: it *is* a "participation in [or communion of] the body of Christ" — not just a symbol of it (1 Cor. 10:16). This sacramental way of speaking, which in my view is thoroughly biblical, is traditionally identified by the Latin words *phraseologia sacramentalis*.

10.8.2 How the Sacraments Work

This is not the place to explain the character of the sacraments any further.[81] For the moment, our most important conclusion must be that, during the administration of water baptism and the Lord's Supper, the Holy Spirit "does" something, or at least *intends* to "do" something. Water baptism is the gracious admission on God's behalf to the spiritual sphere of the king-

---

81. See extensively, Ouweneel (2010b, chapters 5–9).

dom of God,[82] and the Lord's Supper is by nature "eucharist," that is, thanksgiving (1 Cor. 11:24, Gk. *eucharistēsas*), praise to God (10:16, Gk. *eulogia*), and thus a special form of fellowship with God. The traditional Latin phrase for how sacraments work is *ex opere operato* ("through the act performed"), that is, their efficacy belongs to the *nature* of baptism and the Lord's Supper as *accomplishing* initiation and thanksgiving, respectively, apart from the words that we actually think or speak when partaking in these sacraments. Of course, this does not imply anything automatic, as if the inner intention plays no role; after all, it is possible to eat and drink judgment upon oneself by eating and drinking in a way that displeases God (1 Cor. 11:29.)

Water baptism and the Lord's Supper are intended to be, through the work of the Holy Spirit, concrete encounters with God and his grace. Insight into this matter might grow if Protestants would begin to recognize the anointing of the sick with oil (James 5:14-16) as another sacrament (which is an ambiguous and multivalent term).[83] The reason for our claim is that here, if anywhere, the elders are expecting the administration of this very sacrament to effect the flowing of God's healing grace to the sick. It is in this sacrament *par excellence* that God is present in his grace with his Spirit, all symbolized in the oil.

But could it be different in water baptism and the Lord's Supper? In this book, I emphasize several times that conversion, water baptism, and Spirit baptism are closely connected. Consider the examples discussed in §§7.3-7.7 above, especially the three thousand new converts on the Day of Pentecost: "Repent and be baptized every one of you in the name of Jesus Christ for the forgiveness of your sins, and you will receive the gift of the Holy Spirit" (Acts 2:38). It is fascinating to see how Saul in Acts 9:17 receives this promise through Ananias: "Brother Saul, the Lord Jesus who appeared to you on the

---

82. See extensively, Ouweneel (*RT* IV/2, §4.4 and Appendix 1).
83. See extensively, Ouweneel (2010b, chapters 6–7).

road by which you came has sent me so that you may regain your sight and be filled with the Holy Spirit." Compare this with the command in 22:16, "Rise and be baptized and wash away your sins, calling on his name." In a sense, this is the same command.

In Acts 19:5-6, too, water baptism and Spirit baptism are closely connected: "On hearing this, they [i.e., the twelve disciples at Ephesus] were baptized in [or, into, unto] the name of the Lord Jesus. And when Paul had laid his hands on them, the Holy Spirit came on them, and they began speaking in tongues and prophesying." We can imagine how the baptized persons rose from the water, and how Paul immediately laid hands on them—as still happens in many congregations. Water baptism and Spirit baptism occur, or should occur, together.

In Acts 2, the effect of Spirit baptism can be seen very strikingly in, among other things, the celebration of the Lord's Supper:

> So those who received his word were baptized, and there were added that day about three thousand souls. And they devoted themselves to the apostles' teaching and the fellowship, to the breaking of bread and the prayers. . . . And day by day, attending the temple together and breaking bread in their homes, they received their food with glad and generous hearts, praising God and having favor with all the people (vv. 41-42, 46-47).

This is a celebration in the power of the Holy Spirit; this is Jesus who is "known" (or "made known," CEB) to (or "recognized by," GNT) the church "in the breaking of the bread" (Luke 24:35). Such a recognition of the Lord is linked inseparably with the "burning hearts" (v. 32) of those celebrating.

10.8.3 Sacraments and the Spirit

Paul suggested in 1 Corinthians 10:3-4 that the Lord's Supper is "Spirit-ual" food and "Spirit-ual" drink. This seems to be what John Calvin meant:

> But the sacraments properly fulfill their office only when the Spirit, that inward teacher, comes to them, by whose power alone hearts are penetrated and affections moved and our souls opened for the sacraments to enter in. If the Spirit be lacking, the sacraments can accomplish nothing more in our minds than the splendor of the sun shining upon blind eyes, or a voice sounding in deaf ears. Therefore, I make such a division between Spirit and sacraments that the power to act rests with the former, and the ministry alone is left to the latter — a ministry empty and trifling, apart from the action of the Spirit, but charged with great effect when the Spirit works within and manifests his power.[84]

Whereas Roman Catholics and Lutherans were particularly concerned with the "real presence" (Lat. *praesentia realis*) of Christ under the emblems of bread and wine, Calvin emphasized instead the presence of the Holy Spirit. In the *Catechism of Geneva*, written by Calvin in 1542, he does say that Christ "adds reality" to the figures of bread and wine in the Lord's Supper (Q & A 353). To the next question (354): "But how can this be, when the body of Christ is in heaven, and we are still pilgrims on the earth?", the reply is given: "This he accomplishes by the secret and miraculous agency of his Spirit, to whom it is not difficult to unite things otherwise disjoined by a distant space."

The sacraments themselves do not effectuate things automatically; they do not bring about the realities symbolized by these sacraments. Such a view would be purely magical. Conversely, neither are the sacraments just symbolic acts, acts that have no inner performative reality. They do possess performative reality — but this reality has no spiritual meaning apart from the Holy Spirit. Clark Pinnock rightly argued that the anti-sacramentalist attitude of many Protestants, especially Evangelicals, results from the matter-spirit dualism, which sacramental attitude began particularly with Ulrich Zwing-

---

84. Calvin, *Institutes* 4.14.9.

li.[85] As a consequence of this dualism, many Protestants have difficulty appreciating material symbols because they cannot imagine how these could relate to spiritual reality.

There is no true celebration of the Lord's Supper without the Spirit, who is, first, the power and stimulus unto a true eucharist (thanksgiving), and, second, the power unto the concrete personal experience of the "communion of the blood of Christ" and the "communion of the body of Christ" (1 Cor. 10:16 NKJV). The command to "give thanks in all circumstances" is followed immediately by this other command: "Do not quench the Spirit" (1 Thess. 5:18-19). If we better understood water baptism, it would become more self-evident that the fullness of the Spirit begins to be manifested from the moment a person has received this baptism. If we better understood the Lord's Supper, we would, when celebrating it, be more filled with the Spirit unto true thanksgiving (eucharist): "[B]e filled with the Spirit, addressing one another in psalms and hymns and spiritual songs, singing and making melody to the Lord with your heart, giving thanks (Gk. *eucharistountes*) always and for everything to God the Father in the name of our Lord Jesus Christ" (Eph. 5:18-20). And if we better understood the anointing of the sick, under the sign of the oil the healing power of the Holy Spirit would be manifested more significantly.

10.9 The Universal Spirit and Christ
10.9.1 The Spirit's Omnipresence

Although the church is the dwelling place of the Holy Spirit, we should never limit the Spirit's presence on earth to the church. God the Spirit is and remains omnipresent: "Where shall I go from your Spirit? Or where shall I flee from your presence?" (Ps. 139:7). Also compare these deuterocanonical statements: "The Lord's Spirit fills the whole world" (Wisd. 1:7 CEB). "Your imperishable spirit is present in all things"

---

85. Pinnock (1996, 125; cf. 127, the sacraments do not work automatically but derive their efficacy from the presence of the Spirit in relation to faith).

(12:1 CEB). Earlier in §10.7.2 I did assert that ultimately there is no truth to be found outside the church, and this is correct as far as Christian doctrine is concerned. However, what traditional theology calls "general revelation" (Lat. *revelatio generalis*) comprises God's revelation in the cosmos and in nature, in culture and in history (see extensively §5.1 above).

In his monumental work on the Holy Spirit, Clark Pinnock devoted an entire chapter to the universality of the Holy Spirit.[86] This means that the Holy Spirit works far beyond the boundaries of Christianity. Sometimes, however, Pinnock seems to suggest that this can also mean that he works beyond the reach of Christ, or apart from Christ. He pleads for the omission of *filioque* in the Nicene Creed (see §1.6 above) because he fears that the Spirit is being viewed as a gift that is limited to the sphere of the Son's activities.[87] But this is precisely what I wish to emphasize: the Spirit cannot be severed from Christ and his work, precisely as the will of his word, as we know this from God's general revelation (§5.1), cannot be severed from Christ and his work.

In other words, we must speak here of the Christological connection between the *general* work of God's Spirit in nature, culture, and history, and the *particular* work of God's Spirit in effectuating God's salvation in Christ. This is such an important matter that it deserves our closest attention. It is an ancient problem: what is the precise relationship between Jesus' central creational position in the first creation (John 1:3; Col. 1:16; Heb. 1:2) and his central redemptive position in the renewed creation? Or, what is the precise relationship between the Spirit's *universal* position in the first creation and his *special* position in the second creation? Reformed theologian Herman Ridderbos said of it that

> in him [i.e., Christ] God has given to all creation its existing-to-

---

86. Pinnock (1996, 185–214: "Spirit and Universality"); also see Johnson (2002, 124–28).
87. Pinnock (1996, 196–97).

gether, its mutual coherence. Outside Christ, each creature and every power is disintegrated. Only because and insofar as they are borne by Christ, and stand under his rule, they possess their coherent and meaningful relationship to all other creatures. . . . Christ [is] the carrying ground and concentration point of each creature and every power.[88]

The actual *problem* in each interpretation of the Bible passages just mentioned is clearly illustrated here by Ridderbos. It is the problem that many expositors speak vaguely of Christ's power and dominion over all things *without* indicating whether, and how, these are related to the first creation, or whether these are limited to the redeemed world (cf. the same problem with regard to Matt. 28:18, "All authority in heaven and on earth has been given to me"). When we frame the problem in terms of the Holy Spirit, the question becomes: Does the Spirit work universally, that is, in the entire creation, on the basis of *general* revelation, and thus of the first creation, or on the basis of *special* revelation, and thus of Christ's work of redemption, and thus of the new creation? Does the Holy Spirit bring cultural blessing (in whatever form) within the framework of redemption, or apart from this framework, that is, within that of the first creation? Or is this simply an altogether false dilemma?[89]

10.9.2 Barth and Some Opponents

The problem just described was both sharply posited and well answered by Karl Barth.[90] Because of his fierce rejection of any form of natural revelation, he approached each Bible passage concerning creation in and through Christ in an exclusively redemptive-historical, infralapsarian way.[91] However, this implied that his view presupposed the scholastic

---

88. Ridderbos (1960, 139; cf. also 1975, 82, 387–92, on Col. 1:16–17).
89. Resolving this theological problem forms the heart of Ouweneel (2017a); for a more extensive discussion of this crucial matter, I refer the interested reader to this work.
90. See especially Barth (*CD* III/1).
91. Cf. also Ebeling (1979, 251–52).

nature-grace dualism, but with all the emphasis now being placed on the grace component.

This has been called Barth's "Christomonism" (or "Christocentrism," "Christocracy"). He did not want to interpret John 1:3 ("All things were made though him") apart from John 1:14 ("the Word became flesh").[92] According to Barth, this means that God wanted to know and love his Son from eternity in this way, namely, *in view of* the fact that the Son would become the Mediator, the incarnate Word. And as such he was the "motive" (Ger. *Beweggrund*) of creation. In fact, we cannot even speak of the Logos "as such." As Bolkestein has summarized Barth's view: God created the world in order to be able to redeem it. John's prologue is not about cosmology but about soteriology; from verse 1 onward, the subject is not creation but salvation.[93]

No expositor doubts that the prologue of John's Gospel (1:1-13) refers to Jesus, and culminates in the incarnation of verse 14. In this way the soteriological aspect is implied from the outset. However, we cannot *begin* the prologue with verse 14, and then assign every pre-temporal aspect of the prologue a soteriological meaning. I wonder, however, if Berkouwer himself has transcended the cosmological-soteriological dilemma, just as F. W. Grosheide continued to presuppose this dilemma in his claim that John does not sever the soteriological from the cosmic.[94] As long as this dualism is presupposed, there is no effective defense against Barth, no real room for the general revelation,[95] and thus no real room for the idea of the cosmic universality of the Holy Spirit.

One of the central ideas of Neo-Calvinist (philosophical and theological) thought is that Christ is the Root (Gk. *archē*), the Firstborn, of both the first creation (Col. 1:15) and the new creation (Rom. 8:29; Col. 1:18; Heb. 1:6; Rev. 1:5). It is my strong

---

92. Barth (*CD* III/1, 54).
93. Bolkestein (1949, 5).
94. Grosheide (1949, 76; cf. 83, 116).
95. Cf. Troost (1978, 114–15).

impression that here we have the most balanced approach to the biblical claim that all things have been created *in*, and exist *in*, Christ (Col. 1:16-17). In the Bible, this notion is constantly and without any distinction applied both soteriologically and cosmologically (if we may still retain these terms for a moment). Not only is the eternal Son, the divine Logos, the Root (Gk. *archē*) of both creation and re-creation, but the *incarnate* Logos, Christ, the *Man* anointed with the Spirit, is also the cosmological-soteriological Root of the cosmos. The transcendent unity, fullness, and concentration of the *one* cosmos exist in him who "upholds the universe by the word of his power" (Heb. 1:3). This is what Paul expressed in the words: "In him we live and move and have our being," appealing to a pagan poet who had said, "For we are indeed his offspring" — which Paul applied to *all* humanity (Acts 17:28).

10.10 Creation and Re-Creation
10.10.1 No Dualism

Concerning the relationship between God's general revelation and God's special revelation, A. Troost said:

> This placing alongside one another, and then inevitably under and above one another, of the alleged twofold revelation acts of God can, in our view, be arrested in its disastrous theological consequences only by means of the alternative of acknowledging only the single revelation-in-Christ, the Word, that from the beginning was with God. This self-revelation of God in his eternal Word maintains its central position of source, fullness, and transcendence in time when it is manifest after the Fall in the saving and liberating redemptive work of Jesus, the Christ. But then continually *from out of* the divine Origin, who remains faithful to himself and to his creation within and above all times and historical formation, until the "consummation" of "eternity."[96]

A Christian view of reality has no room for the scholastic

---
96. Ibid., 115–16.

nature-grace dualism, and therefore no room for any underlying dualism between general revelation and special revelation. This means as well that a Christian view of reality has no room for any universal work of the Holy Spirit in the created cosmos apart from Christ, and refuses to limit his activity instead to his special redemptive work in connection with the new creation in Christ.[97] Since there is neither contrast, contradiction, conflict, nor tension between God's creational word and his redemptive word, there is also no tension between the Spirit's work in creation and his work in redemption. In Christ these works are absolutely one (in the sense of identical) because Christ is the one Logos of God. Troost argued "that the cross of Christ was manufactured *in* and *from* the creation in order that Christ could carry, redeem, and deliver this creation from its un-nature, and bring it to its fulfillment and consummation."[98]

10.10.2 One Word of God

The implications of the view just summarized are far reaching. There can be no contrast between creation and salvation if we realize that God's good creation—the one that existed before the Fall—in principle contained blessing and bliss, the complete and the perfect. It was the calling of humanity to follow this path of blessing, which was the route of tending and developing the creation, of "subduing and having dominion," of "working and keeping" (Gen. 1:28; 2:15). Before sin entered the creation, *this* was the way of true and real life in the power of the Holy Spirit. And after sin had entered the creation, this remained the same way of life in the power of the Holy Spirit, though now on the basis of redemption in Christ. Therefore the creation as it was "in the beginning" and the eschatological future of Christ cannot be pitted against each other. The

---

97. Kuyper (2008) wanted to eliminate this dualism from all forms of thinking. However, by maintaining the distinction of a *principium speciale* and a *principium naturale* in theology (309–311), his system continued to employ the dualism, although he denied this (335).
98. Troost (1976, 86; cf. 29–30).

great emphasis that the New Testament Gospels place on living in the light of the coming kingdom of God, which breaks through in the Spirit, is not in contrast with God's creational revelation, for the kingdom of God exists in no domain other than *this* created cosmos.[99]

These considerations do not at all conflict with the expectation that a world will ultimately emerge that far surpasses what would have been possible without the Fall and redemption. History is not circular, whereby the end would return to the beginning, but history is a spiral, whereby *this* world is restored, but to a higher level than it existed before the Fall. (I have explained this in several earlier volumes of the present series.)

G. Spykman emphasized that the creational word remains God's first Word for the world. It is also an enduring Word; God did not withdraw it, although this Word for creation now, in a fallen world, has become a double-edged sword, speaking of both the severity of its Author and his goodness. The difficulty arises not from God's Word but from human responses. Therefore, that first Word, though still sufficient for God's original intention, is no longer sufficient for our present need. That first Word, thanks to God's condescending grace, is not his last Word, for God fulfills his creational word through his redemptive word. The gospel is a second, redemptively renewed edition of God's creational word, now in a linguistic form.[100]

The world in which the Holy Spirit is universally active is the same world as the one that God created in the beginning, even though sin has intervened. The goal toward which God is working is still the same goal he had at creation, namely, leading the world to full blessing and bliss, though since the Fall and Christ's death and resurrection, the route toward this has become a *redemptive* path. When Paul describes the "new

---

99. See already (in the wake of Calvin) Kuyper (1900, 1:27–46); further Troost (1969, 12, 35–37; 1982, 189–92).
100. Spykman (1988, 142–43; cf. 1992, 88–90).

person," he indicates how in practice this person flourishes within the spheres of God's created world, namely, within mutual relationships between people, marriage partners, parents and children, masters and slaves (Eph. 4:22–6:9; Col. 3:9–4:1; Titus 2:1–10; cf. 1 Pet. 2:13–3:9). The "new creation" is not a new structure or structural order replacing the old one, but a radical renewal of the *direction* of the human heart through the power of the Holy Spirit, so that regenerated people live within the creational order in a totally *new* way, no longer oriented toward sin but toward Christ.

10.10.3 *Creatio Continua?*

The view just described implies a refutation of two other views (discussed in this and the next section).[101] First, it combats the idea of an ongoing creation (Lat. *creatio continua*), a continuing work of divine creation within history, particularly within the social structures of our time. In this humanistic idea, autonomous human social and historical actions are identified with God's creational activity, supposedly occurring through the Holy Spirit. This view is typical for all kinds of liberation theology, third-world theology, and feminist theology, which all love to be pneumatological (cf. §2.5). The guidelines for such renewal theologies are derived from the new creation, or from the kingdom of God, or directly from the Holy Spirit, but not from the unchangeable creational order, that is, from God's eternal Torah.

I am not discussing here those views in which the idea of an ongoing creation is watered down to little more than providence or the upholding of creation.[102] This idea has been criticized for obscuring the biblical distinction between creation out of nothing (Lat. *creatio ex nihilo*; cf. the term "finished" in Gen. 2:1) and preservation of the already-finished creation (*conservatio post creationem*; see §§5.1 and 5.2).[103] More

---

101. Cf. Berkouwer (1952, 61–74); Troost (1969, 14–15; 1976, 30–31, 148–49).
102. See Bavinck (*RD* 2.604–608); Kuyper (1910, 2.37–39).
103. Berkouwer (1952, 68).

important is *how* exactly human responsibility under God's ordinances in the present sinful world must be understood. Neo-Calvinism has dealt with this problem in the framework of the cultural mandate and common grace.[104] These have led to heated discussions,[105] particularly in connection with whether common grace must be severed from Christ's redemptive work.[106]

Once we are delivered from the scholastic nature–grace dualism this issue disappears. Everything that exists, from spiders to galaxies, manifests the power of the Spirit. He is present in all human experience and beyond. There is no special sacred sphere, no sacred–secular dichotomy. Practically everything within the created order can be a sacrament (read: a manifestation; see §10.8) of God's presence. The Spirit is present in the struggle to make creatures whole, giving hope to the hopeless, and working for reconciliation in order to create newness. The Spirit renews the face of the ground (cf. Ps. 104:30), and works to restore brokenness. For where sin is abundant, grace abounds all the more (Rom. 5:20). The Spirit is the power of redemption only because he is first the power of creation. Only the Spirit of creation is strong enough to be the Spirit of resurrection (cf., e.g., Rom. 1:4; 1 Pet. 3:18 NKJV). Let us stop degrading the Spirit by confining him to the spheres of church and of piety. His role in creation is foundational for these other activities. The entire creation is home for the operations of the Spirit, and the cosmic fruits of these operations anticipate the new creation. The Spirit is the perfecter of God's works in creation.[107]

10.10.4 *Creatio Nova?*

This brings us to the second misunderstanding with regard to the relationship between creation and redemption, namely,

---

104. See Douma's summary of this framework (1966).
105. Cf. Puchinger (1970) regarding the debate in 1936 between Oepke Noordmans and Klaas Schilder.
106. See my recent discussion of these matters in Ouweneel (2017a).
107. Pinnock (1996, 62–63).

the view of a "new creation" (Lat. *creatio nova*), which supposedly is not a restoration of the original creation but *replaces* it altogether.[108] To restore does *not* simply mean repair, as if redemption would merely bring creation back to its pre-Fall state. If this were the case, creation might fall into sin again, and redemptive history might repeat itself in a cyclical way. But this is not the case. To restore the creation is to add tremendous value, in contrast with merely repairing creation — a point that cannot be developed further here.[109]

Restoration means that it is *this* creation that God, through redemption and in the power of the Holy Spirit, restores in order to lead it to its true completion and consummation. God never gives up the present creation. If he were to destroy it by replacing it, he would then surrender the first creation to the power of sin and Satan. He would then admit to having lost his power over the first creation, and to being able to respond to this only by creating an entirely new world. God does not *replace* his creation but *renews* it. This is the force of the word "new" (Gk. *kainos* or *neos*) in the "new person" (Eph. 2:15; 4:24; Col. 3:9-10) and the "new creation" (2 Cor. 5:17; Gal. 6:15).

The real source of the entire problem involving the relationship between creation and re-creation is, as stated earlier, the scholastic nature–grace dualism, in its older form or its newer humanistic form of the nature–freedom dualism. In the latter case, it is manifested in the so-called "twofold order" (Lat. *duplex ordo*), the doctrine of the two realms or kingdoms: the natural kingdom of earthly and human realities, and the supernatural (spiritual) kingdom of God's revelation and the work of the Holy Spirit. This is the well-known dualism of

---

108. Irenaeus (*Adv. Haer.* book II) defended the continuity of creation and re-creation against the Gnostics, who alleged that the Creator-God and the Redeemer-God were not the same God. According to Irenaeus, it is the same Spirit who is working in both the old creation and the new creation.
109. Cf. Ouweneel (2012a; 2017a). This subject touches upon one of the essential differences between the views of Emil Brunner (who defended continuity and restoration) and Karl Barth (who defended discontinuity and replacement); see the summary by Heron (1980, 84-88).

law and gospel, of the two "regiments" (related to Luther's two kingdoms, one on God's left hand and the other on his right hand), of commandment and ordinances,[110] of church and society, of soul and body,[111] of the sacred and the secular, of the Christian and the human, of faith and reason, of general revelation and special revelation, and so forth.[112] Although some of these dualisms are not popular in theology anymore, nevertheless the same fundamental dualism lives on under different names and in different forms.

The thoroughly biblical, vertical antithesis between God and Satan, between the Spirit and the flesh, is being replaced here by a putative horizontal antithesis, with an artificial *structural* antithesis *within* created reality, a supposed antithesis between the old creation and the redeemed part of creation. However, the antithesis between the Spirit's power and sin's power runs *right through* both the so-called "natural" and "supernatural" realms: through both church and society, through both the sacred and the secular, through faith and intellect (if we may still retain these false contrasts for a moment). The Holy Spirit is working hard to bring church *and* society, faith *and* reason, Christians *and* Muslims, Animists, Neo-Pagans, Buddhists and Hindus to acknowledge the universal authority of Christ and to surrender themselves to him.

10.11 The Spirit Blows Where He Wishes
10.11.1 Working Outside the Church

The Holy Spirit does not need the church in order for him to be active in this world, just as he did not need Old Testament Israel for this. Throughout all of history, God has been engaged with all the nations of the world, without any interference from Israel or the church: "'Are you not like the Cushites to me, O people of Israel?' declares the LORD. 'Did I not bring up Israel from the land of Egypt, and the Philistines

---

110. Brunner (1937).
111. See Ouweneel (1986, especially chapters 5–6; 2008a, chapters 7–8).
112. See extensively, Ouweneel (2017a).

from Caphtor and the Syrians from Kir?'" (Amos 9:7). The apostle Paul witnessed to the Gentiles that God "did not leave himself without witness, for he did good by giving you rains from heaven and fruitful seasons, satisfying your hearts with food and gladness" (Acts 14:17).

In Acts 17:22-31 Paul discerned an even deeper connection between the religion of the Greeks and the service of the true God. He could do so because every pagan religion is a response — no matter how distorted, incomplete, and partially treacherous — to God's general revelation, and partly also to his special (Noahic) revelation.[113] God's Spirit worked with Melchizedek and his followers, with Job and his friends, entirely apart from the line of the patriarchs. God's Spirit was working on Cornelius' heart, entirely apart from the apostles; they came in later to round off the Spirit's work (Acts 10). Peter had to acknowledge that "in every nation anyone who fears him and does what is right is acceptable to him" (v. 35). This truth has been far too underappreciated by Christians, one that, if it would be properly discerned, could offer a clearly defined view of the Spirit's work also among people of other religions.

A similar thorough consideration is repeatedly necessary with regard to Paul's remarkable words that God "will render to each one according to his works: to those who by patience in well-doing seek for glory and honor and immortality, he will give eternal life . . . glory and honor and peace for everyone who does good, the Jew first and also the Greek. For God shows no partiality. For . . . the doers of the law . . . will be justified" (Rom. 2:6-7, 10-11, 13). This does *not* imply that salvation could occur apart from Christ and his redemptive work, or apart from the work of the Holy Spirit in human souls. On the contrary: (a) "[T]here is salvation in no one else, for there is no other name under heaven given among men by which we must be saved" (Acts 4:12; cf. John 14:6), and (b)

---

113. See Ouweneel (2003, 315–26).

there is no eternal life without regeneration and justification, and these are given by the Spirit only (John 3:5; 1 Cor. 6:11; Titus 3:5). According to Romans 2:6–13, good works are not an aim in themselves, but a sign of the inner hope for the one, true *God*, whose glory and honor are being sought (v. 7).

10.11.2 Aslan and Emeth

Irenaeus expressed the conviction that the Holy Spirit had been sent "to all the earth" (Lat. *in omnem terram*), and that he was operating among the *entire* human race.[114] And to Ambrose these astonishing words are ascribed: "All that is true, no matter by whom it was said, is from the Holy Spirit" (Lat. *Omne verum, a quocumque dicitur, a Spiritu Sancto est*).[115] The Reformer Ulrich Zwingli wrote that no single good person has lived, no single godly heart or believing soul has existed from the beginning of the world to its end, whom believers will not see in the presence of God.[116]

In his own way, C. S. Lewis placed the following words on the lips of Aslan the Lion (a figure of Christ) spoken to the pagan soldier Emeth:

> Child, all the service thou hast done to [the false god] Tash, I account as service done to me. . . . Not because he and I are one, but because we are opposites, I take to me the services which thou hast done to him. For I and he are of such different kinds that no service which is vile can be done to me, and none which is not vile can be done to him. Therefore if any man swear by Tash and keep his oath for the oath's sake, it is by me that he has truly sworn, though he know it not, and it is I who reward him. And if any man do a cruelty in my name, then, though he says the name Aslan, it is Tash whom he serves and by Tash his deed is accepted. . . . Beloved, . . . unless thy desire had [in fact] been for me thou wouldst not have sought so long and so truly.

---

114. *Adv. Haer.* III.11.8v.; vgl. 17.1–3.
115. MPL 17, 245; cf. Holmes (1977 book title: *All Truth Is God's Truth*).
116. Quoted in Bromiley (1953, 275–76).

For all find what they truly seek.[117]

As we apply this to the real world, we can state that such people are saved only on the basis of Christ's redemptive work. They truly seek God only through the power of the Holy Spirit working in them. But that does not change the fact that there are people who cannot help being ignorant of the gospel of Jesus Christ, but who nevertheless "seek God, and perhaps feel their way toward him and find him" (Acts 17:27), and, touched by his Spirit, long to do his will in accordance with their conscience (Rom. 2:14–15).

The Holy Spirit does not work among Christians alone, but also among Muslims, Hindus, Buddhists, (neo-)Pagans, and atheists. We are told about visions of Jesus Christ granted by the Holy Spirit to Jews and Muslims, so that they come to faith in Christ. In one year, I met an Israeli Jew and a Palestinian Muslim who, independently of each other, had received a vision of Jesus, which was the beginning of their conversion to the God of Jesus Christ. I have spoken with both of them. Both now preach the gospel. We are told by missionaries that in certain areas in North Africa and the Middle East hundreds of Muslims come to Christ, without much influence by missionaries. We are told of regions where missionaries found people who had never heard the gospel, but who apparently had been fully prepared by the Holy Spirit (sometimes also by visions of Jesus, or visions of the missionaries who would visit them).

10.11.3 The Spirit Is Universal

For some Christians, these stories raise a host of questions concerning general or particular atonement, election and reprobation, the necessity of preaching the gospel, and so on— questions that fall outside the scope of the present study.[118] We suffice with establishing that the Holy Spirit is at work

---

117. Lewis (1956, 149); the name Emeth is probably an allusion to the Hebrew term *emeth*, "faithfulness, truth."
118. See extensively, Ouweneel (2009b; RT III/1).

among all people, in all cultures and religions. According to John V. Taylor, the Holy Spirit is the incessant, dynamic communicator and mediator working on each element and every process of the material universe, the immanent and anonymous presence of God.[119]

The Spirit is active not only in all cultural work, but also in every restless quest for the ultimate and firm grounds of human existence. The wisdom of God in his works of creation cannot be ignored (Prov. 3:19-20). It is this same wisdom — which coincides with the Holy Spirit — of which is said, "Does not wisdom call? Does not understanding raise her voice? On the heights beside the way, at the crossroads she takes her stand; beside the gates in front of the town, at the entrance of the portals she cries aloud: 'To you, O men, I call, and my cry is to the children of man'" (Prov. 8:1-4). This is a voice that is still heard, not only in gospel preaching but also in all forms of wisdom that can be perceived within human experience.[120]

Lady *Chokmah* or *Ruach* appeals to people's wise insight, but also to their consciences. She does so because her delighting is "in the children of man":

> And now, O sons, listen to me: blessed are those who keep my ways. Hear instruction and be wise, and do not neglect it. Blessed is the one who listens to me, watching daily at my gates, waiting beside my doors. For whoever finds me finds life and obtains favor from the LORD, but he who fails to find me injures himself; all who hate me love death (Prov. 8:31-36).

Thus, the appeal of Lady Wisdom — that is, the Holy Spirit — still operates throughout the entire world, through a wide variety of channels, sometimes directly in the hearts of people:

> Wisdom has built her house; she has hewn her seven pillars. She has slaughtered her beasts; she has mixed her wine; she

---

119. Taylor (1972, 64).
120. Pinnock (1996, 193).

has also set her table. She has sent out her young women to call from the highest places in the town, "Whoever is simple, let him turn in here!" To him who lacks sense she says, "Come, eat of my bread and drink of the wine I have mixed. Leave your simple ways, and live, and walk in the way of insight." ... The fear of the Lord is the beginning of wisdom, and the knowledge of the Holy One is insight. For by me your days will be multiplied, and years will be added to your life (Prov. 9:1–6, 10–11).

Chapter 11
Being Filled With the Spirit

[W]hen they had prayed,
  the place in which they were gathered together was shaken,
and they were all filled with the Holy Spirit
  and continued to speak the word of God with boldness.

                              Acts 4:31

[D]o not get drunk with wine, for that is debauchery,
  but be filled with the Spirit,
addressing one another in psalms and hymns and spiritual songs,
  singing and making melody to the Lord with your heart,
giving thanks always and for everything
  to God the Father in the name of our Lord Jesus Christ.

                         Ephesians 5:18–20

Summary: *What does it mean to be filled with the Spirit? What are the characteristics of this filling? Terms such as ecstasy, trance, and the root meaning of "prophesying" are investigated, as well as the significance of fasting. The following effects of being filled with the Spirit are discussed: power for one's ministry and for spiritual warfare, true obedience and dedication to the Lord, compassion toward others, worship of God, preaching and prophetic utterances, rendering one's testimony for the Lord, the performance of miraculous works (for the* charismata *see the next chapter). The question is discussed how the power of the Spirit can be transferred; what is the meaning of the laying on of hands? The apparent similarities and differences between the occult and truly Spirit-ual phenomena are investigated. Special attention is given to the psycho-physical relationships involved, with some reference to the natural sciences. Finally, the various Spirit anointings are discussed, including the decrease and increase of the anointing.*

11.1 Filling
11.1.1 What Is It?

IN CERTAIN CIRCLES, the power (Gk. *dynamis*) of the Spirit is described with the term "anointing," referring to the quantity of Spirit-ual power that a believer possesses. Thus, according to Peter Tan, anointing is the ability in the believer's life to do God's work; in other words, it is a tangible measure of God's Holy Spirit.[1] I have a problem with this, not with the matter as such, but with this use of the *term* "anointing." To me it seems that this usage does not agree with New Testament parlance. Here, Christ (Luke 4:18; Acts 4:27; 10:38; Heb. 1:9) and the believer (2 Cor. 1:21; 1 John 2:20, 27) *have been* anointed from the very beginning (§4.5), but there is no question of a smaller or greater anointing. Yet, I can see how useful this way of speaking might be: it is more understandable to speak of a great or small amount of the power of the Spirit than of a great or small anointing.

A more correct image might actually be that of being filled

---

1. Tan (1995, 13, 15; cf. 17).

or not, or being more filled or less filled, with the Holy Spirit. Indeed, it is the quantity of power (Gk. *dynamis*) that is involved. As Peter Tan puts it, the anointing of the Holy Spirit always produces power,[2] and more anointing gives more power. It is undeniable that the power of the Holy Spirit is often given in measures or degrees (see §4.4). To continue with the imagery: a few droplets of oil on someone's forehead is a far smaller amount than the oil that is amply "running down on the beard, on the beard of Aaron, running down on the collar of his robes" (Ps. 133:2).

This measure in which the Holy Spirit can work in believers—say, the quantity of power (Gk. *dynamis*)—can decrease, for instance, when working in a strongly disbelieving or even hostile environment (cf. Matt. 13:57–58; Mark 6:3–6; for a contrast, see Luke 5:17; 6:19). But this power can also increase. Charles G. Finney wrote that, when no more power was left in him, he took a day to fast and to pray until the *dynamis* came back to him in all its freshness.[3] Similar things have been reported of many other servants of the Lord. Jesus said—in my words—that for certain strong demons such a high level of *dynamis* is needed to drive them out "by prayer" only (Mark 9:29).[4] The New Testament provides examples of groups of believers where being filled with the Holy Spirit was *accompanied by* strong outward manifestations, both of which occurred particularly during prayer (see Acts 1:4, 2:2–4, and 4:31).

The book of Acts speaks of some who, apparently more or less permanently, were full (Gk. *plērēs*) of the Holy Spirit: Stephen (Acts 6:3, 10 ["Spirit" rather than "spirit"]; 7:55) and Barnabas (11:24). However, when speaking of being filled (Gk. *plēroō*), the verb is usually in the aorist tense, emphasizing the singular character of the event: the people concerned

---

2. Ibid., 17.
3. Cited in ibid., 93.
4. The Received Text has here "prayer and fasting" (KJV); for this combination see also Luke 2:37; 5:33; Acts 10:30; 13:3; 14:23; see further §11.2.

were filled at that moment (Acts 4:8, 31; 9:17; 13:9). An exception is 13:52 ("the disciples were filled with joy and with the Holy Spirit"), where we find the imperfect tense, which indicates a more continuous state. Being filled with the Holy Spirit is not necessarily permanent, but it can be experienced at many separate moments, as long as the person is open to it (the subjective aspect), and the circumstances demand or allow it (the objective aspect).

11.1.2 Ecstasy

In §4.6, I briefly referred to the phenomenon of ecstasy in a discussion of Ephesians 5:18. We have seen in Acts 2:13 that being filled with the Spirit, and thus with exuberance, plus the accompanying glossolalia, may sometimes create in superficial spectators the impression of intoxication ("they are filled with new wine"), that is, of an ecstatic experience. We find something similar in 1 Corinthians 14:23, "If . . . the whole church comes together and all speak in tongues, and outsiders or unbelievers enter, will they not say that you are out of your minds?" Being "out of your mind" is in Greek *mainomai*, "to rage." An Old Testament example of this is found in Hosea 9:7, where the critics say, "[T]he prophet is a fool, the man of the spirit [Heb. *ruach*; ERV: This man with God's Spirit] is mad [Heb. *meshuggah*]." Quite likely the people spoke about him this way because of his ecstatic behavior.

This prophetic behavior reminds us of New Testament men of God who experienced this kind of ecstasy, such as Peter, who fell into a trance (CEB: had a visionary experience; Darby; DRA: an ecstasy came upon him; Acts 10:10; cf. 11:5). The same happened to Paul in the temple (22:17). John's being "in the Spirit" on Patmos was probably of a similar nature (Rev. 1:10; 4:2; cf. 17:3; 21:10).

Of Jesus we are told, too, that, as he was busy with his ministry of deliverance, he was "out of his mind" (Gk. *exestē*, from *existēmi*, the verb from which the word "ecstasy" was derived; Mark 3:21). Of course, we should not conclude too much from this, but the opposite conclusion—we do not encounter any charismatic phenomena in Jesus' life[5]—cannot be claimed either. Consider Luke 10:21 as well, where the word "rejoiced" is a rather weak rendering of the Greek verb *ēgalliasato* (cf. AMP, TLV "overjoyed"; CEB "overflowed with joy"; ISV "extremely joyful"; MSG "exuberant"; VOICE "elated"). At this moment, Jesus would have looked more like people in a Charismatic church than like those in a traditional Protestant church.

The apostle Paul uses the word "ecstasy" too: "[I]f we are beside ourselves [or out of our minds, Gk. *exestēmen*], it is for God; if we are in our right mind [or sober, Gk. *sōphronoumen*], it is for you" (2 Cor. 5:13). Here, the contrast between "ecstatic" and "sober" is of special interest: being "ecstatic" can give to outsiders the impression that one is drunk, or even mad. We may wonder what many Christians, who are against "wild scenes" in their church services, would say if they could have observed Jesus, Peter, Paul, or John "in ecstasy."[6] And what did the disciples from Emmaus experience when their hearts were "burning" within them (Luke 24:32)? Or was this experienced only on the inside? To allow a "burning" on the inside but to restrict any outward manifestation of this—is this not an attitude arising from a Greek-scholastic dualism between mind and body? Jesus described the house of joy to which the prodigal son returned as one of "music and dancing" (Luke 15:25). In the Bible, inner ecstasy is always connected with outward expressions of it, dancing being one of the most obvious (Exod. 15:20; Judg. 21:21; 1 Sam. 18:6; 2 Sam. 6:14; Ps. 30:11; 87:7; 149:3; 150:4; Jer. 31:4, 13; Matt. 11:17).

11.1.3 "Prophesying"

Another expression of ecstasy is prophecy. It occurred among the elders of Israel upon whom the Holy Spirit had come (§7.2.3): the Lord "took some of the Spirit that was on him

---

5. Erickson (1983, 872).
6. Cf. Bickle (1998, 207–208).

[i.e., Moses] and put it on the seventy elders. And as soon as the Spirit rested on them, they prophesied" (Num. 11:25). In this meaning, prophesying is the utterance of words of God, or magnifying God, or even "getting into a state of ecstasy."[7] We find this with Asaph, Heman, and Jeduthun, "who prophesied [or worshiped ecstatically] with lyres, with harps, and with cymbals . . . who prophesied with the lyre in thanksgiving and praise to the LORD" (1 Chron. 25:1-3). This use of musical instruments that facilitate ecstasy and inspiration is found also in Exodus 15:20 (tambourines), 1 Samuel 10:5 (harps, tambourines, flutes, lyres), and 2 Kings 3:15 (a lyre?). The Greek word *psallō* ("to sing," lit. "to strum") points to an accompaniment by string instruments (1 Cor. 14:15).

Presumably, the Hebrew root *n-b-'*, from which the words for "prophet" and "prophesy" have been derived, is related to phenomena of trance and ecstasy.[8] The clearest examples of ecstatic behavior among prophets are found in 1 Samuel 10:5-6, 10-11, and 19:20, 23-24 (cf. 2 Sam. 6:14-15) (on this, see §5.5.1 above). Ecstasy is one of the common consequences of being filled with the Spirit. Therefore, Clark Pinnock viewed the term virtually as a name for the Spirit: the term suggests that the Spirit is the ecstasy that makes the Triune life an open circle and a source of pure abundance.[9] Yet, ecstasy is no absolute *proof* of the fullness of the Spirit, or of the right attitude toward God of the people involved. In 1 Kings 22:10, an entire group of false prophets was prophesying before the kings of Israel and Judah. But the true prophet Micaiah unmasked their ecstasy (vv. 19-28).

The Lord himself spoke of "every madman [Heb. *ish meshuggah*] who prophesies" (Jer. 29:26), that is, every person who exhibits the outward phenomena of prophecy (frenzy, elation, ecstatic language and actions), either by simulation or by spiritual powers: "You know that when you were pagans

---

7. Welker (1992, 81).
8. Hildebrandt (1995, 160).
9. Pinnock (1996, 38; cf. 55: "God is pure ecstasy").

you were led astray to mute idols, however you were led" (1 Cor. 12:2). Behind the "mute idols" are hidden demonic powers (Deut. 32:17; 1 Cor. 10:19–20; Rev. 9:20), which can induce their servants into ecstasy as well. Thus we read of the Baal priests on Mount Carmel that they "called upon the name of Baal from morning until noon, saying, 'O Baal, answer us!' But there was no voice, and no one answered. And they limped around the altar that they had made. . . . And they cried aloud and cut themselves after their custom with swords and lances, until the blood gushed out upon them. And as midday passed, they raved on [Heb. *wayyitnabb'u*, lit., prophesied; see KJV] until the time of the offering of the oblation" (1 Kings 18:26–29).

In passages where the trance comes from the Lord this in fact means the same as being "in the Spirit" (cf. Eph. 6:18; Rev. 1:10; 4:2; 17:3; 21:10; always "Spirit," not "spirit"). The human spirit is "elated" by the Holy Spirit. It is important not to dismiss these trances as exceptional phenomena. On the contrary, it is apparently quite common that just like what happened to the apostles, when people are in prayer, they enter a trance (see again Acts 10:10 [cf. 11:5]; 22:17; 2 Cor. 5:13; Rev. 1:10; 4:2; cf. 17:3; 21:10).

In Christian literature, parallels have been pointed out between such a trance and erotic elation. The Egyptian (?) (Pseudo-)Macarius compared being filled with the Holy Spirit to the experiences of a bride in the arms of her bridegroom; we may think here of many passages in the Song of Solomon. A similar idea is found among the heretical Messalians.[10] This imagery reminds us of both the fire and the wine metaphors (see §§4.3 and 4.6).

11.2 Fasting
11.2.1 Asceticism

Traditional Protestants have usually been quite suspicious of, on the one hand, ecstasy (trance, frenzy, elation, exuberance)

---

10. Burgess (1989, 147, 214).

and on the other hand, what may seem to be (but is not) the opposite of ecstasy: asceticism. Elation seems to be the opposite of soberness. Such Christians can easily adduce 1 Timothy 4:1–5 in support of their suspicion:

> Now the Spirit expressly says that in later times some will depart from the faith by devoting themselves to deceitful spirits and teachings of demons, through the insincerity of liars whose consciences are seared, who forbid marriage and require abstinence from foods that God created to be received with thanksgiving by those who believe and know the truth. For everything created by God is good, and nothing is to be rejected if it is received with thanksgiving, for it is made holy by the word of God and prayer.

The apostle Paul argues that asceticism is demonic if it becomes a goal in itself, a means to please God, or to even become divine, or if it is enforced ("require abstinence from foods"), or based upon a false dualism of the "good" soul and the "inferior" matter. However, this does not mean that *every* form of asceticism is objectionable. The term "asceticism" is related to another less familiar term, "ascesis," both of which come from the Greek verb *askeō*, which means "to exercise." Paul himself said, "[H]erein do I exercise [Gk. *askō*] myself to have always a conscience void of offense toward God and toward men" (Acts 24:16 KJV). The Greek word *askēsis* means "exercise"; it is comparable to the Greek word *gymnasia*, "exercise, training" (cf. gymnastics), as in 1 Timothy 4:7–8, "[E]xercise yourself [Gk. *gymnaze*] toward godliness. For bodily exercise [Gk. *gymnasia*] profits a little, but godliness is profitable for all things, having promise of the life that now is and of that which is to come."

One important activity belonging to asceticism is fasting, which occurs in the Bible many times in a very positive sense. Jesus apparently viewed fasting as self-evident (Matt. 6:16–18; 9:15). Derek Prince pointed out how significant it is that the promise of the outpouring of the Holy Spirit in Joel 2 followed upon the LORD's call for fasting and praying: "Yet even now, . . . return to me with all your heart, with fasting, with weeping, and with mourning. . . . Blow the trumpet in Zion; consecrate a fast; call a solemn assembly; gather the people. Consecrate the congregation; assemble the elders; gather the children, even nursing infants" (vv. 12, 15–16).[11] Probably the one hundred twenty, who waited at Jerusalem for the outpouring of the Spirit, devoted themselves to prayer *and* fasting (Acts 1:14) because Jesus had foretold, "The days will come when the bridegroom is taken away from them [i.e., the wedding guests, here: the disciples], and then they will fast in those days" (Luke 5:35).

11.2.2 Preparation

Fasting was often a sign of mourning (1 Sam. 31:13; 2 Sam. 1:12; 3:35; Ezra 10:6; Neh. 1:4; Esther 4:3; Ps. 69:10–11) and of humbling oneself (1 Sam. 7:6; 1 Kings 21:27; Ezra 8:21, 23; Neh. 9:1–2; Ps. 35:13; Isa. 58:5; Dan. 9:3–4; Jonah 3:5–8; Acts 9:9). But there is more: fasting often constituted a part of some preparation for transcendent experiences. In times of distress, believers who wished to consult the LORD fasted (Judg. 20:26–27; 2 Sam. 12:16–23; 2 Chron. 20:3–4; Ezra 8:21–23; Joel 1:14). Moses fasted for forty days when he was on Mount Horeb (Exod. 34:28; Deut. 9:9), Elijah did the same when he was on his way to Horeb (1 Kings 19:8); Horeb was the mountain where they encountered the God of Israel. Daniel had fasted for three weeks before he received the wonderful vision of the pre-incarnate Christ (Dan. 10:2–4). Jesus gained his spiritual triumphs over Satan after he had fasted for forty days (Matt. 4:2).

Fasting and praying are part of the common repertoire of people who serve God intensely, also in the New Testament. We read about this in connection with the prophetess Anna (Luke 2:37), with the prophets and teachers in Antioch (13:2), and with Paul (2 Cor. 6:5; 11:27). The Antiochian leaders fasted

---

11. Ibid., 426.

and prayed before they laid their hands on Saul and Barnabas (Acts 13:3), and these two leaders fasted and prayed when appointing elders (14:23). They did so apparently because they were aware of the great responsibility involved in the laying on of hands (1 Tim. 5:22).[12] The words for "fasting" (verb and noun) probably do not belong to the original text of Matthew 17:21, Mark 9:29, and 1 Corinthians 7:5 (compare the KJV with modern translations), nor presumably in Acts 10:30. But the addition of these terms in later manuscripts does provide an indication that the early church attached more and more value to fasting so that later copyists felt a growing drive to insert the words wherever they thought fit.

Indeed, in church history fasting has consistently played a role in the lives of saints who received important Spirit-ual experiences. John Chrysostom reportedly said that fasting makes the soul clearer and furnishes it with wings to fly.[13] In Egypt the ascetic hermit Ammonas taught that those who continually seek God's face with tears and fasting, and deny their own ego, will receive a greater joy than before, and will be confirmed more strongly.[14] Fasting also played an important role in holiness movements, such as early Methodism. And the outpouring of the Spirit among the Moravian Brethren at Herrnhut (1727) occurred during a week of prayer and fasting.

Many more such examples could be mentioned. We are told of the great revival that began in America (1741) through Jonathan Edwards preaching his sermon "Sinners in the Hands of an Angry God," a sermon that he had preached many times without much result. What made the difference? This time his preaching was preceded by three days of prayer and fasting during which he barely slept. We are also told that

---

12. Prince (1995, 428).
13. Quoted in Ferguson (1979, 295); he pointed out that in non-Christian religions, too, fasting is often viewed as a necessary preparation for visionary experiences (294–95).
14. Quoted in Burgess (1989, 153).

before the power of God fell at Azusa Street (1906), the small band of believers united in ten days of prayer and fasting. William Seymour, who led the three-year revival (1906-1909) that spread throughout the world, spent weeks at a time in fasting and prayer.[15]

It seems rather clear that, throughout the centuries, believers who knew the deepest joy of the Spirit and the most powerful experiences with the Spirit were those who gave much attention to prayer *and* fasting in their lives. Bill Bright wrote: "The longer I fasted, the more I sensed the presence of the Lord. The Holy Spirit refreshed my soul and spirit, and I experienced the joy of the Lord as seldom before."[16]

11.3 Effects of Being Filled (1)
11.3.1 Introduction

Being filled with the Holy Spirit is a rather important topic in the New Testament. Every believer *possesses* the Spirit (cf. Acts 10:44-45; Rom. 8:9; 1 Cor. 6:19; 12:13; Eph. 1:13) but this does not mean that every believer experiences being *filled* with the Spirit, which was the ongoing experience of John the Baptist (Luke 1:15), Jesus (4:1), Stephen (Acts 6:3, 5; 7:55), and Barnabas (11:24); or on certain occasions, Elizabeth (v. 41), Zechariah (v. 67), the one hundred twenty (Acts 2:4), Peter (4:8), all the gathered believers (v. 31), Saul just after his conversion (9:17), Paul (13:9), and all the disciples in Antioch (13:52).

All too often in believers' lives, the Spirit is only an ember among the ashes, not a raging fire; a breeze, not a hurricane; a rivulet, not a roaring river (see §§4.1-4.3 above). How can believers know whether they are *filled*, or have ever been filled, with the Holy Spirit? From the New Testament we can distill at least ten characteristics, which we find first in Jesus Christ, and afterward in his followers, beginning with his apostles. Let us briefly consider them one by one.

---

15. http://www.pentecostalpioneers.org/fasting.html.
16. https://www.cru.org/train-and-grow/spiritual-growth/fasting/7-steps-to-fasting.html.

11.3.2 Power[17]

Christ. Being filled with the Holy Spirit entails power in the most general sense, sometimes even including physical strength, as in the case of Samson (Judg. 14:6, 19; 15:14).[18] Jesus himself was "anointed . . . with the Holy Spirit and with power" (Acts 10:38), which is equivalent to being "anointed with the power of the Holy Spirit." Jesus confronted the evil powers through the Holy Spirit (Luke 4:1–13) and walked in the power of the Spirit (v. 14). Of his ministry we read, "[T]he power of the Lord was with him to heal" (5:17; cf. Mark 5:30; 6:14).

Believers. Jesus told his disciples, "[S]tay in the city until you are clothed with power from on high" (Luke 24:49); "you will receive power when the Holy Spirit has come upon you" (Acts 1:8). Paul wrote, "[M]y speech and my message were . . . in demonstration of the Spirit and of power" (1 Cor. 2:4), which means: "in demonstration of the power of the Spirit" (cf. CJB, GNT). "[O]ur gospel came to you not only in word, but also in power and in the Holy Spirit and with full conviction" (1 Thess. 1:5), that is, "in the power of the Holy Spirit" (cf. CEV "with the power and assurance that come from the Holy Spirit"). Paul wished for believers in Rome that "by the power of the Holy Spirit you may abound in hope" (Rom. 15:13). For believers in Ephesus he prayed that God "may grant you to be strengthened with power through his Spirit in your inner being" (Eph. 3:16), after which he stated that God "is able to do far more abundantly than all that we ask or think, according to the power at work within us" (v. 20). According to some manuscripts Peter called the Holy Spirit "the Spirit of the . . . power . . . of God" (1 Pet. 4:14).[19]

---

17. Cf. Duffield and Van Cleave (1996, 327–29).
18. It is interesting that Samson is always depicted as a muscular bodybuilder, whereas his power was due not to his physical strength but to the power of the Holy Spirit.
19. Metzger (1975, 695) argues for omitting the words "and the power."

11.3.3 The Service of God

Christ. Jesus began his ministry with the proclamation that this ministry of his had been foretold in Isaiah 61:1-2, "The Spirit of the Lord God is upon me, because the Lord has *anointed* me to bring good news to the poor; he has sent me to bind up the brokenhearted, to proclaim liberty to the captives, and the opening of the prison to those who are bound; to proclaim the year of the Lord's favor" (cf. Luke 4:17-21). This ministry was based upon the anointing with the Holy Spirit. Compare this earlier word in Isaiah (42:1), "Behold my servant, whom I uphold, my chosen, in whom my soul delights; I have put my Spirit upon him; he will bring forth justice to the nations."

Believers. The Spirit-filled person experiences the power of the Holy Spirit in a particular way in the service of God. We read of both John the Baptist (Luke 1:15) and Saul of Tarsus (Acts 9:17) that they were to be filled with the Holy Spirit in view of their specific ministry. The power of the Spirit is certainly a general condition for any Christian ministry. Yet, this did not mean that, for instance, Saul/Paul was permanently filled with the Spirit. In his case, too, this is mentioned as something special, namely, to resist the evil one (13:9-11). He does say, however, that his ministry took place "by the power of signs and wonders, by the power of the Spirit of God" (Rom. 15:19).

D. M. Lloyd-Jones pointed to the enormous importance of being filled with the Spirit for ministry. He called this an absolute requirement for true service. Jesus did not begin his ministry before the Holy Spirit had descended upon him. His disciples, who had been trained by him for three years, who belonged to the circle of his intimate friends, who had seen his miracles and had heard all his words, even these exceptional men, who enjoyed all possible benefits, received the order from him to wait until they had received the power that the Holy Spirit would give them (Luke 24:49; Acts 1:8). Before this, they were not allowed to undertake their ministry, and to witness of Christ.[20]

11.3.4 Obedience and Dedication

Christ. The person who not only has the Spirit but is with filled with him is also the person who will be led by the Spirit. Thus it was with Christ: as soon as he had received the Holy Spirit, he was led by this Spirit (Luke 3:21–22; 4:1, 14). This implied a life of obedience: "[B]y the one man's [i.e., Christ's] obedience the many will be made righteous" (Rom. 5:19). "And being found in human form, he humbled himself by becoming obedient to the point of death, even death on a cross" (Phil. 2:8). "Although he was a son, he learned obedience through what he suffered" (Heb. 5:8).

Believers. It is the same with Christians: being filled with the Spirit leads to practical obedience: "[A]ll who are led by the Spirit of God are sons of God" (Rom. 8:14) (§9.4), that is, true sons of God are led by the Spirit. Examples of persons in the book of Acts who were obediently led by the Spirit are Philip (8:29), Peter (10:19; 11:12), Paul and Barnabas (13:2, 4), the apostles (15:28), Paul and companions (16:6–7), Paul alone (20:22–23). This experience lies at the trailhead of the pathway of faith: the Holy Spirit is given by God "to those who obey him" (5:32); this is the obedience of faith (John 3:36; Acts 6:7; Rom. 1:5; 16:26). In a wider sense, this is the triumph of the Spirit over the flesh to lead a life of obedience (§9.6). This implies dedication and obedience toward God.

It is remarkable that Ephesians 5:18b ("be filled with the Spirit") is preceded by these words: "Look carefully then how you walk, not as unwise but as wise, making the best use of the time, because the days are evil. Therefore do not be foolish, but understand what the will of the Lord is" (vv. 15–17). Moreover, verse 18 is found in the middle of a passage in which the church's practical behavior is described in the context of the community of faith (4:25–5:21), the community of marriage and family (5:22–6:4), and the community of daily

---

20. Lloyd-Jones (1997, 241–42).

work (6:5-9). Being filled with the Spirit is not only for special occasions but is very important in the believer's circumstances of everyday life. In these very circumstances believers are tested most thoroughly in terms of their love, obedience, and dedication.

11.4 Effects of Being Filled (2)
11.4.1 Compassion

Christ. Being filled with the Spirit also entails compassion (mercy, pity, charity, loving-kindness) toward people. The entire Spirit-filled ministry of Jesus was characterized by his compassion toward the crowds and individuals: "When he saw the crowds, he had compassion for them, because they were harassed and helpless, like sheep without a shepherd" (Matt. 9:36; cf.14:14; 15:32; 20:34).

Believers. Being filled with the Holy Spirit to such extent that the vessel overflows is beautifully described in John 7:38-39, where Jesus says, "'Whoever believes in me, as the Scripture has said, 'Out of his heart will flow rivers of living water.' Now this he said about the Spirit, whom those who believed in him were to receive." Here, the Holy Spirit overflows toward others, namely, out of the heart, or more literally, belly (KJV). In the Bible, the bowels are the seat of compassion (see §§6.6.2). Augustine said, "Interrogate your bowels: if they are full of love, you have the Spirit of God."[21]

The Assyrian Nestorian Abdisho Hazzaya (seventh century) distinguished the following successive signs of the Spirit's work in the soul: the love of God burning in the heart like a fire (cf. §4.3); true humility, from which come forth peace, gentleness, and strength (cf. Gal. 5:22); true kindness toward all people in deep compassion rich in tears; true love toward God; and ultimately the contemplation of God.[22]

---

21. *Ep. Ioan.* VIII.12.
22. Burgess (1989, 99).

11.4.2 Worship

Christ. In Luke 10:21 we read that Jesus "rejoiced in the Holy Spirit," and as a consequence he said, "I thank [or, praise] you, Father, Lord of heaven and earth." In Psalm 45:7 (cf. Heb. 1:9) the oil with which Christ has been anointed is the oil of *gladness*, an oil that is also granted to believers who have experienced sadness (Isa. 61:3). "[T]he joy of the LORD is your strength" (Neh. 8:10) — it is also the basis of all worship.

Believers. Spirit-filled people enthusiastically magnify and worship God, in their own language or in other languages that they have never learned (Acts 2:4, 11; cf. 10:46; 19:6). Thus, Acts 13:53 says, "[T]he disciples were filled with joy and with the Holy Spirit" (cf. 1 Thess. 1:6, "the joy of the Holy Spirit"). Jesus said, "[T]he hour is coming, and is now here, when the true worshipers will worship the Father in spirit [or, Spirit; see §10.6.1] and truth, for the Father is seeking such people to worship him. God is spirit,[23] and those who worship him must worship in s/Spirit and truth" (John 4:23-24).

Ephesians 5:18-20 says, "[B]e filled with the Spirit, addressing one another in psalms and hymns and spiritual songs, singing and making melody to the Lord with your heart, giving thanks always and for everything to God the Father in the name of our Lord Jesus Christ." Notice three things here. First, a passive imperative ("be filled") is quite remarkable: the sovereign work of the Spirit is linked with the believer's responsibility.[24] Second, the Greek phrase *en pneumati* is exceptional; hence sometimes the phrase is rendered "in [your] spirit." Others defend the translation "filled *by* the Spirit,"[25] seen in translations like "let the Spirit fill your life" (CEV). Third, all four participles depend on being filled with the Spirit; they describe the condition of those who are continually filled in the sphere of the Spirit, as Wood put it.[26] Those

---

23. *Not* "is *a* s/Spirit" (KJV); I prefer "God is Spirit" (NKJV) (see §3.1 above).
24. Cf. Versteeg (1976, 25).
25. Salmond (1979, 362–63).
26. Wood (1978, 74).

who are filled with the Spirit will speak to others with blessing (cf. Col. 3:16), will sing, make melody, and give thanks (§4.6); they "worship by the Spirit of God" (Phil. 3:3).[27]

After the Philippian jailor had put Paul and Silas into prison and had "fastened their feet in the stocks," the following happened: "About midnight Paul and Silas were praying and singing hymns to God, and the prisoners were listening to them, and suddenly there was a great earthquake, so that the foundations of the prison were shaken. And immediately all the doors were opened, and everyone's bonds were unfastened" (Acts 16:24–26). This was worship in the power of the Spirit, which not only had an impact on the other prisoners but also had physical consequences (as in Acts 4:31, where "the place was shaken"): the prison's foundations began to shake, the doors sprang open, and the bonds were unfastened. This was a very unusual earthquake: the walls remained standing, while only the doors and the bonds were opened.

We find an Old Testament example in 2 Chronicles 20:18–22, which is about the battle of King Jehoshaphat against his enemies, where we see how, through pure praise, a great victory over his enemies was gained in the heavenly places. Similarly, it is fascinating to see that the word for "strength" (Heb. *oz*) in Psalm 8:2 is rendered as "praise" (Gk. *ainos*) in the Septuagint (cf. the quotation in Matt. 21:16): praise is power! In Psalm 149:5–6, the "high praises" in the throats of the "godly" are poetically parallel with the "two-edged swords in their hands." Here again, praising and fighting go hand in hand (cf. also Isa. 30:31–32, every stroke that the Lord lays on the Assyrians is "to the sound of tambourines and lyres").

11.4.3 Spiritual Warfare

Christ. At the end of the previous section, spiritual battle was mentioned. Jesus said, "[I]f it is by the Spirit of God that I cast out demons, then the kingdom of God has come upon you" (Matt. 12:28). After his anointing, Jesus himself had immedi-

---

27. Müller (1984, 107–108).

ately confronted the devil (4:1-11). The kingdom of God is the manifestation of God's realm that, in the power of the Spirit, has been breaking through violently, against the resistance of the devil and his companions (cf. Matt. 11:12 note; text: "the kingdom ... has suffered violence"; cf. also Luke 16:16)[28] (also see §7.8.1). Jesus did not perform his miracles through his own personal divine power but as a Man through the power of the Spirit with which he had been anointed (Acts 10:38).

Believers. In this respect, Jesus is the example for his followers who, through the same power, extend the kingdom of God ever further in this world, in opposition to the same evil powers (cf. John 14:12; Mark 16:17). This is why casting out demons is a work of the Spirit, and at the same time a special sign of the kingdom of God (Matt. 4:23-24; 10:7-8; 12:28; Acts 8:6-7, 12; 19:8, 11-12). In 1 John 4:2-4 we find a description of a certain form of spiritual warfare in which the Spirit is explicitly involved: "By this you know the Spirit of God: every spirit that confesses that Jesus Christ has come in the flesh is from God, and every spirit that does not confess Jesus is not from God. This is the spirit of the antichrist, which you heard was coming and now is in the world already. Little children, you are from God and have overcome them, for he who is in you is greater than he who is in the world." The precise context and the nature of this spiritual battle—the docetic heresy (cf. 2 John 1:9-11)—are not so relevant right now. What is central here is "he who is in you": God, more specifically, the Spirit of God (v. 2), "and [you] have overcome them, for he who is in you is greater than he who is in the world."

11.5   Effects of Being Filled (3)
11.5.1 Prophecy

Christ. In Luke 4:17-21 Jesus made it clear that he is the proph-

---

28. For various interpretations of this controversial passage (does the violence come from Jesus' followers *or* from his opponents?) see Bruce (1979, 173, 587); Geldenhuys (1983, 421); Carson (1984, 265-69); Liefeld (1984, 989-90).

et who is described in Isaiah 61:1 as the One who has been anointed with the Spirit of God. Elsewhere he claimed the title of prophet, and he was acknowledged as such by many people (see §12.2.3).

Believers. The Spirit-filled person often begins to prophesy, as we read of Elizabeth and Zechariah (Luke 1:41, 67; cf. 2:25-27) and Paul (Acts 13:9-11; cf. 7:55). In Acts 19:6 we read of the Ephesian disciples: "[W]hen Paul had laid his hands on them, the Holy Spirit came on them, and they began speaking in tongues and prophesying." In this sense, prophesying is uttering words of God, or magnifying God (see §11.1.3). Paul writes, "[I]f all prophesy, and an unbeliever or outsider enters, he is convicted by all, he is called to account by all, the secrets of his heart are disclosed, and so, falling on his face, he will worship God and declare that God is really among you" (1 Cor. 14:24-25). Here, a spiritual victory is gained because "all prophesy," that is, they (presumably) ecstatically magnify God. If prophesying by the Spirit (cf. Luke 1:41, 67; Acts 19:6) leads to "upbuilding and encouragement and consolation" of the believers (1 Cor. 14:3), we understand how, according to Paul, Christians can teach and admonish "one another in all wisdom, singing psalms and hymns and spiritual songs, with thankfulness in your hearts to God" (Col. 3:16).

11.5.2 Witnessing

Christ. It was still in the power of the Spirit that Jesus could say: "For this purpose I was born and for this purpose I have come into the world—to bear witness to the truth" (John 18:37). He is the true and faithful witness (Rev. 1:5; 3:14) (cf. §7.8.2).

Believers. Spirit-filled people receive the power of the Spirit to bear witness to unbelievers, even enemies of God; see the difference between John 20:19 ("the doors locked for fear of the Jews") and Acts 4:13 ("when they saw the boldness of Peter and John. . ."; cf. vv. 29) (also see 8:1, 4; cf. Mark 13:11; 1 Cor. 2:4; 4:19-20). A striking example is Acts 4:31, "And when they had prayed, the place in which they were gathered together was shaken, and they were all filled with the Holy Spirit and continued to speak the word of God with boldness."[29] And of Stephen we read, "But he, full of the Holy Spirit, gazed into heaven and saw the glory of God, and Jesus standing at the right hand of God. And he said, 'Behold, I see the heavens opened, and the Son of Man standing at the right hand of God'" (7:55). Paul wrote, "[M]y speech and my message were not in plausible words of wisdom, but in demonstration of the Spirit and of power [read, of the power of the Spirit]" (1 Cor. 2:4).

Derek Prince wrote that the Holy Spirit will never withdraw his supernatural testimony as long as God has a people on earth that believes and obeys the revealed truth of his Word.[30]

11.5.3 Miraculous Works

Christ. Jesus healed the sick and delivered demon-possessed people by the power of the Holy Spirit, and thereby demonstrated the arrival of God's kingdom (Matt. 12:28; cf. 4:23; 9:35): "God anointed Jesus of Nazareth with the Holy Spirit and with power. He went about doing good and healing all who were oppressed by the devil, for God was with him" (Acts 10:38).

Believers. Being filled with the Holy Spirit resulted in experiencing the powers, signs, and wonders of the Spirit (see again Acts 4:31). Paul ministered "by the power of signs and wonders, by the power of the Spirit of God" (Rom. 15:19). He writes about him "who supplies the Spirit to you and [thus] works miracles among you" (Gal. 3:5). Of the apostles and their companions it is said that "God also bore witness by signs and wonders and various miracles and by gifts of the

---

29. The vernacular seems to point to an objective event in Acts 4:31 like a kind of earthquake (cf. Exod. 19:8; Ps. 114:7; Isa. 6:4; Joel 3:16; Amos 9:5; Hag. 2:7; Luke 21:26; Acts 16:26; Heb. 12:26–27); *contra* Bruce (1988, 100).
30. Prince (1995, 397).

Holy Spirit distributed according to his will" (Heb. 2:4; cf. 6:5; Mark 16:20; Acts 2:43; 4:30; 5:12; 6:8; 8:6, 13; 14:3; 15:12; 19:11; 1 Cor. 12:10, 28-29; 2 Cor. 12:12).

Unfortunately, such works can easily be imitated (§11.1.3). The sons of the Pharisees cast out demons (Matt. 12:27); Jesus spoke of those who one day would say to him, "Lord, Lord, did we not prophesy in your name, and cast out demons in your name, and do many mighty works in your name?" and to them he would answer, "I never knew you; depart from me, you workers of lawlessness" (7:22-23). The Antichrist comes "with all power and false signs and wonders" (2 Thess. 2:9; cf. Matt. 24:24; Rev. 13:13). Simon the Magician performed great miracles, and wished to continue them after his baptism (Acts 8:9-11, 18-19). The sons of Sceva tried, just like Paul, to cast out demons (Acts 19:13-16). However, Simon and the sons of Sceva were easily unmasked, and the people of Matthew 7:22-23 can be exposed because they are in fact "workers of lawlessness." The faithful will also see through the works of the Antichrist (cf. Dan. 12:10; Rev. 13:18). By means of the gift of distinguishing between spirits (1 Cor. 12:10), those who themselves possess the Spirit should be able to discern the difference between wonders of the Spirit and wonders of the flesh (or the devil).

11.5.4 Preaching

Christ. Everything Jesus did and everything he said always proceeded through the Holy Spirit: "And Jesus returned in the power of the Spirit to Galilee. . . . And he taught in their synagogues" (Luke 4:14-15).

Believers. Peter describes God's servants as "those who preached the good news to you by the Holy Spirit sent from heaven" (1 Pet. 1:12). There is nothing wrong with natural eloquence and acquired erudition; but the primary characteristic of the true servant of God is that one speaks through the Spirit. Paul writes to the Corinthians: "I was with you in weakness and in fear and much trembling, and my speech and my message were not in plausible words of wisdom, but in demonstration of the Spirit and of power, so that your faith might not rest in the wisdom of men but in the power of God" (1 Cor. 2:3-5). Whether preaching is proceeding from the Spirit or not becomes evident, generally speaking, through its effects, whether positive or negative. When the people heard Peter's message, "they were cut to the heart," and repented (Acts 2:37-41). But when Stephen preached, the members of the Sanhedrin "cried out with a loud voice and stopped their ears and rushed together at him. Then they cast him out of the city and stoned him" (7:57-58). When Peter preached in the house of Cornelius, "the Holy Spirit fell on all who heard the word" (10:44). But when Paul and Barnabas preached in Pisidian Antioch, they were driven out from there (13:50), and after preaching in Lystra Paul was stoned (14:19). If the Word is of the Spirit it leads either to revival or to rebellion; a word that has no effect at all is a bad sign (cf. Isa. 55:11).

Preaching the Word entails a kind of "channeling" of the Spirit. As Derek Prince put it, if Peter had not stood up on the Day of Pentecost and preached a message from God's Word, the Holy Spirit would still have been mightily present among the disciples. But the Spirit would not have had a sword to wield (cf. Eph. 6:17, the Word as sword). Among unbelievers, there would definitely have been awe and wondering, but no conversions would have occurred. It was the sharp, two-edged sword of God's Word that, through the Holy Spirit, was wielded via the lips of Peter. It was this that cut deeply to the hearts of these unbelievers, and brought them to a deep conviction.[31]

It is fitting to finish and summarize our discussion of these features with Paul's important words in Romans 15:18-19, "I will not venture to speak of anything except what Christ has accomplished through me to bring the Gentiles to obedience — by word and deed, by the power of signs and wonders,

---

31. Ibid., 384.

by the power of the Spirit of God."

11.6 The Transfer of the *Dynamis*
11.6.1 Healing Through Hands

In the Bible we often discover remarkable things when it comes to the power of the Holy Spirit. Jesus performed his ministry on the basis of having been anointed with the Holy Spirit (Acts 10:38; cf. 2:22), and the power of this anointing was almost tangibly present (Luke 5:17; 6:19). In his healing ministry, where we find the most frequent and striking examples of the Spirit's power, this power sometimes seemed to flow from his body to the body of the sick person. Concerning the woman with the discharge of blood, Jesus said, "I perceive that power has gone from me" (Luke 8:43–46).

Normally, such a transfer of power takes place by the healing minister laying his hands on the sick so that the *dynamis* goes to the people to be healed: "[T]hey will lay their hands on the sick, and they will recover" (Mark 16:18). "[Saul had] seen in a vision a man named Ananias come in and lay his hands on him so that he might regain his sight. . . . [L]aying his hands on him he [i.e., Ananias] said, 'Brother Saul, the Lord Jesus who appeared to you on the road by which you came has sent me so that you may regain your sight and be filled with the Holy Spirit'" (Acts 9:12, 17). "It happened that the father of Publius lay sick with fever and dysentery. And Paul visited him and prayed, and putting his hands on him, healed him" (28:8).

The meaning of the laying on of hands can hardly be overestimated; where the fullness of the Spirit is present it really involves the *transfer* of blessing (power, healing, restoration, authority). We find this already in the Old Testament. Through the outstretched hands of the priest who blesses the nation, the name of YHWH is placed upon the Israelites (Num. 6:27). Moses laid his hands on Joshua so that the latter was full of the Spirit: "Joshua, son of Nun, was filled with the Spirit of wisdom, because Moses had laid his hands on him" (Deut.

34:9 GW). (Interestingly, in Num. 27:18 the Spirit-filling preceded the laying on of hands: "Take Joshua the son of Nun, a man in whom is the Spirit, and lay your hand on him," that is, Moses laid hands on him *because* the Spirit was already in him.)

In 2 Kings 13:15-17 we see how a person's hands were empowered for the service of God because a man of God laid his hands on this person's hands: "Elisha said to him [i.e., King Joash], 'Take a bow and arrows.' So he took a bow and arrows. Then he said to the king of Israel, 'Draw the bow,' and he drew it. And Elisha laid his hands on the king's hands. And he said, 'Open the window eastward,' and he opened it. Then Elisha said, 'Shoot,' and he shot. And he said, 'The LORD's arrow of victory, the arrow of victory over Syria! For you shall fight the Syrians in Aphek until you have made an end of them.'"

Through the laying on of hands, the Holy Spirit can be transferred as a gift (Acts 8:17-19; 9:17; 19:6), even though the laying on of hands is not an absolute condition (2:4, 38; 10:44). Also through the laying on of hands certain persons are inducted into ministry, whether they are deacons (6:6), missionaries (13:3), or apostolic co-workers (1 Tim. 4:14; 2 Tim. 1:6), and no doubt the same was true for overseers[32] (cf. "appointing" elders in Titus 1:5). The warning, "Do not be hasty in the laying on of hands" (1 Tim. 5:11), implies that without the guidance and the power of the Spirit, the laying on of hands is meaningless, and can even be harmful. Therefore, the prophets and teachers in Antioch observed a time of fasting (see §11.2) and praying before they laid their hands on Saul and Barnabas (Acts 13:3).[33]

---

32. However, according to the lexica, the Gk. noun *cheir*, "hand," in the Gk. verb *cheirotoneō*, "to appoint" (Acts 14:23), can hardly function as evidence for this.
33. Prince (1995, 428).

11.6.2 God's Hands

As I just indicated, nothing magical occurs through the laying on of hands (as if the gesture itself would accomplish anything) because the ritual is effective only if done by a Spirit-filled person. Where this is the case, behind the hands of God's servants are, as it were, God's own hands. Acts 4:30 says, "[W]hile you [i.e., God] stretch out your hand to heal, and signs and wonders are performed through the name of your holy servant Jesus."[34] Recall as well the wonders performed by God's "mighty (or strong) hand" and "outstretched arm."[35]

God's "hand" reminds us of God's "finger" in Luke 11:20, which is identical with the "Spirit of God" in Matthew 12:28 (§4.8.2). By God's "hand," and hence by the "hands" of his servants, signs and wonders are done, which means: through the power of the Holy Spirit (Acts 5:12). In yet another sense, God's hand can be a symbol of the overwhelming power of the Holy Spirit: by the "hand of the LORD," the prophet Elijah ran before Ahab's chariot (1 Kings 18:46), which was an enormous physical achievement. (Or could Elijah have followed a much shorter footpath? In the cases of Elijah and Philip [Acts 8:30] some people have spoken of a "running ministry.")

The prophet Elisha sensed that, at a certain moment, the Spirit of God was not upon him; therefore, he asked for a musician (2 Kings 3:15): "And when the musician played, the hand of the LORD came upon him," and he began prophesying.[36]

---

34. Elsewhere, God stretching out his hand can also have a negative meaning (Exod. 7:5; Isa. 5:25; Jer. 21:5; Ezek. 14:13; 16:27); see Patterson and Austel (1988, 147).
35. Deut. 4:34; 5:15; 7:19; 11:2; 26:8; 1 Kings 8:42; 2 Chron. 6:32; Ezek. 20:33–34; "mighty hand" alone: Ezek. 3:19; 32:11; Deut. 3:24; 6:21; 7:8; 9:26; Dan. 9:15; "outstretched arm" alone: Exod. 6:6; Deut. 9:29; 2 Kings 17:36; Jer. 27:5; 32:17; "strong hand": Exod. 6:1; 13:3, 9, 14, 16; Neh. 1:10; Ps. 136:12; Isa. 8:11; Jer. 32:21; "outstretched hand": Jer. 21:5. See also "the hand of God/the LORD" and "the LORD's hand" (many passages).
36. This does not necessarily prove that Israel's prophets could prophesy only when they were in a trance; rather, the music was needed to bring Elisha to inner rest, which was necessary before the Spirit could come upon him; see

Through that same "hand of the LORD," the prophet Ezekiel received visions and other wondrous experiences (Ezek. 1:3; 3:14, 22; 37:1; 40:1). This sensing of the power of God's Spirit agreed with the prophet's Hebrew name: *Yechezqēl*, "God strengthens."[37] By the hand of God his mouth was closed or opened (33:22). Chapter 37:1 says, "The hand of the LORD was upon me, and he brought me out in the Spirit of the LORD"; in such a verse, God's hand and God's Spirit can hardly be distinguished.

11.6.3 Other Ways of Transfer

How far the power of God can reach without any touching by people is seen, for instance, in Acts 5:15. People "even carried out the sick into the streets and laid them on cots and mats, that as Peter came by at least his shadow might fall on some of them." Of course, this does not mean that the shadow itself has healing power[38] but rather that the sick were brought very near to Peter, so that God's power would, as it were, flow from him to them. It seems that in the bones of the dead Elisha so much *dynamis* was still left that, when a dead man was thrown into his tomb and touched his bones, that man came to life (2 Kings 13:21).

Apparently, the *dynamis* that is present in the body of the healing minister can be transferred to material aids and utensils, and in this way can even bring about healing: "God was doing extraordinary miracles by the hands of Paul, so that even handkerchiefs or aprons *that had touched his skin* were carried away to the sick, and their diseases left them and the evil spirits came out of them" (Acts 19:11–12). The *dynamis* that was in or on his body apparently entered the cloth that had touched his body, specifically through his sweat.[39] From there, the *dynamis* was transferred to the sick. The cloths had

---

Patterson and Austel (1988, 181).
37. Alexander (1986, 755).
38. Cf. the discussion in Knowling (1979, 147).
39. The Gr. noun *soudarion* ("handkerchief") comes from the Latin noun *sudarium*, "sweat cloth," derived from the verb *sudo*, "sweat."

been in contact with the apostle's body, and drawn their healing power from his body, said Knowles.[40] Bruce argued that these cloths had no intrinsic healing effect but this effect lay in the name of Jesus.[41] However, in this way justice is not done to the precise role of the cloths. Indeed, they had no intrinsic healing power, of course, but they certainly possessed a transferred power, as in the case of Jesus' garment (Mark 5:28; 6:56).

Peter Tan compared this with the way electricity can be stored in batteries (see more extensively §11.7.3).[42] We can imagine that, in an analogous way, the power of God's Spirit was in some imperceptible way present in the staff of Elisha (2 Kings 4:29, 31).[43] No prayers, no special formulas, not just any staff, but the prophet's staff should have brought about the miracle. Its failure to do so in this case does not change the fact that Elisha was convinced that, in principle, his staff could have done it. Similarly, in the staff of Moses, sometimes called the "staff of God" (Exod. 4:20; 17:9), the *dynamis* was so strong that the latter could turn a dead piece of wood into a living snake (4:1–4). By the same life-giving *dynamis*, the dead staff of Aaron "had sprouted and put forth buds and produced blossoms, and it bore ripe almonds" (Num. 17:8).

Sometimes, God's servants used their own bodies in their entirety as a "point of contact," especially when raising a dead person (1 Kings 17:21; 2 Kings 4:34–35; Acts 20:10). In all these cases, there was physical connection with the minister, and through him with God,[44] entirely analogous to touching the fringe of Jesus' garment by the woman with the discharge of blood (Luke 8:44; cf. also Mark 6:56).

---

40. Knowling (1979, 405).
41. Bruce (1988, 367–68; cf. Longenecker 1981, 496).
42. Tan (1995, 18; cf. 49–52).
43. From the addition, "but there was no sound or sign of life [in the boy]" (2 Kings 4:31), it is evident that laying the staff on the dead boy was intended to raise him up.
44. See Witt (1959, 190).

11.7 Parallels With the Occult
11.7.1 The Magicians of Egypt

Those who investigate the phenomena just mentioned, and who are somewhat familiar with parapsychology, will be easily reminded of all kinds of parallels with "psi," psychic force, psychokinesis, remote control, "magnetism" (or mesmerism[45]). We find such parallels also in other domains where the power of the Holy Spirit is involved, especially in cases of healings: clairvoyance (foresight), telepathy (mind reading), extra-sensory perception (ESP), psychic trance (cf. 1 Sam. 10:5-11; §11.1.3), astral projection (cf. Ezek. 37:1; 40:1; 2 Cor. 12:2-4; Rev. 4:1-2; 21:10), and even levitation (cf. 1 Kings 18:12; Acts 8:39; in these cases the Spirit is explicitly mentioned).

A biblical example of the intended parallelism is that the divine miracles performed by Moses and Aaron were immediately imitated by Pharaoh's magicians (Exod. 7:11-12, 22; 8:7). However, their abilities were more limited than those of Moses: they could not create life out of inanimate matter (8:18). Their response, "This is the finger of God" (v. 19),[46] reminds us of the parallel between Matthew 12:28 and Luke 11:20, where the "finger of God" refers to the Spirit of God (§4.8.2). The *dynamis* of the magicians came from pagan idolatry (Deut. 18:10), that is, the world of demons (32:16-17; 1 Cor. 10:19-20; Rev. 9:20), whereas the *dynamis* of Moses and Aaron came from God.

This example is of supreme importance because it shows that Spirit-ual and occult phenomena may appear outwardly identical. This is the force of Paul's argument in 1 Corinthians 12:1-3: spiritual utterances in paganism and Christianity may appear identical, but they proceed from very different sources, namely, demons (10:20) and the Holy Spirit, respectively.

---

45. Cf. 2 Kings 5:11, "I thought that he [i.e., Elisha] would ... call upon the name of the LORD his God, and wave his hand over the place and cure the leper." Naaman is referring here to the method of healers whom we today would call magnetizers.
46. Cf. Kaiser (1990, 354).

The methods of Moses and Aaron appeared to be identical to those of the Egyptian magicians, but this was because demonic miracles are nothing but a sophisticated imitation of divine miracles. As Martin Luther said, where God builds a chapel, Satan builds a church next to it.[47]

11.7.2 Simon the Magician

A second example of demonic imitation is Acts 8:9–10, where Simon the Magician is described as "the power [Gk. *dynamis*] of God that is called Great [Power] [Gk. *hē Megalē*]," whereas he was clearly practicing magic (Gk. *mageiai*; vv. 9, 11). When Philip came to Samaria, Simon recognized immediately that a greater *dynamis* was at work here than what he himself possessed (v. 13, Gk. *dynameis megalas*, "great powers," or "great works of power"). The point was that Philip was not at all engaging in magic but functioning with the power of the Holy Spirit (cf. 6:3, 5). When the apostles placed the Holy Spirit upon believers (vv. 17–18), apparently with remarkable, visible consequences (§7.5.2), Simon joined them and asked, "Give me this power [Gk. *exousia*] also, so that anyone on whom I lay my hands may receive the Holy Spirit" (v. 19). This strongly suggests that Simon did not see any phenomenological difference between his own ministry and that of Philip and the apostles, but was merely seeking an extension of his own *dynamis*.

Because of this same confusion, today as well the work of the Holy Spirit is sometimes ascribed to the devil (Matt. 12:22–33) — and the reverse occurs, too. However, for the spiritual Christian it should not be difficult to distinguish between the two: "[T]he tree is known by its fruit" (v. 33; cf. 7:15–23). The seeming parallelism does not have to amaze us; on the contrary, it may be *expected*. Michael Green stated that Almighty God is not limited by natural laws (which are nothing more — nor less — than an extensive series of observed uniformities). For example, if levitation can be practiced in

---

47. Luther (1938, Sermon July 22, 1526).

occultism and Eastern meditation, there is no reason why it would not be available for Christians through the Holy Spirit (cf. 1 Kings 18:12; Acts 8:39).[48] Indeed, levitation is mentioned, for instance, in ancient Coptic hagiographies.[49] The Spanish mystic Teresa of Ávila told of experiencing levitation during states of rapture. One eyewitness, Sister Anne of the Incarnation, said Teresa levitated eighteen inches above the ground for about thirty minutes.[50]

Similar examples of many other psychic phenomena can be given; whatever paganism can do, the Spirit within Christianity can do as well. And he does, if he finds it appropriate. No single psychic phenomenon itself is ever "of the devil" or "of the Spirit"; it must always be tested according to strict criteria. In such testing the Holy Spirit himself is the most important criterion; this involves the gift (Gk. *charisma*) of distinguishing between spirits (1 Cor. 12:10; see §12.3.4 below). A person with psychic gifts may dedicate them to God, and if God accepts them they may be used for God through the Holy Spirit.[51]

11.7.3 The Spirit and the Physical

The contrast between the Spirit and the spirits is as great as that between righteousness and lawlessness, light and darkness, Christ and Belial (cf. 2 Cor. 6:14-15). The only noticeable similarity is that the *work* of the spirits and the *work* of the Spirit often involve similar physical phenomena, such as trembling, quivering, shaking, the phenomenon of fire (sometimes even visible tongues of fire and bolts of lightning), or an electrical current (such as tickling, or even power surges), a tingling sensation, a magnetic force, and so on.[52]

---

48. Green (1975, 179).
49. Burgess (1989, 140).
50. About this and similar phenomena in church history, see the classic work by E. Underhill (2011).
51. M. Parmentier, quoted in Vranckx (n.d., 429).
52. Weisberger (1958, 92); Theron (1969, 158); Hagin (1983, 25); Wimber and Springer (1986, 193, 218, 222-24, 263-64); Hunter (2000, 202); How-

We read that when the woman with the discharge of blood touched Jesus, he noticed that "power" had "gone out" from him (Luke 8:46). On certain occasions this power was apparently available as a supply upon which one could draw (cf. 5:17). Common people sensed that, when they touched Jesus, "power came out from him and healed them all" (6:19). I imagine that this was somewhat comparable to touching an electric fence. During ordinary contact, as in a teeming crowd, nothing special happened (8:45). It was different when a person intentionally touched the Lord in faith, thus mentally opening oneself for the Lord's power.

In the book of Acts, the Holy Spirit was just as tangibly present (cf. 4:31). The effects of receiving the Spirit are either explicitly mentioned (2:2-4; 10:44-46; 19:6) or implied. Simon the Magician saw with his eyes the outward effects of receiving the Spirit (8:17-18). James Dunn said that the Spirit is present in Acts as an almost tangible force, if not perceptible itself, then at least perceptible in its effects.[53]

Long before the modern Pentecostal and Charismatic movement, such phenomena were known in Christian mysticism, especially in Eastern Christianity. John Cassian spoke of experiencing a stronger sense of smell and enjoying the loveliest scents when filled with the Spirit. Abdisho Hazzaya (seventh century) also spoke of holy scents and tastes, and hearing beautiful sounds. According to him and Symeon the New Theologian, Spirit baptism goes hand in hand with the experience of God as light, accompanied by the "gift of tears." Especially Ephrem of Syria is said to have possessed this gift in rich measure, but so did Ignatius of Loyola. Isaac of Nineveh spoke of an unusual warmth of the body during Spirit-filled prayer. Gregory Palamas described the highest encounter with the Spirit as a mystical sensation of the divine

---

ard-Browne (1994, 20, 94); Tan (1995, 45, 50, 52, 85–86); Nathan and Wilson (1995, 21, 26–28); Bickle (1998, 215); Hinn (1999, 29, 67–70). For extensive quotations, see Ouweneel (2005a, 323–29).

53. Dunn (1992, 698).

energies, which fill the entire inner person with glory like the transfiguration of Jesus on the mountain.[54] Ephrem, too, described extensively the characteristics of Spirit baptism. In Western Christianity, we hear of such phenomena among the Montanists (late second century) and the great mystics like the Spanish saints Ignatius of Loyola, John of Ávila, Teresa of Ávila, and John of the Cross.[55]

Because of the *outward* similarities between the work of the spirits and the work of the Spirit, some have often tried to find a common denominator among them, as we saw earlier. The error committed here is that people fail to make any distinction between the outward symptoms and the underlying force. Take a physical example: fire, chemical reactions, and electricity can all cause heat, but this does not mean they are identical phenomena. The physical phenomena in Christian experience may (closely or superficially) resemble those occurring among pagans, but the force from which they originate is either

(a) the unconscious or subconscious element of the person being ministered to, or

(b) the unconscious or subconscious element of the person ministering, or

(c) an occult (read: demonic) spirit, or

(d) the Holy Spirit.

Compare the weaker but materially identical description by M. Parmentier: from a phenomenological viewpoint, something occurs in the ministry of Christian healing that certainly can be compared to magnetism. In both cases a higher power is addressed in order to pass on healing power through the healer to the person concerned. The phenomena resemble each other, but the sources (whether Jesus or a psychic entity)

---

54. All of these phenomena are mentioned in Burgess (1989, 3–5, 59, 71, 98, 106, 186).
55. Burgess (1989, 58–62, 99; 1997, 180, 186, 195). According to some, such as the Egyptians Ammonas and Besa, Spirit baptism is available only to those who are most advanced in sinlessness; see Burgess (1989, 152, 161).

are quite different.[56]

11.8 Special Manifestations
11.8.1 Being "Slain in the Spirit"

Intense physical phenomena and wild scenes that accompany a ministry (§11.7.3) are not necessarily evidence that this ministry is from God, *nor* that something is wrong with it, for that matter. Devilish imitation does not make the work of the Spirit wrong. Nor are such phenomena necessarily evidence of a particularly powerful work of the Spirit. D. du Plessis presumed that usually these phenomena are rather mental resistances against the purely spiritual event.[57] K. Kraan called them symptoms of the effort required for the Spirit to do his work, and he presumed that the associated electric and heat experiences might also be the effects of such resistance. I have trouble believing this because such phenomena occur also among people who *love* to submit themselves to the work of the Holy Spirit, and give no evidence at all of resistance.

Kraan wisely advises, however, that we should pay as little attention as possible to such collateral phenomena.[58] And Peter Tan wisely remarked that there is no biblical basis for establishing a person's spirituality on the basis of his falling down, or not falling down, under the power of the Spirit. The Bible treats such falling down as a by-product (see §11.9.3), and not as an experience that one should seek. Jesus ignored the fact that the men who came to arrest him had fallen down (John 18:6-7). He paid no attention to it. When Ezekiel saw God's glory and fell down under its power, God asked him to stand up so that he could speak with him (Ezek. 2:1).[59]

In my view, this is a sober and balanced position: being "slain in the Spirit," as some call it, can never be a goal but is at most a collateral phenomenon in reaching the actual goal:

---

56. Parmentier (1997, 83–84).
57. Quoted by Kraan (1974, 387).
58. Ibid.
59. Tan (1995, 61–62).

the work of the Holy Spirit who is coming upon people. This simple statement helps us, on the one hand, not to reject *a priori* the Toronto blessing itself as *only* carnal, mental, or even occult, and on the other hand, to reject all striving after being "slain in the Spirit" as a goal in itself. Consider the balanced approach of M. Parmentier, who prefers to speak of a "resting in the Spirit," pointing to fascinating examples of earlier mystics such as David of Augsburg (1272), the Dutch Hadewych (thirteenth century), the Spanish mystics Teresa of Ávila and John of the Cross (1591), and the French Francis of Sales (1622).[60] Ronald Knox also comments on people being "slain in the Spirit" in the revival movements of Jonathan Edwards, George Whitefield (1770), John Wesley, and others.[61]

Mike Bickle, who did not reject such falling down, did condemn any overestimation of it. He pointed out that some people push and pull the person for whom they are praying until the person falls down. For them it has become a personal matter because public opinion is at stake. This is manipulation carried to excess.[62] I myself have seen people fall down who were pushed, and I abhor that. But I have also seen many people who were slain in the Spirit without even being touched. This has happened even in countries where the phenomenon itself was as yet scarcely known, so that it was virtually unexpected.

11.8.2 The Human Spirit Versus the Divine Spirit

In Spirit baptism, the believer's spirit is immersed in the Holy Spirit, and drenched with the Spirit (§§4.6.1 and 8.6.1). Agnes Sanford has tried to express how the divine Spirit might work within the human spirit (or mind, soul), and how the two could be related. This was courageous, for many Pentecostal theologians reject any correlation between the supernatural *charismata* and natural human abilities. In their view, the *cha-*

---

60. Parmentier (1992, 17–24).
61. Knox (1950).
62. Bickle (1998, 60).

rismata come from above, to use an expression of Karl Barth, to intersect vertically the plane that is known to us (Ger. *senkrecht von oben*).[63] Sanford said that *charismata* such as wisdom, knowledge, faith, healing, and prophecy might be viewed as normal human abilities that are simply strengthened and increased by the Holy Spirit. She believed that even those gifts that are usually viewed as supernatural are not entirely foreign to people but are the manifestation and extension of forces latent within them.[64]

Sanford applied this concretely to the phenomenon of speaking in tongues by claiming that, even in glossolalia, the Spirit comes from the outside to arouse and activate potential forces within believers that the Creator had planted in them long ago. Remember that, from the beginning in the Garden of Eden, God had spoken to people. When people could no longer hear the direct speech of God, the Creator spoke to them through the indirect speech of dreams, and he moved mysteriously within the deep unconscious, often using symbols that the conscious mind does not understand until the person's intellect is opened. When one speaks in tongues, one is speaking a language that the conscious mind does not know, but that this deep domain of the unconscious does know. Sanford referred to a psychiatrist who claimed that a spiritual power possibly enters a person with such a force that it reaches and touches something within the deep unconscious. As a consequence, the person speaks a language known not to the conscious mind but only to the unconscious. It seems that this can provide a person with significant deliverance, more so than a number of shock treatments. But this is strong medicine that should not be administered casually.[65]

Sanford claimed that one who is speaking in tongues *knows* what they are saying. That is, the conscious mind may not know it, but the unconscious does. For the first time, a person

---

63. Suurmond (1995, 155); see Barth (1933, 30).
64. Sanford (1966, 136).
65. Sanford (1966, 137–39).

expresses the deep knowledge from that other part of oneself. One speaks directly to God as Adam and Eve did in the Garden of Eden. One's natural connection with one's Creator has been restored; one's soul is brought closer to God. Of course, since people are speaking from the unconscious (or rather, from the spirit), they are in closer contact with the Spirit of God than when they are speaking and thinking by means of the unadorned medium of their own language. Thus, the upbuilding (1 Cor. 14:4a) comes from Spirit to spirit, and this is perceived through the increased ability for praying, thinking, and writing.[66]

Such a discussion about the unconscious and about released energy leaves room for various speculations. This is no surprise; we know so little about the physical and mental significance of the phenomena in view here. Yet, I admire the courage of Sanford and of the psychiatrist she quotes in providing a sketch, no matter how preliminary, of the possible connections between the human spirit and the divine Spirit. Perhaps the human spirit itself—more specifically, the subconscious or the unconscious—does contain paranormal energy. But the important question remains to be asked: Through what external human spirit is this energy being released: through the Holy Spirit or through a demonic spirit?

11.9 Psycho-Physical Relationships
11.9.1 Natural-Scientific

When speaking about the possible relationships between the Holy Spirit and the human spirit, we may, with all carefulness, also leave some room for parapsychological insights. The well-known Christian neurophysiologist and Nobel Prize winner, Sir John Eccles, suggested that the brain works like a highly sensitive detector for very weak paranormal[67] in-

---

66. Ibid., 144–45.
67. Here the term "paranormal" is being used to describe phenomena that are (presumably) in some way physical, though hardly understood or not (yet) understood in terms of contemporary physics.

fluences. Such influences are exerted upon the so-called synaptic knobs, those little structures in the synapses that connect nerve cells. Eccles believed that such neurological signals could be amplified thousands of times through a network of nerve cells in the brain cortex, more or less as an electrical signal is amplified through an amplifier and a loudspeaker. This supposedly works only if these influences exhibit some meaningful pattern, and are not arbitrary.[68]

If Eccles is right, the brain functions as a kind of radio receiver, which is set for transmissions from the spiritual/mental world.[69] Upton Sinclair, too, has suggested an analogy between telepathy and radio waves.[70] It seems to me rather speculative but not inconceivable that any type of spirit may work in an analogous way within human consciousness. Of course, the Holy Spirit and demonic spirits are not physical—but they can certainly *manifest* themselves in physical phenomena, even (supposedly) within biophysical processes in nerve cells. It is therefore an error to separate strictly physical and strictly spiritual/mental phenomena.[71] Mental and spiritual activities affect the body;[72] we need think only of (auto)suggestion, of psychosomatic diseases, and of the physiological excitement (red or white complexion, accelerated breath, palpitations, and in more extreme situations, uncontrolled movements, and even involuntary loss of urine and feces), which are brought about by violent emotions.

Parapsychology has identified indications concerning an intermediate zone between what we call physical and mental phenomena. Elsewhere[73] I have pointed to possible mental aspects of quantum mechanical processes.[74] For years parapsychologists have conducted experiments demonstrating that

---

68. Eccles (1953, 278).
69. Cf. Ouweneel (1978, 114).
70. Sinclair (1971).
71. See Ouweneel (2005a, §3.2).
72. See extensively, Ouweneel (1984, 70–77).
73. Ouweneel (2000b, 519–20).
74. See Broughton (1995, 89, 133–37, 169–83, 290–95).

human consciousness can directly influence physical reality. On the basis of quantum mechanics, some physicists have added human consciousness as a variable in their equations. This is not a passive consciousness but a consciousness that is able to cause selective perception of physical reality. It seems that parapsychologists and physicists have converged at this point.[75]

Some qualified researchers who have devoted special attention in this domain are E. H. Walker, who investigated the possible relationships between quantum mechanics and human consciousness (the mind),[76] and R. Sheldrake, with his theory of formative causation, a non-energetic (mental) principle that influences energetic (material) processes.[77]

11.9.2 Biblical Application

Just as the Holy Spirit can dwell in the (material) body of each believer, demonic spirits can dwell in people. In a collective sense this is indicated in Revelation 18:2, "Fallen, fallen is Babylon the great! She has become a dwelling place for demons, a haunt for every unclean spirit, a haunt for every unclean bird, a haunt for every unclean and detestable beast." The word for "dwelling place" (Gk. *katoikētērion*) is used in Ephesians 2:11 (see §10.2.2 above), so that the connection between God's Spirit dwelling and demons dwelling in people is a fact. As far as the individual person is concerned, Jesus says, ". . . Then it [i.e., the unclean spirit] goes and brings with it seven other spirits more evil than itself, and they enter and dwell [Gk. *katoikei*] there [i.e., in that person], and the last state of that person is worse than the first" (Matt. 12:45; cf. Luke 11:26).

A spiritual power dwelling in the physical body of a person, whether a divine or a demonic power, can be manifested in the deliberations and emotions of that person, and also

---

75. Broughton (1995, 294).
76. See Walker (2000); cf. Ouweneel (2000b, 520).
77. See Sheldrake (1992); Sheldrake and Fox (2014); cf. Ouweneel (2000b, 518–19).

in physical processes, in a way that reminds us of electricity or heat (§11.7.3), or possibly even in biophysical processes in our nerve cells. The Holy Spirit or an evil spirit *is* not that "electricity," that "heat," or those biophysical processes, but apparently he can and does *manifest* himself in such phenomena. In these cases, the activity of the Spirit, or *a* spirit, is carried or borne, and thus made visible, by certain physical phenomena. If we know that mental-spiritual processes in a person are borne by physico-chemical processes, *and* that the human spirit can be saturated with the Holy Spirit *or* with one or more evil spirits, these suggested relationships should not amaze us.

Thus, the *spiritual* can express itself in *physical* phenomena. Just as the Holy Spirit can express himself in physical sounds (words) when a person preaches in a Spirit-filled way (Mark 13:11; Acts 2:4; 1 Cor. 2:13), thus the Spirit can express himself in an "electric" tingling in hands that are laid on the sick. We should remember here again the purely physical foundational meaning of the Hebrew word *ruach* and the Greek word *pneuma*: "current or air," whether in the senses of "breath" or of "wind" (§4.1). These are not just metaphors. The breath of both humans and animals (Eccl. 3:19) is the same *ruach* as the spirit (GW: "breath"), about which we read that, at death, "the dust returns to the earth as it was, and the spirit [Heb. *ruach*[78]] returns to God who gave it" (Eccl. 12:7). The "east wind" (Heb. *ruach qadim*) that turned the Red Sea into dry ground (Exod. 14:21) is just as much *ruach* as the blast of God's nostrils that made the waters of the Red Sea pile up (15:8, 10), and this is the same as God's Spirit.

11.9.3 Trembling and Falling

The Bible, too, knows of the psycho-physical relationships just mentioned. The book of Proverbs has beautiful examples: "Anxiety in the heart of man causes depression" (12:25 NKJV),

---

78. This refers to the life principle in both humans and animals (cf. Ps. 104:29–30); so Ross (1991, 1194).

and "A joyful heart is good medicine, but depression drains one's strength" (17:22 GW), and "A man's spirit will endure sickness, but a crushed spirit who can bear?" (8:14; also see 13:12; 14:30; 15:13, 30). The mind can either impede or promote physical changes in the body. This is even more strongly the case when the Holy Spirit mightily works in the human spirit. Indeed, we have seen that being touched by God's Spirit can lead to intense physical phenomena. One example is intense trembling. It is remarkable that in our Western culture, trembling has become an altogether figurative notion, except in cases of illness. But in the Bible, trembling before God is both a spiritual and a physical reality (Exod. 19:16; Ezra 9:4; Ps. 2:11; 119:120; Isa. 66:5; Jer. 5:22; Matt. 28:4; Mark 5:33; 16:8; Luke 8:47; Acts 7:32; 16:29; 1 Cor. 2:3; 2 Cor. 7:15; Phil. 2:12; Heb. 12:21).

Another example: being "slain in the Spirit" (§11.8.1) may have been discredited by many because of the malpractices of some, but falling down before, or being slain by, the awe of God's glory is not uncommon in the Bible.[79] When King Saul heard the words of Samuel who had come up from Sheol, he "fell at once full length on the ground" (1 Sam. 28:20). When fire descended from heaven on Elijah's sacrifice at Mount Carmel, the Israelites "fell [not, cast themselves] on their faces and said, 'The LORD, he is God; the LORD, he is God'" (1 Kings 18:39). When the soldiers wanted to take Jesus captive, and "Jesus said to them, 'I am he,' they drew back and fell to the ground" (John 18:6). When Saul of Tarsus met Jesus for the first time, "he fell to the ground, and heard a voice" (Acts 9:4 NKJV; cf. 22:6-7). The guards at the tomb "trembled and became like dead men" (i.e., stiffened and fell to the ground) for fear of the radiant angel (Matt. 28:4).

After John had received his vision on Patmos, he said, "When I saw him, I fell at his feet as though dead" (Rev. 1:17).

---

79. Prince (1995, 260–63). Incidentally, demons also caused people to fall to the ground (see Mark 9:20).

When God appeared to Abram, "Abram fell[80] on his face" (Gen. 17:3; cf. v. 17). When Joshua saw "the commander of the army of the LORD," he "fell on his face to the earth and worshiped" (Josh. 5:14). When the Shekinah entered Solomon's temple, "the priests *could not remain standing* to minister because of the cloud, for the glory of the LORD filled the house of God" (2 Chron. 5:14 AMP, italics added; cf. Exod. 40:34-35), which seems to mean that they fell to the ground (though other renderings are also possible; see CEV, GNT).

Ezekiel, too, tells us what happened when he beheld the glory of God: "[W]hen I saw it, I fell on my face" (Ezek. 1:28; see also 3:23; 9:8; 11:13; 43:3; 44:4). Daniel tells us about a divine vision: "I was frightened and fell on my face. . . . [W]hen he had spoken to me, I fell into a deep sleep with my face to the ground" (8:17-18), and: "[A]s I heard the sound of his words, I fell on my face in deep sleep with my face to the ground. And behold, a hand touched me and set me trembling on my hands and knees. . . . And when he had spoken this word to me, I stood up trembling" (10:9-11).

11.9.4 Again: Prophetic Ecstasy

In §5.5.1, I dealt with the special cases in 1 Samuel 10:5-10 and 19:20-24. Here, the rushing of the Holy Spirit upon Saul, and the resulting ecstasy or trance, appear to me to be essentially the same as being "in the Spirit" (cf. Eph. 6:18; Rev. 1:10; 4:2; 17:3; 21:10).

We find similar remarkable experiences with the great prophets. Jeremiah tells us how the prophetic word became "in my heart as it were a burning fire shut up in my bones, and I am weary with holding it in, and I cannot" (Jer. 20:9), and: "My heart is broken within me; all my bones shake; I am like a drunken man, like a man overcome by wine, because of the LORD and because of his holy words" (23:9). This

---

80. It is interesting to see how several translations wish to turn this into a deliberate act of Abram himself: "bowed with his face to the ground" (CEV). Much better is the MSG: "Overwhelmed, Abram fell flat on his face."

is a striking example of the overwhelming effect of the Holy Spirit on one's body, comparable to David's experience: "My heart became hot within me. As I mused, the fire burned" (Ps. 39:3). Or Elihu: "I am full of words; the spirit [or, Spirit; GW, NOG] within me constrains me. Behold, my belly is like wine that has no vent; like new wineskins ready to burst. I must speak, that I may find relief; I must open my lips and answer" (Job 32:18-20). Can this all be reduced simply to poetic exaggeration?

Presumably, these are also the things that occurred to the judges of Israel, when the Spirit of the Lord "was" or "came" upon or over them, "clothed" them, "stirred" them, "rushed" upon them (Judg. 3:10; 6:34; 11:29; 13:25; 14:6, 19; 15:14). The same happened to David when the Lord's Spirit "rushed" upon him (1 Sam. 16:13), and to Ezekiel when the Lord's Spirit "lifted" him up or "fell" upon him (Ezek. 3:12, 14; 8:3; 11:1, 5, 24; 43:5). All of these cases involve powerful physical phenomena with which modern believers are often quite unfamiliar, and *if* these phenomena occur, they are assigned all too quickly to the occult.

Someone has rightly remarked that situations can undoubtedly occur where such phenomena may result from emotionality or fanaticism, or perhaps from a carnal desire to be the center of attention. But who would level such accusations against people like the prophets Moses, Jeremiah, or Daniel, or the apostles John and Paul? Far too often the tendency seems to be to reject all forms of physical responses to the presence and power of God. This rejection arises from preconceived erroneous ideas about what is true holiness or about the way of behavior that is acceptable to God in the worship given by his people,[81] or it arises simply from a strong dualism between mind and body. These are the people who believe that it is possible, in the kingdom of God, to overflow with joy (§11.1.2), or to be touched by the power of God, with-

---

81. Prince (1995, 262).

out any concomitant physical manifestation of that power.

11.10 Empowering
11.10.1 Various Anointings

The anointing with the Holy Spirit always implies both the authority and the capacity and power for the ministry a believer has received. Only when an Old Testament king-to-be or priest-to-be had been anointed could he formally function as a king or a priest. This was his authority. However, to factually act as a good king or priest he also needed capacity and power. The anointing was granted for this as well. The anointing implies power. And conversely, the more dedicated to the Lord a person is, the greater is his power; this is why some say, the greater is his anointing (§11.1.1). Every servant of the Lord may apply Isaiah 61:1 personally: the Spirit of God rests on his servants *because* he has anointed them. He sends them "to bring good news to the poor; he has sent [them] to bind up the brokenhearted, to proclaim liberty to the captives, and the opening of the prison to those who are bound." What is true of the Messiah is true in principle of his anointed followers.

One servant has more a ministry of *preaching*, "to bring good news to the poor [GW: humble]," that is, to experienced and fresh converts who truly humble themselves because of their sins (cf. Matt. 5:3, "Blessed are the poor in spirit"). Another servant has more of a *pastoral* ministry, "to bind up the brokenhearted." Yet another servant has more a ministry of *evangelism* and/or *deliverance*: "to proclaim liberty to the captives, and the opening of the prison to those who are bound." But in all these cases, the ministry in view functions only through the "anointing oil" of the Spirit that rests on the servant concerned. More concretely, it is always the same Spirit with which believers are anointed, but, so to speak, a different anointing is involved, depending on the ministry to which a person has been called. Also, for each new ministry a new anointing is needed.[82] This time, we are referring not to quan-

---
82. Cf. Torrey (n.d., 95, 108).

titative but to qualitative differences in the anointing, if we may put it that way.

Just as a person must learn to recognize the voice of the Lord in one's life (cf. the young prophet Samuel in 1 Sam. 3), so too one must learn to recognize the anointing in one's life. In Luke 5:17, it was very clear that the power of the anointing was present: "On one of those days, as he was teaching, Pharisees and teachers of the law were sitting there, who had come from every village of Galilee and Judea and from Jerusalem. And the power of the Lord was with him to heal." However, in Mark 6:4–6, it was equally clear that the power was *not* available: "Jesus said to them [i.e., his former fellow-citizens], 'A prophet is not without honor, except in his hometown and among his relatives and in his own household.' And he could do no mighty work there, except that he laid his hands on a few sick people and healed them. And he marveled because of their unbelief. And he went about among the villages teaching."

In a similar way, each believer must learn to recognize the power of one's anointing. When the prophet Elisha was still inexperienced, he had to wait and see whether the anointing of Elijah had been transferred to him (2 Kings 2:14). However, in the next chapter we see that he had already received the anointing. Thus, at a certain moment he knew that the power of the anointing was *not* present. Therefore, he called for a musician: "And when the musician played, the hand of the Lord came upon him" (3:15), that is, so to speak, the anointing in all its fullness returned to him. The consequence of this was that he could pass on the word of the Lord. I believe that the rest and the excitement that entered his soul through the musician's playing restored the Lord's power to him.

11.10.2 Vulnerability

In Matthew 10, Jesus gave his twelve disciples "authority over unclean spirits, to cast them out, and to heal every disease and every affliction" (v. 1). He said, "Heal the sick, raise the dead, cleanse lepers, cast out demons" (v. 8), and this is what they did: "The apostles returned to Jesus and told him all that they had done and taught" (Mark 6:30; cf. Luke 9:10).

Nevertheless, sometime later, these same disciples who had healed the sick, had raised the dead, had cleansed lepers, and had cast out demons, did not have the power to deliver a boy from his unclean spirit. The reason was that power (Gk. *dynamis*) is not always present in the believers in equal measure: this power must be *sustained*. Time and again believers must *pray* for this power (Luke 11:13). Therefore, Jesus reproached the disciples for their "little faith" (Matt. 17:20), and said of the demons in this poor boy: "This kind cannot be driven out by anything but prayer" (Mark 9:29). Time and again, a believer's humbling, surrender, and dedication must be renewed. This is a condition for a powerful anointing in *every* type of ministry that believers have received.

Especially after great victories in spiritual warfare, believers can be particularly vulnerable. With his three hundred and eighteen men, Abram gained a great victory over the four hostile kings, and even withstood the temptation from the king of Sodom (Gen. 14). But shortly afterward, the LORD came to him in a vision and said, "*Fear not*, Abram" (15:1). With the jawbone of a donkey, Samson slew one thousand Philistines—but shortly afterward, he was extremely weak, almost dying of thirst, and he called upon the LORD for help (Judg. 15:14–19). And after Elijah on Mount Carmel had led the people back to the LORD, and had executed eight hundred and fifty false prophets (1 Kings 18), he fled because of one single threatening message from Queen Jezebel (19:1–3).

A servant of the Lord is never more vulnerable than right after a great spiritual victory. Therefore, after *each* battle believers must reload spiritually and renew their anointing. "Therefore take up the whole armor of God, that you may be able to withstand in the evil day, and *having done all, to stand firm*" (Eph. 6:13). After Samson had surrendered the secret of his power, and his hair was cut, the LORD left him (Judg. 16:19-20). This was not because his power was in his hair; rather, his power lay in his dependence upon the LORD. In his final hour, he called to the LORD and said, "O LORD God, please remember me and please strengthen me only this once, O God, that I may be avenged on the Philistines for my two eyes" (v. 28). Through humble supplication his strength was renewed once more in an exceptionally powerful way.

11.10.3 Oppression

There is yet another means by which spiritual power (Gk. *dynamis*) can increase tremendously, and this is external pressure. Sometimes, spiritual warfare *itself* can contribute to the increase of the Spirit's power in his servant: "If you are insulted for the name of Christ, you are blessed, because the Spirit of glory [some insert: and of power] and of God rests upon you" (1 Pet. 4:14). The very fact that God's servants are insulted (negatively criticized, slandered, mocked) is evidence that they are standing in God's favor, for the Holy Spirit rests upon them. Yes, the more they are insulted, the greater will God's glory and the power of his Spirit be manifested in them.

Persecution and oppression do not necessarily decrease a person's anointing—for instance, because one allows oneself to feel discouraged—but they may rather strengthen one's anointing. Precisely when all resistance is lacking, believers should be worrying: "Woe to you, when all people speak well of you, for so their fathers did to the false prophets" (Luke 6:26). Every true ministry flourishes and is strengthened under pressure. Resistance increases the *dynamis*. The very pressure that was exerted upon Peter became the occasion for his being filled with the Holy Spirit and giving his testimony (Acts 4:8). The very pressure that was exerted upon the Jerusalem believers became the occasion for their being filled with the Holy Spirit, and "the place where they were gathered together was shaken" (v. 31). The very resistance that Paul experienced became the occasion for his being filled with the Holy Spirit and properly answering his opponent (Acts 13:9–11).

The very difficulties that Paul expected in Corinth gave him the right spiritual preparation for his evangelism campaign in this city: "I was with you in weakness and in fear and much trembling, and my speech and my message were not in plausible words of wisdom, but in demonstration of the Spirit and of power, so that your faith might not rest in the wisdom of men but in the power of God" (1 Cor. 2:3–5). As he says elsewhere (2 Cor. 12:9–10), the Lord "said to me, 'My grace is sufficient for you, for my power is made perfect in weakness.' Therefore I will boast all the more gladly of my weaknesses, so that the power of Christ may rest upon me. For the sake of Christ, then, I am content with weaknesses, insults, hardships, persecutions, and calamities. For when I am weak, then I am strong."

When believers are resisted, even imprisoned and interrogated, these may be the very occasions when the Holy Spirit will speak more clearly through them than on any other occasion: "[W]hen they bring you to trial and deliver you over, do not be anxious beforehand what you are to say, but say whatever is given you in that hour, for it is not you who speak, but the Holy Spirit" (Mark 13:11). Of the apostles we read, "[T]hey left the presence of the council, rejoicing that they were counted worthy to suffer dishonor for the name. And every day, in the temple and from house to house, they did not cease teaching and preaching that the Christ is Jesus" (Acts 5:41–42).

Chapter 12
The Gifts of the Holy Spirit[1]

Now there are varieties of gifts,
  but the same Spirit;
and there are varieties of service,
  but the same Lord;
and there are varieties of activities,
  but it is the same God
  who empowers them all in everyone.
To each is given the manifestation of the Spirit
  for the common good.
For to one is given through the Spirit the utterance of wisdom,
  and to another the utterance of knowledge according to the same Spirit,
    to another faith by the same Spirit,
    to another gifts of healing by the one Spirit,
    to another the working of miracles,
    to another prophecy,
    to another the ability to distinguish be-

---
1. See Ouweneel (2005a, chapter 5).

> tween spirits,
>> to another various kinds of tongues,
>> to another the interpretation of tongues.
>
> All these are empowered by one and the same Spirit,
>> who apportions to each one individually as he wills.
>
> 1 Corinthians 12:4–11

Summary: *This chapter deals with the* charismata *(Rom. 12; 1 Cor. 12) and the ministries (1 Cor. 12; Eph. 4). They come from the Triune God, and they are gifts of his grace. Precursors of them are found already in the Old Testament. 1 Corinthians 12 speaks of "gifts of illumination" (words of wisdom and knowledge, discerning the spirits), "gifts of action" (faith [exceptional confidence in God], healings, and other miraculous works), and "gifts of communication" (prophecy, glossolalia, and its interpretation). They are not gifts to individuals as such but to the entire church, but all individual believers can receive them (although the gifts do not make them more spiritual for it). In the ideal case, all the* charismata *function in each of the five ministries. Cessationism (the gifts were only for the apostolic age) cannot stand the test of theological scrutiny. Gifts must be practiced in an attitude of love (1 Cor. 13); one day they will cease, but love will remain. Finally, attention is given to the way the gifts ought to function during the church's worship services: in both order and freedom (1 Cor. 14).*

12.1 Gifts and Ministries
12.1.1 *Pneumatika*

AMONG ALL THE NEW TESTAMENT CHURCHES, the one at Corinth seems to have been particularly blessed with the gifts of the Spirit. Later Clement of Rome wrote to this church (1 Clem. 2:2b), "[A] full outpouring of the Holy Spirit was upon you all."[2] Paul could say, "I give thanks to my God always for you

---

2. http://www.ewtn.com/library/patristc/anf1-1.htm.

The Gifts of the Holy Spirit

because of the grace of God that was given you in Christ Jesus, that in every way you were enriched in him in all speech and all knowledge—even as the testimony about Christ was confirmed among you—so that you are not lacking in any gift" (1 Cor. 1:4-7).

At a later point Paul writes, "Now concerning spiritual gifts [Gk. *pneumatika*], brothers, I do not want you to be uninformed" (1 Cor. 12:1). The first thing of which the Corinthian Christians should be aware was that the *pneumatika* (spiritual [things, gifts, manifestations, utterances]) that had been so richly granted to them were by themselves no proof of the work of the Holy Spirit; such phenomena could come from the demonic world as well. Therefore the apostle continues, "You know that when you were pagans you were led astray to mute idols, however you were led. Therefore I want you to understand that no one speaking in the Spirit of God ever says 'Jesus is accursed!' and no one can say 'Jesus is Lord' except in the Holy Spirit" (vv. 2-3). In other words, according to their phenomenal form, identical *pneumatika* may come from the Spirit but also from the world of idols (read: demons; cf. §§11.1.3, 11.5.3, and 11.7.1). Decisive in this respect is a person's attitude toward Jesus; if this person actively lives under the Lordship of Christ, he may be sure that his *pneumatika* are from the right source.

In the time before their conversion, it had been very different. The Corinthians had served idols. The idolatrous images were indeed mute, but the demons hiding behind them (10:19-21), expressing themselves through psychic persons, definitely were not. A statement like "Jesus is accursed!" did not come from the Holy Spirit but from such demons, whether before the conversion of these Corinthian believers, or because false spirits had nestled within the Corinthian church.[3] By contrast, the perilous statement "Jesus is Lord!" the Christian confession that was being made in the face of the pagan

---

3. Regarding the various interpretations, see Fee (1987, 579–81).

emperor cult—the emperor was venerated as "lord and god" (Lat. *dominus et deus*)—could come only from the Holy Spirit working in the believer.

Presumably, in verses 2–3 Paul also wanted to express that, in paganism, the Corinthians had been accustomed to a great diversity of spirits, each of which produced its own type of spiritual phenomenon. However, they now had to realize that the *pneumatika* within Christianity, no matter how diverse they were, came from one and the same Holy Spirit (cf. v. 4).

12.1.2 Trinitarian Involvement

In 1 Corinthians 7, these *pneumatika*, "spiritual things," or more clearly, "things of the Spirit," are summarized as "the manifestation [Gk. *phanerōsis*] of the Spirit," and in verses 4–6 they are organized as follows: "Now there are varieties of gifts [Gk. *charismata*], but [it is] the same Spirit; and there are varieties of service [one Greek word, plural: *diakoniai*; NKJV: ministries], but [it is] the same Lord; and there are varieties of activities [Gk. *energēmata*; NASB: effects], but it is the same God who empowers [Gk. *energōn*][4] them all in everyone." The Trinitarian involvement is remarkable: the Holy Spirit, the Lord (Jesus, the Son of the Father), and God (the Father). In Romans 12:6 (cf. v. 3b), God (the Father) is the giver of all the gifts, in Ephesians 4:7–11 the glorified Christ is the giver, and in 1 Corinthians 12 especially the Holy Spirit is the giver.

In the gifts (Gk. *charismata*, from *charis*, "grace," and thus literally, "portions of grace"), granted by the one Spirit, it is the power of God that comes to the fore. These *charismata* do not necessarily conflict with natural capacities or theological education, but they do transcend these to a considerable extent.

A preacher must have both natural eloquence and divine equipping. A pastor (shepherd, counselor) must have both a

---

4. The Gk. words *energēmata* . . . *energōn* can be rendered as "varieties of workings . . . God who works them."

natural ability to listen and divine equipping. A teacher must have both a natural ability to explain ideas and divine equipping.

In the ministries that are granted by the one Lord, the authority under which the servant stands seems to be what the apostle is targeting. These ministries do not necessarily conflict with human appointment, but the authority of the Master transcends to a considerable extent all human consecration. Notice Acts 13:1-3, where the Lord through his Holy Spirit does the sending, and the Antiochian prophets and teachers merely testify to their agreement. In Acts 20:28 it is primarily the Holy Spirit, not any humans, who has made certain men overseers in the church of Ephesus.

In the effects of these ministries, granted by the one *God*, the apostle seems to be focusing on the outcome of serviceability of all the gifts. These outcomes do not necessarily conflict with human methods of creating certain effects: eloquence, vivacious music, and the like. However, God's operations within the human soul transcend all these natural effects. The Holy Spirit can work *through* musical instruments (e.g., Exod. 15:20; 1 Sam. 10:5; 2 Sam. 6:5; 1 Kings 10:12; 2 Kings 3:15; 1 Chron. 15:16; 25:1, 3, 6; 2 Chron. 5:12; 20:28; 29:25; Neh. 12:27; Ps. 68:25; 92:3; 149:3; 150:3-5; Isa. 30:29; Matt. 11:17), but they are always only means, never goals.

12.1.3 Enumeration

A number of *pneumatika* that were important for the Corinthians are enumerated in 1 Corinthians 12:8-10, introduced with these words: "[T]he manifestation of the Spirit is given to each one for the profit of [all]" (v. 7 NKJV; cf. 6:12; 7:35; 10:23, 33). Notice four things here. First, the expression "of the Spirit" (Gk. *tou pneumatos*) is either a subjective genitive ("by/through the Spirit," namely, it is the Spirit who manifests), or an objective genitive ("concerning [the presence and working of] the Spirit," namely, something of the Spirit is manifested).

Possibly both meanings are included.[5] Second, Paul says "is given" (Gk. *didotai*), not "has been given," thus referring to a continual, repeatedly momentaneous, granting of the *charismata*.[6] Third, the *charismata* are given to each member of the body of Christ; each believer can receive a *charisma* any moment it is needed: "[G]race was given to each one of us according to the measure of Christ's gift" (Eph. 4:7). Fourth, "profitable" is what contributes to the upbuilding of the church (cf. vv. 12, 16, 29; Rom. 14:19; 1 Cor. 14:3-4, 12, 26; 2 Cor. 12:9; 1 Thess. 5:11; Jude 1:20).

After this we have the following enumeration (vv. 8-10):

> For to one is given through the Spirit [1] the utterance of wisdom, and to another [2] the utterance of knowledge according to the same Spirit, to another [3] faith by the same Spirit, to another [4] gifts [charismata] of healing by the one Spirit, to another [5] the working [plur.: *energēmata*, operations] of miracles [Gk. *dynameōn*, NIV: miraculous powers], to another [6] prophecy, to another [7] the ability to distinguish between spirits, to another [8] various kinds of tongues [others: languages], to another [9] the interpretation of tongues [languages].

In verses 28-30, five of the Nine Gracious Gifts are summarized again: [6] prophets, [5] miracles (lit., powers), [4] *charismata* of healings, [8] various kinds of tongues, and [9] interpreters (of tongues). This occurs in addition to the enumeration of some ministries: apostles, teachers (is this ministry linked with [2], knowledge?), helpers (plural!) (perhaps to be linked with some of the *charismata* in Rom. 12:7-8: service, generosity, mercy[7]), administrators. Because of these four ministries, it is possible that the five *charismata* mentioned here in fact also refer to ministries characterized by these *cha-*

---

5. Grosheide (1957, 323).
6. Findlay (1979, 885).
7. Dunn (1997, 252); Fee (1987, 621); cf. also the good works of the "real" widows: hospitality, washing the saints' feet, caring for the afflicted (1 Tim. 5:10).

rismata (see §12.6.1).

In 1 Corinthians 13:1-2 five of the Nine Gracious Gifts are mentioned again: [8] tongues/languages, [6] prophecy, [1] "mysteries" (this reminds us most strongly of the "word of wisdom" of v. 8; see the interpretation below), [2] knowledge, [3] faith. Thus, in 1 Corinthians 12:28-13:2, eight of the Nine Gracious Gifts are identified once again, while [7], discernment of spirits, seems to be alluded to in 14:29-32 (see the interpretation below). In 13:8, [6] prophecies, [8] tongues/languages, and [2] knowledge are mentioned again.

In addition to this, we find in Ephesians 4:11 the five well-known ministries (cf. the Gk. word *diakonia* in v. 12): apostles, prophets, evangelists, shepherds, and teachers. Further, Romans 12:6-8 gives an enumeration of seven *charismata*: prophecy, serving, teaching, exhorting, contributing, leading, and showing mercy. 1 Peter 4:10-11 mentions two of them (or summarizes all *charismata* mentioned in these two terms): serving and speaking. Of course, with these lists the total array of possible *charismata* and ministries is not necessarily exhausted.

12.2 Charismata
12.2.1 Gifts of Grace

As noted earlier, a *charisma*, from the Greek word *charis*, "grace," is a "portion of grace" in the widest conceivable sense, whether it is the salvation of the sinner (Rom. 5:15; 6:23), or sexual abstinence (1 Cor. 7:7), or deliverance from distress (2 Cor. 1:11), or in the form of privileges like those given to Israel (Rom. 11:29), or in the form of a certain ministry (1 Tim. 4:4; 2 Tim. 1:6). The "*charismata* of healing" (1 Cor. 12:9 plural; in v. 28 even "*charismata* of healings") are "portions of grace" as well, granted at certain moments.[8]

---

8. See Dunn (1992, 703); Fee (1994, 169, 887); *contra* Esser (1976, 121). Parmentier (1992, 12) rightly said, "Charismata and everything connected with it are 'gratis grace," in which "gratis" ("free") and "grace" both come from Latin *gratia*.

Unfortunately, the common translation of *charis* as "gift" loses this notion of grace; every *charisma* is a piece of grace bestowed by the Holy Spirit. (In the next section we will find a second reason why the rendering "gift" is unfortunate.) As Paul wrote, "Having gifts [*charismata*] that differ according to the grace [*charis*] given to us..." (Rom. 12:6), and, "I give thanks to my God always for you because of the grace [*charis*] of God that was given you in Christ Jesus... so that you are not lacking in any gift [Gk. *charisma*]" (1 Cor. 1:4, 7). By way of comparison, consider these words: "[G]race [*charis*] was given to each one of us according to the measure of Christ's gift [Gk. *dōrea*].... And he gave the apostles, the prophets, the evangelists, the shepherds and teachers" (Eph. 4:7, 11).

All *charismata* flow forth from the one, basic *charisma*, namely, the gracious gift of God's salvation in Christ: "But the free gift [one word: *charisma*] is not like the trespass. For if many died through one man's trespass, much more have the grace [*charis*] of God and the free gift [one word: *dōrea*] by the grace [*charis*] of that one man Jesus Christ abounded for many" (Rom. 5:15). "For the wages of sin is death, but the free gift [one word: *charisma*] of God is eternal life in Christ Jesus our Lord" (6:23). This led E. Käsemann to write that Paul's doctrine of the *charismata* is an elaboration of his doctrine of justification by faith, and indicates the enormous scope of this doctrine.[9] Therefore, those who emphasize the *charismata* are moving entirely along the lines of the Reformation's adage "by grace alone" (Lat. *sola gratia*).[10]

The *charismata* in 1 Corinthians 12 are, without any exception, miraculous gifts. We mean by this that each of them is supernatural, or if we wish to avoid the confusing nature–supernature dualism,[11] we mean that none of them can be explained in terms of the natural sciences and the humanities,

---

9. Käsemann (1964, 75).
10. Suurmond (1995, 163).
11. Cf. Bavinck (n.d., 61); Green (1975, 156); Floor (1982, 165–66; 1999, 35–37); Pinnock (1996, 137).

though they are linked with natural human abilities (§11.8.2). It is quite important to see that this is true not for just a few of the Nine Gracious Gifts but for each of them. Especially in the case of the *pneumatika*, it is dangerous to make a distinction between supernatural and natural utterances.[12] What is worked by the Holy Spirit is by definition supernatural or, in more careful terms, miraculous.[13]

12.2.2 What Is "Gift"?

If along with many expositors,[14] I properly understand the term *charisma* within the context of 1 Corinthians 12, then no single believer possesses any of the Nine Gracious Gifts of verses 8-10 in the sense of a permanent capacity. Rather, each believer can, in a given situation and for that specific moment, receive one of these gifts. In my view, in order to understand the meaning of the *charismata*, this is an essential point. Thus, a "gift" (Gk. *charisma*) is not at all a continual talent or capacity or ability, like a musical or a technical "gift."

Therefore, the NLT rendering is completely mistaken: ". . . to someone else the one Spirit gives the gift of healing" (v. 9). Such a translation suggests a permanent capacity, ignoring the plural: *charismata* (so also in v. 28). These are gifts, granted by the Spirit not once and for all, but repeatedly, as the situation demands. *Charismata* are not ongoing ministries, like those of teachers or elders,[15] but gifts of God at a certain moment, received by a person to pass on to others. A beautiful example, mentioned by Findlay,[16] is Luke 7:21 (AMP), "He

---

12. As Mare does (1976, 272).
13. Cf. Vranckx (n.d., 32): supernatural = animated by the Spirit.
14. See extensively, Price (1997, 85–107); cf. Sanford (1966, 135); Watson (1973, 89); Wimber and Springer (1991, 173–74, 177); Duffield and Van Cleave (1996, 353).
15. *Contra* Belder (1997, 19): "Also the offices in the church belong to the 'charismata'"; and Floor (1999, 39), who claimed: "In 1 Corinthians 12:28 and Ephesians 4:11 Paul called . . . his own apostolic office a charisma." Paul simply did *not* do this. Grudem (1994, 1020), too, hardly seemed to distinguish between *charismata*, ministries, and offices.
16. Findlay (1979, 888).

gave [the gracious gift of] sight to many [who were] blind." The phrase "he gave" is expressed by the Greek verb *echarisato*, in which we recognize the root *charis*: Jesus gave sight to the blind as a gift of grace. This is why *charisma* is used in the plural in 1 Corinthians 12:9 and 28: every healing, at a certain place and time, is a gift of grace in itself.[17] In the *charismata* we have to do with manifestations of the Spirit (cf. 1 Cor. 12:7); this expression, too, points to the incidental character of the *charismata*.

At the same time, we find that some believers receive certain *charismata* much more often than other believers: according to 1 Corinthians 12:28, there are apostles, prophets (persons who frequently receive prophecies), teachers, *dynameis* (people in whom God's miraculous power frequently manifests itself), healing ministers, and so on. Thus, believers can have a healing or prophetic ministry. But at the same time, we maintain, on the one hand, that, in principle, all believers can occasionally receive *gifts* of healing or prophetic words without having a healing or prophetic *ministry*. On the other hand, even in the ministry of healing not all sick people are indeed healed, and even prophets do not have prophetic words for all people who come under their ministry. In other words, healing ministers and prophets do not have a permanent gift of healing or prophetic gift in the sense of an ability that is constantly at their disposal.

Confusing *charismata* and ministries[18] has obstructed much potential blessing from reaching God's people. Examples include these: many believers have refused, or stopped, laying hands on people (in spite of Mark 16:17-18) with the argument that they have no gift of healing. But in this sense of the term, nobody on earth has a gift of healing. Many Christians are not open for occasionally passing on a prophetic word, us-

---

17. Bittlinger (1967, 37); Fee (1987, 594). Totally unfounded is the exegesis of Grosheide (1957, 325–26), who explains the plural "gifts" as "healings of various diseases, in which each disease presupposes its own charisma."
18. Floor (1982, 186–87).

ing the argument that they have no prophetic gift. The problem, as I see it, is that they do not understand the meaning of *charismata* in 1 Corinthians 12.

The occasional, momentaneous character of the *charismata* has been properly grasped by the Belgian Roman Catholic theologian, philosopher, and psychologist Antoon Vergote. He called visions *charismata* or "gifts of the Spirit" as well, and thus "signs of God to humanity."[19] At the same time, visions fit less well into the category of *charismata* if we realize that the *charismata* in 1 Corinthians 12 always seem to be gifts of the Spirit that a person receives for another person. But perhaps we cannot maintain this claim with regard to glossolalia (see below).

12.2.3 Old Testament Gifts

The miraculous gifts are "for the common good," that is, they are given "unto profit" (1 Cor. 12:7 DRA; cf. 14:3; Eph. 4:12). The gospel announces the ultimate wholeness of the whole person: wholeness of the body through the casting out of demons and the healing from diseases, and wholeness of the soul through regeneration, and the transformation unto conformity to the image of Christ. In God's kingdom, this wholeness is, and was, always one inextricable totality.[20] When Jesus sent out his disciples, first the twelve and later the seventy(-two), casting out demons and healing the sick were mentioned first among their tasks (Matt. 10:1; Mark 6:7; Luke 9:1-2; 10:1, 9).

If the miraculous gifts are profitable for the people of God, one may expect to find at least some of them already in the Old Testament. This indeed turns out to be the case. It was not the case that the miraculous gifts of the Spirit were possible only after the outpouring of the Holy Spirit in Acts 2. However, there is this big difference. The New Testament message based on Joel 2:28-29 (prophesying, dreaming dreams, seeing visions) implies that the *charismata* can be manifested in the

---

19. Quoted in Vranckx (n.d., 216).
20. See Ouweneel (2005a, §3.2-3).

lives of all believers. However, in the Old Testament we find them only here and there—actually only among those who are called prophets. In the next sections, I will also regularly point to corresponding phenomena in the Old Testament. Similarly, I will also point to the way the *charismata* functioned in the ministry of Christ himself.

One of the details in Joel 2:28–29 is, first, that young people and old people are being distinguished. Samuel was only a boy when he was called by the LORD (1 Sam. 3:1; cf. v. 15, Eli was ninety-eight years old), and Jeremiah was "only a youth" (Jer. 1:7; cf. v. 5). Conversely, when Ahijah's "eyes were dim because of his age" (1 Kings 14:4; cf. the "old prophet" in 13:11), he was still used by the LORD.

Second, Joel emphasizes that God uses not only men but also women ("daughters," "female servants"). Of them, too, we find examples in biblical history before Acts 2. The prophetess Deborah (Judg. 4:4) pronounced prophecies (vv. 9, 14), including an entire prophetic song (Judg. 5). Further, we know four more prophetesses of God: Miriam "the prophetess" (Exod. 15:20), Huldah (2 Kings 22:14; 2 Chron. 34:22), the unnamed wife of Isaiah (Isa. 8:3[21]), and Anna (Luke 2:36). In Luke 1:41–55, Elizabeth and Mary pronounced prophetic words, too. Among the one hundred twenty who in Acts 2:4 were filled with the Spirit and spoke in tongues were "the women and Mary the mother of Jesus" (1:14). Among these women, some are known by name: Mary Magdalene, Mary of Bethany (unless these two are the same) and her sister Martha, Joanna, the wife of Chuza (Herod's household manager), Susanna (Luke 8:2–3; John 11:1), Mary the mother of James the younger and of Joses, and Salome (Mark. 15:40; cf. John 11:25).

After Acts 2, we hear about Philip who "had four unmarried daughters, who prophesied" (21:9). 1 Corinthians 11:5 speaks of "every woman/wife who prays or prophesies...."

---

21. Perhaps she was called a prophetess only because she was the wife of a prophet.

Any believing woman can receive prophetic words, and the same is true for each of the other *charismata*. None of them is withheld from Christian women, unless they themselves are a hindrance (through ignorance or sin) — but that is true for Christian men as well.

12.3 Gifts of Illumination
12.3.1 Introduction

Agnes Sanford has described the Nine Gracious Gifts of the Spirit as the tools in the tool box, with which believers have to do God's work on earth.[22] Such a positive assessment is so refreshing in comparison, for instance, with that of Vellenga and Kret, who claimed that these gifts already in the first century were of incidental importance.[23] I would rather claim the opposite: no true work of God, also after the first century, was ever done without these Nine Gracious Gifts. What can the carpenter do without his saw, his hammer, his pliers, or his screwdriver? Similarly, how poorly would God's work be done without the believers' tools: words of wisdom and knowledge, discerning the spirits, faith that moves mountains, and even healings and deliverances. Notice that the carpenter can properly do his work only if he has all his tools at his disposal. Notice that God's people can properly do God's work only if they have all their tools at their disposal.

The Nine Gifts remind us of the ninefold fruit of the Spirit in Galatians 5:22-23 (see §9.7). We could describe their relationship as follows: the ninefold fruit of the Spirit constitutes the moral condition for receiving and applying the Nine Gracious Gifts.

Each of the first, second, third, and fourth *charismata* are explicitly associated with the Spirit, each time in a different way: they are "through [Gk. *dia*] the Spirit," "according to [one Gk. word: *kata*[24]] the same Spirit," "by [Gk. *en*, in the

---

22. Sanford (1966, 135).
23. Vellenga and Kret (1957, 20).
24. The Gk. preposition *kata* can sometimes mean "through" as well; see Fee

power of] the same Spirit," and "by [Gk. *en*] the one Spirit."

Let us now have a closer look at the Nine Gracious Gifts. Any arrangement of them is rather arbitrary, but I have some preference for that by William R. Jones.[25] He distinguished between the gifts of illumination (the word of wisdom, the word of knowledge, the gift of discerning the spirits), of action (faith, gifts of healing, miracle works), and of communication (prophecy, tongues, interpretation of tongues). The only point where Jones deviated from Paul's order in 1 Corinthians 12 is that he gives number [7] (discerning the spirits) an earlier place in the lineup. I follow the ordering by Jones, but I do maintain the numbering of the *charismata* according to the enumeration in 1 Corinthians 12.

12.3.2 [1] A Word of Wisdom

Wisdom and knowledge themselves are not called *charismata*, although they too undoubtedly are gifts of the grace of God. But that is not the point here. In the present context, it is the utterance (Gk. *logos*, "word") of wisdom or knowledge that is a gracious gift of the Lord through the believer to the benefit of others.[26] In 1 Corinthians we find especially the wisdom that God has revealed in and through the crucified Christ (see 1:17, 19–22, 24, 30; 2:1, 4–7, 13; 3:19). Therefore, Gordon Fee assumed that, in 12:8, Paul is speaking of utterances that presented the crucified Christ in this rather "wisdom" oriented church.[27] However, it is not necessary to limit the meaning to this. Paul spoke wisdom "among the mature [Gk. *teleiois*]" (2:6), and "the mature" are "those who have their powers of discernment trained by constant practice to distinguish good from evil" (Heb. 5:14). "Behold, the fear of the LORD, that is wisdom, and to turn away from evil is understanding" (Job

---

(1987, 592n51).
25. Jones (1976). Tan (1995, 7–8) and Howard-Browne (2005, 9) give the same arrangement and speak of revelational gifts, power gifts, and vocal gifts (or gifts of utterance).
26. Dunn (1997, 221).
27. Findlay (1979, 888); Fee (1987, 592; 1994, 166–67).

28:28). Wisdom is the Spirit-given light on good and evil, that is, the understanding of how, in a given situation, one must speak or act according to God's will, and avoid all that is against it. In my view, this exegesis is supported by 1 Corinthians 13:2, one "understand[s] all mysteries," that is, the hidden will of God is revealed in a "word of wisdom."

Very practically, wisdom is needed even in view of the elementary question how, where, and when the following *charismata* that we have enumerated must be exercised. Examples in 1 Corinthians of words of wisdom are the advice that Paul gives on the basis of his own understanding, led by the Spirit (7:8, 12, 25, 40), and what he (supernaturally) received (Gk. *parelabon*) concerning the Lord's Supper (11:23) and concerning Christ's death and resurrection (15:3).

Other examples are the following: in Acts 6:1-4, the twelve apostles, in a troublesome situation in the church, received wisdom from the Holy Spirit to arrive at a good solution. In 10:15, the apostle Peter received a word of wisdom concerning relationships between Jews and Gentiles (cf. vv. 19 and 28). In Acts 15, the elders through the Spirit received insight about what they were to require from Gentile Christians (v. 28). Several times, the apostle Paul received words of wisdom, of both a practical nature (Acts 18:9-10; 23:11; 27:23; Gal. 1:12) and a doctrinal nature (Eph. 3:3). The Lord promised a word of wisdom to all his disciples who would be taken captive and would have to testify before their judges (Matt. 10:17-20; cf. Acts 4:7-21; 6:9-10; 2 Tim. 4:16-17).

Old Testament. Some striking examples are found in the ministry of Moses who, whenever necessary, sought God's face, and received words of wisdom concerning what had to be done (e.g., Exod. 14:15-16, 26; Lev. 24:10-23; Num. 15:32-36). Such words are received in a dependent, prayerful attitude. At a given moment, Joshua could not speak the word of wisdom because he "did not ask counsel from the LORD" (Josh. 9:14).

Christic. He who was himself "the wisdom of God" (1 Cor. 1:24) supplies us with many examples of spoken wisdom from his life on earth. One example is the various ways recorded in Luke 20 in which he responded to the various groups of his opponents. The people were stunned and asked, "Where did this man get this wisdom and these mighty works [one Gk. word: *dynameis*, powers]?" (Matt. 13:54; cf. Mark 6:2); note the combination of wisdom and powers. Jesus said, "The queen of the South . . . came from the ends of the earth to hear the wisdom of Solomon, and behold, something greater than Solomon is here" (Luke 11:31).

12.3.3 [2] A Word of Knowledge

In 1 Corinthians 13:2, knowledge is a gift that follows upon mysteries, and in verse 8 it is something that, in the consummation of the ages, will cease together with prophecies and tongues. In 14:6, "knowledge" appears between "revelation" and "prophecy." We can therefore safely conclude that the "word of knowledge," just like the "word of wisdom," has a revelatory character.[28] In the wider sense, some think here of inspired doctrinal teaching (cf. NLV: "the gift of teaching"; TLB: "someone else may be especially good at studying and teaching"; cf. CEV: "can speak with knowledge"; ERV: "the ability to speak with knowledge"). But J. H. Bavinck goes too far in naturalizing wisdom and knowledge here: "In general, wisdom is an innate gift, knowledge is usually the product of study and reflection. Both are viewed here as being in service of the Spirit, included in his blessed work for the benefit of the church."[29]

Within the context of 1 Corinthians 12, it seems more obvious to think of the supernatural knowledge of facts concerning the past and present of persons and facts, as well as insight into Biblical principles from whose viewpoint we must look at these facts (cf. Rom. 15:14, ". . . filled with all knowledge

---

28. Fee (1987, 593; 1994, 167–68); *contra* Gee (1963, 27–34, 110–19).
29. Bavinck (n.d., 62).

The Gifts of the Holy Spirit

and able to instruct one another"). This interpretation must be preferred because, according to 1 Corinthians 13:8, this is a kind of knowledge that will one day pass away, whereas knowledge of the truth will exist forever.

We find that Peter received a word of knowledge when, on the mount of transfiguration, he "knew" in a miraculous way that Jesus' companions were Moses and Elijah (Luke 9:33). In another word of knowledge, Peter revealed that Ananias and Sapphira had lied about the price they had received for the piece of land they had sold (Acts 5:1–11). In Acts 9:10–16, another Ananias received a word of knowledge about Saul of Tarsus, about the place where he was staying, and about his condition. In Acts 14:9, Paul "saw" that the paralyzed man "had faith to be made well."

Old Testament. The blind prophet Ahijah knew that it was King Jeroboam's wife who was coming in, and with what message (1 Kings 14:5). Elisha received a word of knowledge concerning what his servant Gehazi had done (2 Kings 5:25–27), and even about what the king of Syria said in his bedroom (6:12).

Christ. Notice this statement: "And immediately Jesus, perceiving in his spirit that they thus questioned within themselves . . ." (Mark 2:8; cf. Luke 5:22; 9:47). Jesus "knew" many things and states of affairs through the Spirit (Matt. 12:15; 26:10; 27:18; John 2:25; 5:6; 6:15, 61, 64; 13:1, 3, 11; 16:19; 18:4; 19:28). In a wider sense, "the crowds were astonished at his teaching, for he was teaching them as one who had authority, and not as their scribes" (Matt. 7:28–29); that is, his teaching was supernatural, not natural like that of ordinary theologians. This is why his teaching was saturated with miraculous signs (John 3:2).

12.3.4 [7] Discerning the Spirits

The "ability to distinguish between spirits" goes much further than a kind of psychological insight into human nature, and is far more than theological knowledge; it is a miraculous knowledge of spirits. In my view, J. H. Bavinck here again naturalizes the *charisma* too strongly:

> [T]he church could not do without people who had been adorned by the Spirit with the gift of discerning the spirits. The early church had at this point produced so little theology. . . . It is that indispensable gift that, during the first centuries, kept the church on the right track, or drew it back to it, in the midst of all kinds of heresies that were arising.[30]

Notice the similarities and contrasts between this quotation and the remarks by Derek Prince, with reference to 1 Corinthians 2:1-5. Prince pointed out that, according to some, a high level of erudition and education of God's servants renders the special supernatural testimony of the Holy Spirit superfluous. However, the great example of the apostle Paul shows that this is not correct. Intellectual knowledge, no matter how useful on a natural level, can never replace, or even compete with, the supernatural power and ministry of the Holy Spirit.[31]

Here the word "spirit" can mean the inner man (1 Cor. 14:2, 14-16 [?]; Heb. 12:9, 23; 1 John 4:2-3 [?]; Rev. 22:6), a spiritual utterance, or gift ("utterance/gift of the Spirit") (1 Cor. 14:12, "manifestations of the Spirit," one word: "spirits"; so also v. 32), an angel (Heb. 1:7, 14), or a demon (Mark 1:27; Luke 10:20; 1 Tim. 4:1; 1 John 4:2-3 [?]; Rev. 16:13-14). Paul also speaks of receiving "a different spirit from the one you received" (2 Cor. 11:4), that is, a wrong attitude, or even a demon. Presumably, within the context of 1 Corinthians 12(-14), we must think primarily of distinguishing the utterances of the Spirit from those that came from all kinds of other spirits. Compare the ERV: ". . . the ability to judge what is from the Spirit and what is not" (cf. GNT); the NLT: ". . . to discern whether a message is from the Spirit of God or from another spirit." Particularly prophecy and glossolalia can come from

---

30. Ibid., 64.
31. Prince (1995, 395).

wrong sources; therefore, few gifts are more important than discerning the spirits.[32]

Humans do not know the hearts of other humans (cf. Acts 1:24), but those who receive, at moments when this is needed, the *charisma* of discerning the spirits can fathom in a supernatural way what goes on in the spirit (mind) of a person, whether good or bad, whether from the Spirit or from the flesh. They can also fathom whether the Holy Spirit or the flesh is active behind a person's innermost feelings.[33]

What is additionally important in this gift is discerning whether angels or demons are playing a role in a certain situation. Therefore, this gift is important when a person wishes to cast out demons: one must first discern them before one can cast them out. Paul apparently received this gift in Acts 16: it seemed the fortune-telling girl gave a nice-sounding testimony concerning Paul and his companions, but through the Spirit Paul discerned that a false spirit was involved (vv. 16–18). Inexperienced Christians may think that in certain psychiatric disorders evil spirits must surely be involved, but these disorders may simply be somatic illnesses, which demand healing, not exorcism. The reverse can be true as well: ordinary somatic diseases may, in certain cases, have a demonic origin (perhaps more often than people think; see examples in Mark 9:25; Luke 13:11, 16; Acts 10:38; 19:12).

This gift of discernment is very important for distinguishing between, on the one hand, the "power and all signs and wonders" of Satan in the end times (2 Thess. 2:9; cf. Matt. 24:24) and, on the other hand, the signs and wonders of the Holy Spirit (Acts 2:22, 43; 4:30; 5:12; 6:8; 14:3; 15:12; Rom. 15:19; 2 Cor. 12:12; Heb. 2:4). In too many cases the proper distinguishing between spiritual powers was not discerned,

---

32. Green (1975, 192).
33. Cf. the same Gk. root *diakrin-* underlying the verb "weigh" (1 Cor. 14:29), that is, distinguish what in the prophet is of God, and what not; cf. also "test" (Gk. *dokimazō*) in 1 Thess. 5:21.

so that unfortunately they were not cast out.[34]

Old Testament. In Deuteronomy 13:1-5 and 18:15-22, Moses gives instructions about discerning the spirits of (false) prophets. Several times, true prophets unmasked such false prophets (1 Kings 22:8-28; Jer. 28), but sometimes even they did not properly discern a particular false prophecy (1 Kings 13:18). Incidentally, Balaam is sometimes called a false prophet, but in fact we know only true prophecies from him (Num. 22-24).

Christ. (a) Jesus knew the inner feelings and deliberations of people (e.g., Matt. 16:22-23; Mark 2:8; Joh. 2:25; 6:15, 64), and (b) he recognized the demons active in certain diseases (Matt. 8:14-15; Mark 1:23-25; Luke 13:11-17) or in rebellious people, even if they were his own disciples. Thus he said to Peter, "Get behind me, Satan!" (Matt. 16:23); and concerning Judas, "Did I not choose you, the twelve? And yet one of you is a devil" (John 6:70; cf. 13:27).

12.4   Gifts of Action
12.4.1 [3] Faith

From 1 Corinthians 13:2 it is clear that Paul refers to the faith that, figuratively speaking, casts mountains into the sea: "[I]f I have all faith, so as to remove mountains, . . ."; as Jesus said, "Have faith in God. Truly, I say to you, whoever says to this mountain, 'Be taken up and thrown into the sea,' and does not doubt in his heart, but believes that what he says will come to pass, it will be done for him" (Mark 11:23-23; cf. Matt. 17:20; 21:21). This kind of practical, ordinary faith must be carefully distinguished from what is called saving faith, which is that faith by which a person comes to salvation.[35] Rather, here it is the God-given conviction that God is able and willing to do a certain miraculous work through the person who, in that

---

34. Cf. Sanford (1966, 155–56, 159–160). In contrast with this, some people believe to discern false spirits being present where they are not at all.
35. Although Graafland (1999, 315) seems to think otherwise: "Wisdom, knowledge and faith, these gifts we do recognize. With some modesty we may say that we have received these gifts."

given situation and at that given moment, receives the gift of faith to this end, that is, who entrusts oneself entirely to God in this matter.[36] The receiving aspect is a matter of God's sovereign grace; the entrusting aspect is a matter of the believer's personal responsibility.

"Gifts of healing" [4] and the "working of miracles" [5] are hardly conceivable without this gift of faith. Even in order to speak aloud a word of wisdom [1] or of knowledge [2], or a prophecy [6], or to cast out demons on the basis of discerning spirits [7], faith is needed—not to mention obeying the most demanding order that the Lord could possibly give: "[R]aise the dead" (Matt. 10:8).

Faith may be described here as receptiveness to a miracle, the expectation that God will do something special in a given situation. Take, for example, the ministry of healing: faith is not an absolute condition for healing (cf. 2 Kings 5:11–14; John 5:6–9; Acts 3:4–8), but it does play a greater role than many people think. Faith plays an active role in (a) the one who administers healing (Acts 3:16; James 5:15), (b) the sick person (Matt. 9:22, 28–29; Mark 10:52; Luke 17:19; Acts 14:9–10), (c) friends or relatives accompanying him/her (Matt. 8:10, 13; 9:2; 15:21–28; Mark 5:36; 7:32; 9:23–24), and (d) (usually negatively) the bystanders (Mark 5:40; 6:5–6; 7:33; 8:23).

Old Testament. Although the word is not mentioned, it was Elijah's faith that, despite all the risks of failure (humanly speaking), boldly challenged the false prophets, built his altar, rendered his sacrifice soaking wet, and asked God to make fire come down from heaven (1 Kings 18:20–46). Hebrews 11:33–35 speaks of Old Testament believers "who through faith conquered kingdoms, . . . stopped the mouths of lions, quenched the power of fire, escaped the edge of the sword, were made strong out of weakness, became mighty in war, put foreign armies to flight. Women received back their dead by resurrection." In Hebrews 11, the momentaneous

---

36. See more extensively, Ouweneel (2005a, §§5.4, 8.1, and 10.2).

character of receiving the gift of faith at an important moment is seen especially in Noah, Abraham, Isaac, Jacob, Joseph, Moses, and Rahab.

Christ. Some think here of the expression "faith of Jesus (or Christ)" (cf. Rom. 3:22, 26; Gal. 2:16; 3:22; Phil. 3:9; Rev. 14:12 KJV), but in my view (and that of most translators and expositors) this always means "faith in Jesus" (cf. KJV and NKJV).[37] A better example is the statement from Isaiah 8:17 (Septuagint) that in Hebrews 2:13 is placed on Jesus' lips: "I will put my trust in him [i.e., God]." A beautiful example of this is his prayer to the Father, just before the resurrection of Lazarus: "Father, I thank you that you have heard me. I knew that you always hear me, but I said this on account of the people standing around, that they may believe that you sent me" (John 11:41–42).

12.4.2 [4] Gifts of Healing

Through his servants, by the power of the Holy Spirit, God sometimes grants a healing miracle, especially (but not exclusively) to people who open themselves for this. Among believers, this can occur through the elders of the church (James 5:14–16), but in light of 1 Corinthians 12 this can happen in principle through every Christian, in agreement with Mark 16:17–18 ("And these signs will accompany those who believe: . . . they will lay their hands on the sick, and they will recover"). Healing miracles occurred not only through the twelve apostles (cf. 2 Cor. 12:12) and through the apostle Paul (cf. Rom. 15:19), but also through the seventy(-two) ordinary disciples (Luke 10:1–9), and through the non-apostles Stephen (Acts 6:8), Philip (8:6–7), and Ananias (9:17–18).

Of course, usually healing miracles will take place only through Christians who believe in healing miracles occurring today, who make themselves available to the Holy Spirit to

---

37. Here the genitive phrase "of Jesus" is not subjective (the faith with which Jesus himself believed) but objective (the faith whose object is Jesus); see Ouweneel (2005a, §5.4.1).

work through them, and who have faith in God in view of the desired miracle (cf. Acts 3:16; James 5:15). Please note that such miracles have occurred throughout all of church history. The bad spiritual condition of God's people was never an impediment, as in Israel during the times of Elijah and Elisha. Note as well that such miraculous healings are not intended for unbelievers only (e.g., on the mission fields) but also for believers, such as Saul of Tarsus (Acts 9:9, 17–18), Aeneas (vv. 32–35), Dorcas (vv. 36–42), and Eutychus (20:9–10).

Of course, God can perform healing miracles without the intervention of people, but apparently he loves to use people (Mark 16:17–18; 1 Cor. 12:9, 28; James 5:12–16). And of course, God heals through doctors as well; Jesus himself stated that sick people need a doctor (Matt. 9:12). Paul was glad to have a doctor with him (Col. 4:14) – but on Cyprus, all the sick people came running not to doctor Luke but to the apostle Paul (Acts 28:9). Medical healings may be miracles, too (cf. Job 37:14; Ps. 139:14, where ordinary natural phenomena are called "wonders"). We praise God, for instance, for surgery and medicines. Yet, we do see people healed through the ministry of healing who could not be healed through regular medicine.

Evidently, many more miraculous healings occur through some than through others; apparently, they have a ministry of healing, just as the apostles did (Matt. 10:7–8; 2 Cor. 12:12). On all these and many other points I have written extensively elsewhere.[38] Please note that the gifts of healing clearly illustrate how all Nine Gracious Gifts are interrelated within the ministry of healing: the healing minister sometimes receives [1] words of wisdom or [2] words of knowledge regarding the sick or [6] a prophecy; if one must [7] discern the spirits behind the disease, one needs [3] faith; sometimes we observe [5] the working of miracles, and [8, 9] even tongue-speaking may be important (some healing ministers have claimed that they saw more miracles happen when they prayed in tongues

---

38. Ouweneel (2005a, especially chapter 6 and following).

during the ministry).[39]

Old Testament. The prophets Abraham (Gen. 18:10-14; 20:17; 21:1-7), Moses (Exod. 4:6-7; Num. 12:10-15; 21:5-9), the man of God from Judah (1 Kings 13:4-6), Elijah (1 Kings 17:17-24), Elisha (2 Kings 4:18-37; 5:1-19; 13:20-21), and Isaiah (2 Kings 20:1-11; 2 Chron. 32:24-26; Isa. 38) were all involved in miraculous healings.[40]

Christ. In the Gospels we read fifteen general (Matt. 4:23) and twenty specific mentions of healings (Matt. 8:1-15), and we learn about three people raised from the dead by Jesus (Luke 7:11-17; 8:40-46; John 11:1-44).[41]

12.4.3 [5] Performing Miracles

Here the term "miracles" renders the Greek word *dynameis*, literally "powers," that is, power works of the Spirit (cf. 1 Cor. 2:4-5; 2 Cor. 12:12; Gal. 3:5; Heb. 2:4; 6:5). We may think here of the miraculous works summed up in Mark 16:17-18,[42] "And these signs will accompany those who believe: in my name they will cast out demons [cf. gift (7); see Mark 9:38-39; Acts 16:16-18]; they will speak in new tongues [cf. gifts (8) and (9); see §§12.5.2 and 12.5.3]; they will pick up serpents with their hands [cf. Luke 10:19; Acts 28:3-6; cf. Rom. 16:20]; and if they drink any deadly poison, it will not hurt them; they will lay their hands on the sick, and they will recover [cf. gift (4); see §12.4.2]."

There seems to be a close connection between [4] the "gifts of healing" and [5] these miraculous works (see especially Mark 5:30; Acts 4:7; 10:38; 19:11-12). Indeed, the two gifts overlap. In addition to the miracles mentioned in Mark 16:17-18, these miraculous works may also contain miraculous dislocations (Acts 8:39-40; 9:36-42; 20:9-12; 13:8-11), and

---

39. See examples in Ouweneel (2005a, §9.5.2 and note 72). Regarding tongues, see Wimber and Springer (1986, 217).
40. See Ouweneel (2005a, Appendix 1).
41. See ibid., Appendix 2.
42. See ibid., chapter 4.

The Gifts of the Holy Spirit

in addition to resurrections (9:36-42; 20:9-10) there may also be the execution of a sentence of death (5:5, 10) or of blindness (13:8-11). Today, too, cases have been described in which believers in emergency situations have commanded the winds, as Jesus did (Matt. 8:26-27).[43]

Old Testament. The plagues of Egypt, dividing the waters of the Red Sea, granting the manna, the quail, and the water from the rock (Exod. 7-17), the sprouted staff of Aaron (Num. 17:8), and so on, were miraculous works by the hand of Moses. I further mention the sun and moon standing still at the prayer of Joshua (Josh. 10:12-13), multiplying the oil, purifying the pot, and the floating iron in Elisha's ministry (2 Kings 4:1-7, 38-44; 6:1-7).

Christ. With Jesus we see miraculous works (apart from healings) in changing water into wine (John 2:6-11), multiplying the bread (Matt. 14:19), walking on water (v. 25), calming the storm (v. 32; Mark 4:39), and the like.

12.5 Gifts of Communication
12.5.1 [6] Prophecy

Prophecy entails spontaneous, understandable, edifying, encouraging, and consoling utterances of the Holy Spirit (cf. 1 Cor. 13:2, 8-9; 14:1, 3-6, 22, 24, 29, 31-32, 37, 39; 1 Thess. 5:20). The prophet is the "man of the Spirit" (Hos. 9:7 YLT), "filled with power, with the Spirit of the LORD" (Micah 3:8). In Acts 2:17 prophecy is parallel with "seeing visions," and elsewhere (2:30-31; 3:18, 21-24; 11:27-28; 21:10-11) it means looking into the future. Prophecies can be given to a person to strengthen one in view of spiritual warfare (1 Tim. 1:18; cf. 4:14).

There are various levels in prophecy:[44] first, there were those who laid the foundation of the church (Eph. 2:20): "apostles and prophets." Second, prophets are one of the five basic ministries in the church ("apostles, prophets, evange-

---

43. Cf. Sanford (1966, 171); for other examples, see Ouweneel (2005a, §4.4.1).
44. Cf. Bickle (1998, 121–23), who distinguishes four levels: simple prophetic words, prophetic gifts, prophetic ministry, and prophetic office.

lists, shepherds, teachers," Eph. 4:11–12; cf. Acts 15:32; 1 Cor. 12:28). Agabus (Acts 11:27–28; 21:10–11) was an example of such a prophet, who reminds us strongly of the Old Testament prophets.[45] Third, in principle, each believer in every church can receive prophetic words to pass on to others.

Notice the remarkable statement in 1 Corinthians 14:24, "if all prophesy. . ." (cf. 11:4–5; 14:5, 31; Acts 21:9; also Num. 11:29). Here, prophecy may not mean anything other than ecstatically praising God (cf. §§11.1.3, 11.5.1, and 11.9.4).

Usually, prophecies are conditional: they will not be fulfilled if the person over whom the prophecy was pronounced runs away from it, does not stay close to the Lord, does not wait in faith, does not remain in the sphere of practical sanctification, and so on.

Prophecies may never lead a believer; that is, they do not tell him what he must do; else the danger of manipulation by the so-called "prophet" would be too great. Prophecies are given only to encourage and comfort the person (1 Cor. 14:3). They must confirm what the person already knows in their heart, or will know.

Gordon Fee believes that prophecy can never refer to the very personal circumstances in the lives of individuals.[46] However, to me this seems to conflict with other passages (Acts 21:10–11; 1 Tim. 1:18; 4:14), not to mention many Old Testament examples.

Old Testament. With Abraham (Gen. 20:7), Moses (Deut. 18:15, 18; 34:10), and Samuel (1 Sam. 3:20; Acts 3:24; 13:20), as well as Elijah and Elisha (1 Kings 17:1–2 Kings 13:21), and the sixteen writing prophets (from Isaiah to Malachi),[47] and many other, minor prophets, whose names are not always mentioned, we encounter a large number of Old Testament prophets.

---

45. Knowling (1979, 270, 446); Longenecker (1981, 517); Bruce (1988, 401).
46. Fee (1994, 170–71).
47. The rabbis do not recognize Daniel as a prophet, but Jesus did (Matt. 24:15).

Christ. Jesus referred to himself as a prophet (Matt. 13:57; Luke 13:33), the crowds saw him as a prophet (Matt. 14:5; 21:46; Mark 6:15; Luke 7:16; 9:8, 19; 24:19; John 4:19), including in the sense of Deuteronomy 18:15, 18 (Matt. 21:11; John 6:14; 7:40; 9:17; Acts 3:22-23; 7:37). Jesus is compared with the great prophets of the Old Testament (Matt. 16:14), and at the same time he is presented as One who surpasses them (Heb. 1:1-3).

12.5.2 [8] Various Kinds of Tongues

In 1 Corinthians 12-14, the actual highlight to which Paul's argument is leading is the abuse of glossolalia. From chapters 6 and 7 (the Corinthians' attitude toward sexuality and marriage) and 15 (their attitude toward the bodily resurrection), the over-spiritual tendency of Christians in Corinth to despise the bodily and the natural was apparent. This attitude also explains their great preference for, and their childish bragging about, the "language of angels" (13:1; 14:20). In these chapters, Paul attempts to assign to glossolalia its correct place in the church's life.

Of all the *charismata*, glossolalia is the one about which people have written the most.[48] Here are some of the basic insights on glossolalia as accepted by many. Glossolalia entails speaking in a known language that one has not learned, and thus is of a miraculous nature; or, more precisely, it is of the Spirit.[49] True glossolalia occurs through the Holy Spirit, but not beyond the control of the person speaking in tongues (see 1 Cor. 14:27-28, 32). Such persons therefore can quietly wait upon each other, and upon interpreters. To put it more strongly, it is not so much that the Spirit speaks through the one speaking in tongues, but rather that the one speaking

---

48. Fee (1994, 172n336) gave a survey of the literature up to his day. In his day, Congar (1997, 2.173) noted 400 books and articles on glossolalia in the Pentecostal and Charismatic movement.
49. Some think that Rom. 8:26 refers to this: "[W]e do not know what to pray for as we ought, but the Spirit himself intercedes for us with groanings too deep for words"; but see §9.9.3 above.

does so in the power of the Spirit. This is important for those who claim that they have prayed to God so often for this gift but did not yet receive it. The reason might simply be that they never began speaking in the confidence that the Spirit would be fully present in their glossolalia.

Let me explain this important point a little further. One cannot pray that God will witness or prophesy through the one praying; no, the one praying must open one's mouth in order to witness and to prophesy, prayerfully confident that the Spirit will be fully present in these things. The same pertains to glossolalia. God gives the praying person the right words, but only when the person begins to speak.

Glossolalia addresses God, and thus entails prayer or praise; as the Jews from foreign countries said about the one hundred twenty whom they heard on Pentecost: "[W]e hear them telling in our own [foreign] tongues the mighty works of God" (Acts 2:11; cf. 1 Cor. 14:2, 14–15, 28). Thus, the tongues were not (primarily) intended for preaching the gospel, but for praising God, in languages that the missionaries had not learned. This possible meaning and function of glossolalia on the mission fields cannot be excluded, though. For instance, it strikes us that Paul understood what was said in the Lycaonian language (Acts 14:11). The miraculous speaking and understanding of non-learned languages seem to have been observed regularly on the mission fields.

Glossolalia may be unintelligible to the person speaking in tongues (1 Cor. 14:13–14) but not necessarily so (v. 15).[50] The "tongues" mentioned in 1 Corinthians 14 are utterances in the church, and therefore should possibly be distinguished from what in Charismatic circles is called a person's own "prayer language" (cf. 1 Cor. 14:2, 4; also see Rom. 8:26–27; Eph. 6:18 [cf. 5:18–20]; Jude 1:20).

Glossolalia may involve ordinary human languages (Acts

---

50. *Contra* Fee (1987, 598).

2:11)⁵¹ but possibly also heavenly ones (cf. John 3:31–32; 1 Cor. 13:1). 1 Corinthians 14:10–12 draws a parallel between glossolalia and earthly languages, so that here glossolalia may be, but need not be, different from earthly languages. If this is the case, the expression "various kinds of tongues" might refer to this diversity. Pinnock suggested that tongues are not intelligible languages but a way of responding to God's inexpressibility, a way of crying to God out of the depths (Ps. 130:1) and of expressing groanings that are too deep for words (Rom. 8:26). Glossolalia is prayer without formulating ideas, prayer at a deep, non-cognitive level. We give ourselves to God when praying in tongues, and surrender to him control over our speaking. Perhaps, suggests Pinnock, praying in tongues relates to common praying as abstract painting relates to ordinary painting. It is a way that God uses to challenge control strategies. It is a humble but also a humiliating gift, for which we should be open.⁵²

Through glossolalia that is not understood by others, a person builds up only oneself (1 Cor. 14:4). Yet, like all *charismata*, this one too is intended primarily for building up others, namely, when the latter (a) understand the languages involved, (b) hear an interpretation of them, (c) are healed by the laying on of hands together with glossolalia, and so on.

In unbelievers and believers led by the flesh, glossolalia can also be of a demonic origin. However, practice shows that believers who receive gifts of discerning the spirits can easily distinguish between the two.⁵³

The most controversial question concerning glossolalia is the claim of many Pentecostal and Charismatic leaders that Spirit baptism can be genuine only if it is followed by glos-

---

51. Sanders (1973, 115–16), Bruce (1988, 52), and Longenecker (1981, 271, 394) believe that Acts 2 and 1 Cor. 12–14 refer to two different kinds of glossolalia, but Mare (1976, 263) and others have argued that the same phenomenon is quite possibly involved—in my view rightly so.
52. Pinnock (1996, 173).
53. Howard-Browne (2005) gives various remarkable examples of this.

solalia; in other words, all true Christians ought to speak in tongues. Suurmond wrote of this, "Moreover, this doctrine [of baptism in the Spirit] divides Christians into two classes: those who are only reborn, and those who in addition are at the same time said to be baptized with the Spirit."[54] As I stated earlier, on the one hand it is an exaggeration to claim that we are dealing with genuine Spirit baptism only when the person involved speaks in tongues (for this is not mentioned in Acts 2:41 and 8:17). On the other hand, all believers may pursue all Nine Gracious Gifts, including glossolalia (see §12.6.2 on the often misunderstood 1 Cor. 12:30).

Old Testament. See §12.5.3.

Christ. Often, glossolalia is mentioned as the only miraculous gift that did not occur in Jesus' ministry. If Romans 8:26 refers to glossolalia (but see §9.9.3), the connection between "groaning" (Gk. *stenagmos*) and "sighing" (Gk. *stenazō*) in Mark 7:34 might be taken to suggest that Jesus spoke in tongues when healing the deaf person. However, perhaps Jesus did not need this gift because, in a certain sense, it presupposes a deficiency: it might be intended for cases in which ordinary language fails.

12.5.3 [9] Interpretation of Tongues

Just as glossolalia is a gracious gift of the Spirit, so too is interpretation (Gk. *hermēneia*). The interpreter translates and explains words that have been spoken in a language that the interpreter has not learned either. The interpreter of such tongues may be the same person as the speaker (1 Cor. 14:5, 13), or it may be another person (vv. 27-28).

During a church service, many may be praising God in tongues. These tongues do not have to be interpreted; people are speaking to God, not to the church. Moreover, there are no limitations: all can speak in tongues, even at the same time, just as all can prophesy, even at the same time (ecstatically praising God, v. 24). However, if a person addresses

---

54. Suurmond (1995, 99).

The Gifts of the Holy Spirit

the church in a tongue, first, there may be no more than two or three of them (v. 27-28), just as in the case of prophetic addresses (v. 29). Second, the message must be interpreted in a language that the church understands. Such messages have the same purposes and functions as prophetic messages; that is, they must be for the edification, encouragement, and consolation of the church (vv. 5, 26-28).

Verse 27, "If anyone speaks in a tongue, [let there be] two or at the most three, [each] in turn, and let one interpret" (NKJV), might be taken to mean that one particular person in the church has the ministry of interpreting tongues.

Old Testament. Daniel 5 gives an example of the miraculous interpretation of a written language, which King Belshazzar and his scholars could not read, let alone interpret, but the prophet Daniel could.

Christ. See §12.5.2. In passing, notice that what the crowd experienced as a thunderbolt, or possibly as the (not understood) voice of an angel, Jesus understood as intelligible words spoken by the Father (John 12:28-30).

12.6 Gifts of the Church
12.6.1 The Five Ministries

Gordon Fee suggested that we follow the division of the Nine Gracious Gifts that Paul himself seems to indicate by using the Greek word *heteros* ("different") with gifts [3] and [8], and the Greek word *allos* ("other") with the other gifts.[55] This yields the following division: [1] wisdom and [2] knowledge come first because they were highly regarded in Corinth; then follow the special miraculous gifts ([3] through [7]), and finally the Corinthian "problem gift": [8] tongues and [9] its companion. Earlier than Fee, George G. Findlay gave the same division, which he described as follows: in the first two of the Nine Gifts, the Spirit works through the mind or through thought (Gk. *nous*); in the next five Gifts, he works apart from the mind, and in the last two, he works beyond the mind. I am

---
55. Fee (1994, 165; cf. 886-87).

sympathetic to such an approach, as long as we realize that all the Nine Gracious Gifts are basically miraculous gifts, so that in this sense they all operate beyond the mind.[56]

Let us now compare these Nine Gracious Gifts with the five ministries of the church: "[H]e gave the apostles, the prophets, the evangelists, the shepherds and teachers, . . ." (Eph. 4:11). If these five ministries reach their fullness, we find all Nine Gifts back in all five ministries. It thus becomes clear that these ministries, too, are produced and empowered by the Spirit.

(1) The ministry of the apostle (pioneers on the mission fields, church builders in new territories;[57] cf. Rom. 15:18-21; 2 Cor. 10:13-17) is characterized by apostolic signs: "The signs of a true apostle were performed among you with utmost patience, with signs and wonders and mighty works" (2 Cor. 12:12; cf. Luke 9:1, 10; Acts 5:12; Rom. 15:18-19; Heb. 2:3-4). Each believer may receive gifts of healing and the working of miracles, but these belong specifically to the ministry of the apostle. If this distinction is not maintained, people might be tempted to call each person who has a healing ministry an apostle. Practice teaches us that a healing ministry may be connected with each of the five ministries, as we will presently see.

(2) The ministry of the prophet is particularly characterized by one of the Nine Gracious Gifts: prophecy, often connected with a word of wisdom, or of knowledge, and with discerning the spirits. (Often, a word of knowledge combined with a word of wisdom can hardly be distinguished from a prophecy; messages expressed in tongue speaking in the church, if interpreted, clearly overlap with prophecy.) The *charisma* of prophecy is not the same as the ministry of the prophet (cf. §12.5.1). Each believer can receive a prophetic word to pass on to others, but that does not make each believer a prophet. The

---

56. Findlay (1979, 888).
57. Perhaps even broader: leaders of national and international spiritual ministries.

The Gifts of the Holy Spirit

prophet (cf. Acts 11:27-28; 13:1; 15:32; 21:10; 1 Cor. 12:28-29; 14:29, 32; Eph. 2:20; 3:5; Rev. 10:7; 11:18; 16:6; 18:20, 24; 22:6, 9) receives such *charismata* much more often than ordinary believers; they are characteristic of his ministry.

(3) The ministry of the evangelist makes use of the Nine Gracious Gifts as a great support in preaching the gospel. Philip is specifically called an "evangelist" (Acts 21:8); in Samaria we see how his ministry was linked with signs and wonders (8:6-7, 13). Paul explains that he had "fulfilled the ministry of the gospel of Christ" "by the power of signs and wonders" (Rom. 15:16). The message of salvation "was declared at first by the Lord, and it was attested to us by those who heard, while God also bore witness by signs and wonders and various miracles and by gifts of the Holy Spirit distributed according to his will" (Heb. 2:3-4).

(4) The ministry of the shepherd makes use of the Nine Gracious Gifts as a support for all pastoral work, which is literally the work of the shepherd. The apostle Peter received the command to feed and tend the Lord's lambs and sheep (John 21:15-17), and thus presented himself as a shepherd (1 Pet. 5:1-4). He performed great signs in public (Acts 3:4-8; 5:14-15), but also in a more pastoral setting (9:32-42). Everyone can understand how useful — even indispensable — words of wisdom and knowledge, faith and prophecy, and even miraculous works, can be in any pastoral ministry.

(5) In his ministry, the teacher can receive the Nine Gracious Gifts because he binds the Word of God not only upon the intellect but also upon the heart of his hearers. Thus, Nicodemus said to Jesus, "Rabbi, we know that you are a teacher come from God, for no one can do these signs that you do unless God is with him" (John 3:2). Apparently, to him it was self-evident that, among God's people, teaching belonged to the supernatural world of the Spirit.

It is important to emphasize that the Nine Gracious Gifts of 1 Corinthians 12 are given to the body of Christ, and not to individual believers apart from the body. Thus, the gifts function primarily within the framework of the local church, and more broadly in the universal church.[58] Verse 28 says that persons with special gifts are "appointed in the church." In Ephesians 4:11, this is expressed in an even stronger way because here it is not gifts (*charismata*) that are given to persons, but the persons themselves are given (Gk. *edōken*) to the church, "for building up the body of Christ" (v. 12). This ministry is oriented "to the unity of the faith and of the knowledge of the Son of God" (v. 13). First, exercising the gifts proceed from the authentic church; and second, they are aimed at the building up and functional unity of the church. The gifts are, so to speak, from the church to the church.

12.6.2 The Gifts Are for All

The fact that the gifts belong to the church does not change the fact that, in principle, *each* believer has at his or her disposal each of the Nine Gracious Gifts, as a carpenter has at his disposal all the tools in his toolbox. This claim may seem to conflict with this word by Paul: "Are all apostles? Are all prophets? Are all teachers? Do all work miracles? Do all possess gifts of healing? Do all speak with tongues? Do all interpret?" (1 Cor. 12:29–30). The implied answer seems to be: Of course not. But what does Paul intend to say here? There are basically two interpretations, which both seem to fit well into the context.

(a) The emphasis is not on "all" but on "languages." Thus it is not: "Do *all* speak with tongues?" (answer: No, *some* do *not* speak with tongues), but: "Do all speak with *tongues*?" (answer: No, in addition to glossolalia we find all the other gracious gifts). Paul emphasizes that not all in the church are *only* apostles or teachers or healing ministers or speakers in tongues, but that there must be a great *diversity* in the church: prophecies and miracles and tongues are needed, and so on. In a body, eyes are needed; but if every organ were an eye, the

---

58. See Du Plessis (1964, 119–20).

body would not be able to function (cf. v. 17).[59]

(b) Paul is not referring here to the *charismata* — for these can be received by all believers at all times when needed at a certain moment — but to ministries; for instance, at a given moment, all could receive a prophetic word (that is, a *charisma*, intended for building up another person) but not all have a prophetic ministry.[60]

According to both interpretations, in the light of the entire chapter, Paul is not saying that not all in the church could receive prophecies, or gifts of healing, or glossolalia. They certainly can. Nothing hinders a believer from pursuing all Nine Gracious Gifts.

There is another problematic statement here: "[E]arnestly desire the higher gifts," says Paul (v. 31). This does not mean, as some think, that there is a certain order among the gracious gifts and ministries: apostles at the top of the list, tongues at the bottom (vv. 28-30). If that were right, Paul would be saying that all believers must earnestly desire to become apostles, which is absurd.[61] (Of course, the opposite idea — that glossolalia would belong to the "higher gifts" of 1 Cor. 12:31 — is equally absurd.[62]) Rather Paul seems to be saying that the gifts that are understandable by, and thus edifying for, the church must be preferred above glossolalia in the church that is unintelligible and thus unedifying. This is further explained in 1 Corinthians 14 (see §12.9).[63] Generally speaking, Paul apparently views it as normal that all prophesy in church (14:24, 31), but he also says, "I want you all to speak in tongues" (v. 5; cf. v. 23).

It has often been asserted that Paul presents love here as the highest *charisma*,[64] but this cannot be correct. The "still

---

59. So Fee (1987, 622).
60. So Mare (1976, 266–67); Findlay (1979, 895); Prince (1995, 247).
61. Fee (1987, 619, 623 including note 34); *contra* Green (1975, 193).
62. Erickson (1983, 878).
63. See the solid argumentation of Fee (1994, 195–97).
64. Green (1975, 120).

more excellent way" of 1 Corinthians 12:31 does not refer to a still higher gift, but to the true Christian attitude with which the gifts must be exercised (§12.8).[65] Believers who are led by love will realize that intelligible utterances in church are more edifying than unintelligible utterances (see the entire scope of 1 Cor. 14). However, if these unintelligible utterances are interpreted, they can build up the church just as well as prophecy.

12.6.3 Are Miracle Workers More Spiritual?

We have come to the conclusion that each believer may and must pursue all gifts through which they can be a blessing for their fellow-believers: "I want you all to speak in tongues" (1 Cor. 14:5); "if all prophesy..." (v. 24); "you can all prophesy one by one, so that all may learn and all be encouraged" (v. 31). Two kinds of serious misunderstanding may be identified here, which entail great dangers for the church (for the second one, see §12.7).[66]

The first misunderstanding is that believers in whose ministry signs and wonders occur by the power of the Holy Spirit would therefore automatically be higher, more spiritual, more mature than believers who do not know any, or know hardly any, signs and wonders in their ministry. Generally speaking, it may be quite true that more mature believers experience more signs and wonders than less mature believers, but this is not an immutable law.

A few examples may clarify this. On the one hand, we see in 1 Corinthians 14:18-20 that, apparently, some Corinthian Christians, when speaking in tongues, behaved like spiritual babies. Their glossolalia was not a sign of spiritual maturity at all; on the contrary, the way they used it rather pointed to spiritual immaturity.

On the other hand, there have been numerous mature, spiritual believers who experienced hardly any, or no, mirac-

---

65. Fee (1987, 625); *contra* Grosheide (1957, 339).
66. See Wimber and Springer (1991, 180–81).

ulous gifts in their ministry, and they were not inferior because of that. A remarkable example is John the Baptist. We read of him that he would "be filled with the Holy Spirit, even from his mother's womb," and he went before the Lord "in the s/Spirit and power of Elijah," who did perform quite a few miracles (Luke 1:15, 17). Jesus even said that "among those born of women there has arisen no one greater than John the Baptist" (Matt. 11:11). Yet, the people said of him, strikingly enough, "John did no sign" (John 10:41; GW: "didn't perform any miracles").[67] Thus, a person may be a powerful servant of God, and yet perform no signs and wonders.

If we see that the point of the miraculous gifts is not to honor the persons exercising the gifts, there is no reason why any false modesty should stop believers from earnestly desiring whatever *charisma* there is (cf. 1 Tim. 3:1, where we find something similar: aspiring to the office of overseer). As long as the motives are pure and loving—and this is the entire point of 1 Corinthians 13 (see §12.8)—a believer may aspire to any of the Nine Gracious Gifts. The believer will "decrease" by this (cf. John 3:30 for this vernacular). But if the Lord is to "increase" by it, it would be tremendous if believers were to experience something of the miraculous gifts in their lives and ministries.

12.7 Were the Gifts Only for the Apostolic Age?
12.7.1 Cessationism

The second misunderstanding (see §12.6.3) is the idea that the Nine Gracious Gifts were intended only for the apostolic period, that is, for the first century of church history. This mistaken notion is called cessationism (the gifts "ceased"; see §§2.3.2 and 2.3.3).[68] Those who hold this idea either do not know the miraculous gifts by experience, or their church denomination has condemned the continuation of the gifts decades or centu-

---

67. It is all the more striking that people said that even John the Baptist had a demon (Matt. 11:18; cf. 12:24).
68. See Ouweneel (2005a, §4.1).

ries ago,[69] or they have heard only one-sided stories from (extreme) Pentecostal and Charismatic circles. Conclusion: the gifts cannot have been intended for our own time. C. Graafland said of this,

> Calvin... finally arrives at the solution: as we do not recognize today what we find in 1 Corinthians 12, we leave it out of consideration. But this is letting our own context reign over Scripture. What ought to be done is that Scripture will reign over our context, even if this brings about a radical correction. It is precisely then that it will turn out that our own contextual position is not harmed but, on the contrary, is enriched and renewed.[70]

On the basis of the bias we have identified—what one does not know (or what the fathers rejected) apparently cannot exist—it is not so difficult to read *a posteriori* arguments into the New Testament that seem to confirm one's own position. I found a striking example with Bernard of Clairvaux, who said in a Pentecostal sermon, "A first time [Acts 2] the invisible Spirit makes his coming known through visible signs, because it had to be this way, but nowadays these signs are of a spiritual nature, and all the more appropriate; thus they seem all the more worthy of the Holy Spirit."[71] So is it the case that today the external signs of the Spirit's presence are no longer needed? As if the signs of Acts 2 were not spiritual, too! And is the absence of these external signs more worthy of the Spirit? But it is not unworthy of the Holy Spirit, who deigns to dwell in our physical bodies, to manifest himself in physical phenomena such as are linked with (some of) the miraculous gifts.

One of the *a posteriori* arguments is that the *charismata* cannot be that important because among the New Testament

---

69. As a Reformed lady once told me: "If God had really intended the gifts for our time, my denomination would certainly have them." But it does *not* have them, therefore they were not intended for our time.
70. Graafland (1999, 313).
71. Bernardus (1992, 10).

letters they are mentioned only in 1 Corinthians. Using this argument, we might as well dispense with the Lord's Supper, for among the New Testament letters this is mentioned only in 1 Corinthians, too.

The real situation is that an unbiased study of the New Testament does not yield the slightest proof that the Nine Gracious Gifts were limited to the apostolic age. This conclusion is a typical example of eisegesis. On the contrary, especially miraculous healings and deliverances have occurred in literally every century of church history[72] (see §2.3 above).

12.7.2 Historical Notes

Stanley Burgess has mentioned many examples throughout church history of the *charismata* both in Eastern and in Western Christianity. In the Eastern churches, he begins with the Egyptian desert fathers (healings, casting out of demons, even levitation, miraculous protection against fire and water, miraculous nourishment, miraculous icons). John Cassian mentioned various examples from his own time: raising a dead person by Macarius of Egypt (viz., of a mummy from the times of the Pharaohs!), healing by him of a breast infection in a nursing mother, and of a crippled man, as well as predictions of the future. As the highest *charisma* Cassian mentioned discerning the spirits.

Severus of Antioch reported prophecies, miraculous healings, and casting out demons. Of the Armenian Gregory of Narek many miracles have been reported. Symeon the New Theologian claimed for his own time the same measure of experiences with the Holy Spirit as in the time of the apostles. Gregory Palamas mentioned in his own time healings and other miracles, foreknowledge, glossolalia, and its interpretation, especially during intense silent prayer. Nicholas Cabasilas, too, reported that in his time some experienced the miraculous gifts. Many miraculous healings of the famous Russian

---

72. Ouweneel (2005a, chapter 2).

starets, Seraphim of Sarov, have been reported.[73]

Examples in the history of the Western church are fewer, but they are not lacking. Stanley Burgess speaks of "signs of charismatic vitality" (healings, raising the dead, casting out demons, prophetic predictions, miraculous deliverances, discerning the spirits, sometimes even levitation) in the lives and writings of such outstanding figures as Benedict of Nursia, Gregory the Great, Augustine of Canterbury, Cuthbert, Bernard of Clairvaux, Francis of Assisi, Bonaventure, Thomas Aquinas, Ignatius of Loyola, and Teresa of Ávila. The *charismata* were even more important for apocalyptic writers like Rupert of Deutz, Joachim of Fiore, and Thomas Müntzer, and for prophetesses like Hildegard of Bingen, Gertrud of Helfta, Birgitta of Sweden, Catherine of Siena, Juliana of Norwich, and Margery Kempe.

Most Catholic theologians taught that the *charismata* of 1 Corinthians 12–14 were reserved for the most godly—the saints. Many saints are reported to have spoken in languages that they had not learned, but which could often be identified as existing languages. Even more often we hear about prophecy, miraculous healings, and other miraculous works. Many later critics have rejected this kind of miracle stories, but this tells us more about their own Enlightenment prejudices than about the saints involved. The important thing is that their contemporaries apparently did believe these stories, not necessarily because they were so gullible but because they were personally familiar with such miracles. It is significant that, whereas both Catholics and radical Reformers were familiar with the *charismata*, Luther, Zwingli, and Calvin emphasized them much less, or even rejected them—though even among their followers such miraculous gifts were not absent.[74]

Clark Pinnock emphasized, over against cessationism, that, even if the apostles' ministry were foundational and

---

73. Burgess (1989, 30, 59, 71, 76, 80, 126, 138–40, 142, 206).
74. Burgess (1997, 9, 17–20, 24–25, 57–60, 74–75, 81–82, 89–90, 95, 102, 107–108, 117, 151, 167, 181, 205–208).

unrepeatable, their signs and wonders were aimed at human needs that continue to exist until this very day. He wondered why the relevance of the kingdom would change in view of these needs. Why would the sick not always need prayer, and the possessed not always need deliverance? The Spirit has not withdrawn himself, nor has the power departed from the kingdom (cf. 1 Cor. 4:20). Unfortunately, the cessationist view is self-fulfilling (if you do not expect miracles, you will hardly experience them). If one does not take seriously the possibilities that the Bible offers, people will eventually come under the influence of secular modernity through the backdoor. The cessationist position leads to an experiential deficiency, which obstructs people from entering into the full reality of the Spirit.[75]

12.8 The Spirit in 1 Corinthians 13
12.8.1 The "More Excellent Way"

The chapter about love (1 Cor. 13) stands in the middle of Paul's argument about the proper use of the *charismata*, especially glossolalia, or his argument about the proper operation of the Holy Spirit in church life. Within the direct context of the latter formulation alone, I am offering some remarks on this chapter of the Bible. We have already seen that, if Paul says, "[E]arnestly desire the higher gifts" (12:31a), he does not mean that there is a certain ranking in the gifts and ministries enumerated in 12:8-10 and 28-30. In both passages glossolalia and its interpretation appear last, not because they are the least in ranking[76] but because they created the greatest problems in Corinth (see 1 Cor. 14). For a different order, note that in chapter 13:1 they are mentioned first.

From the context we learn that the "still more excellent way" to which Paul points (1 Cor. 12:31b) is the way by which the believer earnestly desires the gifts. The excellent way requires that building up one's fellow believers comes before

---
75. Pinnock (1996, 132–33).
76. This has been suggested many times, recently by K. Runia (2000, 121).

anything else. This is possible only through the love (Gk. *agapē*) that thinks of others first. The point is not that such love itself would be the highest gift. Nor is the point that striving for love would be a more excellent way than striving for the gifts.[77] Paul's real claim is that the gifts can be exercised only through genuine love. Tongues, prophecy that builds up (cf. 14:3), declaring mysteries or knowledge, and even the greatest acts of faith, mean nothing if they are not motivated by love. This is the attitude that "does not insist on its own way" (13:5), but looks "to the interests of others" (Phil. 2:4).

Love is not an abstract notion here; the term itself can easily be replaced by the concrete person of Jesus or of the Holy Spirit:[78] "Jesus/the Spirit is patient and kind; Jesus/the Spirit does not envy or boast; Jesus/the Spirit is not arrogant or rude. Jesus/the Spirit does not insist on its own way; he is not irritable or resentful; he does not rejoice at wrongdoing, but rejoices with the truth. Jesus/the Spirit bears all things, believes all things, hopes all things, endures all things" (cf. 1 Cor. 13:4-7). Being led by true divine love is the same as being led by the Spirit (cf. Rom. 5:5). What is described here does not differ fundamentally from what in Galatians 5:22 is called the "fruit of the Spirit," in which love is the very first thing mentioned.

One day, all *charismata* and all ministries will come to an end, but "love never ends" (1 Cor. 13:8). One day, prophecies, glossolalia, and words of knowledge will no longer be needed because they function in the present (broken) world. They are the Spirit's provisions for building up the church as long as it is on earth. But love itself is everlasting. From the use of different verbs, "to pass away" and to "cease" (v. 8), some have tried to derive the conclusion that glossolalia would cease prior to prophecies and words of knowledge.[79] However, first, this does not follow from these verbs at all; and second, this

---

77. *Contra* Grosheide (1957, 340); Kelly (n.d.-a, 218).
78. Fee (1987, 628).
79. Gromacki (1963, 311–16); Findlay (1979, 900); cf. Kelly (n.d.-a, 223–24).

The Gifts of the Holy Spirit

overlooks entirely the actual intention of Paul's argument, whereby he is emphasizing the temporal as contrasted with the eternal (cf. 2 Cor. 4:18), not the question whether A is perhaps more temporal than B.[80]

12.8.2 "The Perfect"

The fiercely debated question concerning verses 8–10 involves when the *charismata* mentioned will pass away. This question is directly related to the question concerning "the perfect" in verse 12, and the "then" in verse 12. The latter ought to be the easiest: how could it be denied that "then I shall know fully, even as I have been fully known" (v. 12) can refer only to our eternal state? However, "then" refers back to the "when the perfect comes" in verse 10, and "the perfect" here cannot be anything else than what belongs to the eternal.[81] This is the common view of expositors as far as I can assess.[82] Our prophesying and knowing are deficient, but in the consummation of the age, all that is deficient (partial, incomplete, imperfect) will have been done away with (vv. 9–12).

Others have ardently argued that the phrase "the perfect" refers to some much earlier time: to the full maturation of either the individual believer or the church as a whole (which supposedly took place when the church got an established clergy! cf. §1.4.1), or to the completion of the New Testament canon (cf. §§1.4.2, 2.3.2).[83] In the latter two cases, this would have occurred near the end of the first century. Nothing in the text itself supports these views; on the contrary. We get the strong impression that such views have been invented because people want it to be true that the *charismata* ceased by the end of the first century. This is claimed despite the fact that church history clearly shows that the *charismata* did not

---

80. Fee (1987, 643–44n17); Erickson (1983, 880–81).
81. Phil. 3:12 (but in v. 15 the Gk. word *teleios* means "mature"!).
82. Grosheide (1957, 347); Mare (1976, 269); Findlay (1979, 900); Fee (1987, 644–45n23); Kelly (n.d.-a, 224); *contra* Maris (1992, 248–250). Notice MSG: "when the Complete arrives . . . ."
83. Vine (1985, 149–50); Legrand (1994); Harinck (2006).

cease at an earlier time. On the contrary, they have functioned throughout the centuries of church history. It is true that Paul relativizes the *charismata*: they may function in a deficient way, and one day they will pass away (TLB: "[W]hen we have been made perfect and complete, then the need for these inadequate special gifts will come to an end, and they will disappear"). However, until the time of the "perfection" (VOICE: the "fullness of God's kingdom"), they remain gracious gifts that we should not despise as long as they are exercised in love.

Gordon Fee summed up the matter this way:

> It is perhaps an indictment of Western Christianity that we should consider "mature"[84] our rather totally cerebral and domesticated — but bland — brand of faith, with the concomitant absence of the Spirit in terms of his supernatural gifts! The Spirit, not Western rationalism, marks the turning of the ages, after all; and to deny the Spirit's manifestations is to deny our present existence to be eschatological, as belonging to the beginning of the time of the End.[85]

This hits the nail on its head. Cessationists, limiting the gifts to the first century of Christian history, never tire of assuring us that at that time the gifts were needed, but now we have the complete Word of God. Of course, cessationists are not claiming that, now that we have the complete Bible, we no longer need the Spirit. Yet, in fact this is the import of what they are saying, at least as far as church life is concerned. The Spirit is needed to understand the Bible (and to regenerate people), but for the rest, the Bible is sufficient for Christian life. This is a form of biblicism: overemphasizing the Bible, in this case, at the expense of the Holy Spirit.

Far worse is the view that the church needed the *charismata* at the beginning, but not today because today we have

---

84. In a recent interview, Netherlands Reformed pastor A. T. Vergunst (USA) argued that the gifts belonged to the "childhood" of Christianity!
85. Fee (1987, 645n23).

science. For instance, Reformed theologian Abraham Kuyper argued that John 14:12 ("whoever believes in me will also do the works that I do; and greater works than these will he do") is now fulfilled especially through modern medicine.[86] To me, such an assertion is just as strange as arguing that we no longer need words of knowledge because we have modern theology, or no longer need discerning of spirits because we have modern psychology. (This despite the fact that certain diseases that were incurable in New Testament times remain incurable today, such as many forms of paralysis and of blindness and deafness—diseases that are sometimes cured by miraculous healing.[87]) Such ideas are products of Enlightenment thinking, defended by not only liberal theologians but also orthodox theologians.[88]

12.9 The Spirit in 1 Corinthians 14
12.9.1 *Pneuma, Pneumata, Pneumatikos*

In 1 Corinthians 14, Paul picks up the thread of chapter 12. In chapter 12:31 he says, "[E]arnestly desire the higher gifts [Gk. *ta charismata ta meizona*]," and in 14:1, "Pursue love, and earnestly desire the spiritual gifts [Gk. *ta pneumatika*]." Although in the church Paul prefers prophecy to glossolalia—for "the one who prophesies speaks to people for their upbuilding and encouragement and consolation" (v. 3)—this is not his pivotal point. The crucial point of his argument is that the church is to be built up in whatever way; this building up can occur just as well through glossolalia as through prophecy, as long as the former is interpreted (v. 5). "So, my brothers, earnestly desire to prophesy, and do not forbid speaking in tongues" (v. 39)—for, if glossolalia is interpreted, it builds up the church just the same. As we continue now, our focus is not the exegesis of the chapter itself but the light that it sheds on the Spirit-led application of the *charismata*.

---

86. Kuyper (2016, 1:164–65).
87. Ouweneel (2005a, 311).
88. See notes 29 and 30 above.

Allow me to list a few lexicographic starting points. 1 Corinthians 14 contains the following meanings of the Greek word *pneuma* ("s/Spirit"):

A. *Pneumata*, "spirits"
   (1) *Pneumata*, in the sense of "spiritual [gifts, utterances, operations]" (v. 12, here especially glossolalia[89]).
   (2) *Pneumata*, "spirits" ("spiritual [utterances]" or "spiritual minds/inward parts," namely, of the prophets, v. 32).
B. *Pneuma*, "s/Spirit"
   (3) *Pneumati*, "in/by [the] s/Spirit" (v. 2).
   (4) *Tōi pneumati*, "in/by [the] s/Spirit" (v. 15, 2x).
   (5) *En pneumati*, "in/with/by [the] s/Spirit" (v. 16).
   (6) *To pneuma mou*, "my spirit" (v. 14).

In category A, point (2) is remarkable. "Spirit" can refer here to the inner person (mind, heart) but also to "spiritual (Spirit-worked) utterances."[90] In light of verse 12, it would be more consistent to understand verse 32 this way. Just as *pneuma* means "s/Spirit," *pneumata* can mean "spirits" but also "spiritual utterances/operations." Thus verse 32 means: the Spirit-led utterances (or possibly, the Spirit-led minds) of prophets are subject to prophets in the sense that they themselves can decide how and when they express these Spirit-worked utterances.

In category B, only verse 14 (point 6) clearly refers to the human spirit because of the addition "my," even though the Holy Spirit is involved in "my spirit's" praying. It is different in verse 2 and 15–16. In verse 2 (point 3) we read, "[O]ne who speaks in a tongue speaks not to men but to God; for no one understands him, but he utters mysteries in/through the s/Spirit." The context suggests that, in our mind, we add, "One who speaks to the church in a tongue without any interpretation. . . ." Such a person does not speak "to men" because they cannot understand this "language." Only God can under-

---

89. Fee (1987, 666).
90. Ibid., 666, 696.

stand it; the person in this situation is speaking "mysteries," which here (other than in 13:2?) presumably simply means, "things hidden to people." To God we do not have to communicate hidden things; it is he who, through the Spirit, communicates hidden things to us.[91] Such speaking in tongues occurs through the Spirit (v. 15).[92] Of course it occurs "in the [human] spirit," but this "spirit" in the Spirit-filled believer is saturated with the Holy Spirit.

Since verses 15–16 (points 4 and 5) speak of "my spirit," one could think that again the human spirit is intended; this is the way most translations render it.[93] However, the CEB translates twice "in the Spirit." Gordon Fee argued that spiritual utterances issuing from the "spirit" of the believer can never be severed from the working of the Holy Spirit.[94] In paraphrase this means (vv. 14–16):

> For if I pray in a tongue, the Spirit prays through my spirit but my mind does not understand this.[95] What am I to do? I will pray with my spirit [or, in/through the Spirit], but I will pray with my mind also; I will sing praise with my spirit [or, in/through the Spirit], but I will sing with my mind also [i.e., in a language that I do understand]. Otherwise, if you give thanks with your spirit [or, in/through the Spirit], how can anyone in the position of an outsider say "Amen" to your thanksgiving when he does not know what you are saying?

This entire argument must never be understood as scorning glossolalia itself, for else Paul could never say, "I want

---

91. *Contra* Mare (1976, 272); Findlay (1979, 902).
92. Thus BRG, CEB; most other translations read "spirit"; AMP combines: "I will pray with the spirit [by the Holy Spirit that is within me]." Cf. Grosheide (1957, 355): ". . . the believer's *pneuma* sanctified and especially driven by the Holy Spirit."
93. See also Mare (1976, 272).
94. Fee (1987, 204–205 [on 1 Cor. 5:3–4], 596-97 [on 12:10], 670–71 [on 14:14–16], 696 [on 14:32]).
95. And thus does not share in my blessing in an intelligent way (Mare (1976, 273).

you all to speak in tongues" (v. 5), and, "I thank God that I speak in tongues more than all of you" (v. 18). No, what Paul scorns is uninterpreted glossolalia addressed to the church. Verse 14 does not hint at some disadvantage of glossolalia but simply describes how glossolalia works. Obviously, there is no *a priori* reason why praying with the intellect would be better than praying in the Spirit apart from the intellect; perhaps under certain circumstances the latter must even be preferred. The only point Paul wishes to make here is that the church can be built up only if the church members hear intelligible language; whether this occurs through prophecy or through interpreted glossolalia is irrelevant. In my view, this is the entire tenor of verses 1-19.

12.9.2 1 Corinthians 14 on Glossolalia

There are various other points in 1 Corinthians 14 that demand our attention. First there is verse 4: "The one who speaks in a tongue builds up himself, but the one who prophesies builds up the church." In my view, this means again: one who addresses the church in a language that is not interpreted is building up only oneself, not others. The question is what Paul means with this "building up oneself." It has been argued that he means this in a disapproving, or even sarcastic way.[96] But the text does not necessarily suggest such an interpretation. Paul does not deny that glossolalia might serve the purpose of building up the speaker personally—for this is not at all his subject here—but that, in church, the speaker must ask first and foremost what will build up the entire church, and not just oneself. Paul's statement, "All things are lawful, but not all things build up" (10:23), can easily include one's own person. Jude speaks explicitly of building oneself up in one's most holy faith, and immediately continues with praying in the Holy Spirit (Jude 1:20). It is understandable that people have thought here of glossolalia, but this cannot be

---

96. See O. Michel, R. G. Gromacki, J. F. MacArthur, quoted by Fee (1987, 657n24).

proven from the context. At any rate, 1 Corinthians 14:15-16 speaks of praying and praising "by (or in) the s/Spirit" (Gk. *tōi* [or *en*] *pneumati*), which clearly refers to glossolalia—and in this way one builds up oneself. This is not inherently wrong; but in church people must seek primarily to build up others.

In this connection, Findlay has made the interesting observation that when someone spoke in tongues, this mightily confirmed his faith, since it left behind a lasting awareness of possessing the Spirit of God (cf. 2 Cor. 12:1-10).[97] Our deepest feelings often enter our mind below surface consciousness—as is indeed the case with glossolalia.

Another point demanding our attention is 1 Corinthians 14:21-23:

> In the Law it is written, "'By people of strange tongues and by the lips of foreigners will I speak to this people, and even then they will not listen to me,' says the Lord." Thus tongues are a sign not for believers but for unbelievers, while prophecy is a sign not for unbelievers but for believers. If, therefore, the whole church comes together and all speak in tongues, and outsiders or unbelievers enter, will they not say that you are out of your minds?

Here, Paul supplies us with yet another argument to relativize the significance of glossolalia in church if it is not interpreted—although we must add that this passage, especially verse 22, has led to a plethora of interpretations.

Glossolalia is a "sign for unbelievers" (1 Cor. 14:22). This is not the case when unbelievers understand the languages that are spoken, as in Acts 2:11, where it led to the conversion of many of them. According to 1 Corinthians 14:1 (a quotation from Isa. 28:11-12), the Israelites heard foreign languages that were a (bad) "sign" for them. In Isaiah 28:11-12 it was the Assyrians who spoke to Judah in languages that the people did not understand, and this—despite this speaking, or due to not

---

97. Findlay (1979, 902); cf. also Grosheide (1957, 356).

understanding this speaking—did not lead the Judeans to repentance. If they did not want to listen to their own prophets, then they certainly would not listen to the strange sounds that the Assyrians would address to them. Right now, the point is not how Isaiah may have meant this, but the (rather free) way Paul uses this quotation within the context of 1 Corinthians 14. He says, as it were, tongues are not a sign that you, Corinthians, are so spiritual (cf. v. 20), or that God is in your midst (cf. vv. 24–25, where this is the very effect of prophecy!). Rather, they are a "sign" for unbelievers. This sign must be understood in the negative sense, just as in verse 21: tongues that are not understood do not lead people to repentance.

This interpretation is supported by what follows: "If, therefore, the whole church comes together and all speak in tongues, and outsiders or unbelievers enter, will they not say that you are out of your minds?" (v. 23). Thus, the word "sign" refers here to something that creates a negative effect.[98] Therefore, it would be better for the Corinthians if they would prophesy because intelligible, edifying utterances have a positive effect, both upon believers (vv. 3, 22b) and upon unbelievers (vv. 24–25): "But if all prophesy, and an unbeliever or outsider enters, he is convicted by all, he is called to account by all, the secrets of his heart are disclosed, and so, falling on his face, he will worship God and declare that God is really among you."

12.9.3 The Spiritual Utterances in Verses 6 and 26

Let me add a few words on the enumeration of spiritual utterances in verse 6b ("revelation or knowledge or prophecy or teaching"), verses 14–15 (prayer, praise), and verse 26 ("When you come together, each one has a hymn, a lesson, a revelation, a tongue, or an interpretation. Let all things be done for building up"). We find here nine *pneumatika*:

---

98. See extensively, Fee (1987, 680–83); much more concisely but with the same result: Mare (1976, 274); Findlay (1979, 910); Mallone (1983, 86); cf. J. P. M. Sweet in Mills (1986, 141–64).

(1) Revelation (vv. 6, 26, 29–30; Gk. *apokalypsis* ["unveiling"], different from *phanerōsis* ["appearance"] in 12:7); here probably mainly identical with a prophetic utterance (cf. Gal. 2:2); verse 30 would then mean: "to another [prophet]."[99] Findlay therefore argued that the second pair of utterances in verse 6 corresponds with the first pair: revelations come from prophets, words of knowledge come from teachers.[100] The problem with this view is that the four categories are apparently juxtaposed in such a way that they suggest four different matters.

(2) Knowledge (v. 6; cf. 13:2, 8); apparently the same as "word of knowledge" in 12:8.

(3) Prophecy (v. 6 and throughout; see §12.5.1).

(4) Teaching (vv. 6, 26; this refers back to the "teacher" in 12:28).

(5) Hymn (v. 26), every sung spiritual utterance (cf. vv. 15–16; Eph. 5:19; Col. 3:16).[101]

(6) Tongue (v. 6 and throughout; this refers to a language that one has not learned; glossolalia; see §12.5.2).

(7) Interpretation (v. 26 and throughout; see §12.5.3).

(8) Prayer (vv. 14–15; cf. 11:4–5); prayer is a common element in every church service.

(9) Praise (v. 15), whether in sung form (cf. [5]) or otherwise.

12.9.4 Order and Freedom

1 Corinthians 14 is of great importance for the functioning of the *charismata* in church. One could not imagine the Corinthian church as a place where, apart from the singing, only one person—the priest or pastor—is heard during the entire service. "Now the Lord is the Spirit, and where the Spirit of

---

99. Cf. the discussion in Grosheide (1957, 358 including n16).
100. Findlay (1979, 903).
101. Fee (1987, 671, 690–91). In Luke's writings the Gk. word *psalmos* refers to the Old Testament Psalms, but this is not the case in Paul's writings.

the Lord is, there is freedom" (2 Cor. 3:17), and this is true in a special way with regard to the church service. Freedom is not debauchery, for here the Spirit is Lord over all words and deeds of the believers who are present. We therefore might render this statement to read "Where the Spirit is Lord, there is freedom."[102] But whereas debauchery lurches to the "left" (so to speak), a straitjacket lurches to the "right." The Holy Spirit works in all (spiritual) believers in the church, and therefore he must be free to work through all, as it pleases him. "To each is given the manifestation of the Spirit for the common good.... All these [i.e., the *charismata*] are empowered by one and the same Spirit, who apportions to each one individually as he wills" (1 Cor. 12:7, 11), and not insofar as human rules allow.

Such a general participation does not at all exclude a (Spirit-led) leading and order in the church services, and self-discipline is excluded even less. This might seem a paradox: where the freedom of the Spirit reigns, the Spirit is the Lord, the Leader, and believers must submit to this guidance. There is no true spiritual freedom without the Spirit's leadership, nor is there any genuine Spiritual leadership without the true freedom of God's people.

Paul expresses this as follows:

> If any speak in a tongue, let there be only two or at most three, and each in turn, and let someone interpret. But if there is no one to interpret, let each of them keep silent in church and speak to himself and to God. Let two or three prophets speak, and let the others weigh what is said. If a revelation is made to another sitting there, let the first be silent. For you can all prophesy one by one, so that all may learn and all be encouraged, and the spirits of prophets are subject to prophets. For God is not a God of confusion but of peace (1 Cor. 14:27–33).

Here we have the two sides of the freedom of the Spirit during church services. On the one hand, the starting point is

---

102. Prince (1995, 355–56; see 355–60, 367–76).

that each believer has a contribution to make, and that there must be optimal room for this (v. 26a).[103] This implies the opportunity to raise or recite a hymn, produced in the heart by the Spirit, to speak a prayer or a word of praise, to pass on a word of knowledge or of wisdom, or a prophecy, or a message in tongues if it is interpreted. This is the freedom of the Spirit. This ought not to be restricted by a "one man show" in any form. According to 1 Corinthians 14, the believer goes to church not primarily to receive something (although the believer will be blessed), but to contribute something for the benefit of the entire congregation.

On the other hand, this freedom is placed under norms, and thus restricted, by the consideration that all things must "be done for building up" the congregation (v. 26b). (Actually, this ought to be a superfluous exhortation, for if a contribution is really of the Spirit, it will always build up; 1 Cor. 12:7; cf. 14:3–5, 12, 17.) Because of this norm of edification, there should not be too many messages in glossolalia (because they must all be interpreted), nor too many prophecies. First, the church cannot handle too many exhortations. Second, the meeting should not be dominated by one type of ministry. Where the Holy Spirit works in God's people there will be wide diversity. Many other, different forms of service are demanded to have a full, complete worship service.[104]

Another point is that the various contributions must not all be shouted out at the same time. Such behavior is very confusing, and certainly not edifying. "[A]ll things should be done decently and in order" (1 Cor. 14:40). Therefore, believers must never defend any disorderly behavior with the excuse that they were "driven" by the Holy Spirit. In extreme cases, one might even become suspicious about whether wrong spirits are involved, as in paganism, where demons

---

103. In my view, v. 34 ("the women should keep silent in the churches") is no exception to this, and thus is not meant in an absolute sense. This is evident from 11:5, where women, too, pray and prophesy in church.
104. Prince (1995, 373).

"lead" people against their own will (cf. 12:2). In the church, the prophet always maintains control over what goes on within one's person, and over what comes out of one's mouth. "For you can all prophesy one by one, so that all may learn and all be encouraged, and the spirits of prophets are subject to prophets. For God is not a God of confusion but of peace" (vv. 31-33).

With what more powerful term could we finish this book than this word "peace" in connection with the Holy Spirit? Consider and take to heart, from the letter to the Romans, these concluding exhortations:

> [T]o set the mind on the flesh is death, but to set the mind on the Spirit is life and peace (8:6).

> For the kingdom of God is not a matter of eating and drinking but of righteousness and peace and joy in the Holy Spirit (14:17).

> May the God of hope fill you with all joy and peace in believing, so that by the power of the Holy Spirit you may abound in hope (15:13).

> Therefore, since we have been justified by faith, we have peace with God through our Lord Jesus Christ. Through him we have also obtained access by faith into this grace in which we stand, and we rejoice in hope of the glory of God. . . . and hope does not put us to shame, because God's love has been poured into our hearts through the Holy Spirit who has been given to us (5:1-5).

Bibliography

Aalders, C. 1977. "Botsende oer-ervaringen." *Kerk en Theologie* 28.2:89–112.

Adamson, J. 1976. *The Epistle of James.* NICNT. Grand Rapids, MI: Eerdmans.

Aeppli, E. 1984. *Der Traum und seine Deutung.* Zürich: Eugen Rentsch Verlag.

Alexander, R. H. 1986. *Ezekiel.* EBC 6. Grand Rapids, MI: Zondervan.

Althaus, P. (1914) 1967. *Die Prinzipien der deutschen reformierten Dogmatik im Zeitalter der aristotelischen Scholastik.* Darmstadt: Wissenschaftliche Buchgesellschaft.

_____. 1952. *Die christliche Wahrheit: Lehrbuch der Dogmatik.* 3rd ed. Gütersloh: Bertelsmann.

Anrich, G. 1914. *Martin Bucer.* Strassburg: Trübner.

Ashley, T. R. 1993. *The Book of Numbers.* NICOT. Grand Rapids, MI: Eerdmans.

Badcock, G. D. 1997. *Light of Truth and Fire of Love: A Theology of the Holy Spirit.* Grand Rapids, MI: Eerdmans.

Bakker, H. 2005. *"Ze hebben lief, maar worden vervolgd": Radicaal christendom in de tweede eeuw en nu.* Zoetermeer: Boekencentrum.

Barker, G. W. 1981. *1 John.* EBC 12. Grand Rapids, MI: Zondervan.

Barker, K. L. 1985. *Zechariah*. EBC 7. Grand Rapids, MI: Zondervan.

Barth, K. 1933. *The Epistle to the Romans*. Translated by E. C. Hoskyns. New York: Oxford University.

_____. 2009. *Church Dogmatics. Study Edition*. Translated by G. W. Bromiley et al. Vols. I/1–IV/1. New York, NY: T&T Clark. (Editor's Note: The original fourteen volumes have been published in the *Study Edition* as thirty-one volumes. For citation purposes, the original volume enumeration is followed by the number of the equivalent new volume: e.g., III/3=18. The sections [§] are identical in both editions. The final number[s] refer[s] to the page[s] in the new *Study Edition*. Sample citation convention: CD III/3=18, §51.2:130.)

Bavinck, H. 2002–2008. *Reformed Dogmatics*. Edited by John Bolt. Translated by John Vriend. 4 vols. Grand Rapids, MI: Baker Academic.

Bavinck, J. H. n.d. *Ik geloof in de Heilige Geest*. Den Haag: J. N. Voorhoeve.

_____, P. Prins, and G. Brillenburg Wurth. 1949. *De Heilige Geest*. Kampen: J.H. Kok.

Belder, J. 1997. *Wat geloof ik van de Heilige Geest?* Heerenveen: J. J. Groen and Zoon.

Berdayev, N. 1964. *Spirit and Reality*. London: G. Bles.

Berkhof, H. 1964. *The Doctrine of the Holy Spirit*. Atlanta, GA: John Knox Press.

_____. 1982. "Het hedendaagse zoeken naar de Heilige Geest en het antwoord van de bijbel." *Bulletin voor Charismatische Theologie* 9: 15–25.

_____. 1986. *Christian Faith: An Introduction to the Study of the Faith*. Translated by S. Woudstra. Rev. ed. Grand Rapids, MI: Eerdmans.

Berkhof, L. 1996. *Systematic Theology*. New edition. Grand Rapids, MI: Eerdmans.

Berkouwer, G. C. 1952. *The Providence of God*. Translated by L. B. Smedes. Studies in Dogmatics. Grand Rapids, MI: Eerdmans.

———. 1971. *Sin*. Translated by P. C. Holtrop. Studies in Dogmatics. Grand Rapids, MI: Eerdmans.

Bermejo, L. 1989. *The Spirit of Life: The Holy Spirit in the Life of the Christian*. Chicago: Loyola University Press.

Bernard, J. H. 1979. *The Second Epistle to the Corinthians*. EGT 3. Grand Rapids, MI: Eerdmans.

Bernard of Clairvaux. 1992. *Pinkstergeest en heilsgeschiedenis*. Brugge: Zevenkerken.

Bickle, M. with M. Sullivant. 1998. *Groeien in de profetische bediening*. Vlissingen: Bread of Life.

Bittlinger, A. 1967. *Gifts and Graces: A Commentary on I Corinthians 12–14*. London: Hodder and Stoughton.

Bloch-Hoell, N. 1964. *The Pentecostal Movement: Its Origin, Development, and Distinctive Character*. New York: Humanities Press.

Block, D. I. 1989. "The Prophet of the Spirit: The Use of RWH in the Book of Ezekiel." *Journal of the Evangelical Theological Society* 32: 27–49.

Bloesch, D. G. 1992. *A Theology of Word and Spirit: Authority and Method in Theology*. Carlisle: Paternoster Press.

Blum, E. A. 1981a. *1 Peter*. EBC 12. Grand Rapids, MI: Zondervan.

———. 1981b. *Jude*. EBC 12. Grand Rapids, MI: Zondervan.

Boice, J. M. 1976. *Galatians*. EBC. Grand Rapids, MI: Zondervan.

Bolkestein, M. H. 1949. "Het Woord Gods en de kosmos." *Nederlands Theologisch Tijdschrift* 1949: 1–11.

Bönker, J. and T. Wintels, with M. Nota. 2004. *Macht en manipulatie . . . toch niet onder christelijke leiders?* Hoornaar: Gideon.

Bouma, C. 1927. *Het evangelie naar Johannes.* KV. Kampen: J.H. Kok.

———. 1937. *De brieven van den apostel Paulus aan Timotheus en Titus.* KV. Kampen: J.H. Kok.

Bromiley, G. W., ed. 1953. *Zwingli and Bullinger.* Library of Christian Classics 24. Philadelphia: Westminster Press.

Broughton, R. S. 1995. *Parapsychologie: Een wetenschap in beweging.* Deventer: Ankh-Hermes.

Brown, R. E. 1970. *The Gospel According to John, XIII-XXI.* Anchor Yale Bible Commentaries. New Haven, CT: Yale University Press.

Bruce, A. B. 1979. *The Synoptic Gospels.* EGT 1. Grand Rapids, MI: Eerdmans.

Bruce, F. F. 1964. *The Epistle to the Hebrews.* NICNT. Grand Rapids, MI: Eerdmans.

———. 1984. *The Epistles to the Colossians, to Philemon, and to the Ephesians.* NICNT. Grand Rapids, MI: Eerdmans.

———. 1988. *The Book of the Acts.* NICNT. Grand Rapids, MI: Eerdmans.

Bruner, F. D. 1970. *A Theology of the Holy Spirit: The Pentecostal Experience and the New Testament Witness.* Grand Rapids, MI: Eerdmans.

Brunner, E. 1937. *The Divine Imperative: A Study in Christian Ethics.* Translated by O. Wyon. New York: Macmillan.

Bultema, H. 1981. *Commentary on Isaiah.* Grand Rapids, MI: Kregel.

Burdick, D. W. 1981. *James.* EBC 12. Grand Rapids, MI: Zondervan.

Burgess, S. M. 1989. *The Holy Spirit: Eastern Christian Traditions.* Peabody, MA: Hendrickson.

———. 1997. *The Holy Spirit: Medieval Roman Catholic and Reformation Traditions.* Peabody, MA: Hendrickson.

Buri, F. 1978. *Dogmatik als Selbstverständnis des christlichen Glaubens.* Vol. 3: *Die Transzendenz der Verantwortung in* der dreifachen Schöpfung des dreieinigen Gottes. Bern: Paul Haupt; Tübingen: Katzmann.

Buse, I. 1956. "The Markan Account of the Baptism of Jesus and Isaiah LXIII." *Journal of Theological Studies* n.s. 7:74-75.

Calvin, J. 1960. *Institutes of the Christian Religion*. Edited by John T. McNeill. Translated by Ford Lewis Battles. 2 vols. Library of Christian Classics 20-21. Philadelphia: Westminster Press.

Candlish, R. S. 1973. *A Commentary on 1 John*. Geneva Series. London: Banner of Truth.

Carson, D. A. 1984. *Matthew*. EBC 8. Grand Rapids, MI: Zondervan.

Cerfaux, L. 1967. *The Christian in the Theology of Paul*. London: G. Chapman.

Chafer, L. S. 1983. *Systematic Theology*. 8 vols. 15th ed. Dallas: Dallas Seminary Press.

Chase, F. H. 1902. *The Credibility of the Book of the Acts of the Apostles*. London: Macmillan.

Cobb, J. B., Jr. and D. R. Griffin. 1976. *Process Theology*. Philadelphia: Westminster Press.

Cohen, A., ed. 1957. *The Twelve prophets*. The Soncino Books of the Bible. London: Soncino Press.

_____, ed. 1980. *The Twelve Prophets*. The Soncino Books of the Bible. London etc.: Soncino Press.

_____, ed. 1982. *Joshua and Judges*. The Soncino Books of the Bible. London etc.: Soncino Press.

_____, ed. 1983. *The Soncino Chumash*. The Soncino Books of the Bible. London etc.: Soncino Press.

Comblin, J. 1989. *The Holy Spirit and Liberation*. Maryknoll, NY: Orbis.

Congar, Y. 1997. *I Believe in the Holy Spirit*. 3 vols. New York: Crossroad Herder.

Conzelmann, H. 1987. *Acts of the Apostles: A Commentary on the Acts of the Apostles*. Edited by E. J. Epp with C. R. Matthews. Translated by J. Limburg, A. T. Kraabel, and D. H. Juel. Philadelphia: Fortress Press.

Cunneen, S. 1997. *Maria: Relikwie uit het verleden of baken voor de toekomst?* Houten: Van Reemst.

Dabney, D. L. 1997. *Die Kenosis des Geistes: Kontinuität zwischen Schöpfung und Erlösung im Werk des Heiligen Geistes.* Neukirchen-Vluyn: Neukirchener Verlag.

Da Costa, I. 1968. "Bezwaren tegen den geest der eeuw." In *Vrijmoedige bedenkingen: Een eeuw essays en beschouwingen 1766–1875.* Edited by M. C. A. Van der Heiden, 123–88. Spectrum van de Nederlandse letterkunde 20. Utrecht/Antwerpen: Het Spectrum.

Darby, J. N. n.d. *Synopsis of the Books of the Bible.* Kingston-on-Thames: Stow Hill.

Davids, P. 1990. *The First Epistle of Peter.* NICNT. Grand Rapids, MI: Eerdmans.

Dee, S. P. 1918. *Het geloofsbegrip van Calvijn.* Kampen: J.H. Kok.

De Graaf, S. G. 1940. *Hoofdlijnen in de dogmatiek.* Kampen: J.H. Kok.

De Graaff, F. 1987. *Jezus de Verborgene: Een voorbereiding tot inwijding in de mysteriën van het Evangelie.* Kampen: J.H. Kok.

De Groot, D. J. 1949. "Het werk van de Heilige Geest." In *Het dogma der kerk.* Edited by G. C. Berkouwer and G. Toornvliet, 407–444. Groningen: Jan Haan.

Den Boer, C. and W. J. Bouw, eds. 1986. *Het werk van de Heilige Geest en de gemeente.* Amersfoort: Echo.

Dengerink, J. D. 1986. *De zin van de werkelijkheid.* Amsterdam: VU Uitgeverij.

Denney, J. 1979. *St. Paul's Epistle to the Romans.* EGT 2. Grand Rapids, MI: Eerdmans.

Dijk, K. n.d. *Korte dogmatiek.* Kampen: J.H. Kok.

Dods, M. 1979. *The Gospel of John.* EGT 1. Grand Rapids, MI: Eerdmans.

Doornenbal, R. J. A. and P. A. Siebesma. 2005. *Gaven voor de gemeente: Over het werk en de gaven van de Heilige Geest*. Zoetermeer: Boekencentrum.

Douma, J. 1966. *Algemene genade*. 2nd ed. Goes: Oosterbaan and Le Cointre.

Drescher, K. et al, ed. 1883–1925. *Martin Luthers Werke*. Vols. I-X. Weimar: Böhlau.

Dreyer, E. A. 1998. "Resources for a Renewed Life in the Spirit and Pneumatology: Medieval Mystics and Saints." *Advent of the Spirit: Orientations in Pneumatology*. Readings held during a symposium at Marquette University, 17–19 april 1998 (unpublished).

Duffield, G. P. and N. M. Van Cleave. 1996. *Woord en Geest: Hoofdlijnen van de theologie van de Pinksterbeweging*. Kampen: J.H. Kok/Rafaël Nederland.

Dunn, J. D. G. 1970. *Baptism in the Holy Spirit*. London: SCM.

_____. 1992. "Spirit, Holy Spirit (part)." *NIDNTT*. 3.693–707.

_____. 1993. "Baptism in the Spirit: A Response to Pentecostal Scholarship on Luke-Acts." *Journal of Pentecostal Theology* 1.3: 3–27.

_____. 1997. *Jesus and the Spirit*. Grand Rapids, MI: Eerdmans.

_____. 1998. *Christ and the Spirit*. 2 vols. Edinburgh: T. and T. Clark.

Du Plessis, D. J. 1964. *De Geest maakt levend*. Emmen: Gideon.

Ebeling, G. 1979. *Dogmatik des christlichen Glaubens*. Vol. 1. Tübingen: Mohr (Siebeck).

Eccles, J. C. 1953. *The Neurophysiological Basis of Mind: The Principles of Neurophysiology*. Oxford: Clarendon Press.

Edersheim, A. 1979. *The Life and Times of Jesus the Messiah*. 2 vols. Grand Rapids, MI: Eerdmans.

Edwards, J. 2011. *The Distinguishing Marks of a Work of the Spirit of God*. Amazon Digital Services LLC.

Eichrodt, W. 1967. *Theology of the Old Testament*. Translated by J. A. Baker. Vol. 2. Philadelphia, PA: Westminster.

Ensley, E. 1977. *Sounds of Wonder: A Popular History of Speaking in Tongues in the Catholic Tradition.* Ramsey: Paulist.

Erickson, M. J. 1985. *Christian Theology.* 2nd ed. Grand Rapids, MI: Baker Book House.

Esser, H.-H. 1976. "Grace, Spiritual Gifts." *NIDNTT* 2.115–24.

Evdokimov, P. 1959. *L'Orthodoxie.* Paris: Desclée de Brouwer. 2011. ET: *Orthodoxy.* Hyde Park, NY: New City Press.

Fee, G. D. 1987. *The First Epistle to the Corinthians.* NICNT. Grand Rapids, MI: Eerdmans.

———. 1994. *God's Empowering Presence: The Holy Spirit in the Letters of Paul.* Peabody, MA: Hendrickson.

Ferguson, J. 1979. *Encyclopedie van de mystiek en de mysteriegodsdiensten* (abridged by S. Vinkenoog). Baarn: Het Wereldvenster.

Findlay, G. G. 1979. *St. Paul's First Epistle to the Corinthians.* EGT 2. Grand Rapids, MI: Eerdmans.

Floor, L. 1982. *De doop met de Heilige Geest.* Kampen: J.H. Kok.

———. 1999. *De gaven van de Heilige Geest in bijbels-theologisch perspectief.* Heerenveen: Groen.

Fung, R. Y. K. 1988. *The Epistle to the Galatians.* NICNT. Grand Rapids, MI: Eerdmans.

Gaebelein, A. C. 1910. *The Gospel of Matthew.* Vol. 1. Wheaton, IL: Van Kampen Press.

———. 1980. *Wij hebben zijn heerlijkheid aanschouwd: Aantekeningen bij het evangelie naar Johannes.* Apeldoorn: Medema.

Gee, D. 1963. *Spiritual Gifts in the Work of the Ministry Today.* Springfield: Gospel Publishing House.

Geisler, N. L. 2011. *Systematic Theology.* Minneapolis, MN: Bethany House.

Geldenhuys, N. 1983. *Commentary on the Gospel of Luke.* NICNT. Grand Rapids, MI: Eerdmans.

Gelpi, D. J. 1992. "The Theological Challenge of Charismatic Spirituality." *Pneuma* 14/2: 185–197.

Gispen, W. H. 1974. *Genesis*. COT. Kampen: J.H. Kok.

Godet, F. 1978. *Commentary on the Gospel of John*. Grand Rapids, MI: Kregel.

Goldmann, S. 1983. *Samuel*. The Soncino Books of the Bible. London: Soncino Press.

Goldstein, K. 1995. *The Organism: A Holistic Approach to Biology Derived from Pathological Data in Man*. New York: Zone Books.

Goslinga, C. J. 1951. *Het boek der Richteren*. Vol. 1. KV. Kampen: J.H. Kok.

_____. 1968. *Het eerste boek Samuël*. COT. Kampen: J.H. Kok.

Graafland, C. 1999. *Gedachten over het ambt*. Zoetermeer: Boekencentrum.

Grant, F. W. 1890. *The Numerical Bible: The Pentateuch*. New York: Loizeaux Brothers.

_____. 1897. *The Numerical Bible: The Gospels*. New York: Loizeaux Brothers.

_____. 1901. *The Numerical Bible: Acts to 2 Corinthians*. New York: Loizeaux Brothers.

_____. 1902. *The Numerical Bible: Hebrews to Revelation*. New York: Loizeaux Brothers.

Green, J. and M. Pasquarello, eds. 2003. *Narrative Reading, Narrative Preaching: Reuniting New Testament Interpretation and Proclamation*. Grand Rapids, MI: Baker Academic.

Green, M. 1975. *I Believe in the Holy Spirit*. London: Hodder and Stoughton.

_____. 2005. *The Books the Church Suppressed: Fiction and Truth in the Da Vinci Code*. Oxford: Monarch Books.

Greeven, H. 1968. "*Peristera, trygōn*." TDNT 6.63–72.

Greijdanus, S. 1925. *De brief van den apostel Paulus aan de Epheziërs*. KV. Kampen: J.H. Kok.

_____. 1931. *De eerste brief van den apostel Petrus*. KV. Kampen: J.H. Kok.

———. 1934. *De brieven van den apostel Johannes.* KV. Kampen: J.H. Kok.

———. 1941. *Het evangelie naar Lucas.* Vol. 2. KV. Kampen: J.H. Kok.

———. 1950. *De brief van Jakobus.* KV. Kampen: J.H. Kok.

———. 1955. *Het evangelie naar Lucas.* Vol. 1. 2nd ed. KV. Kampen: J.H. Kok.

Grenz, S. J. and J. A. Franke. 2000. *Beyond Foundationalism: Shaping Theology in a Postmodern Context.* Westminster: John Knox Press.

Griffith Thomas, W. H. 1930. *Principles of Theology.* New York: Longmans, Green and Company.

Groen van Prinsterer, G. 2018. *Unbelief and Revolution.* Bellingham, WA: Lexham Press.

Grogan, G. W. 1986. *Isaiah.* EBC 6. Grand Rapids, MI: Zondervan.

Gromacki, R. G. 1967. *The Modern Tongues Movement.* Philadelphia: Presbyterian and Reformed Publishing Company.

Groothuis, D. R. 1986. *Unmasking the New Age.* Downers Grove, IL: InterVarsity Press.

Grosheide, F. W. 1949. *Het heilig evangelie volgens Johannes.* Vol. 1. Amsterdam: H. A. van Bottenburg.

———. 1954. *Het heilig evangelie volgens Mattheüs.* 2nd ed. CNT. Kampen: J.H. Kok.

———. 1955. *De brief aan de Hebreeën en de brief van Jakobus.* CNT. Kampen: J.H. Kok.

———. 1957. *De eerste brief aan de kerk te Korinthe.* CNT. Kampen: J.H. Kok.

———. 1960. *De brief van Paulus aan de Efeziërs.* CNT. Kampen: J.H. Kok.

———. 1962–1963. *De Handelingen der Apostelen.* 2 vols. KV. Kampen: J.H. Kok.

Grudem, W. 1988. *1 Peter.* Tyndale New Testament Commentary. Grand Rapids, MI: Eerdmans.

———. 1994. *Systematic Theology: An Introduction to Biblical Doctrine*. Grand Rapids, MI: Zondervan.

Grundmann, W. 1964. "Dynamai, etc." *TDNT* 2.284–317.

Hagin, K. E. 1983, 2004. *Understanding the Anointing*. 17th ed. Tulsa, OK: Faith Library Publications.

Halkes, C. J. M. 1984. *Zoekend naar wat verloren ging: Enkele aanzetten voor een feministische theologie*. Baarn: Ten Have.

Haller, M. 1925. *Das Judentum: Geschichtsschreibung, prophetie und Gesetzgebung nach dem Exil*. 2nd ed. Die Schriften des Alten Testaments II/3. Göttingen: Vandenhoeck and Ruprecht.

Hamilton, V. P. 1990. *The Book of Genesis Chapters 1–17*. NICOT. Grand Rapids, MI: Eerdmans.

Harinck, C. 2006. *De Geestesgaven: Een bezinning op de opkomst van de charismatische beweging*. Houten: Den Hertog.

Harris, M. J. 1976. *2 Corinthians*. EBC 10. Grand Rapids, MI: Zondervan.

Harrison, E. F. 1976. *Romans*. EBC. Grand Rapids, MI: Zondervan.

Hart, J. H. A. 1979. *The First Epistle General of Peter*. EGT 5. Grand Rapids, MI: Eerdmans.

Hartvelt, G. P. 1977. *Het gebinte van de tijd: Een historische studie over constructies van de geschiedenis, met name in de tijd der Reformatie*. Kampen: J.H. Kok.

———. 1978. "De balans." In *Op het spoor van de Geest: Theologische opstellen. Vragen aan en kanttekeningen bij de charismatische beweging*, edited by J. Veenhof et al. 31–53. Kampen: J.H. Kok.

Hasenhüttl, G. 1979. *Kritische Dogmatik*. Graz: Styria.

Hendriksen, W. 1968. *Galatians and Ephesians*. New Testament Commentary. Grand Rapids, MI: Baker Book House.

Henry, C. F. H. 1982. *God Who Stands and Stays*. Part One. *God, Revelation, and Authority*. Vol. 5. Waco, TX: Word Books.

Hermann, I. 1961. *Kyrios und Pneuma: Studien zur Christologie der paulinischen Haptbriefe*. München: Kösel.

Heron, A. I. C. 1980. *A Century of Protestant Theology*. Philadelphia: Westminster Press.

Hess, K. 1976. "*Latreuō.*" *NIDNTT* 3.549-551.

Heyns, J. A. 1976. *Brug tussen God en mens: Oor die Bybel*. Pretoria: NG Kerkboekhandel.

_____. 1988. *Dogmatiek*. Pretoria: NG Kerkboekhandel.

Hiebert, D. E. 1978. *Titus*. EBC 11. Grand Rapids, MI: Zondervan.

Hilberath, B. J. 1992. "Pneumatologie." In *Handbuch der Dogmatik*. Edited by Th. Schneider. 2 vols. Düsseldorf: Patmos.

_____. 1998. "Identity through Self-Transcendence: The Holy Spirit and the Communion of Free Persons." *Advent of the Spirit: Orientations in Pneumatology*. Readings held during a symposium at Marquette University, 17-19 April 1998 (unpublished).

Hildebrandt, W. 1995. *An Old Testament Theology of the Spirit of God*. Peabody, MA: Hendrickson.

Hinn, B. 1999. *He Touched Me: An Autobiography*. Nashville, TN: Thomas Nelson.

Hodge, C. A. 1872. *Systematic Theology*. Vol. 1. New York: Scribner, Armstrong and Company.

Hoek, J. 2006. "Terug naar het midden en zo vooruit." *Ellips* 268:8.

Hoenderdaal, G. J. 1968. *Geloven in de Heilige Geest*. Wageningen: Veenman.

Hollenweger, W. J. 1969. *Enthusiastes Christentum: Die Pfingstbewegung in Geschichte und Gegenwart*. Wuppertal/Zürich: Brockhaus.

Hommes, N. J., J. L. Koole, P. G. Kunst, H. N. Ridderbos, and R. Schippers. 1946. *Het Nieuwe Testament van verklarende aanteekeningen voorzien*. Kampen: J.H. Kok.

Hoskyns, E. 1947. *The Fourth Gospel*. Edited by F. N. Davey.

London: Faber and Faber.

Howard-Browne, R. M. 1994. *The Touch of God: A Practical Workbook on the Anointing*. Louisville, KY: R.H.B.E.A. Publications.

———. 2005. *Flowing in the Holy Spirit: A Practical Handbook on the Gifts of the Spirit*. Shippensburg, PA: Destiny Image Publishers.

Hughes, P. E. 1962. *Paul's Second Epistle to the Corinthians*. NICNT. Grand Rapids, MI: Eerdmans.

Hunter, C. and F. 2000. *How To Heal the Sick*. New Kensington, PA: Whitaker House.

Hutten, G. 2004. *Verrast door de Geest*. Heerenveen: Barnabas.

Hutten, K. 1957. *Geloof en sekte: Het sektarisme als anti-reformatorisch geloofsverschijnsel, zijn doelstrelling en zijn tragiek*. Franeker, T. Wever.

Jenson, R. W. 1982. *The Triune Identity: God According to the Gospel*. Philadelphia: Fortress Press.

Johnson, A. F. 1981. *Revelation*. EBC 12. Grand Rapids: Zondervan.

Johnson, E. 2002. *She Who Is: The Mystery of God in Feminist Theological Discourse*. New York: Crossroad.

Johnson, L. T. 1991. *The Gospel of Luke*. Collegeville, MN: Liturgical Press.

Jones, W. R. 1976. "The Nine Gifts of the Holy Spirit." In *Pentecostal Doctrine*. Edited by P. S. Brewster, 47–61. Cheltenham: Elim Pentecostal Church Headquarters.

Joyce, G. H. 1912. "Trinity." *The Catholic Encyclopedia* 18: 47–57.

Kaiser, W. C., Jr. 1990. *Exodus*. EBC 2. Grand Rapids, MI: Zondervan.

Kamlah, E. 1976. "Spirit, Holy Spirit" (part). *NIDNTT* 3.689–693.

Kärkkäinen, V.-M. 2002. *Pneumatology: The Holy Spirit in Ecumenical, International, and Contextual Perspective*. Grand

Rapids, MI: Baker Academic.

———. 2003. *Christology: A Global Introduction*. Grand Rapids, MI: Baker Academic.

Karsawin, L. P. 1925. "Der Geist des russischen Christentums." In *Philosophie*. Vol. 2: Östliches *Christentum: Dokumente*. Edited by N. von Bubnoff and H. Ehrenberg. 307–377. München: C. H. Beck.

Käsemann, E. 1964. "Ministry and Community in the New Testament." *Essays on New Testament Themes*. Translated by W. J. Montague. 63–94. London: SCM Press.

———. 1971. *Perspectives on Paul*. Translated by M. Kohl. Philadelphia, PA: Fortress Press.

Kasper, W. 1974. *Jesus der Christus*. Mainz: Grünewald.

———. 1983. *The God of Jesus Christ*. London: SCM Press (orig.: *Der Gott Jesu Christi*. Mainz: Matthias Grünewald Verlag, 1982).

Keener, C. S. 1997. *The Spirit in the Gospels and Acts: Divine Purity and Power*. Peabody, MA: Hendrickson.

Kelly, W. 1869. "Notes on the Epistle to the Romans (Chap. vii. 14–20)." *The Bible Treasury* 7: 326–327.

———. 1896. *Lectures on the Gospel of Matthew*. London: A. S. Rouse.

———. 1923. *The Epistles of Peter*. London: C. A. Hammond.

———. 1952. *An Exposition of the Acts of the Apostles*. 3rd ed. London: C. A. Hammond.

———. 1966. *An Exposition of the Gospel of John*. London: C. A. Hammond.

———. 1970. *An Exposition of the Epistles of John the Apostle*. Winschoten: H. L. Heijkoop.

———. n.d.-a. *Notes on the First Epistle to the Corinthians*. Sunbury, PA: Believers Bookshelf.

———. n.d.-b. *Lectures on the Doctrine of the Holy Spirit*. Sunbury, PA: Believers Bookshelf.

Kent, H. A., Jr. 1978. *Philippians*. EBC 11. Grand Rapids, MI:

Zondervan.

Kettler, F. H. 1986. "Trinität. III. Dogmengeschichtlich." *RGG* 6.1025-1032.

Kittel, G. et al., eds. 1964-1976. *Theological Dictionary of the New Testament*. Translated by G. W. Bromiley. 10 vols. Grand Rapids, MI: Eerdmans.

Kline, M. G. 1980. *Images of the Spirit*. Grand Rapids, MI: Baker Book House.

Knowling, R. J. 1979. *The Acts of the Apostles*. EGT 2. Grand Rapids, MI: Eerdmans.

Knox, R. A. 1950. *Enthusiasm: A Chapter in the History of Religion*. Oxford: Clarendon Press.

Koole, J. L. 1955. *De boodschap der genezing*. Kampen: J.H. Kok.

Kraan, K. J. 1970. *Ruimte voor de Geest?* Kampen: J.H. Kok.

_____. 1974. *"Opdat u genezing ontvangt": Handboek voor de dienst der genezing*. 3rd ed. Hoornaar: Gideon.

_____. 1978. "Kerk en pinkstergemeenten over de doop." In *Op het spoor van de Geest: Theologische opstellen. Vragen aan en kanttekeningen bij de charismatische beweging*, edited by J. Veenhof et al. 54-76. Kampen: J.H. Kok.

_____. 1983-1984. *Genezing en bevrijding*. 2 vols. Kampen: J.H. Kok.

Kroeze, J. H. 1962. *Strijd bij de schepping*. Exegetica III/6. Den Haag: Van Keulen.

Krusche, W. 1957. *Das Wirken des Heiligen Geistes nach Calvin*. Göttingen: Vandenhoeck and Ruprecht.

Kuyper, A. 1893. *E Voto Dordraceno: Toelichting on den Heidelbergschen Catechismus*. 3rd ed. Vol. 2. Kampen: J.H. Kok.

_____. 1899. *Calvinism: Six Stone Lectures*. Chicago, IL: Fleming H. Revell Company. Available at https://www.ccel.org/ccel/kuyper/lecture.html.

_____. 1900. *The Work of the Holy Spirit*. 3 vols. New York: Funk and Wagnalls. Available at http://www.ccel.org/ccel/kuyper/holy_spirit.html.

———. 1910. *Dictaten Dogmatiek.* Vol. 2: *Locus de Sacra Scriptura, Creatione, Creaturis.* Kampen: J.H. Kok.

———. 1918. *To Be Near Unto God.* Trans. by J. H. de Vries. Grand Rapids, MI: Eerdmans-Sevensma Company. Available at https://www.ccel.org/ccel/kuyper/near.

———. 2008. *Encyclopedia of Sacred Theology: Its Principles.* Translated by J. H. De Vries. Edited by B. C. Richards. Vol. 1, 1–53, and Vol. 2 of the original. Available at www.reformingscience.com.

———. 2016. *Pro Rege: Living Under Christ's Kingship.* Vol. 1: *The Exalted Nature of Christ's Kingship.* Edited by John Kok and Nelson D. Kloosterman. Translated by Albert Gootjes. Abraham Kuyper Collected Works in Public Theology. Acton Institute for the Study of Religion and Liberty / Lexham Press.

Lacoue-Labarthe, P. and Nancy, J.-L., eds. 1981. *Les fins de l'homme: A partir du travail de Jacques Derrida* (Colloque de Cerisy). Paris: Galilée.

Ladd, G. E. 1975. *A Theology of the New Testament.* Grand Rapids, MI: Eerdmans.

Lalleman, P. J. 2005. *1, 2 en 3 Johannes: Brieven van een kroongetuige.* Commentaar op het Nieuwe Testament, Derde serie. Kampen: J.H. Kok.

Lampe, G. W. H. 1951. *The Seal of the Spirit: A Study in the Doctrine of Baptism and Confirmation in the New Testament and the Fathers.* London: Longmans, Green and Company.

———. 1969. *St. Luke and the Church of Jerusalem.* London: Athlone.

———. 1977. *God as Spirit.* Oxford: Clarendon Press.

Lane, W. L. (1974) 1979. *The Gospel of Mark.* NICNT. Grand Rapids, MI: Eerdmans.

Lang, A. 1900. *Der Evangelienkommentar Martin Butzers und die Grundzüge seiner Theologie.* Leipzig: Dietrich.

Laurentin, R. 1977. *Catholic Pentecostalism.* London: Darton,

Longman and Todd.
Legrand, F. 1994. *Het teken van de talen.* Vaassen: Medema.
Lewis, C. S. 1956. *The Last Battle.* Harmondsworth: Puffin Books.
Liefeld, W. L. 1984. *Luke.* EBC 8. Grand Rapids, MI: Zondervan.
Lloyd-Jones, D. M. 1997. *God the Holy Spirit.* Vol. 2: Great Doctrines of the Bible. Wheaton, IL: Crossway Books.
Longenecker, R. N. 1981. *The Acts of the Apostles.* EBC 9. Grand Rapids, MI: Zondervan.
Lossky, V. 1985. *In the Image and Likeness of God* (J. H. Erickson and T.E. Bird, eds.). Crestwood, NY: St. Vladimir's Seminary Press.
Luther, M. 1938. *Luthers Evangelien-Auslegung.* Vol. 1: *Die Weihnachts- und Vorgeschichten bei Matthäus und Lukas.* Göttingen: Vandenhoeck and Ruprecht.
Lyotard, J.-F. 1979. *La condition postmoderne: Rapport sur le savoir.* Paris: Minuit.
_____. 1983. *Le Différend.* Paris: Minuit.
MacArthur, J. F., Jr. 1992. *Charismatic Chaos.* Grand Rapids, MI: Zondervan.
Macdonald, J. 1964. *The Theology of the Samaritans.* London: SCM.
McDonnell, K. 1996. *The Baptism of Jesus in the Jordan: The Trinitarian and Cosmic Order of Salvation.* Collegeville, MN: Liturgical Press.
McGrath, A. 1992. *Bridge-building: Effective Christian Apologetics.* Leicester: Inter-Varsity Press.
_____. 1996. *A Passion for Truth.* Leicester: Apollos.
_____. 2017. *Christian Theology: An Introduction.* 6th ed. Sussex, UK: John Wiley & Sons Ltd.
Mackintosh, C. H. n.d. *Notes on the Book of Leviticus.* CreateSpace Independent Publishing Platform.

Mallet, M. L., ed. 1993. *Le passage des frontiers: Autour du travail de Jacques Derrida*. Colloque de Cerisy. Paris: Galilée.

Mallone, G. 1983. *Those Controversial Gifts*. Downers Grove, IL: InterVarsity Press.

Mare, W. H. 1976. *1 Corinthians*. EBC 10. Grand Rapids, MI: Zondervan.

Maris, J. W. 1992. *Geloof en ervaring: Van Wesley tot de pinksterbeweging*. Leiden: J.J. Groen and Zoon.

Marshall, I. H. 1970. *Luke: Historian and Theologian*. Grand Rapids, MI: Zondervan.

———. 1978. *The Epistles of John*. NICNT. Grand Rapids, MI: Eerdmans.

Martin, R. P. 1984. *The Spirit and the Congregation: Studies in 1 Corinthians 12–15*. Grand Rapids, MI: Eerdmans.

Mauerhofer, E. 1980. *Der Kampf zwischen Fleisch und Geist bei Paulus*. Frutigen: Trachsel Verlag.

Medema, H. P. 1989. *Geestelijke rijkdom: Bijbelstudies over de eerste brief van Paulus aan de Korinthiërs*. Vaassen: Medema.

———. 1993. *Het leven is geopenbaard: Bijbelstudies bij de Eerste Brief van Johannes*. Vaassen: Medema.

Meijering, E. 2002. *God Christus Heilige Geest: Achtergrond en bedoeling van de leer van de drieëenheid*. Amsterdam: Balans.

Menzies, W. W. and R. P. Menzies. 2005. *Geest en kracht: De theologie van de pinksterbeweging*. Urecht: Sjofar.

Metzger, B. M. 1975. *A Textual Commentary on the Greek New Testament*. 2nd ed. New York: United Bible Societies.

Meyer, F. B. n.d. *Love to the Utmost: Expositions of John XIII-XXI*. London: Morgan and Scott.

Meyer, M. 1983. "Das 'Mutter-Amt des Heiligen Geistes' in der Theologie Zinzendorfs." *Evangelische Theologie* 43: 415–430.

Mills, W. E., ed. 1986. *Speaking in Tongues: A Guide to Research on Glossolalia*. Grand Rapids, MI: Eerdmans.

Moffatt, J. 1979. *The First and Second Epistles to the Thessalo-*

nians. EGT 4. Grand Rapids, MI: Eerdmans.

Molenaar, D. G. 1963. *De doop met de Heilige Geest.* Kampen: J.H. Kok.

Moltmann, J. 1992. *The Spirit of Life: A Universal Affirmation.* Minneapolis: Fortress Press.

Moo, D. J. 1996. *The Epistle to the Romans.* NICNT. Grand Rapids, MI: Eerdmans.

Morris, L. 1959. *The First and Second Epistles to the Thessalonians.* NICNT. Grand Rapids, MI: Eerdmans.

_____. 1971. *The Gospel According to John.* NICNT. Grand Rapids, MI: Eerdmans.

Moule, H. C. G. 1893. *The Epistle of St. Paul to the Romans.* London: Hodder and Stoughton.

Mounce, R. H. 1977. *The Book of Revelation.* NICNT. Grand Rapids, MI: Eerdmans.

Mueller-Fahrenholz, G. 1995. *God's Spirit: Transforming a World in Crisis.* New York: Continuum.

Mühlen, H. 1969. *Der Heilige Geist als Person: In der Trinität bei der Inkarnation und im Gnadenbund: Ich-Du-Wir.* 3rd ed. Münster: Verlag Aschendorff.

_____. 1974. *Die Erneuerung des christlichen Glaubens: Charisma – Geist – Befreiung.* München: Don-Bosco-Verlag.

Müller, J. J. 1984. *The Epistle of Paul to the Philippians.* NICNT. Grand Rapids, MI: Eerdmans.

Murray, A. 1888. *The Spirit of Christ: Thoughts on the Indwelling of the Holy Spirit in the Believer and in the Church.* New York: Anson D. F. Randolph and Company.

Murray, J. 1968. *The Epistle to the Romans.* NICNT. Grand Rapids, MI: Eerdmans.

Nathan, R. and K. Wilson. 1995. *Empowered Evangelicals: Bringing Together the Best of the Evangelical and Charismatic Worlds.* Ann Arbor, MI: Vine Books (Servant Publications).

Neumann, E. 1955. *The Great Mother: An Analysis of the Archetype.* New York: Pantheon.

Newbigin, L. 1954. *The Household of God: Lectures on the Nature of the Church.* New York: Friendship Press.

Neve, L. 1972. *The Spirit of God in the Old Testament.* Tokyo: Seibunsha.

Noordmans, O. 1949. *Het koninkrijk der hemelen: Toelichting op de zondagen 7–22 van den Heidelbergsen Catechismus.* Nijkerk: G. F. Callenbach.

_____. 1955. *Gestalte en Geest.* Amsterdam: Holland.

Noordtzij, A. 1957. *De boeken der Kronieken.* Vol. 2. Kampen: J.H. Kok.

Nuttall, G. F. 1992. *The Holy Spirit in Puritan Faith and Experience.* Chicago: University of Chicago Press.

Odeberg, H. 1929. *The Fourth Gospel.* Uppsala: Almquist and Wicksell.

Oeming, M. 1998. *Biblische Hermeneutik: Eine Einführung.* Darmstadt: Wissenschaftliche Buchgesellschaft.

Oesterley, W. E. 1979. *The General Epistle of James.* EGN 4. Grand Rapids, MI: Eerdmans.

Oswalt, J. N. 1986. *The Book of Isaiah Chapters 1–39.* NICOT. Grand Rapids, MI: Eerdmans.

Ouweneel, W. J. 1978. *Het domein van de slang: Christelijk handboek over occultisme en mysticisme.* Amsterdam: Buijten and Schipperheijn.

_____. 1981. *Glaube und Werke: Eine Auslegung des Jakobusbriefes.* Schwelm: Heijkoop-Verlag.

_____. 1982. *"Wij zien Jezus": Bijbelstudies over de brief aan de Hebreeën.* 2 vols. Vaassen: Medema.

_____. 1984. *Psychologie: Een christelijke kijk op het mentale leven.* Amsterdam: Buijten and Schipperheijn.

_____. 1986. *De leer van de mens.* Amsterdam: Buijten and Schipperheijn.

_____. 1988/90. *De Openbaring van Jezus Christus: Bijbelstudies over het boek Openbaring.* 2 vols. Vaassen: Medema.

_____. 1994. *Godsverlichting: De evocatie van de verduisterde*

God: Een weg tot spiritualiteit en gemeenteopbouw. Amsterdam: Buijten and Schipperheijn.

———. 1997. *De vrijheid van de Geest: Bijbelstudies bij de Brief van Paulus aan de Galaten*. Vaassen: Medema.

———. 1998. *De zevende koningin: Het eeuwig vrouwelijke en de raad van God*. Metahistorische triologie. Vol. 2. Heerenveen: Barnabas.

———. 1999a. *Heiliging*. Vol. 5 of Geloofsleven series. Vaassen: Medema.

———. 2000a. *Het Jobslijden van Israël: Israëls lijden oplichtend uit het boek Job*. Vaassen: Medema.

———. 2000b. *De zesde kanteling: Christus en 5000 jaar denkgeschiedenis: Religie en metafysica in het jaar 2000*. Metahistorische trilogie. Vol. 3. Heerenveen: Barnabas.

———. 2001a. *"Hoe lief heb ik uw wet!": De Eeuwige Torah tussen Oude en Nieuwe Verbond*. Vaassen: Medema.

———. 2001b. *Hoogtijden voor Hem: De bijbelse feesten en hun betekenis voor Joden en christenen*. Vaassen: Medema.

———. 2004. *Meer Geest in de gemeenten*. Vaassen: Medema.

———. (2003) 2005a. *Geneest de zieken!: Over de bijbelse leer van ziekte, genezing en bevrijding*. 4th ed. Vaassen: Medema.

———. 2005b. *Sta op, laat je dopen*. Vaassen: Medema.

———. 2006a. *Seks in de kerk*. Vaassen: Medema.

———. 2007a. *De Geest van God*. EDR 1. Vaassen: Medema.

———. 2007b. *De Christus van God: Ontwerp van een christologie*. EDR 2. Vaassen: Medema.

———. 2008. *De schepping van God: Ontwerp van een scheppings-, mens- en zondeleer*. EDR 3. Vaassen: Medema.

———. 2009a. *Het zoenoffer van God: Ontwerp van een verzoeningsleer*. EDR 5. Heerenveen: Medema.

———. 2009b. *Het heil van God: Ontwerp van een soteriologie*. EDR 6. Heerenveen: Medema.

———. 2010a. *De kerk van God I: Ontwerp van een elementaire ecclesiologie*. EDR 7. Heerenveen: Medema.

———. 2010b. *De kerk van God II: Ontwerp van een historische en praktische ecclesiologie*. EDR 8. Heerenveen: Medema.

———. 2012a. *De toekomst van God: Ontwerp van een eschatologie*. EDR 10. Heerenveen: Medema.

———. 2012b. *Het Woord van God: Ontwerp van een openbarings- en schriftleer*. EDR 9. Heerenveen: Medema

———. 2013. *De glorie van God: Ontwerp van een godsleer en van een theologische vakfilosofie*. EDR 1. Heerenveen: Medema.

———. 2014. *Wisdom for Thinkers: An Introduction to Christian Philosophy*. Edited by N. D. Kloosterman. St. Catharines, ON: Paideia Press.

———. 2015. *What Then Is Theology? An Introduction to Christian Theology*. Edited by N. D. Kloosterman. St. Catharines, ON: Paideia Press.

———. 2016. *Searching the Soul: An Introduction to Christian Psychology*. Edited by N. D. Kloosterman. St. Catharines: Paideia Press.

———. 2017a. *The World Is Christ's: A Critique of Two Kingdoms Theology*. Edited by N. D. Kloosterman. Toronto, ON: Ezra Press.

———. 2017b. *The Eternal Torah: An Evangelical Theology of Living Under God*. Edited by N. D. Kloosterman. Vol. I/2 of *An Evangelical Introduction to Reformational Theology*. St. Catharines, ON: Paideia Press.

———. Forthcoming. *An Evangelical Introduction to Reformational Theology*. Edited by N. D. Kloosterman. 13 vols. Jordan Station, ON: Paideia Press.

———. 2017f (forthcoming). *The Ninth King: The Last of the Celestial Empires: The Triumph of Christ over the Powers*. Edited by N. D. Kloosterman. Jordan Station, ON: Paideia Press.

Owen, J. (1680) 2012. *John Owen on the Holy Spirit: Pneumatologia*. Waymark Books.

Pannenberg, W. 1991. *Systematic Theology*. Translated by G. W. Bromiley. 3 vols. Grand Rapids, MI: Eerdmans.

Parmentier, M. 1992. *Rusten in de Geest: God houdt ons de spiegel voor*. Hilversum: Stg. 'Vuur'.

———. 1997. *Heil maakt heel: De bediening tot genezing*, Zoetermeer: Meinema.

Patterson, R. D. 1985. *Joel*. EBC 7. Grand Rapids, MI: Zondervan.

——— and H. J. Austel. 1988. *1,2 Kings*. EBC 4. Grand Rapids, MI: Zondervan.

Paul, M. J. 1997. *Vergeving en genezing: Ziekenzalving in de christelijke gemeente*. Zoetermeer: Boekencentrum.

———, ed. 2002. *Geestelijke strijd: Demonie en bevrijding in christelijk perspectief*. Zoetermeer: Boekencentrum.

———. n.d. *Handoplegging en ziekenzalving: Vijf bijbelstudies*, Amersfoort: IZB.

Pew Forum on Religion and Public Life. 2011. *Global Christianity: A Report on the Size and Distribution of the World's Christian Population*. Washington, DC: Pew Research Center.

Phypers, D. B. D. 1973. *Spiritual Gifts and the Church*. London: InterVarsity Press.

Pierson, A. T. (1913) 1996. *The Acts of the Holy Spirit*. Camp Hill, PA: Christian Publications.

Pink, A. W. 1970. *The Holy Spirit*. Grand Rapids, MI: Baker Book House.

Pinnock, C. 1996. *Flame of Love: A Theology of the Holy Spirit*. Downers Grove, IL: InterVarsity Press.

Plummer. A. 1894. *The Epistles of St John*. Cambridge Greek Testament for Schools and Colleges. Cambridge: Cambridge University Press.

Prenter, R. 1954. *Spiritus Creator: Studien zu Luthers Theologie*. München: Chr. Kaiser.

Price, D. 1997. *Is Anyone of You Sick? What Should Happen When a Christian is Ill?* Fearn: Christian Focus Publications.

Prince, D. 1995. *De pijlers van het christelijk geloof.* Beverwijk: Derek Prince Ministries.

Puchinger, G. 1970. *Een theologische discussie.* Kampen: J.H. Kok.

Putnam, H. 1990. *Realism with a Human Face.* Cambridge, MA: Harvard University Press.

Quispel, G. 1979. *The Secret Book of Revelation: The Last Book of the Bible.* New York: McGraw-Hill.

Rahner, K. 1966. "Löscht den Geist nicht aus!" *Schriften zur Theologie.* Vol. 7. 77–90. Zürich: Benziger.

———. 1978. *Foundations of Christian Faith: An Introduction to the Idea of Christianity.* New York: Seabury Press.

Ratzinger, J. 1968. *Introduction to Christianity.* 2nd ed. San Francisco, CA: Ignatius Press.

———. 1998. "The Holy Spirit as *Communio:* Concerning the Relationship of Pneumatology and Spirituality in Augustine." *Communio* 25.2: 324–339.

Regan, P. 1977. "Pneumatological and Eschatological Aspects of Liturgical Celebration." *Worship* 51.7 (1977) 4: 332–350.

Reinmuth, E. 1985. *Geist und Gesetz: Studien zu Voraussetzungen und Inhalt der paulinischen Paränese.* Berlin: Evangelische Verlagsanstalt.

Rendall, F. 1979. *The Epistle to the Galatians.* EGT 3. Grand Rapids, MI: Eerdmans.

Ridderbos, H. N. 1959. *Aan de Romeinen.* CNT. Kampen: J.H. Kok.

———. 1960. *Aan de Kolossenzen.* CNT. Kampen: J.H. Kok.

———. 1975. *Paul: An Outline of His Theology.* Translated by J. R. De Witt. Grand Rapids, MI: Eerdmans.

———. 1967. *De pastorale brieven.* CNT. Kampen: J.H. Kok.

———. 1984. *The Epistle of Paul to the Churches of Galatia.* NICNT. Grand Rapids, MI: Eerdmans.

Ridderbos, J. 1935. *De kleine profeten*. Vol. 3: *Haggaï, Zacharia, Maleachi*. KV. Kampen: J.H. Kok.

———. 1958. *De Psalmen*. Vol. 2: *Psalm 42–106*. COT. Kampen: J.H. Kok.

———. 1984. *Deuteronomy*. Translated by E. M. van der Maas. Bible Student's Commentary. Grand Rapids, MI: Zondervan.

Roberts, A. and J. Donaldson, eds. 1995. *Ante-Nicene Christian Library: Translations of the Writings of the Fathers Down to A.D. 325*. Vol. 2: *The Apostolic Fathers*. Peabody, MA: Hendrickson.

Ross, A. P. 1991. *Ecclesiastes*. EBC 5. Grand Rapids, MI: Zondervan.

Runia, K. 2000. *Op zoek naar de Geest*. Kampen: Kok.

Ryle, J. C. 1993. *Expository Thoughts on the Gospels: Mark*. Wheaton, IL: Crossway Books.

Sailhamer, J. H. 1990. *Genesis*. EBC 2. Grand Rapids, MI: Zondervan.

Salmond, S. D. F. 1979. *The Epistle of Paul to the Ephesians*. EGT 3. Grand Rapids, MI: Eerdmans.

Sanders, J. O. 1973. *By the Power of the Holy Spirit*. Downers Grove, IL: InterVarsity Press.

Sanford, A. 1966. *Healing Gifts of the Spirit*. Evesham: Arthur James.

Scheepers, J. H. 1960. *Die Gees van God en die gees van die mens in die Ou Testament*. Kampen: J.H. Kok.

Schep, J. A. 1972. *Baptism in the Spirit According to Scripture*. 3rd ed. Plainfield, NJ: Logos.

Schilder, K. n.d. *Dictaat Encyclopaedie*. Vol. 5. Kampen: Van den Berg.

Schipflinger, Th. 1988. *Sophia-Maria: Eine ganzheitliche Vision der Schöpfung*. München/Zürich: Verlag Neue Stadt.

Schlink, E. 1983. *Oekumenische Dogmatik: Grundzüge*. Göttingen: Vandenhoeck and Ruprecht.

———. 1986. "Trinität. IV. Dogmatisch." In *RGG* 6.1032–1038.
Schmidt, M. A. 1986. "Geist. V. Heiliger Geist, dogmengeschichtlicht." *RGG* 2.1279–1283.
Schmidt-Clausing, F. 1965. *Zwingli*. Berlin: W. de Gruyter.
Schneemelcher, W. 1972. "*Huios, huiothesia*." *TDNT* 8.392–397.
Scholem, G. 1977. *Von der mystischen Gestalt der Gottheit: Studien zu Grundbegriffen der Kabbala*. Frankfurt: Suhrkamp.
Schult, A. 1986. *Maria-Sophia: Das Ewig-Weibliche in Gott, Mensch und Kosmos*. Bietigheim: Turm Verlag.
Schulz, S. 1971. "*Skia, aposkiasma, episkiazō*." *TDNT* 7.394–400.
Schweizer, E. 1968. "*Pneuma, pneumatikos*." *TDNT* 6.389–455.
Sellin, E. 1930. *Das Zwölfprophetenbuch: Nahum–Maleachi*. Leipzig: A. Deichert.
Sheldrake, R. 1981. *A New Science of Life: The Hypothesis of Formative Causation*. London: Icon Books.
——— and M. Fox. 2014. *The Physics of Angels: Exploring the Realm Where Science and Spirit Meet*. Rhinebeck, NY: Monkfish Book Publishing.
Shulam, J. (with H. Le Cornu). 1998. *A Commentary on the Jewish Roots of Romans*. Baltimore: Messianic Jewish Publishers.
Sinclair, U. 1971. *Mental Radio*. New York: Collier-Macmillan.
Sirks, G. J. 1957. "The Cinderella of Theology: The Doctrine of the Holy Spirit." *Harvard Theological Review* 50: 77–89.
Sjöberg, E. 1968. "*Pneuma, pneumatikos*." *TDNT* 6.375–89.
Slotki, I. W. 1983. *Isaiah*. SBB. London: Soncino Press.
Smail, T. A. n.d. *De glorie van God: Het werk van de Heilige Geest*. Kampen: J.H. Kok.
———, A. Walker and N. T. Wright. 1993. *Charismatic Renewal: The Search for a Theology*. London: SPCK.
Smeaton, G. 2010. *The Doctrine of the Holy Spirit*. Whitefish, MT: Kessinger Publishing.
Smick, E. B. 1988. *Job*. EBC 4. Grand Rapids, MI: Zondervan.

Smit, J. H. 1980. "Skeppingsopenbaring en wetenskap." *Tydskrif vir Christelike Wetenskap* 16: 174–200.

Smith, D. 1979. *The Epistles of John*. EGT 5. Grand Rapids, MI: Zondervan.

Smith, J. B. 1961. *A Revelation of Jesus Christ: A Commentary on the Book of Revelation*. Scottsdale, PA: Herald Press.

Smith, J. K. A. 2006. *Who's Afraid of Postmodernism? Taking Derrida, Lyotard, and Foucault to Church*. Grand Rapids, MI: Baker Academic.

Soltau, G. n.d. *The Person and Mission of the Holy Spirit*. Kilmarnock: John Ritchie.

Spitta, F. 1890. *Christi Predigt an die Geister (1. Petr. 3:19ff): Ein Beitrag zur neutestamentlichen Theologie*. Göttingen: Vandenhoeck and Ruprecht.

Spykman, G. J. 1988. "Christian Philosophy as Prolegomena to Reformed Dogmatics." In *'n Woord op sy tyd: 'n Teologiese feesbundel aangebied aan Professor Johan Heyns ter herdenking van sy sestigste verjaarsdag*. Edited by C. J. Wethman and C. J. A. Vos. 137–55. Pretoria: NG Kerkboekhandel.

_____. 1992. *Reformational Theology: A New Paradigm for Doing Dogmatics*. Grand Rapids, MI: Eerdmans.

Stafleu, M. D. 1987. *Theories At Work: On the Structure and Functioning of Theories in Science, in Particular During the Copernican Revolution*. Lanham: University Press of America.

Stephens, W. P. 1970. *The Holy Spirit in the Theology of Martin Bucer*. Cambridge: Cambridge University Press.

Stern, D. H. 1992. *Jewish New Testament Commentary*. Clarksville: Jewish New Testament Publications.

Stott, J. 2006. *Baptism and Fullness: The Work of the Holy Spirit Today*. 3rd ed. IVP Classics. Downers Grove, IL: IVP.

Stronstad, R. 1984. *The Charismatic Theology of S. Luke*. Peabody, MA: Hendrickson.

Suenens, L. J. 2001. *De Heilige Geest, levensadem van de Kerk*. 3 vols. Oppem-Meise: FIAT-Vereniging.

Suurmond, J.-J. 1986. "De pneumatologie van Karl Barth." *Bulletin voor Charismatische Theologie* 18 (Christus Koning): 42–53.

———. 1995. *Word and Spirit at Play: Towards a Charismatic Theology*. Translated by J. Bowdon. Grand Rapids, MI: Eerdmans.

Tabbernee, W. 1997. *Montanist Inscriptions and Testimonia: Epigraphic Sources Illustrating the History of Montanism*. Patristic Monograph Series 16. Macon, GA: Mercer University Press.

Tan, P. 1995. *De zalving van de Heilige Geest*. Roermond: Dynamis Publ.

Taylor, J. V. 1972. *The Go-Between God: The Holy Spirit and the Christian Mission*. London: SCM.

Teilhard de Chardin, P. 1999. *Writings*. Modern Spiritual Masters Series. Maryknoll, NY: Orbis Books.

Tenney, M. C. 1981. *The Gospel of John*. EBC 9. Grand Rapids, MI: Zondervan.

———. 1985. *Interpreting Revelation*. Grand Rapids, MI: Eerdmans.

Theron, J. P. 1969. *Gebed en genesing in die pastorale sorg*. Pretoria: diss. Universiteit van Pretoria.

Thigpar, P., ed. 1997. *Celebrate 2000! Reflections on the Holy Spirit*. Ann Arbor, MI: Servant Publ.

Thiselton, A. C. 1992. *New Horizons in Hermeneutics: The Theory and Practice of Transforming Biblical Reading*. Grand Rapids, MI: Zondervan.

———. 1995. *Interpreting God and the Postmodern Self: On Meaning, Manipulation and Promise*. Grand Rapids, MI: Eerdmans.

———. 2015. *Systematic Theology*. Grand Rapids, MI: Eerdmans.

Tholens, C. J. A. 1987. *In de spiegel van de stilte: Meditaties rondom de schepping*. Delft: Meinema.

Thomas, R. L. 1978. *1,2 Thessalonians*. EBC 11. Grand Rapids, MI: Zondervan.

Tiessen, L. 1996. *De werkelijkheid van Maria: Geschiedenis en mysterie*. Aalsmeer: Dabar-Luyten.

Tillich, P. 1968. *Systematic Theology*. 3 vols. Digswell Place: Nisbett and Company.

Torrey, R. A. 1910. *The Person and Work of the Holy Spirit as Revealed in the Scriptures and in Personal Experience*. New York: Fleming H. Revell Company.

Troost, A. 1969. "De openbaring Gods en de maatschappelijke orde." *Philosophia Reformata* 34 (1969): 1–37.

_____. 1976. *Geen aardse macht begeren wij*. Amsterdam: Buijten and Schipperheijn.

_____. 1978. "De relatie tussen scheppingsopenbaring en woordopenbaring." *Philosophia Reformata* 43 (1978): 101–129.

_____. 1982–1983. "Theologische misverstanden inzake een reformatorische wijsbegeerte." *Philosophia Reformata* 47 (1982): 1–19, 179–92; 48 (1983): 19–49.

_____. 2005. *Antropocentrische totaliteitswetenschap: Inleiding in de reformatorische wijsbegeerte*. Budel: Damon.

Troost, Ph. 2006. *Christus ontvangen: Gereformeerd en charismatisch: Leren van elkaar*. Kampen: J.H. Kok.

Underhill, E. 2011. *Mysticism*. CreateSpace Independent Publishing Platform.

Unger, M. F. 1944. "The Baptism with the Holy Spirit." *Bibliotheca Sacra* 101.404: 483–499.

Van Bruggen, J. 1984. *Ambten in de apostolische kerk: Een exegetisch mozaïek*. Kampen: J.H. Kok.

Van de Beek, A. 1987. *De adem van God: De Heilige Geest in kerk en kosmos*. Nijkerk: G. F. Callenbach.

Van der Kooi, A. 1992. *Het heilige en de Heilige Geest bij Noordmans: Een schets van zijn pneumatologisch ontwerp.* Kampen: J.H. Kok.

Van der Kooi, C. 2003. *In de school van de Geest.* Gorinchem: Ekklesia.

———. 2018. *This Incredible Benevolent Force: The Holy Spirit in Reformed Theology and Spirituality.* Grand Rapids, MI: Eerdmans.

Van der Laan, C. 1989. *De Spade Regen: geboorte en groei van de pinksterbeweging In Nederland 1907–1930.* Kampen: J.H. Kok.

Van der Linde, S. 1943. *De leer van den Heiligen Geest bij Calvijn: Bijdrage tot de kennis der reformatorische theologie.* Wageningen: H. Veenman and Zonen.

Van Genderen, J. 1958. "Heilige Geest." In *Christelijke Encyclopedie.* Kampen: J.H. Kok. 3.403–408.

Van Genderen, J. and W. H. Velema. 2008. *Concise Reformed Dogmatics.* Translated by G. Bilkes and E. M. van der Maas. Phillipsburg, NJ: Presbyterian and Reformed Publishing Company.

Vanhoozer, K. J. 1998. *Is There a Meaning in This Text?* Grand Rapids, MI: Zondervan.

Van Leeuwen, P. C. 1989. *Inleiding tot de dienst der genezing.* Den Haag: Boekencentrum.

Van Niftrik, G. C. 1961. *Kleine dogmatiek.* Nijkerk: Callenbach.

Van Ruler, A. A. 1969. "Structuurverschillen tussen het christologische en het pneumatologische gezichtspunt." *Theologisch Werk.* Vol. 1. 175–190. Nijkerk: Callenbach.

———. 1973. "Hoofdlijnen van de pneumatologie." *Theologisch Werk.* Vol. 6. 9–40. Nijkerk: Callenbach.

Van 't Spijker, W. 1970. *De ambten bij Martin Bucer.* Kampen: J.H. Kok.

———. 1991. *De verzegeling met de Heilige Geest: Over verzegeling en zekerheid van het geloof.* Kampen: De Groot Goudriaan.

Van Veldhuizen, A. 1922. *Paulus' brieven aan de Korinthiërs. Tekst en uitleg.* Groningen: J. B. Wolters.

Veenhof, J. 1978. "Pontifex maximus." In *Op het spoor van de Geest: Theologische opstellen. Vragen aan en kanttekeningen bij de charismatische beweging.* Edited by J. Veenhof et al. 4–15. Kampen: J.H. Kok.

_____. 1992. "Geschiedenis van theologie en spiritualiteit in de gereformeerde kerken." In *100 jaar theologie: Aspecten van een eeuw theologie in de Gereformeerde Kerken in Nederland (1892–1992).* Edited by M. E. Brinkman. 14–95. Kampen: J.H. Kok.

_____, J. P. Versteeg, G. P. Hartveld, K. J. Kraan, and J. Firet. 1978. *Op het spoor van de Geest: Theologische opstellen. Vragen aan en kanttekeningen bij de charismatische beweging.* Kampen: J.H. Kok.

Velema, W. H. 1957. *De leer van de Heilige Geest bij Abraham Kuyper.* 's-Gravenhage: Van Keulen.

Vellenga, G. Y. and A. J. Kret. 1957. *Stromen van kracht: De nieuwe opwekkingsbeweging.* Kampen: J.H. Kok.

Verhoef, W. W. 1974. *Er waait weer wat: De charismatische beweging.* 's-Gravenhage: Boekencentrum.

_____. 1977. "Over de charismatische vernieuwing van de kerk." In *Charismatisch Nederland: Overzicht van de ontwikkeling van de Pinkstervernieuwing.* Edited by F. Rutke. 9–26. Serie Nieuw Leven. Kampen: J.H. Kok.

Verkuil, J. 1992. *De kern van het christelijk geloof.* Kampen: J.H. Kok.

Versteeg, J. P. 1973. *De Heilige Geest en het gebed.* Kampen: J.H. Kok.

_____. 1976. *De Geest en de gelovige: De verhouding van het werk van de Geest en het werk van de gelovigen volgens het Nieuwe Testament.* Kampen: J.H. Kok.

———. 1978. "Christus en de Geest: Enkele exegetische opmerkingen." In *Op het spoor van de Geest: Theologische opstellen. Vragen aan en kanttekeningen bij de charismatische beweging*. Edited by J. Veenhof et al. 16–30. Kampen: J.H. Kok.

———. 1979. "Het ontvangen van de Heilige Geest in Samaria (Hand. 8:14–17)." In *Uw knecht hoort*. Edited by J. Kruis et al. Amsterdam: Bolland.

———. 1980. *Christus en de Geest: Een exegetisch onderzoek naar de verhouding van de opgestane Christus en de Geest van God volgens de brieven van Paulus*. 2nd ed. Kampen: J.H. Kok.

———. 1984. *De Geest schrijft wegen in de tijd: Opstellen over samenleven in kerk en wereld*. Kampen: J.H. Kok.

Vine, W. E. 1985. *1 Corinthians. The Collected Writings of W.E. Vine*. Vol. 2. Glasgow: Gospel Tract Publications.

Volf, M. 1991. *Work in the Spirit: Toward a Theology of Work*. New York: Oxford University Press.

Von Balthasar, H. U. 1993. *Explorations in Theology*. Translated by A. V. Littledale with A. Dru. Vol. 3: *Creator Spirit*. 2nd edition. San Francisco: Ignatius Press.

———. 2005. *Theo-logic: Theological Logical Theory*. Translated by A. J. Walker. Vol. 3: *The Spirit of Truth*. San Francisco, CA: Ignatius Press.

Vonk, C. 1977. *I en II Koningen*. Vol. Ig of *De Voorzeide Leer*. Barendrecht: Wesdijk, Liebeek en Hooijmeijer.

Vranckx, J. n.d. *De terugkeer van het wonder: Het bovennatuurlijke op het einde van de eeuw*. Leuven: Davidsfonds/Kampen: J.H. Kok.

Wagner, C. P. 1988a. "Church Growth." In *Dictionary of Pentecostal and Charismatic Movements*. Edited by S. M. Burgess and G. B. McGee. 181–95. Grand Rapids, MI: Zondervan.

———. 1988b. *The Third Wave of the Holy Spirit*. Ann Arbor: Vine Publications.

———. 1988c. *How to Have a Healing Ministry Without Making*

Your Church Sick. Eastbourne: Monarch.

———. 2000. *Acts of the Holy Spirit*. Ventura, CA: Gospel Light.

Walker, E. H. 2000. *The Physics of Consciousness: The Quantum Mind and the Meaning of Life*. Cambridge, MA: Perseus.

Wallace, M. I. 1996. *Fragments of the Spirit: Nature, Violence and the Renewal of Creation*. New York: Continuum.

Walvoord, J. F. 1966. *The Revelation of Jesus Christ*. Chicago: Moody Press.

———. 1991. *Major Bible Prophecies: 37 Crucial Prophecies that Affect You Today*. Grand Rapids, MI: Zondervan.

Warfield, B. B. 1953. *Counterfeit Miracles*. New York: Charles Scribner and Sons. Reprinted as *Miracles: Yesterday and Today: True and False*. Grand Rapids, MI: Baker Book House.

———. 1909. *Calvin as a Theologian and Calvinism Today: Three addresses in commemoration of the four hundredth anniversary of the birth of John Calvin*. Philadelphia: Presbyterian Board of Publication.

———. 1929. *Biblical Doctrines*. New York: Oxford University Press.

———. 1948. *The Inspiration and Authority of the Bible*. Philadelphia: Presbyterian and Reformed Publishing Company.

Watson, D. 1973. *One in the Spirit*. London: Hodder and Stoughton.

Weber, O. 1981. *Foundations of Dogmatics*. Translated by D. L. Guder. Vol. 1. Grand Rapids, MI: Eerdmans.

Weber, H. E. 1965. "Das innere Leben der altprotestantischen Orthodoxie." In *Gesammelte Aufsätze*. Edited by U. Seeger. 130–153. Theologische Bücherei 28. München: Chr. Kaiser.

Weisberger, B. A. 1958. *They Gathered at the River*. Boston: Little, Brown and Company.

Welker, M. 1992. *Gottes Geist: Theologie des Heiligen Geistes*. Neukirchen-Vluyn: Neukirchener Verlag.

Wentsel, B. 1981. *Dogmatiek*. Vol. 1: *Het Woord, de Zoon en de dienst*. Kampen: J.H. Kok.

_____. 1987. *Dogmatiek.* Vol. 3a: *God en mens verzoend: Godsleer, mensleer en zondeleer.* Kampen: J.H. Kok.

Westermann, C. 1974. *Genesis, 1: Genesis 1–11.* Neukirchen-Vluyn: Neukirchener Verlag des Erziehungsvereins.

Westcott, B. F. (1883) 1966. *The Epistles of St John: The Greek Text with Notes.* Edited by F. F. Bruce. Grand Rapids, MI: Eerdmans.

Westphal, M. 1993. *Suspicion and Faith: The Religious Uses of Modern Atheism.* Grand Rapids, MI: Eerdmans.

White, N. J. D. 1979. *The Epistle to Titus.* EGT 4. Grand Rapids, MI: Eerdmans.

Wielenga, B. n.d. *Het wezen van het christendom.* Kampen: J.H. Kok.

Williams, J. R. 1977. *The Pentecostal Reality.* Plainfield, NJ: Logos International.

Wimber, J. and K. Springer. 1986. *Power Healing.* London: Hodder and Stoughton.

_____. 1991. *Kracht om te groeien.* Hoornaar: Gideon.

Witt, O. 1957, 1959. *Krankenheilung.* 2 vols. Marburg a/d Lahn: Rathman.

Wolff, H. W. 1973. *Anthropologie des Alten Testaments.* München: Chr. Kaiser.

Wolston, W. T. P. 1893. *Simon Peter: His Life and Letters.* London: J. Nisbet and Company.

_____. 1926. *Another Comforter: Thirteen Lectures on the Operations of the Holy Ghost.* 3rd edition. London: Pickering and Inglis.

Wood, A. S. 1978. *Ephesians.* EBC 11. Grand Rapids, MI: Zondervan.

Wuest, K. S. 1953. *Ephesians and Colossians.* Grand Rapids, MI: Eerdmans.

_____. 1973a. *Untranslatable Riches.* Wuest's Word Studies 3. Grand Rapids, MI: Eerdmans.

_____. 1973b. *Great Truths to Live by.* Wuest's Word Studies 3.

Grand Rapids, MI: Eerdmans.

Young, E. J. 1972. *The Book of Isaiah*. Vol. 3. Grand Rapids, MI: Eerdmans.

Zerwick, M. 1969. *The Epistle to the Ephesians*. London: Burns and Oates.

Zizioulas, J. D. 1985. *Being as Communion: Studies in Personhood and the Church*. Crestwood, NY: St. Vladimir's Seminary Press.

———. 2009. *Lectures in Christian Dogmatics*. London: T. and T. Clark.

Scripture Index

OLD TESTAMENT

Genesis

1	13, 79, 175, 179, 180, 182, 184	3:9-19	444	17:3	543
		3:15-16	188	17:7	300, 543
		3:18	147	18:10-14	574
		3:24	449	19:6	294
1:1-3	9, 178	4:23	179	20:7	155, 199, 346, 576
1:2	31, 86, 97, 99, 101, 108, 112, 134, 169, 178, 179, 180, 181, 187, 189, 218, 336	5:1	90		
		6:1-4	242	20:17	574
		6:3	86, 97, 108, 112, 134, 186, 187, 219, 242	21:1-7	574
				26:15	58
				26:18	58
		6:4	227	41:38	192, 215, 219
		6:5	186	41:38-39	116
1:26-27	75, 90	6:6	90	45:8	246
1:28	492	6:8-9	160	49:25	113, 181
1:28-30	444	7:11	181, 187		
2:1	494	8:1	134, 213	**Exodus**	
2:2-3	187	8:2	181	3:2-5	143
2:7	91, 124, 186, 228, 273, 366	8:6-11	170	3:8	176
		8:8-12	187	3:17	176
		8:9	447	4:1-4	529
2:8	204	8:21	186, 187	4:6-7	574
2:15	492	9:6	90	4:12	245
2:16-17	444	9:21	187	4:20	529
2:9-13	204	9:25	188, 397	4:22-23	169
2:28	124	10:6	284	7-17	575
3	13	11:1-9	294	7:11-12	530
3:5	75, 412	14	547	7:22	530
3:6	187	15:1	547	8:7	530
3:8	136, 166, 191	15:6	328	8:18	530
3:9	448				

8:19	174, 530	
9:3	174	
12:12	189, 449	
13:21-22	120, 146, 382	
14:15-16	565	
14:20	120	
14:21	30, 541	
14:24	146	
14:30	188	
15:1-18	178	
15:2	445	
15:3-10	449	
15:4-5	189	
15:8	30, 135, 189, 202, 541	
15:10	30, 189, 202, 541	
15:13,17	444, 445	
15:17	191, 451	
15:20	200, 507, 508, 555, 562	
15:21	200	
16:3	174	
16:8	246	
16:10	120, 146	
17:6	255	
17:9	529	
19-20	290	
19:4	112, 179, 202	
19:6	290, 331	
19:9	120	
19:11	168	
19:16	168, 290, 542	
19:18	168, 290	
20	122, 290	
20:18-22	120	
23:16	354	
24:15-18	120, 445	
24:16	120	
24:17	146	
25:2	445	
25:8	451	
25:8-9	445	
25:22	192	
25:31-36	191	
25-29	445	
28:3	110, 214	
29:7	235	
29:43-45	451	
29:45	451	
31:2-5	193	
31:3	191	
31:3-4	116	
31:13	191, 214	
31:17	191	
31:18	174, 291	
33:9-10	120	
33:11	199	
33:15-16	205	
33:21-23	147	
34:5	120	
34:6	427	
34:22	354	
34:28	511	
34:29	147	
35-40	445	
35:31	149, 191, 193, 214	
37:17-22	191	
40:29	119	
40:34	120, 122	
40:34-35	168, 190, 543	
40:34-38	120, 192, 452	
40:36-37	168	
40:38	146, 168, 190	

Leviticus

1-7	230
1:14	170
2:4	230
2:12	354
6:12-13	438
8:12	235
9:23-24	438, 452
9:24	143
11:15	170
11:44-45	436
14:14	154
14:17-18	154
15:31	450
16:2	120
17:14	138
23	255
23:10	354
23:10-14	289
23:15-16	284
23:17	354
23:20	354
24:10-23	565
25:1-7	204
26:11-12	451

Numbers

6:27	161, 525
7:89	121, 192
8:7	141, 142
9:15-22	120, 393, 394
9:15-23	168
9:17-22	382, 383
10:11-12	120, 383
10:34	120, 383
11	200
11:1	144
11:3	144
11:10-14	190
11:16-30	217
11:17	150, 151, 190, 201, 213, 235, 345
11:23	174
11:25	120, 149, 150, 151, 235, 295, 345, 508
11:25-26	190, 213
11:29	108, 190, 213, 288, 576
11:31	135, 137, 200
12:5	120
12:10-15	574
14:14	120, 383
14:18	427
15:20-21	354
15:30	249
15:32-36	565
17:8	529, 575

Scripture Index

18:13 354	26:2 354	13:25 104, 112, 194, 217, 514, 544
19:9, 11-12 142	26:10 354	
21:5-9 574	30:6 330, 341	14:6 104, 112, 194, 195, 217, 514, 544
21:16-18 255	31:9 186	
22-24 570	31:15-16 120	
24:2 194, 220, 357	32:2 140	14:19 104, 112, 194, 195, 217, 514, 544
24:4 357	32:10 179	
27:18 214, 526	32:11 112, 134, 179	
28:26 354	32:11-12 202	15:14 104, 194, 217, 514, 544
31:23 142	32:16-17 530	
33:4 449	32:17 509	15:14-19 547
	32:18 114	16:19-20 547, 548
Deuteronomy	32:46-47 210	16:28 548
1:30-31 384	33:1 201	20:26-27 511
1:31 169	33:13 181	21:21 507
1:33 120, 383	33:16 143	
2:15 174	34:9 110, 116, 152, 209, 214, 260, 525, 526	**Ruth**
5:22 120		2:12 112
8:5 169		3:9 112
8:5-6 291	34:10 199, 576	
8:7 166	40:38 143	**1 Samuel**
9:9 511		1:7 203
9:10 174, 291	**Joshua**	1:9 203
10:16 330, 341	2 218	1:12-15 162
12:10 191	4:24 174	1:24 203
12:17 354	5:14 543	2:1-10 200
12:23 138	9:14 565	3 546
13:1-5 54, 570	10:12-13 575	3:1 562
13:21 143	21:44 191	3:3 203
14:1 169		3:15 203, 562
14:14 170	**Judges**	3:20 195, 576
16:9 284	2:15 174	4:4 192
16:9-10 354	3:10 104, 108, 112, 194, 217, 544	4:11 203
16:16 286		5:6 174
18:4 354	4 218	5:9 174
18:10 530	4:4 200, 562	7:6 195, 511
18:15 198, 199, 234, 576, 577	4:9 562	7:15 195
	4:14 562	8:1 195
18:15-18 287	5 562	8:6 195
18:15-22 570	5:1 200	9:6-9 195
18:18 234, 576, 577	6:34 104, 193, 217, 544	10 197
18:18-19 198		10:5 508, 555
19:18 143	9:23 200	10:5-6 196, 508
22:6 112	11:29 104, 112, 194, 217, 544	10:5-10 543
24:17 143		10:5-11 530

643

10:6 104, 149, 194, 220, 357	22:16-17 203	532
10:9-10 196	23:1-2 155, 202, 208, 217, 235	18:17 279
10:10 194, 220, 357	23:1-3 327	18:20-46 571
10:10-11 508	23:2 30, 104, 152, 220	18:26-29 509
11:6 194, 220	24:14 174	18:38 143, 144
13:14 158		18:39 542
14:3 203	**1 Kings**	18:46 174, 527
16:13 152, 155, 163, 166, 194, 202, 208, 235, 544	3:4-5 203	19:1-3 547
16:13-14 104	4:29 232	19:8 511
16:13-16 197	6-8 445	19:11 136
16:14 152, 194, 200, 202, 355, 357	6:12-13 451	19:11-12 133, 137
16:15 200	6:18 204	19:12 166
16:16 213	6:29 204	19:16 155
16:23 213	6:32 204	19:16b 154, 155
18:6 507	6:35 204	20:23 137
19 197	7:18 204	20:28 138
19:20 194, 508	7:20 204	21:20-24 279
19:20-24 196, 543	7:22 204	21:27 511
19:23 194, 197, 220	7:24 204	22:8-28 570
19:23-24 508	8 122	22:10 508
21:1 203	8:10-11 120, 122, 203	22:17-28 54
21:6 203	8:10-12 452	22:19-22 200
28:20 542	8:11 452	22:19-28 508
31:13 511	8:12 217	22:24 31, 104, 198
	8:27 218	
2 Samuel	8:30 218	**2 Kings**
1:12 511	8:39 218	1:9-12 279
2:4 155	8:43 218	2:3 389
3:35 511	8:49 218	2:5 389
5:3 155	9:3 90	2:9 150, 152, 155, 213
5:24 137	10:12 555	2:9-10 260
6:5 555	13:4-6 574	2:14 546
6:14 507	13:11 562	2:15 152, 155, 213, 260
6:14-15 508	13:18 570	2:16 104, 213
7:14 31, 410	14:4 562	3:15 174, 508, 527, 546, 555
12:7 156	14:5 567	4:1-7 575
12:16-23 511	17:1 279	4:18-37 574
14:14 138	17:1-2 576	4:29 529
22 202	17:17 28	4:31 529
22:11 202	17:17-24 574	4:34-35 529
22:16 202	17:21 529	4:38-44 575
	18 547	5 218
	18:12 104, 137, 530,	

Scripture Index

5:1-19 574
5:11-14 571
5:25-27 567
6:1-7 575
6:12 567
13:15-17 526
13:20-21 574
13:21 528, 576
19:15 192
20:1-11 574
20:23 389
22:14 201, 562

1 Chronicles
12:18 193
12:32 398
15:16 555
16:22 155
16:39 203
21:18-30 203
21:29 203
25:1 555
25:1-3 508
25:1-6 473
25:3 555
25:6 555
28-29 203
28:2 203
28:11-12 197
28:12 173, 203
28:19 173

2 Chronicles
2:16 137
2-7 445
3:1 203, 445
5:12 555
5:13-14 120, 122, 203
5:14 452, 543
6:1 217, 218
7:1 143
7:1-3 452
15:1 194
16:9 208
18:18-21 200

18:23 104, 198
20:3-4 511
20:7 199
20:14 104, 194
20:18-22 519
20:28 555
24:20 194
29:25 555
30:27 105
32:24-26 574
34:22 201, 562
35:18 195
36:20-21 204

Ezra
1:2 207
1:3 207
1:4-5 207
2:68 207
3-6 445
8:21 511
8:21-23 511
8:23 511
9:4 542
10:6 511

Nehemiah
1:4 511
1:4-5 207
6:14 201
8:10 426, 518
9:1-2 511
9:17 427
9:20 110, 199
9:30 108, 198
12:24 201
12:27 555
12:36 201

Esther
4:3 511

Job
1:6 227
1-2 218

2:1 227
4:9 134
4:15 112
9:13 181
11:7 v
15:30 30
26:12 181, 182, 188
26:13 134, 183
27:3 30, 91, 273
28:14 181
28:28 232, 564, 565
32:7-10 116
32:8 91
32:18 30, 91, 145, 183, 214
32:18-20 544
32:19-20 214
33:4 30, 89, 91, 101, 134, 180
33:7 181
34:14 30, 91
37:14 573
38:7 227
38:8-11 182
38:16 181
38:30 181
38:33 183
41:19 146
41:21 138
41:31 181
42:5-6 214
42:8 181

Psalms
2:1-2 289
2:7 31, 227
2:11 542
8:2 519
8:3 174
17:8 112
18 202
18:8 133
18:10 133, 137, 202
18:11 133
18:13-14 133

18:15 133, 183, 202	74:13-14 188, 189	95:10-11 192
18:15-16 203	78:8 100	95:11 204
18:16 133	78:10 186	99:1 192
19:1-6 185	78:14 120, 384	99:7 120, 384
19:9 291	78:16 166	103:8 427
19:10 176	78:17 100	103:13 114
22:9-10 115, 309	78:39-41 291	104 180, 183, 185
22:10 113	78:40 100	104:3 137
23:5b 153	78:56 100	104:4 166, 189
28:9 384	78:60-61 203	104:6 181, 189
29 133, 185, 211	78:65 164	104:7 189
30:11 507	78:66 164	104:15 411
31:5 272	80:1 121, 192	104:29-30 89, 91
33 135	80:8-9 191	104:30 101, 108, 135,
33:6 30, 101, 134,	86:5 427	149, 174, 180,
174, 180	86:15 427	181, 183, 210,
33:7 181	87:1 110	495
33:9 180, 181	87:4 188	105:9-10 235
35:13 511	87:7 507	105:9-15 199, 346
36:7 112	89:1-5 185	105:15 155, 235
36:7-9 204	89:2-3 183, 186	105:23 235
36:8-9 164	89:5 183	105:26 235
36:9 253	89:6 186	105:32 166
39:3 163, 544	89:9 186	105:39 120, 384
40:17 236	89:9-10 188	105:41 255
42:8 181	89:10 182, 189	106:7 100
45:7 159, 518	89:12 188	106:16 235
48:8 104	89:19-20 233	106:23 235
51:2 331	89:19-21 158, 235	106:33 108, 199
51:4 229	89:20 156	106:43 100
51:7 115	89:26-27 31	107:11 100
51:10-11 212, 327	89:28-29 185	107:20 210
51:11 24, 110, 152,	89:29-30 186	109:27 174
201, 205, 216,	89:36-37 185	110:1 122
217, 220, 355	89:37 183	111:10 232
51:13 134	89:37-38 186	115:16 219
55:4-8 171	90:1 201, 235	119:89 183
56:13 210	91:4 112	119:91 183
57:1 112	92:3 555	119:93 291
61:4 112	93:4 140	119:103 176
63:7 112	95:1 103	119:105 210
68:25 555	95:1-2 106	119:120 542
69:10-11 511	95:6 103	119:130 210
72:12-14 236	95:7-11 103	130:1 579
74:9 225	95:8-9 105, 106	131:2 115

Scripture Index

132:8   203
132:14 203
133:2   140, 154, 166, 505
139:1-4 101
139:7   108, 487
139:7-10 100
139:13 115
139:14a 335
139:14 573
143:10 110, 200, 287
145:8   427
147   185
147:15 183
147:18 183
148:5   180
148:6   183
148:8   183
149:3   507, 555
149:5-6 519
150:3-5 555
150:4   507

Proverbs
1:4   232
1:7   232
1:22   232
1:23   116, 209
1:29   232
2:3a   232
2:5   232
3:5   232
3:12   161, 410
3:19   209
3:19-20 501
4:20-22 210
4:23   90, 348
8:1-4   501
8:14   232, 542
8:15   129
8:22-31 116, 118, 232
8:22-41 209
8:27-28 181
8:31-36 501
9:1   116
9:1-6   502
9:10   232
9:10-11 502
9:13   116
12:25   541
13:12   542
13:14   253
14:30   542
15:13   542
15:30   542
15:33   232
16:23   210
17:22   542
20:27   145
31:6   164

Ecclesiastes
1:10   395
3:1   397
3:11   90
3:19   541
7:10   395
9:7   426
11:5   335
12:7   91, 112, 541

Song of Solomon
        118, 509
1:3   161
1:15   171
2:12   170
2:14   171
4:1   171
4:12   449
4:12-13 204
4:15   449
4:16   136
5:2   171
5:12   171
6:9   171

Isaiah
        576
1:6   153
1:14   134
1:31   166
4:2   231
4:4   115, 133, 144, 233
5:1-2   191
5:7   191
5:20   249
6:1-5   452
6:3   103
6:5   103
6:9   103, 106
7:13-14 231
8:3   201, 562
8:7   182
8:11   174
8:17   572
9:6   232
9:6-7   231, 317
9:8   210
10:8-14 231
10:33-34 231
11   230, 318
11:1-2 197, 230
11:1-5 234, 317
11:1-12 228
11:2   24, 96, 104, 109, 110, 116, 156, 180, 209, 213, 214, 232, 431
11:3   232
11:3-5 233
11:4   146
12:3   141, 255
16:5   231
17:13   182
22:22   231
28:6   110, 233
28:11-12 599
29:18   288
30:1   24
30:1b   97
30:7   188
30:25   166
30:27-28 133

30:28 183	45:12 183	545
30:29 555	45:18 182	61:1-2 515
30:31-32 519	45:25 296, 331	61:1-3 234, 235
32 318	46:3-4 384	61:3 213, 518
32:1 318	48:16 24, 96, 108,	61:21 236
32:15 24, 132, 139,	198, 210	63 189
168, 282, 284	48:20-21 168, 206	63:7 113
32:15-16 233, 234	49:3 234	63:9 190, 384
32:15-17 318	49:9 236	63:10 96, 192
33:11 146	49:10 168	63:10-11 24, 110, 134,
33:24 288	49:15 115	201
34:16 24, 180	49:25 301	63:10-12 177
35:5-6 288	51:9 182	63:10-14 168
35:6-7 206	51:9-10 188, 189	63:11 168, 207, 217
35:10 236	51:9-11 205, 206, 206	63:11-12 201
38 574	51:10 181	63:14 104
38:4 210	51:11 236	63:15 113
38:14 171	51:14 236	63:16 114, 189
40:3 168	52-53 234	63:20-21 291
40:7 30, 135, 183	53 239	64:1 103
40:11 384	54:1 301	64:8 114
40:13 24, 88, 96, 104,	54:16 166	66:5 542
180, 355	55:1 255	66:12 141
41:8 199	55:3-4 231	66:13 115
41:18 141, 206	55:8-9 150	
42 233, 234	55:9 396	**Jeremiah**
42:1 24, 134, 151,	55:10-11 211	1:2 210
158, 159, 197,	55:11 524	1:4 210
210, 228, 239,	56:7 471	1:5 309, 562
283, 515	57:15 236	1:7 562
42:1b 234	57:19 301	1:9 245
42:1-9 233	58:5 511	1:11 210
42:3b 234	58:11 255	1:13 210
42:4b 234	59:19 96, 133, 183	2:13 141, 253
42:5 134	59:21 24, 134, 150,	3:16 206
42:14 114	151, 198, 210,	4:4 330, 341
42:22 236	211, 301	5:9 134
43:3-4 236	60:9 301	5:22 542
43:16-21 206	60:21 296	5:29 134
43:19 141	61 234	6:8 134
43:19-20 168	61:1 104, 108, 151,	7:12 203
43:24 204	153, 155, 156,	7:14 203
44:3 24, 134, 139,	157, 198, 208,	9:9 134
168, 282, 284	210, 213, 228,	9:25-26 341
44:3-4 132	283, 347, 521,	13:23 330

15:1 134	3:22 528	273
15:17 174	3:23 543	37:9-10 336
16:3 114	3:24 31, 199	37:14 30, 104, 134, 135, 282, 284, 296, 327, 336, 447
17:13 141, 204, 253	7:16 171	
20:9 162, 543	8:3 137, 163, 199, 544	
23:5 231		
23:9 162, 163, 543	9-11 205	37:24-25 447
23:29 291	9:8 543	37:25 301
28 570	10:3-4 122	37:26-28 451
29:26 508	11:1 137, 163, 199, 544	37:27 451
30:20 301		39:29 134, 139, 447
31:4 507	11:5 104, 163, 194, 198, 210, 544	40-43 447
31:13 507		40:1 528, 530
31:17 301	11:13 543	40:16 448
31:20 113	11:15 199	40:22 448
31:33 103, 291, 351, 353, 451	11:19 327, 330, 341	40:26 448
	11:24 137, 163, 199, 544	40:31 448
31:34 232, 353		40:34 448
31:35 183	18:31 327	40:37 448
32:41 134	20:12 191	41:18-20 204, 448
33:15 231	20:20 191	41:25-26 448
33:20 183, 186	26:19 181	43 122
33:25 183, 186	28:2 90	43:1-4 205
35 218	28:6 90	43:1-5 122
38 218	29:3 188	43:1-7 448
	33:22 528	43:1-12 446
Lamentations	34:23-24 447	43:2 140
1:13 147	34:26 141	43:3 543
4:20 135	34-39 447	43:3-5 124
	36 178, 282, 327, 328	43:5 137, 163, 199, 212, 452, 544
Ezekiel		
1 293	36:25 333	43:7 452
1:3 210, 528	36:25-26 327, 332	43:7-9 451
1:4 135, 137, 143, 293	36:25-27 139	43:19 452
	36:26 330, 341	44:4 124, 543
1:12 135	36:27 134, 282, 284, 296, 318, 327, 447	44:7 341
1:13 143		47:1 255
1:24 140		47:1-12 140, 204, 255, 448
1:28 143, 543	37 178	
2:1 535	37:1 30, 104, 199, 528, 530	
2:2 31, 199		**Daniel**
3:12 137, 163, 199, 544	37:1-14 135,	2:18-19 207
	37:5-6 30, 135, 331	2:37 207
3:14 137, 163, 173, 199, 528, 544	37:8-10 30	4:8 219
	37:9 104, 135, 166,	4:8-9 192

4:18	192	3:18	141, 166, 255	4:12-14	208
5	581			6:8	96, 97, 134
5:5	174	**Amos**		6:12	231
5:11	192, 219	7:4	181	6:12-13	208
5:14	192, 219	9:7	498	7:12	108, 198
7:9	166			10:1	141
7:9-10	143	**Jonah**		10:7	301
8:17-18	543	2:6	181	10:9	301
9:3-4	511	3:5-8	511	12:10	101, 111, 139,
10:2-4	511	4:2	427		343, 471
10:9-11	543			13:1	141, 142, 255
12:10	523	**Micah**		14:8	140, 255
		2:7	96		
Hosea		3:8	104, 131, 193,	**Malachi**	
1:1	210		210, 575	1:6	114
1:10	169	5:7	140	2:10	114
6:3	141			2:15	24
6:6	232	**Habakkuk**		3:2	143, 144
9:7	506, 575	2:4b	328	3:16	122, 123
10:1	191	3:10	181	4:2	112
11:1-3	169				
13:8	115	**Zephaniah**		**Matthew**	
14:2b	452	3:12	236	1	226
14:5	140			1:18	102, 225, 226
		Haggai		1:20	12, 102, 110,
Joel		1-2	445		114, 225, 226
1:14	511	2:3-5	206	2:12	410
1:15	296	2:4	445	2:22	410
2	282, 510	2:5	97, 134, 210	3:2	297, 329
2:1	296	2:8	446	3:6	297, 359
2:11	296	2:10	446	3:7-10	279
2:12	511			3:11	133, 144, 215,
2:13	427	**Zechariah**			278, 279, 359
2:15-16	511	3:8	231	3:12	136, 280
2:17	294	3:9	101, 146, 208	3:14	281
2:23	141	4	146, 207, 208	3:16	108, 167, 215
2:28	149, 158, 258,	4:1-6	155	3:16-17	102, 228
	328	4:2	207	3:17	159, 160, 233
2:28-29	134, 139, 141,	4:2-3	208	4:1	287
	201, 213, 282,	4:3	207, 208	4:1-11	520
	284, 561, 562	4:6	134, 193, 208	4:2	511
2:28-32	295	4:7-9	208	4:10	105
2:31	296	4:9-10	208	4:23	70, 288, 522,
3	296	4:10b	101, 146, 208		574
3:14	296	4:12	207, 208	4:23-24	520

Scripture Index

5:3 236, 545	10:16 170, 171	15:32 517
5:4 236, 259	10:17-20 565	16:3 398
5:12 420	10:19-20 244, 245, 321	16:4 398
5:13-14 367	10:20 26, 31, 97, 105,	16:14 577
5:13-16 480	108, 246, 357	16:19 306
5:48 416	10:28 89,	16:22-23 570
6:4 420	11:9 235	16:23 570
6:6 420	11:11 221, 346, 587	17:4-5 229
6:9 105	11:12 520	17:5 120, 159, 233
6:9-15 251	11:17 507, 555	17:10-13 214
6:16-18 510	11:27 33	17:20 424, 547, 570
6:18 420	11:29 429	17:21 512
6:31-33 317	12 248	18:18 306
7:7-11 251	12:15 567	18:20 122, 123, 474
7:11 251	12:17-18 245	20:4 428
7:11-12 251	12:22-33 531	20:13 428
7:15-23 531	12:28 527, 530	20:15 428
7:21-22 318, 319	12:33 531	20:20 237
7:22-23 221, 523	12:24 247	20:34 517
7:28-29 567	12:27 248, 523	24:24 523, 569
8:1-15 574	12:28 70, 108, 173,	21:5 429
8:2 237	237, 245, 247,	21:11 234, 577
8:8 210	319, 519, 520,	21:12 429, 430
8:10 571	522, 527, 530	21:16 519
8:12 318	12:31 100	21:21 424, 570
8:13 571	12:31-32 100, 247, 248	21:46 577
8:14-15 570	12:32a 248	22:29 481
8:26-27 575	12:34 480	22:44 297
9:1-6 237	12:39-40 398	23:23 429
9:2 571	12:45 540	24:14 392
9:12 573	13:30 280	24:24 569
9:15 510	13:38 318	24:29 296
9:18 237	13:44 176	25:8 145
9:22 571	13:46 175	25:11-12 318, 319
9:28-29 571	13:54 566	25:21 161
9:35 70, 288, 522	13:57 234, 577	25:23 161
9:36 517	13:57-58 505	25:35-40 319
10 246	14:5 577	25:41 182
10:1 546, 561	14:14 517	26:10 567
10:1-4 220	14:19 575	26:28 298, 331
10:4 357	14:25 575	26:41 240
10:5-6 302	14:32 575	26:64 122, 297
10:7 357	14:33 237	26:65-66 268
10:7-8 520, 573	15:21-28 571	27:18 567
10:8 546, 547, 571	15:25 237	27:50 135, 272

27:66	172, 328	8:12	98		121, 225, 226,
28:4	542	8:23	571		227, 228, 229,
28:18	489	9:5	229		244, 245, 283,
28:18-19	298	9:7	120, 159, 229		475
28:18-20	360	9:23-24	571	1:36	281
28:19	98, 100, 245	9:25	569	1:41	151, 193, 200,
40	479	9:29	505, 512, 547		225, 235, 245,
		9:38-39	574		251, 521

Mark

		9:48	145	1:41-55	562
1:4	229, 280, 297,	10:52	571	1:46	200
	333, 475	11:17	471	1:46-55	200
1:7-8	278	11:23	570	1:67	151, 193, 200,
1:8	279	13:11	31, 244, 245,		225, 235, 245,
1:10	103, 167, 229		246, 321, 478,		251, 521
1:10-11	228		481, 521, 541,	1:78	283
1:11	160		549	1:80	98
1:12	96, 169	14:15	258	2:22-50	446
1:23-25	570	14:16	350	2:25	194
1:27	568	14:36	350	2:25-27	225, 235, 245,
2:8	567, 570	15:37	272		251, 410, 521
3:5	430	15:40	562	2:25-32	235
3:21	506	16:8	542	2:27	194
3:22	247	16:15	246	2:36	235, 562
3:38	248	16:16	358	2:37	511
3:29	247, 248, 250	16:17	299, 520	2:40	286
4:39	575	16:17-18	157, 478,	2:49	286
5:28	529		560, 572, 573,	2:52	286
5:30	514, 574		574	3:3	297
5:33	542	16:17-20	247	3:7-9	279
5:36	571	16:18	525	3:13-17	116
5:40	571	16:19	297	3:16	133, 144, 277,
6	154	16:20	323, 324, 523		278, 279
6:2	566			3:17	144, 145
6:3-6	505	**Luke**		3:21	287
6:4-6	167, 546	1	226	3:21-22	81, 102, 121,
6:5-6	571	1:2	320		228, 244, 516
6:7	561	1:11-12	251, 252	3:22	86, 160, 167,
6:13	153	1:15	151, 161, 162,		229, 247, 410,
6:14	514		193, 225, 235,		447
6:15	577		245, 251, 280,	3:23	228, 285
6:30	547		309, 513, 515,	3:38	228
6:56	529		587	4	236
7:32	571	1:17	214, 279, 587	4:1	81, 96, 121,
7:33	571	1:20-22	286		151, 193, 237,
7:34	580	1:35	102, 110, 114,		239, 245, 247,

	287, 384, 410, 513, 516	9:19	577	13:16	569
		9:26	109	13:33	234, 577
4:1-2	236, 288	9:31	237	14:13	236
4:1-13	237, 514	9:33	229, 567	14:21	236
4:14	81, 96, 121, 235, 236, 237, 239, 245, 247, 287, 410, 514, 516	9:34	120	15	146
		9:35	159, 229	15:8	146
		9:47	567	15:20	363
		9:52-54	303	15:25	458, 507
		10	153	16:16	221, 520
4:14-15	223, 523	10:1	561	16:20	236
4:16-21	155, 157, 198, 234	10:1-9	572	16:22	236
		10:9	561	16:25	259
4:17-21	287, 515, 520	10:19	574	17:10	161, 420
4:18	235, 245, 247, 504	10:20	367, 568	17:19	571
		10:21	236, 237, 245, 247, 287, 411, 426, 507, 518	17:21	318
4:31-41	288			17:21b	319
5:17	166, 167, 505, 514, 525, 533, 546			18:1-8	373
		10:34	153	18:9	268
		11	251	18:22	236
5:22	567	11:2	252, 318	19:8	236
5:35	511	11:5-10	373	19:17	420
6:19	505, 525, 533	11:11-12	152	20	566
6:20	236	11:13	116, 152, 220, 236, 245, 247, 250, 251, 252, 287, 373, 547	21:2-3	236
6:26	548			21:11	296
6:35	427			21:15	321
6:36	416			21:25	296
6:46	319	11:15	247	22:12	258
7:11-17	574	11:19	248	22:15	418
7:16	577	11:20	173, 247, 291, 319, 527, 530	23:34	249
7:21	559, 560			23:46	98, 136, 272
7:22	236	11:26	540	24:19	234, 577
7:28	221	11:31	566	24:21	241
7:29	230	11:48	116	24:32	485, 507
8:2-3	562	12:10a	248	24:33-49	275
8:11	334	12:10	248, 250	24:35	485
8:40-46	574	12:11-12	244, 245, 321	24:39	241
8:43-46	525	12:12	236, 246, 250, 252	24:48	320
8:44	529			24:49	58, 151, 216, 251, 282, 286, 287, 320, 375, 514, 515
8:45	533	12:47-48	249		
8:46	533	12:49	280,		
8:47	542	12:50	237		
9:1	582	12:56	398	24:51	297
9:1-2	561	13:2	511	24:52-53	286
9:8	577	13:11	569	24:53	286, 293
9:10	547, 582	13:11-17	570		

John
1-12 258
1:1 209, 224
1:1-3 116
1:1-13 490
1:1-18 209
1:3 488, 490
1:4 210
1:7 264
1:10 261, 262
1:11 261
1:12 228
1:12-13 31
1:13 114, 115, 228
1:14a 446
1:14 116, 121, 209, 224, 227, 261, 262, 490
1:17 221, 257
1:18 33, 116, 227, 229, 456
1:25-33 333
1:26 279, 281
1:26-27 281
1:29 168
1:31 281
1:31-34 281
1:32 167, 168, 287
1:32-33 81, 215, 228
1:32-34 102
1:33 121, 212, 281
1:35-40 285
1:43-48 301
1:45 198, 234
2:6-11 575
2:16 286
2:19-21 348, 447
2:19 121
2:25 567
3 332, 334, 371
3:1 332
3:2 567, 583
3:3 332
3:4 114
3:5 17, 92, 102, 114, 142, 176, 211, 228, 253, 265, 299, 327, 328, 332, 334, 335, 338, 341, 358, 475, 483, 499
3:5-6 325, 330
3:6 332, 341, 343, 419
3:8 31, 96, 101, 135, 150, 273, 332
3:10 332
3:11 260, 264
3:15-16 330
3:16 240
3:17 33, 330
3:18-19 268
3:25 333
3:30 587
3:31-32 579
3:32 260, 264
3:33 172, 282, 328
3:34 33, 150, 355
3:34b 345
3:36 268, 340, 516
4 224, 252, 253, 254, 471, 472, 474
4:8 101
4:10 252
4:14 166, 252, 256, 334
4:16 101
4:19 577
4:23-24 86, 472, 473, 518
4:24 26, 86
4:25 234
4:34 33
4:39 264
4:40-42 301
4:44 198
5:6 567
5:6-9 571
5:19 33
5:23-24 33
5:26 33
5:30 33
5:31-32 263
5:34 263
5:36 264
5:36-38 33
5:37 263
5:39 264
5:45-47 264
6:14 198, 234, 287, 577
6:15 567
6:26 172
6:27 328, 476
6:37 250
6:44 254
6:51-56 265
6:53-54 454
6:56 260, 479
6:59 260
6:61 567
6:63 89, 101, 150, 178, 210, 240, 327, 328, 334, 336, 337
6:64 567
6:70 570
6:70-71 220,
7 224, 252, 253, 254, 255, 257
7:14 260
7:21-26 342
7:28 260
7:37-38 254
7:37-39 140, 252, 253, 254, 272
7:38-39 166, 267, 334, 449, 517
7:38 256
7:39 81, 218, 222, 251, 256, 257, 274, 315

Scripture Index

7:39b 215
7:40 198, 234, 577
8:2 260
8:14 260, 264
8:18 260, 263, 264, 264
8:20 260
8:26 260, 261
8:28 33
8:32 330
8:36 330, 342
8:37 264
8:40 260, 261
8:54 257
9:17 577
9:24 268
10:7 176
10:9 176
10:10 253, 282, 372, 456
10:17-18 136, 237, 272
10:25 264
10:28-29 172
10:41 587
11:1 562
11:1-44 574
11:4 257
11:25 562
11:33 98, 254
11:41-42 572
11:52 218
12:16 257
12:17 264
12:23-24 257
12:28-30 581
12:31 261, 269, 270
12:41 106
12:47 330
12:49 33
13:1 567
13:3 567
13:1-11 258
13:7 321
13:10 331
13:13 260

13:21 98, 254
13:27 570
13:31-32 257
13:34 422
14-16 224, 257, 258, 261
14 258, 274
14:2 286, 454
14:6 33, 101, 176, 261, 478, 498
14:10 33
14:10-11 454
14:11 264
14:12 157, 237, 257, 260, 476, 478, 520, 595
14:14-17 217
14:15 422
14:16 23, 96, 97, 101, 109, 152, 258, 261, 274, 355
14:16-17 85, 258
14:16-20 258
14:17 96, 101, 110, 151, 168, 212, 258, 260, 261, 262, 265, 287, 425, 473
14:17c 261
14:18 98
14:20 260, 454
14:21 422
14:23 439, 454, 455
14:24 261
14:25 260
14:25-26 258
14:26 33, 81, 85, 96, 101, 109, 122, 258, 260, 261, 270, 274, 283, 291, 321
14:27 478
14:30 261, 270
15 96, 224, 263
15-16 112

15:3 211, 216, 291, 367
15:3-5 260
15:3-7 454
15:4 454
15:9-10 425, 455
15:10 422
15:11 425
15:12 422
15:15 260, 261
15:20 478
15:21 261
15:22 268
15:24 264
15:25 98
15:26 28, 29, 33, 81, 96, 101, 109, 110, 122, 218, 251, 258, 260, 261, 264, 265, 270, 274, 283, 473, 478
15:26-27 263, 321
15:27 264
16 96, 266, 274
16:5 261
16:7 101, 109, 258, 261, 274, 283
16:7-8 96
16:7-15 266
16:8 268, 291
16:8-9 261
16:8-11 93
16:9 268
16:10 230, 269
16:11 261, 269, 270
16:13a 270
16:13 31, 96, 101, 110, 258, 260, 261, 265, 274, 291, 321, 390, 473, 478
16:13b 271
16:13-14 33, 96, 98
16:13-15 81, 98, 264

16:14	257	20:22	33, 124, 136, 216, 224, 239, 273,	1:24	569
16:14-15	15, 246, 258, 267			2	3, 29, 69, 79, 104, 122, 164, 213, 218, 222, 224, 251, 257, 258, 263, 285, 287, 289, 290, 293, 295, 301, 306, 30, 308, 313, 328, 329, 340, 355, 361, 367, 385, 410, 449, 453, 561, 562, 588
16:19	567	20:23	274, 378		
16:21	114, 228	20:25	124		
16:24-27	267	20:28	351		
16:33	269	21:15-17	583		
17	258	21:24	264		
17:1	257	21:26	264		
17:3	38, 253, 261, 456	21:27	264		
17:4	33	**Acts**			
17:4-5	269	1	367		
17:5	257	1-7	283		
17:6	33	1:2	410	2:1	289
17:6-19	367	1:3	284, 316	2:1-4	147, 277
17:8	33	1:4	216, 300, 320, 505	2:2	28, 122, 136, 137, 143, 166, 167, 293, 295
17:10	257				
17:18	273, 479	1:4-5	151, 216, 282, 283, 284, 286, 316, 375		
17:20-23	iii			2:2-3	294, 304, 370
17:21-23	454			2:2-4	290, 505, 533
17:22-23	415	1:5	57, 251, 279, 295, 299, 313, 359	2:3	143, 144, 280, 281, 290, 291
17:23	479				
17:24	425			2:4	57, 151, 193, 290, 295, 299, 303, 305, 309, 310, 336, 356, 370, 374, 377, 513, 518, 526, 541, 562
17:25	269	1:6	284, 316		
17:26	415, 455, 479	1:7-8	316		
18:4	567	1:8	68, 131, 150, 151, 246, 251, 282, 283, 286, 287, 302, 307, 309, 316, 320, 377, 476, 478, 514, 515		
18:6	542				
18:6-7	535				
18:37	477, 521				
19:28	567				
19:30	135, 224, 237, 240, 254, 269, 271, 272			2:6	290, 336
				2:6-12	295
				2:11	370, 518, 578, 579, 599
		1:9	297		
19:34	266, 272	1:13	293, 301, 302	2:13	162, 506
19:35	264	1:13-14	286	2:14	321
19:41-20:17	448	1:14	251, 287, 511, 562	2:16	295
20	124, 271, 273			2:17	108, 258, 296, 303, 328, 575
20:3-10	303	1:15	275, 293		
20:12-13	449	1:16	202, 295	2:17-18	139, 165, 287
20:15	448	1:16-26	293	2:19-20	296
20:19	321, 521	1:18	256	2:20	296
20:20	124	1:20	464	2:22	288, 525, 569
20:21	274, 479	1:21-22	264, 320	2:23	171
20:21-23	273	1:22	283, 321	2:29	321

Scripture Index

2:30-31 575
2:32 283, 321
2:33 33, 111, 139, 165, 216, 257, 300, 346
2:37 369
2:37-41 284, 524
2:38 81, 298, 299, 305, 313, 379, 484, 526
2:38-39 298, 300
2:38-41 303, 367
2:39 346
2:41 312, 370, 580
2:41-42 485
2:41-47 370
2:43 288, 523, 569
2:46 293, 304, 305
2:46-47 485
3:1-11 288, 303
3:4-8 571, 583
3:14 230
3:14-15 269
3:15 283, 321
3:16 299, 571, 572, 573
3:17 249
3:18 295-296, 575
3:20-26 234
3:21-24 575
3:22 198
3:22-23 287, 577
3:24 195, 576
4:7 574
4:7-21 565
4:8 57, 151, 193, 245, 321, 356, 374, 377, 480, 505, 506, 513, 548
4:11 296
4:12 330, 498
4:13 321, 480, 521
4:25 202
4:25-28 289
4:27 286, 347, 504
4:27-30 477
4:28 174
4:29 321, 521
4:30 174, 288, 523, 527, 569
4:31 57, 123, 151, 193, 267, 321, 356, 371, 372, 374, 377, 480, 503, 505, 506, 513, 519, 521, 522, 533, 548
4:33 321, 322
5 321
5:1-11 567
5:3 193, 248
5:3-4 99
5:3-5 249
5:5 575
5:9 108, 248
5:10 575
5:12 523, 527, 569, 582
5:12-16 288
5:14-15 583
5:15 528
5:28 322
5:32 283, 321, 340, 345, 516
5:41 267
5:41-42 549
6 301
6:1-2 314
6:1-4 565
6:3 151, 193, 505, 513, 531
6:3-6 460
6:5 151, 193, 324, 513, 531
6:5-6 301
6:6 526
6:7 314, 516
6:8 324, 523, 569, 572

6:9-10 565
6:10 505
6:13-14 122
6:17-18 531
6:19 531
7:9 215
7:27 215
7:32 542
7:35 215
7:37 198, 234, 287, 576
7:38-51 291
7:39 215
7:51 100, 215, 248
7:52 230
7:55 151, 193, 505, 513, 521
7:57-58 524
7:59 105, 272
8 278, 304, 306, 307, 312, 322, 323, 327, 370, 385
8:1 521
8:5-8 301
8:6-7 288
8:8 322
8-11:18 284
8:5-12 70
8:6 523
8:6-7 323, 520, 572, 583
8:9 531
8:9-10 531
8:9-11 301, 523
8:11 531
8:12 301, 302, 307, 316, 520
8:12-13 288
8:12-17 313
8:13 323, 357, 358, 523, 531, 583
8:14-17 303, 312
8:15-18 308
8:16 298, 303, 470

8:17 300, 305, 316, 370, 580	9:32-35 573	10:45-46 303
8:17-18 314, 533	9:32-42 583	10:46 303, 310, 370, 518
8:17-19 526	9:36 314	
8:18 304	9:36-42 573, 574, 575	10:48 298, 307
8:18-24 357, 358	9:38 314	11:1-18 312
8:18-19 523	10 306, 307, 310, 312, 370	11:5 196, 506, 509
8:20 299		11:12 100, 516
8:26 308, 385	10:1-2 371	11:15 303, 312
8:26-39 284	10:1-4 287	11:15-18 311
8:29 100, 385, 516	10:2 310	11:16 57, 283
8:30 527	10:3 385	11:16-17 287, 295
8:36 307	10:10 196, 506, 509	11:17 299, 312, 345
8:38 307, 359	10:14 385	11:24 151, 193, 505, 513
8:38-39 307, 308, 312	10:15 565	
8:39 137, 289, 308, 367, 370, 385, 530, 532	10:19 100, 385, 516, 565	11:26 314, 428
		11:27-28 287, 461, 575, 576, 583
	10:22 310, 371, 410	11:28 53
8:39-40 574	10:24 310	11:29 314
9:1 314	10:28 565	11:30 458
9:4 542	10:30 287, 512	13:1 271, 287, 583
9:4-5 479	10:34-43 368	13:1-3 306, 460, 461, 465, 555
9:9 367, 368, 369, 511, 573	10:35 498	
	10:38 102, 151, 155, 157, 166, 210, 223, 229, 235, 236, 237, 279, 283, 286, 347, 375, 476, 504, 514, 520, 522, 569	13:1-4 386
9:10 314		13:2 96, 97, 516
9:10-16 309, 567		13:2-4 459
9:11 287		13:3 386, 511, 512, 526
9:12 306, 525		
9:15-16 309		13:4 516
9:16 389		13:8-11 574, 575
9:17 57, 151, 193, 300, 305, 306, 310, 313, 356, 367, 370, 374, 377, 484, 485, 505, 506, 513, 515, 525, 526, 572	10:39 283, 321, 525, 574	13:9 57, 151, 193, 245, 356, 374, 377, 505, 506, 513
	10:41 283, 321	
	10:43 310, 311	
	10:43-44 379	
	10:43-46 369	13:9-11 515, 521, 548, 549
	10:44 303, 305, 312, 524, 526	
		13:20 576
	10:44-45 513	13:22 158
9:17-18 309, 573	10:44-46 284, 298, 303, 312, 313, 314, 363, 370, 533	13:30 195
9:17-19 370		13:31 283, 321
9:19 314		13:33-34 296
9:20 310		13:44 322
9:22 310		13:50 524
9:25-26 314	10:44-48 300, 311, 368	13:52 57, 151, 163, 176, 308, 314,
9:31b 260	10:45 81, 139, 299	

Scripture Index

	356, 374, 377, 411, 506, 513	17:22-31	498	20:28	22, 102, 458, 459, 555
13:53	518	17:25	28	20:30	314
14:3	323, 523, 569	17:25-28	184	21:4	314, 388
14:4	306	17:27	500	21:8	301, 367, 583
14:9	567	17:28	127, 491	21:9	562, 576
14:9-10	571	17:30	249, 340	21:9-10	287
14:11	578	18:9-10	565	21:9-11	461
14:14	306	18:23	314	21:10	583
14:15	101	18:25	145, 315	21:10-11	575, 576
14:17	498	18:27	314	21:11	53, 388
14:19	524	19	278, 323, 387	21:12	389
14:20-22	314	19:1-7	313, 314	21:16	314
14:22	478, 479	19:2	3, 215, 256, 257, 314, 364, 377	21:18	458
14:22b	324			22:6-7	542
14:23	458, 460, 512	19:2-7	285	22:7-8	479
14:28	314	19:5	298, 470	22:10	367
15	390, 565	19:5-6	367, 485	22:12-16	367
15:1-21	305	19:6	287, 299, 300, 303, 305, 310, 314, 316, 370, 518, 521, 526, 533	22:15	283
15:2-23	458			22:16	298, 307, 309, 310
15:8	312				
15:8-9	312			22:17	196
15:8-10	313			22:18	283
15:10	314	19:8	316, 520	22:14	230
15:12	523, 569	19:9	314	22:14-15	309
15:15-18	296	19:10-12	323, 324	22:16	485
15:28	96, 385, 477, 516, 565	19:11	523	22:17	506, 509
		19:11-12	520, 528, 574	22:21	301
15:31-32	259	19:12	569	22:20	283
15:32	287, 461, 576, 583	19:13-16	248, 523	23:11	283, 565
		19:21	387, 388	24:1	245
16	387	19:29	322	24:16	510
16:1	314	19:30	314	24:25	430
16:4	458	20:1	314	26:14-15	479
16:6	97, 387	20:7	304	26:16	283
16:6-7	386, 387, 516	20:9-10	573, 575	26:22	283
16:7	26, 97, 108, 262	20:9-12	574	27:23	565
		20:10	529	28:3	106
16:16-18	299, 300, 322, 569, 574	20:12	259	28:3-6	574
		20:16	305	28:4-6	323
16:24-26	519	20:17	458	28:8	525
16:25-26	372	20:22	388	28:9	573
16:29	542	20:22-23	388, 516	28:23	317
16:31	330	20:23	388	28:25	103, 106
17:6	322	20:25	316, 317	28:30-31	317

Romans

Ref	Pages
1:3-4	241, 243
1:4	12, 81, 101, 102, 110, 227, 244, 477, 495
1:5	516
1:11	465
1:16	314, 330
2:4	427
2:6-7	498
2:6-13	499
2:7	184, 434, 499
2:10-11	498
2:13	498
2:14-15	501
2:29	45, 330, 340, 341, 342, 353
3:2	478
3-8	331
3:3	429
3:4	229
3:20	291
3:22	572
3:24	330
3:26	572
4:5	159, 160, 339
4:11	172, 328
4:17	91
4:24-25	240
4:24-5:1	368
5:1	407, 426, 449
5:1-2	340, 413
5:1-5	604
5:1-11	371
5:2	468
5:3	427
5:5	27, 93, 139, 150, 151, 169, 199, 345, 352, 414, 425, 592
5:7	428
5:9-10	339
5:10-11	331
5:13	407, 408
5:15	557, 558
5:17-18	407
5:18b	339
5:19	516
5:20	291, 495
5:21	407, 408, 434
6:3	450
6:3-4	358
6:4	240, 241, 407, 447, 483
6:6	330, 432
6:7	343, 366
6:12-14	407
6:13	343
6:14-15	421, 422
6:16	450
6:18	366
6:22	343, 366, 456
6:22-23	408, 434
6:23	557, 558
7	326, 363, 364, 366
7:1	450
7:5	421
7:5-24	408
7:6	45, 328, 330, 342, 353, 407
7:7	341
7:7-11	291
7:8-11	421
7:12	343, 421
7:14	424
7:14-19	365
7:14-24	364, 365, 366
7:15-24	371, 417
7:17	365, 419
7:20	419
7:21	366
7:22	89, 90, 365
7:23	366
7:26	366
8	195, 326, 364, 382, 406, 407, 419, 438
8:1	479
8:2	343, 366, 422
8:1-2	330, 342
8:1-14	241
8:1-17	57, 371
8:2	89, 101, 110
8:3	241
8:3b	342
8:4	290, 291, 342, 421, 423, 431
8:4-9a	407
8:4-9	418
8:4-26	178
8:5	407
8:5-8	408
8:5-14	366
8:6	89, 101, 407, 604
8:7	407
8:8	407
8:9	26, 97, 108, 151, 212, 216, 218, 257, 258, 261, 262, 273, 299, 305, 347, 408, 458, 513
8:9b	362
8:9-10	99
8:10	479
8:11a	212
8:11	91, 93, 103, 150, 151, 178, 210, 216, 218, 240, 257, 258, 261, 458
8:12-14	407, 418
8:13a	407
8:13b	407
8:13	408
8:13-14	409
8:14	287, 291, 419, 420, 477, 516
8:14-16	381
8:15	31, 93, 100, 110, 343, 350, 351, 355, 371, 440, 468, 477

8:15-16 349
8:16 48, 96, 321, 420
8:18-25 439
8:23 31, 172, 353, 355
8:23b 355
8:23-25 339
8:26 147, 246, 260, 440, 579, 580
8:26-27 100, 439, 578
8:27 19, 96, 439
8:29 75, 160, 490
8:29-30 414
8:30 340
8:32 240
8:34 260, 264, 439
8:37 365
9:4 473
9:17 227
9:26 169
10:9-10 330, 339
10:12 468
11:2 450
11:8 350
11:22 427
11:26 296
11:29 557
11:34 181
12 552
12:1 348, 474
12:2 330, 336, 412
12:3b 554
12:4-8 467
12:5 479
12:6 554, 558
12:6-8 557
12:7-8 556
12:8 463
12:11 145, 166
12:12 427
12:18 426
13:8-10 352
13:14 352
14:2 317

14:5-6 317
14:7 426
14:10-13 317
14:15 426
14:17 176, 308, 317, 318, 425, 426, 604
14:19 556
15:13 131, 132, 426, 514, 604
15:14 566
15:16 339, 583
15:18 582
15:18-19 524
15:18-21 582
15:19 101, 324, 372, 515, 522, 569, 572
15:29 282
15:30 27, 96, 101, 115, 169, 344, 426
16:20 426, 574
16:26 100, 516
18-19 131, 132

1 Corinthians
1:2 331, 450
1:4 558
1:4-7 553
1:7 558
1:13 298
1:13-17 307
1:15 298
1:17 564
1:18 330
1:19-22 564
1:24 564, 566
1:30 330, 564
2:1 564
2:1-5 568
2:3 542
2:3-5 524, 549
2:4 279, 321, 481, 514, 521, 522

2:4-5 322, 574
2:4-7 564
2:6 564
2:9-11 v
2:10 19
2:10-11 96
2:11 87, 101, 145
2:12 29, 87
2:13 541, 564
2:14 346, 408
2:14-16 337
2:15 347, 408
2:15-16 273, 274, 287
2:16 181
3:1 347, 408, 424
3:1-3 408
3:3 347, 424
3:4 427, 428
3:9 450
3:12-15 356
3:14 420
3:16 27, 96, 100, 103, 122, 151, 202, 210, 212, 216, 217, 218, 257, 258, 261, 347, 443, 444, 453, 476
3:16-17 436, 450
3:17 450
3:19 299, 564
4:19-20 521
4:20 319, 324, 591
4:21 110, 344, 350, 430
5:1-10 300
5:3-4 344
5:5 296, 418
5:6 450
6-7 577
6:2-3 450
6:2-4 300
6:9 450
6:9-10 319
6:11 93, 102, 108,

	299, 331, 338, 358, 450, 499	11:4-5	576		470, 513
6:12	555	11:5	562	12:14-26	467
6:15-16	450	11:7	75, 90	12:17	584, 585
6:16	258	11:8	475, 476	12:25-27	361
6:18-19	436	11:23	565	12:28	271, 463, 465, 557, 559, 560, 573, 576, 584
6:19	96, 100, 102, 151, 202, 216, 218, 257, 261, 346, 347, 348, 355, 443, 450, 458, 513	11:24	484		
		11:26	237		
		11:29	484	12:28-29	288, 523, 583
		12	47, 63, 299, 358, 361, 552, 554, 558, 559, 560, 561, 564, 566, 572, 583, 588, 595	12:28-30	585, 591
				12:28-13:2	557
				12:29-30	584
				12:30	580
7	554			12:31a	591
7:4-6	554			12:31	344, 426, 585, 586, 595
7:5	430, 512	12-14	461, 568, 577, 590		
7:7	557			12:31b	591
7:8	565	12:1	299, 553	13	344, 552, 587, 591
7:9	430	12:1-2	466		
7:12	565	12:1-3	530	13:1	577, 579, 591
7:25	565	12:2	361, 509, 603, 604	13:1-2	557
7:35	555			13:2	424, 565, 566, 570, 575, 596
7:40	565	12:2-3	553		
7:40b	346	12:3	33, 319, 351	13:4-6	427
8:1	426	12:4	81, 299	13:4-7	592
8:13	426	12:4-6	99	13:5	592
9:2	172, 328	12:4-11	102, 361, 461, 552	13:8	557, 566, 567, 592
9:13	450				
9:17-18	420	12:5-6	361	13:8-9	575
9:21	342, 422	12:7	344, 555, 560, 561, 602, 603	13:13	344, 426, 431
9:24	450			14	440, 467, 552, 578, 585, 586, 591, 595, 598, 601, 603
9:25	430	12:7-11	440		
9:25-27	430	12:8	564		
10:1-11	384, 449, 477	12:8-10	300, 555, 559, 591		
10:1-4	237			14:1-19	598
10:2	120, 168	12:9	423, 424, 557, 559, 560, 573	14:1	299, 575, 595, 599
10:2-3	554				
10:3-4	485	12:10	288, 523, 532	14:2	568, 578, 596
10:4	554	12:11	96, 101, 150, 344, 602	14:3	23, 463, 521, 561, 576, 592, 595, 600
10:11	284, 477				
10:16	483, 484, 487	12:12	361, 479		
10:19-20	509, 530	12b	165	14:3-4	240, 556
10:19-21	553	12:13	164, 305, 306, 326, 358, 359, 360, 361, 362, 379, 467, 468,	14:3-5	603
10:20	530			14:3-6	575
10:23	555, 598			14:4a	538
10:33	555			14:4	578, 579, 598

Scripture Index

14:5   576, 580, 581, 585, 586, 595, 597, 598
14:6   566
14:6b 600
14:10-12 579
14:12 556, 568, 596, 603
14:13 580
14:13-14 578
14:14 440, 596, 598
14:14-15 372, 578, 600
14:14-16 473, 568, 597
14:15 440, 441, 508, 578, 596, 597
14:15-16 344, 597, 599
14:16 596
14:17 603
14:18 310, 370, 598
14:18-20 586
14:19 440
14:20 372, 577, 600
14:21 600
14:21-23 599
14:22 575, 599
14:22b 600
14:23 464, 506, 585, 600
14:24 155, 287, 288, 575, 576, 580, 585, 586
14:24-25 521, 600
14:25 123
14:26a 602, 603
14:26 556, 600
14:26b 603
14:26-28 581
14:27 581
14:27-28 577, 580, 581
14:27-33 602
14:28 578
14:29 462, 466, 575, 580, 581, 583
14:29-30 23
14:29-32 557
14:31 288, 576, 585, 586
14:31-32 575
14:31-33 604
14:32 162, 466, 568, 577, 583, 596
14:33 17, 426, 467
14:37 575
14:39 575, 595
14:40 603
15   577
15:1-2 240, 330
15:1-3 314, 328
15:1-4 368
15:3   565
15:17 240
15:22 242
15:24 319
15:34 167
15:44 241
15:45 81, 89, 98, 178, 228, 244, 273
15:45b 241
15:47-49 254
15:49 75
15:50 319
16:8   305
16:14 426
16:24 426

2 Corinthians
1:1   476
1:4   259
1:14   296
1:6   259, 427
1:11   557
1:21   93, 102, 347, 504
1:21-22 155, 156, 171, 287, 299, 476
1:22   93, 172, 328, 353
2:4   426
2:7   259
2:7-8 426
2:15   330
3:3   108, 174, 291, 352, 353
3:5-6 343
3:6   45, 101, 291, 337, 352, 353
3:7   343
3:7-9 352
3:9   343
3:17   80, 81, 100, 108, 244, 262, 273, 291, 330, 341, 343, 351, 422, 602
3:17-18 57, 98, 412
3:18   75, 108, 412
4:8   v
4:13   110, 343, 344
4:16   89, 90
4:18   v, 593
5:5   172, 353
5:13   167, 507, 509
5:17   479, 496
6:4   427
6:5   511
6:6   424, 427
6:10   426, 427
6:14-15 532
6:14-16 450, 451
6:16   103, 122, 212, 218, 249, 258, 261
6:17-18 160, 409
7:1   418, 436
7:15   542
8:2   426
10:1   430
10:3-6 449
10:5   58
10:13-17 582
11:4   568
11:27 511
12:1-10 599
12:2-4 530

12:9	556	5	195, 366, 382,	1:7	330, 331
12:9-10	549		407, 417, 419,	1:9-10	173
12:12	522, 523, 569,		430	1:13	93, 111, 172,
	572, 573, 574,	5:4	339		240, 299, 305,
	582	5:5	339		314, 325, 326,
13:5	479	5:5-6	344		328, 328, 329,
13:11	426	5:13-26	178		355, 363, 365,
13:13	99	5:13-6:2	291		367, 368, 371,
13:14	105, 148, 467	5:16	421, 434		376, 476, 513
		5:16-18	366, 382	1:13-14	103, 171, 353
Galatians		5:16-25	57, 171, 241,	1:15	426
1:12	565		417	1:17	110, 116, 156,
1:15	309	5:16-26	371		157, 209, 214,
1:17	480	5:17	418		231, 232, 343
1:22	479	5:18	287, 419, 420,	1:17-18	291, 344, 396
2:2	601		421, 434, 477	1:20	264
2:16	423, 572	5:19	430	1:22-23	476, 479
2:20	432	5:19-22	419, 422	1:23	127
3	331	5:21	430	2:1	331
3:2	304, 423	5:22	93, 101, 110,	2:4-5	337
3:2-3	345		132, 162, 175,	2:5	328, 330
3:3	339, 417, 420,		176, 308, 317,	2:5-6	242, 243
	421		423, 424, 433,	2:6	479
3:4	420, 421		449, 517, 592	2:7	427
3:5	324, 345, 372,	5:22-23	422, 431, 563	2:8	330, 424, 428
	423, 522, 574	5:23	430	2:11	540
3:10	423	5:23b	431	2:13	301
3:13-14	345	5:24	432	2:15	419, 496
3:14	111	5:25	432, 434	2:16	479
3:19	291	6:1	110, 344, 350,	2:17	301
3:22	572		408, 430	2:18	350, 456, 468,
3:23-24	222	6:2	342, 421, 422		469, 470
3:23-25	257	6:7-8	434	2:19	467, 468
3:27	358, 483	6:8	132, 175, 339,	2:20	575, 583
3:28	468, 479		449	2:20-22	27, 347, 443,
4:4	17, 114, 228	6:15	496		444, 452, 470
4:6	439, 440	6:19	421	2:21	453
4:5	31	6:22	421	2:21-22	96, 103, 122,
4:5-6	350				217, 218
4:6	26, 27, 97, 102,	**Ephesians**		2:22	100, 212, 257,
	105, 108, 239,	1	364		258, 261, 453,
	262, 271, 273,	1:1	479		476
	348, 352, 371,	1:4	159	3:3	565
	468, 477	1:5	31, 409	3:5	583
4:19	416	1:6	160	3:12	468

3:14   26, 97, 108
3:14-17 348, 439
3:14-19 414
3:16   26, 89, 90, 97, 108, 514
3:17   102, 262, 352, 453
3:18   396
3:19   415
3:20   150, 514
4   552
4:1   427
4:3   27
4:3-6 469
4:4   109, 468, 479
4:5   358
4:7   556, 558
4:7-11 554, 558
4:10   127
4:10-12 190
4:11   288, 459, 461, 463, 557, 582, 584
4:11-12 575, 576
4:11-13 271
4:11-14 396
4:11-16 467
4:12   479, 556, 557, 561, 584
4:13   iii, 412, 584
4:13-16 372
4:15   426
4:15-16 479
4:16   453, 556
4:22   330
4:22-6:9 494
4:23   336
4:23-24 330
4:24   419, 431, 496
4:25-5:21 516
4:29   556
4:30   93, 96, 103, 172, 190, 248, 291, 328, 329, 355, 363, 376, 424
4:32   331, 427
5:1   427
5:1-2 416
5:2   426
5:9   428
5:14   167
5:15-17 411, 516
5:17-32 57
5:18   122, 151, 161, 165, 167, 193, 356, 376, 411, 506
5:18b 516
5:18-20 246, 487, 503, 518
5:19   601
5:22-6:4 516
5:23   479
5:26   102, 142, 211, 253, 291, 331, 333, 338, 358
5:26-27 336
5:30   479
6   440
6:12   178, 289, 449
6:13   547
6:17   209, 337, 437, 524
6:18   372, 437, 440, 509, 543, 578

Philippians
1:1   458
1:19   26, 97, 108, 262, 273, 438
1:23   418
1:27   467
1:27-30 449
2:1-2 470
2:1-5 470, 471
2:3-5 471
2:4   592
2:5   471
2:7   15, 104, 239
2:8   516
2:12   542
2:12-13 329
2:13   420
2:27-28 426
3   474
3:1   426
3:1-6 421
3:3   104, 341, 421, 473, 474, 519
3:9   572
3:20-21 414
4:4   426
4:6-7 426
4:7   449
4:9   426
4:13   259

Colossians
1:2   479
1:8   96, 101, 169, 344, 411, 426
1:9-10 411
1:10   372
1:14   330, 331
1:15   490
1:16   488
1:16-17 491
1:17   183
1:18   479, 490
1:19   238, 348
1:21-22 331
1:24   479
1:27   262, 479
1:27-28 372
1:28   479
2:2   426
2:2-3 372
2:7   453, 479
2:8   415
2:9   238, 348
2:10   479
2:9-10 415
2:11   330, 341
2:12   358, 483

2:13	328, 331, 337	5:20	462, 575	5:22	512
2:19	372, 469, 479	5:21	462	6:12	434, 449, 456
3:1	264	5:23	426	6:13	477
3:4	253			6:16	471, 472
3:5	409, 433	**2 Thessalonians**		6:19	434
3:9	330	1:4	427		
3:9-10	496	2:2	296	**2 Timothy**	
3:9-4:1	494	2:8	135, 146	1:6	526, 557
3:10	75, 90, 160, 330, 412	2:9	523, 569	1:7	111, 344, 350
		2:10	330	1:9	330
3:10-11	419	2:13	331, 339	1:14	151, 210, 212, 216, 257, 258, 261, 347, 458
3:11	468	3:2	429		
3:12	427, 431				
3:12-14	425	**1 Timothy**		2:16-22	356
3:14	469	1:11	416	2:19	172, 328
3:15	449, 479	1:13	249	2:20	122, 449
3:16	163, 210, 519, 521, 601	1:15	330	3:4	172
		1:16	434	4:5	167
3:24	420	1:17	471, 472	4:16-17	565
4:14	573	1:18	575, 576	4:17	246
		2:1-2	471, 472		
1 Thessalonians		2:3-4	330	**Titus**	
1:5	279, 327, 514	2:8	471, 472	1:1	418
1:6	176, 308, 411, 426, 518	3	230	1:2	434
		3:1	464, 587	1:5	458, 526
2:14	479	3:1-2	458	1:5-9	460
2:18	387	3:1-7	458	1:7	458
4:7-8	248, 435	3:1-13	460	1:8	430
4:8	345, 436	3:15	122, 449, 468, 471, 474, 478	2:1-10	494
4:13-17	447			2:10	429
5:2	296	3:15-4:3	356	3:4	427
5:6	167	3:16	81, 229, 241, 339	3:4-5	330
5:8	167			3:4-6	335
5:11	556	4:1	568	3:5	93, 102, 176, 211, 299, 328, 358, 499
5:12-13	465	4:1-5	510		
5:14	427, 465	4:4	557		
5:16	426	4:5	471, 472	3:5-6	139, 150, 151, 330, 338
5:16-18	461	4:7-8	510		
5:16-21	461	4:14	458, 460, 526, 575, 576	3:6	165
5:17-19	438			3:7	434
5:18-19	487	5:5	471, 472		
5:19	41, 145, 151, 166, 248, 424, 462, 469,	5:11	526	**Hebrews**	
		5:17	458, 459	1:1-2	198
		5:19	458	1:1-3	577
5:19-21	54	5:21	109	1:2	284, 488

Scripture Index

1:2-3	183
1:3	264, 491
1:5	31
1:6	490
1:7	109, 568
1:9	159, 356, 504, 518
1:13	264
1:14	109, 568
2:3	323
2:3-4	582, 583
2:4	321, 323, 372, 522, 523, 569, 574
2:11	102
2:13	572
2:14	232
2:15	330
2:19	429
3:1	356
3:6	468, 474
3:7	106
3:7-11	103
3:7-19	384
3:7-4:11	449, 477
3:10-11	192
3:14	356
4:3	192
4:5	192
4:12	146
5:2	249
5:8	516
5:9	330
5:12-14	372
5:14	564
6:4	221, 318
6:4-5	357
6:4-6	356
6:5	522, 523, 574
7:5	464
7:23	464
7:25	439
8:1	264, 265
8:10	291, 351, 451
9	238
9:8	100
9:12	330
9:14	7, 12, 99, 100, 102, 110, 237, 238, 240, 271, 331
10:10	331
10:12	264, 265
10:14	331
10:15-17	103
10:19-22	456, 468
10:20	249
10:21	468
10:26-29	356
10:29	111, 248, 343
10:33	356
10:34	420
11	571, 572
11:32-38	195
11:33-35	571
12:2	169, 264, 265
12:6	161
12:9	418, 568
12:14	436
12:21	542
12:23	568
12:29	144
13:7	458
13:15	155, 452
13:17	458
13:20	426
13:24	458

James

1:2-3	427
1:5-8	116
1:15b	115
1:17	115
1:18	115
1:25	291, 342, 422
2	331
2:12	291, 342, 422
2:14-16	433
2:23	199
3:9	90
4:5	348
5	153, 154
5:6	230
5:12-16	573
5:14	458
5:14-15	153
5:14-16	484, 572
5:15	571, 573

1 Peter

1:2	93, 331, 339
1:9	330
1:10-11	102, 280
1:11	26, 97, 108
1:12	523
1:13	167
1:14	249
1:15-16	436
1:18	330
1:23	211, 333, 334
2:2	176, 372
2:4-5	468
2:5	155, 452, 453, 474
2:7-8	340
2:9	155, 331
2:11	418, 424
2:13-3:9	494
3	243
3:18	12, 102, 230, 240, 241, 242, 243, 468, 495
3:19-20	242, 337, 338
3:20-21	447
3:21	299, 358, 483
3:22	243, 265
4:6	328, 337
4:7	167
4:10-11	557
4:14	111, 121, 212, 343, 373, 478, 514, 548
4:17	122, 449, 468
4:18	420
5:1	458

5:1-4	583		476, 504	1:20	372, 440, 556, 578, 598
5:5	458	3:1	262	1:20-21	437
5:8	167	3:2	173		
		3:9	334		
2 Peter		3:24	212, 260, 287, 345, 455	**Revelation**	
1:3-4	412			1-3	454
1:4	75, 457	4:2	96	1:3	462
1:5-7	423, 431	4:2-3	265, 568	1:4	109, 233, 266
1:10	46	4:2-4	520	1:5	330, 477, 490, 521
1:17	121	4:4	96		
1:20-21	72	4:6	110, 265, 473	1:6	155, 452
1:21	102, 137, 174	4:8	27, 101, 425	1:8	266
2:12b	434	4:12	27, 169	1:10	196, 506, 509, 543
2:15	220	4:12-13	260, 455		
2:21	357	4:13	27, 150, 169, 212, 345	1:14-15	166
3:3	296			1:15	140
3:9	330, 427	4:15	415	1:17	542
3:10	296	4:15-16	455	2	19, 231, 305, 385
3:11	436	4:16	27, 101, 169, 425		
3:18	372, 412			2:5	329
		5	266	2:7	19, 43, 96, 124, 389, 462
1 John		5:6	96, 101, 263, 265		
1:1	320, 446			2:11	19, 462
1:1-3	253, 372	5:6-8	224, 265	2:13	479
1:1-4	38, 456	5:8	96, 265, 272	2:14	220
1:2	456	5:11-12	454	2:17	19, 462
1:3	345, 457	5:16	249	2:20	201
1:3-4	458	5:20	101, 253, 456	2:23	406
1:6-7	345			2:29	19, 462
1:7	331	**2 John**		3	19, 231, 305, 385
1:8	366	1:2	520		
1:9	250, 329, 331, 371	1:7	265	3:1	109, 233
		1:9-11	520	3:6	19, 462
2:1	109, 230, 259, 260, 261, 439	1:8	420	3:13	19, 462
				3:14	169, 447, 477, 479, 521
2:5-6	455	**3 John**			
2:13a	372	1:6	454	3:22	19
2:14a	372	1:9	454	3:29	462
2:18	284			4:1-2	530
2:20	102, 155, 156, 286, 287, 332, 347, 476, 504	**Jude**		4:2	506, 509, 543
		1:1	102	4:5	109, 146, 210, 233
		1:3	330		
2:24	454, 458	1:3-4	437	4:6	175
2:27	102, 155, 156, 286, 287, 347,	1:11	220	4:8	101, 266
		1:19	346	4:11	183

5:1-2	172	20:4	155
5:1-9	328	20:6	155, 452
5:5	172	20:10	182, 270
5:6	101, 109, 146, 209, 233	21	125, 126, 447
		21:1	182
5:9	172	21:2	124
5:9-10	155	21:3	125, 451
6:1	172	21:4	115
6:10	452	21:6	255
6:12	296	21:7	160, 409
7:2-8	172	21:9	124
7:3	328	21:10	506, 509, 530, 543
7:17	115, 255		
8:2	109	21:23	182
8:3-8	172	22	182
9:4	172, 328	22:1	140, 204
9:20	509, 530	22:1-2	255
10:4	172	22:5	155
10:7	583	22:6	568, 583
11:4	208	22:7	462
11:18	420, 583	22:9	105, 583
12	125, 126	22:9-10	462
12:1	118, 125	22:10	172
13:6	100	22:16	454
13:13	523	22:16-17	43
13:18	523	22:17	124, 125, 255
14:2	140	22:18-19	462
14:12	572		
14:13	124		
15:2	175		
15:3	449		
16:6	583		
16:12-16	146		
16:13-14	568		
17:3	506, 509, 543		
17:14	146		
17:15	182		
18:2	540		
18:20	583		
18:24	583		
19:6	140		
19:7	124		
19:10	105, 111		
19-22	126		
20:3	172		

Subject Index

A
Aaron 154, 166, 190, 235, 451, 452, 505, 529, 530, 531, 575
Abraham 199, 345, 346, 572, 574, 576
Abrahamic 300
Adam 114, 128, 147, 174, 178, 187, 188, 192, 205, 228, 273, 290, 448, 449, 538
Anabaptist 17, 43, 46, 52, 53, 54, 55
Anglican 64, 106
Anointing 93, 102, 132, 152, 153, 154, 155, 156, 157, 158, 159, 161, 166, 201, 202, 208, 219, 220, 225, 228, 229, 230, 233, 234, 235, 271, 285, 286, 287, 299, 328, 329, 346, 482, 484, 487, 504, 505, 515, 519, 525, 545, 546, 547, 548, 615, 617
Anthropology 10, 80, 89
Apostles vi, 10, 53, 60, 70, 76, 96, 141, 164, 243, 270, 273, 275, 278, 284, 287, 288, 293, 295, 297, 298, 303, 304, 306, 307, 308, 311, 312, 320, 321, 322, 323, 324, 327, 375, 377, 385, 396, 458, 460, 461, 463, 465, 480, 485, 498, 509, 513, 516, 522, 531, 544, 547, 549, 556, 557, 558, 560, 565, 572, 573, 575, 582, 584, 585, 589, 590, 609, 618, 619, 621
Apostolic 11, 59, 60, 270, 304,

306, 322,
526, 552,
559, 582,
587, 589,
629
Apostles' Creed
10, 76, 243
Asceticism
430, 509,
510
Aspect 32, 36, 58,
75, 86, 95,
118, 125,
127, 129,
132, 156,
227, 231,
261, 289,
313, 326,
328, 329,
330, 348,
370, 393,
396, 406,
409, 414,
423, 224,
426, 427,
429, 435,
438, 451,
454, 458,
466, 473,
474, 490,
506, 539,
571, 628,
625
Athanasius
13, 21, 25,
94, 229,
412, 416
Atonement
56, 238,
334, 343,
500,
Augustine
9, 11, 15,
16, 18, 26,
27, 28, 30,

35, 44, 95,
187, 242,
248, 262,
266, 308,
359, 364,
395, 455,
479, 517,
628

B

Baptism i, 57, 60, 66,
68, 71, 72,
98, 102,
113, 119,
120, 121,
133, 144,
145, 147,
164, 165,
168, 170,
171, 175,
211, 215,
228, 229,
230, 231,
237, 247,
264, 265,
266, 278,
279, 280,
281, 282,
283, 284,
285, 294,
295, 297,
298, 299,
300, 302,
303, 304,
305, 306,
307, 308,
309, 310,
312, 313,
315, 320,
326, 329,
332, 333,
335, 336,
338, 346,
358, 359,
360, 361,

362, 366,
367, 368,
370, 374,
375, 376,
377, 378,
379, 380,
391, 393,
411, 436,
447, 469,
470, 475,
476, 482,
483, 484,
485, 487,
523, 533,
534, 536,
579, 580,
609, 611,
620, 621,
629, 631,
633
Baptist
5, 65, 67,
70, 133,
144, 161,
157, 168,
214, 215,
235, 251,
264, 278,
279, 281,
282, 285,
294, 297,
309, 314,
346, 359,
476, 513,
515, 587
Barth, Karl
x, 38, 39,
40, 49, 50,
51, 56, 73,
94, 95, 109,
110, 395,
401, 402,
489, 490,
496, 537,
606, 632

Subject Index

Bavinck, Herman	291, 292,	477, 479,
	29, 30, 35,	293, 299,	480, 499,
	37, 38, 58,	303, 305,	505, 506,
	59, 60, 61,	306, 307,	511, 513,
	99, 148,	310, 311,	514, 515,
	248, 458,	312, 313,	516, 517,
	459, 482,	316, 319,	518, 520,
	494, 558,	323, 324,	521, 522,
	566, 568,	326, 327,	523, 524,
	606	328, 337,	531, 537,
Beautiful	47, 89, 107,	338, 339,	544, 545,
	129, 158,	241, 343,	547, 548,
	197, 329,	345, 346,	549, 552,
	405, 438,	347, 348,	553, 560,
	517, 533,	349, 350,	562, 563,
	541, 559,	352, 353,	571, 572,
	572	354, 355,	573, 575,
Believers	47, 55, 60,	356, 359,	579, 580,
	68, 71, 72,	361, 367,	583, 584,
	75, 96, 100,	369, 373,	585, 586,
	102, 103,	374, 375,	587, 591,
	114, 115,	382, 384,	599, 600,
	132, 141,	385, 386,	602, 603,
	142, 143,	390, 391,	618
	151, 156,	408, 409,	Beloved 102, 106,
	157, 158,	411, 412,	159, 160,
	159, 160,	414, 415,	173, 229,
	168, 171,	416, 420,	292, 297,
	173, 176,	423, 424,	410, 416,
	178, 185,	425, 431,	437, 476,
	199, 210,	432, 433,	499
	211, 212,	434, 435,	Bible vii, viii, ix,
	215, 216,	436, 437,	x, xi, 7, 19,
	217, 218,	438, 439,	23, 26, 31,
	220, 221,	440, 449,	35, 50, 52,
	225, 228,	450, 452,	53, 54, 57,
	229, 235,	453, 454,	60, 65, 72,
	236, 242,	455, 456,	79, 86, 95,
	246, 251,	461, 462,	96, 97, 104,
	254, 256,	464, 465,	111, 112,
	257, 258,	466, 467,	114, 117,
	260, 261,	468, 469,	118, 132,
	262, 268,	470, 472,	140, 154,
	271, 272,	473, 474,	171, 178,
	275, 288,	475, 476,	182, 199,

673

212, 225,
238, 239,
296, 300,
315, 338,
357, 377,
382, 389,
392, 394,
395, 396,
399, 401,
402, 403,
405, 412,
444, 478,
489, 491,
507, 510,
517, 525,
535, 541,
542, 591,
594, 608,
609, 610,
618, 621,
622, 628,
629, 637

Blessing 24, 71, 72,
74, 105,
113, 139,
141, 161,
163, 174,
255, 256,
280, 282,
286, 324,
326, 345,
346, 354,
355, 356,
361, 262,
396, 374,
375, 376,
378, 387,
393, 413,
480, 482,
489, 492,
493, 519,
525, 536,
560, 586,
597

Body 11, 40, 74,

90, 91, 114,
118, 121,
142, 145,
164, 168,
216, 217,
238, 241,
279, 285,
305, 306,
311, 331,
333 335,
341, 347,
348, 355,
358, 359,
360, 361,
362, 365,
379, 407,
408, 409,
418, 433,
436, 438,
443, 444,
446, 447,
450, 453,
467, 468,
469, 470,
475, 476,
479, 482,
483, 486,
487, 497,
507, 525,
528, 529,
533, 539,
540, 542,
544, 556,
560, 561,
583, 584,
585

Breath 19, 28, 29,
30, 31, 88,
89, 90, 91,
97, 101,
104, 105,
107, 109,
124, 132,
133, 134,
135, 136,

138, 144,
146, 148,
165, 166,
174, 176,
180, 181,
183, 184,
186, 202,
203, 228,
272, 273,
274, 293,
331, 366,
539, 541

C
Calvinism 14, 54, 55,
72, 78, 495,
619, 637
Calvin, John
3, 43, 46,
47, 48, 49,
55, 186,
187, 243,
265, 326,
350, 359,
396, 468,
485, 486,
493, 588,
590, 609,
619, 637
Cessationism
59, 60, 62,
552, 587,
590
Charismata
13, 16, 21,
22, 47, 56,
59, 62, 73,
81, 299,
300, 344,
361, 372,
379, 423,
461, 464,
465, 466,
467, 504,
536, 552,

	554, 556,	181, 182,	412, 413,
	557, 558,	183, 184,	414, 415,
	559, 560,	186, 187,	416, 417,
	561, 562,	190, 209,	419, 421,
	563, 564,	217, 218,	422, 426,
	565, 577,	221, 222,	428, 430,
	579, 583,	223, 224,	432, 434,
	584, 585,	228, 229,	435, 437,
	588, 589,	230, 232,	438, 439,
	590, 591,	233, 235,	443, 447,
	592, 593,	238, 239,	450, 451,
	594, 595,	240, 241,	452, 453,
	601, 602	242, 243,	455, 456,
Charismatics		244, 246,	457, 458,
	2, 6, 17, 20,	253, 254,	461, 468,
	21, 45, 54,	257, 258,	469, 470,
	65, 69, 74,	260, 261,	471, 473,
	75, 76, 78,	264, 265,	474, 476,
	309, 326,	271, 273,	478, 479,
	374, 394,	281, 282,	482, 483,
	395	288, 291,	484, 486,
Christ	i, ii, iii, 12,	295, 296,	487, 488,
	13, 14, 15,	297, 298,	489, 490,
	38, 45, 47,	301, 302,	491, 492,
	60, 62, 63,	305, 306,	493, 494,
	64, 69, 70,	310, 311,	495, 497,
	74, 77, 78,	312, 316,	498, 499,
	80, 81, 89,	317, 322,	500, 503,
	97, 98, 100,	326, 238,	504, 511,
	101, 102,	333, 335,	513, 514,
	103, 104,	336, 337,	515, 516,
	105, 106,	338, 339,	517, 518,
	108, 109,	340, 342,	519, 520,
	114, 116,	343, 344,	521, 522,
	119, 121,	345, 346,	523, 524,
	122, 123,	348, 350,	532, 548,
	126, 128,	351, 352,	549, 553,
	131, 136,	359, 360,	554, 556,
	138, 139,	361, 362,	558, 561,
	155, 156,	363, 365,	562, 564,
	157, 159,	366, 368,	565, 566,
	160, 163,	372, 373,	567, 570,
	167, 171,	379, 384,	572, 574,
	173, 174,	390, 391,	575, 577,
	175, 176,	410, 411,	580, 581,

583, 584,
604, 626,
631, 637
Christian 28, 35, 36,
38, 39, 40,
41, 46, 50,
54, 57, 59,
66, 67, 68,
69, 73, 78,
80, 83, 92,
94, 102,
106, 113,
118, 119,
126, 147,
149, 160,
166, 169,
171, 173,
175, 182,
187, 218,
246, 250,
252, 274,
285, 286,
287, 298,
299, 306,
315, 332,
346, 357,
364, 365,
366, 370,
373, 376,
379, 396,
397, 400,
402, 405,
409, 412,
415, 418,
421, 424,
426, 429,
433, 435,
436, 437,
446, 457,
461, 468,
469, 470,
473, 477,
481, 488,
491, 492,
497, 509,

512, 515,
531, 533,
534, 538,
553, 563,
572, 586,
594, 606,
607, 608,
609, 612,
621, 626,
627, 628,
629, 631,
632, 639
Christianity
iii, 13, 14,
21, 35, 36,
37, 67, 69,
75, 86, 129,
147, 392,
488, 530,
532, 355,
534, 554,
589, 594,
627, 628
Christology
13, 73, 77,
79, 80, 81,
239, 240,
618,
Church ii, vi, viii, x,
1, 2, 3, 4, 5,
6, 7, 9, 10,
11, 12, 13,
14, 15, 16,
17, 18, 19,
20, 21, 22,
23, 24, 25,
27, 28, 29,
35, 36, 37,
38, 39, 40,
41, 43, 44,
45, 46, 47,
50, 51, 53,
54, 55, 56,
58, 59, 60,
61, 62, 63,

64, 66, 67,
68, 69, 72,
73, 74, 75,
76, 78, 79,
82, 85, 88,
92, 93, 96,
100, 101,
103, 104,
107, 118,
122, 123,
125, 126,
128, 129,
147, 153,
175, 205,
211, 217,
218, 219,
221, 224,
240, 244,
245, 258,
260, 261,
274, 275,
278, 285,
286, 287,
288, 290,
294, 301,
304, 305,
306, 311,
312, 318,
319, 330,
333, 346,
347, 361,
362, 364,
373, 376,
379, 382,
384, 385,
386, 389,
390, 391,
392, 393,
394, 398,
399, 400,
437, 444,
447, 449,
450, 451,
452, 453,
456, 457,

Subject Index

458, 459,
460, 561,
462, 363,
464, 465,
466, 467,
468, 469,
471, 472,
474, 475,
476, 477,
478, 479,
480, 482,
485, 487,
488, 495,
497, 506,
507, 512,
516, 531,
532, 552,
553, 555,
556, 559,
564, 565,
566, 568,
572, 573,
575, 576,
577, 578,
580, 581,
582, 584,
585, 586,
587, 589,
590, 591,
592, 593,
594, 595,
596, 598,
599, 600,
601, 602,
603, 604,
606, 613,
617, 620,
623, 624,
627, 628,
631, 636,
637, 639

Church History
3, 6, 11, 16,
17, 21, 53,
69, 73, 79,

88, 125,
129, 245,
312, 330,
382, 389,
394, 453,
512, 532,
573, 587,
589, 593,
594

Circumcision
312, 326,
330, 340,
341, 474

City 36, 104,
151, 196,
216, 282,
289, 292,
295, 301,
320, 322,
388, 389,
477, 480,
514, 524,
549, 612

Cleansing 141, 142,
154, 211,
327, 331,
333, 334,
335, 338,
358

Commandments
210, 293,
318, 390,
419, 422,
454

Communion
26, 38, 148,
437, 454,
455, 457,
467

Congregation
iv, 6, 55, 64,
65, 66, 71,
73, 142,
218, 356,
359, 392,

393, 458,
459, 461,
462, 463,
465, 466,
474, 480,
485, 511,
603, 622

Constantinople
9, 24, 92

Conversion
10, 51, 56,
71, 229,
278, 298,
299, 303,
304, 305,
309, 312,
313, 329,
339, 344,
366, 367,
371, 375,
379, 380,
413, 484,
500, 513,
553, 599

Covenant viii, 77, 120,
158, 183,
186, 191,
203, 206,
210, 249,
290, 291,
292, 298,
300, 343,
346, 351,
352, 353,
391

Creation 39, 56, 76,
91, 101,
124, 128,
169, 170,
174, 177,
178, 179,
180, 182,
183, 184,
185, 186,
187, 188,

	190, 191, 192, 202, 246, 273, 444, 447, 456, 457, 474, 488, 489, 490, 491, 492, 493, 494, 495, 496, 497, 501, 620, 637		223, 230, 235, 237, 240, 241, 242, 243, 249, 257, 262, 265, 266, 271, 290, 326, 328, 330, 331, 336, 337, 338, 342, 343,		306, 307, 309, 313, 314, 315, 316, 319, 327, 333, 367, 420, 480, 485, 506, 507, 511, 513, 514, 515, 518, 521, 524, 546,
Culture	38, 70, 184, 185, 186, 322, 400, 404, 444, 488, 501, 542		346, 352, 365, 366, 398, 407, 408, 409, 410, 432, 434, 448,	Divine	547, 561, 565, 570, 572 10, 16, 24, 25, 26, 28, 29, 32, 34,
Curse	345, 397		493, 501, 516, 541,		35, 39, 40, 47, 52, 53,
D			558, 565,		75, 85, 88,
Daughter	117, 118, 125, 129	Deity	575, 604 94, 99, 101,		90, 92, 93, 94, 95, 99,
David	30, 43, 49, 115, 139, 142, 152, 155, 156, 158, 163, 166, 173, 177, 194, 195, 196, 197, 201, 202, 203, 205, 212, 216, 217, 219, 220, 231, 232, 233, 235, 241, 242,	Disciples	103, 132, 148, 224, 227, 238, 239, 271, 351, 415 ix, 3, 124, 153, 163, 167, 215, 216, 217, 220, 256, 258, 260, 262, 263, 264, 266, 267, 269, 270, 272, 273, 274, 275, 278, 284, 285,		100, 101, 103, 105, 108, 109, 111, 112, 113, 116, 118, 121, 123, 124, 125, 127, 128, 129, 147, 148, 149, 158, 160, 163, 171, 195, 212, 220, 224, 226, 227, 228, 230, 232, 233, 234,
	243, 317, 327, 335, 338, 536, 544, 610		286, 287, 293, 295, 297, 298,		238, 239, 240, 242, 243, 244,
Death	28, 61, 91, 102, 122,		302, 303,		253, 254,

Subject Index

	267, 268, 270, 275, 281, 285, 312, 328, 373, 390, 394, 397, 404, 406, 413, 416, 419, 422, 432, 434, 439, 446, 452, 453, 454, 455, 456, 457, 460, 482, 491, 494, 510, 520, 530, 531, 533, 536, 538, 540, 543, 554, 555, 592, 608, 618		141, 146, 150, 157, 159, 170, 171, 173, 175, 179, 182, 187, 189, 202, 208, 209, 210, 211, 215, 216, 218, 219, 222, 224, 226, 236, 243, 246, 251, 252, 255, 256, 257, 258, 264, 265, 266, 269, 271, 280, 283, 284, 286, 287, 289, 291, 292, 293, 297, 298, 317, 320, 324, 338, 356, 392, 399, 409, 426, 433, 438, 439, 444, 447, 448, 453, 456, 458, 472, 478, 480, 486, 487, 489, 496, 499, 518, 522, 541, 543, 560, 563, 566, 579, 579, 592	Egypt Egyptian Elders Elements	78, 275, 370, 389, 398 120, 168, 174, 176, 177, 179, 188, 189, 191, 206, 207, 210, 382, 384, 444, 449, 452, 497, 512, 530, 575, 589 66, 118, 120, 163, 176, 179, 188, 189, 509, 531, 534, 589 150, 153, 155, 190, 194, 213, 217, 294, 295, 345, 385, 430, 458, 459, 460, 461, 462, 484, 507, 508, 511, 512, 526, 559, 565, 572 16, 52, 123, 132, 133, 185, 379, 382, 425, 451, 462, 463
Dooyeweerd, Herman	89, 184				
Dualism	37, 38, 39, 90, 91, 241, 444, 486, 487, 490, 491, 492, 495, 496, 497, 507, 510, 544, 558				
Duty	161, 399, 420, 480				
E					
Earth	9, 31, 55, 87, 88, 90, 97, 106, 114, 119, 121, 122, 125, 131, 132, 140,	Ecclesiastical	20, 54, 74,	Elijah	137, 143, 150, 152, 155, 156, 213, 229, 237, 260, 279, 511,

679

Empire 527, 542,
546, 547,
567, 571,
573, 574,
576, 587
213, 393,
626

Enlightenment
35, 39, 51,
52, 73, 395,
590, 595

Epoch 322, 329,
389, 448

Eschatology
10, 77, 80

Eternal v, 12, 25,
29, 30, 31,
32, 33, 34,
35, 36, 40,
41, 92, 93,
99, 100,
102, 106,
107, 108,
110, 112,
117, 123,
128, 129,
159, 160,
166, 175,
199, 227,
238, 239,
240, 250,
252, 253,
254, 257,
261, 271,
293, 327,
329, 339,
340, 391,
408, 434,
437, 455,
456, 457,
491, 494,
498, 499,
558, 593,
626,

Evangelical
68, 71, 72,
75, 77, 78,
82, 221,
280, 377,
392, 400,
403, 413,
414, 474,
483, 607,
623, 626

Evangelism
44, 68, 69,
545, 549

Exodus 119, 122,
168, 169,
174, 177,
186, 188,
189, 190,
191, 192,
202, 206,
207, 214,
223, 237,
246, 290,
382, 445,
449, 508,
617

Ezekiel 104, 122,
124, 135,
137, 140,
163, 173,
178, 199,
204, 205,
212, 273,
283, 293,
327, 328,
333, 341,
447, 528,
535, 543,
544, 605,
607

F

Faith iii, 13, 23,
34, 35, 38,
39, 40, 41,
44, 46, 47,
49, 50, 52,
55, 56, 57,
70, 71, 72,
76, 82, 92,
110, 136,
153, 161,
172, 176,
183, 185,
194, 195,
221, 222,
240, 299,
302, 305,
307, 313,
314, 315,
322, 324,
325, 326,
327, 328,
329, 338,
339, 340,
343, 344,
345, 348,
351, 352,
354, 355,
360, 362,
364, 365,
367, 368,
369, 371,
372, 373,
374, 376,
378, 391,
393, 399,
404, 412,
413, 414,
415, 420,
421, 423,
424, 426,
428, 429,
431, 432,
433, 435,
437, 468,
469, 470,
476, 497,
500, 510,
516, 524,

Subject Index

	533, 537,		115, 118,		410, 414,
	547, 549,		119, 128,		415, 416,
	551, 552,		136, 139,		439, 440,
	556, 557,		146, 147,		446, 454,
	558, 563,		148, 149,		455, 456,
	564, 567,		151, 152,		457, 458,
	570, 571,		156, 157,		459, 468,
	572, 573,		158, 159,		469, 470,
	576, 583,		160, 161,		472, 473,
	584, 592,		163, 175,		474, 476,
	594, 598,		176, 178,		478, 479,
	599, 604,		182, 189,		480, 487,
	606, 615,		191, 198,		503, 518,
	624, 628,		199, 206,		525, 548,
	638		215, 216,		554, 572,
Family	2, 32, 115,		217, 218,		581, 588,
	118, 171,		221, 224,		589, 620,
	243, 308,		227, 229,		629
	357, 452,		230, 231,	Feast	12, 140,
	467, 468,		232, 236,		164, 204,
	470, 516		238, 240,		254, 255,
Fasting	373, 386,		241, 244,		289, 295,
	460, 504,		245, 246,		354, 449
	505, 509,		251, 252,	Festivals	255, 305,
	510, 511,		253, 254,		354
	512, 513,		257, 258,	Figurative	132, 134,
	526		259, 261,		165, 204,
Father	9, 11, 12,		262, 263,		208, 278,
	13, 15, 16,		264, 265,		542
	24, 25, 26,		266, 267,	Fire	v, vi, 55,
	27, 28, 29,		268, 269,		57, 86, 109,
	30, 31, 32,		270, 271,		122, 132,
	33, 35, 36,		272, 273,		133, 137,
	37, 38, 39,		274, 282,		138, 142,
	45, 64, 67,		283, 286,		143, 144,
	78, 81, 85,		287, 294,		145, 146,
	86, 91, 92,		297, 298,		147, 148,
	93, 94, 95,		318, 320,		150, 151,
	97, 98, 99,		348, 349,		153, 162,
	100, 102,		350, 351,		163, 164,
	103, 105,		357, 362,		166, 170,
	106, 107,		363, 364,		176, 182,
	108, 109,		371, 372,		190, 207,
	111, 112,		375, 381,		210, 211,
	113, 114,		385, 409,		277, 278,

681

279, 280, 282, 290, 291, 293, 294, 296, 303, 304, 359, 382, 383, 384, 483, 461, 509, 513, 517, 532, 534, 542, 543, 544, 571, 589, 605

Flood 74, 77, 138, 141, 170, 177, 179, 182, 186, 187, 188, 189, 190, 191, 192, 202, 205, 242, 447,

Food 152, 189, 252, 485, 498, 510, 152, 189, 252, 485

Forgiveness 11, 72, 229, 250, 273, 274, 275, 280, 297, 298, 299, 300, 311, 329, 331, 333, 371, 475, 484

Foundation 35, 58, 70, 77, 159, 183, 203, 206, 292, 301, 338, 405, 453,

478, 495, 519, 541, 575, 590, 628, 637

Framework 347, 379, 489, 495, 584

Freedom 78, 79, 291, 342, 343, 364, 411, 496, 552, 601, 602, 603

Fulfilled 172, 198, 205, 213, 236, 257, 287, 288, 291, 295, 296, 407, 576, 583, 595

Function 21, 22, 51, 59, 74, 80, 81, 90, 116, 153, 182, 183, 186, 191, 260, 263, 301, 344, 355, 379, 398, 401, 403, 422, 469, 463, 465, 526, 531, 539, 545, 552, 562, 578, 581, 584, 585, 592, 594, 601, 631

Future 3, 73, 173, 194, 260, 268, 296, 301, 305,

306, 310, 354, 390, 413, 414, 417, 492, 575, 589

G

Garden 136, 170, 187, 191, 192, 204, 444, 448, 449, 537, 538

Gentile 53, 131, 139, 219, 255, 289, 296, 301, 302, 305, 307, 310, 311, 312, 313, 339, 341, 345, 368, 388, 390, 468, 477, 498, 524, 565

Glorification 257, 264, 269, 296, 297, 414

Glossolalia 2, 5, 21, 24, 56, 59, 71, 72, 299, 370, 372, 374, 438, 440, 441, 461, 462, 475, 506, 537, 552, 561, 568, 577, 578, 579, 580, 584, 585, 586, 589,

Subject Index

	591, 592,	139, 140,	237, 238,
	595, 597,	141, 142,	239, 240,
	598, 599,	143, 144,	242, 243,
	601, 603,	147, 148,	244, 245,
	622	149, 150,	246, 247,
God	i, ii, v, vi,	151, 153,	248, 249,
	vii, viii, ix,	154, 155,	250, 251,
	x, 6, 9, 10,	156, 157,	252, 253,
	11, 13, 14,	158, 159,	254, 256,
	16, 17, 18,	160, 161,	257, 258,
	19, 22, 23,	162, 163,	260, 264,
	24, 25, 26,	164, 166,	267, 268,
	27, 28, 29,	167, 168,	269, 271,
	30, 31, 32,	169, 170,	272, 273,
	33, 38, 46,	171, 172,	278, 281,
	48, 49, 51,	173, 174,	283, 284,
	52, 54, 57,	175, 176,	285, 286,
	59, 61, 62,	178, 179,	288, 289,
	63, 64, 70,	180, 181,	290, 291,
	74, 75, 76,	182, 183,	292, 293,
	78, 79, 80,	184, 185,	294, 295,
	81, 82, 85,	186, 187,	296, 297,
	86, 87, 88,	188, 189,	298, 299,
	89, 90, 91,	190, 191,	300, 301,
	92, 93, 94,	192, 193,	302, 303,
	95, 96, 97,	194, 195,	306, 309,
	98, 99, 100,	196, 197,	310, 311,
	101, 102,	198, 199,	312, 313,
	103, 104,	200, 201,	316, 317,
	105, 106,	202, 203,	318, 319,
	107, 108,	204, 205,	321, 322,
	109, 111,	206, 207,	323, 324,
	112, 113,	208, 209,	325, 326,
	114, 115,	210, 211,	327, 328,
	116, 117,	212, 213,	329, 330,
	118, 119,	214, 215,	331, 332,
	120, 121,	216, 217,	333, 334,
	122, 123,	218, 219,	335, 336,
	124, 125,	220, 221,	337, 338,
	126, 127,	222, 223,	339, 340,
	128, 129,	224, 225,	342, 434,
	131, 132,	226, 227,	344, 345,
	133, 134,	228, 229,	346, 347,
	135, 136,	230, 233,	348, 349,
	137, 138,	235, 236,	350, 351,

352, 353, 354, 355, 356, 357, 360, 361, 362, 363, 365, 366, 368, 370, 371, 372, 373, 375, 376, 381, 383, 384, 385, 387, 389, 390, 391, 392, 393, 396, 399, 401, 402, 404, 406, 407, 408, 409, 410, 411, 412, 413, 414, 415, 416, 417, 419, 420, 422, 424, 425, 246, 427, 429, 430, 431, 432, 433, 434, 435, 436, 437, 438, 439, 440, 443, 444, 445, 446, 447, 448, 449, 450, 451, 452, 453, 454, 455, 456, 457, 459, 460, 461, 464, 466, 467, 468, 669, 470, 471, 472, 473, 474, 476, 477, 478, 479, 480, 481, 482, 483, 484, 485, 487, 488, 490, 491, 492, 493, 494, 495, 496, 497, 498, 499, 500, 501, 503, 504, 506, 507, 508, 510, 511, 512, 514, 515, 516, 517, 518, 519, 520, 521, 522, 523, 524, 525, 526, 527, 528, 529, 530, 531, 532, 533, 535, 537, 538, 540, 541, 542, 543, 544, 545, 547, 548, 549, 551, 552, 553, 554, 555, 558, 559, 560, 561, 562, 563, 564, 565, 566, 568, 569, 570, 571, 572, 573, 574, 576, 578, 579, 580, 583, 584, 587, 588, 590, 594, 596, 597, 598, 599, 600, 602, 603, 604, 607, 611, 612, 615, 616, 617, 618, 620, 621, 622, 623, 624, 625, 626, 629, 630, 632, 633, 636, 638

Godhead 11, 25, 32, 33, 85, 88, 92, 94, 95, 98, 101, 108, 109, 178, 183, 239, 240, 469

Godly 220, 225, 499, 519, 590

Gospel ii, 44, 68, 81, 98, 119, 121, 126, 159, 171, 175, 224, 236, 240, 244, 245, 246, 250, 258, 268, 270, 278, 281, 282, 285, 286, 288, 300, 301, 302, 307, 310, 314, 315,

Subject Index

	316, 323,	356, 358,	254, 255,
	325, 327,	359, 360,	256, 268,
	329, 332,	361, 363,	271, 291,
	333, 337,	364, 387,	297, 299,
	358, 363,	388, 410,	327, 330,
	368, 371,	412, 413,	341, 345,
	372, 380,	418, 424,	348, 349,
	387, 390,	428, 429,	350, 351,
	391, 392,	434, 436,	352, 353,
	399, 416,	440, 454,	354, 357,
	490, 493,	458, 464,	358, 362,
	497, 500,	468, 470,	369, 385,
	501, 514,	471, 473,	393, 396,
	561, 574,	476, 498,	404, 406,
	578, 583,	506, 507,	410, 411,
	608, 610,	508, 510,	414, 415,
	612, 613,	518, 541,	418, 419,
	616, 617,	554, 557,	423, 425,
	618, 620,	560, 574,	426, 428,
	623, 624,	581, 596,	429, 430,
	629, 632,	622, 627,	431, 439,
	636, 637	638	440, 444,
Greek	xi, 15, 35,	Guilt 13, 51, 72,	472, 473,
	74, 87, 88,	95, 154,	475, 476,
	91, 94, 95,	342, 343,	480, 481,
	96, 111,	371	485, 486,
	112, 114,		487, 489,
	119, 121,	**H**	494, 498,
	135, 142,	Heart	499, 501,
	169, 199,	v,vii, 12,	503, 507,
	221, 226,	19, 27, 48,	511, 517,
	227, 229,	49, 55, 89,	518, 521,
	241, 250,	90, 91, 92,	524, 541,
	256, 259,	102, 105,	542, 543,
	273, 274,	113, 119,	544, 569,
	275, 278,	139, 140,	570, 576,
	279, 280,	142, 144,	583, 596,
	286, 301,	147, 156,	600, 603,
	305, 308,	158, 162,	604
	319, 323,	163, 166,	
	334, 335,	171, 172,	Heaven
	339, 345,	174, 189,	9, 87, 101,
	346, 347,	190, 192,	103, 105,
	349, 350,	196, 202,	107, 113,
	351, 352,	203, 215,	117, 119,
		217, 236,	122, 134,

685

136, 140,
143, 150,
152, 167,
168, 173,
174, 179,
180, 183,
207, 211,
217, 218,
219, 225,
229, 234,
236, 247,
251, 252,
254, 255,
257, 260,
262, 264,
265, 267,
269, 271,
277, 281,
286, 287,
289, 292,
293, 296,
298, 303,
311, 334,
346, 351,
356, 357,
397, 416,
434, 439,
447, 453,
456, 480,
486, 489,
498, 518,
519, 522,
523, 542,
571, 579

Hebrew 17, 88, 112,
113, 117,
120, 126,
133, 138,
181, 186,
189, 225,
228, 247,
293, 426,
445, 500,
508, 528,
541

Hermeneutics
400, 402,
404, 632
History
3, 6, 8, 9,
11, 15, 16,
17, 18, 21,
28, 53, 66,
69, 70, 73,
79, 80, 88,
125, 129,
143, 147,
184, 185,
218, 222,
224, 231,
343, 245,
285, 290,
312, 330,
379, 382,
389, 394,
400, 404,
444, 453,
488, 493,
494, 496,
497, 512,
532, 562,
573, 587,
589, 590,
593, 594
Hodge, Charles
47, 243,
350, 399,
616
Holy Spirit
26, 27, 28,
29, 33, 34,
38, 40, 41,
43, 44, 45,
46, 47, 48,
49, 51, 52,
53, 55, 56,
57, 58, 60,
63, 64, 65,
67, 69, 72,
73, 74, 75,

76, 77, 78,
82, 85, 86,
89, 91, 92,
93, 94, 95,
96, 97, 98,
99, 100,
101, 102,
103, 104,
105, 106,
107, 108,
109, 110,
111, 112,
113, 114,
115, 116,
117, 119,
121, 122,
124, 125,
126, 127,
129, 131,
132, 133,
134, 136,
137, 138,
139, 140,
141, 142,
144, 145,
146, 147,
148, 149,
150, 151,
152, 153,
154, 155,
156, 157,
160, 161,
162, 163,
164, 165,
166, 167,
168, 169,
170, 171,
172, 173,
174, 175,
176, 177,
178, 180,
181, 182,
183, 184,
186, 187,
189, 190,

Subject Index

192, 194, 197, 198, 199, 200, 201, 203, 205, 206, 207, 208, 209, 210, 211, 212, 213, 214, 215, 216, 217, 218, 219, 220, 221, 222, 223, 224, 225, 226, 227, 228, 229, 230, 231, 232, 233, 234, 235, 236, 237, 238, 239, 240, 241, 244, 245, 246, 247, 248, 249, 250, 251, 252, 253, 254, 256, 257, 258, 259, 260, 261, 262, 263, 264, 265, 266, 267, 268, 270, 271, 272, 273, 274, 275, 277, 278, 279, 280, 281, 282, 283, 284, 285, 286, 287, 288, 290, 291, 293,

294, 295, 296, 297, 298, 300, 302, 303, 304, 305, 306, 308, 309, 310, 311, 312, 313, 314, 315, 316, 317, 318, 319, 320, 321, 322, 323, 324, 325, 326, 327, 328, 329, 331, 332, 333, 334, 335, 336, 337, 338, 339, 340, 341, 342, 343, 344, 345, 346, 347, 348, 349, 351, 353, 354, 355, 356, 357, 359, 360, 361, 363, 364, 365, 367, 368, 369, 370, 371, 372, 373, 374, 375, 376, 377, 378, 381, 382, 384, 385, 386, 387, 388, 389, 390, 391, 392, 393, 395, 396,

398, 399, 400, 401, 402, 403, 404, 406, 407, 408, 409, 410, 411, 413, 414, 417, 418, 419, 421, 422, 423, 424, 425, 426, 428, 431, 432, 433, 434, 435, 436, 437, 438, 439, 440, 443, 444, 445, 446, 447, 449, 450, 451, 452, 453, 454, 456, 457, 458, 459, 460, 461, 463, 465, 467, 468, 469, 470, 471, 472, 473, 474, 476, 477, 478, 479, 480, 481, 482, 483, 484, 485, 486, 487, 488, 489, 490, 492, 493, 494, 496, 497, 498, 499, 500, 501, 503, 504, 505, 506,

507, 509, 510, 513, 514, 515, 516, 517, 518, 521, 522, 523, 524, 525, 526, 527, 530, 531, 532, 533, 534, 535, 536, 537, 538, 539, 540, 541, 542, 543, 544, 545, 548, 549, 551, 552, 553, 554, 555, 558, 559, 561, 565, 568, 569, 572, 575, 577, 583, 586, 587, 588, 589, 591, 592, 594, 596, 597, 598, 602, 603, 604, 605, 606, 607, 608, 609, 611, 612, 613, 616, 617, 618, 619, 621, 623, 624, 626, 627, 628, 629, 630, 631, 632, 633, 634, 637

Humanity v, 10, 16, 118, 170, 182, 183, 186, 187, 219, 224, 227, 232, 238, 239, 271, 352, 446, 456, 457, 491, 492, 561

I
Idol 247, 327, 361, 451, 466, 509, 530, 553
Idolatry 409, 422, 530
Isaac 235, 407, 572
Isaiah 30, 88, 103, 104, 106, 114, 115, 133, 134, 135, 139, 144, 146, 155, 156, 157, 158, 159, 177, 180, 188, 189, 198, 199, 201, 205, 206, 212, 214, 217, 223, 230, 231, 232, 233, 234, 235, 236, 239, 255, 318, 431, 515, 521, 545, 562, 572,

574, 576, 599, 600, 608, 609, 614, 624, 630, 639
Israel i,74, 100, 114, 120, 126, 137, 139, 140, 146, 150, 155, 156, 158, 161, 168, 169, 171, 177, 179, 188, 189, 190, 191, 192, 193, 194, 195, 199, 200, 202, 204, 205, 207, 208, 209, 210, 217, 218, 220, 225, 231, 234, 235, 237, 273, 281, 282, 283, 284, 287, 289, 290, 292, 294, 297, 302, 316, 331, 332, 352, 354, 359, 382, 383, 391, 392, 393, 398, 408, 410, 445, 446, 447, 448, 449, 451, 452, 465, 475, 477,

Subject Index

Israelite
478, 497, 507, 508, 511, 526, 527, 544, 557, 573, 625
117, 118, 120, 217, 218, 302, 351, 352, 354, 525, 542, 599

J

Jacob
113, 140, 155, 179, 187, 193, 202, 209, 210, 235, 292, 445, 572

Jesus Christ
i, ii, iii, 15, 38, 63, 64, 97, 105, 106, 108, 109, 123, 139, 156, 157, 159, 163, 186, 221, 222, 224, 243, 265, 288, 297, 298, 302, 311, 312, 316, 317, 335, 336, 338, 362, 365, 368, 412, 437, 438, 452, 458, 474, 484, 487, 500, 503, 513,
518, 520, 558, 604, 618, 631, 637

Jerusalem
53, 125, 131, 139, 140, 142, 144, 182, 207, 208, 216, 235, 237, 255, 256, 283, 289, 292, 301, 303, 322, 362, 387, 388, 389, 445, 446, 447, 453, 471, 472, 477, 480, 511, 546, 548, 620

Jew
53, 91, 225, 284, 290, 295, 297, 301, 310, 312, 323, 332, 341, 358, 361, 370, 388, 390, 393, 447, 472, 498, 500, 521, 565, 578

John, The Apostle
106, 121, 125, 209, 221, 224, 244, 245, 250, 254, 256, 258, 265, 266,
270, 282, 303, 306, 316, 327, 332, 454, 455, 456, 460, 462, 490, 506, 507, 544

John the Baptist
3, 133, 144, 161, 167, 168, 214, 215, 251, 264, 278, 279, 281, 282, 285, 294, 297, 309, 314, 346, 476, 513, 515, 587

Judaism 117, 234

Judge
iv, 57, 122, 144, 163, 177, 192, 193, 194, 195, 200, 217, 231, 233, 246, 252, 266, 269, 314, 317, 319, 337, 544, 565, 568, 609

Judgement
23, 53, 96, 109, 110, 134, 144, 171, 174, 186, 233, 242, 266, 268, 269, 279, 280, 291, 296,

Justice
429, 432,
449, 484

14, 15, 16,
20, 60, 79,
158, 193,
195, 197,
230, 233,
234, 240,
261, 274,
317, 318,
323, 351,
429, 515,
529

Justification
ii, viii, 3, 5,
10, 44, 46,
55, 56, 240,
326, 331,
338, 339,
340, 368,
382, 391,
393, 395,
412, 413,
414, 435,
499, 558

K
Kind (s) 1, 12, 13,
17, 29, 34,
52, 57, 58,
71, 88, 99,
115, 126,
153, 158,
259, 260,
268, 318,
374, 395,
426, 427,
428, 444,
452, 462,
468, 475,
494, 499,
506, 522,
524, 530,
539, 547,
552, 556,
567, 568,
570, 577,
579, 586,
590, 592

Kingdom 64, 70, 102,
142, 164,
173, 185,
195, 204,
221, 233,
247, 248,
252, 255,
278, 280,
282, 284,
288, 298,
301, 302,
306, 316,
317, 318,
319, 324,
325, 331,
332, 333,
340, 346,
360, 391,
392, 393,
422, 425,
426, 434,
446, 447,
452, 479,
493, 494,
496, 497,
519, 520,
522, 544,
561, 571,
591, 594,
604, 626

Kuyper, Abraham
3, 14, 44,
48, 55, 56,
57, 59, 60,
492, 493,
494, 595,
619, 620,
635

Kuyperian
5, 57, 58, 63

L
Latin 12, 18, 28,
69, 94, 106,
112, 113,
221, 259,
308, 319,
408, 412,
426, 460,
483, 484,
528, 557

Law i, viii, 99,
146, 174,
183, 184,
185, 186,
210, 221,
222, 234,
257, 260,
289, 290,
291, 292,
293, 326,
339, 341,
342, 343,
345, 353,
364, 365,
366, 371,
382, 407,
417, 420,
421, 422,
423, 430,
431, 449,
497, 498,
531, 546,
586, 599

Lewis, C.S.
416, 499,
500, 621

Liberalism
17, 239

Light vii, 7, 9, 13,
31, 32, 74,
80, 86, 107,
118, 120,
122, 127,
129, 136,

Subject Index

	142, 143, 147, 148, 149, 161, 171, 174, 179, 182, 188, 204, 206, 208, 210, 249, 282, 284, 293, 298, 306, 335, 353, 357, 373, 378, 379, 380, 382, 384, 399, 404, 412, 432, 446, 451, 480, 493, 532, 533, 565, 572, 585, 595, 596, 605, 637	164, 169, 171, 173, 199, 204, 210, 229, 249, 262, 272, 319, 337, 341, 344, 345, 346, 349, 350, 352, 365, 410, 411, 414, 415, 416, 417, 422, 423, 424, 425, 426, 427, 430, 431, 437, 444, 453, 455, 457, 465, 470, 490, 494, 499, 501, 517, 533, 535, 552, 573, 585, 586, 591, 592, 594, 595, 604, 605, 622, 627	627
		M Measures	353, 355, 390, 505
		Messiah	104, 114, 125, 126, 146, 156, 157, 158, 159, 169, 177, 197, 198, 205, 208, 209, 226, 227, 228, 230, 231, 232, 233, 224, 235, 247, 255, 280, 281, 282, 286, 298, 410, 446, 475, 545, 611
Logos	116, 128, 147, 209, 211, 224, 227, 239, 240, 290, 291, 292, 564, 629, 638		
		Metaphor	17, 30, 31, 86, 88, 89, 91, 111, 113, 132, 133, 136, 137, 139, 140, 141, 142, 144, 145, 146, 147, 148, 149, 150, 151, 152, 153, 156, 166, 170, 174, 175, 176, 211, 217, 223, 228, 254, 282, 283,
Love	i, ii, v, 16, 26, 27, 28, 30, 56, 57, 64, 70, 86, 93, 101, 102, 105, 106, 111, 114, 115, 119, 129, 136, 139, 141, 144, 152, 159, 160, 161,	Lutheran	10, 45, 46, 51, 54, 55, 63, 67, 75, 76, 128, 374, 394, 413, 486
		Luther, Martin	21, 44, 45, 46, 48, 187, 213, 259, 265, 395, 401, 497, 531, 590, 611, 621,

691

294, 330,
347, 354,
360, 384,
404, 411,
423, 437,
450, 451,
461, 467,
509, 541

Miracles 2, 56, 61, 62,
69, 213,
237, 285,
288, 299,
232, 324,
515, 520,
522, 523,
528, 530,
531, 551,
556, 571,
572, 573,
574, 582,
583, 584,
587, 589,
590, 591,
637

Missions 44, 68, 391

Montanus 23

N

Netherlands
2, 5, 6, 44,
50, 58, 61,
62, 63, 64,
82, 89, 124,
394, 594

New Garden
187, 191,
448

New Nature
330, 334,
336, 341,
417, 419,
420, 423

New Testament
xi, xii, 16,
20, 31, 53,
54, 59, 70,
72, 82, 83,
86, 97, 100,
103, 104,
111, 112,
120, 121,
126, 127,
135, 139,
144, 149,
152, 155,
156, 159,
172, 178,
192, 193,
195, 200,
201, 202,
209, 210,
212, 215,
216, 217,
218, 220,
221, 227,
235, 242,
246, 254,
264, 270,
280, 282,
285, 288,
290, 293,
305, 308,
311, 327,
329, 330,
331, 338,
343, 349,
354, 358,
361, 378,
382, 384,
385, 390,
391, 428,
429, 435,
437, 444,
449, 452,
458, 459,
463, 464,
467, 475,
479, 493,
504, 505,
506, 511,
513, 552,
561, 588,
589, 593,
595, 608,
613, 614,
615, 618,
619, 620,
622, 631

Nicaea 24, 94, 390,
396

Nicene Creed
10, 24, 28,
36, 37, 41,
390, 488

O

Obedience
46, 54, 58,
63, 131,
154, 224,
340, 346,
373, 417,
504, 516,
517, 524

Old Testament
xi, 24, 45,
54, 99, 100,
102, 104,
105, 112,
116, 133,
134, 137,
139, 142,
143, 149,
152, 154,
155, 156,
162, 177,
178, 189,
192, 195,
199, 200,
201, 202,
206, 208,
209, 212,
213, 215,
216, 217,
218, 219,

Subject Index

220, 221,
225, 227,
228, 235,
253, 256,
257, 279,
282, 288,
290, 326,
327, 328,
337, 355,
367, 379,
427, 452,
465, 497,
506, 519,
525, 545,
552, 561,
562, 565,
567, 570,
571, 574,
575, 576,
577, 580,
581, 601,
611, 616,
624

Orthodox
    x, 5, 11, 15,
    34, 38, 45,
    67, 68, 71,
    75, 78, 92,
    107, 170,
    175, 275,
    382, 389,
    391, 400,
    405, 412,
    413, 438,
    595

P
Paul, The Apostle
    54, 63, 80,
    81, 87, 89,
    105, 120,
    156, 162,
    166, 167,
    171, 172,
    174, 181,

184, 195,
210, 211,
216, 221,
240, 261,
270, 304,
306, 310,
313, 314,
315, 316,
317, 322,
323, 324,
329, 333,
337, 338,
340, 341,
342, 343,
346, 347,
349, 352,
353, 354,
355, 358,
359, 361,
362, 366,
368, 370,
378, 379,
380, 387,
388, 389,
397, 406,
407, 408,
413, 414,
417, 420,
421, 422,
425, 430,
431, 432,
433, 434,
436, 437,
438, 450,
452, 453,
456, 458,
459, 461,
462, 463,
465, 466,
467, 468,
473, 476,
480, 481,
485, 491,
493, 498,
506, 507,

510, 511,
513, 514,
515, 516,
519, 521,
522, 523,
524, 525,
528, 544,
448, 449,
552, 554,
556, 558,
559, 564,
565, 567,
568, 569,
570, 572,
573, 577,
578, 581,
583, 584,
585, 591,
594, 595,
597, 598,
599, 600,
602, 609,
612, 618,
623, 628,
629

Pentateuch
    192, 613
Pentecostalism
    2, 4, 5, 6,
    10, 17, 20,
    44, 45, 47,
    50, 53, 54,
    55, 57, 62,
    64, 65, 66,
    67, 68, 69,
    71, 72, 73,
    74, 75, 76,
    78, 240,
    295, 304,
    307, 326,
    362, 376,
    378, 379,
    393, 394,
    513, 533,
    536, 577,

　　　　　　　　579, 588,
　　　　　　　　607, 608,
　　　　　　　　611, 617,
　　　　　　　　620, 636,
　　　　　　　　638
Pentecost 3, 5, 12, 60,
　　　　　　　　69, 76, 78,
　　　　　　　　100, 107,
　　　　　　　　143, 215,
　　　　　　　　220, 222,
　　　　　　　　245, 246,
　　　　　　　　254, 257,
　　　　　　　　260, 261,
　　　　　　　　267, 274,
　　　　　　　　277, 278,
　　　　　　　　284, 286,
　　　　　　　　289, 290,
　　　　　　　　295, 296,
　　　　　　　　307, 310,
　　　　　　　　311, 312,
　　　　　　　　315, 318,
　　　　　　　　327, 328,
　　　　　　　　346, 351,
　　　　　　　　354, 355,
　　　　　　　　361, 362,
　　　　　　　　367, 375,
　　　　　　　　447, 449,
　　　　　　　　475, 476,
　　　　　　　　484, 524,
　　　　　　　　578
Peter, The Apostle
　　　　　　　　72, 120,
　　　　　　　　157, 229,
　　　　　　　　235, 240,
　　　　　　　　263, 270,
　　　　　　　　293, 294,
　　　　　　　　295, 296,
　　　　　　　　297, 300,
　　　　　　　　301, 303,
　　　　　　　　306, 307,
　　　　　　　　310, 311,
　　　　　　　　312, 313,
　　　　　　　　316, 321,
　　　　　　　　327, 337,
　　　　　　　　346, 351,

　　　　　　　　368, 371,
　　　　　　　　373, 377,
　　　　　　　　385, 412,
　　　　　　　　418, 431,
　　　　　　　　447, 449,
　　　　　　　　480, 498,
　　　　　　　　504, 505,
　　　　　　　　506, 507,
　　　　　　　　513, 514,
　　　　　　　　516, 521,
　　　　　　　　523, 524,
　　　　　　　　528, 529,
　　　　　　　　535, 548,
　　　　　　　　565, 567,
　　　　　　　　570, 583,
　　　　　　　　607, 610,
　　　　　　　　614, 615,
　　　　　　　　618, 638
Philosophy
　　　　　　　　39, 40, 403,
　　　　　　　　415, 626,
　　　　　　　　631
Pietism　50, 54, 393
Pinnock, Clark
　　　　　　　　6, 12, 16,
　　　　　　　　30, 36, 39,
　　　　　　　　55, 67, 77,
　　　　　　　　83, 86, 91,
　　　　　　　　94, 95, 96,
　　　　　　　　112, 113,
　　　　　　　　118, 224,
　　　　　　　　228, 229,
　　　　　　　　239, 240,
　　　　　　　　248, 359,
　　　　　　　　370, 371,
　　　　　　　　375, 376,
　　　　　　　　389, 394,
　　　　　　　　399, 404,
　　　　　　　　405, 416,
　　　　　　　　456, 457,
　　　　　　　　464, 474,
　　　　　　　　479, 480,
　　　　　　　　486, 487,
　　　　　　　　488, 495,
　　　　　　　　501, 508,

　　　　　　　　558, 579,
　　　　　　　　590, 591,
　　　　　　　　627
Pneuma　28, 29, 30,
　　　　　　　　31, 32, 80,
　　　　　　　　81, 88, 90,
　　　　　　　　91, 92, 96,
　　　　　　　　112, 133,
　　　　　　　　135, 136,
　　　　　　　　138, 226,
　　　　　　　　239, 250,
　　　　　　　　257, 272,
　　　　　　　　273, 274,
　　　　　　　　335, 335,
　　　　　　　　343, 349,
　　　　　　　　350, 351,
　　　　　　　　353, 360,
　　　　　　　　407, 408,
　　　　　　　　418, 436,
　　　　　　　　440, 541,
　　　　　　　　596, 597,
　　　　　　　　612, 616,
　　　　　　　　630
Pneumatology
　　　　　　　　v, viii, 10,
　　　　　　　　11, 12, 13,
　　　　　　　　14, 15, 18,
　　　　　　　　20, 28, 43,
　　　　　　　　44, 48, 57,
　　　　　　　　58, 61, 67,
　　　　　　　　73, 76, 77,
　　　　　　　　78, 79, 80,
　　　　　　　　81, 82, 83,
　　　　　　　　95, 126,
　　　　　　　　149, 379,
　　　　　　　　380, 611,
　　　　　　　　616, 517,
　　　　　　　　628
Prayer　6, 56, 59,
　　　　　　　　63, 70, 104,
　　　　　　　　105, 111,
　　　　　　　　118, 140,
　　　　　　　　147, 152,
　　　　　　　　153, 205,
　　　　　　　　220, 252,

Subject Index

 261, 287,
 289
Preaching
 44, 45, 51,
 60, 65, 68,
 268, 288,
 301, 310,
 314, 316,
 323, 329,
 368, 369,
 372, 377,
 387, 416,
 458, 478,
 481, 482,
 500, 501,
 504, 512,
 523, 524,
 545, 549,
 578, 583,
 613
Presbyterian
 ii, iii, 67,
 462, 614,
 634, 637
Prophet vi, 14, 20,
 21, 22, 23,
 54, 59, 96,
 102, 104,
 124, 137,
 143, 149,
 151, 152,
 154, 155,
 157, 158,
 162, 173,
 174, 177,
 180, 190,
 192, 193,
 195, 196,
 197, 198,
 199, 200,
 201, 202,
 206, 207,
 210, 213,
 215, 217,
 220, 221,

 225, 228,
 231, 234,
 235, 245,
 279, 282,
 287, 288,
 294, 295,
 306, 309,
 346, 372,
 386, 387,
 388, 389,
 393, 396,
 408, 444,
 459, 460,
 461, 462,
 463, 465,
 466, 467,
 504, 506,
 508, 511,
 521, 526,
 527, 528,
 529, 543,
 544, 546,
 547, 548,
 555, 556,
 557, 558,
 560, 562,
 563, 567,
 569, 570,
 571, 574,
 575, 576,
 577, 581,
 582, 584,
 585, 590,
 596, 600,
 601, 602,
 604, 607,
 609, 615
Protestant
 viii, 2, 3, 4,
 5, 6, 14, 35,
 37, 39, 45,
 46, 50, 51,
 53, 54, 63,
 67, 68, 69,
 75, 82, 88,

 126, 259,
 374, 382,
 393, 394,
 396, 398,
 400, 414,
 462, 484,
 486, 487,
 507, 509,
 616
Puritanism
 50, 54, 393

Q
Quakers 17, 50
Quantification
 165
Question vi, 3, 4, 13,
 24, 28, 32,
 35, 36, 39,
 48, 49, 50,
 53, 60, 62,
 87, 93, 96,
 97, 98, 99,
 138, 178,
 186, 202,
 219, 221,
 243, 248,
 252, 253,
 263, 284,
 295, 300,
 305, 315,
 316, 326,
 332, 340,
 342, 349,
 356, 362,
 367, 368,
 375, 378,
 388, 392,
 395, 398,
 401, 402,
 403, 433,
 456, 459,
 463, 466,
 486, 489,
 500, 504,

R

Rebirth 4, 46, 56, 326, 327, 328, 329, 330, 332, 333, 335, 338, 340, 341, 363, 366, 367, 368, 369

Reformational viii, xii, 48, 78, 626, 631

Reformers 5, 43, 44, 46, 52, 364, 391, 392, 590

Regeneration 3, 5, 10, 92, 102, 139, 178, 211, 229, 253, 299, 325, 327, 328, 329, 330, 335, 336, 363, 369, 499, 561

Religion 3, 39, 47, 78, 128, 403, 498, 501, 512, 609, 619, 620, 627

Renewal 2, 5, 6, 44, 57, 61, 64, 65, 66, 73, 74, 76, 93, 102, 139, 178, 211, 538, 565, 567, 579, 593, 598 220, 273, 328, 330, 335, 336, 376, 398, 412, 475, 494, 630, 637

Repentance ii, 143, 229, 250, 278, 280, 297, 311, 313, 333, 360, 362, 368, 372, 375, 600

Resurrection 11, 93, 102, 103, 223, 227, 237, 240, 241, 242, 243, 244, 257, 266, 272, 273, 274, 282, 290, 296, 320, 321, 322, 328, 337, 355, 356, 398, 410, 447, 493, 495, 565, 571, 572, 575, 577

Roman Catholic 3, 10, 11, 17, 18, 20, 29, 36, 37, 50, 53, 65, 66, 67, 68, 75, 76, 78, 80, 107, 128, 271, 391, 438, 482, 561, 608

S

Sacrament 4, 16, 22, 44, 46, 47, 50, 55, 77, 153, 265, 332, 374, 444, 481, 482, 483, 484, 485, 486, 487, 495

Salvation 10, 13, 34, 58, 62, 93, 106, 141, 171, 185, 255, 280, 297, 299, 314, 325, 328, 329, 330, 338, 339, 341, 344, 363, 365, 367, 368, 369, 371, 372, 379, 380, 432, 482, 488, 490, 492, 498, 557, 558, 570, 583, 621

Samaritans 278, 301, 302, 303, 306, 367, 370, 472, 621

Samuel 156, 177, 195, 196, 197, 201,

Subject Index

    202, 207,
    217, 542,
    546, 562,
    576, 613
Sanctification
    3, 5, 10, 44,
    46, 50, 56,
    93, 102,
    154, 326,
    331, 338,
    339, 340,
    379, 382,
    424, 435,
    436, 576
Satan   75, 247,
    261, 268,
    269, 270,
    323, 330,
    387, 412,
    430, 451,
    496, 497,
    511, 531,
    569, 570
Schism   10, 12, 28,
    35, 36, 37
Scholastic
    18, 23, 38,
    39, 46, 51,
    405, 489,
    491, 495,
    496, 507
Scholasticism
    50
Scripture ii, vi, 3, 10,
    17, 23, 35,
    45, 46, 47,
    48, 49, 50,
    51, 52, 53,
    54, 55, 62,
    63, 72, 82,
    89, 90, 93,
    101, 104,
    105, 112,
    129, 132,
    133, 140,

    144, 148,
    153, 168,
    184, 198,
    236, 240,
    248, 249,
    254, 255,
    264, 271,
    273, 295,
    330, 348,
    349, 354,
    355, 360,
    368, 389,
    390, 391,
    393, 395,
    396, 397,
    398, 401,
    402, 404,
    459, 481,
    517, 588,
    629, 633
Second Blessing
    71, 72, 326,
    362, 374,
    375, 376,
    378, 393
Sin   10, 11, 56,
    58, 72, 93,
    142, 147,
    192, 193,
    201, 204,
    205, 220,
    229, 237,
    240, 244,
    248, 249,
    250, 261,
    266, 268,
    269, 273,
    274, 275,
    280, 291,
    297, 298,
    299, 300,
    310, 311,
    314, 326,
    329, 330,
    331, 333,

    335, 338,
    342, 343,
    353, 364,
    365, 366,
    368, 371,
    372, 407,
    419, 422,
    436, 438,
    475, 484,
    485, 492,
    493, 494,
    495, 496,
    497, 545,
    558, 563,
    607
Sinai   120, 143,
    168, 205,
    278, 289,
    290, 291,
    292, 383,
    444, 445,
    449
Solomon   116, 118,
    119, 120,
    122, 136,
    170, 173,
    177, 191,
    197, 201,
    203, 204,
    218, 232,
    292, 341,
    410, 451,
    509, 543,
    566
Soteriology
    10, 13, 46,
    47, 57, 77,
    329, 490,
Spirit Baptism
    66, 68, 71,
    72, 120,
    145, 147,
    215, 278,
    280, 285,
    287, 297,

298, 299,
302, 303,
304, 305,
306, 308,
309, 310,
313, 315,
326, 329,
336, 358,
359, 360,
361, 362,
366, 367,
368, 370,
374, 375,
376, 377,
378, 379,
380, 393,
484, 485,
533, 534,
536, 579,
580

Spirituality
6, 9, 17, 18,
20, 68, 71,
413, 535,
612, 628,
634

Spiritual Gifts
17, 56, 299,
466, 553,
595, 612,
627

Systematic Theology
3, 10, 11,
14, 77, 80,
606, 609,
612, 615,
616, 627,
632, 633

T
Tehom 177, 181,
182, 187,
188, 189
Temple 27, 90, 100,
102, 103,

120, 121,
122, 140,
143, 177,
178, 191,
193, 197,
201, 203,
204, 205,
206, 207,
208, 209,
212, 216,
217, 218,
225, 226,
235, 255,
258, 261,
286, 289,
293, 311,
347, 348

Terminology
94, 189,
239, 326,
375, 454

Tertullian
23, 266,
319, 482

Theology i, ii, v, vi,
vii, xii, 3,
9, 10, 11,
12, 13, 14,
23, 25, 38,
39, 40, 44,
46, 47, 48,
50, 52, 60,
64, 70, 73,
74, 77, 78,
79, 80, 82,
83, 111,
224, 227,
300, 376,
389, 392,
395, 399,
400, 404,
405, 406,
413, 414,
463, 488,
492, 494,

497, 668,
595, 605,
606, 607,
608, 609,
611, 612,
614, 615,
616, 620,
621, 626,
627, 628,
630, 631,
632, 633,
634, 636

Thomas Aquinas
28, 45, 334,
422

Tongues 22, 56, 65,
66, 71, 73,
122, 143,
157, 162,
165, 247,
277, 290,
293, 294,
303, 304,
310, 311,
313, 314,
316, 370,
440, 478,
485, 506,
521, 532,
537, 552,
556, 557,
564, 566,
573, 574,
577, 578,
579, 580,
581, 584,
585, 586,
592, 595,
597, 598,
599, 600,
603

Torah 116, 117,
123, 176,
209, 234,
253, 278,

Subject Index

	289, 290, 291, 292, 293, 342, 351, 352, 354, 390, 421, 429, 431, 432, 494, 625, 626, 355, 410, 429, 436, 338, 443, 444, 445, 446, 447, 448, 450, 451, 452, 453, 470, 471, 472, 473, 474, 476, 485, 506, 543, 549		455, 456, 458, 470, 554, 621,	**U**	
		Trinity	3, 10, 12, 25, 26, 28, 32, 35, 47, 78, 85, 92, 93, 94, 98, 101, 118, 132, 178, 238, 246, 416, 457, 617	Unity	ii, iii, 25, 27, 32, 41, 90, 99, 360, 361, 362, 390, 412, 426, 444, 454, 467, 468, 469, 470, 491, 584
		Truth	ii, 20, 23, 28, 35, 52, 85, 86, 98, 101, 107, 110, 129, 156, 168, 171, 178, 217, 221, 258, 260, 261, 263, 265, 266, 267, 270, 271, 325, 328, 341, 363, 390, 396, 399, 401, 404, 405, 406, 427, 437, 446, 470, 472, 473, 477, 478, 488, 498, 499, 500, 510, 518, 521, 522, 567, 592, 605, 609, 613, 621, 636, 638	**V** Virgin Birth	115, 226, 228, 229
Toronto Blessing	24, 536, 612, 614, 622			**W** Water	v, 9, 31, 43, 96, 101, 102, 112, 113, 119, 120, 127, 132, 133, 137, 138, 139, 140, 141, 142, 144, 145, 148, 150, 153, 164, 165, 166, 167, 169, 170, 171, 175, 176, 179, 180, 184, 187, 188, 189, 190, 200, 202, 203, 204, 206, 211, 212, 216, 218, 237, 252, 253, 254, 255, 256,
Tradition	6, 12, 14, 26, 27, 31, 35, 39, 45, 47, 54, 57, 65, 66, 75, 78, 79, 82, 109, 113, 114, 118, 119, 124, 203, 206, 225, 227, 292, 293, 395, 401, 404, 415, 446, 475, 608, 612				
Trinitarian	12, 24, 77, 87, 91, 189, 390, 454,				

	265, 266,		179, 180,		125, 126,
	272, 277,		183, 200,		162, 228,
	278, 279,		202, 213,		252, 253,
	280, 281,		273, 277,		264, 322,
	283, 291,		282, 291,		326, 355,
	295, 297,		293, 294,		398, 448,
	298, 299,		304, 335,		472, 525,
	303, 304,		541, 575		529, 533,
	305, 307,	Wisdom	50, 56, 86,		562, 563
	308, 310,		90, 96, 100,	World	ii, vi, x, 1,
	311, 312,		101, 110,		2, 3, 5, 36,
	313, 315,		116, 117,		38, 39, 40,
	325, 327,		118, 120,		50, 53, 55,
	332, 333,		125, 128,		60, 61, 62,
	334, 335,		129, 148,		63, 65, 67,
	338, 357,		156, 169,		68, 69, 70,
	358, 359,		180, 192,		72, 75, 76,
	360, 367,		197, 198,		81, 88, 96,
	368, 375,		199, 209,		100, 117,
	447, 448,		210, 214,		118, 126,
	449, 470,		215, 230,		127, 128,
	482, 483,		231, 232,		129, 159,
	484, 485,		240, 245,		164, 168,
	487, 494,		246, 292,		169, 170,
	517, 541,		293, 300,		171, 173,
	575, 589		322, 343,		178, 179,
Warfield, Benjamin			387, 395,		181, 182,
	99, 149		396, 411,		183, 203,
Wimber, John			431, 460,		214, 217,
	69, 163,		481, 501,		224, 227,
	376, 377,		502, 521,		246, 258,
	378, 532,		522, 524,		261, 262,
	559, 574,		525, 537,		266, 268,
	586, 638		549, 551,		269, 270,
Wind	28, 30, 31,		552, 556,		273, 274,
	88, 91, 105,		557, 563,		282, 283,
	122, 132,		564, 565,		284, 292,
	133, 134,		566, 570,		311, 322,
	135, 136,		571, 573,		335, 357,
	137, 138,		581, 582,		362, 378,
	140, 143,		583, 603,		391, 392,
	144, 148,		626		397, 400,
	155, 163,	Woman	17, 79, 86,		402, 412,
	165, 166,		87, 114,		415, 444,
	167, 176,		115, 118,		447, 449,

Subject Index

        457, 459,
        447, 479,
        480, 481,
        487, 489,
        490, 493,
        494, 495,
        496, 497,
        499, 500,
        501, 513,
        520, 521,
        530, 539,
        553, 583,
        592, 623,
        626, 627
Worldview
        14, 405
Worship 5, 6, 25, 55,
        64, 70, 71,
        73, 74, 86,
        87, 104,
        105, 106,
        107, 108,
        148, 162,
        237, 246,
        286, 351,
        372, 386,
        438, 444,
        451, 460,
        471, 472,
        473, 474,
        475, 504,
        508, 518,
        519, 521,
        543, 544,
        552, 600,
        603, 628

Y
YHWH 78, 86, 88,
        100, 103,
        104, 105,
        106, 108,
        120, 156,
        212, 213,
        218, 231,
        232, 233,
        235, 239,
        525

Z
Zechariah
        140, 142,
        146, 155,
        193, 194,
        200, 201,
        207, 208,
        225, 235,
        251, 513,
        521, 606
Zion 125, 140,
        141, 144,
        206, 210,
        278, 289,
        290, 292,
        511
Zwingi, Ulrich
        46, 499,
        608, 630